The Developing Person
Through Childhood and Adolescence

The Developing Person
Through Childhood and Adolescence

SECOND EDITION

Kathleen Stassen Berger

Bronx Community College
City University of New York

Worth Publishers, Inc.

The Developing Person Through Childhood and Adolescence, SECOND EDITION

Copyright © 1980, 1986 by Worth Publishers, Inc.

Printed in the United States of America

Library of Congress Catalog Card Number: 85-051771

ISBN: 0-87901-241-2

Second Printing, July 1987

Editors: Peter Deane, Judith Wilson

Illustrator: Angie Lloyd

Picture Editor: Elaine Bernstein

Production: Sarah Segal, Margie Brassil

Design: Malcolm Grear Designers

Composition: York Graphic Services

Printing and Binding: R. R. Donnelley & Sons

Cover: *Children's Games* (Detail), Pieter Bruegel, The Elder
    Kunsthistorisches Museum, Vienna

Worth Publishers, Inc.
33 Irving Place
New York, New York 10003

Preface

When I wrote the first edition of this book, it was my intention to produce a text that was accurate and current, that reflected the most significant theories and research in developmental psychology, and that, at the same time, was sensitive to students' interests, concerns, and motivation. The response to the first edition suggested that, in large measure, I had achieved my goals.

The second edition, *The Developing Person Through Childhood and Adolescence,* represents a reaffirmation of those goals. I have attempted to make every aspect of this text as fresh and up-to-date as possible while retaining those features that seemed to work most successfully in the first edition. Due largely to instructors' and students' response to the first edition, the overall organization of the book remains the same. Two introductory chapters, one on definitions and methodology and one on the three major theories, are followed by five parts that correspond to the five major periods of child development—the prenatal period, infancy, early childhood, middle childhood, and adolescence. With the exception of the prenatal section, each part consists of a trio of chapters dealing with, respectively, physical development, cognitive development, and psychosocial development. This topical organization within a chronological framework fosters students' appreciation of how the various aspects of development are interrelated—of how body, mind, and personality develop through interaction rather than separately.

New Research and Emphases

Within this retained framework, however, many important changes reflect new research discoveries and theoretical shifts. Most important overall is the increased emphasis on interaction—within the family, between the family and the community, and between developing individuals and the economic, cultural, and historical conditions that affect their growth. For example, a comparison of this book with its predecessor would reveal that the distinctive contribution of fathers is now more consistently highlighted, that the roles of siblings and family support networks are included, and that various family structures—the single-child family, the single-parent family, the blended family—are examined in detail. Further, the role of the larger society, both in contributing to, and preventing, such problems as birth defects, child abuse, school failure, lonely and friendless children, language deficits, and teenage pregnancy, is examined more explicitly than before. One change in theoretical emphasis is also apparent: while Piaget's insights continue to form the foundation for every chapter on cognition, a substantial part of each of these chapters is devoted to neo-Piagetian and non-Piagetian approaches, resulting in an increased emphasis on perception, memory, language, information-processing, learning contexts, and educational techniques.

Because recent scientific research and public attention have focused on particular areas of importance to the study of development, some topics in this edition are entirely new, including the latest methods of fetal monitoring and fetal surgery, the possible effects of accelerated learning in infants, the interplay of brain development and motor and language skills, the pros and cons of various methods of bilingual education, the role of social cognition and training in social skills, the causes and consequences of sexual abuse (including incest), gender differences in moral thinking, the cohort factor in identity formation, and many others.

In addition to the more obvious changes in subject matter, much of the text has been revised for greater clarity and liveliness. Even the illustrations have been thoroughly reconsidered, and more than half of the photographs in this edition are new ones.

Supplementary Materials

Because they seemed to work so well in the first edition, the original pedagogical aids have been retained. Thus, at the end of each chapter there is a chapter summary, a list of key terms (along with page numbers indicating where the term was introduced), a series of key questions for reviewing important concepts, and a list of recommended readings—paperback books that students can understand and enjoy without an extensive background in psychology. New to this edition are full-page charts that come at the end of each part of the book and provide an overview of the significant physical, cognitive, and psychosocial events covered in that part. Finally, all the supplements to the book, including the *Study Guide,* the *Test Bank,* and the *Instructor's Resource Manual* have been thoroughly revised with the intention of providing both instructors and students with a greater variety of ways in which to teach, or learn, the material in the text.

Personal Influences

Within all the social sciences, there is increased recognition of the ways in which scientists' theoretical perspectives, personal values, and background experiences may shape their work. These factors are equally influential in the work of the social science writer. For instance, decisions about which topics are to be discussed or omitted, and how each topic is to be framed for the reader, are affected by the writer's own values. Therefore, it would seem helpful to have an author set forth his or her background and leanings at the outset so that the reader may take them into account.

My own theoretical roots are diverse: I have been taught by gifted teachers who studied directly with Erik Erikson, B. F. Skinner, and Jean Piaget. I share with my mentors much respect and admiration for these great theorists, although I do not consider myself a follower of any of them. I have found Erikson's psychosocial formulations to be insightful (although I think they are more art than science), and I have used behaviorist techniques in my own family, classroom, and life, and found them effective. However, the perspective that seems to me to be the most persuasive is the cognitive one, with its insights into the ways in which what we think and how we think shape our construction of reality.

As great an influence on my thinking as those who have taught me have been those whom I have taught, for my students have had a powerful effect on how I interpret and envision the material I study and write about. I have been a teacher at several institutions, from the United Nations High School to Fordham University Graduate School, and I have been a member of the psychology department at

Bronx Community College of the City University of New York for the past twelve years. My students have come from a great diversity of ethnic, economic, and educational backgrounds, and my work with them and my close observation of their interests and concerns have greatly broadened my own understanding of human development.

Of special significance to my writing has been my family, especially in terms of the personal changes that have occurred within it since this book was first published. At that time, the eldest of my three children was just approaching adolescence: within the past few years, Bethany, now 17, and Rachel, now 16, have given me plenty of front-line experience in adolescent behavior and parental response. The last three chapters of this book undoubtedly reflect some of the insights gained first-hand.

My third child, Elissa, is now 9. Her first attempts to talk were noted in the earlier edition; since then, her unique development has reinforced my appreciation of genetic diversity, even within a family. The most dramatic change in my family has been the addition of Sarah, born almost four years ago, slowing down the revision schedule for this book but deeply enriching our lives. She also has provided, as her older siblings have, examples, anecdotes, and photos that help this book to reflect actual as well as theoretical child development.

All told, my theoretical orientation, my students, and my personal experiences have led me to believe that a broad, eclectic approach to human development is the most useful. Further, the current emphasis among developmentalists on the ecological, or systems, approach is reflected in my own thinking, for I continually see the interaction among family members, and between individuals and their social systems, as pivotal in channeling human development.

Thanks

I have often been asked by those familiar with *The Developing Person,* "How did you do it all yourself?" The answer is, I didn't. I have had a great deal of help from many quarters, all of which has considerably strengthened my own efforts. Hundreds of instructors offered criticisms and suggestions based on their classroom experience with the first edition. For this edition, twenty-four academic reviewers provided not only helpful criticism and equally helpful support, but also a great many inspiring suggestions and hot leads. I am very grateful to each of them.

Patricia P. Barker, Schenectady County Community College
Eda Bower, Marycrest College
Joseph J. Campos, University of Denver
Margaret K. Cass, University of Michigan, Ann Arbor
Vicky Fong, Sacramento City College
Janet Fritz, Colorado State University
Mary Gauvain, University of Pennsylvania
Hill Goldsmith, University of Oregon
Anita L. Greene, West Virginia University
James N. Greene, Ricks College
Robert J. Hoffnung, University of New Haven
Sybillyn Jennings, Russell Sage College
Murray Krantz, Florida State University
John J. Mitchell, University of Alberta (Edmonton)
Philip J. Mohan, University of Idaho
Roberta H. Morgan, University of Alaska, Anchorage

Kathryn Quina, University of Rhode Island
Harriette Ritchie, American River College
Gary L. Schilmoeller, University of Maine at Orono
Ross A. Thompson, University of Nebraska-Lincoln
Kenneth A. Tokuno, University of Hawaii at Manoa
Daniel J. Tomasulo, Brookdale Community College
Cynthia Whitfield, Merritt College
Robert H. Woodson, University of Texas at Austin

Even more important to the final realization of this book are the people at Worth Publishers, who have lavished the careful attention to editing, design, and art work that is apparent on every page. Worth is a company devoted to excellence, with a genuine concern for the quality of the books they publish, and this concern is manifest in each step of the publishing process, from the first draft to the final page.

I particularly want to thank Judith Wilson and her assistant, Patty Nankervis, for their very intelligent and very patient help throughout, and Elaine Bernstein, the art editor, for her contributions to this book's distinctive visual appeal. Most of all I want to acknowledge the efforts of my editor, Peter Deane, who not only knows and cares as much about this book as I do, but whose countless contributions are visible on every page—from refinement of virtually every paragraph to the organization of key sections that had sometimes seemed to defy my getting them right.

One final word of thanks is overdue. The first edition of this book was dedicated to my students, and my life-span book, *The Developing Person Through the Life Span* (Worth, 1983), was dedicated to my parents. It is time to give credit to the man without whom I could not be teacher, mother, and writer simultaneously. This book is dedicated, with love, to my husband, Martin.

New York City
February, 1986

Kathryn Stassen Berger

Contents

Preface   v

Chapter 1   **Introduction**   1

The Study of Human Development   3

The Three Domains   3

The Context of Development   4
    The Ecological, or Systems, Approach   4

David's Story: Domains and Systems at Work   5
    The Early Years: Heartbreaking Handicaps,
      Slow Progress   6
    Middle Childhood: Heartening Progress   7
    Adolescence and Beyond: New Problems,
      New Hopes   8

Three Controversies   9

Nature or Nurture?   10

Continuity or Discontinuity?   11

Deficit or Difference?   13

A CLOSER LOOK   Stages in History   14

The Scientific Method   17

RESEARCH REPORT   Ways to Make Research
    More Valid   18

Naturalistic Observation   18
    A Naturalistic Study   18
    Limitations of Natural Observation   20

A CLOSER LOOK   Correlation: What It Does,
    And Does Not, Mean   21

The Experiment   22
    An Experiment with Newborns   22
    Limitations of Experiments   23

The Interview   24

The Case Study   24

Designing Developmental Research   25
    Cross-Sectional Research   25
    Longitudinal Research   26
    Cohort Effects   26

A Look at the History and Ethics of
    the Study of Children   27

Scientific Child Study   29

Ethics and Values   29

Chapter 2   **Theories**   33

What Theories Do   34

Three Possible Explanations   35

Psychoanalytic Theories   37

Origins   37

Freud's Ideas   39
    Id, Ego, and Superego   40
    Defense Mechanisms   40

Erikson's Ideas   41
    Eight Crises of Life   42
    Psychosocial Development   43
    Cultural Differences   43

RESEARCH REPORT   "Combat Crisis" in a
    Marine   44

Evaluations of Psychoanalytic Theories   44

Learning Theories   45

Emphasis on Behavior   46

Laws of Behavior   46
    Classical Conditioning   47
    Operant Conditioning   47
    Reinforcement   48
    Laws of Reinforcement   48

Social Learning Theory   49
    Modeling   50
    Effects of Social Learning   51

Evaluations of Learning Theories   51

RESEARCH REPORT   Children Who Are Out
    of Control   52

Cognitive Theories   54

Piaget's Ideas   54
    How Cognitive Development Occurs 54
    Thirst For Knowledge 56

RESEARCH REPORT The Clinical Method   58

Evaluations of Cognitive Theories   60

The Theories Compared   **61**

Part I **The Beginnings**   **65**

───────────────────────────────

Chapter 3 **Conception and
Heredity**   **67**

Culture and Conception   **69**

The Biology of Conception   **71**

The Moment of Conception   71

Genes and Chromosomes   **71**

The Twenty-third Pair   72

Genetic Uniqueness   73
    Twins 73

A CLOSER LOOK Twins and Research   74

Dominant and Recessive Genes   77
    X-Linked Recessive Genes 77

Polygenic Inheritance   78

Heredity and Environment   **78**

Multifactorial Characteristics   79

Abnormal Genes and Chromosomes   **80**

Chromosomal Abnormalities   80

RESEARCH REPORT Genes and IQ   82
    Causes of Chromosomal Abnormalities 84

Harmful Genes   84

Genetic Counseling   **85**

Two Success Stories   85

Who Should Be Tested?   88

A CLOSER LOOK Compulsory Genetic Testing   88

Testing for Genetic Conditions   89

Predicting Genetic Problems   90

Many Alternatives   91

───────────────────────────────

Chapter 4 **Prenatal Development**   **97**

From Zygote to Newborn   **99**

The Germinal Period: The First Fourteen Days   99
    Implantation 99
    Four Protective Membranes 100
    The Placenta 100

The Period of the Embryo: Two Weeks to
  Eight Weeks   101
    The Second Month 101

The Period of the Fetus: Two Months to Birth   102
    The Second Trimester 102
    The Third Trimester 103

Preventing Complications   **103**

Teratology   103
    The Critical Period 104

Diseases   104

A CLOSER LOOK Rubella   106

Drugs   107
    Thalidomide 107
    Other Medicines 107
    Social Drugs 107

Environmental Hazards   109
    Radiation 110
    Pollution 110
    Risk Factors 111

The Expectant Parents   **111**

The Psychological Impact of Pregnancy   112
    The First Trimester 113
    The Second Trimester 115

A CLOSER LOOK The Fetus as Patient   116
    The Third Trimester 118

Nutrition   118

Preparation for Birth   119

───────────────────────────────

Chapter 5 **Birth**   **123**

The Normal Birth   **124**

The Newborn's First Minutes   125
    The Newborn's Appearance 127

Variations, Problems, and Solutions   **127**

The Low-Birth-Weight Infant   127

RESEARCH REPORT The Problems of the
  Preterm Infant   128
    Causes of Low Birth Weight 130
    Consequences of Low Birth Weight 130

Stressful Birth   131

The Birth Experience   **133**

The Baby's Experience   133
    Gentle Birth 134

The Parents' Experience   135
    Preparation for Childbirth 135

A CLOSER LOOK Prepared Childbirth   136
    Hospital and Home 137
    Birth Attendants 137
    The Father's Participation 138

The Older Sibling's Experience 140

Bonding Between Baby, Mother, and Father 141

Animals and Bonding 141

Bonding in Humans 141

RESEARCH REPORT Mother-Infant Contact 142

A CLOSER LOOK Engrossment 143

Adoption 144

Part II **The First Two Years: Infants and Toddlers** 149

Chapter 6 **The First Two Years: Physical Development** 151

Size and Shape 152

Proportions 153

Brain Growth and Maturation 154

Development of the Sensory and Motor Areas 155

Regulating Physiological States 156

A CLOSER LOOK Sudden Infant Death 156

Sensation and Perception 158

Research on Infant Perception 158

Vision 159

Hearing 160

RESEARCH REPORT Depth Perception 161

The Other Senses 161

The Development of Motor Abilities 162

Motor Skills 164

The Sequence of Motor Skills 164
Locomotion 165

Variations in Timing 166

Reasons for Variation 167

Nutrition 168

The Early Months 168

Nutrition After Weaning 168

A CLOSER LOOK Breast Versus Bottle 169

Serious Malnutrition 170

Serious Malnutrition in the United States 171

Chapter 7 **The First Two Years: Cognitive Development** 175

How Cognitive Development Occurs 177

Interaction Between Maturation and Learning 177

Difference in Emphasis 177

Piaget's Theory 177

Sensorimotor Intelligence 178

Stage One: Reflexes (Birth to 1 Month) 178
Stage Two: The First Acquired Adaptations (1 Month to 4 Months) 179
Stage Three: Procedures for Making Interesting Sights Last (4 Months to 8 Months) 180
Stage Four: New Adaptation and Anticipation (8 Months to 12 Months) 181

A CLOSER LOOK Piaget's Test of Object Permanence 182

Stage Five: New Means Through Active Experimentation (12 Months to 18 Months) 184
Stage Six: New Means Through Mental Combinations (18 Months to 24 Months) 185
Pretending 186
Full Object Permanence 186
The Significance of Stage Six Behavior 187

Postscripts to Piaget 187

Perception and Cognition 188

"The American Question" 189

Teaching and Learning in Infancy 189

RESEARCH REPORT Infant Memory 191

Special Programs for High-Risk Infants 191

Teaching the Privileged Infant 192

Language Development 194

Theories of Language Development 195

Learning Theory: Skinner 195
A Structural View: Chomsky 196
Later Research 197

Steps in Language Development 197

First Communications 197
Cooing 198
Babbling 198

A CLOSER LOOK Babbling and Language Development in Deaf Babies 199

Meaningful Sounds 200
Comprehension 201
First Spoken Words 201

RESEARCH REPORT Strategies for Learning Language: Referential and Expressive 202

Combining Words 204

Teamwork: Adults and Babies Teach Each Other to Talk 204

A CLOSER LOOK Berger Learns the Rules of Baby Talk 206

A Social Interaction 207

Chapter 8 The First Two Years: Psychosocial Development 211

Emotional Development 212
The First Half Year 213
RESEARCH REPORT Measuring Emotion 214
8 Months to 2 Years 215
    Emotion and Cognition 216
    Self-Awareness 216

Personality Development 218
Traditional Views: The Omnipotent Mother 218
A CLOSER LOOK Overcoming Fears and Hiding Tears 219
Freud: Oral and Anal Stages 220
Erikson: Trust and Autonomy 221
Mahler: Symbiosis and Separation-Individuation 223
    Separation-Individuation 223
Temperament 224
    Other Research 225
    The Parents' Role 227

Parent-Infant Interaction 227
The Beginning of the First Year: Synchrony 228
    A Typical Interaction 229
The End of the First Year: Attachment 231
    Measuring Attachment 231
    Attachment and Care-Giving 232
RESEARCH REPORT Fathers and Infants 234
    The Importance of Attachment 236
The Second Year: Caring for Toddlers 237
    HOME 237

Child Abuse and Neglect 242
Causes of Child Abuse and Neglect 244
    The Social Context 244
    Problems in the Parents 245
    Problems in the Child 246
Treatment and Prevention 247

Part III The Play Years 253

Chapter 9 The Play Years: Physical Development 255

Physical Play 256
Sensorimotor Play 256
Mastery Play 257
Rough-and-Tumble Play 258
The Importance of Play 259

Size and Shape 260
Height and Weight 261
    Eating Habits 262
Growth Problems 263
    Treatment of Growth Problems 264

Brain, Eyes, and Other Organs 265
Brain Maturation 265
A CLOSER LOOK The Left-Handed Child 266
The Two Halves of the Brain 267
Eye Maturation 269
Body Changes 269
A CLOSER LOOK Readiness for School 270

Mastering Motor Skills 270
Gross Motor Skills 271
Fine Motor Skills 273
    The Value of Fine Motor Skills 273
A CLOSER LOOK Very Nice! What Is It? 274
Children's Art 274

Activity Level 276
Accident Rates 276

Sex Differences and Similarities 278
RESEARCH REPORT Girls and Boys Together 280
Implications 281

Chapter 10 The Play Years: Cognitive Development 285

How Preschoolers Think 287
Symbolic Thought 287
    Pretend Play 287
Preoperational Thought 288
    Centration 289
    The Problem of Conservation 290
    Egocentrism 291
    Piaget's Three Mountains 293
Revising Piaget 294
    Perspective-Taking in Preschoolers 294
    Instruction in Conservation 295
A CLOSER LOOK Preoperational Conceptions of Death, Illness, and Divorce 296

Language Development 298
Language and Thought 299
Vocabulary 300
RESEARCH REPORT The Critical Period for Language Development 300
    Difficulties with Vocabulary 302

Grammar   302
   Difficulties with Grammar 304
Pragmatics   305
A CLOSER LOOK Articulation   306
   Inner Speech 307
   Difficulties with Pragmatics 308
Differences in Language Development   309

Teaching and Learning   **311**
Headstart   311
   Long-Term Benefits 312
Parent Involvement   313

Chapter 11 The Play Years:
Psychosocial Development   **317**

The Self and the Social World   **318**
The Development of Self-Concept   319
   Theories of Self and Others 319
Social Skills and Self-Understanding   320

Play   **322**
Categories of Social Play   322
Dramatic Play   324
Sibling Interaction   325
The Importance of Social Play   326
RESEARCH REPORT Self and the Social World
   of Primates   326

Parenting   **328**
Hostility and Affection   328
Patterns of Parenting   328
   An Example 329
Punishment   330
   Effects of Physical Punishment 330
A CLOSER LOOK It Sounds Easy But . . .   331
   The Effects of Criticism 331
   Suggestions 333
RESEARCH REPORT Television: A Dilemma for
   Parents   334

Possible Problems   **336**
Aggression   336
   Developmental Trends 336
   Adult Intervention 337
Fantasy and Fear   338
Serious Psychological Disturbances   340
   Causes 341
   Cures 341

Sex Roles and Stereotypes   **342**
RESEARCH REPORT Sexual Stereotypes in
   3-Year-Olds   343

Three Theories of Sex-Role Development   344
   Psychoanalytic Theory 344
   Learning Theory 345
A CLOSER LOOK Berger and Freud   346
   Cognitive Theory 348
A New Theory: Androgyny   349

Part IV **The School Years**   **355**

Chapter 12 The School Years:
Physical Development   **357**

Size and Shape   **358**
Variations in Physique   359
Childhood Obesity   360
   Help for Overweight Children 360
A CLOSER LOOK Causes of Childhood Obesity   362

Motor Skills   **362**
Differences in Motor Skills   364
   Games Children Play 365

Children with Handicaps   **366**
Separate Education   366
Mainstreaming   367
Learning Disabilities   369
   What Causes a Learning Disability? 370
A CLOSER LOOK The Learning-Disabled Child
   in School   372
Hyperactive Children   372
   Causes of Hyperactivity 375
   Help for Hyperactive Children 376

Chapter 13 The School Years:
Cognitive Development   **381**

Concrete Operational Thought   **383**
The 5-to-7 Shift   383
Logical Ideas   383
   Classification and Class Inclusion 384
   Seriation 385
Application of Concrete Concepts   386
   Mathematics 386
   Time and Distance 387
Modifying Piaget   388
   The Legacy of Piaget 388
A CLOSER LOOK Piaget in the Classroom   390

An Information-Processing View   **392**

Memory   393
    Memory Capacity 393
Metamemory   393
    Selective Attention 393
    Memory Techniques 394
Learning How to Learn   395

Language   398
Vocabulary   398
A CLOSER LOOK   Thinking and Joking   400
Grammar   400
Pragmatics   402
    Code-Switching 403
Nonstandard English   404
Learning a Second Language   406

Measuring Cognitive Development   408
Achievement Tests   408
A CLOSER LOOK   Test Construction   409
Aptitude Tests   410
    Intelligence Tests 410
A CLOSER LOOK   The Gifted Child   412

Chapter 14   The School Years: Psychosocial Development   419

The Three Theories and Middle Childhood   420
Psychoanalytic Theory   420
Learning Theory   421
    Social Learning Theory 422
Cognitive Theory   423

Social Cognition   424
Understanding Others   424
Self-Understanding   426
    Learned Helplessness 426
    Developing Positive Self-Esteem 427
The Peer Group   428
    The Society of Children 430
    Friendship 431
    The Rejected Child 433

Moral Development   435
Thinking about Right and Wrong   435
    Kohlberg's Stages of Moral Development 435
    Customs and Principles 437
Moral Behavior   438
    Prosocial Behavior 438

Problems and Challenges   440
The Expanding Social World   440

Socioeconomic Status   441
Problems in the Family   442
    Divorce 443
A CLOSER LOOK   Custody and Visitation   445
    Children in Single-Parent Households 446
    Blended Families 447
    Maternal Employment 449
Coping with Stress   451
    Competence 452
    The School 452
    Social Support 453
RESEARCH REPORT   The Children of Kauai   454

Part V   Adolescence   459

Chapter 15   Adolescence: Physical Development   461

The Stormy Decade?   462
Psychoanalytic Theory   463
A More Balanced View   465

Puberty   466
Physical Growth   467
    Sequence of Growth 468
    Nutrition 470
Sexual Growth   471
    Changes in Sex Organs 471
    Secondary Sex Characteristics 471
RESEARCH REPORT   Menarche and Self-Concept   472
A CLOSER LOOK   Body Image   474
The Timing of Puberty   474
    Factors Affecting When Puberty Occurs 475
Gender Differences in Sex Drive   476
    Masturbation 478

Storm and Stress: Who, When, and Why?   478
Early and Late Puberty   478
    Early-Maturing Girls 478
    Late-Maturing Boys 479
Boys' Problems, Girls' Problems   480
A CLOSER LOOK   Delinquency   482
A CLOSER LOOK   Anorexia Nervosa and Bulimia   484

Chapter 16   Adolescence: Cognitive Development   489

Adolescent Thought   490

Development of Scientific Reasoning 491
Logic in Other Domains 493
   True, False, or Impossible to Judge? 493
Piaget Reevaluated 495
A CLOSER LOOK Implications for Education 496

Adolescent Egocentrism 497
Fantasies and Fables 499

Moral Development 500
Stages of Moral Development 500
   Kohlberg and His Critics 500
   Conclusion 503

Decision-Making: Two Contemporary Issues 503
Sexual Behavior 504
   Sexually Transmitted Disease 505
   Adolescent Pregnancy 505
   Possible Explanations 506
Adolescent Drug Use 508
   Why Do Adolescents Use Drugs? 510
Helping Adolescents Find Answers 510

Chapter 17 Adolescence: Psychosocial Development 515

Identity 516
Identity Statuses 517
   Research on Identity Status 519
A CLOSER LOOK The Rite of Passage 520

Social Influences on Identity 521
   Identity in Modern Societies 522

Friends and Family 524
The Role of Peers 525
   Friendship 526
   Peer Groups 526
   Boys and Girls Together 528
Parental Influence 530
   Parenting Styles 531

Special Problems 533
Psychosomatic Disease 533
Sexual Abuse 534
   Typical Abuse 535
   Consequences of Abuse 536
   Prevention 537
Adolescent Suicide 539
   Contributing Factors 539
   Warning Signs 542

Jobs and Careers 543
Career Selection 543
   Girls and Careers 545

Conclusion 546

Glossary 551
Bibliography 567
Acknowledgments 607
Name Index 611
Subject Index 619

The Developing Person
Through Childhood and Adolescence

Introduction

Chapter 1

To be what we are, and to become what we are capable of becoming, is the only end of life.

Robert Louis Stevenson

All cases are unique, and very similar to others.

T. S. Eliot
The Cocktail Party

The Study of Human Development
The Three Domains
The Context of Development
David's Story: Domains and Systems at Work

Three Controversies
Nature or Nurture?
Continuity or Discontinuity?
Deficit or Difference?

The Scientific Method
Naturalistic Observation
The Experiment
The Interview
The Case Study
Designing Developmental Research

A Look at the History and Ethics of the Study of Children
Scientific Child Study
Ethics and Values

Chapter 1

Often we are aware of our lives and those of others only as a series of points in time, like snapshots, moments that are, for a myriad of reasons, particularly important or memorable for each of us. But how do we come to an understanding of all the events and interactions of our lives that lead us to becoming who we are and to behaving in the ways that we do? To understand the physical, intellectual, and emotional capacities of the three children pictured here, for example, a social scientist studying development would be interested in their genetic inheritance, their ages, their socioeconomic background, their relationship with their parents and with the culture into which they were born. Topics such as these and those that follow are the subject of developmental psychology, the field of study introduced by this chapter and examined in this text.

What effect can a person's physical characteristics have on his or her intellectual and social development?

Individuals and cultures vary in the pace and patterns of development that are considered normal for them. What are some of the reasons for the differences that are found?

What methods do researchers use to study the development of individuals, both at particular points in time and throughout the life span?

In what specific ways do characteristics of the larger society affect the lives of individuals?

What are some of the ethical questions that arise when people, especially children, are the subject of research?

David, my brother's son, is 17 now. Like most other boys his age, he is developing in typically adolescent ways. Self-conscious about his body, he lifts weights to develop his slight build. As a junior in high school and a bright student, he is looking forward to going to college, and gives a good deal of thought to selecting the one that will be right for him. A late-bloomer socially, he looks at females in general with new interest, but for one reason or another remains aloof from most of the girls in his classes.

In these and many other ways, David's physical, intellectual, and social development is much like that of the typical children and adolescents we will encounter throughout this book. In one very basic way, however, David is not typical. He began life severely handicapped, with little hope even for survival, let alone for a life approaching normality.

Although most of this book is about "normal" development—that is, development that follows the usual patterns of growth and change—we will begin with David's story for two reasons. First, the extremity of his handicaps and the extent of his triumphs over them highlight the central issues and concerns of the study of human development. Second, David's story demonstrates what the study of human development is about: using our understanding of human growth to help the developing person fulfill his or her potential.

Before looking more closely at David, we need to explain what development means and what the study of it involves.

The Study of Human Development

Briefly, *the study of human development is the study of how people change over time.* Like all scientists, developmentalists seek to understand and objectively describe the phenomena they study. But they are motivated by another goal as well: to help people develop to their fullest capacity. In the course of this endeavor developmentalists study people at all periods of life, and look at all kinds of change—simple growth, radical transformations, improvements and declines. One of their fundamental quests is to identify those circumstances that enhance development and those that diminish it. While a developmental perspective is valid at all points in the life span, most of the interest and research in the field has been on development from conception and infancy through adolescence, that is, on the years that have traditionally been regarded as the "formative" period of life. It is this particular part of the life span that is the focus of this book.

The Three Domains

To make it easier to study, human development is often separated into three domains: the **physical domain,** including body changes and motor skills; the **cognitive domain,** including intellect, thought processes, and language; and the **psychosocial domain,** including emotions, personality, and relationships with other people (see Figure 1.1).

All three domains are important at every age. For instance, understanding an infant involves studying his or her physical well-being, curiosity, and temperament, as well as dozens of other aspects of physical, cognitive, and psychosocial development. Similarly, to understand an adolescent, we consider physical changes that mark the transition from the body of a child to that of an adult; intellectual development that leads to thinking about moral issues and future goals; and the emerging patterns of friendship and courtship that prepare for the intimate relationships of adulthood. Each of these domains is affected by the other two: whether or not an

Figure 1.1 *The division of development into three domains makes it easier to study, but we must remember that very few factors belong exclusively to one domain or another. Development is not piecemeal but holistic: each aspect of development is related to all three domains.*

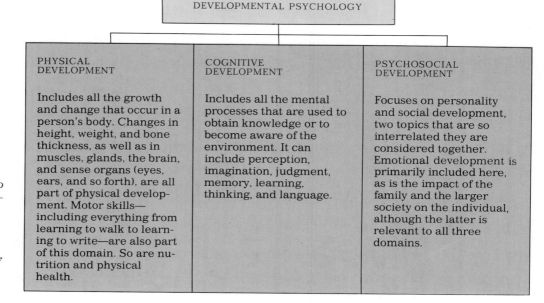

DEVELOPMENTAL PSYCHOLOGY

PHYSICAL DEVELOPMENT

Includes all the growth and change that occur in a person's body. Changes in height, weight, and bone thickness, as well as in muscles, glands, the brain, and sense organs (eyes, ears, and so forth), are all part of physical development. Motor skills—including everything from learning to walk to learning to write—are also part of this domain. So are nutrition and physical health.

COGNITIVE DEVELOPMENT

Includes all the mental processes that are used to obtain knowledge or to become aware of the environment. It can include perception, imagination, judgment, memory, learning, thinking, and language.

PSYCHOSOCIAL DEVELOPMENT

Focuses on personality and social development, two topics that are so interrelated they are considered together. Emotional development is primarily included here, as is the impact of the family and the larger society on the individual, although the latter is relevant to all three domains.

Figure 1.2 *This photo reflects the influence of all three domains. While the physical changes of puberty are behind the development of this boy's biceps, the culture's emphasis on masculine strength is behind his urge to display them. At the same time, the increased self-consciousness that is part of adolescent cognitive development was revealed by the question the boy asked when he first saw this photo: "Is my nose really that big?"*

infant is well-nourished, for instance, may well affect the baby's learning ability and social experiences. For many adolescents, their perception of their bodies—the way they *think* their bodies look—affects their eating and exercise habits, and these, in turn, affect their physical health and their emotional and social development.

Indeed, no moment of life can be fully understood without considering all three domains. The constant interaction and overlapping among the domains means that, although different aspects of development are sometimes studied piece by piece, human development is conceptualized as **holistic,** that is, as an integrated whole. Similarly, while the study of development is pursued by researchers from a variety of academic disciplines—including biology, education, and psychology—all agree that the field of human development is an interdisciplinary one.

The Context of Development

Until recently, the focus of developmental study was primarily on the individual. In the past ten years, this narrow focus has widened markedly. We now are much more aware of how the individual is affected by, and affects, myriads of other individuals and groups of individuals, and also how the individual is shaped by social forces such as history, culture, politics, and economics.

The Ecological, or Systems, Approach   This broader approach to understanding development is sometimes called an **ecological approach,** for, just as the naturalist looking at a flower or a squirrel needs to study the ecosystem that supports that plant or animal, a developmentalist needs to look at the ecosystem in which the human being seeks to thrive. The systems that support human development can be depicted as occurring at four levels, each nested within the next (Bronfenbrenner, 1979; Bronfenbrenner and Crouter, 1983):

1. *the microsystem:* the immediate systems, such as the family and the classroom, that affect the individual's daily life;

2. the *mesosystem:* the interlocking systems, such as parent-teacher relations, that link one microsystem to another;

3. *the exosystem:* neighborhood and community structures (including newspapers, television, and government agencies) that affect the functioning of the smaller systems;

4. *the macrosystem:* the overarching patterns of culture, politics, the economy, and so forth.

Another name for this multifaceted way of looking at development is the **systems approach,** a term that highlights the interaction between and among various elements in each system (Sameroff, 1983). Consider this approach in the study of the family, for example. Not too long ago, child psychologists looking at family influences focused almost exclusively on how mothers affect their children (Sigel et al., 1984). Now that researchers have broadened their study of the family, they have found that fathers are as influential as mothers (Lamb, 1982) and that brothers and sisters and grandparents can be powerful shaping forces as well (Lamb and Sutton-Smith, 1982; Kornhaber and Woodward, 1981). Further, they now acknowledge that each child influences the family's development just as the family affects the child's (Bell and Harper, 1977; Lerner and Spanier, 1978; Maccoby and Martin, 1983).

A systems approach also provides insight into the ways the larger systems of society affect the smaller systems. Thus the interaction within a family is affected by the male and female roles prevalent in the culture, by the national and regional economic picture and its impact on employment, by the customs and laws governing divorce, and so on. A period of high inflation, such as that of the 1970s, may affect family stability, which in turn may contribute to an increase in the divorce rate and a decrease in the birth rate, with a variety of repercussions for individual family members. The reverse may also be true: a high divorce rate leads to more maternal employment, which, in turn, may affect the economy.

Figure 1.3 *As cross-cultural comparisons reveal, even a family interaction as simple as game playing can be affected by a society's larger systems. For example, three generations getting together to enjoy a game of cards is much more common among the Japanese than among Americans because the intergenerational ties, socially and geographically, are closer in Japan.*

David's Story: Domains and Systems at Work

To better understand the interaction of the three domains, as well as the larger systems that support, direct, or hinder development, let us return to David. David's story begins with an event that seems clearly from the physical domain. In the fourth week of his prenatal life, his mother contracted rubella (German measles), a disease that almost always causes physical damage to a developing embryo, sometimes causing devastating physical handicaps, and sometimes causing more subtle learning problems (Hardy, 1973), (see the Closer Look on rubella, page 106).

The Early Years: Heartbreaking Handicaps, Slow Progress In David's case, major problems were obvious at birth. David was born with a life-threatening heart defect and thick cataracts covering both eyes. Other damage caused by the virus became apparent as time went on, including minor malformations of the thumbs, feet, jaw and teeth, and brain injury.

From a systems perspective, the larger medical and political systems had already had a major impact. Had David been born a decade later, the development and widespread use of the rubella vaccine would probably have prevented his mother's contracting the disease. On the other hand, had he been born a few years earlier, the medical technology that saved his life would not have been available.

In fact, heart surgery in the first days of life was successful, and it was thought that David would have at least a few years of life. However, surgery to open a channel around one of the cataracts failed, causing damage that completely blinded the eye.

It soon became apparent that David's physical handicaps fostered cognitive and psychosocial liabilities as well. Not only did his blindness make it impossible for him to learn by looking at his world, but his parents overprotected him to the point that he spent almost all his early months in their arms or in his crib. An analysis of the family system would have revealed that David's impact on his family, and their effect on him, were harmful in many ways. Like most parents of seriously impaired infants (Featherstone, 1980), David's parents felt guilt, anger, and despair; they were initially unable to make constructive plans to foster normal development.

Luckily, the larger social system helped rescue David and his family. The first step occurred when a teacher from the Kentucky School for the Blind visited David's home and gave his parents some much-needed encouragement and advice. They were told to stop blaming themselves for David's condition and to stop overprotecting him because of it. If David was going to learn about his world, he was going to have to explore it. To this end, it was suggested that, rather than confining David to a crib or playpen, his parents should provide him with a large rug for a play area. Whenever he crawled off the rug, they were to say "No" and place him back on in the middle of it, thus enabling him to use his sense of touch to learn where he could explore safely without bumping into walls or furniture. David's mother dedicated herself to this and the many other tasks that various specialists suggested, including exercising his twisted feet and cradling him frequently in her arms as she sang lullabies to provide extra tactile and auditory stimulation.

Figure 1.4 *The support system comes easily into play when the new baby is physically perfect and temperamentally easy, as this infant seems to be. However, when an infant is handicapped or difficult, genuine help from friends, neighbors, and community agencies can make the difference between parents who are unable to cope and those who do what is necessary to help the child.*

His father helped too, taking over much of the housework and care of the two older boys, who were 2 and 4 when David was born. When he found an opportunity to work in Boston, he took it, partly because the Perkins School for the Blind had just begun an experimental program for blind toddlers and their mothers. At Perkins, David's mother learned specific methods for developing physical and language skills in multihandicapped children, and she, in turn, taught the techniques to David's father and brothers. Every day the family spent hours rolling balls, doing puzzles, and singing with David.

Thus the family system and the educational system collaborated to help young David develop his physical and cognitive skills. However, progress was slow. It became painfully apparent that rubella had damaged much more than his eyes and heart, for at age 3, David could neither talk, nor chew solid food, nor use the toilet, nor coordinate his fingers well, nor even walk normally. An IQ test showed him to be severely mentally retarded. Fortunately, although 72 percent of 3-year-olds with rubella syndrome have hearing defects (Chess et al., 1971), David's hearing was normal. However, the only intelligible sounds he made mimicked the noises of the buses and trucks that passed by the house.

At age 4, David said his first word, "Dada." Open-heart surgery corrected the last of his heart damage, and an operation brought partial vision to his remaining eye. While sight in that eye was far from perfect, David could now recognize his family by sight as well as by sound, and could look at picture books. By age 5, when the family returned to Kentucky, further progress was obvious: he no longer needed diapers or baby food.

David's fifth birthday occurred in 1972, just when the idea that the education of severely handicapped children could take place in school rather than at home was beginning to be accepted. David's parents found four schools that would accept him and enrolled him in all of them. He attended two schools for victims of cerebral palsy: one had morning classes, and the other—forty miles away—afternoon classes. (David ate lunch in the car with his mother on the daily trip.) On Fridays these schools were closed, so he attended a school for the mentally retarded, and on Sunday he spent two hours in church school, his first experience with "mainstreaming"—the then new idea that children with special needs should be educated with normal children.

Middle Childhood: Heartening Progress By age 7, David's intellectual development had progressed to the point considered adequate for the normal educational system. In some skills, he was advanced; he could multiply and divide in his head. He entered first grade in a public school, one of the first severely handicapped children to be mainstreamed. However, he was far from a normal first-grader, for rubella continued to have an obvious impact on his physical, cognitive, and social development. His motor skills were poor (among other things, he had difficulty controlling a pencil); he was legally blind even in his "good" eye, and his social skills were seriously deficient (he pinched people he didn't like and cried and laughed at inappropriate times).

During the next several years, David's cognitive development proceeded rapidly. By age 11, he had skipped a year and was a fifth-grader. He could read with a magnifying glass—at the eleventh-grade level—and was labeled "intellectually gifted" according to tests of verbal and math skills. At home he began to learn a second language and to play the violin. In both areas, he proved to have extraordinary auditory acuity and memory.

David's greatest problem was in the psychosocial domain. Schools generally ignore the social skills of mainstreamed children (Gottlieb and Leyser, 1981), and David's experience was no exception. For instance, David was required to sit on the sidelines during most physical-education classes, and to stay inside during most recess periods. Without a chance to experience the normal give-and-take of schoolboy play, David remained more childish than his years. His classmates were not helped to understand his problems, and some teased him because he still looked and acted "different."

David had one advantage that many handicapped children do not. He had two older brothers who treated him normally, playing with him, fighting with him, and protecting him. At one point, David desperately wanted to play basketball, so his brothers took him out to their backyard hoop and showed him the basics. He was not very good, but his enthusiasm was high, and he eagerly joined an after-school basketball program at the Y, which was advertised as "just for fun, not for competition—anyone can participate." On the first day, however, the other kids teased David, calling him a "retard," and the coach asked that David not come back because, he said, he might injure himself.

Adolescence and Beyond: New Problems, New Hopes Because of David's problems with outsiders and classmates, his parents decided to send him to a special school when he was ready for junior high. In the Kentucky School for the Blind, his physical, cognitive, and psychosocial development all advanced: David learned to wrestle and swim, mastered algebra with large-print books, and made friends whose vision was as bad or even worse than his.

As this book goes to press, David's severe physical and cognitive problems are a thing of the past. Doctors no longer doubt that he will survive to adulthood, and are helping to improve the quality of his future life: he now has an artificial eye in place of the blind one; he wears a back brace to help correct his posture; and he recently had surgery to correct his misaligned jaw. Teachers no longer doubt that David will be able to cope, intellectually, in the normal world, and he takes some classes at the regular high school to supplement the education at his special school.

His family delights in him, appreciating his many talents. Notably, he is the most musical family member (he plays with a group that makes electronically synthesized music), and he has a gift for speaking foreign languages (when the family spent a year in Germany, David's vocabulary and accent developed faster than anyone else's). In fact, the very success of David's life allows David and his parents to bicker about such things as the cleanliness of his hair and the carelessness of his homework, much as other parents and adolescent boys do.

However, David's psychosocial development is still a problem. For instance, his poor vision makes him inclined to come very close to people he is talking with, perhaps putting his arm around them to draw them nearer—a behavior that causes most adolescents and many adults to draw back. He continues to be hindered by an educational system that rarely teaches social skills (in an English class in the regular high school, the teacher let him interrupt and "correct" her and the other students because she was "making allowances," even though she had been told to treat him like a normal student). He is also affected by the adolescent subculture, which treats even minor physical blemishes as serious defects. Consequently, David is missing many normal adolescent experiences with peers.

Thus, in looking at David's life, we can see how the domains and systems interact to affect development, both positively and negatively. We can also see the impor-

Figure 1.5 *Adolescence is a time when acceptance by peers seems of particular importance. Teenagers who are liked and respected are likely to develop a healthy self-concept. On the other hand, teenagers who are continually belittled and rejected—especially for characteristics over which they have no control—may develop a poor self-image and also be deprived of opportunities to develop important social skills.*

tance of research and application of developmental principles. For example, without research that demonstrated the importance of sensory stimulation to an infant's development, David's parents might not have been taught how to keep his young mind actively learning. Nor would David have been educated in schools had not the previous efforts of hundreds of developmental scientists proved that schools could provide effective teaching even for severely handicapped children. David might instead have led an overly sheltered and restricted life, as many children born with David's problems once did. Indeed, many children with David's initial level of disability formerly spent their lives in institutions.

And what of David's future? One goal of the study of development is to predict its future course. If we look again at domains and systems, we have reason to be optimistic. As David reaches adulthood, the various systems are likely to be supportive. Certainly his family will continue to help him, and the laws of the land now safeguard his right to a normal life, in college, employment, housing, and the like.

However, in predicting anyone's future or interpreting anyone's past, we must remember that each person is a unique individual, who is uniquely affected by, and affects, the constellation of systems that impinges on his or her development. Thus the most important factor in David's past successes may have been David himself, for his determination, stubbornness, and stoic courage helped him weather the physical trauma of repeated surgery and the psychological devastation of social rejection. While thousands of scientists, dozens of teachers, and both parents deserve to be proud of David's accomplishments, the one who should be most proud is David himself. In the final analysis, more than anyone else, David is responsible for his future.

Three Controversies

As David's case makes abundantly clear, the study of development requires taking into account the interplay of the physical, cognitive, and psychosocial domains, and the effects of familial, cultural, political, and economic forces. Not surprisingly, assessing the relative impact of all of these factors is no simple matter. In fact, developmentalists often find themselves on one side or another of three controversies that have been debated since the study of development began.

Nature or Nurture?

The **nature-nurture controversy,** also known as the heredity-environment controversy, is the central dispute of the study of human development. It is the continuing debate over whether the individual's various traits and characteristics are influenced more by inborn factors or by experience.

Nature refers to the range of traits, capacities, and limitations that each person inherits genetically from his or her parents at the moment of conception. Body type, eye color, and inherited diseases are obvious examples. Nature also includes those inherited traits, such as athletic ability or memory, that appear after a certain amount of maturation has occurred.

Nurture refers to all the environmental influences that come into play after conception, beginning with the mother's health during pregnancy and running through all one's experience with the outside world—in the family, the school, the community, and the culture at large. Nurture also includes all learning, from the obvious learning in classrooms to the less obvious, but equally powerful, learned patterns of social interaction.

Thus the nature-nurture question, in its broadest form, becomes, How do individuals develop into the people they are? Are a person's characteristics and behaviors determined by genes, or are they the result of the myriad experiences and influences that occur after conception? Of course, no developmentalist believes that these questions can be answered with a simple nature or nurture answer. Both nature and nurture are essential to development: the interaction between them is the crucial factor.

However, the controversy over the relative importance of nature and nurture (or heredity and environment, or maturation and learning) continues because it is often difficult to prove which is more responsible for a particular developmental change. David's facility with words could be innate, an inherited verbal strength that was unaffected by the rubella virus. (Suggestive evidence for this possibility

Figure 1.6 *Most subway commuters spend the waiting time watching others, chatting, or impatiently checking for the train, but this family is obviously different. Why? Is it a genetic tendency that makes them a family of nearsighted readers, or is it nurture—a family culture that encourages intellectual pursuits and discourages "impolite staring," "idle talk," or "time-wasting"?*

comes from his father's and brother's verbal-ability SAT scores, which were in the 99th percentile.) On the other hand, David's verbal ability could be largely the result of nurture: he may have focused on language because the verbal encouragement he received from his family and the many adults who knew him offered a counterbalance to the uncertainty of his social world.

In some instances, the practical implications of one's answer to the nature-nurture controversy are enormous. For example, although boys and girls in elementary school show the same math aptitude, beginning at about the eighth grade, the average mathematical achievement of boys is higher than that of girls, a difference that continues throughout high school, college, and adult life (Maccoby and Jacklin, 1974; Benbow and Stanley, 1980). Is this discrepancy a result of maturation? Does some sex-based difference in brain development during adolescence make it harder for girls to grasp the concepts of advanced math (Waber, 1976)? Or does the discrepancy arise from experience? Perhaps girls somehow learn that mathematical achievement is not "feminine" and therefore shy away from it (Sherman, 1982). Or perhaps parents expect less of their daughters in math and thus lower their daughters' expectations of themselves (Entwisle and Baker, 1983).

If, in fact, the difference in the math ability of adolescent males and females is the result of nature, it is foolish and frustrating to expect young women to do as well in math as young men. On the other hand, if the difference is the result of learning, we are wasting precious mathematical talent by not encouraging girls to develop their full math potential.

With many nature-nurture questions, the differences between individuals make the issue even more complex: genetic factors might play a major role in one person's level of achievement, while learning might be primarily responsible for the same ability in another. One girl might not have the intellectual capacity to master trigonometry as fast as her brother can. Her younger sister, on the other hand, might have more aptitude than the brother, yet might do less well because, say, she feels uncomfortable excelling at what she perceives to be a "masculine" pursuit. Thus neither sister does well in math, but in one case the reason is largely nature, in the other, largely nurture.

Continuity or Discontinuity?

How would you describe human growth? Would you say we develop gradually and continually, the way a seedling becomes a tree? Or do you think we undergo sudden changes, like a caterpillar becoming a butterfly?

Many developmental researchers emphasize the **continuity** of development. They believe that there is a continual progression from the beginning of life to the end. Accomplishments that may seem abrupt, such as a baby's first step, can actually be viewed as the final event in weeks of growth and practice. In the same way, learning to talk or read, or the physical changes that occur in adolescence, can be seen as gradual processes rather than as abrupt changes.

Other theorists emphasize the **discontinuity** of development. They see growth occurring in identifiable stages, each with distinct problems and characteristics. Terms such as the "terrible twos" or "teenage rebellion" reflect the popular version of the stage concept. Those who focus on stages of development believe that, at certain times during life, a person moves from one level to another, as though climbing a flight of stairs. Often a pivotal event, such as beginning to walk, learning to talk, or beginning the sexual changes of puberty, signals the beginning of a new stage. Such events are thought to change the individual quite suddenly and in many specific ways, leading to new patterns of thought and behavior.

Figure 1.7 *Development can be envisioned* (a) *as a continuous, steady progression or* (b) *as a series of distinct stages, separated by transitional periods during which rapid change occurs.*

(a)

The stage view of development has been the dominant one in the twentieth century. Indeed, this textbook, like most of its kind, reflects the stage view, at least implicitly, by treating development in terms of distinct periods—infancy, early childhood, middle childhood, and adolescence. There is, of course, good reason for this organization. To begin with, physical maturation occurs according to a biologically determined timetable, with the result that children of roughly the same age have many physical abilities and limitations in common. As we shall see, children also share age-related patterns in the way they think about their world and about themselves. Correspondingly, according to many theorists, children at various ages also experience similar kinds of psychosocial needs and conflicts.

Recently, however, a number of developmentalists have cautioned against an overemphasis on distinct stages of development. As Flavell (1982) expresses it, strict stage views "gloss over differences, inconsistencies, irregularities, and other real but complexity-adding features." Although it would be convenient to approach human development as a "neat 'ages and stages' developmental story," Flavell notes that actual development is much more complex, for children grow in varied ways—sometimes in sudden leaps and bounds, sometimes step by step, and sometimes with such continuity that they seem not to change at all.

As with the nature-nurture controversy, the implications of stage theory can have profound practical consequences. Consider adolescence, for example. At the moment, in the eyes of the law, minors are to be treated quite differently from adults. In every state, they are prohibited from purchasing alcohol and cigarettes, and, in some states, from engaging in sexual intercourse. At the same time, they are treated more leniently than adults when arrested for stealing, carrying a gun, or selling illegal drugs. If convicted, their sentences are lighter; if they are under 16, they escape the adult court and prison system entirely. The premise behind this legal stance is that adolescence is a stage of greater vulnerability and less responsibility than adulthood. As the Closer Look on page 14 makes clear, however, societal stage views of adolescence, and of childhood, are as much a product of cultural assumptions as they are of biological imperatives.

(b)

Deficit or Difference?

Is there one pattern of human development that is the usual, normal one? Or are there as many paths of development as there are individuals?

The idea that there was one universal pattern was held by many of the first scientists interested in development. Consequently, a number of early research projects were concerned with determining what constituted "normal" development. They began with a large group of children of various ages, tested them on one characteristic or another, and averaged the results. This average was used as the **norm**, that is, the typical case. Norms were established for everything from walking without holding onto something to speaking in two-word sentences, from reading simple words to falling in love for the first time (e.g., McCarthy, 1954; Bayley, 1935, 1955; Gesell, 1926; Gesell and Ilg, 1946; Hall, 1904).

One of the most influential of these researchers was Arnold Gesell (1926), who tested over 500 children between the ages of 3 months and 5 years to find the norms for various behaviors and abilities. Among other things, Gesell determined that, by age 3, the average child can be "trusted with breakables . . . such as carrying china, glassware, or grandmother's spectacles from one part of the house to another. A moderate capacity in this direction is, therefore, characteristic of three-year-old maturity." Gesell also found that 3-year-olds use plurals and pronouns correctly, draw circles, put on shoes (lacing them at age 4 and tying them at age 5) and perform dozens of other normative behaviors.

The establishment of norms such as these led, quite logically, to another idea—that children who did not follow the usual path were abnormal and probably deficient or deprived in some way. If a child's development differed from the norms, the assumption was that something must be wrong, either in the child, the family, or the culture.

Recently, however, differences have increasingly come to be seen as alternative paths of development rather than inferior ones. Contemporary developmentalists are much more likely to recognize the unique characteristics of each child, each family, each culture, than they are to stress the universal generalities that apply to all of them. The 2-year-old who carries breakables or the 4-year-old who drops them may both be developing perfectly well.

A CLOSER LOOK   **Stages in History**

Whenever we take a stage view of development, we should bear in mind that the stages themselves are, to a certain degree, cultural creations. We tend to think of the stages of childhood and adolescence as inevitable consequences of biological maturation, but at various times, in various cultures, these stages have been nonexistent, or barely recognizable as such. For example, the idea that childhood is a tender stage of life, and that children need protection from hard work, sexual knowledge, and harsh punishment, has not always been with us. Indeed, Philippe Ariès (1962) contends that childhood as we think of it was unknown in Europe throughout much of history. Children were cared for until they could take care of themselves—at about age 7—and then they entered the adult world.

This phenomenon was most apparent during the Middle Ages, when children dressed as adults, drank with them, and worked beside them at home and in the fields. Children could be married, employed, crowned as monarchs, or hanged as thieves. Evidence for this comes from church documents, prison records, and the detailed descriptions of the lives of the very privileged. For instance, King Louis XIV of France became king at age 5 and played sexual games with his nursemaids throughout childhood. Many of the folktales of earlier times were designed to entertain adults as well as children, and many children's games were played by people of all ages. The distinction we now make between activities that are appropriate for children and those appropriate for adults did not exist.

While some educators and clergy began to see childhood as a special stage several centuries ago, legal recognition of childhood and of the special needs of children was a long time in coming. Not until the twentieth century were laws passed to regulate child labor, mandate education for all children, and delineate parental responsibility for minors. (Indeed, the first cases of child abuse in the United States were brought to court in the late 1860s under statutes protecting domestic animals, because laws pertaining specifically to children did not exist.)

Similarly, adolescence as a separate stage of life— especially as a stage in which the individual is supposed to develop a sense of independence—is essentially a phenomenon of the twentieth-century industrial nation. In many preindustrial societies, puberty marked the beginning of adulthood. (The transition from child to adult was usually accomplished through a single initiation ceremony.) By contrast, in the United States, before the twentieth century, teenagers were expected to labor like

(a)

Although there are obvious class differences reflected in the historical illustrations shown here, they clearly reflect the idea of the children as miniaturized adults— clothed and consorting in the manner of their elders or working full-time as day laborers. Today the specialness of childhood is taken for granted, and the child's particular needs are

adults, and, if they still lived at home, to be obedient like children. Their parents made them pay for their room and board, told them what to wear and whom to date, insisted on respectful behavior, and accepted no "back talk" (Kett, 1977).

Discipline and dependence, not rebellion and "self-discovery," characterized the life of most American teenagers until they moved away to begin their own families, an event that often occurred in the mid-teens for girls, and the mid-twenties for boys. In the early twentieth century, middle-class teenage boys were granted some measure of independence (they could, at least, regulate

(b)

(c)

the focus of much parental and scientific attention. Adolescence is a somewhat different story. Although teenagers are recognized as a special population, they are often left in limbo with respect to the opportunities they are provided to develop a sense of responsible independence. Research suggests that adolescents who work part-time during high school have an improved morale as well as a cash supply.

(d)

their own social lives), even if they remained financially dependent on their parents. Middle-class girls and lower-class youth of both sexes attained this measure of freedom even later. Gradually, teenagers' obligation to contribute financially to their parents while still obeying their commands gave way to the current notion that teenagers should make more and more of their own decisions, even while their parents pay for them.

In fact, it was not until the rising affluence of mid-twentieth century brought high-school education, the mobility and privacy afforded by automobiles, the youth-affirming messages of teen music, and the creation of a distinct "youth market" that adolescence became a time for American teenagers to be "understood" rather than held in check (Boxer et al., 1984). These same forces transformed adolescence in other countries as well, with other developed countries experiencing intergenerational conflicts quite similar to those encountered in the United States in the 1960s. Many developing countries are now trying to combat the disrespect and delinquency that economic change and "Americanization" seem to foster (Johnson, 1983; Tesfaye, 1976).

Figure 1.8 *For this 3½-year-old, one advantage of his preschool class will be that someone will soon show him the proper grip for effective scissoring. He will enter first grade with above-average scissors skills, one of the abilities expected of elementary school children. However, those children who do not attend a preschool program or who get little practice with scissors at home may later be judged clumsy, rather than merely lacking in scissoring experience. Similarly, and much more significantly, children whose backgrounds have given them less than average experience in speaking English, playing with other children, or writing the alphabet may be judged deficient rather than merely different.*

One important reason for this shift is that researchers realized that much of the early research on development was done by white, middle-class American researchers, using white, middle-class children as their sample. For instance, most intelligence tests were standardized using the scores of such children (Anastasi, 1982; Hollander, 1982), as were the norms of physical, cognitive, and social development widely disseminated by Gesell. Some researchers even attempted to describe the normal course of development for both sexes on the basis of studies that involved only males (e.g., Kohlberg, 1966).

Not surprisingly, non-Americans, nonwhites, and females were found to be different from white American males. Interpreting these differences as deficiencies has been vigorously challenged in recent years (Myers, 1982; Gilligan, 1982; Guthrie, 1976; Segall, 1980; Hale, 1982; Laosa, 1984). For example, if black children score below average on standard tests of learning ability, it may well be because these tests emphasize the abstract, analytic thinking valued by the white culture and neglect other, possibly more creative and expressive, modes of thought that appear to be more typical of the black culture (Hale, 1982). Or if females score lower than males on a particular series of tests of moral reasoning (Kohlberg, 1963), it may be that females, socialized to be nurturing and concerned with others, tend, more than males do, to concentrate on the practical, humane issues rather than on the abstract principles that are more highly rated by the test (Gilligan, 1982). Similarly, if personality tests suggest that Asian-American children are withdrawn, dependent, and passive, it may be because these children are developing the characteristics fostered by families and subcultures that value deference, family loyalties, and serenity much more than the outgoing, individualistic, assertiveness encouraged by many families of Western European ancestry (Endo et al., 1980; Super and Harkness, 1982). Indeed, the realization that behavior that is desirable and healthy in one culture might be rude and disruptive in another has broadened the scope and the direction of developmental research, and led to an appreciation of cultural and individual differences (Laosa, 1984). This is a trend welcomed by developmentalists, both men and women, of every color and background. It has led to more flexible patterns of teaching in the classroom (as David experienced when he entered the mainstream of public education), and to less judgmental interpretations of children who are atypical.

The Scientific Method

As the above controversies show, developmentalists are no different from other people; they have opinions, too, opinions that are partly the result of their own background and biases. However, as scientists, they are committed to consider insights and evidence from the available research before they draw conclusions and to change their view when new data indicate they should. When doing research, they are expected to follow a general procedural model often referred to as the **scientific method,** which helps them overcome whatever biases they have. Procedures and techniques, not theories and assumptions, are what make the study of development a science (Scarr, 1985).

The scientific method involves four basic steps, and sometimes a fifth:

1. *Formulate a research question:* Build on previous research, or on one of the theories of development, or on personal observation and reflection, and pose a question that has relevance for the study of development.

2. *Develop a hypothesis.* Reformulate the question into a hypothesis, which is a specific prediction that can be tested.

3. *Test the hypothesis.* Design and conduct a specific research project that will provide evidence about the truth or falsity of the hypothesis. As the Research Report on the following page indicates, the research design often includes many specific elements that help make the test of the hypothesis a valid one.

4. *Draw conclusions.* Formulate conclusions directly from the results of the test, avoiding general conclusions that are not substantiated by the data.

5. *Make the findings available.* Publishing the results of the test is often the fifth step in the scientific method. In this step, the scientist must describe the test procedures and the resulting data in sufficient detail that other scientists can evaluate the conclusions and, perhaps, **replicate** the test of the hypothesis—that is, repeat it and obtain the same results—or extend it, using a different but related set of subjects or procedures. In this way, the conclusions from each test of every hypothesis accumulate, leading to more definitive and extensive conclusions and generalizations. In this way, science progresses.

Figure 1.9 *The scientific method often reveals the unexpected. Popular wisdom usually blames teenage drinking habits on the youth culture and/or state drinking laws. Scientific research has shown that the most influential factor in adolescents' use or nonuse of alcohol or other drugs is the closeness of their relationship with their parents.*

RESEARCH REPORT   **Ways to Make Research More Valid**

In scientific investigation, there is always the possibility that the researcher's procedures and/or biases can compromise the validity of their findings. Consequently, scientists often take a number of steps to ensure that their research is as valid as possible. Four of them are explained here.

Sample Size

To begin with, in order to make any valid statement about people in general, the scientist must study a group of individuals that is large enough so that a few extreme cases will not distort the picture of the group as a whole. Suppose, for instance, that researchers wanted to know the age at which average American children begin to walk. Since they could not include all 3 million American infants in their study, they would work with a large sample group—*a sample population*—determining the age of walking for each member of the sample and then calculating the average for the group.

The importance of **sample size** can be seen if we assume for the moment that one of the infants in their sample was severely mentally retarded, and did not walk until 24 months. If the sample size were less than ten infants, that one late walker would, relative to the current standard of 12 months, add more than a month to the age when the "average" child was said to walk. However, if the sample were more than 500 children, one abnormally late walker would not change the results by even one day.

Representative Sample

Since the data collected on one group of individuals might not be valid for other people who are different in significant ways, such as gender, ethnic background, and

Why is this child taking her first step now, and not two weeks earlier or two weeks later? Scientific study of thousands of other babies reveals that dozens of factors are relevant, including her genes, her body size, her foot formation, her parents' encouragement, and her diet.

the like, it is important that the sample population be a **representative sample,** that is, a group of subjects who are typical of the general population the researchers wish to learn about. In a study of when the average American infant begins to walk, the sample population should reflect—in terms of sex ratio, economic and ethnic background, and so forth—the entire population of American children. Ideally, other factors might be taken into consideration. For instance, if there is some evidence that first-born children walk earlier than later- or last-born children, then the sample should include a representative sample of each birth order.

There are many ways to test hypotheses. Among the most common are naturalistic observation, laboratory experiments, and interviews. Each has advantages and disadvantages.

Naturalistic Observation

Scientists can test hypotheses by using **naturalistic observation,** that is, by observing people in their natural environments. When observing children, this usually means going to a home, a school, or a playground, and recording the children's behavior and interactions in detail. Typically, the scientist tries to be as unobtrusive as possible, so the children will act as they normally do.

A Naturalistic Study The uses of naturalistic observation, as well as the steps of the scientific method, become clearer with an example. Two scientists, Harvey Ginsberg and Shirley Miller, became interested in the widely held belief that

The importance of representative sampling is revealed by its absence in two studies of age of walking (Gesell, 1926; Shirley, 1933) undertaken in the 1920s. Both studies used a relatively small and unrepresentative sample (all the children were white and most were middle-class), and, consequently, both arrived at a norm that is 3 months later than the current one, which was derived from a much more representative sample.

"Blind" Experimenters

A substantial body of evidence suggests that when experimenters have specific expectations of the outcome of their research, those expectations can affect their perception of the events of the research itself. As much as possible, then, the people who are carrying out the actual testing should be **"blind,"** that is, unaware of the purpose of the research. Suppose one hypothesis is that first-born infants walk sooner than later-borns. Ideally, the examiner who tests the infants' walking ability would not know what the hypothesis is, and would not even know the age or birth order of the toddlers under study.

Experimental Group and Control Group

In order to test a hypothesis adequately, researchers must compare two study groups that are similar in every important way except one: they must compare an **experimental group**, which receives some special experimental treatment, and a **control group**, which does not receive the experimental treatment.

Suppose a researcher hypothesized that children who use "walkers" walk earlier than children who spend several hours a day in a playpen. In order to find out if this is true, the researcher would select two representative groups of children and arrange that one group (the experimental group) be placed in walkers for a certain amount of time each day while the other group (the control group) would be put in their playpens for the same length of time. If the infants in the experimental group, in fact, walked *significantly* earlier on average than the infants in the control group, then the hypothesis would be confirmed.

Determining Significance

Whenever researchers find a difference between two groups, they have to consider the possibility that the difference might have occurred purely by chance. For instance, in any group of infants, some would walk relatively early and some relatively late. When the researchers in the "walker versus playpen" study were dividing the sample population into the experimental and control groups, it would have been possible that, by chance, a preponderance of early walkers ended up in one group or the other. To determine whether their results are, in fact, simply the result of chance, researchers use a statistical test, called a test of **significance.** This test takes into account many statistical factors, including the sample size and the average difference between the groups, and yields the *level of significance,* a numerical indication of exactly how unlikely it is that the particular difference occurred by chance. Generally, in order to be called *significant,* the possibility of the results occurring by chance has to be less than one chance in twenty, which is written in decimals as a significance of .05. Often the likelihood of a particular finding's occurring by chance is even rarer, perhaps one chance in a hundred (the .01 level) or one in a thousand (the .001 level).

"males demonstrate a greater willingness to take risks or chances than females" (Ginsberg and Miller, 1982). In reading a famous review of sex differences (Maccoby and Jacklin, 1974), they learned that whether or not males are actually more daring than females is not yet known.

Ginsberg and Miller developed a hypothesis: that preschool and school-age boys take more risks than girls. To give the hypothesis a fair test (one in which there would be ample opportunity for finding evidence against the hypothesis as well as for it), they did a naturalistic study in a place where boys and girls, in roughly equal numbers, would have the opportunity to take various risks.

They chose the San Antonio Zoo, where they watched to see which children would take any of four "risks": riding on the elephants, feeding the animals, petting the burro (a sign said "Careful, he bites"), and climbing up a steep concrete embankment to walk along on a narrow ledge. The researchers sat on a bench, far enough away so that the children were not aware of them, but close enough to keep careful tabs of the sex and approximate age of each child who engaged in any of these "risky" activities.

They found that although boys and girls entered the zoo in almost equal numbers, more than two-thirds of the children who rode the elephant, fed the animals, petted the burro, or climbed the embankment were boys (See Figure 1.10). These sex differences were significant, at the .001 level, which means that there was less than one possibility in a thousand that these sex differences were found only because an unusual sequence of children happened to be observed.

Figure 1.10 *As you can see, the data show that some girls do take risks, but that boys are more likely to take them. Interestingly, the "risks" girls are relatively likely to take are "risks" their parents had to approve, and pay for.*

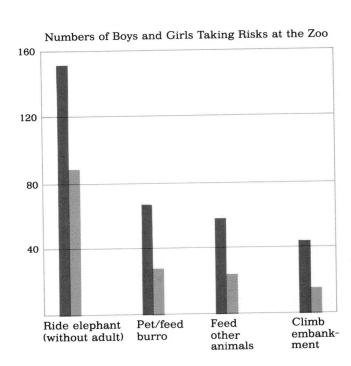

Numbers of Boys and Girls Taking Risks at the Zoo

■ boys
■ girls

Further examination of the results showed that older children took more of these risks than did younger children, but the sex ratio held no matter what the age: more preschool boys, school-age boys, and preadolescent boys were risk-takers than were girls of the same age.

One way to describe these results is to say that there was a **correlation** between sex and risk-taking, as well as between age and risk-taking. Correlation is a statistical measure used to describe the relationship between two variables. It indicates whether or not one variable (e.g., risk-taking) is likely to occur when another variable (e.g., maleness) occurs, or whether a change in one variable (e.g., increasing willingness to take risks) is related to a change in another (e.g., increasing age). For a further explanation of correlation, see the Closer Look on the opposite page.

Limitations of Natural Observation   Naturalistic observation is an excellent method, but it has one main disadvantage. Because the variables in a natural setting are numerous and uncontrolled, it is difficult to pinpoint precisely which of them could explain a particular event. Perhaps the sex differences in risk-taking are the result of biologically governed impulses in males or inhibitions in females.

A CLOSER LOOK   **Correlation: What It Does, and Does Not, Mean**

Correlation is a statistical term that indicates that two variables are somehow related, that is, that one particular variable is likely, or unlikely, to occur when another particular variable does. For instance, there is a correlation between height and weight, because, usually, the taller a person is, the more he or she weighs. There is also a correlation between wealth and education, and perhaps even between springtime and falling in love.

Note that the fact that two variables are correlated does not mean that they are related in every instance. Some tall people weigh less than people of average height; some wealthy people never finished high school; some people fall in love in the depths of winter.

Nor does correlation indicate cause. The correlation between education and wealth does not necessarily imply that more education leads to greater wealth. It may be instead that more wealth leads to greater education, since wealthier people are more likely to be able to afford the expense of college. Or there may be a third variable, perhaps intelligence or family background, that accounts for the level of both income and education.

There are two types of correlation, positive and negative. Whenever one variable changes in the same direction as another variable changes (for example, both increase or both decrease), the correlation is said to be *positive*. All the examples given so far are examples of positive correlation. Thus, when education increases, income tends to increase as well; when education is low, so is income likely to be.

When two variables are inversely related (one increasing while the other decreases), the correlation is said to be *negative*. Snow and summertime, maleness and motherhood, and blue eyes and black hair are negatively correlated.

When there is no relationship between the two variables, the correlation is said to be *zero*. It is hard to think of any two variables that have no relationship to each other at all. Probably the correlation between eye color and age is zero (except in infancy, when many babies have blue eyes), as is the correlation between how much milk you drank yesterday and whether it is raining today (unless seasonal variations in rainfall are related to your thirst).

Correlations can be expressed numerically. They range from plus one (+1.0), the highest positive correlation, to minus one (-1.0), the most negative correlation. Halfway between plus one and minus one is zero, which, as you just learned, indicates no correlation at all.

Correlations are one of the most useful tools in psychology and, at the same time, one of the most often misused. They are useful because knowing how variables are related helps us understand the world we live in. However, as the respected researcher Sandra Scarr (1985) notes, "the psychological world . . . is, a cloud of correlated events to which we as human observers give meaning." Unless we are cautious in giving that meaning, we are likely to seize on one or another particular correlation as an explanation, without looking for other possible explanations. For instance, in the 1960s many psychologists noted the correlation between "broken" homes and maladjustment in children and concluded that single parents necessarily put their children at risk. In the 1980s, psychologists looking at the same kinds of homes (now called single-parent families) note that many children in them do quite well, and that other factors that correlate with such homes (e.g., low income, disrupted education) may be the explanation for children's problems when they occur. The lesson is clear: we need to be very cautious in jumping from the discovery of correlations to conclusions about causes.

The correlation between height and weight is clear in this photo of members of a Polar Bear Club as they pose before their ocean swim in sub-freezing weather. Apparently, there is also a correlation between being a Polar Bear and being heavier than average. Did some members put on weight to insulate themselves from the cold, or did they pick this sport because they were already well-padded? Since correlation indicates nothing about causation, we cannot say why these particular bodies gravitate toward the icy ocean.

Or the explanation may lie with nurture rather than nature. For instance, even at their young age, these children may have been responding to cultural stereotypes of daring heroes and helpless heroines; or perhaps their parents were saying such things as "Be a brave boy, pet the burro" or "Be a good girl and hold my hand; I don't want to lose you." It is even possible that some variable that had little to do with sex influenced the result: for instance, some of the girls may have been wearing shoes with soles too slippery for climbing embankments.

To help solve the problem of sorting out variables and to better establish cause and effect, another method, the laboratory experiment, is sometimes used.

The Experiment

In a **laboratory experiment,** the scientist tests his or her hypothesis in a *controlled* environment, that is, in a setting in which the relevant variables are limited and subject to manipulation by the experimenter. Because the variables are controlled, the link between cause and effect is much clearer than in naturalistic observation.

An Experiment with Newborns In addition to the obvious impact of nutrition, naturalistic observation suggests that factors in the early mother-child interaction also affect children's growth and development. This is most clear in studies of motherless infants raised in institutions (Spitz, 1945; Dennis, 1973). It is also apparent in home-reared children who suffer from psychological dwarfism (Gardner, 1972; Tanner, 1978), a condition in which growth is retarded even though there is no medical abnormality that would slow development. Some investigators have speculated that stress and neglect might cause the child to eat inadequately, even when adequate nutrition is available. Others have suggested that lack of physical stimulation due to not being held and caressed might lower the production of growth hormones.

In an attempt to isolate factors that might account for such instances of slow growth, scientists first studied rats in the laboratory (Schanberg and Kuhn, 1980; Schanberg et al., 1984). One group of mother rats was anesthetized—so that they could nurse their pups but not stimulate them by nuzzling or grooming. Another group of rats had their nipples ligated—so that they could groom their infants but not nurse them. Researchers found that those pups who had had normal physical interaction with their mothers (but were not nursed by them) were close to normal in the production of growth hormones and that those pups who were fed by their mothers, but not nuzzled or groomed, had abnormally low levels.

To further isolate the effects of physical stimulation, some rat pups were separated from their mothers and were either left untouched or were "stroked vigorously on the back and head for 2 hours with a moist, one-inch camel hair paint brush in a matter roughly similar to that used by the mother in grooming the pups" (Schanberg and Kuhn, 1980). After two hours, the levels of growth hormone in the separated and untouched pups averaged only 25 percent that of a control group left with their mothers, while the stroked group overall had a nearly normal level.

This finding was particularly interesting to scientists working with tiny, preterm infants, for whom gaining a few ounces can mean the difference between life and death. Because these infants are deprived of normal mother-infant contact by virtue of being continuously hooked-up to intensive-care machinery, it was thought that they might be responsive to a program of physical stimulation. Accordingly, an interdisciplinary team of scientists (Field et al., 1984) selected forty infants, all born at least a month early and all weighing less than 1,500 grams (about 3 pounds) at birth, and divided them evenly into experimental and control groups. The average weight, length, number of birth complications, and so forth was the same for infants in both groups, and infants in both groups were in the same nursery, given the same care by the same nurses.

The only difference between the groups was the experimental treatment, which consisted of gentle massaging of head, back, and limbs for thirty minutes per day, and rhythmic moving of the infants' arms and legs for fifteen minutes a day. This treatment was carried out for ten days, over a two-week period (weekends were a time of rest for the infants and the experimenter).

At the end of the two-week period, the experimental group had gained an average of 25 grams per day, while the control group had gained only 17 grams per day. Thus the experimental group gained 47 percent more weight than the control group, a difference that was significant at the .001 level. The experimental group also tended to spend more time awake and moving around, and to score higher on a test of maturation given by testers who were "blind" to whether a particular infant was in the control group or the experimental group. Finally, infants in the experimental group were released from the hospital an average of six days earlier than those in the control group, because, in the judgment of their pediatricians, they had reached sufficient maturity and weight to go home.

The scientists then tried to determine why the infants had responded so well to the special handling. Had it stimulated their appetites, thus causing greater food consumption and weight gain, or had it triggered more fundamental body changes that affect the growth rate? Tabulating the amount of food all the infants in both groups had consumed, they found no significant differences between the groups. Thus they concluded that the massage and exercises provoked biochemical processes that promoted growth.

Figure 1.11 *Traditionally, premature infants were kept isolated from all but medical personnel. Because recent research has shown that mothers are more responsive to their premature babies if they hold and touch them soon after birth, many hospitals now encourage contact between new mothers and their premature infants. If the tactile-stimulation experiments described in the text are supported by further research, such interaction will be encouraged for the baby's benefit as well.*

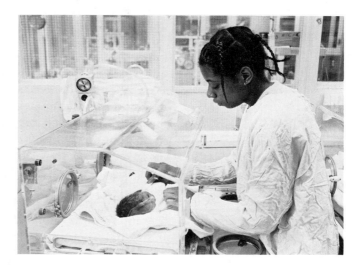

Limitations of Experiments   While the research on the effects of tactile stimulation on infants' growth rate is valuable as an example of the strengths of the experimental approach, it does not reveal two of the limitations that commonly beset experiments with humans.

One of these problems is that, in almost any experiment with people (except, of course, young infants), the subjects are aware that they are being studied and might act differently than they normally would, thereby invalidating the findings. Furthermore, even if the subjects in an experiment behave normally, the carefully controlled situation of an experiment may not readily apply in the much less controlled circumstances of everyday life. As Urie Bronfenbrenner, the leading advocate of the ecological approach reminds us, there are many experiments

> that are elegantly designed but often limited in scope. This limitation derives from the fact that many of these experiments involve situations that are unfamiliar, artificial, and short-lived and that call for unusual behaviors that are difficult to generalize to other settings . . . a variety of approaches are needed if we are to make progress toward the ultimate goal of understanding human development in context. [Bronfenbrenner, 1977]

For this reason, naturalistic observation and laboratory experiments are often used to complement each other. The lack of precision in naturalistic observation is balanced by the control of the laboratory experiment; the artificiality of the laboratory is balanced by the realism of naturalistic observation. Often both methods are combined. For example, a researcher can perform an experiment in a natural setting, or observe, rather than experiment, in a laboratory.

The Interview

In an **interview,** the scientist asks a number of people for information about themselves or for their opinions. This seems to be an easy, quick, and direct research method. However, it is more difficult to get valid interview data than it seems, because the interview is particularly vulnerable to bias, on the part of the interviewer and the interviewee. To begin with, the very phrasing of the interview questions can influence the answers. An interview on the issue of abortion, for instance, might prompt different responses depending on whether it asked about "terminating an unwanted pregnancy" or "taking the life of an unborn child."

In addition, many people who are interviewed give answers that they think the interviewer will want to hear, or that they think will make them look good in the interviewer's eyes, or that will perhaps make them feel good about themselves. Even when people wish to give completely accurate information, their responses may be flawed because their opinion on a particular question varies from day to day, or because their recollection of events is distorted. For example, if you wanted to find out how parents share the household work, whom would you ask? According to one study that asked both parents, fathers generally report doing more of the work than their wives think they do (Condron and Bode, 1982).

The Case Study

The interview is often the heart of a **case study,** which is an intensive study of one individual. Typically, both the person's background and his or her present thinking and actions are reported, often with interviews of parents, teachers, and others who know the individual. Naturalistic observation and standardized tests may furnish additional case-study material.

Case studies can provide a wealth of detail and therefore are rich in possible insights. However, not only are case studies susceptible to the usual problems of the interview, the interpretation of case-study data depends on the wisdom as well as the biases of the interpreter. Even if the interpretation is valid, it may apply only to the particular individual being studied. In general, the case study is not used to do basic research, because no conclusions about people in general can be drawn from a sample size of one.

Designing Developmental Research

Thus, there are many ways to test hypotheses. Researchers can find out what children are like by observing them in natural settings, or by experimenting with them in a laboratory; they can compare one group with another and find out correlations and significant differences; they can interview hundreds of people or study one or two cases in depth.

However, for research to be truly developmental, scientists must discover and describe how people change with time. To learn about the pace and process of change, developmentalists use two basic research designs, cross-sectional and longitudinal.

Cross-Sectional Research The more convenient, and thus more common, way researchers study development is by doing a **cross-sectional** comparison of people of various ages. In this kind of study, groups of people who are different in age but similar in other important ways (such as their level of education, economic status, ethnic background, and so forth) are compared on the characteristic or tendency that is of interest. Any differences on this dimension that exist among the people of one age and the people of another are, presumably, the result of age-related development.

One cross-sectional study (Field et al., 1984) compared infants, toddlers, and preschoolers (average ages, 9, 12, and 24 months) to see if distress at being dropped off at nursery school fluctuated with the child's age. Children in all three groups attended the same all-day nursery school, and came from similar middle-class families of a range of ethnic backgrounds. The ratio of boys to girls was about the same for all three age groups.

Figure 1.12 *Since this preschooler is 3 years old, it is unlikely that he is crying because his mother has just left. More probably, he has just hurt his hand, or lost a toy, or wet his pants.*

An observer, "blind" to the purpose of the study, noted precisely how the children behaved when the parents dropped them off. The results showed definite age differences: the toddlers were significantly more likely than older or younger children to cry, cling, and complain when their parents left.

Presumably, the differences in the behavior of the three groups of children occurred because of their age differences, suggesting that some developmental factor makes toddlers less willing to be parted from their parents than infants or preschoolers are. It might be, for instance, that the memory capacity of these toddlers had matured enough that they realized what their parents' good-byes signified but had not matured enough for them to remember that previous leave-takings were followed by several hours of fun with classmates and teachers. However, in a cross-sectional study, it is always possible that some variable other than age differentiates the groups of children. Perhaps this group of toddlers happened to have several particularly difficult children, or perhaps the toddlers' teachers were not as friendly as the teachers of the younger and older children were, or perhaps one particular child, who happened to be a toddler, was so obviously upset about being left by a parent that all the other toddlers picked up on the emotion and became similarly upset.

Longitudinal Research   To help find out if age, rather than some other personal or situational variable, is the reason for an apparent developmental change, researchers, when it is feasible, study the *same* people over a period of time. This type of research, known as **longitudinal research,** allows information about people at one age to be compared with information about them at another age, thus enabling researchers to find out how those particular people changed with time.

In the study of nursery-school children discussed above, the researchers added a longitudinal component: they reexamined the children in all three groups six months after the initial observation. They found that the relatively docile infants of the first study had become toddlers who were likely to protest at being left, and that those who had been protesting toddlers had, over the six-month period, become less likely to fuss when their parents departed. This longitudinal finding confirms the developmental trends suggested by the cross-sectional research: as children approach their second birthday, they become more likely to cry and cling when their parents leave them in nursery school, and then, after about age 2, they gradually take these separations in stride.

Longitudinal research is particularly useful in studying developmental trends that occur over a long age span. It has produced valuable and sometimes surprising findings on such questions as (1) children's adjustment to divorce (the negative effects linger, especially for school-age and older boys [Wallerstein and Kelly, 1980; Wallerstein, 1984]); (2) the long-term effects of serious birth problems (remarkable resiliency is often apparent, even among infants of low-income families [Werner and Smith, 1982]); and (3) the adult lives of "genius" children (contrary to the popular wisdom that "genius is akin to madness," these individuals are happier and more successful than most adults [Terman and Oden, 1959]).

However, although longitudinal research is "the lifeblood of developmental science," the actual number of longitudinal studies is "woefully small" (Applebaum and McCall, 1983). The primary reason for this is a very practical one: to follow the development of a group of people over a number of years usually requires great effort, considerable foresight, and substantial funding. Thus, while most developmental researchers consider longitudinal research far more revealing than cross-sectional studies, they are forced to rely heavily on cross-sectional research.

Cohort Effects   One fact that both longitudinal and cross-sectional researchers must bear in mind as they assess their findings is that each **cohort,** or group of people born in a particular generation, may experience social conditions and attitudes that are different from those of other cohorts. Thus research on people developing in one era may not be valid for people developing earlier or later. This is particularly true in a society such as ours, in which rapid social change occurs. For

Figure 1.13 *The long time span of longitudinal research provides a revealing view of how individuals change and how they remain the same. Longitudinal research on this woman would reveal whether her view of woman's role over the years has changed as readily as her sense of hair style, and whether her outgoing personality has remained as stable as her engaging smile would seem to suggest.*

example, research on adolescence based on young people growing up ten years ago may not be valid for today's teenagers, who use fewer drugs, for instance, are more conservative politically, and are more concerned about material possessions. In fact, in this century the experience of American adolescence changes notably about every decade (Boxer et al., 1984).

Researchers have a variety of complex ways to take cohort effects into account, often using a combination of cross-sectional and longitudinal techniques (Wohlwill, 1973). Nonetheless, future cohorts of children or adults may well differ in unknown ways from those studied in the past.

A Look at the History and Ethics of the Study of Children

It is fitting to end this chapter on the scientific study of child development with a longitudinal look at child-rearing. As the Closer Look on page 14 points out, in some periods of history, childhood, after age 6 or so, was nonexistent as a distinct stage of life. Such special attention as children received consisted mostly of frequent punishment, because it was assumed that they would otherwise go astray

(Borstelmann, 1983). Biblical advice from Proverbs was to "spare not the rod and spoil not the child"; Plato described boys as the "craftiest, most mischievous, and unruliest of brutes"; and the Pilgrims in Massachusetts were reminded from the pulpit that the child's "natural pride must be broken and beaten down." Except for a few dissenters (such as the eighteenth-century radical Jean-Jacques Rousseau, who thought that children should be allowed to grow "naturally," without any adult direction), most people were much more interested in disciplining children to keep them from becoming sinners or degenerates than in nurturing them so they would preserve their natural curiosity and enthusiasm. According to the historian Lloyd deMause (1975):

> Children were always felt to be on the verge of turning into actual demons, or at least to be easily susceptible to "the power of the Devil." To keep their small devils cowed, adults regularly terrorized them with a vast army of ghostlike figures, from the Lamia and Striga of the ancients, who ate children raw, to the witches of Medieval times, who would steal bad children away and suck their blood. One 19th-century tract described in simplified language the tortures God had in store for children in Hell: "The little child is in this red-hot oven. Hear how it screams to come out . . . "

The policies of the first schoolmasters likewise seem astonishingly harsh by contemporary standards. DeMause cites one nineteenth-century German schoolmaster who kept meticulous records of his disciplinary measures: "911,527 strokes with a stick, 124,000 lashes with a whip, 136,715 slaps with his hand, and 1,115,800 boxes on the ear." According to deMause, the severity of those punishments was not atypical: "The beatings described in most historical sources began at an early age, continued regularly throughout childhood, and were severe enough to cause bruising and bloodying."

The attitude toward children today is, for the most part, quite different from that of earlier centuries. The disciplinary measures that were commonly accepted in the past would now be considered abuse, and child abuse itself is recognized as one of our most serious problems. Today's children are encouraged to play and to imagine, as well as to develop their self-esteem—quite unthinkable at many earlier historical periods, when hard work and humility were expected of every child.

Figure 1.14 *Unsparing application of the rod was once thought to be necessary to tame the devil in every child. However, contemporary longitudinal research has linked physical punishment with later self-doubt, anger, and violence. Other ways of preventing misbehavior and alternate modes of discipline are more likely to result in confident, competent, and compassionate adults.*

Scientific Child Study

One reason for these changes is the impact of a new science, the science of child development, which began about 100 years ago. For example, G. Stanley Hall (1883) asked 400 first graders in Massachusetts some 134 questions to ascertain their understanding of words and concepts. On the basis of his findings, he advised teachers to recognize the immaturity of the child's thinking, and to become more responsive and less demanding in their teaching methods. In France, in the early 1900s, Alfred Binet, who developed the first IQ test, emphasized the individual differences between one child and another, pointing out that teachers and parents should not assume that every child who did not perform perfectly was either lazy, spoiled, or deliberately disobedient (Binet, 1909).

As a logical outcome of their research, many early developmentalists became reformers, advocating laws against child labor and child abuse, and proposing educational and social welfare reforms (Cairns, 1983). Advice to parents, generally recommending careful attention to the child's needs and problems, was penned and published by many developmental psychologists.

In recent years, researchers continue to uncover new findings on the nature of children and childhood, findings that continue to lead to reform. From influencing the way hospitals deal with birth, or the way the courts arrive at their decisions in child-custody cases, to championing tax credits for day-care or recommending approaches to sex education in the schools, developmentalists are among the most articulate advocates of new policies.

Ethics and Values

Because the conclusions of developmental science often lead directly (and sometimes too hastily) to practical application, and because the participants in basic research are a sample of the very children whom developmentalists seek to help, contemporary researchers in the field are very concerned about the ethics of what they do.

At the most basic level, researchers must ensure that the children and families who are the subjects of their research are not harmed by the research process. Among the precautions urged by the Society for Research in Child Development (1973) are the following:

> No matter how young the child, he has rights that supersede the rights of the investigator . . .

> The investigator should respect the child's freedom to choose to participate in research or not, as well as to discontinue participation at any time . . .

> The informed consent of the parents . . . should be obtained, preferably in writing. Informed consent requires that the parent or other responsible adult be told all features of the research that may affect his willingness to allow the child to participate . . .

> The investigator uses no research operation that may harm the child either physically or psychologically . . .

Researchers spend considerable time, and experience notable frustration, in order to assure the informed consent and confidentiality of all the parents and children involved (Charlesworth, 1984). In experiments, the experimental intervention—such as providing extra stimulation to premature infants—is often one that the researchers have good reason to think will be beneficial. If the researchers suspect that some harm might possibly come from an experiment, the experiment is not done. Indeed, one reason naturalistic observation is often used in developmental research is that the scientist merely observes and hence does not inadvertently harm anyone.

However, the most difficult ethical question raised by the study of human development is not safeguarding the participants, which is fairly straightforward, but attending to larger implications of the research. Readily acknowledging the complex ethical issues raised by research findings, the Society for Research in Child Development stipulates that "caution should be exercised in reporting results, making evaluative statements, or giving advice" and that "the investigator should be mindful of the social, political, and human implications of his [or her] research."

Likewise, each reader of this book should try to be mindful of the implications of the various findings, theories, and examples found in the study of human development. As we examine the mechanisms and patterns of development, you will, time and time again, be confronted with both practical and ethical issues—from family-planning and prenatal care to parent education and child abuse, from mainstreaming and prejudice to adolescent sexuality and suicide—many of which may touch on some aspect of your own life. Your own growing involvement in the practical and philosophical questions of development is important whether you plan to become a researcher or a practitioner, a teacher or a parent, or simply a more involved and better-informed member of the human family.

CHAPTER SUMMARY

The Study of Human Development

1. The study of development is the study of how people change as they grow older, from the beginning of life to the end.

2. Development is often divided into three domains, the physical, the cognitive, and the psychosocial. However, while research projects often center on one particular domain, development is thought to be holistic. Researchers from many academic and practical disciplines, particularly biology, education, and psychology, study human development.

3. An ecological, or systems, approach stresses the context of development, particularly the influence of family, community, and culture. Each individual is seen as part of many systems, affecting them as well as being affected by them.

4. The interaction of domains is clearly seen in the example of David, a handicapped teenager, whose problems originating in the physical domain quickly affected the other two domains. His example also shows how the individual is affected by, and also affects, the surrounding systems of family, society, and culture.

Three Controversies

5. All types of development are guided by innate biological forces as well as by the particular experiences a person has. The relative importance of these factors is a topic of debate, called the nature-nurture controversy.

6. Another controversy exists between those who think that development is smooth and continuous, and those who think it occurs in stages. While the stage view is common today, in past centuries childhood and adolescence were not recognized as stages.

7. Traditionally, many researchers searched for the averages, or "norms," of development, and considered children who differed from those norms deviant. Current researchers are much more likely to accept differences, considering them alternative paths of development.

The Scientific Method

8. The scientific method is used, in some form, by most developmentalists. They observe, pose a question, develop a hypothesis, test the hypothesis, and draw conclusions based on the results of the tests.

9. To check their conclusions and to try to remain as objective as possible, researchers use a variety of methods, among them, selection of a representative sample population, "blind" experimenters, control groups, and tests of statistical significance.

10. One common method of testing hypotheses is naturalistic observation, which provides ecologically valid information but does not pinpoint cause and effect. The laboratory experiment pinpoints causes but is not

necessarily applicable to daily life. The interview and case study are also useful.

11. In developmental research, ways are needed to detect change over time. Cross-sectional research compares people of different ages, longitudinal research (which is preferable but more difficult) studies the same individuals over a long time period. Both are valid for the cohorts under examination, but not necessarily for other cohorts.

A Look at the History and Ethics of the Study of Children

12. Contemporary researchers in the social sciences give considerable thought and attention to safeguarding the rights and well-being of the participants in their research. A more difficult ethical problem is the accurate reporting of research and understanding and dealing with all of its implications.

KEY TERMS

physical domain *(3)*	naturalistic observation *(18)*
cognitive domain *(3)*	blind experimenter *(19)*
psychosocial domain *(3)*	experimental group *(19)*
holistic development *(4)*	control group *(19)*
ecological, or systems, approach *(4)*	significance *(19)*
nature-nurture controversy *(10)*	correlation *(20)*
nature *(10)*	laboratory experiment *(22)*
nurture *(10)*	interview method *(24)*
continuity *(11)*	case study *(24)*
discontinuity *(11)*	cross-sectional research *(25)*
norm *(13)*	longitudinal research *(26)*
scientific method *(17)*	cohort *(26)*
replicate *(17)*	
sample size *(18)*	
representative sample *(18)*	

KEY QUESTIONS

1. What is developmental psychology?

2. What is included in the study of developmental psychology?

3. What are the three domains of developmental psychology?

4. Give examples of the interaction among the various systems that affect an individual's development.

5. What are the steps of the scientific method?

6. What are the advantages of the scientific method?

7. What are the advantages and disadvantages of testing a hypothesis by naturalistic observation?

8. What are the advantages and disadvantages of testing a hypothesis by experiment?

9. Compare the advantages of longitudinal research and cross-sectional research.

10. What ethical precautions should developmental psychologists take?

RECOMMENDED READINGS

Books in the recommended readings sections that follow each chapter are always paperbacks, and chosen partly because they are interesting and accessible to students who have no special background in the topic.

Kett, Joseph F. *Rites of passage.* New York: Basic Books, 1979.

Filled with fascinating historical detail, this book describes the changes in teenage life in America over the past two centuries and raises interesting points. For example, adolescents are as crucial to the economy as they ever were, but their role has changed from worker to consumer.

Gilligan, Carol. *In a different voice: Psychological theory and women's development.* Cambridge, Mass.: Harvard University Press, 1983.

Hale, Janice E. *Black Children: Their roots, culture, and learning styles.* Brigham Young University Press, Provo, Utah. 1982.

Both these books make clear why the "difference versus deficit" question is as emotional as it is. Gilligan shows that women approach moral issues differently than men do, and thus standards set by research on males should not be applied to females. Hale notes the many differences in family patterns and learning styles of black American children, arguing that these patterns often originate in Africa and are adaptive in contemporary America. Both of these works are provocative, but not always based on rigorous scientific research.

Bronfenbrenner, Urie. *The ecology of human development: Experiments by nature and design.* Cambridge, Mass.: Harvard University Press, 1981.

Written for researchers and for graduate students, this is a somewhat difficult but rewarding book. Bronfenbrenner writes well, with humor and with a consistent point of view.

Garbarino, James (Ed.) *Children and families in the social environment.* Aldine, 1982.

As a leading advocate of the ecological approach, Garbarino and many of his former students have written a book that emphasizes the importance of culture and society in many of the pivotal issues concerning child development. Among the issues discussed are birth customs, child abuse, and foster care. This book is not easy reading, but the careful reader will find it well worth the effort.

Theories

Chapter 2

Perhaps the most incomprehensible thing about the world is that it is comprehensible.

Albert Einstein

It is a capital mistake to theorize before one has the data.

Sherlock Holmes

Never trust an experimental result until it has been confirmed by theory.

Sir Arthur Eddington

What Theories Do
Three Possible Explanations

Psychoanalytic Theories
Origins
Freud's Ideas
Erikson's Ideas
Evaluations of Psychoanalytic Theories

Learning Theories
Emphasis on Behavior
Laws of Behavior
Social Learning Theory
Evaluations of Learning Theories

Cognitive Theories
Piaget's Ideas
Evaluations of Cognitive Theories

The Theories Compared

Chapter 2

The patterns of human interaction in everyday life are often complex and not simply explained. Over the past hundred years, social scientists have devised several theoretical perspectives that offer insight into why we behave in the ways that we do and how we learn to act in new ways. In this chapter, we will see how these perspectives suggest answers to such questions as:

How does children's understanding of self and others progress from the egocentrism of infancy to the realization that other's needs are as real as their own?

Are humans, including children, motivated by hidden erotic impulses?

How does conscience develop?

Which is more effective in changing behavior—punishments or rewards?

Since an infant, at first, understands the world only through the senses and motor abilities, how does the ability to think logically develop?

Picture this scene. It is early Sunday morning. A woman sleepily descending the stairs comes to a halt as she notices the rubble heap of toy soldiers, airplanes, tanks, trucks, and wooden blocks that occupies her living room. In the middle of it all sits her 5-year-old son, Jack, in a fort he has just made of up-ended chairs draped with a tablecloth, singing to himself as he shares some orange juice with his G.I. Joe doll. His mother says, "Jack, what do you think you are doing?"

Jack pokes his head out of his fortress, smiling broadly. "Want to come into my house?"

His mother tries a different approach, putting her hands on her hips and shouting, "Jack, pick up that mess right now before Tom sees it!"

Jack stops smiling, puts his hands on *his* hips, and says "No!"

"Pick it up!" Jack's mother screams.

"No! You can't tell me what to do," Jack screams back.

Suddenly, Tom, Jack's new stepfather appears, takes in the scene at a glance, puts his arm around his wife's shoulders, and says, "You let that kid get away with murder. I wish you'd let me take charge."

Jack's mother starts to cry, and Jack charges out of his fort, pointing his G.I. Joe rifle at his stepfather and shouting, "Don't touch my mother!"

What Theories Do

How would you interpret this family scene? Would you approach it in terms of a power struggle among the participants? Or would you analyze it in terms of the apparent interpersonal inadequacies it represents—say, the boy's lack of discipline, the mother's lack of self-control, and the step-father's poor mediation skills?

Or would you say that this scene could be characterized as a drama involving a culprit, a victim, and an innocent observer who is drawn into a conflict that really doesn't involve him directly?

Any of these approaches would be plausible and might lead to partial explanations. But a moment's reflection makes it apparent that none of them provides a comprehensive view of the conflict that is going on. In order to analyze this scene, and other situations in real life, we need some way to clarify what we see, a way that takes us deeper than our first (probably biased) speculations and organizes our assumptions and guesses into hypotheses that can be tested and proven valid or invalid. In short, we need a theory, for a theory provides a framework of general ideas that permits a broad and cohesive view of the complexities that may be involved in any given human interaction.

Figure 2.1 *A theory provides a frame of reference that organizes particular experiences, observations, ideas, and guesses about given phenomena.*

Three Possible Explanations

In this chapter, we will briefly examine three theories that have had particular influence in the study of human development: psychoanalytic theory, learning theory, and cognitive theory. Each theory emphasizes different aspects of human development, and each would approach our family scene in a very different way.

For example, psychoanalytic theory—the first perspective in developmental psychology to be formally elaborated—holds that we are largely ruled by unconscious forces of the mind—that is, by impulses and emotional conflicts that are hidden from our awareness. According to this perspective, nearly all our behaviors—from the most significant to the most trivial—are, in one form or another, expressions of these impulses and conflicts. Thus, if we were to consider the foregoing family scene in terms of psychoanalytic theory, we would search for the underlying motivations of the parties involved.

A psychoanalytic thinker might explain that the boy is trying to establish his masculinity amid difficult circumstances, for the prime object of his affection, his mother, has turned away from him and from his father to another man. The living room this particular morning is literally strewn with clues to Jack's inner struggle. Feeling insecure and dependent and wishing to gain his mother's attention, he makes a total mess the way a baby would. At the same time wanting to seem manly, he fantasizes himself as a soldier. Most tellingly, he builds a fort in which to hide (as in the womb), into which to invite his mother (so he can have her all to himself again), and finally from which to attack the intruder who threatens to steal his mother away.

A psychoanalytic explanation might also say that Jack's mother is torn between her sexual need for her new husband, her guilt for having left her son's father, and the intensification of her relationship with her son that resulted from her divorce. (Indeed, she may even have encouraged her son's jealous feelings by telling him "You're the man of the house now" during the interlude between husbands.) Now she is caught in the middle. Unable to command her son (as his father might have), unwilling to let her new husband fully replace her old one by taking over, she falls back on the behavior that helped her escape difficult decisions when she was a girl—crying.

Meanwhile, the new stepfather feels threatened by the influence Jack has over his mother, as well as by the evidence Jack represents of his mother's having loved another man. Unable to deal with this small boy man-to-man or father-to-son, he tries to intimidate him indirectly, by laying blame on his mother.

According to psychoanalytic theory, most human interactions are similarly freighted with tangled emotions and hidden meanings. Other theories in psychology are founded on quite different general laws or principles and would lead to quite different interpretations of this scene. Learning theory would maintain that the behaviors exhibited in this family drama express, not unconscious motives and hidden meanings, but learned responses to particular kinds of situations. After Jack's father was out of the house, for instance, Jack's mother may have found that having quiet weekend mornings to herself reduced stress more than being a vigilant guardian of neatness did, so she got into the habit of letting Jack play however he wished. In turn, Jack learned that he was free to turn the house upside-down as long as he did it without making noise. The introduction of a new authority figure into the household has brought about pressure for changes in this behavior pattern, pressure that both mother and child are having difficulty adjusting to. The stepfather, meanwhile, may never have learned how to deal with young children, but may have learned on the job that subordinates respond to criticism and a "tough" stance.

Cognitive theorists would approach this family scene with an interest in how the individuals' conscious thought processes and their understanding of themselves and others affects their behavior. In particular, they would point out that 5-year-olds have great difficulty taking the perspective of others, and that Jack, therefore, is probably genuinely perplexed at the trouble his play has caused. They would also probably come to the conclusion that both adults in this instance are likewise having trouble seeing the other's point of view.

Figure 2.2 *No matter what interaction developmentalists study, they can make their observations from three theoretical perspectives—psychosocial, which emphasizes unconscious drives and motives; learning theory, emphasizing learned responses to particular situations; and cognitive, emphasizing the individual's understanding of self and others.*

Whatever their differences in approach or emphasis, all theories of human development perform the same function: they take us beyond isolated incidents of human interaction and toward an understanding of the full context in which the interactions occur.

Unfortunately, theory and practice are often discussed as opposites—as though we had to choose between them. In fact, theories arise from experience, and once a theory is formulated, it leads to practical applications (Miller, 1983). The value of a theory can be measured by how "useful" it is—that is, how productive it is in generating hypotheses to test and in inspiring new insights into behavior (Lee, 1976). This will become clear as we discuss psychoanalytic, learning, and cognitive theories in detail, in this chapter and throughout the book.

Psychoanalytic Theories

As we have seen, **psychoanalytic theory** interprets human development in terms of unconscious drives and motives. These unconscious impulses are viewed as influencing every aspect of a person's thinking and behavior, from the crucial choices of a lifetime, including whom and what to love or hate, to the smallest details of daily life, including manner of dress, eating habits, what we say and how we say it, what we daydream about—in fact, the entire gamut of our personal preferences, dislikes, and idiosyncrasies.

Origins

To understand the tenets of this theory, it is helpful to know something about the intellectual climate in which it arose. In the Europe of the 1870s, when the psychoanalytic perspective began to take shape, thought about human behavior included the ideas that men are governed for the most part by reason; that children are "innocent," devoid of all sexual feelings; and that women are particularly susceptible to "hysteria," a nervous disorder that produced such symptoms as paralysis of a limb, or deafness, or loss of feeling, and was believed to originate in the uterus. (The term "hysteric" derives from the Greek *hustera*, meaning "womb." The common treatment for hysteria was a hysterectomy, that is, the removal of the uterus.)

Against the grain of these notions, a number of intellectuals were developing an explanation of human behavior that emphasized the controlling power of emotional forces and the subordinate position of reason. In particular, Sigmund Freud (1856–1939), the founder of the psychoanalytic approach, began to evolve a theory that pointed specifically to the irrational basis of human behavior, to the hidden emotional content of our everyday actions, and to the ways in which the individual is driven by powerful sexual and aggressive impulses, and by fear of them.

Figure 2.3 *Many of Freud's students and patients spoke about his penetrating gaze, which, they said, helped them uncover their hidden thoughts and fantasies. Indeed, some critics contend that much of Freud's success as a psychoanalyst could be credited to his personality and insight, rather than to his methods or theories.*

Freud, who began his career as a medical doctor, formulated his theory while treating some of those women who were considered "hysterics." Freud suspected that the origin of their symptoms was in the mind, not in the uterus. In an effort to uncover the hidden causes of their problems, Freud hypnotized his first patients, suggesting that they talk about events and feelings related to their hysteria. Sometimes these treatments were successful: patients would eventually reveal the events that had precipitated their illness, and when this occurred, their symptoms would be much relieved.

Freud was not satisfied with hypnosis, however. Some patients did not know what troubled them; others did not respond to hypnotic suggestion. Gradually, Freud developed an ingenious new way to uncover the thoughts and feelings of his patients. He would have them recline on his office couch and talk about anything and everything that came into their minds—daily events, dreams, childhood memories, fears, desires—no matter how seemingly trivial or how unpleasant. From these disclosures and such things as the patient's slips of the tongue and unexpected associations between one word and another, Freud discerned clues to the usually unconscious emotional conflicts that paralyzed one person or terrified another. Once the patient, under Freud's guidance, came to understand the nature of these hidden conflicts, the patient's symptoms often diminished or disappeared altogether.

The medical establishment ridiculed Freud's "talking cure," especially when he reported that many emotional problems were caused by unconscious sexual desires, some of which originated in infancy. But patients flocked to Freud's door, and as they revealed their problems and fantasies, Freud listened, interpreted, and formulated an influential theory of the human psyche.

Freud's Ideas

One of Freud's basic ideas is that children have sexual pleasures and fantasies long before they reach adolescence. According to this theory of **infantile sexuality,** development in the first five or six years occurs in three **psychosexual stages.** Each stage is characterized by the focusing of sexual interest and pleasure in a particular part of the body, respectively, the mouth (the **oral stage**), the anus (the **anal stage**), and the penis (the **phallic stage**). In each stage, the child strives for satisfaction through activities centered on these organs—feeding and sucking; defecation and toilet training; and masturbation. It was Freud's contention that the parent-child interaction during these stages—especially how the child experiences the conflicts that these stages imply—determines the child's basic personality. In other words, in the Freudian view, personality is essentially fixed by age 5 or so. Then, after a five- or six-year period of **sexual latency,** during which sexual forces are dormant, the individual enters a final psychosexual stage, the **genital stage,** which lasts throughout adulthood.

Figure 2.4 *This girl's interest in the statue's anatomy may reflect simple curiosity, but Freudian theory would maintain that it is a clear manifestation of the phallic stage of psychosexual development, in which girls are said to feel deprived because they lack a penis.*

Figure 2.5 *Freud developed this model of human mental processes to explain why people have conflicting ideas of what to do or think. The id, ego, and superego are not actually parts of the mind, but they represent the conscious and unconscious forces within the human psyche.*

Id, Ego, and Superego   To help explain the dynamics of the individual's psychological development, Freud proposed three theoretical components of personality: the id, ego, and superego. The **id** is the source of our unconscious impulses toward fulfillment of our needs. It operates according to the *pleasure principle,* that is, the striving for immediate gratification. In other words, the id wants whatever seems satisfying and enjoyable—and wants it *now.* The impatient, greedy infant screaming for food in the middle of the night is all id.

Gradually, as babies learn that other people have demands of their own, and that gratification therefore must sometimes wait, the **ego** begins to develop. It is the role of the ego to mediate between the unbridled demands of the id and the limits imposed by the real world. The ego is said to operate according to the *reality principle:* it attempts to satisfy the id's demands in ways that recognize life as it is, not as the id wants it to be.

The ego also strives to keep another irrational force at bay. At about age 4 or 5, the **superego** starts to develop, as children begin to identify with their parents' moral standards. The superego is like a *relentless conscience* that distinguishes right from wrong in no uncertain terms. Its prime objective is to keep the id in check. In this regard, it is the function of the ego to mediate between the primal desires of the id and the superego's unbending effort to inhibit those desires.

By elementary school, many children have internalized the standards of right and wrong that they learned from their parents. They no longer need someone to tell them that they have been bad because they are already aware of their misdeeds and feel guilty and ashamed, imagining terrible punishments. A child who tells a lie might have nightmares about the fires of hell; another child who steals a candy bar might shudder every time a policeman comes into view.

Defense Mechanisms   When the superego becomes so overbearing, or the id's demands so insistent, that the ego feels in danger of being overwhelmed, people involuntarily defend themselves against the superego's attack and against the frightening impulses of the id by using one of dozens of **defense mechanisms.** Three common defense mechanisms are regression, repression, and displacement.

Regression occurs when someone retreats to a form of behavior typical of a younger person, allowing the individual to avoid dealing with reality in an age-appropriate way. An adult might slip back to dependence on his or her parents; a 10-year-old might start wetting the bed again; a 5-year-old might talk baby talk and want to sleep with a bottle. **Repression** is the pushing of a disturbing idea or memory or impulse into the unconscious, where it will not be actively threatening. Adolescents who are not interested in anything to do with sex, or abused children who forget how they got hurt, are probably repressing powerful feelings that would be deeply distressing if they were to surface. **Displacement** is the shifting of a drive or emotion from a threatening or unavailable object to a substitute object. An infant who is frustrated in the quest for oral gratification during the first psychosexual stage might develop an ongoing need for oral satisfaction. When deprived of a breast or a bottle, the baby might displace the oral drive to thumb-sucking. As the child grows older, the social unacceptability of thumb-sucking might cause the need to be displaced by some activity such as chewing on fingernails or pencil erasers. In adulthood, displacements might take such forms as heavy smoking or drinking, or overeating.

According to psychoanalytic theory, psychologically healthy children gradually develop strong egos, able to cope with the demands of the id and superego. Defense mechanisms help regulate this process throughout life by deflecting or countering the demands of the id or superego when they threaten to become overwhelming. At any point, however, defense mechanisms can be overused, preventing the ego from ever confronting the unconscious drives directly. As a result, the individual is handicapped in dealing with reality.

Psychoanalytic theory holds that each person inherits a legacy of problems from the conflicts of his or her childhood, along with particular ways of coping with them. Depending on our early experiences, some of us are more able to cope with the stresses of daily life than others.

Erikson's Ideas

Dozens of Freud's students became famous theorists in their own right. Although they acknowledged the importance of the unconscious, of sexual urges, and of early childhood, each in his or her own way expanded and modified Freud's ideas. Many of these neo-Freudians, including Karen Horney, Otto Rank, Margaret Mahler, Helene Deutsch, and Anna Freud, are mentioned at various points in this book. One of them, Erik Erikson (1902–   ), formulated a comprehensive theory of development that will be outlined here and discussed in later chapters.

Figure 2.6 *Erik Erikson has continued to write and lecture on psychosocial development throughout his long life. His most recent work emphasizes psychohistory—the relationship between historical factors and personality development.*

Eight Crises of Life   Whereas Freud remained rooted in Vienna for most of his life, Erikson spent his childhood in Germany, his adolescence wandering throughout Europe, his young adulthood in Vienna under the tutelage of Freud and in analysis with Freud's daughter Anna, and finally his adulthood in the United States. As an American citizen, he studied students at Harvard, soldiers who suffered emotional breakdowns during World War II, civil rights workers in the South, and Native Americans from the Sioux and Yurok tribes. Partly as a result of this diversity of experience, Erikson came to think of Freud's stages of development as too limited and too few. He proposed instead eight developmental stages, each one character- ized by a particular conflict, or crisis, that must be resolved.

As you can see from Table 2.1, Erikson's first five stages are closely related to Freud's stages. Freud's last stage occurs at adolescence, however, whereas Erikson sees adulthood as having three stages. One particularly significant difference is that all of Erikson's stages are centered, not on a body part, but on each person's relationship to the social environment.

TABLE 2.1   **Comparison of Psychosexual and Psychosocial Stages**

Approximate Age	Freud (Psychosexual)	Erikson* (Psychosocial)
Birth to 1 year	*Oral Stage* The mouth is the focus of pleasurable sensations in the baby's body, and feeding is the most stim- ulating activity.	*Trust vs. Mistrust* Babies learn either to trust or mistrust that oth- ers will care for their basic needs, including nour- ishment, sucking, warmth, cleanliness, and physi- cal contact.
1–3 years	*Anal Stage* The anus is the focus of pleasurable sensations in the baby's body, and toilet training is the most important activity.	*Autonomy vs. Shame and Doubt* Children learn either to be self-sufficient in many activities, including toileting, feeding, walking, and talking, or to doubt their own abilities.
3–6 years	*Phallic Stage* The phallus, or penis, is the most important body part. Boys are proud of their penis but ashamed when they masturbate, and girls are envious and wonder why they don't have one. Children of both sexes have sexual fantasies about their parents, for which they feel guilty.	*Initiative vs. Guilt* Children want to undertake many adultlike activ- ities, sometimes overstepping the limits set by parents and feeling guilty.
7–11 years	*Latency* Not a stage but an interlude, when sexual needs are relatively quiet and children can put psychic energy into learning skills.	*Industry vs. Inferiority* Children busily learn to be competent and pro- ductive, or feel inferior and unable to do anything well.
Adolescence	*Genital Stage* The genitals are the focus of pleasurable sensa- tions, and the young person seeks sexual stimu- lation and sexual satisfaction.	*Identity vs. Role Confusion* Adolescents try to figure out "Who am I?" They establish sexual, ethnic, and career identities or are confused about what future roles to play.
Adulthood	Freud believed that the genital stage lasts throughout adulthood. He also said that the goal of a healthy life is "to love and to work."	*Intimacy vs. Isolation* Young adults seek companionship and love with another person or become isolated from other people.
		Generativity vs. Stagnation Adults are productive, performing meaningful work and raising a family, or become stagnant and inactive.
		Integrity vs. Despair People try to make sense out of their lives, either seeing life as a meaningful whole or despairing at goals never reached and questions never an- swered.

*Although Erikson describes two extreme resolutions to each crisis, he recognizes that there is a wide range of solutions between these extremes and that most people probably arrive at some middle course.

Figure 2.7 *It seems quite clear that the young boy here is in the thick of the psychosocial stage Erikson referred to as autonomy versus shame and doubt. Whether he emerges from this stage feeling independent or inept depends in part on whether his parents encourage his efforts to feed himself or, instead, regularly criticize him for the mess he is making. It seems equally clear that this young woman is trying to negotiate the stage Erikson called identity versus role confusion. In this stage, teenagers try out a number of roles (sometimes mostly through costume) in an effort to discover who they really are.*

Psychosocial Development To highlight this emphasis on social and cultural influences, Erikson calls his theory the **psychosocial theory** of human development.

According to Erikson, there are three major aspects in the study of development:

Somatic. Physical strengths and weaknesses.

Personal. Life history and current developmental stages.

Social. Cultural, historical, and social forces.

He believes that psychologists should study all three areas, not to find cause and effect, but to find relationships and interdependence. For example, if analyzing a teenager who is a loner because he is wary and withdrawn, Erikson would not only take into account the problems typically associated with the stage of life referred to as adolescence but would also consider the boy's physique (Is he unusually short or thin or fat?), his family history (Was he neglected in infancy when he was learning to trust or mistrust?), and his culture (Is he a member of a minority group that is discriminated against, or does his peer group place a premium on abilities he doesn't possess?). (Erikson's use of this theoretical framework is shown in greater detail in the Research Report on "combat crisis" in a marine.)

Cultural Differences Central to Erikson's theory is his conviction that each culture faces particular challenges and, correspondingly, promotes particular paths of development that are likely to meet those challenges. Erikson suggests, for example, that the traditional German stress on early toilet training and cleanliness prepared adults for a society where law and order were paramount, just as the stress on independence and self-assertion in pioneer America prepared adults to explore new territory and ignore traditional laws and conventions—precisely what that society needed at the time (Erikson, 1963). A problem arises when a society's traditional methods of upbringing no longer prepare its children to cope with the demands they face as adults. No culture anticipates the future so well that each child is prepared to live in it without problems. Each society provides better preparation for some crises than for others.

"Combat Crisis" in a Marine

A young patient at the veteran's clinic where Erikson worked as a therapist suffered such severe headaches that he couldn't work. Erikson described the origins of the problem:

A group of marines, just ashore, lay in the pitch darkness of a Pacific beachhead within close range of enemy fire. Somehow it had always contradicted the essential spirit of their corps to have "to take it lying down." Yet it had happened in this war. And when it happened, it exposed them not only to damnable sniping from nowhere, but also to a strange mixture of disgust, rage, and fear—down in their stomachs.

Here they were again. The "supporting" fire from the Navy had not been much of a support. . . . Among these men lay our patient . . . a medical soldier. . . .

Our medical soldier never quite remembered what happened that night. . . . He claims that the medical corps were ordered to unload ammunition instead of setting up a hospital; that the medical officer, somehow, became very angry and abusive, and that sometime during the night somebody pressed a sub-machine gun into his hands. Here his memory becomes a blank.

The following morning the patient . . . found himself in the finally improvised hospital. Overnight he had developed a severe intestinal fever. He spent the day in the twilight of sedatives. At nightfall the enemy attacked from the air. All the able bodied men found shelter or helped the sick to find one. He was immobilized, unable to move, and, much worse, unable to help . . .

From then on his life was made miserable by raging headaches. His fever (or whatever had caused it) was cured; but his headaches and his jumpiness made it necessary for him to be returned home to the States and to be discharged.

Where was the seat of his neurosis? For a "war neurosis" it was, if we accept his doctors' diagnosis . . . .

He had not seen his mother, it appeared, since he was fourteen years old. His family had then been on an economic and moral decline. He had left home abruptly when his mother, in a drunken rage, had pointed a gun at him. He had grabbed the gun, broken it, and thrown it out of the window. Then he had left for good. He secured the secret help of a fatherly man—in fact, his [high-school] principal. In exchange for protection and guidance, he had promised never to drink, or swear, or to indulge himself sexually—and then, never to touch a gun. He had become a good student and teacher, and an exceptionally even tempered man, at least on the surface, until that night on the Pacific beachhead.

Several factors combined to cause a real crisis and make it a lasting one. [Erikson, 1963]

According to Erikson, a combination of somatic, personal, and social factors caused the crisis. Without the fever (somatic) or the family problems in adolescence (personal) or the war (social), he might never have become sick.

The marine had resolved the crisis of adolescence (trying to find an identity of one's own) by adopting a rigid code of behavior, usually not the best solution. Then he temporarily solved the crisis of young adulthood—intimacy versus isolation—by joining the marines. When his troop could no longer attack and he could no longer help the wounded, he felt isolated, cut off from the security of a joint enterprise. Then when his officer cursed him and someone put a gun in his hands, his identity was shattered and he fell apart. This breakdown would not have happened if his identity had been less rigid and his attachment to the marines less strong.

Erikson thinks that at every stage people experience both sides of each crisis—a negative as well as a positive side. Every toddler sometimes feels shame; every adolescent experiences role confusion; all mature people know despair. The critical question is how to resolve each developmental crisis, not how to avoid it.

Evaluations of Psychoanalytic Theories

All psychologists owe a debt of gratitude to Freud, and to the neo-Freudians who extended and refined his concepts. Many of Freud's ideas are so widely accepted today that they are no longer thought of as his—for example, that unconscious motives affect our behavior, that we use defense mechanisms to avoid conflicts, and that sexuality is a powerful drive in humans. While few psychologists accept his ideas completely, many have learned from his insights.

Developmentalists have been influenced by three psychoanalytic ideas in particular. Stage theory is one of them. Although poets and playwrights had previously written about the "ages" of man, Freud was the first to use his observations and insights to construct a coherent theory regarding our different needs and problems at various ages, or stages, of life.

Another influential idea concerns the importance of certain parts of the life span. Freud centered our attention on the critical first five years, a time previously neglected in education and psychology. Erikson led us to recognize that adolescents and adults also experience developmental changes.

Finally, psychoanalytic theory has helped us to realize that human thoughts and actions are likely to be far more complicated than might at first be apparent. Indeed, it is difficult to imagine that there was once a world in which it was assumed that human beings act on the basis of reason alone, so clear does it seem to us now that the forces of impulse and fantasy, and the influences and pressures applied by parents and society, shape and direct our behavior throughout our lives.

Although the general concepts and implications of psychoanalytic theory are very much part of our current thinking about development, most contemporary developmentalists find many psychoanalytic ideas to be inadequate or wrong. For instance, Freud's notion that the child's experiences during the first three psychosexual stages form the basis for character structure and personality problems in adulthood has found little support in studies of normal children. It seems that the nature of the parent-child relationship, rather than any specific event of early childhood, is the primary factor in later emotional development (Caldwell, 1964; Martin, 1975).

Some aspects of Freud's theory strike many as anachronistic today. His depiction of the struggle between the id and the superego—that is, between a torrent of impulses seeking immediate release and a ceaselessly judgmental agency trying to check those impulses—seems more an outgrowth of the Victorian morality of nineteenth-century Vienna than a valid depiction of a universal process.

Erikson's interpretation of development has fared better than Freud's, perhaps because Erikson's ideas, though arising from Freudian theory, are more comprehensive and apply to a wider range of behavior. Even so, most of the sources of Erikson's theory are, like Freud's, subjective, grounded in Erikson's own experiences, the recollections of his patients in therapy, and the insights of classical literature. Psychoanalytic theory does not lend itself to laboratory testing under controlled conditions, which leads to the accusation by some that this theory is more myth than science, with the validity of psychoanalytic ideas "evaluated by dogma, not data" (Cairns, 1983). Certainly, evaluations of psychoanalytic theory are more personal than scientific. And they are also highly varied. Some psychologists find psychoanalytic theory illuminating and insightful; others find it provocative nonsense; most think it a combination of both.

Learning Theories

Early in the twentieth century, John B. Watson (1878–1958) decided that if psychology was to be a true science, psychologists should study only what they could see and measure. In Watson's words: "Why don't we make what we can *observe* the real field of psychology? Let us limit ourselves to things that can be observed, and formulate laws concerned with only those things . . . We can observe behavior—what the organism does or says" (Watson, 1967; originally published 1930). Many American psychologists agreed with Watson. Thus began a major theory of American psychology, **behaviorism,** now more commonly called **learning theory** because of its emphasis on how we learn specific behaviors.

Emphasis on Behavior

Learning theorists focus on what people do, and what particular circumstances make people likely to behave the same way again. Consider the following example:

> . . . a three-year old girl had regressed to an excessive amount of crawling . . . By "excessive" is meant that after three weeks of school she was spending most of her morning crawling or in a crouched position with her face hidden. Her parents reported that for some months the behavior had been occurring whenever they took her to visit or when friends came to their home . . .
>
> Observations recorded in the third week at school showed . . . that more than 80 percent of the child's time was spent in the off-feet positions. The records also showed that the crawling behavior frequently drew the attention of the teachers. On-feet behaviors, such as standing and walking . . . seldom drew such notice. [Harris, et al., 1964]

The emphasis in this description is on the girl's crawling and on the teachers' response to this odd behavior, not on the thoughts of either child or teachers. Nowhere in their report do the authors try to analyze the unconscious forces that might have caused this regression, because learning theorists think that unconscious urges are either irrelevant or nonexistent.

Instead, when trying to account for a given behavior, learning theorists try to figure out the immediate causes and consequences of that behavior. Behavior therapists want to know what can be done in the immediate environment to change problem behavior. In the little girl's case

> a program was instituted in which the teachers no longer attended to the child whenever she was crawling or crouching, but gave her continuous warm attention as long as she was . . . standing, running, or walking. Initially the only upright behavior . . . occurred when the child pulled herself almost to her feet in order to hang up or take down her coat from her locker, and when she pulled herself up to wash her hands in the wash basin. Within a week of the initiation of the new attention-giving procedure, the child acquired a close-to-normal pattern of on-feet behavior. [Harris, et al., 1964]

Laws of Behavior

Unlike the other theorists in this chapter, learning theorists have not developed a stage theory of human development. Instead, they have formulated laws of behavior that can be applied to any individual at any age, from fetus to octogenarian.

The basic laws of learning theory explore the relationship between **stimulus** and **response,** that is, between any behavior or event (the stimulus) and the behavioral reaction (the response) that it elicits. Some responses are automatic, like reflexes. If someone suddenly waves a hand in your face, you will blink; if a hungry dog smells food, it will salivate. But most responses do not occur spontaneously; they are learned.

Learning theorists emphasize that life is a continual learning process, as new behavior patterns become appropriate responses to current stimuli, while old, unproductive responses tend to fade away. This learning process, called **conditioning,** occurs in two basic ways: classical and operant.

Classical Conditioning   More than eighty years ago, a Russian scientist named Ivan Pavlov (1849–1936) began to study the link between stimulus and response. While doing research on salivation in dogs, Pavlov had noted that his experimental dogs began to salivate not only at the sight of food but, eventually, at the sound of the approaching attendants who brought the food. This observation led him to perform his famous experiment in which he taught a dog to salivate at the sound of a bell. Pavlov began by ringing the bell just before feeding the dog. After several repetitions of this routine, the dog began salivating at the sound of the bell even when there was no food. This simple experiment in learning was one of the first scientific demonstrations of **classical conditioning** (also called *respondent conditioning*), in which an animal or person comes to associate a neutral stimulus with a meaningful one, and then *responds* to the former stimulus as if it were the latter. In this case, the dog associated the bell (the neutral stimulus) with food and responded to its sound as though it were the food itself. This part of the conditioning process is called *learning by association.*

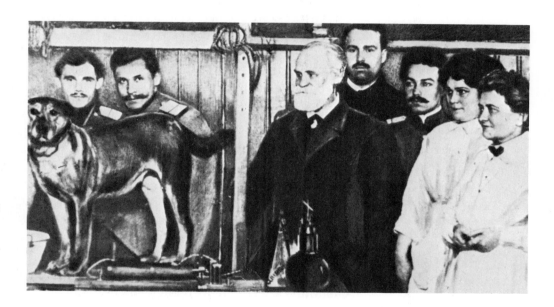

Figure 2.8 *Pavlov, his assistants, and one of his famous dogs are shown in this photo taken in Czarist Russia in 1911. Despite the war, revolution, and the purges of the next two decades, Pavlov's laboratory continued to receive government support.*

There are many everyday examples that suggest classical conditioning you yourself may have experienced: imagining a lemon might make your mouth pucker; reading the final-exam schedule might make your palms sweat; seeing a sexy photograph might make your heart beat faster. In each instance, the stimulus is connected, or associated, with another stimulus that produced the physiological response in the past. Reading the exam schedule might make you sweat, for instance, if actually taking tests has made you anxious on earlier occasions.

Operant Conditioning   The most influential contemporary proponent of learning theory is B. F. Skinner (1904–   ). Skinner agrees with Pavlov that the processes of classical conditioning explain some of behavior, especially behavior that is reflexive. However, Skinner believes that another type of conditioning—**operant conditioning**—plays a much greater role, especially when trying to explain more complex learning. Whereas in classical conditioning, the animal is merely responding to prior cues, in operant conditioning, the animal learns that a particular behavior

Figure 2.9 *B. F. Skinner is best known for his experiments with rats and pigeons, but he has also applied his knowledge to a wide range of human problems. For his daughter, he designed a glass-enclosed crib in which temperature, humidity, and perceptual stimulation could be controlled to make time spent in the crib as enjoyable and educational as possible. He has also speculated and written about an ideal society where, for example, workers at the less desirable jobs earn greater rewards.*

produces a particular response and then performs that behavior to achieve that response. (The term ''operant'' comes from the Latin word meaning work, and is intended to emphasize the work done to get a particular response.)

In operant conditioning, then, a system of rewards might be used to train a dog to perform a specific behavior that is not in the dog's usual repertoire—fetch newspapers, jump through hoops, capture suspected criminals. Once the behavior has been learned, the dog will continue to do the work—for example, fetching the newspaper—even when a reward is not always forthcoming. Similarly, almost all the adult's daily behavior, from putting on socks to earning a paycheck, can be said to be the result of operant conditioning. (Operant conditioning is also referred to as *instrumental conditioning,* calling attention to the fact that the behavior in question has become an instrument for achieving a particular response.)

Reinforcement   In operant conditioning, the process whereby a particular behavior is strengthened, making it more likely that the behavior will occur more frequently, is referred to as **reinforcement** (Skinner, 1953). A stimulus that *increases* the likelihood that a particular behavior will be repeated is called a **reinforcer.** Reinforcers may be either positive or negative. A **positive reinforcer** is something pleasant—a good feeling, say, or the satisfaction of a need, or something received from another, such as a piece of candy or a word of praise. For a grade-conscious student, who has studied hard for an exam, getting an ''A'' would be a positive reinforcer of scholarly effort. A **negative reinforcer** is the removal of an unpleasant stimulus as the result of a particular behavior. When a student's anxiety about test-taking is reduced by extra preparation, or, counterproductively, by ''getting high,'' the reduction of anxiety is a negative reinforcer of either behavior. Note that a negative reinforcer differs from a **punishment,** in that a punishment is an unpleasant event that makes behavior *less* likely to be repeated.

Laws of Reinforcement   Learning theorists judge the effectiveness of a reinforcer or a punishment by how well it strengthens or changes behavior. Not all reinforcers or punishments have equal significance for those experiencing them. For instance, some children would work very hard to earn an allowance; others might not be at

Figure 2.10 *According to learning theory, the boy on the left is likely to develop good hygiene habits, largely because he is reinforced frequently for his efforts at cleanliness and is aware of the link between behavior and consequence. By contrast, punishment of the boy on the right will result in improved behavior only if he knows precisely why he is being punished and how he can avoid repeating his offense. But an even more important consideration is whether he is often reinforced for good behavior.*

all motivated by money but would work to earn a special privilege, such as being allowed to stay up an hour later on weekends. Similarly, the threat of being sent to one's room may be very effective in getting one child to stop misbehaving but have no effect on another, who may even seem to enjoy this particular "punishment."

Among the general rules pertaining to reinforcement, learning theorists have determined that basic reinforcers (food, physical comfort) are usually more effective with young children, while more complex and symbolic reinforcers (a college degree, an expensive car) are very effective for adults. At every stage, **social reinforcers,** such as praise or affection, can be powerful.

Timing is important when reinforcement is being used to promote learning (Ferster and Skinner, 1957). Especially for young children, immediate reinforcement for each step in the right direction is usually best at first. Later, occasional reinforcement for larger accomplishments is more effective. For example, a 6-year-old boy learning to read might be congratulated for each word sounded out; later, an occasional word of praise as he reads a story might be enough; later still, he might sometimes be allowed to buy a new book when he finishes an old one. Eventually, the act of reading becomes reinforcing in itself, and he will read everything, from cereal boxes to textbooks, without external reinforcers.

To create lasting changes, behaviorists prefer reinforcers to punishments (Skinner, 1953). Hitting a child or jailing an adult might work for a short while, but research has shown that these are not the best ways to alter behavior permanently, partly because punishment does not teach a desirable alternative behavior to replace the one that is being punished. Punishment can also have destructive side effects: someone who is punished frequently can become an apathetic or aggressive person (Skinner, 1972).

Social Learning Theory

Traditionally, with both classical and operant conditioning, learning theorists have sought to explain behavior in terms of the organism's direct experience, for they believe that each individual's current behavior results from the accumulated bits of learning acquired through past conditioning. Theoretically, this conditioning process could explain complex patterns of human interaction, as well as simpler behaviors. For example, according to this theory, adults smile at other people because in infancy smiling is associated with, and then reinforced by, food and comfort. And then, once the social smile is learned, it is reinforced, at least occasionally, by the pleasant responses of others. Further variations and subtleties are all the result of different patterns of reinforcement (Bijou and Baer, 1978).

However, a more recent group of learning theorists has focused on less direct, though equally potent, learning. They emphasize the many ways in which people learn new behaviors merely by observing the behavior of others, without themselves experiencing any personal reinforcement. Smiling, then, particularly the development of variant smiles—"winning" smiles, flirtatious smiles, questioning smiles, sickened smiles—could be the result of seeing other people smile and noting the responses they get. These theorists have developed an extension of learning theory called **social learning theory.**

Modeling   An integral part of social learning is **modeling,** the process whereby people pattern their behavior after that of specific others. We are more likely to model our behavior after people we consider admirable, or powerful, or similar to us, particularly if we have seen them reinforced for what they do (Bandura, 1977). While modeling occurs at every age, most of the research has focused on children, who seem very susceptible to social learning processes. Because parents are the most powerful figures in a child's life, the child is likely to model much of his or her behavior on that of the same-sex parent. Children also model their behavior after that of their teachers, their favorite friends, sports heroes, rock stars, and even television characters.

Often the modeling process is patently obvious: when a teacher conducts class calmly and talks in a quiet voice, the children in the class tend to be self-controlled and to respond quietly, while if the teacher seems to be disorganized, frantic, and

Figure 2.11 *Social learning theory tends to validate the old maxim, "Practice what you preach." If the moments pictured here are typical for each child, the girl on the left will acquire the skills and attitudes that contribute to good parenting. On the other hand, the actions of the parents of the girl on the right are likely to speak more loudly than words. Though they may warn her that smoking is an unhealthy habit that should be avoided, it is likely that she will be a cigarette smoker, too.*

loud, the children are likely to behave in a similar fashion. Even in the artificiality of a laboratory, a child who sees another child disobey orders, or share a snack, or play with a toy in an unusual way is likely to follow the example. Indeed, as one review concludes, "under the right circumstances, children will imitate almost anything, from physical aggression to moral judgment, from taste in candy to patterns of speech" (Hetherington and McIntyre, 1975).

Effects of Social Learning Social learning theory helps explain how children learn complex characteristics, such as values and social skills, which are rarely taught directly but are often acquired as children observe the world around them. Many grown children still follow thinking and behavioral patterns acquired through observation of their parents, either because new patterns were never learned or because the old patterns have become habitual and rewarding in themselves (Sears, 1965). This provides a social learning explanation for the fact that many adults find themselves thinking and acting as their parents did, even to the point of repeating their parents' mistakes. For example, a man whose father never displayed physical affection might well realize that he missed an important experience; but nevertheless when he himself becomes a father, he might find it difficult to hug his own son.

Indeed, as you will see in later chapters, this theory provides a plausible explanation for many phenomena noted by developmentalists. For example, parents who use physical punishment as a form of discipline are likely to raise children who become physically aggressive later on (Martin, 1975); children who watch "educational" television shows such as "Mr. Rogers" tend to act more creatively, and those who watch violence-packed cartoons and dramas tend to act more aggressively (Liebert et al., 1982; Sprafkin et al., 1983). Boys and girls tend to follow whatever sex roles their culture promotes, even if alternative roles seem more fulfilling (Maccoby, 1980). In adolescence, drug use is affected by the attitudes and examples of peers, to the point that many teenagers will "go along with the crowd" even when the crowd is using drugs the teenager knows to be dangerous (Sutker, 1982).

Social learning theory in no way contradicts the findings of earlier classical or operant conditioning. In fact, as the research report on the following page shows, when psychologists attempt to apply the insights provided by learning theory, they typically look at all three types of learning.

Evaluations of Learning Theories

The study of human development has benefited from learning theory in at least two ways. First, the emphasis on the causes and consequences of a specific behavior has led researchers to see that many behavior patterns that may seem to be inborn or the result of deeply rooted emotional problems may actually be the result of the immediate environment. And even when the immediate environment cannot be used to explain a problem completely, altering that environment in a significant way may nevertheless remedy the problem.

This realization has encouraged many scientists to approach particular problem behaviors, such as temper tantrums, fear of school, or reluctance to study, by analyzing, and attempting to change, the stimulus-response patterns they entail. The success achieved in eliminating such behaviors has astonished many psychologists who, believing these problems to be deep-seated or even constitutional, would have regarded them as requiring long-term treatment or perhaps even as being untreatable. Many people trained in the application of learning theory now work in schools, clinics, and hospitals, helping people to change their behavior patterns.

Children Who Are Out of Control

One of the most serious problems that developmentalists have been called upon to solve is that of disruptive, antisocial children. Such children not only cause havoc at home and trouble at school, they also tend to grow up to be juvenile delinquents and even career criminals (Hirschi, 1969).

One social learning researcher, Gerald Patterson, has spent his professional life trying to understand and help "out-of-control" children, that is, children who behave in aggressive and antisocial ways that neither family nor school seems able to control. For the past two decades, Patterson has led a team of scientists at the Oregon Social Learning Center in providing behavioral analysis as well as practical help to families in which one child is disruptively aggressive (Patterson et al., 1967; Patterson, 1980; 1982).

In the tradition of learning theorists, Patterson and his research team have spent thousands of hours observing the moment-by-moment sequences of behavior in hundreds of normal families and families with an out-of-control child. They have produced a vast amount of data on the frequency of aversive behavior (defined as unpleasant acts such as hitting, yelling, teasing, scolding), as well as on the events leading up to, and the consequences of, such acts.

It was found that out-of-control children behaved aversively at least three times as often as normal children (the record for frequency was set by a 6-year-old boy who behaved aversively, on average, four times a minute). Patterson determined that the problem is not just in the child but also in the social learning provided by the family. For one thing, in problem families the other family members also have higher-than-average rates of aversive behavior, often responding to aggression with aggression,

in a way that sets up an escalating cycle of retaliations. Typically, a problem child and a sibling might begin exchanging increasingly nasty names with each other and end up exchanging blows. In time, these patterns of attack and counterattack become so well learned that the parties involved become blind to alternative ways of resolving conflict.

Another factor highlighted by Patterson's research is that mothers of problem children are often unwitting perpetrators of aversive behavior once it occurs. When a child does something aversive, mothers of problem children are about twice as likely to end up responding positively—that is, by giving in to the child—or neutrally, allowing the child to continue the aversive behavior, than they are to respond negatively by punishing the behavior. Thus they buy their children candy to stop them from screaming and crying in the supermarket, or they let a child stay up later if he or she vehemently refuses to go to bed. As Patterson analyzes it, the immediate result of such maternal behavior is reinforcing for both the child and the mother. The child gets candy or the chance to stay up later, and the mother is spared further screaming or other unmanageable behavior that calls attention to her ineffectiveness. In essence, the child becomes operantly conditioned to go out of control in order to get his or her way, and the mother becomes operantly conditioned to avoid confronting the child's behavior in order to avoid intensifying it.

The mother's short-term solution creates a long-term problem, however. Patterson found that mothers are the victims of aversive behavior ten times as often as fathers, and three times as often as siblings. As his research clearly shows, the mother's role is typically that of family caretaker and "crisis manager," the one who is almost

Second, learning theory has provided a scientific model for developmentalists of all theoretical backgrounds. It encourages them to define terms precisely, test hypotheses, and publish supporting data as well as conclusions.

At the same time, learning theorists are often criticized for ignoring human emotions and ideas because these cannot be readily tested through controlled experiments. They do not accept the existence of the unconscious, and this, their critics believe, limits their understanding of behavior, particularly abnormal behavior. Many think that focusing only on that which can be observed provides too narrow a perspective to allow a full understanding of the complexities of human behavior and development.

Finally, much of the original elaboration of learning theory was based on re-always at the front lines when problems occur. This is in marked contrast to the role taken by the typical father:

The role most appropriate for fathers might be that of "guest." They expend much effort on activities which they find reinforcing (e.g., reading the newspaper). They may function as reinforcer, spectator, and participant in games, that is, "the resident good guy." They may even enter into some lightweight child management activities. However, given real crisis or high rate of aversives, they tend to drop out. [Patterson, 1980]

Patterson also notes that mothers who do not generally deal effectively with aversive behavior also tend to respond inappropriately to good behavior, either ignoring it or, about 20 percent of the time, actually punishing it. (One explanation for this involves classical conditioning: the mother becomes so conditioned to interpret her child's behavior as negative that she doesn't notice positive behavior.) Since the child is neither reinforced for good behavior nor punished for bad, the child doesn't learn to do anything other than what he or she pleases.

The solution, as Patterson sees it, is for the mothers to become more skilled at management techniques. They must reinforce positive behavior in their children, and, when punishing negative behavior, they must make sure that the punishment is sufficient to stop the outburst, rather than simply escalating and extending it. Here is an observer's account of Patterson's approach to training mothers in appropriate management techniques:

The child went to bed only when he felt like it, insisted on sleeping with his mother (she had no husband), rarely obeyed even the most reasonable commands, spread his excrement all over the living room walls, was a terror to other children who tried to play with him, and seemed destined to be a terror to his teachers. The first task was to make the mother realize that he was not minding her

in important ways because he was not minding her in small ones. Every day for one hour she was to count the number of times the boy failed to obey an order within fifteen seconds of its being issued and report the results to the therapist. This led the mother to become aware of how many times she was issuing orders and how long she was waiting to get results. . . .

At the third session, the mother was taught how to use "time out" as a means of discipline. She was told that whenever her son did something wrong she should immediately tell him why it was wrong and order him to go to time out—five minutes alone in the bathroom. She resisted doing this, because it forced her to confront all of her son's rule-breaking, and to do so immediately. She preferred to avoid the conflicts and the angry protests. She especially resisted using this means to enforce her son's going to bed at a stated, appropriate time; she was a lonely, not particularly attractive woman, and it was clear to the therapist that she wanted her son to sleep with her. In time, the woman was persuaded to try this new form of discipline and to back up a failure to go to time out by the withdrawal of some privilege ("no TV tonight"). As the weeks went by, the woman became excited about the improvement in the boy's behavior and came to value having him sleep alone in his own room. [Wilson, 1983]

However, retraining is not easy. It takes a skilled trainer, and several weeks or months to undo the habits learned over many years. Ideally, mother, father, and siblings should be brought into the project to change the social network of the family and to become models of appropriate rather than inappropriate behavior. They can also practice specific techniques to condition the problem child. Patterson finds that if the entire family works to improve their interaction, a family that has been at war with itself can learn to function in a supportive way for every member.

search with lower animals—generally dogs, rats, and pigeons—on the assumption that all animals, including humans, follow the same laws of behavior. If researchers had begun instead with the study of human learning, their findings might have led them to different conclusions (Stevenson, 1983). Learning theorists ignored, for example, the importance of our assessment of the meaning of others' behaviors, and, in turn, the effect that that assessment can have on our own behavior. For instance, verbal praise, such as "That was a job well done," may be very reinforcing if it is thought to be genuinely given, but not at all reinforcing if it is interpreted as mechanical. The fact that few learning theorists recognized the importance of cognition has meant that their laws of behavior have proved to be much more limited than was once believed (Cairns, 1983).

Cognitive Theories

The prime focus of **cognitive theory** is the structure and development of the individual's thought processes and the ways in which those processes can affect the person's understanding of, and expectations of, his or her world. In turn, cognitive theory considers how these understandings and expectations can affect the individual's behavior.

Piaget's Ideas

Jean Piaget (1896–1980), the most famous of cognitive theorists, first became interested in thought processes while field-testing questions that were being considered for a standard intelligence test for children. Piaget was supposed to find the age at which most children could answer each question correctly, but eventually he became more interested in the children's *wrong* answers. What intrigued him was that children who were the same age made similar types of mistakes, suggesting that there was a developmental sequence to intellectual growth. He began to believe that *how* children think is much more important, and more revealing of their mental ability, than tabulating what they know (Flavell, 1963; Cowan, 1978).

How Cognitive Development Occurs   Piaget held that there are four major stages of cognitive development. Each one is age-related and has structural features that permit certain types of thinking.

According to Piaget, infants think exclusively through their senses and motor abilities: their understanding of the objects in their world is limited to the actions they can perform on them. Preschool children can think about objects independently of their actions on them, and they can begin to think symbolically, as reflected in their ability to use language and to pretend. However, they cannot think logically in a consistent way. School-age children can begin to think logically in a consistent way, but only with regard to specific features of their world. Adolescents and adults, in varying degrees, are able to think abstractly: that is, they can think about thinking and can coordinate ideas (see Table 2.2). Each of these ways of thinking is explained in detail later in this book.

Figure 2.12 *All his life Jean Piaget was absorbed with studying the way children think. He is shown here on one of his trips to America, interviewing some school-children in New York's Harlem. Despite Piaget's age and French accent, these children are giving him what children everywhere have given him: illuminating answers to Piagetian questions.*

TABLE 2.2 **Piaget's Periods of Cognitive Development**

Approximate Age	Name	Characteristics	Major Acquisitions
Birth–2 years	Sensorimotor	Infant uses senses and motor abilities to understand the world. This period begins with reflexes and ends with complex coordinations of sensorimotor skills.	The infant learns that an object still exists when it is out of sight (*object permanence*) and begins to remember and imagine experiences (*mental representation*).
2–6 years	Preoperational	The child uses *symbolic thinking,* including language, to understand the world. Most thinking is *egocentric,* which means that children understand the world from only one perspective, their own.	The imagination flourishes. Children gradually begin to *decenter,* or become less egocentric, and to understand other points of view.
7–11 years	Concrete Operational	The child understands and applies logical operations, or principles, to help interpret specific experiences or perceptions.	By applying logical abilities, children learn to understand the basic ideas of conservation, number, classification, and many other concrete ideas.
From 12 on	Formal Operational	The adolescent or adult is able to think about abstractions and hypothetical concepts. During adolescence, this glimpse of the vast complexity of knowledge leads some to believe they understand nothing and others to believe they are on the verge of understanding everything.	There evolves the idea that there are many answers to every question, and many questions about every answer. Ethics, politics, and all social and moral issues become more interesting and involving.

The way children progress from one phase of cognitive development to another, or from one concept to another within a given phase, is the same throughout the life span. Piaget believed that everyone seeks mental **equilibrium,** that is, a balance of opposing forces (Piaget, 1970). What he meant by this is that each person needs to make sense of conflicting experiences and perceptions.

People achieve this equilibrium through mental concepts, or in Piaget's terms, **schemas,** that strike a harmony between their ideas and their experiences. A schema is a general way of thinking about, or interacting with, ideas and objects in the environment. The infant first comes to know the world through a sucking schema and a grasping schema; by adulthood the schemas through which the individual knows the world are beyond counting, ranging from something as simple as the schema for doing and undoing a button to the abstract moral schema that a human life is more valuable than any material thing. When existing schemas do not seem to fit present experiences, the individual falls into a state of **disequilibrium,** a kind of imbalance that initially produces confusion and then leads to growth as the person modifies old schemas and constructs new ones to fit the new conditions.

These ideas become clearer with an example. In one of Piaget's experiments, a child is shown two identical glasses, each containing the same quantity of liquid (Piaget and Inhelder, 1974). Next, the child pours the liquid from one of these glasses into a third glass, which is taller and narrower than the other two. The experimenter then asks the child which glass contains more. Almost every child younger than 6 says the taller glass contains more, because preschool children use the schema that taller is bigger. They are unshakable in this conviction, even when the experimenter points out that the taller glass is narrower and that the amount of water in each of the original identical glasses was obviously the same.

Most children older than 7, on the other hand, have developed the schema that Piaget called **conservation of liquids:** that is, they realize that pouring the liquid into a taller glass does not change the amount of liquid. They remain steadfast in this conviction even when the experimenter attempts to convince them otherwise.

Figure 2.13 *Although the experimenter has poured identical quantities of liquid into the two containers, this preschool boy will probably be guided more by appearance than logic, so he will decide that the taller, narrower container necessarily holds more than the shorter, wider one.*

In both these cases, the children's ideas and perceptions are in a state of equilibrium. They have managed to construct a mental structure that enables them to interpret what they see. Children progress from the first state of equilibrium to the second by passing through a transitional period of disequilibrium in which they begin to be able to recognize that some of their ideas conflict with their experiences. In the tall-glass experiment, for instance, they become aware that the idea that the identical glasses originally contained the same amount of liquid is inconsistent with the idea that taller glasses always hold more. They resolve this dilemma in a variety of ways. Some imagine that water was magically added to the tall glass. Some even say that the tall glass contains less because it is narrower, reversing their previous schema in their confusion. Some are puzzled, some are distressed, some say the question is impossible. All these reactions are evidence of disequilibrium.

Thirst For Knowledge Periods of disequilibrium can be disquieting to a child or an adult who suspects that accepted ideas no longer hold true. But they are also exciting periods of mental growth. By seeking out new experiences, children are constantly challenging their current schema. Babies poke, pull, and taste everything they get their hands on; preschool children ask thousands of questions; school-age children become avid readers and information collectors; and adolescents try out a wide variety of roles and experiences—all because people at every age want cognitive challenges. Recognition of this active searching for knowledge is the essence of the cognitive theory of human development.

Active searching is also the essence of intelligence, according to Piaget. It is part of human nature to seek to clarify and understand the myriad sensations and ideas that bombard the mind. The result of this quest for comprehension, according to Piaget, is intelligence, which, in his view, comprises two interrelated processes, **organization** and **adaptation.** People organize their thoughts so that they make sense, separating the more important thoughts from the less important ones, as well as establishing links between one idea and another. In the process of learning about various animals, for example, a child may organize them mentally in clusters according to whether they are birds, mammals, or fishes. At the same time, people adapt their thinking to include new ideas, as new experiences provide additional information. This adaptation occurs in two ways, through **assimilation** and **accom-**

modation. In the process of assimilation, information is simply added to the cognitive organization already there. In the process of accommodation, the intellectual organization has to adjust to the new idea. Thus, in watching a nature film, a child may extend his or her understanding of animals by discovering new animals to add to existing clusters (assimilation); or the child may be led to rearrange old clusters or create new ones as a result of seeing, say, whales, which are mammals that look like, and live like, fishes (accommodation).

These basic cognitive processes are at work even in the first weeks of life. Consider the grasping reflex, for instance. Newborns curl their fingers tightly around anything that crosses their palm. Soon, however, their grasping reflex becomes organized in specific ways as their particular experiences provide them with new knowledge: they grasp Mother's sweater one way, their bottle another way, a rattle another, and the cat's tail not at all. They have thus adopted their inborn grasping schema to their environment, first by assimilation (grasping everything that comes their way) and then by accommodation (adjusting their grasp to the "graspability" of the object).

The process of assimilation and accommodation continues throughout life. Consider the concept of Santa Claus. When 2-year-olds are taken to see a store Santa Claus, many cry or sit mute on his lap, for the typical toddler assimilates Santa into a schema that strange-looking men are frightening. With repeated experiences, however, children quickly come to realize that Santa Claus has something to do with the arrival of presents. They accommodate by forming a more favorable concept of Santa Claus, perhaps using another schema such as "getting presents is fun." With time, many come to believe that Santa Claus is really the source of Christmas presents. Once formed, this concept often becomes strengthened, as the child assimilates all the evidence that Santa Claus brings presents and resists all claims to the contrary offered by older children. Eventually, however, the notion of a real Santa Claus crumbles, as the child's increasing reasoning ability must confront the obvious impossibility of one man bringing presents to all the children in the world—especially by coming down the chimney. Some time later a new Santa schema may develop, perhaps one that centers on the idea of the Christmas spirit or of the commercialization of religious occasions. In any case, intelligence involves the continual adaptation of old organizational structures to assimilate, and, if need be, accommodate new ideas and experiences.

Figure 2.14 *Children between 6 months and 2 years are fearful of, or at least wary of, strangers. This fear is most powerful if the stranger is large, male, bearded, oddly dressed, and in a public place.*

RESEARCH REPORT   **The Clinical Method**

Piaget's interest in children's thought processes led him to be dissatisfied with naturalistic observation and with standardized laboratory tests. He needed to ask children probing questions, which a mere observer would not do, and to follow the lead of the child's answers, which would be impossible in a tightly controlled experiment. Thus he developed the clinical method, so named because, like a doctor with a patient, the researcher asks certain initial questions and then, on the basis of the child's responses, determines what questions to ask next.

The clinical method has produced many fascinating glimpses into the child's mental development. In one series of investigations, Piaget decided to explore children's understanding of family relationships (Piaget, 1962; originally published 1928). He began by asking 140 boys aged 4 to 11 their definition of what a brother is. He then posed several questions about their responses.

Boy, age 7: All boys are brothers.
Piaget: Is your father a brother?
Yes, when he was little.
Why was your father a brother?
Because he was a boy.
Do you know your father's brother?
He doesn't have a brother.

Boy, only child, age 6: A brother is a boy. (He has just said that he himself is not a brother.)
Piaget: Are all boys brothers?
[No] because some of them are little.
If anyone is little, isn't he a brother?
No, you can only be a brother if you are big.

Even older children often made mistakes:

Boy, age 9: When there is a boy and another boy, when there are two of them.
Piaget: Has your father got a brother?
Yes.
Why?
Because he was born second.
Then what is a brother?
It is the second brother that comes.
Then the first is not a brother?
Oh no. The second brother that comes is called a brother.

Almost every 4- and 5-year-old knew whether or not he was a brother, but few understood what a brother is. Girls were similarly limited in their understanding about sisters.

Indeed, most young siblings think that all girls are sisters and all boys are brothers. Not until age 9 did 75 percent of the children Piaget interviewed define "brother" or "sister" correctly, presumably because not until then were they able to understand and follow the logic of the categories used to designate family members.

This basic finding, that children's ability to understand their world depends partly on their comprehension of logical categories and their use of logical thought processes, has been confirmed by many other researchers using the clinical method.

One recent example comes from Ronald and Juliette Goldman (1982), who became interested in how children's thinking processes affect their understanding of sexuality and how that understanding might affect their behavior. They began by questioning 838 public school children aged 5 to 15, from Australia, England, North America (the United States and Canada), and Sweden. They chose only children who lived with both parents and who had at least one younger sibling, because they thought such children would have had a natural opportunity to learn something about sex differences and about pregnancy.

The Goldmans found that children's misconceptions about sexual questions were widespread and consistent with the cognitive patterns described by Piaget. For example, before children reach the cognitive stage when they begin to reason logically about concrete matters (concrete operational thinking), they tend to make assumptions on the basis of a single, not necessarily relevant, characteristic and ignore all others. When the Goldmans asked children, "How can anyone know if a newborn baby is a boy or a girl?" many of the younger children centered on a physical feature such as hair, or on a particular behavior, or on some other feature such as clothing. For example, a 7-year-old Australian girl said, "Because mum dressed her in a dress. There's no other way to tell," and a 7-year-old Swedish boy answered, "If it cries a lot it's a boy." As shown by the chart, more than half of the children 7 or younger evidenced no understanding that differences in the sex organs could be a major clue to gender.

In many cases, the interviewers followed Piaget's clinical method by asking additional questions, which often revealed the child's attempt to "logically" extend his or her illogical premise. One 7-year-old North American boy, for example, replied as follows:

Interviewer: How can anyone know if a newborn baby is a boy or a girl?
Boy: By the hair.
How by the hair?
My mum told me it was a boy.
How did she know?
The doctor tells her.
How does the doctor know?
He looks through a magnifying glass at their eyes, and he can tell by the eyebrows.

By contrast, the older children, who had reached the stage of concrete reasoning, usually showed some understanding that sex organs distinguish male from female and were not misled in their thinking by irrelevant features such as attire.

Significantly, Swedish children arrived at a fuller understanding of sexual matters earlier than their contemporaries from the other countries, a difference that was most apparent during the elementary school years. This was due in large measure to the fact that they had begun sex education in public school at age 8. According to cognitive theory, the English-speaking children could have done as well if sex education had been part of their curriculum too, for once children reach the stage at which they can begin to reason concretely, they are able to understand and organize basic sexual information within a biological framework.

Like many cognitive theorists, the Goldmans argue that children's attitudes and behavior are affected by their understanding of the world. In this case, the children

By school age, children no longer show babies hatching from eggs, or purchased at stores. But note that the first child, age 6, has imagined the fetus standing up with long hair, and although the second, age 8, is correct about position, she still imagines much more belly than baby.

whose sexual understanding was most limited also had the most limited ideas of male and female roles (insisting, for example, that daddies work and mommies stay home) and the most stereotyped ideas of their classmates, believing that members of the opposite sex were so different that they were unsuitable to be chosen as friends.

In this research, as well as in countless other studies, it is apparent that the clinical method is a useful tool for revealing children's thought patterns. It provides some of the control of laboratory research as well as some of the realism of naturalistic studies. While this method is not as. objective as a tightly structured experiment would be, it is systematic, and the results are replicable; thus it qualifies as one more approach to the scientific study of the child (Cowan, 1978).

Evaluations of Cognitive Theories

Cognitive theory has revolutionized developmental psychology by focusing attention on the child's active mental processes. The attempt to understand the mental structures of the child's thought, and to appreciate the child's internal need for new mental structures when the old ones become outmoded, has led to a new understanding of certain aspects of children's behavior. Thanks to the insights provided by cognitive theory, researchers, parents, and educators now have a greater appreciation of the capacities and limitations of children's thinking at various ages—and of the ways these capacities and limitations can affect behavior.

Cognitive theory has also profoundly affected education throughout England and North America, allowing teachers and students to become partners in the educational process once the child's own capacities and needs are recognized. For instance, elementary-school math is now taught with objects the child can manipulate, because we now know that the thinking of school-age children is better suited to working out solutions by concrete activities, such as measuring blocks or counting pennies, than to the more abstract learning tasks involved in reading about, and memorizing, mathematical facts.

Figure 2.15 *Manipulating math cubes may be especially helpful to a child during the development of the basic ideas of logic and number. For example, familiarity with the nines table is enhanced more by counting the cubes and observing the pattern they make than by simply memorizing the numbers.*

Finally, cognitive theory has helped researchers in many fields to reexamine their assumptions, for we have learned that the way we think colors what we see. In order to be more objective as scientists, we need to become aware of our subjectivity—an awareness that cognitive theory has helped to foster.

Piaget's theories at first met with indifference and criticism in North America. He seemed too uninterested in emotions for Freud's followers and too unscientific for the behaviorists. But his ideas have gradually won over many professionals, especially educators.

At the same time, many people think Piaget was so absorbed by the child's active search for knowledge that he ignored external motivation or teaching. While it is comforting to think that children develop their own schemas when they are ready, this implies that teachers should not intervene when a child seems uninterested in learning to add or spell. To some extent, the "back to basics" movement in American education is a reaction against Piagetian ideas carried to their logical extreme. And even some of those who most admire Piaget believe that he underestimated the role of society and home in fostering cognitive development. Partly for this reason, Jerome Kagan (1971) has called Piaget "a developmental idealist." Many psychologists believe that culture and education can be crucial in providing the proper mix of equilibrium and disequilibrium to help the child develop. In Bruner's (1973) words, "Some environments push cognitive growth better, earlier, and longer than others . . . it makes a huge difference to the intellectual life of a child simply that he was in school."

A number of critics have also found fault with Piaget's depiction of cognitive stages as universal. For example, there are many adults who never develop the capacity for abstract thinking that Piaget described as being typical of adolescence. Further, Piaget's description of intelligence focused mainly on scientific and logical thinking, with little attention given to the development of language, art, and personal understanding (Gardner, 1983; Miller, 1983).

A final point is less a quibble than a qualification. As a number of researchers have pointed out, Piaget's description of cognitive development tends to make it seem as though once a new stage of cognition has been achieved, it will be reflected in all aspects of the individual's thinking. In fact, the cognitive advance may occur in some areas of thinking and not in others. And particularly with children, the advance in a given area may be evident on one occasion and not on another. Most cognitive theorists now generally believe that "unevenness is the rule in development" (Fischer, 1980; Flavell, 1982).

The Theories Compared

Each of the three theories presented here has contributed a great deal to the study of human development. Psychoanalytic theory has made us aware of the importance of early childhood experiences and of the possible impact of the "hidden dramas" that influence our daily lives. Learning theory has shown us the effect that the immediate environment can have on behaviors; cognitive theory has brought us to a greater understanding of how our thinking affects our actions.

Each theory has also been criticized: psychoanalytic theory for being too subjective; learning theory for being too mechanistic; and cognitive theory for undervaluing the power of direct instruction and overemphasizing rational, logical thought.

Each theory by itself is, in fact, too restricted to grasp the breadth and diversity of human development (Cairns, 1983; Thomas, 1981). As one researcher explains, we now see people as "so complex and multifaceted as to defy easy classification . . . [and] multiply influenced by a host of interacting determinants . . . It is an image that highlights the shortcomings of all simplistic theories that view behavior as the exclusive result of any narrow set of determinants, whether these are habits, traits, drives, reinforcers, constructs, instincts, or genes, and whether they are exclusively inside or outside the person" (Mischel, 1977).

For this reason, most developmentalists describe themselves as having an **eclectic perspective,** meaning that rather than adopting any one of these theories exclusively, they make use of all of them. Indeed, many developmentalists who, in the past, had been identified with particular theories have become increasingly aware of the limitations of any one theoretical system and now incorporate some of the ideas from the other perspectives into their thinking (Cairns, 1983; Kuhn, 1978; Sameroff, 1982).

In subsequent chapters, as echoes and elaborations of the psychoanalytic, learning, and cognitive theories appear, you can form your own opinion of the validity of each theory. The best challenge you can set for yourself, the same one that faces developmental researchers, is the integration of theory, research, and applications into an increasingly comprehensive picture of human development.

SUMMARY

What Theories Do

1. A theory provides a framework of general principles that can be used to interpret our observations. Each theory interprets human development from a somewhat different perspective, but all theories attempt to provide a context in which to understand individual experiences and behaviors.

Psychoanalytic Theories

2. Psychoanalytic theory emphasizes that our actions are largely ruled by the unconscious—the source of powerful impulses and conflicts that usually lie below the level of our conscious awareness.

3. Freud, the founder of psychoanalytic theory, developed the theory of psychosexual stages to explain how unconscious impulses arise and how they affect behavior during the development of the child.

4. Freud interpreted behavior in terms of three components of personality: the id seeks immediate gratification of its desires; the superego acts as a conscience to suppress the id; the ego moderates the demands of the id and superego and copes with the recognition that other people have needs, too.

5. Erikson's theory of psychosocial development describes individuals as being shaped by the interaction of physical characteristics, personal history, and social forces. Culture plays a large part in each person's ability to deal with the most significant tasks, or crises, of psychological development.

Learning Theories

6. Learning theorists believe that psychologists should study only behavior that can be observed and measured.

They are especially interested in the relationship between behaviors or events and the reactions they elicit, that is, between the stimulus and the response.

7. Learning theory emphasizes the importance of various forms of conditioning, a process by which particular stimuli become linked with particular responses. In classical conditioning, one stimulus becomes associated with another to produce a particular response. In operant, or instrumental, conditioning, reinforcement makes a behavior either more or less likely to occur.

8. Social learning theory recognizes that much of human behavior is modeled after the behavior of others. For children, models of behavior include parents, peers, popular heroes, and celebrities.

Cognitive Theories

9. Cognitive theorists believe that a person's thought processes—the understanding and expectations of a particular situation—have an important effect on behavior. Piaget, the leading cognitive theorist, proposed that people learn by a process of organization and adaptation.

10. At each age, people develop schemas—general ways of thinking about ideas and objects. When a person becomes aware of perceptions or experiences that do not fit an existing schema, a new schema is created, and cognitive growth occurs.

The Theories Compared

11. Psychoanalytic, learning, and cognitive theories have all contributed to the understanding of human development, yet no one theory is adequate to describe the complexity and diversity of the human experience. Most developmentalists incorporate ideas from several developmental perspectives into their thinking.

KEY TERMS

psychoanalytic theory *(37)*
infantile sexuality *(39)*
psychosexual stages *(39)*
oral stage *(39)*
anal stage *(39)*
phallic stage *(39)*
sexual latency *(39)*
genital stage *(39)*
id *(40)*
ego *(40)*
superego *(40)*
defense mechanism *(40)*
regression *(40)*
repression *(40)*
displacement *(41)*
psychosocial theory *(43)*
behaviorism *(45)*
learning theory *(45)*
stimulus *(46)*
response *(46)*
conditioning *(46)*

classical conditioning *(47)*
operant conditioning *(47)*
reinforcement *(48)*
reinforcer *(48)*
positive reinforcer *(48)*
negative reinforcer *(48)*
punishment *(48)*
social reinforcer *(49)*
social learning theory *(50)*
modeling *(50)*
cognitive theory *(54)*
equilibrium *(55)*
schema *(55)*
disequilibrium *(55)*
conservation of liquids *(55)*
organization *(56)*
adaptation *(56)*
assimilation *(56)*
accommodation *(56)*
eclectic perspective *(62)*

KEY QUESTIONS

1. What functions does a good theory perform?

2. What is the major premise of psychoanalytic theory?

3. According to Freud's theory, what is the function of the ego?

4. What is the major difference between Erikson's theory and Freud's theory?

5. According to Erikson, which factors influence human development?

6. What insights of psychoanalytic theory have proved particularly valuable to developmentalists?

7. What is the major premise of learning theory?

8. What are the differences between classical and operant conditioning?

9. What factors should be considered when choosing reinforcers to promote learning?

10. What factors influence the modeling of children's behavior after the behavior of others?

11. What is the major premise of cognitive theory?

12. According to Piaget, how do periods of disequilibrium lead to mental growth?

13. What is the difference between assimilation and accommodation?

14. What are the main differences between the psychoanalytic, learning, and cognitive theories?

RECOMMENDED READINGS

Miller, Patricia H. *Theories of developmental psychology.* San Francisco: Freeman, 1983.

An excellent source for a thorough examination of the theories outlined in this chapter, as well as reflections on the role of theories in developmental psychology.

Freud, Sigmund. *The sexual enlightenment of children.* New York: Collier Books, 1963.

This book contains several essays by Freud. In one, Freud advocates telling children the truth when they ask questions about sexual matters. In other essays, he analyzes the sexual implications of some of the fantasies that children have and some of the lies they tell.

Erikson, Erik. *Childhood and society* (2nd ed.). New York: Norton, 1963.

Erikson's beautifully written classic, which explains his theory of psychosocial development and his reinterpretation of Freud. The discussion of several American subcultures, as well as the childhoods of Hitler in Germany and Gorky in Russia, is fascinating.

Skinner, B. F. *About behaviorism.* New York: Random House, 1976.

The most famous American behaviorist defends behaviorism in clear and definite terms.

Piaget, Jean, and Inhelder, Barbel. *The psychology of the child.* New York: Basic Books, 1969.

Relatively brief, yet comprehensive, which is why it is recommended. However, it is also quite difficult (as is all of Piaget).

Gould, Stephen J. *The panda's thumb: More reflections in natural history.* New York: Norton, 1982.

Calvin, W. H. *The throwing madonna: From nervous cells to the hominid brain.* New York: McGraw-Hill, 1983.

Both these books are fascinating examples of the relationship between theory and fact, although neither is directly relevant to developmental psychology.

The Panda's Thumb is a series of essays by a naturalist, who begins with surprising facts (for example, that pandas have thumbs) and proposes intriguing theories.

The Throwing Madonna begins with a question: why are most humans right-handed? The traditional explanation is that men had to protect their hearts in battle, which was best done by gripping a shield in the left hand and a club or spear in the right. However, Calvin suggests that female nurturance is a more likely explanation. Since the beginning of time, mothers have held their infants near their hearts, a task done more easily with the left hand. Thus the right hand was free to perform most of the tasks of daily life, including the hunting of small game by stone-throwing.

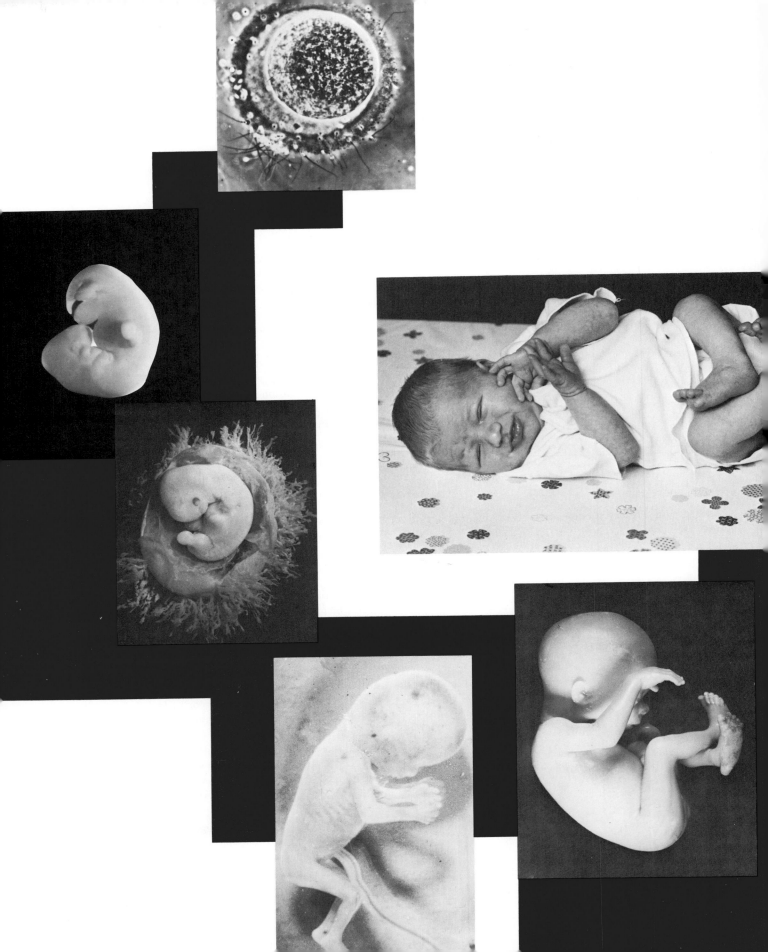

The Beginnings

Part I

When considering the human life span, most people ignore or take for granted the time from conception through birth. Indeed, among all the cultures of the world, China seems to have been the only one to have ever included the prenatal period when reckoning age. Yet, these 266 or so days could not be more crucial. On the very first day, for instance, our entire genetic heritage is set, affecting not only what we see when we look in the mirror but also many of the abilities, talents, and disabilities that characterize each of us. Survival is much more doubtful and growth much more rapid during the prenatal period than at any other time in our lives. Finally, each child's day of birth usually provides the occasion for more anticipation, worry, excitement, and joy on the part of parents than any other day of childhood. Indeed, the impact of the physiological and emotional events of that day can be felt for weeks, months, even years.

These early days, usually uncounted and underemphasized, are the focus of the next three chapters.

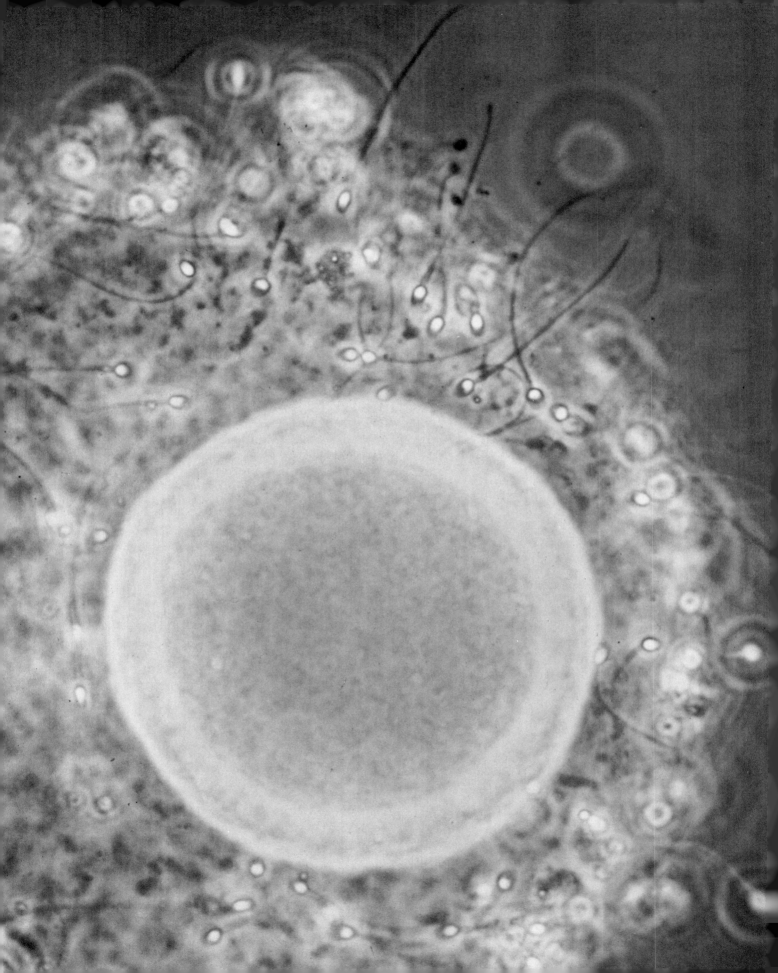

Conception and Heredity

A million, million spermatozoa,
*   All of them alive*
Out of their cataclysm but one poor Noah
*   Dare hope to survive*
And among that billion minus one
*   might have chanced to be*
Shakespeare, another Newton, a new Donne
*   But the One was Me.*

Aldous Huxley
"Fifth Philosopher's Song"

Culture and Conception

The Biology of Conception
The Moment of Conception

Genes and Chromosomes
The Twenty-third Pair

Genetic Uniqueness

Dominant and Recessive Genes

Polygenic Inheritance

Heredity and Environment
Multifactorial Characteristics

Abnormal Genes and Chromosomes
Chromosomal Abnormalities

Harmful Genes

Genetic Counseling
Two Success Stories

Who Should Be Tested?

Testing for Genetic Conditions

Predicting Genetic Problems

Many Alternatives

Chapter 3

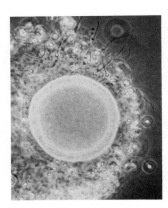

If any one of the hundreds of sperm surrounding this ovum manages to penetrate its surface, genetic messages from both parents will combine to create the pattern of instructions required for the growth and development of a unique new person. Although the direction this person's life takes will be strongly influenced by his or her genetic inheritance, its ultimate course will depend on many factors, from the mother's health and nourishment during the pregnancy to the society's systems of social and economic support.

In this chapter, we will discuss the interactions between genetics and environment that affect the developing person, including answers to the following questions:

What is the sequence of events that results in conception?

What determines the sex of the fetus?

Why are some pairs of twins identical in every way while others are no more alike than other pairs of brothers and sisters?

How does environment interact with genetic endowment to influence physical and psychological characteristics?

Which parents are most at risk of having a child with genetic or chromosomal abnormalities?

What advances are being made in the diagnosis and treatment of genetic diseases?

Conception—that moment when a sperm and ovum join to begin a new human being—might seem a simple topic in the study of development, a miracle to be briefly mentioned. But much depends on that moment, for within a very short time the genes contained in the sperm and ovum combine to form a developmental "blueprint" that will influence virtually everything about the person-to-be, not only physical attributes, such as gender and appearance, but every intellectual and personality characteristic as well.

Many environmental influences are also set at conception. Some of these, such as the mother's health, age, and life style, have a direct impact on the uterine environment where the embryo will live or die. Other environmental factors, such as the parents' education, income, and social class, also have a powerful, although indirect, impact.

Beyond that, like a stone tossed into a quiet pond, the beginning of each life alters the future for those who are closest to the prospective baby, and sends ripples that may eventually be felt by a vastly larger circle of people. One couple may be delighted with the addition to their lives, another may find a child to be just one more source of stress and anger, a thing to be ignored or even abused.

Thus, conception is much more than a brief biological miracle; it is the foundation upon which a life is built.

Culture and Conception

Throughout most of human history, married couples did not plan their families; they simply had as many babies as chance provided (Rudel et al., 1973). For one thing, they had little choice in the matter, since contraceptive methods were, at best, unreliable. For another, children were generally considered an economic asset, first as unpaid labor in the home or the shop or the field, and later, as a source of support for parents in their old age. Reinforcing these two factors was the pervasive cultural pressure to "be fruitful and multiply." Bearing as many children as possible was usually regarded as a woman's duty, as well as her major source of fulfillment. All told, the childless couple was to be pitied.

Recently, there have been changes in all three of these areas. (1) Important refinements in contraceptive methods now make it possible for a couple to determine how many children they will have, and when. (2) Children today are no longer perceived as an economic asset. Indeed, in the United States, each child represents a financial liability of approximately $167,000* between birth and the end of high school. (3) Psychologists and lay people alike acknowledge that having children does not necessarily guarantee fulfillment, nor does not having them necessarily preclude it. In some instances, in fact, nonparents are envied rather than pitied. Largely as a result of these changes, adults in developed nations are having fewer children. In the United States, for instance, couples are having their first child later, and are currently limiting their family size to an average of 1.8 children, as compared to 3.8 in 1957 (Glick, 1984).

Figure 3.1 *When this photograph was taken in 1880, a family with nine children was the envy of the neighborhood.*

---

*Based on an estimate by Lawrence Olson (1983). The estimate includes public schools and does not take into account wages lost by the care-taking parent.

Figure 3.2 *The $167,000 price tag seems high until one totals up all the food, clothing, shelter, medical, and play costs of raising an average child. Not only does each child personally consume many items, but each child also increases the amount needed for family expenses, such as rent, electricity, paper goods, telephone, vacations, laundry, and so forth. When a child has special medical or educational needs, the cost is much higher than this estimate.*

These changes are welcomed by most developmental researchers, who believe that prospective parents' increasing ability to make decisions about conception allows them to plan a good family life. For example, in general, the healthiest and happiest families include relatively mature parents and relatively few children, who are not too close in age. In addition, the fact that a child is planned for implies that the child is truly wanted and that the parents feel ready to take on the responsibilities of child-rearing. Planning also allows parents to help ensure their future child's health by making changes, if necessary, in their diet and drug use (the importance of this factor will be explained in the next chapter). Finally, increased knowledge about how a child inherits physical characteristics and developmental predispositions from his or her parents, and new techniques for gaining information about this genetic heritage, allow parents to know, in advance, how their age, family and ethnic background, or other factors, might affect their child.

With this background in mind, let us now examine the genetic interaction that occurs at conception and the biological events that set it in motion.

Figure 3.3 *Similarities in facial characteristics and skin and hair color create the impression of family resemblance apparent in this portrait. However, it is the less-obvious hereditary characteristics—personality traits, intellectual abilities, and possibly even genetic diseases—that are likely to be of greater significance to the next generation.*

The Biology of Conception

Human reproductive cells are called **gametes.** Female gametes are **ova** (singular, ovum). Sometimes they are called eggs. An ovum is the largest cell in the human body, about one-quarter the size of the period at the end of this sentence. Male gametes are **spermatozoa** (singular, spermatozoon), usually abbreviated to sperm. A spermatozoon is only about one twenty-fifth the size of an ovum.

Usually an ovum is released from one of the woman's two ovaries about fourteen days after the beginning of each menstrual period. This process is called ovulation (see Figure 3.4). Most of the time, the ovum travels uneventfully through one of the Fallopian tubes, whereupon, if it has not been fertilized by a sperm, it passes into the uterus and disintegrates.

The Moment of Conception

At his climax during sexual intercourse, a man ejaculates about 350 million sperm into the vagina. Only a few thousand of these sperm will survive long enough to make their way to the Fallopian tubes. If intercourse occurs a few days before or after ovulation, the surviving sperm might meet an ovum, and one sperm might penetrate the egg's lining. (This penetration triggers a chemical reaction that prevents the other nearby sperm from fertilizing the ovum.) Within hours, the sperm and ovum fuse to form a one-celled organism called a **zygote:** the development of a human life has begun (see Figure 3.4).

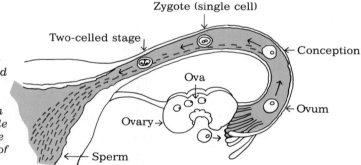

Figure 3.4 *One of the millions of sperm that entered the uterus has found and fertilized the ovum in the Fallopian tube. This union produces a zygote, a single cell which contains all the genes and chromosomes of the person-to-be.*

Genes and Chromosomes

The differences between a zygote and a newborn are, obviously, vast. Yet the tiny zygote shares one crucial element with the human being it may become. It contains all the biologically inherited information—the genes and chromosomes—that will influence the development of the person for the rest of his or her life. Virtually every human characteristic, from hair texture to blood type, from foot size to heart shape, from memory to moodiness, is affected, though not determined, by our genes. Each cell of the human body contains a copy of the original genetic material that was inherited from the parents by way of the sperm and ovum and organized into a set of unique instructions in the zygote.

A **gene** is a segment of a DNA (deoxyribonucleic acid) molecule that provides the biochemical instructions a cell needs to perform a specific function in the human body. Genes are arranged in specific locations like, speaking loosely, beads on a string. The "string" is the long, exquisitely thin DNA molecule that, together with other materials, makes up a **chromosome.** Every human body cell has forty-six chromosomes in the form of twenty-three chromosome pairs, one pair member coming from each parent. Since each chromosome carries several thousand genes (some chromosomes have more, some less), the fusion of sperm and ovum produces millions of genetic instructions.

Shortly after the zygote has been formed, it begins a process (*mitosis*) of duplication and division. The single cell first divides into two cells; then the two cells divide into four, the four into eight, and so on. Just before each cell division, the forty-six chromosomes duplicate themselves, forming two complete sets of chromosomes. These two sets separate from each other, move to opposite sides of the cell, and the cell then divides in the middle. Each new cell thus has the same twenty-three pairs of chromosomes, and therefore the same genetic information, that was contained in the zygote. This process continues throughout the development of the individual, creating new cells and replacing old ones. At birth, a baby is made up of about 10 trillion cells. By adulthood, the number has increased to between 300 and 500 trillion. But no matter how many cells a person may have, no matter what their specific function, each cell carries the genetic message of the original zygote.

The Twenty-third Pair

Twenty-two of the twenty-three pairs of chromosomes found in human beings are identical in both males and females. They are called **autosomes**, and they control the development and the functioning of most of the body. The twenty-third pair, which is the one that determines the individual's sex, is a special case. In the male, the twenty-third pair is designated XY (so named because of its appearance—see Figure 3.5), and in the female, it is designated XX.

When the male germ cells in the testes and the female germ cells in the ovaries divide to produce gametes, they do so in a way different from that of body cells; that is, the chromosomes do not merely duplicate themselves. Instead, through a complex process (*meiosis*), the chromosomes divide in such a way that each sperm or

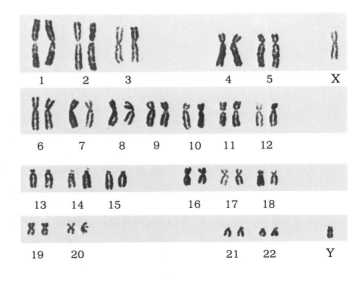

Figure 3.5 *A picture of the forty-six chromosomes from one individual, in this case a normal male. In order to produce a chromosomal portrait such as this one, a cell is removed from the person's body (usually from inside the mouth), processed so that the chromosomes become visible, magnified many times, photographed, and then arranged in pairs according to length of the upper "arms."*

Figure 3.6 *Whether a fertilized ovum will develop into a male or female depends on whether the ovum, which always has an X chromosome, is fertilized by a sperm carrying an X chromosome (a female will result) or a sperm carrying a Y chromosome (a male will result).*

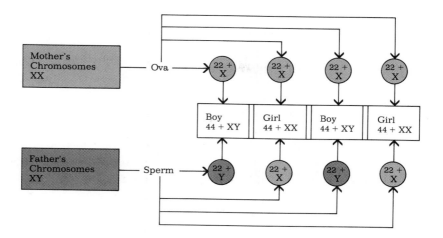

ovum receives only one member of each chromosome pair. (In other words, each sperm or ovum has only twenty-three chromosomes, half as many as the original cell.) Since in females the twenty-third chromosome pair is XX, each ovum carries one X chromosome. And since in males the twenty-third pair is XY, approximately half of the sperm will have an X chromosome and the other half, a Y. If an ovum is fertilized by a sperm bearing a Y chromosome (*XY* zygote), a male will develop. If it is fertilized by a sperm bearing an X chromosome (*XX* zygote), a female will develop (see Figure 3.6).

Genetic Uniqueness

On the basis of what you have been told so far, you might well wonder why all children in a given family do not look exactly alike, inasmuch as they each have twenty-three chromosomes from their father and twenty-three from their mother. One reason is that each member of a chromosome pair carries a different genetic message. When the chromosome pairs divide during the formation of gametes, which of the two pair members will wind up in a particular gamete is a matter of chance, and many combinations are possible. In fact, the laws of probability show that there are 2^{23}—that is, about 8 million—possible outcomes. In other words, approximately 8 million different ova or sperm can be produced by a single individual. In addition, corresponding segments of a chromosome pair are sometimes exchanged in the first stages of gamete production, a crossing-over, or "reshuffling," of genes that can create a new genetic interaction because of the new placement (Emery, 1983). And finally, when the genes of the ovum and the sperm combine, they interact to form combinations not present in either parent. All things considered, any given mother and father can form over 64 trillion genetically different offspring, a number "far greater than the number of humans who have ever lived on earth!" (Klug and Cummings, 1983). Thus it is no exaggeration to say that every conception represents the beginning of a genetically unique individual.

Twins Not all individuals are born genetically unique, however. Occasionally a zygote splits apart during its initial division, and the two separate, identical cells begin to develop independently, becoming identical twins. They are called **monozygotic twins** because they come from one (mono) zygote. Monozygotic twins are the same sex, look alike, and share all other inherited characteristics, because each has the same genes that were in the original zygote.

A CLOSER LOOK   **Twins and Research**

Monozygotic and dizygotic twins have been studied extensively, partly because they provide much-needed data on the interaction between nature and nurture. The basic idea is that if, for any given characteristic, monozygotic twins are much more alike than dizygotic twins, this would suggest that genes rather than environment (growing up in the same household) determine that characteristic.

Note, however, that this way of differentiating the influence of genes from the influence of environment makes the assumption that children growing up in the same family will have the same experiences. In fact, children in the same household often have quite different experiences, and the extent of these differences depends partly on how parents and others react to each child (McCall, 1983). It is quite probable that parents and teachers will treat monozygotic twins much more alike than dizygotic twins, if only because it is so hard to tell monozygotic twins apart. Thus, when research data finds monozygotic twins to be more alike than dizygotic twins, both genes and environment might be responsible.

One presumed way to separate the effect of genes and experience is to look at monozygotic twins who have been raised in different households. Several studies that have done this (Shields, 1962; Juel-Nielson, 1980; Bouchard, 1981) provide a wealth of suggestive evidence for the influence of genes. In fact, the similarities that they have found between twins reared apart has sometimes been startling.

Take the case of Robert Shafran, who while walking across the campus of the university in which he had recently enrolled, was suddenly greeted by a young woman who kissed him warmly on the mouth and exclaimed, "Where have you been?" That Robert didn't even know this woman was a fact he admitted somewhat reluctantly, since she was just his type. As it turned out, she was also his brother Eddy Galland's type: in fact, it was Eddy, Robert's long-lost twin, whom the woman had taken Robert to be. And it was soon clear that the resemblance between Robert and Eddy was not limited to physical characteristics. Among other striking similarities, the brothers wore the same kinds of clothes; had similar hairstyles; laughed in the same way at the same jokes; drank the same brand of beer; smoked the same brand of cigarettes (which they held in the same way); engaged in the same sports, including team wrestling (in which they had almost identical records); and listened to the same music, at similar volumes.

When the story of Robert and Eddy hit the press, David Kellman looked at their photo and thought he was seeing mirror images of himself—and, in fact, he was, for in this case, monozygotic triplets rather than twins had been separated at birth. When the three brothers were reunited, they (and the psychologists who studied them) were amazed at the number of experiences, tastes, and interests they had in common (*New York Times*, 1981).

The sources of triple confusion, from top to bottom: Edward Galland, David Kellman, and Robert Shafran.

Similar amazement was recently registered, a bit less publicly, by a group of researchers beginning the Minnesota Study of Twins Reared Apart, an extensive study of monozygotic twins who were separated early in life (Holden, 1980; Bouchard, 1981). One pair of identical twins, Oskar Stohr and Jack Yufe, were born of a Jewish father and German mother in Trinidad in the 1930s. Soon after their birth, Oskar was taken to Nazi Germany by his mother to be raised as a Catholic in a household consisting mostly of women. Jack was raised as a Jew by his father, spending his childhood in the Caribbean, and some of his adolescence in Israel.

Since Oskar Stohr (left) and Jack Yufe (right) are monozygotic twins, it is not surprising that they look very much alike. However, since they have been separated almost from birth, it is more difficult to explain their similarities in many of those characteristics that are usually considered to be acquired, for example, their preference for moustaches and their tastes in food and drink.

On the face of it, it would be difficult to imagine more disparate cultural backgrounds. In addition, the twins certainly had their differences. Oskar was married, an employee, and a devoted union member. Jack was divorced and owned a clothing store in Southern California. But, when the brothers met for the first time in Minnesota,

similarities started cropping up as soon as Oskar arrived at the airport. Both were wearing wire-rimmed glasses and mustaches, both sported two-pocket shirts with epaulets. They share idiosyncrasies galore: they like spicy foods and sweet liqueurs, are absentminded, have a habit of falling asleep in front of the television, think it's funny to sneeze in a crowd of strangers, flush the toilet before using it, store rubber bands on their wrists, read magazines from back to front, dip buttered toast in their coffee. Oskar is domineering toward women and yells at his wife, which Jack did before he was separated. [Holden, 1980].

Their scores on several psychological tests were very similar, and they struck the investigator as remarkably similar in temperament and tempo. Other pairs of twins in this study likewise startled the observers by their similarity, not only in appearance and on test scores, but in mannerisms and dress. One pair of female twins, separated since infancy, arrived in Minnesota, each wearing seven rings (on the same fingers) and three bracelets, a coincidence that might be explained by pure

chance, but more likely was partly genetic—that is, genes endowed both women with beautiful hands and, possibly, contributed to an interest in self-adornment.

The evidence from monozygotic twins suggests that genes affect a much greater number of characteristics than most psychologists, including the leader of the Minnesota study, Thomas Bouchard, suspected. Says Bouchard,

No matter what trait we look at—psychological interest, personality, temperament, across the whole spectrum—almost everything has a hereditary effect. Some psychologists concluded a while back from other studies that it looked like all traits were about equally genetically influenced. I always thought that was kind of foolish. But now, with these studies of identical twins reared apart, I'm starting to become a believer. [Quoted in Cassill, 1982]

However, while studies of monozygotic twins astonish researchers with the extent of genetic influence, they also furnish ample evidence for environmental impact. For example, while monozygotic twins often share the same fears, their reaction to the fear may be different; one will feel anxious when riding an escalator or swimming in deep water, while the other will avoid escalators or deep water altogether (Cassill, 1982). Another factor to be considered is that even twins reared apart have generally had quite similar home experiences. Typically they are raised by close relatives in neighboring communities, and only rarely are they separated by language, culture, and religion, as Oskar and Jack were. Even in their case, says Bouchard, beneath the more dramatic differences in background, their upbringing was basically quite similar. Finally, in all the studies in which one twin had experienced "extreme deprivation or unusual enrichment," the result has been to "lessen the resemblance of identical twins reared apart" (Scarr and McCartney, 1983).

Obviously, the question of the relative importance of nature and nurture cannot be settled by evidence drawn from a few pairs of twins. The Minnesota researchers plan to study dozens of twins over a five-year period before drawing conclusions, and they expect that the data will provide ample evidence for the role of nurture as well as nature. At this point, however, it seems likely that genes have a broader range of general influence than many theorists and researchers had previously thought. At the same time, it also seems clear that the question of the specific contributions of nature and nurture may never be settled precisely, partly because the answer, as you will soon see, appears to vary from individual to individual, and from trait to trait.

Figure 3.7 *Since monozy-gotic twins (left) share all the same genes, their simi-larity is apparent in every detail, from their height to the shading of their hair and the slope of their eye-lids, and the hairiness of their arms. While dizygotic twins (right) sometimes look quite different and may not even be of the same sex, they may also look quite alike, as these Cuban-American sisters do. However, a closer look reveals many differences—in noses, hair color, and height for instance.*

Of course, not all twins are identical. In fact, most twins are **dizygotic,** or frater-nal. Dizygotic twins begin life as two separate zygotes created by the fertilization of two ova that were ovulated at the same time. Dizygotic twins share no more genes than any other two offspring of the same parents. They may be of different sexes and very different in appearance. Or they may look a great deal alike, just as broth-ers and sisters sometimes do.

Other multiple births, such as triplets and quadruplets, can likewise be monozy-gotic, dizygotic, trizygotic, quadrazygotic, and so forth. (See Table 3.1 for factors that can affect the incidence of multiple births.)

TABLE 3.1 **Factors Affecting the Incidence of Dizygotic Twinning**

Monozygotic twins are born about once in every 270 pregnancies, a rate that is seemingly unaffected by environmental factors. The incidence of dizygotic twins, however, is subject to a number of influences, including the following:

Family History   If a woman's mother was a twin, or if the woman had twins in a previous pregnancy, there is 1 chance in 8 that a new pregnancy will produce twins.

Ethnic Group   Among North Americans, black women have approximately 1 chance in 75 of having twins; whites, 1 chance in 93; and Chinese, Japanese, and Native Americans, 1 chance in 150.

Age and Childbearing History   Older women, and women who have had several children, are more likely to have dizygotic twins. For example, a 40-year-old woman in her eighth preg-nancy is three times more likely to have fraternal twins than a 20-year-old in her first preg-nancy. The primary reason is that toward the end of the reproductive years ovulation be-comes less regular, some cycles occurring without ovulation and others with double ovulation.

Fertility Drugs   Couples who are infertile because the woman does not ovulate spontane-ously can be helped by a fertility drug that triggers ovulation—sometimes of several ova. In this case, couples who have been childless for years may find that they are suddenly blessed with several children at once.

Sources: Scheinfeld, 1973; Cassill, 1982.

Dominant and Recessive Genes

In the simplest form of heredity, a pair of genes, one from each parent, determines a particular inherited characteristic. However, the interaction between the two members of a gene pair is not always fifty-fifty. Sometimes one member of the pair has a greater influence in determining the specific characteristic. Genes that act in this controlling manner are called **dominant genes;** those genes whose influence is obscured when paired with the more powerful genes are called **recessive genes.**

Hundreds of physical characteristics follow the dominant-recessive pattern. Let us consider eye color. To simplify somewhat, let's say that a person inherits two eye-color genes, one from each parent, and that the gene for brown eyes is dominant and that the gene for blue eyes is recessive. (Following traditional practice, we will indicate the dominant gene with an upper-case letter—"B" for dominant brown—and the recessive gene with a lower-case letter—"b" for recessive blue.) If both genes are for brown eyes (BB), the person's eyes will be brown. If one gene is for brown eyes and the other for blue (Bb), the person's eyes will be brown, since the brown-eye gene is dominant. If both genes are recessive genes for blue eyes (bb), the person will have blue eyes.

The sum total of all the genes a person inherits—that is, his or her genetic potential—is called the person's **genotype.** The result of the interaction of the genes with each other and with the environment—that is, that part of a person's appearance and behavior that expresses his or her genetic inheritance—is called the **phenotype.** As you can see in the example of brown eyes, although two people have the same phenotype with respect to a particular trait, they may have different genotypes—in this case, one brown-eye gene and one blue-eye gene (Bb) producing the same eye-color as two brown-eye genes (BB).

It is also possible for parents to have offspring whose phenotype for a particular characteristic is completely different from theirs, if the parents both have the necessary recessive genes. For example, if each of two brown-eyed parents has a recessive gene for blue eyes (Bb and Bb), there is one chance in four that a particular child of theirs will inherit the recessive blue-eye gene from both of them and will therefore have blue eyes. (The four possible combinations in their offspring would be BB, Bb, Bb—all yielding brown eyes—and bb, yielding blue eyes.) A person who has a recessive gene as a part of his or her genotype is called a **carrier** of that gene. In fact, we are all carriers of dozens of recessive genes that are in our genotypes but not in our phenotypes. Usually we are unaware of which recessive genes we carry until we have a child with a surprising phenotype (see Figure 3.8).

It should be noted that the interaction of dominant and recessive genes just described is a simplified model. The actual interaction of all the pairs of genes that could be inherited is more complicated. In some cases, a dominant gene is not completely dominant and may interact with the recessive gene to influence the phenotype. For example, although many textbooks list blue eye color as recessive, this is somewhat misleading. Many a hazel-eyed child has one parent with blue eyes and the other parent with brown. In this case, the child's light-brown eye color bears witness to the recessive gene in his or her genotype. In addition, most people have several pairs of genes that affect eye color, so shades of blue, green, and brown develop, following more complicated laws of inheritance.

Figure 3.8 *Phenotype and genotype are not always the same. Since both parents here have curly black hair, a dominant characteristic, we know from looking at their phenotype that they both have the genotype for this characteristic. But we know that they also have the genotype for straight red hair, a recessive characteristic, only because they have a child who has this phenotype. She must have inherited the necessary recessive genes from both parents.*

X-Linked Recessive Genes Some recessive genes are called **X-linked** because they are located only on the X chromosome. For example, the genes for most forms of color blindness, certain allergies, several diseases, and perhaps some perceptual skills are recessive and are carried only by the X chromosome. This means that if a male inherits a gene for color blindness on the X chromosome he receives from his mother, he will be color blind, since his Y chromosome carries no corresponding dominant gene for normal color vision to countermand the instructions of the recessive gene for color blindness. On the other hand, if a female (XX) inherits a harmful recessive gene on one of her X chromosomes, but also inherits a corresponding dominant gene for the normal characteristic on her other X chromosome, only the normal characteristic will manifest itself. She will not show the effects of the harmful recessive gene unless she inherits two of them.

Polygenic Inheritance

Most human characteristics are the product of **polygenic inheritance;** that is, they are affected by many genes rather than by a single pair. One example is human skin color, which is the result of the interaction of a dozen or so genes. Thus skin can be any of hundreds of tones, depending on which genes are inherited. A light-skinned person and a dark-skinned person will usually have children who are some shade between light and dark, each child inheriting half of his or her skin-color genes from the light-skinned parent and half from the dark-skinned parent. However, since each parent's genotype contains a range of skin-color genes, the child may inherit mainly light-skin genes, or, alternatively, mainly dark-skin genes, from both parents and therefore have lighter or darker skin than either of them. Similarly, height, weight, and body shape are polygenic, as are almost all complex human characteristics, such as intelligence, behavioral patterns, and special talents.

Heredity and Environment

Don't be misled by this focus on genes. Heredity is of basic importance, but nurture always affects nature. Both are vital to development. As Scarr and Weinberg (1980) put it, "No genes, no organism; no environment, no organism." Genes influence the direction of development and often set the boundaries for the expression of particular traits, but the impact of environment is crucial.

Figure 3.9 *Is it heredity or environment that explains the fact that several generations of the Flying Wallendas have pursued the perfection of incredible high-wire feats of balance and coordination? Obviously, body type and a hearty attitude toward danger must play a role, together with family encouragement and practice that begins almost in infancy.*

When social scientists discuss the effects of the **environment** on the individual, they are referring to the impact of everything in the outside world that impinges upon the individual—from food, clothing, shelter, climate, and the like, to social, economic, political, and cultural patterns. Broadly defined in this way, environment affects the expression of almost any genotype.

Multifactorial Characteristics

Another way of saying this is that most characteristics are **multifactorial**, that is, caused by the interaction of many genetic and environmental factors.

Even physical characteristics are often multifactorial rather than purely genetic. Take height, for example. An individual's maximum possible growth is genetically determined, yet most North Americans are taller than their grandparents, but virtually the same height as their full-grown children. Why? Because to reach the maximum height set by his or her genes, an individual must have adequate nutrition and good health. In the nineteenth century, these two crucial factors were much less common than they are now, and Americans were, on the average, about 6 inches shorter than they are today (Tanner, 1971). Throughout most of the twentieth century, as nutrition and medical care improved, each generation grew slightly taller than the previous one. Over the past two decades, however, this trend for the children to be taller than their parents has stopped. The reasons may include the fact that most Americans now receive sufficient nourishment to reach their maximum potential height, and, possibly, that few recent developments in health care have had a significant effect on growth.

Just as there have been shown to be environmental effects on physical characteristic previously thought to be almost completely determined by genetics, the reverse has also been found: psychological traits that have often been considered mainly the result of nurture—shyness and extroversion, phobias, schizophrenia—show definite genetic influence (Goldsmith, 1983; Loehlin et al., 1982; Cohen et al., 1972; Walker and Emory, 1983). If one monozygotic twin becomes schizophrenic or manic-depressive, for example, chances are (estimates range from 80 percent to 20 percent, depending on definition) that the other twin will have similar psychological problems—a risk far greater than would be the case for dizygotic twins.

The research question is no longer whether nature and nurture interact for any particular trait, because the answer almost always is that they do. Instead, the question revolves around how that interaction varies from individual to individual, and, within each individual, how particular traits are affected by the individual's experiences and stage of development. Consider the importance of one's stage of development, for instance. According to Robert McCall (1981), in the first months of life, nature has a stronger influence on development than at any other period. Perception and cognition develop according to genetic instructions, and only massive environmental deprivation (such as being constantly isolated in a dark room) prevent the normal development of intelligence. (An instance of this kind of deprivation is discussed in Chapter 10, page 300.) Later, however, variations in nurture can have a substantial impact: quantity and quality of education may profoundly affect how a person thinks.

The relationship between genes and environment also varies from person to person: some individuals, for instance, are genetically more vulnerable than others to certain aspects of their environment—to, say, bee stings, or alcohol, or emotional losses. Some traits—shyness and fearfulness, for instance—have a stronger genetic component than others. And some traits can express themselves in quite different ways, depending on the environment. For example, the inherited characteristics that help to account for abilities with higher mathematics are also involved in musical creativity, but whether an individual possessing these characteristics becomes a mathematician or a composer—or something else altogether—is determined by the interaction of a great number of environmental influences (Gardner, 1983). Similarly, researchers have suggested that some children appear to have a "genetically-based early sensitivity to cues of parental warmth or rejection," which may make them particularly likely to thrive in a loving home but also particularly likely to suffer in a bad one (Loehlin et al., 1982). Whenever we look at polygenic and multifactorial traits, such as emotional health or intelligence, the complexity of nature-nurture interaction becomes apparent (see the Research Report on genes and IQ).

Abnormal Genes and Chromosomes

Half or more of all zygotes have abnormal genes or chromosomes. Almost all of these are aborted spontaneously, usually so early that the woman never knew she was pregnant. Most of the others die later in pregnancy. The remainder, some 3 to 5 percent, develop to full-term (National Institute of Child Health, 1979). This means that each year in the United States, between 100,000 and 150,000 infants are born with a chromosomal abnormality, a clearly defined genetic disorder, or a genetically influenced defect, such as a malformation of the spine, the head, or the foot. Chromosomal abnormalities are, in general, the most serious, but they are also the easiest to detect and prevent.

Chromosomal Abnormalities

Sometimes when sperm or ova are formed, the forty-six chromosomes divide unevenly, producing a gamete that has too few or too many chromosomes. About 8 percent of all conceptions involve this kind of gamete (Moore, 1982). In most of these cases, a spontaneous abortion occurs in the first days or weeks after conception. But sometimes, about once in every 200 births, a baby is born with one chromosome too many or one too few (Goad et al., 1976).

Many chromosomal abnormalities involve the twenty-third pair, the sex chromosomes. Males, normally XY, are sometimes born with two or three Y chromosomes (XYY or XYYY), or two or three X chromosomes (XXY or XXXY) or two of each (XXYY). In addition, males who seem to have a normal pair of sex chromosomes (XY) occasionally, in fact, have a "fragile X," an X chromosome that is present in only some of the cells, not all of them. Females, normally XX, are sometimes born with only one X chromosome (XO) or three, four, or five (XXX, XXXX, XXXXX). In every case, these abnormalities result in, among other things, impaired mental abilities (see Table 3.2).

Chromosomal abnormalities do not always involve the sex chromosomes. Sometimes a sperm or ovum contains twenty-three autosomes instead of twenty-two. In the formation of a zygote, the extra autosome attaches itself as a third chromosome to the eighth, thirteenth, fourteenth, fifteenth, eighteenth, twenty-first, or twenty-second pair of chromosomes, forming syndromes known as trisomy-8, trisomy-13, and so forth.

TABLE 3.2 **Common Sex-Linked Chromosomal Abnormalities**

Name	Chromosomal Pattern	Physical Appearance*	Psychological Characteristics*	Incidence
Kleinfelter's syndrome	XXY (extra sex chromosome)	Male. At adolescence, secondary sex characteristics do not develop. For example, penis does not grow, voice does not change. Breasts may develop.	Retarded in language skills.	1 in 1,000 males
(No name)	XYY (extra sex chromosome)	Male. Prone to acne. Unusually tall.	More aggressive than most males. Mildly retarded, especially in language skills.	1 in 1,000 males
(No name)	XXX	Female. Normal appearance.	Retarded in almost all intellectual skills.	1 in 1,000 females
Turner's syndrome	XO (only one sex chromosome)	Female. Short, "webbed" neck. At adolescence, secondary sex characteristics (breasts, menstruation) do not develop.	Mildly retarded, especially in abilities related to math and science.	1 in 10,000 females

*There is some variation in the physical appearance, and considerable variation in the psychological characteristics, of these individuals. For example, several studies of prison populations have found a higher percentage of XYY men than is found in the general population. At the same time, many XYY men are normal, law-abiding citizens, and some children in each group seem completely normal. For psychological characteristics, much depends on the family environment of the child.
Sources: Goad et al., 1976; Hier et al., 1980; Pennington et al., 1982; Moore, 1982.

The most common chromosomal problem that results from abnormalities in the autosomes, rather than the sex chromosomes, is trisomy-21, the main cause of **Down's syndrome.** This disorder affects about 1 baby in every 800 (National Institute of Child Health, 1979).

Figure 3.10 *This Down's syndrome child has the round face, almond-shaped eyes, and thick tongue that characterize those who have an extra chromosome at the twenty-first pair. (His parents are also typical in at least one way, namely, their age.) This young man is fortunate, however, in that his family's affectionate care and support should help to make him comparatively self-sufficient by young adulthood.*

RESEARCH REPORT   ## Genes and IQ

The intelligence-test score is far from perfect as a measure of innate intellectual ability, as you will learn in Chapter 13. Nevertheless, as a measure of some of the various mental skills that comprise intelligence, it is a useful research tool. One common way to study the impact of genes and environment on IQ (intelligence quotient) scores is to compare the IQ scores of relatives.

Substantial research indicates that intelligence is partly genetic. In general, a child who scores high on an intelligence test usually has parents and siblings who also score above average in IQ, and a child who scores relatively low on an intelligence test has near relatives who tend to score low. The correlation between IQ scores of siblings is about .45, as is the correlation between the IQ of parent and child (Erlenmeyer-Kinling and Jarvik, 1963). (If you need to refresh your understanding of correlation, see the Closer Look on page 21.) Since siblings have about half their genes in common, as do a parent and child, this positive correlation can be used as evidence that genes affect IQ. Similarly, grandparents and grandchildren, first cousins, and other blood relatives show some correlation in IQ scores, but not as much as parents and children or siblings do.

Further evidence for the heritability of IQ comes from the study of twins. Monozygotic twins, who have identical genes, often have IQ scores within a few points of each other; dizygotic twins, on the other hand, have scores that are only slightly closer than those of nontwin siblings (Wilson, 1983). In addition, monozygotic twins show very similar performance patterns over various intelligence-test tasks, both scoring, say, high in arithmetic and picture completion and low in vocabulary (see chart below).

But as we saw in the Closer Look on twin research, evidence like this does not necessarily distinguish the influence of genes from the influence of environment. Parents and children may have similar scores because parents with higher IQs may provide more stimulating environments for their children than parents with lower IQs. Identical twins could be more similar in IQ than dizygotic twins because they often receive identical treatment from parents and teachers, who, as we noted previously, cannot always tell them apart.

The best way to distinguish genetic and environmental influences is, once again, to study children who have the same genes but different environments, and children who have the same environments but different genes. In practice, this means comparing IQ scores of monozygotic twins who grew up in separate homes, or comparing the IQ scores of adopted children with those of both their biological and their adoptive parents. Such studies have found strong evidence for the influence of both heredity and environment. For instance, in a classic study of identical twins reared apart, James Shields (1962) found that most of the twin pairs were very close in IQ scores (evidence for the strength of genes) but that three pairs were 23, 24, and 30 points apart, a wide enough point spread to differentiate average IQ from genius. (IQ scores between 85 and 115 are considered average; those below 70 indicate retardation; scores above 130 indicate gifted

This chart shows the ten subtest scores of the Wechsler Preschool-Primary Scale of Intelligence (WPPSI) for a pair of twins. An average score on a subtest is 10, so, as you can see, these twins are amazingly similar in their patterns, scoring above average on some tests and below on others. Wilson (1975) found that subtest patterns are much more similar in monozygotic twins than in dizygotic twins, although not all pairs in his study were as similar as the two represented here.

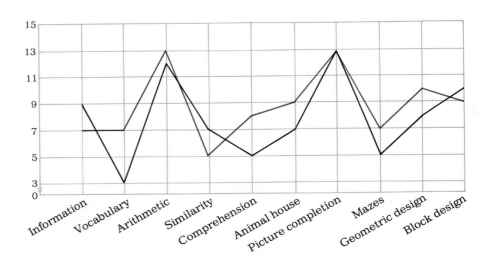

intelligence.) Significantly, the twins who had the lower scores in these cases had been raised in deprived circumstances, while their identical siblings who scored higher had been raised in enriched circumstances. Similar findings have been reported by a more recent study of a larger number of Scandinavian twins (Juel-Nielson, 1980).

In one of the most recent and best studies of adopted children, Sandra Scarr and Richard Weinberg (1983) studied black children who had been adopted by white parents. (The children averaged 7 years in age and had been in the adoptive family since infancy.) The researchers found the following correlations between the adopted children and their parents:

IQ of adoptive mother	.21
IQ of adoptive father	.27
Education* of biological mother	.33
Education of biological father	.43

These data show a strong genetic influence in IQ scores, for the children's IQ can be predicted more accurately by knowing the biological parents' educational achievements than by knowing the adoptive parents' IQs.

These same researchers also compared the IQ scores of the adopted children with those of the children born into the adopting families. For instance, one such family might have had two biological children and two adopted children who were not biologically related to each other. They tested 230 sibling pairs consisting of adopted and biological children, 107 pairs of biological siblings, and 140 pairs of biologically unrelated adopted siblings. The correlations between the IQ scores of sibling pairs were as follows:

Adopted child and biological child in same family	.25
Biological sibling pairs	.42
Two unrelated adopted children in same family	.44

These results show the impact of the specific environment on IQ scores. First of all, the .25 correlation between adopted children and biological children raised in the same family is substantially higher than the zero correlation ordinarily found between genetically unrelated children. The home environment has already had an impact on these adopted children, bringing their scores closer to that of the siblings born into that family.

*IQ scores were not available for biological parents, so education was used as a rough measure of intelligence, since there is a strong positive correlation between IQ and educational attainment.

The second correlation, .42 between biological siblings, is higher than .25, as one would expect for children who share many of the same genes as well as the same home. However, the third correlation, .44 for adopted children who are unrelated by blood but who grow up in the same adoptive home, is both surprising and intriguing. It suggests that the general impact of interracial adoption, coupled with the specific experience within a particular home, may make genetically unrelated children as close in IQ as siblings who share the same home and about half the same genes.

Is this effect typical for adopted children generally, and does it hold throughout childhood? The same two researchers explored these questions by looking this time at white adolescent adoptive children. Here the influence of genes was much more apparent, for the correlation between their IQs and those of their adoptive parents was very low (.10), whereas the correlation between their IQs and those of their biological parents was about .35. In contrast to the case of the black adoptees in the earlier study, for these white adolescents the correlation between unrelated adoptees raised in the same family was essentially zero. It may be, as the authors of the adopted children's study speculate, "older adolescents are largely liberated from their families' influences and have made choices that are in keeping with their own talents and interests. Thus, the unrelated siblings have grown less and less alike" (Scarr and Weinberg, 1983).

This research suggests that intellectual development may be especially vulnerable to either genetic or environmental influences at particular periods in the life span. For instance, early development is dependent mainly on genetic instructions, so that, given reasonable care, most 1-year-old babies begin to talk and walk on about the same schedule. Adults, on the other hand, are more vulnerable to experience; consequently their development is much more varied. Some 30-year-olds, for instance, are completing research that will win them a Nobel prize; others born with the same abilities may never realize them because of the lack of educational opportunities, or because life circumstances led, or forced, them in other directions, or, possibly, because environmental influences such as malnutrition or drug abuse diminished their potential. In no case is intellectual development simply the result of genetic programming. Instead, radically different lives after birth lead to diverse paths in adulthood.

People who have Down's syndrome usually exhibit distinguishing features of the eyes, nose, and tongue. (Because of the very superficial resemblance between their eyelids and those of people from Mongolia, they are, unfortunately, sometimes called mongoloid.) They often suffer heart defects, and they usually develop more slowly, physically and intellectually, than other children. How well they function as adolescents and adults seems to depend a great deal on early experience. Typically, those who are raised at home are able to care for themselves, to read, and to write, while those who are institutionalized remain much more retarded (Edgerton, 1979). If individuals with Down's syndrome survive to middle age, they often develop a particular form of senility that is characterized by forgetfulness and unpredictable bad temper (Kolata, 1985).

Causes of Chromosomal Abnormalities   What accounts for chromosome-based defects? Sometimes one parent may have an extra or a missing chromosome in some cells. A parent with this condition—known as **mosaicism** because the person's cells, including reproductive cells, are like a mosaic of different patterns, some normal, some not—has a high probability of contributing an abnormal gamete to the formation of a zygote.

A more common finding is that chromosomal abnormalities, especially Down's syndrome and Kleinfelter's syndrome, occur much more frequently when the parents are middle-aged or older. One possible explanation for this is the aging of the ova. Since the female is born with all the ova she will ever have, a 45-year-old woman has ova that are 45 years old. Perhaps degeneration of the ova leads to chromosomal abnormalities (Fuhrmann and Vogel, 1983). However, this cannot be the only reason older parents have more offspring with chromosomal problems, because no matter what the age of the mother, there is a positive correlation between the age of the father and the birth of a child with an extra chromosome. Perhaps the male reproductive system functions less efficiently with age, producing a higher percentage of malformed sperm. It may also be that the sexual activity between husband and wife is implicated. Older couples generally have intercourse less frequently than they did when they were younger, increasing the likelihood of a relatively old sperm fertilizing an ovum that has been in the Fallopian tube for a relatively long time and may be defective because it is close to the point of degeneration (Emery, 1983).

Harmful Genes

While abnormal chromosomes are relatively rare, everyone is a carrier of several genes that could produce serious diseases or handicaps (Milunsky, 1977). Among the more common of these are cystic fibrosis, spinal defects, cleft palate, and club feet (see Table 3.3 for a detailed listing of these and other genetic disorders). Fortunately, many genetic problems are recessive, so a person will not have a particular condition unless he or she has inherited the genes for it from both parents. In addition, some serious genetic conditions are polygenic, so several specific genes must be present in the genotype before the problem appears in the phenotype. Still others are multifactorial; they do not become apparent unless something in the prenatal or postnatal environment fosters their expression. Thus, most babies have no apparent genetic problems, although all carry some of the destructive genes that their parents have. About one baby in every thirty, however, is not so lucky, and is born with a serious genetic problem (Roberts, 1973).

Genetic Counseling

For most of human history, couples at risk for having a child with a genetic problem did not know it. Indeed, if a child of theirs was born with a serious defect or died very young, the couple often had a "replacement" child soon after—unaware of the risk they were taking. More recently, if a genetic problem was suspected in the family, couples could either avoid pregnancy or hope that they would be lucky; there was not much else they could do.

Today, a combination of testing and counseling before and during pregnancy, as well as immediate medical attention at birth, has transformed the dilemmas faced by prospective parents. Through **genetic counseling** couples can learn more about their genes, and make informed decisions about their childbearing future.

Two Success Stories

Genetic counseling brings good news to many couples, who learn that their risk of having a child with a genetic problem is no higher than the average. They also learn that, with early diagnosis and treatment, most common serious genetic problems can be avoided or minimized. One particularly encouraging example involves **phenylketonuria (PKU)**, a recessive-gene defect that prevents a person from metabolizing protein normally. Left untreated, PKU causes serious mental retardation and emotional disturbance. PKU can now be detected at birth, and treated with a special diet that greatly reduces the symptoms.

Even more striking has been the success in treating **erythroblastosis**, or **Rh disease,** a blood disorder that can kill the infant or cause such defects as deafness, cerebral palsy, and mental retardation. Rh disease can occur in conceptions involving a woman whose blood type is Rh negative and a man whose blood type is Rh positive. (This combination exists in about 12 percent of all American marriages.) Since the gene for Rh positive blood is dominant, most children from those marriages inherit the father's blood type. During childbirth, some of the child's positive blood, which had been circulating in the placenta, might enter the mother's bloodstream, especially if the birth is a difficult one. This causes the mother to develop antibodies to the positive blood, in much the same way a vaccination causes a person to develop antibodies against a disease. In any subsequent pregnancy, these antibodies cross the placenta, attacking and destroying some of the fetus's blood. The more antibodies the mother has, the stronger the attack. In the most severe cases, antibodies destroy the fetus months before the baby would have been born. Until 1968, 10,000 Rh positive babies born to Rh negative women died each year in the United States, and 20,000 had serious birth defects.

Medical advances have now made this disease rare. Since the beginning of the 1960s, doctors have been able to give ill newborns a series of blood transfusions, removing all the blood with its destructive antibodies and replacing it with new blood. Most impressive of all, if the fetal blood supply is attacked, even months before birth, the fetus can be given a blood transfusion in the uterus.

Since 1968, there has been a way to avoid the formation of Rh antibodies. In the first days after giving birth, women are given Rhogam (Rh negative blood that already contains antibodies), which stops their bodies from forming additional antibodies. The injected antibodies disappear within a few weeks. When the woman becomes pregnant again, she has no antibodies to destroy the blood cells of the new fetus.

TABLE 3.3 **Common Genetic Diseases and Conditions**

Name	Description	Prognosis	Method of Inheritance	Incidence*	Carrier Detection?†	Prenatal Detection?
Cleft palate, cleft lip	The two sides of the upper lip or palate are not joined.	Correctable by surgery.	Multifactorial. Drugs taken during pregnancy or stress may be involved.	One baby in every 700. More common in Japanese and Native Americans; rare in blacks.	No.	Yes, in some cases.
Club foot	The foot and ankle are twisted, making it impossible to walk normally.	Correctable by surgery.	Multifactorial.	One baby in every 300. More common in boys.	No.	Yes.
Cystic fibrosis	Lack of an enzyme. Mucous obstructions in body, especially in lungs and digestive organs.	Few victims survive to adulthood.	Recessive gene.	One baby in every 2,000. One in 25 white Americans is a carrier.	No.	Possible in near future.
Diabetes	Abnormal metabolism of sugar because body does not produce enough insulin.	Usually fatal if untreated. Controllable by insulin and diet.	Recessive gene, but exact pattern hard to predict because environment is crucial.	About 7 million Americans. Most develop it in late adulthood. One child in 2,500 is diabetic. More common in Native Americans.	No.	No.
Hemophilia	Absence of clotting factor in blood. Called "bleeder's disease."	Crippling and death from internal bleeding. Now transfusions can lessen or even prevent damage.	X-linked. Also spontaneous mutations.	One in 1,000 males. Royal families of England, Russia, and Germany had it.	Yes.	Yes.
Huntington's disease	Deterioration of body and brain in middle age.	Death.	Dominant gene.	Rare.	Yes.	Possible in near future.
Hydrocephalus	Obstruction causes excess water in brain.	Can produce brain damage and death. Surgery can make survival and normal intelligence possible.	Multifactorial.	One baby in every 100.	No.	Yes.
Marfan's syndrome	Long bony limbs, heart malformation, hearing loss, eye weakness.	Depends on severity; possibly death.	Dominant gene of varying strength.	Rare.	Yes.	Yes.

*Incidence statistics vary from country to country; those given here are for the United States. All these diseases can occur in any ethnic group of Americans. When certain groups have a higher incidence, it is noted here.
†Studying the family tree can help geneticists spot a possible carrier of many genetic diseases or, in some cases, a definite carrier. However, here "Yes" means that a carrier can be detected even without knowledge of family history.

Name	Description	Prognosis	Method of Inheritance	Incidence*	Carrier Detection?†	Prenatal Detection?
Muscular dystrophy (13 separate diseases)	Weakening of muscles. Some forms begin in childhood, others in adulthood.	Inability to walk, move; wasting away and sometimes death.	Duchenne's is X-linked; other forms are autosomal recessive or multifactorial.	One in every 4000 males will develop Duchenne's (about 600 per year). About 100,000 Americans have some form of MD.	Yes, for some forms.	Yes, for some forms.
Neural tube defects (open spine)	Two main forms: anencephaly (part of the brain and skull is missing) and spina bifida (the lower portion of the spine is not closed over).	Often, early death. In some cases, surgery may prolong life for several years. Anencephalic children are severely retarded; children with spina bifida have trouble with walking and with bowel and bladder control.	Multifactorial; defect occurs in first weeks of pregnancy.	Anencephaly: 1 in 1000 births; spina bifida: 3 in 1000.	No.	Yes, usually.
Phenylketonuria (PKU)	Abnormal digestion of protein.	Mental retardation, hyperactivity. Preventable by diet.	Recessive gene.	One in 15,000 births; one in 80 whites is a carrier.	No.	Yes.
Pyloric stenosis	Overgrowth of muscle in intestine.	Vomiting, loss of weight, eventual death; correctable by surgery.	Multifactorial.	One male in 200; one female in 1000.	No.	No.
Sickle-cell anemia	Abnormal blood cells.	Possible painful "crises" (see page 88), heart and kidney failure.	Recessive gene.	One in 400 black babies is affected. One in 10 black Americans is a carrier; one in 20 Latin Americans is a carrier.	Yes.	Yes.
Tay-Sachs disease	Enzyme disease.	Apparently healthy infant becomes progressively weaker, usually dying by age 3.	Recessive gene.	One in 30 American Jews is a carrier.	Yes.	Yes.
Thalassemia (Cooley's anemia)	Abnormal blood cells.	Paleness and listlessness, low resistance to infection; treatment by blood transfusion.	Recessive gene.	One in 10 Greek- or Italian-Americans is a carrier; one in 400 of their babies is affected.	Yes.	Yes.

Sources: Apgar and Beck, 1973; Nyhan, 1976; Milunsky, 1977; Moss, 1979; Omenn, 1978; Moore, 1982.

Who Should Be Tested?   In spite of successes like these, there are still many genetic disorders that can result in serious problems. In addition, many high-risk couples are unaware of their situation, and therefore unable to avoid potential problems. Even with genetic counseling, many couples must still make difficult choices about conception and pregnancy.

These facts lead to the question of who should receive genetic counseling. Certainly everyone who plans to become a parent should probably know something about their genetic inheritance. But genetic counseling is strongly recommended for couples in five situations: those who already have a child with a genetic disease; those who have relatives with genetic problems; those who come from the same genetic stock (as first cousins do) or whose ancestors come from regions where certain genetic problems are common; those who have had previous pregnancies

---

A CLOSER LOOK   **Compulsory Genetic Testing**

Most couples who need genetic counseling do not get it (Harsanyi and Hutton, 1981). Whose responsibility is it to see that they do?

Perhaps obstetricians should provide more advice to women about their risk of carrying an abnormal fetus, or perhaps gynecologists should tell them that they should be tested for particular genetic diseases before they become pregnant. In several cases, parents of children with Down's syndrome or with Tay-Sachs have successfully sued their doctors for "wrongful life," arguing that proper advice could have prevented the birth of a seriously impaired child.

Some psychologists (e.g., McIntire, 1973) and physicians (e.g., Milunsky, 1977) suggest that all people about to be married or become parents should be required to undergo genetic testing, just as applicants for a marriage license must, in some states, be tested for syphilis.

Before you agree with them, consider the controversy surrounding sickle-cell anemia, a blood disorder caused by recessive genes. In serious cases, victims of sickle-cell have periodic "crises," during which their joints swell and they experience intense pain. Often they die of complications affecting the heart or kidneys. About 2.5 million Americans carry the recessive sickle-cell gene, sometimes called the sickle-cell *trait*.

A simple blood test can spot carriers of the sickle-cell trait. Since the disease is serious, the recessive gene common, and the genetic test easy, you might expect everyone to endorse mass screening for sickle cell. In 1972, almost everyone did. Congress appropriated $115 million for a three-year, nationwide testing program. Several states passed laws requiring testing for all high-risk people (Nyhan, 1976).

But two additional facts make mass testing for the sickle-cell trait controversial. The first is that people who have the sickle-cell trait usually have ancestors from Africa. One out of every ten black Americans has the sickle-cell trait, as does one out of every twenty Americans from the Caribbean and Central America, and a smaller proportion of people from countries around the Mediterranean (Maugh, 1981). There is a good reason why the recessive gene is common among these ethnic groups. The sickle-cell trait gives some protection against malaria, so carriers of the gene in malaria-prone areas (central Africa, Central America, and parts of the Caribbean) were among those most likely to survive to become parents, and thereby to pass the gene on to their children.

Thus, mass screening for the sickle-cell trait meant, in effect, mass screening of all black Americans. This led many to the conclusion that such screening was, in fact, a subtle form of genocide—that is, a means of psychologically coercing the 2 million black Americans who have the trait to remain childless (Linde, 1972).

Another problem with compulsory testing is that the presence of the sickle-cell trait could be used as new justification for discrimination in certain circumstances. For eight years, for example, the Air Force Academy disqualified all carriers of the sickle-cell trait on the grounds that individuals with the trait may be more susceptible to passing out when their oxygen supply is reduced—as might happen under some conditions in high-altitude flights. One young black man sued the Academy, after he was expelled when medical tests revealed that he carried the sickle-cell trait. The young man argued that the academy's rationale was a flimsy reason to disqualify all carriers of the trait from positions

that ended in spontaneous abortion; those in which the woman is 35 or older or the man is 45 or older.

The process of genetic counseling varies from couple to couple, depending on the genetic background of each prospective parent. However, the basic procedure is the same: testing, predicting, and deciding.

Testing for Genetic Conditions

Detecting some genetic conditions is relatively simple. A blood test can reveal the recessive genes for sickle-cell anemia, Tay-Sachs disease, PKU, hemophilia, and thalassemia (Cooley's anemia). Analyzing a few cells from the prospective parents' bodies (easily obtained by lightly scraping the inside of the mouth) indicates the possibility of some chromosomal abnormalities. In some cases, minor physical ab-

of responsibility in the Air Force. In 1981, two years after his suit was filed, the Academy agreed to drop its ban on sickle-cell carriers.

A final factor in the controversy was the tendency of people to panic if they learned they had the trait, an understandable reaction when counseling is not provided. People need to know that having one gene for sickle-cell anemia is generally harmless, since the disease occurs only when a person has two sickle-cell genes, one from each parent. Carriers also need to know that even the disease itself is not always crippling. Many people with sickle-cell anemia live almost normal lives. In its mildest form, it causes little more than fatigue and shortness of breath, although fatal complications can occur during pregnancy or surgery if the attending physician does not know that the patient has sickle-cell disease and therefore needs a variety of special measures.

The important point is that carriers of the trait need not worry, unless they are considering parenthood with another carrier. In this case, a genetic counselor can explain the odds of their conceiving a fetus with the disease, the probable severity of the disease if their child inherits it (a prediction based on analysis of other genes they may carry), the possibility of prenatal diagnosis and elective abortion, and the latest research on care for sickle-cell victims. The counselor can also put them in touch with other carrier couples, including some who have a sickle-cell child. Talking with someone who shares the same genetic problem often helps in decision-making.

Even with counseling, couples who are both carriers of serious genetic disease have a difficult choice to make. However, without sensitive and informative counseling, compulsory screening for sickle-cell anemia or any other genetic disease might do more harm than good.

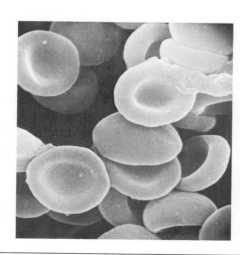 

The blood cells in the photo at left show the characteristic roundness of normal cells. The curved and flattened shapes of the cells in the photo at right reveals the presence of a recessive gene for sickle-cell anemia.

Figure 3.11 *Rare genetic conditions become more common when blood relatives marry, because the chance of a child's inheriting the same recessive genes from both parents increases. This child is a six-fingered dwarf, a condition extremely rare in the general population. However, at least sixty-one cases have occurred among the Old Order Amish, a religious group founded by three couples over 200 years ago. Members of this group are forbidden to marry outsiders, despite the fact that approximately one out of every eight members is a carrier of this gene.*

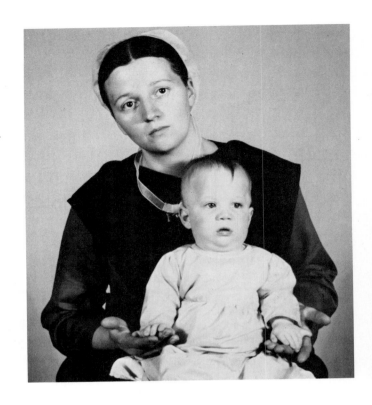

normalities, such as an oddly shaped little finger or unusual ear lobes, signal that a person may be a carrier of certain harmful recessive genes (Fuhrmann and Vogel, 1983).

Family medical history, already-born children, and knowing where one's ancestors came from provide important clues. For example, Tay-Sachs disease is most common among Jews whose ancestors came from Eastern Europe (especially one part of Poland); sickle-cell anemia, among blacks whose roots go back to Central Africa; thalassemia, among descendents of Greeks or Italians (especially from Sicily); PKU, among Scandinavians; and so on.

Predicting Genetic Problems

Once a genetic counselor knows that a problem may be present, the next step is calculating the odds that a child could inherit the condition. Sometimes the prediction is simple. If two carriers of the same recessive gene marry, each of their children has one chance in four of having the disease, because each child has one chance in four of inheriting the recessive gene from both parents. (The same principle applies as in the case (page 77) of the two brown-eyed parents who had recessive genes for blue eyes and a one-in-four probability of having blue-eyed offspring.) It is important to remember that "chance has no memory," which means that *each time* two carriers have another child, the odds of that child's inheriting the disease are one in four. Each child born into the family also stands a one-in-four chance of avoiding the gene altogether and a 50-50 chance of inheriting one recessive gene, making the child a carrier like the parents.

In sex-linked diseases, such as color blindness, Duchenne's muscular dystrophy, or hemophilia, a male who inherits the recessive gene on his X chromosome will always have the disease. A woman who is a carrier will transmit the gene to about half of her ova, so it is probable that about half of her sons will have the disease, and

Figure 3.12 *A genetic counselor explains a karotype to an expectant couple. In all likelihood, he is also telling them about their chances of having a baby with serious genetic or chromosomal abnormalities, as well as answering their questions about the many alternatives they should consider.*

half of her daughters will be carriers like their mother. The other half of her children are likely not to inherit the gene at all.

Some genetic diseases are carried by dominant rather than recessive genes. In fact, a catalogue of genetic disease lists 1,489 dominant-gene disorders as compared to 1,117 recessive and 213 X-linked problems (McKusick, 1979). Each offspring of a carrier of a dominant-gene disorder has a 50-50 chance of inheriting the disorder. Luckily, deadly dominant diseases are rare, because carriers always have the disease as well as the gene, and therefore usually die before they are old enough to have children. Huntington's disease, a dominant-gene disorder that causes gradual deterioration of the nervous system, leading to physical weakness, emotional disturbance, mental retardation, and eventually, death, is an exception. The symptoms of the disease do not appear until the person is over 30, so a person can have many children before dying. Fortunately, carrier detection is now possible, so this tragic disease may become increasingly rare (Pines, 1984).

Many genetic conditions follow neither the recessive nor the dominant gene pattern. Some are caused by mutation, that is, a spontaneous change in a gene's formation. In this case, the problem cannot be predicted from the genotype of either parent. In other cases, dominance is partial, or the problem is polygenic or multifactorial. Cleft palate and cleft lip, club feet, spina bifida (a malformation at the end of the spine), diabetes, emphysema, many forms of cancer, hardening of the arteries, and high blood pressure are probably among this group of genetic diseases (Dronamraju, 1974; McAuliffe and McAuliffe, 1983). At the moment, they are hard to predict, because the interaction of genes and environment may be responsible for their appearance. New genetic-screening techniques, however, will soon aid markedly in the detection of genetic susceptibility for such problems; nevertheless, environment and life style will probably continue to exert a strong influence on whether a specific multifactorial disease will develop and how severe it will be (McAuliffe and McAuliffe, 1983).

Many Alternatives

The last step of genetic counseling is the most difficult, for, once the couple has been tested for genetic problems and knows the odds of their bearing a child with a problem, they must decide what risks they are willing to take. Most learn that the risks are not great, and they become pregnant and give birth to a normal baby. For others, the risk is substantial. Some avoid pregnancy, perhaps choosing sterilization and adoption. Others simply prepare themselves for the possibility of having a fatally ill or seriously handicapped child.

Others have another option, becoming pregnant and then aborting the fetus if prenatal diagnosis reveals that it is seriously handicapped. Prenatal diagnosis is now possible for chromosomal abnormalities, sickle-cell anemia, Tay-Sachs disease, spina bifida, malformations of the head, and many other major problems. (Table 3.4 describes several of the diagnostic techniques currently in use.) While

---

TABLE 3.4 **Methods of Prenatal Diagnosis**

Amniocentesis
In **amniocentesis,** which can be performed after the fifteenth week of pregnancy, about half an ounce of amniotic fluid is withdrawn through the mother's abdominal wall with a syringe. This fluid contains sloughed-off fetal cells that can be analyzed to detect major chromosomal abnormalities and many genetic problems. Amniocentesis also reveals the sex of the fetus (useful knowledge if an X-linked genetic disease is likely) and provides clues about fetal age and health.

Sonogram
The **sonogram** uses high-frequency sound waves to outline the shape of the fetus. Sonograms can reveal problems such as an abnormally small head (anencephaly), fluid on the brain (hydrocephaly), body malformations, and several diseases of the kidney. In addition, a sonogram can be used to guide the needle in amniocentesis, diagnose twins, estimate fetal age, locate the position of the placenta, and, if repeated sonograms are performed, reveal the rate of growth. Almost half of all North American pregnancies are now scanned with ultrasound.

Fetoscopy
Fetoscopy is performed using a very narrow tube that is inserted into the woman's abdomen, piercing the uterus. Then a fetoscope, a viewing instrument, is inserted, allowing the physician to observe the fetus and the inside of the placenta directly. Fetoscopy is most commonly performed when a malformation is suspected. It can also be used for taking a sample of blood from the placenta to test for blood abnormalities.

Alphafetoprotein assay
If a fetus has a neural-tube defect (see page 87), the level of *alphafetoprotein* (AFP) in the mother's blood will be higher than normal. (The level of this protein is determined by a simple blood test.) However, an elevated AFP level does not necessarily indicate a problem, for the level also varies depending on the age of the fetus and the number of fetuses present. High AFP levels do indicate that amniocentesis, a sonogram, or fetoscopy should be performed.

Chorion villi sampling
At this writing, *chorion villi sampling* is an experimental method of analyzing a sample of the membrane that surrounds the embryo, providing information similar to that obtained through amniocentesis. This test, unlike amniocentesis, can be performed in the eighth week of pregnancy, thus allowing an early abortion of a defective fetus. Early abortions are somewhat safer for the woman, as well as being easier psychologically.

Risks
With the exception of chorion villi sampling, none of these four tests is considered particularly risky to either the mother or the fetus. However, none of them is routinely recommended for all pregnancies, for even a low risk should be avoided if possible.

The AFP assay can needlessly alarm a woman, if it shows a high level that is actually due to normal causes. In some cases it has even led to an unnecessary abortion because further tests were not performed (Sun, 1983; Hooker et al., 1984).

The sonogram has no proven risks (most research finds it harmless), but British studies suggest a possible link between repeated sonograms and later childhood leukemia (Boffey, 1983; Stark et al., 1984).

Both amniocentesis and fetoscopy are relatively painless for the mother, and usually produce no harm to the fetus. Occasionally, the woman feels cramps for a few hours after the procedure; and though they are rare, complications—including spontaneous abortion—can occur.

For chorion villi sampling, the risk of spontaneous abortion may be higher, so this technique is not yet considered a replacement for amniocentesis.

Sources: Kitzinger, 1983; Scher and Dix, 1983; Mahoney, 1984; Kolata, 1983.

abortion of a fetus is never an easy choice, many couples would rather face that alternative, knowing they can conceive again, than to avoid pregnancy or knowingly giving birth to a child who must live a severely limited life.

Still others limit their family to one child, hoping that their first child will not be affected and reconciling themselves, if necessary, to the child's early death or difficult life. Others postpone pregnancy, hoping that medical research will be as successful in other diseases as in PKU or Rh disease.

Genetic engineering, now in an early experimental stage, may someday make it possible to add a dominant, healthy gene to counteract the damage done by recessive genes, thus curing children with genetic defects, or possibly even preventing damage while the fetus is still in the uterus. Progress in this area is sufficiently rapid that some geneticists think that a breakthrough may be near (Baskin, 1984). In every case, the choice is up to the couple. And, as the decision tree below shows, the great majority of couples end up having a healthy and normal baby.

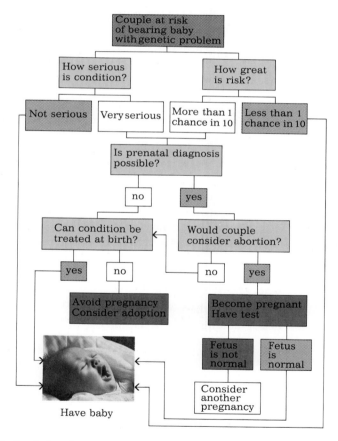

Figure 3.13 *With the help of a genetic counselor, even couples who know they run a risk of having a baby with a genetic defect might decide to have a child. Although the process of making that decision is more complicated for them than it is for a couple with no family genetic illness and no positive tests for harmful recessive genes, the outcome is usually a healthy baby. In each case, the genetic counselor provides facts and alternatives; every couple must make their own decision. In fact, two couples who have the same potential for producing a child with a genetic defect, and are aware of the same facts regarding the situation, sometimes make opposite decisions because they differ in their attitudes about abortion, in their willingness to raise a child with a genetic abnormality, or in their desire to have their own child rather than an adopted one.*

SUMMARY

Culture and Conception

1. With the increasing reliability of contraceptive methods, the rising costs of raising children, and changing attitudes toward family size, more couples are planning smaller families.

The Biology of Conception

2. Conception occurs when a sperm penetrates an ovum, creating a single-celled organism called a zygote.

Genes and Chromosomes

3. Genes, which provide the information cells need to perform specific functions in the body, are arranged on chromosomes. Every human cell contains 23 pairs of chromosomes, one member of each pair contributed by each parent. Every cell contains a duplicate of the genetic information in the first cell, the zygote.

4. Twenty-two pairs of chromosomes control the development of most of the body. The twenty-third pair determines the individual's sex: zygotes with an XY combination will become males; those with two X chromosomes will become females.

5. Each person has a unique combination of genes, with one important exception. Identical (monozygotic) twins are formed from one zygote that splits in two, creating two zygotes with identical genes.

6. Genes can interact in many ways. In the simplest type of heredity, a person who inherits a dominant gene and a recessive gene for a particular characteristic develops the phenotype of the dominant gene. If two recessive genes are present, then the phenotype expresses the recessive form of the characteristic.

7. Males inherit just one X chromosome from their mother, and so, through X-linked inheritance, they have a greater chance than females of inheriting certain harmful recessive genes, including the gene for colorblindness.

8. Most inherited characteristics are polygenic, the result of the interaction of many genes rather than of a single pair.

Heredity and Environment

9. Most physical and psychological characteristics are multifactorial, the result of the interaction of many genetic and environmental influences. Heredity tends to have a greater effect early in life, while the environment tends to have more influence as the individual grows older.

Abnormal Genes and Chromosomes

10. Chromosomal abnormalities occur when the zygote has too few or too many chromosomes. Most of these defects involve the sex chromosomes. The most common autosomal abnormality occurs when an extra chromosome attaches itself to the twenty-first pair, causing Down's syndrome. Middle-aged couples are more likely than younger parents to produce a child with a chromosomal abnormality.

11. Every individual carries some genes for genetic handicaps and diseases. However, since many of these genes are recessive, and many of the diseases involved are polygenic, or multifactorial, most babies will not inherit a combination of genes that will result in a serious genetic defect.

Genetic Counseling

12. Genetic testing and an evaluation of family background can help predict whether a couple will have a child with a genetic problem. If there is a high probability that they will, they can consider several options, such as adoption, remaining childless, obtaining prenatal diagnosis and, if necessary, abortion. In some cases, appropriate postnatal treatment may remedy or alleviate the problem.

KEY TERMS

gametes *(71)*	X-linked genes *(77)*
ova *(71)*	polygenic inheritance *(78)*
spermatozoa *(71)*	environment *(79)*
zygote *(71)*	multifactorial characteristics *(79)*
gene *(72)*	
chromosome *(72)*	Down's syndrome *(81)*
autosomes *(72)*	mosaicism *(84)*
monozygotic twins *(73)*	genetic counseling *(85)*
dizygotic twins *(76)*	phenylketonuria (PKU) *(85)*
dominant genes *(77)*	
recessive genes *(77)*	erythroblastosis (Rh disease) *(85)*
genotype *(77)*	amniocentesis *(92)*
phenotype *(77)*	sonogram *(92)*
carrier *(77)*	fetoscopy *(92)*

KEY QUESTIONS

1. Why are some parents deciding to have small families?

2. How do chromosomes determine the sex of a zygote?

3. In what ways do identical twins differ from fraternal twins?

4. What is the difference between a dominant and a recessive gene?

5. What effects can environment have on genetically inherited traits?

6. What are some of the causes of chromosomal defects?

7. How can genetic counseling help those parents who are at risk of bearing a child with genetic problems?

8. What are some of the factors that genetic counselors examine to determine if a couple is at risk of bearing a child with genetic abnormalities?

9. Who should receive genetic counseling?

RECOMMENDED READINGS

Boston Women's Health Book Collective. *Our bodies, ourselves.* Rev. ed. New York: Simon and Schuster, 1976.

Discusses many aspects of female physiology and psychology, and includes comments by many women on contraception, sex, pregnancy, birth, and motherhood. Some of the medical advice does not agree with that commonly given by most health professionals (for example, the side effects of the "pill" are overemphasized, and its comparative effectiveness underrated), but as a feminist view of female health, this book has no equal.

Jimenez, Sherry Lynn Mims. *The other side of pregnancy.* Englewood Cliffs, N.J.: Prentice Hall, 1982.

Writing with sensitivity and wisdom, Sherry Jiminez discusses the causes and consequences of miscarriage and still-birth. As a birth-education instructor, she is particularly aware of the parents' emotions. For instance, she explains why well-intentioned comments such as "It was probably for the best" do more harm than good, for they deny the grief many parents feel. This book is particularly recommended for parents who have experienced fetal death, as well as for health professionals who might serve them.

Walters, William, and **Singer, Peter** (Eds.). *Test-tube babies.* New York: Oxford University Press, 1982.

The focus of this book is on the ethics of *in vitro* fertilization, the procedure that has now allowed many previously infertile couples, from several countries, to have a baby even though the woman's Fallopian tubes are blocked. Although varying viewpoints are expressed, the thrust of the book is in favor of *in vitro* fertilization. Cloning and surrogate motherhood are also debated.

Fox, Greer Litton (Ed.). *The childbearing decision: Fertility attitudes and behavior.* Beverly Hills, California: Sage, 1982.

Conception is clearly a sociological and emotional phenomena, as well as a biological one. This book contains many articles that are relevant to this point, with special emphasis on how and why people decide to become sexually active, to use contraception, and to have a baby.

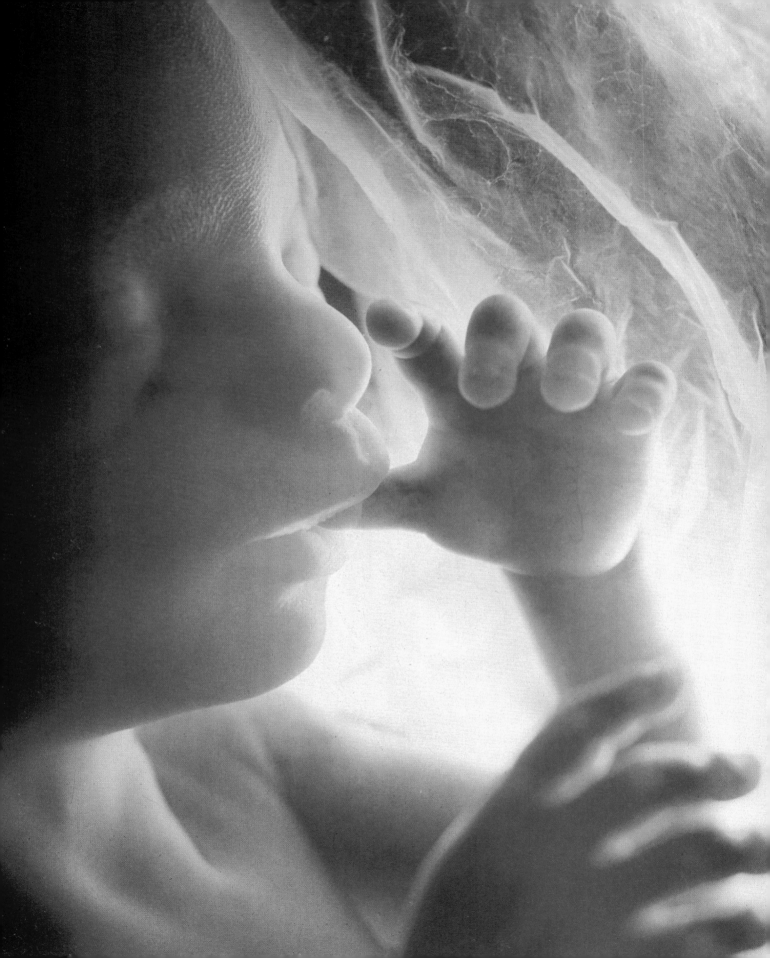

Prenatal Development

Chapter 4

*"I don't care whether it's a boy or a girl;
I just want it to be healthy."*

*Every pregnant woman says that. Or
thinks it. Or prays it. Or incants it like a
charm in the secret core of her soul. So
does every prospective father, every
grandparent-to-be.*

Virginia Apgar and Joan Beck
Is My Baby All Right?

*Yes, the history of a man for the nine
months preceding his birth would,
probably, be far more interesting, and
contain events of greater moment, than
all three score and ten years that follow it.*

Samuel Taylor Coleridge

From Zygote to Newborn
The Germinal Period: The First Fourteen Days
The Period of the Embryo: Two Weeks to Eight Weeks
The Period of the Fetus: Two Months to Birth

Preventing Complications
Teratology

Diseases

Drugs

Environmental Hazards

The Expectant Parents
The Psychological Impact of Pregnancy

Nutrition

Preparation for Birth

Chapter 4

At 4½ months from conception, midway through pregnancy, this fetus is only about 7 inches (18 centimeters) long and weighs about 1 pound (454 grams). By now, all major body organs are formed, although they are not yet ready to meet the demands of survival outside the womb.

Are those really fingernails, and is the fetus already able to suck its thumb at this tender age?

Which parts of the body are continuing to undergo significant development?

How many more months must pass before this fetus has a chance of surviving if born prematurely?

Which foods and drugs consumed by the mother might harm the fetus? If she has been careful in the early months of pregnancy, can she stop worrying now?

By mid-pregnancy, how are the parents-to-be likely to feel about their future baby and about each other?

Development in the first nine months of life has always been a topic of wonder and speculation. For most of human history, knowledge about prenatal development consisted mainly of myths and old wives' tales.

Then about 300 years ago, the first crude microscopes were invented, and living sperm were seen for the first time. This caused new speculations about prenatal development, for some scientists believed they saw within each human sperm a homunculus, or "little man," who was already formed and active, a future human being in miniature. During the same decade (the 1670s), the ovarian follicle, the structure in which the human egg forms, was also described for the first time. Consequently, another school of thought arose to maintain that the female egg, not the male sperm, contains the tiny future person. These "ovists," as they were called, believed that the sperm merely stimulates the fully formed human being within the egg to begin growing.

Both ovists and spermists soon carried the argument a logical step further. Each homunculus, they contended, had within it another perfectly formed homunculus, and in that was still another one, and so on—children, grandchildren, great-grandchildren—all stored away for the future. Some ovists even went so far as to say that Eve had contained within her body all the unborn generations yet to come.

Today we know that each person begins life as a single cell formed by the equal genetic contributions of two parent cells. Far from being fully formed at conception, the developing organism does not resemble a human until eight weeks after conception, and the brain and lung maturation necessary for survival takes at least six months. We also know that many circumstances during prenatal development affect the growing organism. As we will see, the facts of prenatal development are much more complicated, though no less miraculous, than the seventeenth-century natural scientists imagined.

From Zygote to Newborn

As explained in Chapter 3, each newborn begins life as a zygote, a tiny single-cell organism barely visible to the human eye. The growth of this organism into a fully developed baby has been divided into three main periods. The first two weeks of development are called the **germinal period** (also called the period of the ovum); from the third week through the seventh week is the **period of the embryo;** and from the eighth week until birth is the **period of the fetus.***

The Germinal Period: The First Fourteen Days

Within hours after conception, the one-celled zygote divides into two separate cells, which soon become four, then eight, then sixteen, and so on. About five days later, the multiplying cells divide into two distinct masses, a circular mass of outer cells enclosing a mass of inner cells. The outer cells will become membranes that protect and nourish the inner cells, which become the developing person.

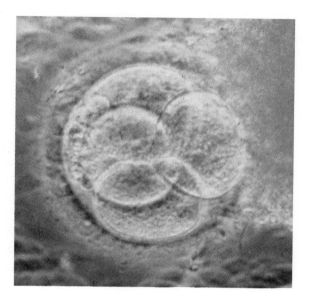

Figure 4.1 *Within 36 hours after fertilization, the one-celled zygote divides into two cells, and then, about one day later, it divides into four cells, as shown here. At the time of implantation, about 6 days after fertilization, the developing organism consists of more than one hundred cells, each one much smaller than the original cell, but each containing exact copies of the genes and chromosomes in the zygote.*

Implantation   The organism, now containing more than a hundred cells, travels down the Fallopian tube and arrives at the uterus just at the time in the menstrual cycle when the lining of the uterus is covered with tiny blood vessels. About ten days after conception, it burrows into this lining, rupturing the blood vessels to obtain nourishment and initiating the hormonal changes that will prevent its being expelled during the next menstrual cycle (Moore, 1982).

This process, called **implantation,** is not routine. It has been estimated that 55 percent of all conceptions never achieve implantation, usually because of some abnormality in the organism or in the lining of the uterus (Grobstein et al., 1983). A successful implantation marks the end of the most rapid growth and the most hazardous transition of the entire life span.

---

*Technically speaking, the name of the developing human organism changes several times depending on the precise stage of development. While there is no need for the student to know them all, the curious might be interested that the organism that begins as a zygote becomes a morula, a blastocyst, a gastrula, a neurula, an embryo, and a fetus before it finally becomes an infant (Moore, 1982).

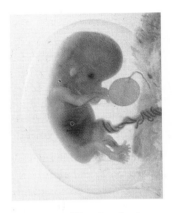

Figure 4.2 *The developing embryo is encased in the amnion, which holds the amniotic fluid. The yolk sac, the round structure visible immediately in front of the embryo, produces blood cells until the embryo can produce its own. It will then disappear.*

Four Protective Membranes   During the germinal period the outer cells, called the **trophoblast** (from the Greek *trophe*, "to nourish"), grow more rapidly than the future embryo. The trophoblast begins to form four protective membranes that make human prenatal development possible.

One membrane, the *yolk sac*, produces blood cells for the embryo until the embryo can produce blood cells on its own, and then disappears. Another membrane, the *allantois*, forms the umbilical cord and the blood vessels in the placenta. A third membrane, the *amnion* (also called "the bag of waters"), holds the **amniotic fluid,** which keeps the temperature of the prenatal environment fairly stable, and cushions the future baby against sudden movement or shock, like a surrounding water bed. The fourth membrane is the *chorion*, which becomes the lining of the placenta.

The Placenta   The **placenta** makes it possible for the embryo (and, later, the fetus) to have its own independent blood supply and, at the same time, to obtain nourishment from the mother's blood (see Figure 4.3). In the placenta, blood vessels from the mother are interwoven with blood vessels that lead to the developing person. These two sets of blood vessels are separated by membranes that prevent mixture of the two bloodstreams, while allowing some substances to pass from one bloodstream to the other. For example, oxygen and nourishment from the mother pass into the developing organism's bloodstream. Carbon dioxide and other waste products pass from the organism into the mother's bloodstream and are then removed through her lungs and kidneys. The pregnant woman is literally breathing, eating, and urinating for two.

The organism is connected to the placenta by the umbilical cord, which contains three blood vessels—one that carries nourishment and two that remove waste products. The movement of blood through the umbilical cord acts like water at high pressure in a hose, keeping the cord taut and making it almost impossible for the cord to become knotted or tangled or squeezed during prenatal development, no matter how many somersaults the developing baby or its mother does.

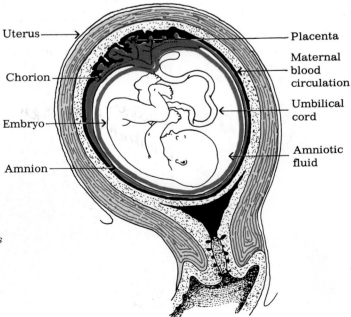

Figure 4.3 *This diagram shows the placenta and the fetus in the last months of pregnancy. At full term, the fetus weighs about five times as much as the placenta. In the first weeks of development, the ratio is reversed.*

The Period of the Embryo: Two Weeks to Eight Weeks

Figure 4.4 *During the first months of life, growth is rapid and from the center outward. (a) At 4 weeks past conception, the embryo is only about ⅕ inch long (5 millimeters), but already the head (top right) has taken shape. (b) At 5 weeks past conception, the embryo has grown to twice the size it was at 4 weeks. Its heart, which has been beating for a week now, is visible, as is what appears to be a primitive tail, which will soon be enclosed by skin and protective tissue at the tip of the backbone (the coccyx). (c) By 7 weeks, the organism is about an inch long (2 centimeters). Facial features, the digestive system, and even the first stage of toe formation are readily seen. (d) At 8 weeks, the overall proportions of the developing person are close enough to those of a full-term baby that we can recognize this 1½-inch-long (4-centimeter) creature as a well-formed human fetus.*

While the trophoblast is forming the various structures necessary to support prenatal life, some of the inner cells form a simple flat structure known as the **embryonic disc.** This initiation of the period of the embryo is followed by the separation of the embryonic disc into three layers: an outer layer *(ectoderm),* which will become the skin and the nervous system; an inner layer *(endoderm),* which will become the digestive system and lungs; and a middle layer *(mesoderm),* which will become muscles, bones, and the circulatory, excretory, and reproductive systems.

The early growth of the embryo is rapid and orderly. During the first days of the embryonic period, a fold occurs down the middle of the embryonic disc, which, 21 days after conception, forms the **neural tube**—the beginning of the central nervous system (the spinal cord and brain). This is the point at which the organism is called an embryo. After the neural tube is formed, growth proceeds in two directions: from the head downward—referred to as **cephalo-caudal development** (literally, "from head to tail")—and from the center, that is, the spine, outward—referred to as **proximo-distal development** (literally, "from near to far"). Thus the most vital organs and body parts form first.

Following this pattern, in the third week after conception the head and blood vessels begin to develop. In the fourth week, the heart begins to beat, making the cardiovascular system the first organ system to begin to function (Moore, 1982). At the end of the first month, eyes, ears, nose, and mouth start to form, and buds that will become arms and legs appear. The embryo is now about ⅕ of an inch long (5 millimeters), about 7,000 times the size of the zygote it was twenty-eight days before.

The Second Month Following the proximo-distal sequence, the upper arms, then the forearms, the hands, and the fingers appear. Legs, feet, and toes, in that order, follow a few days later, each having the beginning of a skeletal structure. By the end of the second month, the fingers and toes, which originally were webbed together, are separate.

Eight weeks after conception, the embryo weighs about ⅟₃₀ of an ounce (1 gram) and is about 1 inch (2.5 centimeters) long. The head has become more rounded and the features of the face are fully formed. The embryo has all the basic organs (except sex organs) and features of a human being, including elbows and knees, fingers and toes, and even buds for the first baby teeth. It is now ready for another name, the fetus.

(a)

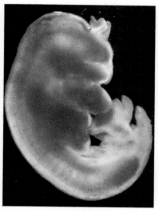

(b)

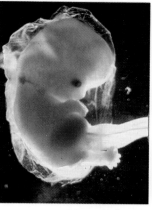

(c)

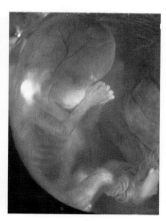

(d)

Figure 4.5 *At the end of 4 months, this fetus, now 6 inches long, looks fully formed, down to the details of eyebrows and finger-nails. However, brain de-velopment is not yet suffi-cient to sustain life outside the uterus; for many more weeks, the fetus must de-pend on the placenta and umbilicus for survival.*

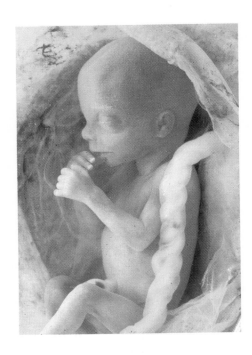

The Period of the Fetus: Two Months to Birth

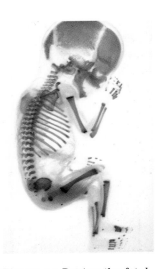

Figure 4.6 *During the fetal period, cartilage becomes bone, as can be seen in this x-ray of a fetus at 18 weeks. The skull and the spine are most clearly de-veloped and the bones of the fingers and toes are visible. Even buds for the teeth will soon begin to harden, although the first "baby" tooth will not emerge until 6 months after birth.*

During the third month, muscles develop and cartilage begins to harden into bone. All the major organs complete their formation, including stomach, heart, lungs, and kidneys.

It is also during this period that the sex organs take discernible shape. The first stage of their development actually occurs in the sixth week, with the appearance of the *indifferent gonad,* a cluster of cells that can develop into male or female sex organs (Jirasek, 1976). If the fetus is male (XY), genes on the Y chromosome send a biochemical signal late in the embryonic period that triggers the development of male sex organs, first the testes at about seven weeks and then the other male organs during the early fetal period. If the embryo is female and therefore has no Y chromosome, no signal is sent, and the fetus begins to develop female sex organs. By the twelfth week after conception, the external male or female genital organs are fully formed (Moore, 1982).

By the end of the third month, the fetus can and does move almost every part of its body, kicking its legs, sucking its thumb, and even squinting and frowning. The 3-month old fetus swallows amniotic fluid, digests it, and urinates, providing its tiny organs with practice for the day when it will take in nourishment on its own. This active little creature is now fully formed—including its fingerprint pattern—and weighs approximately 3 ounces and is about 3 inches long.*

The Second Trimester   Pregnancy is often divided into 3-month-long segments, each called a **trimester.** In the second trimester (the fourth, fifth, and sixth months), hair, including eyebrows and eyelashes, begins to grow. Fingernails, toenails, and buds for adult teeth form. The heartbeat can be heard with a stethoscope, and at about the fifth month the woman can feel the flutter, and later the bump, of fetal arms and legs.

---

*During early prenatal development, growth is very rapid and considerable variation occurs between one fetus and another, so numbers given for length and especially for weight are only rough guidelines. For example, at 12 weeks after conception the average fetus weighs 45 grams (about 1½ ounces), while at 14 weeks, the average weight is 110 grams (about 4 ounces) (Moore, 1982).

Figure 4.7 *On Mother's Day, 1983, tiny DeAnna McWhorter was born sixteen weeks early, weighing only 20 ounces, and the odds against her survival were great. According to her mother, DeAnna "was so tiny that I was almost afraid that I could hurt her just by looking at her. Her face was no bigger than a half dollar. Her legs and arms were just a few inches long and no thicker than pencils. Her skin seemed thinner than tissue paper." DeAnna was one of the lucky ones. Although she had to spend the first four months of life in an isolette and undergo heart surgery when she was only 3 weeks old, one year later, she was a healthy toddler weighing close to 20 pounds.*

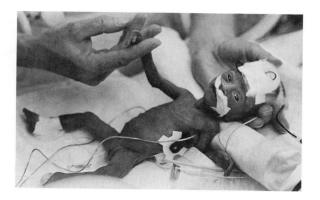

During the second trimester the development of the brain is appreciable. This development, which is essential to the regulation of basic body functions, may be the critical factor in the fetus's attaining the **age of viability** (sometime between the twentieth and twenty-sixth weeks after conception), at which point the fetus has at least some slight chance of survival outside the uterus, if expert care is available.

The Third Trimester During the last trimester the lungs and heart become increasingly capable of sustaining life without the placenta. Brain development is particularly notable during this period, and beginning at about 29 weeks after conception, brain activity gradually takes on patterns of sleeping and waking (Parmelee and Sigman, 1983).

In these final prenatal months, the fetus gains about 5½ pounds (2,500 grams). This gain includes an insulating layer of fat that will protect the newborn in the world outside the uterus, and that will also provide a source of nourishment in the first days after birth until the mother is producing breast milk.

Preventing Complications

Despite the complexity of prenatal development, 97 percent of all babies are born without serious congenital abnormalities (Heinonen et al., 1977). They are healthy and capable, ready for eighty years or so of life on earth.

Part of the reason for this, as we have seen, is that most malformed organisms either never become implanted or are aborted spontaneously during the embryonic period. In addition, recent research has provided insights into the causes of birth defects, ways to prevent prenatal problems, as well as ways to reduce the impact of those problems that occur.

Teratology

Until recently, the placenta was thought to be a barrier that protected the fetus against any disease the mother might contract or any harmful substance that might enter her system. However, within the last forty years, we have learned a great deal through **teratology,** the study of birth defects.* We know now that hundreds of **teratogens,** that is, substances that cause birth defects, can cross the placenta and harm the embryo.

---

*The term *teratology* derives from the Greek *tera*, or "monster."

The Critical Period   The particular harm that can be done by any given teratogen depends on many factors, among them the intensity, duration, and timing of the exposure to the teratogen. Timing is particularly important, because as the embryo and fetus develop, there is a particular time span, called the **critical period,** for the formation of each organ and body part. This critical period for each body part is also the time when that part is most susceptible to damage. As can be seen in the chart opposite, malformations of the heart, central nervous system, and spinal column are most likely to occur in the third through the fifth week; of the eyes, ears, arms and legs from the fourth through the seventh week; of the teeth and palate in the seventh and eighth weeks. Because most body parts form during the first two months, the period of the embryo is sometimes called the critical period of pregnancy.

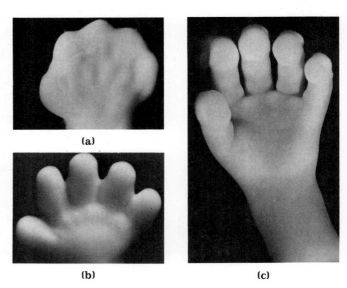

Figure 4.8 *Three stages in finger development: (a) notches appear in the hand at day 44; (b) fingers are growing but webbed together at day 50; and (c) fingers have separated and lengthened at day 52. By day 56, fingers are completely formed, and the critical period for hand development is over. Other parts of the body, including the eyes, heart, and central nervous system, take much longer to complete development, so they are vulnerable to teratogens for months rather than days.*

(a)

(b)

(c)

In fact, however, all nine months can be considered critical. One careful study of 50,282 pregnancies found structural malformation in 6 percent of the babies born (Heinonen et al., 1976). According to these researchers, two-thirds of the defects were probably caused in the first trimester. The remaining one-third were dubbed **anytime malformations** because they could have originated anytime during the nine months of pregnancy. There were thirty-seven different anytime malformations, affecting 911 children.

While the cause of such malformations is often not easy to pinpoint, much is known about several diseases and drugs that can be teratogenic.

Diseases

One of the first teratogens to be recognized was **rubella** (sometimes called German measles), which had long been considered a harmless disease that generally occurred in childhood. It is now well established that rubella, if contracted early in pregnancy, may cause many birth handicaps, among them blindness, deafness, heart abnormalities, and brain damage (see Closer Look page 106). Some of these problems and their effects were apparent in David's story in Chapter 1.

Once the link between rubella and birth defects was established, researchers began looking for other diseases that might affect unborn babies. They found dozens, including mumps, chickenpox, polio, measles, genital herpes (herpes simplex 2), and some strains of flu.

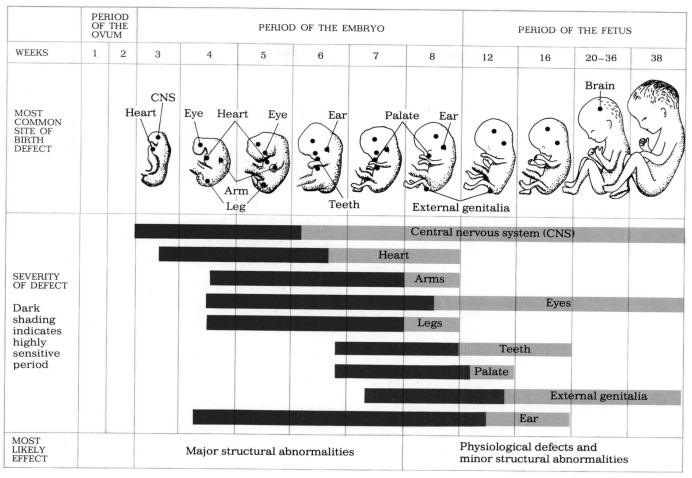

	PERIOD OF THE OVUM		PERIOD OF THE EMBRYO						PERIOD OF THE FETUS			
WEEKS	1	2	3	4	5	6	7	8	12	16	20–36	38

Figure 4.9 *As this chart shows, the most serious damage from teratogens is likely to occur in the first eight weeks after conception. However, damage to many vital parts of the body, including the brain, eyes, and genitals, can occur during the last months of pregnancy as well.*

As with rubella, the woman need not be very ill for the embryo or fetus to be affected. For example, **toxoplasmosis,** a disease caused by a parasite commonly present in uncooked meat and in cat feces, is hardly noticeable in an adult but can cause prenatal blindness and serious brain damage. (If a blood test early in pregnancy indicates that the mother-to-be is among the two-thirds of the population that is not immune [Larsen, 1982], she should not eat rare meat nor change the cat's litter box.) Indeed a woman may not have to be sick at all for prenatal damage to occur: even the disease organisms present in certain vaccines, smallpox and rubella among them, are sometimes teratogenic if the exposure to them occurs just before or during early pregnancy (O'Brien and McManus, 1978).

Syphilis is another teratogenic disease for which good prenatal care is critically important in order to avoid serious harm to the fetus. In the first months of pregnancy, the organisms that produce the disease cannot cross the placenta, so syphilis, which is diagnosed by a simple blood test, can be cured with antibiotics before the fetus is affected. But if a woman does not get early prenatal care (and many, especially teenagers, do not) her fetus may die or suffer bone, liver, and brain damage.

A CLOSER LOOK   Rubella

In 1941 an Australian physician named McAllister Gregg noticed a sudden increase in the number of blind newborns that he and his colleagues were delivering. At first, there seemed to be no explanation for this tragedy. Then Gregg recalled a local epidemic of rubella in July and August of 1940—a period in which most of the mothers of the blind infants would have been pregnant. Struck by this coincidence, Gregg asked the mothers of the blind babies if they had had rubella symptoms during early pregnancy. Many of them remembered having had a pink stomach rash, a sore throat, and swollen glands, the typical symptoms of the disease. Gregg published his suspicion that prenatal rubella might cause congenital blindness (Gregg 1941; reprinted in Persaud, 1977).

Subsequently, doctors throughout the world began to note whenever a newly pregnant patient had the symptoms of rubella. They were amazed and saddened when many of these women gave birth to babies with serious defects. Follow-up research has shown that, in fact, 80 percent of women who have rubella in early pregnancy give birth to babies with clear signs of damage (Hardy, 1973). The rubella virus attacks whatever part of the embryo or fetus is developing at the onset of the disease. Thus rubella in the first two months of pregnancy is likely to cause blindness, deafness, and abnormalities of the heart. Damage to the central nervous system, causing later emotional and behavioral disturbances, is also likely to occur at this time, as well as later (Chess et al., 1971). In the second trimester, after the fetus is completely formed, rubella almost never causes obvious physical defects, but it can cause hearing problems and language retardation (Hardy et al., 1969).

Rubella epidemics occur approximately every twenty-five years. Following the most recent outbreak in the United States, in 1964–1965, about 11,000 women who had had rubella early in pregnancy had therapeutic abortions, and another 20,000 women gave birth to infants with rubella-caused defects (Franklin, 1984).

Within the past twenty years, the birth of a rubella-syndrome baby has become a rare event. (In 1983, fewer

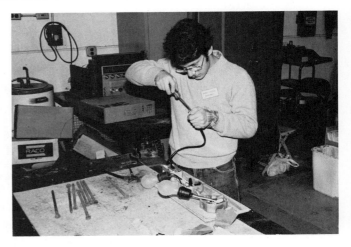

Rubella syndrome children often have a number of handicaps, but with proper attention, many of these children can live relatively full lives. This teenager, whose disabilities include severely impaired hearing and vision, is at work in his building-maintenance class at the New York Institute for the Education of the Blind.

than 100 fetuses were damaged by rubella [Franklin, 1984]). The primary reason for this is the development of a rubella vaccine that has greatly reduced the incidence of the disease among preschool children, the group most likely to spread it. In addition, there is a simple blood test, which a woman can now have before pregnancy, to see if she is immune to the disease. If she is not (about 5 million North American women aren't), she can be immunized up to three months before becoming pregnant (Behrman and Vaughan, 1983). (The three month's safety period is to ensure that the vaccine itself can't cause prenatal damage.)

Ironically, the success of the rubella vaccine in eliminating outbreaks of the disease has led to a decrease in the awareness of its dangers and, consequently, a drop in the inoculation rate. This means there is a possibility that the rubella epidemic due in 1989–1990 may actually occur.

Prenatal care is also crucial in the last weeks of pregnancy when there is a possibility of the mother's developing **eclampsia,** a disease that arises when the mother has difficulty ridding her system of fetal wastes. Women who are malnourished or bearing multiple fetuses are particularly likely to develop this problem. The early stage of this disease, called *toxemia* or *preeclampsia,* occurs during the last trimester in about 6 percent of all pregnancies. The symptoms in the mother include sudden weight gain and swollen fingers and ankles due to increased water retention, high blood pressure, and protein in the urine. In its early stages, preeclampsia can usually be controlled by diet and rest. If such measures do not work, the fetus is delivered prematurely, preventing fetal and maternal brain damage and even death.

Drugs

It is not routinely possible to test the teratogenic effects of drugs in humans, so, until fairly recently, a drug was presumed safe if it produced no ill effects when administered to pregnant animals. One drug provided tragic proof that this assumption is false and thereby revised medical opinion about the use of drugs during pregnancy.

Thalidomide In 1960, thousands of pregnant women were pleased at the introduction of thalidomide, a new mild tranquilizer, supposedly effective against nausea and insomnia. The drug had been tested on pregnant rats with no side effects and was duly pronounced safe. Many women took this tranquilizer in early pregnancy, especially in England and Germany, where they could buy it without a prescription.

Virtually every woman who took thalidomide in the second month of pregnancy gave birth to a seriously deformed baby. If a woman took the drug between the thirty-fourth and thirty-eighth day, her baby had no ears; if she used it between the thirty-eighth and forty-sixth day, her infant had deformed arms or none at all; if she took it between the fortieth and forty-sixth day, her baby had deformed legs. As a result of thalidomide, approximately 8000 deformed babies were born in twenty-eight countries (Schardein, 1976). The clear-cut tie between thalidomide and specific defects proved beyond any doubt that drugs could cross the placenta.

Other Medicines The thalidomide tragedy has made physicians more cautious in prescribing drugs for pregnant women. They now assume that all drugs enter the fetal bloodstream and try to make sure that the benefits of an indicated drug outweigh the risks (Pritchard and MacDonald, 1976). Drugs with proven harmful effects on the human fetus include streptomycin, tetracycline, anticoagulants, bromides, Thorazine, Valium, iodine, most hormones, and phenobarbital (O'Brien and McManus, 1978; Gupta et al., 1982). Several nonprescription drugs, including aspirin, antacids, and megadoses of vitamins C, D, and A have also been implicated in birth defects (Scher and Dix, 1983). Doctors now recommend that pregnant women take no drugs, unless the drug has been proved safe for use during pregnancy and is necessary for the woman's health.

Social Drugs Many of the drugs that harm the fetus, however, are not purchased at the drug store, but instead are bought at the supermarket, liquor store, or on the street. Unfortunately, if they are part of the woman's life style prior to pregnancy, such drugs are often used during pregnancy as well. In a recent survey of 417 pregnant women, mostly middle-class and fairly well educated (more than half had attended college), three-fourths of the women reported drinking alcohol during pregnancy (five drinks a week, on average), and a third reported smoking cigarettes (an average of sixteen a day) (Streissguth et al., 1983).

Alcohol. The most prevalent drug in our society, alcohol, can have serious teratogenic consequences. Each year in the United States about 1,500 babies are born physically deformed and mentally retarded because their mothers consumed alcohol during pregnancy (Smith, 1978). One study found that 43 percent of the babies born to severe alcoholics had the distinctive symptoms of the **fetal alcohol syndrome (FAS),** including small heads, abnormally spaced eyes, and malproportioned faces (Jones, 1975).

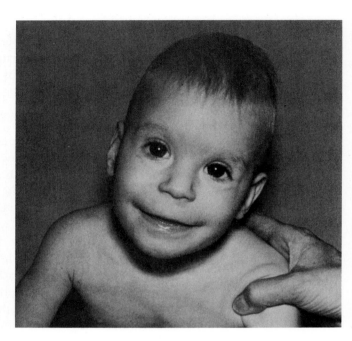

Figure 4.10 *This boy's widely spaced eyes, underdeveloped upper jaw, and flattened nose are three of the typical facial characteristics of children with fetal alcohol syndrome. Many babies born to women who drank alcohol during pregnancy show no signs of FAS; others have more obvious deformities of the eyes and head.*

In some cases, even moderate drinking may be harmful. A study of fifty-four women who were social drinkers found that nine had had babies with at least two of the half dozen or so facial characteristics of FAS (Hanson et al., 1978). None of the women in this study were alcoholics; in fact, many of them said they took only an occasional drink once the pregnancy was confirmed. However, these fifty-four women consumed between one and two ounces of absolute alcohol (that is, about three or four cocktails) per day during the month before they knew they were pregnant. For the nine whose infants were affected, this level of drinking in early pregnancy may have been the crucial factor, since extrapolation from animal research suggests that the third week of prenatal development (just when the woman becomes aware that she is "late") is the time when alcohol affects facial features most noticeably (Sulik et al., 1981).

Another study found that newborns born to women who drink moderately during pregnancy tend to be somewhat more excitable and irritable than the average newborn (Streissguth et al., 1983). Again, animal research suggests an explanation: alcohol in the maternal bloodstream temporarily reduces oxygen to the fetus, a deprivation that can cause minimal brain damage (Mukherjee and Hodgen, 1982), and minimal brain damage has been shown to be associated with hyperactivity and readiness to anger (Ross and Ross, 1982).

These studies need to be interpreted cautiously. While no serious researcher doubts that alcohol abuse sometimes harms an embryo, some researchers believe that serious damage can occur only if the woman drinks heavily and the embryo is genetically predisposed to FAS (Kolata, 1981). However, the March of Dimes and the Surgeon General of the United States both advise that pregnant women avoid alcohol completely.

Cigarettes. There is no controversy about the physical effects of maternal cigarette smoking during pregnancy. As the United States Surgeon General concluded in his summary of the results of thousands of studies in the United States, Canada, and Europe, "Children of women who smoke are more likely to have measurable deficiencies in physical growth and development" (U.S. Department of Health, Education, and Welfare, 1979). Babies born to mothers who smoke are more likely to be underweight, premature, and in need of special care in the hours, days, and months after birth. According to a longitudinal British study, children whose mothers smoked during pregnancy are also more likely to develop learning and behavioral problems as measured by test scores and school reports (Butler, 1974), although an American study does not confirm this (Lefkowitz, 1981).

Figure 4.11 *The habit of lighting up a cigarette with the morning coffee and newspaper may be hard to break, but the price of continuing to smoke during pregnancy may be a smaller, more vulnerable newborn.*

Heroin and Methadone. Babies whose mothers are addicted to either heroin or methadone are born addicted themselves. If they do not receive the drug soon after birth, they may die of severe withdrawal symptoms. Addicted babies also suffer from a variety of problems, among them low birth weight, jaundice, and various malformations. Compared to infants born to other mothers from the same socioeconomic class, addicted newborns are twice as likely to die within days after birth, primarily because they have trouble breathing (Ostrea and Chavez, 1979).

Other Common Drugs. Definitive research on the teratogenic effects of other common drugs has yet to be done. To the best of our present knowledge, moderate amounts of caffeine (the equivalent to three cups of coffee a day) are not harmful. However, even moderate amounts of marijuana or cocaine have been associated with complications, including low birth weight (Scher and Dix, 1983).

Given our limited present knowledge, and the evidence that drugs once thought safe are not, many expectant mothers are rightly cautious about all the drugs they consume.

Environmental Hazards

Pregnant women who are sufficiently cautious can avoid taking drugs. With a little luck and planning, they may even avoid getting sick. But without adopting a very different lifestyle, it would be virtually impossible for most of them to avoid all cosmetics, food additives, and pollutants in the air and water. Could these be harmful as well? The answer is yes, sometimes. A few are known to cause serious damage. Most of the rest are probably harmless, but no one knows for certain.

Radiation Massive doses of radiation from the atmosphere can cause many congenital problems. The best evidence of this, unfortunately, comes from the results of the atom-bomb explosions in Hiroshima and Nagasaki in 1945; none of the surviving pregnant women who were within a mile of the center of the explosion gave birth to live babies. Three-fourths of the pregnant women who were between one and four miles of the center had spontaneous abortions, stillborn babies, or severely handicapped infants (Apgar and Beck, 1973).

Another problematic source of radiation is x-rays. Use of x-rays, especially in the first trimester, increases the risk of leukemia during childhood (Stewart and Kneale, 1970). Prenatal exposure has also been associated with an increased incidence of respiratory diseases and infectious illnesses (Kitzinger, 1983). If a medical emergency makes x-rays advisable, the woman should consult with her doctor about the specific benefits to her and the risks to the fetus. Obviously, x-rays are no longer used to diagnose obstetrical problems, such as a narrow pelvis or multiple births; a sonogram provides the same information in a much safer way.

Pollution When exposure to them is extensive, several environmental pollutants can be teratogenic, among them, carbon monoxide, lead, and mercury. Although these teratogens are well known, tracking them to their source is often difficult. For example, many severely deformed and retarded babies were born to the women of Minamata Bay in Japan over a seven-year period. No one could figure out why. Finally, doctors realized that a nearby industrial plant was discharging mercury into the water. By way of the food chain, the mercury was passed in increasingly concentrated amounts from fish to the women and their babies. Since then, Minamata disease has become a synonym for mercury poisoning (Milunsky, 1977).

For several years, scientists have been aware that the manufacturing chemicals known as PCBs are teratogenic to animals (Allen et al., 1980) and, in high levels, to humans (Harada, 1976). Recently, evidence of the teratogenic effects of low levels of PCBs has been found. Pregnant women in Michigan were compared

Figure 4.12 *A woman who ate too much mercury-contaminated fish during pregnancy now cares for the result, her deformed and retarded daughter. She is one of 181 known victims of Minamata disease.*

on their levels of consumption of PCB-polluted fish from Lake Michigan, and then their newborns were examined. Women who had eaten more fish had newborns with more problems: their infants tended to be smaller, preterm, and have slowed and depressed reactions to stimuli. As the authors point out, however, the effect of any teratogen depends on a variety of factors, and small amounts of PCB alone may not seriously damage a fetus (Jacobson et al., 1984).

Risk Factors The effects of a particular teratogen are the result of the interaction of many factors. Some babies are more likely to have serious congenital problems than others (see Table 4.1), and it is rare for any teratogen to harm every embryo or fetus that is exposed to it. Among the factors affecting susceptibility are the baby's genetic structure (for instance, some seem especially vulnerable to cleft palate), gender (males are more vulnerable), and the mothers's age, health, social class, and nutrition. Birth order is also a factor: later-borns are more vulnerable.

TABLE 4.1 **Risk Factors**

	A specific teratogen is more likely to harm a particular embryo or fetus if several of the following conditions prevail.
Family Background	Several children already born to the family.
	Low socioeconomic status.
Inborn Characteristics	Genetic predisposition to certain problems.
	The fetus is XY (male).
Mother's Characteristics	Undernourished.
	Over 40 or under 18.
Nature of Teratogen	Occurs early in pregnancy.
	High dose or exposure.
	Occurs over a period of several days or weeks.
	Other teratogens also present.
Nature of Prenatal Care	Woman is several months pregnant before prenatal care begins.
	Prenatal visits to doctor are more than four weeks apart.

The *interaction* among factors is crucial (Fein et al., 1983). Most pregnant women experience some of the potential hazards to normal prenatal development, and have healthy babies nonetheless. Most of the hazards—malnutrition, diseases, drugs, pollution, chemicals—probably affect only fetuses that are already vulnerable for some other reason.

The Expectant Parents

As we will see throughout the rest of this book, the child affects the development of his or her parents just as much as the parents affect the development of the child. The beginnings of this parent-child interaction, in fact, occur almost from the moment a pregnancy becomes known.

**The Psychological
Impact of Pregnancy**

Pregnancy is an intense emotional experience for most parents-to-be. As one study of healthy, married women who were having their first babies reports, "the overall findings support a view of pregnancy as a turbulent, difficult period rather than one of calm bliss" (Leifer, 1980). This is not surprising, for any change, even a joyous one, necessitates adjustment and thereby causes some degree of stress. Obviously, the stress caused by any pregnancy depends on the particular circumstances surrounding it (see Table 4.2).

TABLE 4.2   Some Factors Affecting Parents' Stress During Pregnancy

Less Stress	More Stress
Planned and wanted baby	Unplanned, unwanted baby
Entire family wants baby	Not everyone in family wants baby
Sufficient income for baby	Insufficient income for baby
Sufficient space for baby	Insufficient space for baby
No other children under 3	Has another infant
Good maternal nutrition	Poor maternal nutrition
Good prenatal care	Poor prenatal care
No physical complications for the mother	Physical complications for the mother (nausea, swelling, high blood pressure, etc.)
No fear of birth process	Fear of birth process
Birth will not mean change of plans or life style	Birth will mean loss of job, schooling, or personal freedom
Assured that there is a very low risk of problem birth or diseased infant	Concern over high risk of problem birth or diseased infant
Mother's age is between 18 and 35	Mother is younger than 18, older than 35

As we shall soon see, each trimester of pregnancy tends to be characterized by particular challenges, emotions, and stresses. In addition, especially for first-time parents-to-be, pregnancy changes the marital relationship and transforms the couple's status in the generational sequence: no longer are they primarily husband and wife and someone's children; they are soon to be someone's parent. First pregnancies may also change the way the parents-to-be think about themselves: many young adults do not consider themselves truly adult until they are cast into the role of parent (Leifer, 1980).

Couples having their second or third child experience stress during pregnancy as well. Indeed, one study found that women experienced second and subsequent pregnancies more negatively than first ones (Westbrook, 1978). One reason for this is that the parents were much more aware of the costs and responsibilities of parenthood than they were as first-time parents-to-be. Another reason is that relatives and friends tend to take a greater interest in, and to be more supportive during, the first pregnancy (Kitzinger, 1983).

Given what we have learned about factors that can influence prenatal development, the obvious question is, can the emotional stress occasioned by pregnancy affect the fetus directly? Since stress can produce a number of physiological changes—including muscular tension, shallow breathing, and alterations in blood chemistry—it would seem possible that maternal stress could affect the fetus. In addition, nervous, worried women may digest food less well or smoke more than relaxed confident women do, and these factors may affect the fetus too. However, a direct cause-and-effect relationship between the woman's psychological state and the newborn's health or mood is virtually impossible to prove (Sameroff and Chandler, 1975). Nevertheless, it is certainly safe to assume that a relaxed and easy pregnancy is beneficial for the mother and probably for the child too, so factors that increase stress should be avoided if possible. In this respect it should be noted that the way the father-to-be reacts to his own stress as well as to his wife's will, of course, affect his interactions with his wife—and thus may indirectly affect the well-being of his future child.

Figure 4.13 *The relationship between father and child can begin during pregnancy. This father can feel the fetus's movements and even hear the heartbeat of his future daughter or son. (The same father and child, several months later, are shown again on page 148.)*

The First Trimester   The first adjustment to pregnancy is accepting the fact that pregnancy has actually occurred. Many couples may have already thought themselves to be "expectant" several times, only to be disappointed, or relieved, when the woman's next menstrual period arrived. Thus, when pregnancy does occur, it often takes time to accept the fact. As one woman said:

> I keep waiting for any sign that I'm pregnant, but my stomach looks flatter than it was at puberty. I can't feel a thing! If I could just feel something stirring. I'd even be glad to wake up sick in the morning. Then maybe I could really believe I'm pregnant. [quoted in Galinsky, 1981]

Usually women do begin to feel "something" by the end of the first month—sometimes morning sickness, but more commonly signs such as tenderness in the breasts, increased need to urinate, or a slight aversion to certain foods or smells. For the prospective father, the conviction that new life is on the way may be even harder to come by until the pregnancy actually becomes visible.

Once the reality of pregnancy sets in, many couples experience conflicting emotions in the first trimester. Even those who wanted the baby sometimes consider an abortion, feeling they have entered a new stage of life without being ready. Problems that never occurred to them before now loom large. As one woman explained,

"Sometimes big worries hit me. Oh, my God—what are we going to do? We don't have seventy thousand dollars in the bank. How will we pay for college?" (quoted in Galinsky, 1981).

In the stress and mixed emotions typical of the first trimester, many future fathers and mothers find that they become divided by their different responses to the pregnancy and draw apart. Not surprisingly under these circumstances, the sexual relationship between husband and wife often ebbs in early pregnancy (Masters and Johnson, 1966).

One common worry concerns miscarriage. Since the actual rate of spontaneous abortion in the first trimester is much higher than most people realize—perhaps about one pregnancy in three (Scher and Dix, 1983)—fears of miscarriage are, in fact, quite rational. However, many women needlessly fear that something they might *do*, like exercising or having intercourse, will cause a miscarriage. As we have seen, spontaneous abortions usually occur because something was wrong with the embryo, so it is not necessary to restrict most normal physical activities for fear of losing the baby. However, pregnant women should avoid those activities that raise body temperature much above normal, such as an overly long stay in a sauna or hot tub. High maternal body temperature for more than a few minutes can cause fetal brain damage, according to some reports (Smith et al., 1978; Miller et al., 1978).

Figure 4.14 *While overexertion should be avoided, physical fitness is especially important during pregnancy. Maintaining and improving general health and muscle tone assure an easier birth for both mother and baby. An added benefit is that exercise, especially in a class with other pregnant women, is good for the spirits as well as the body.*

Finally, many prospective parents begin thinking seriously about the responsibilities of motherhood or fatherhood, and about their own relationship with their mothers or fathers. They become more understanding of their parents' failings while resolving not to repeat their parents' mistakes (Galinsky, 1981). As one father-to-be put it, he, unlike his father, was not going to expect his child to be perfect:

> If my kid has a problem, my kid has a problem. I'll ask myself what I've done to aggravate it and what I can do to alleviate it. I'm sure this is all very easy in theory. I'm sure that on a day-after-day basis, it's hard to stay on top. But that's what I'm going into it hoping.

Fathers can, in fact, begin to take paternal responsibility for their offspring early in pregnancy. The mother's ability to take care of her body and to avoid teratogens depends a great deal on the support of her husband. It is much harder for the mother to stop drinking and smoking, for instance, if her mate continues to imbibe and light up.

The Second Trimester In the second trimester, the fetus seems more of a reality to its parents. The worst fears of miscarriage are over. During the early part of this trimester, fetal development is far enough along that the various prenatal tests available (see page 92) will yield clear information about the fetus's health if there has been any reason to worry about it. When the test results are known (immediately for the sonogram or fetoscope, several days or weeks later for tests of the blood or the amniotic fluid), chances are that all is well, and the parents are relieved to know that their baby will probably be normal. Often they also learn whether to expect a son or a daughter, one baby or more.

Figure 4.15 *Naming the baby is an activity that often brings many members of the family together—either in pleased agreement or in a heated discussion. In addition to pleasing parents and relatives, a particular name must be weighed with regard to its effect on the future child. Boys with unusual names tend to have a harder time getting along with their peers. On the other hand, a child with a popular name might not enjoy finding that he or she is just one of several Jonathans or Jennifers in the kindergarten class.*

The availability of techniques for the early evaluation of fetal health has greatly increased the number of decisions that parents must make if a serious problem is diagnosed. If tests show that the fetus is severely impaired, the parents must decide whether or not to abort. If they choose to carry the pregnancy to term, new lifesaving measures, including direct treatment, even surgery, for the fetus may be included among the options for care (see Closer Look).

In the fifth month, the pregnancy becomes clearly visible, fetal movements are felt, the age of viability is reached, and abortion is no longer an option. All these developments give the husband and wife a deeper sense of the reality of the impending birth.

This change is often reflected in the dreams reported by pregnant women. As one woman noted, not long after she first felt the baby move, "I used to dream that I would give birth to cats. Now I'm beginning to dream of actually having a baby" (quoted in Galinsky, 1981). This is often the time when husbands and wives draw closer, as they realize more forcefully that they are in the pregnancy together.

The Fetus as Patient

Recent medical breakthroughs have made it possible to treat the fetus while it is still in the womb. For instance, transfusions can be given directly to a 23-to-31 week-old whose life might be threatened by a blood disorder (Queenan and Hobbins, 1982). Similarly, the fetoscope and special surgical instruments make possible the repair of heart or kidney defects. Even certain kinds of brain surgery are possible. For example, when a fetus suffers from hydrocephalus (a condition in which fluids collect abnormally in the brain), a shunt, or drainage tube, can be inserted into the fetal skull, allowing the brain fluid to drain into the amniotic fluid. Without such surgery, the pressure from the fluid in the skull causes irreparable brain damage.

This new ability to deliver medical intervention directly to a fetus raises questions about the rights of the woman carrying that fetus. At the moment, the demand for fetal surgery far exceeds the supply of surgeons trained to do it. But what will happen when such surgery becomes readily available, and improved sonograms, fetoscopes, and other diagnostic techniques reveal more and more fetuses who could benefit from direct intervention? Would women be expected, or even legally required, to submit to surgery that might save their fetus's life? What if the surgery entails substantial risk to the woman? Or what if fetal surgery merely prolongs the life of a seriously impaired fetus?

These questions, which have only begun to be addressed, are actually part of an even larger issue: What is the proper role of mother, physician, and society at large in safeguarding and promoting the health of the fetus generally? This issue was recently highlighted by a medical team's report on a troubling case (Mackenzie et al., 1982). A pregnant woman with a 16-year history of alcohol and phenobarbital abuse was hospitalized in a state of stuporous intoxication, with bruises and other signs that she might have been physically abused. In response to the medical staff's concerns, she denied that she was trying to get rid of the fetus, saying she and her husband wanted the baby "very much." Nevertheless she admitted to two phenobarbital overdoses during the first two months of pregnancy.

Two months later the woman was hospitalized because of premature labor. The pregnancy was successfully prolonged, but the medical staff became more concerned about the fetus, for blood tests revealed that the woman was continuing to abuse phenobarbital, and while she was in the hospital, she covertly took an overdose of diuretics.

With their fears for the well-being of the fetus mounting, the medical team referred the woman to the local Child Protection Service. She attended several counseling sessions, and thereafter no further episodes of drug abuse were reported. The woman subsequently gave birth to a girl who, though low in birth weight, was full-term and seemingly healthy.

As the authors of the report make clear, a case such as this is likely to have aspects that make the decision to

---

Many women grow concerned with their husband's safety, becoming fearful of an auto accident, for instance, if he is a little later than usual arriving home (Colman and Colman, 1977). Many men become more directly interested in the pregnancy, and try to help their wives avoid unnecessary drugs, eat nutritious food, and get enough rest. Some become very concerned with building a nest and a nest egg, searching for a bigger place to live, for example, or asking for a promotion at work.

Unfortunately, the undeniable reality of the pregnancy, and the responsibilities and limitations it implies, trigger a destructive reaction in a minority of fathers-to-be. According to one study:

> The most common behavioral problem for the expectant father is simply that of "running away." But it is rarely recognized as such by the man himself or by the people around him. There always seems to be an explanation: business trips, new casual acquaintances, ball games; the pattern develops gradually and extends itself into long absences from home or sexual affairs with other women. [Colman and Colman, 1977]

intervene prenatally a highly complex one:

At no time could fetal damage be demonstrated. Further, it could not be established conclusively that [the mother's] behavior, if continued, would have caused significant harm to the fetus. Yet this behavior indisputably increased the risk of neonatal morbidity and mortality and threatened to compromise the child's postuterine developmental capacities.

Further complicating the issue is the fact that, in this particular case, the baby appeared to have escaped harm. Nevertheless, the authors believe that in cases like this one, it is (1) the clear responsibility of the physician to take action on behalf of the fetus and (2) the responsibility of society to make provisions for such action. They suggest that, now that more is known about harm that can occur prenatally, the laws that permit "protective custody" of an abused child be extended to include the fetus. Indeed, such measures have already been upheld in certain cases where, over the parents' religious objections, the courts have ordered that the fetus be given the blood transfusions it needed to live. However, arriving at a workable general policy raises questions that have yet to be addressed:

What sorts of behavior constitute abridgement of the right to be well-born? Must actual damage be demonstrated? To whom should the physician report the abridgement? What implications does abridgement have for privileged communication? How can intervention provide for a graded response, beginning with education and psychosocial support and escalating to custody of the fetus (and hence mother) as a last resort?

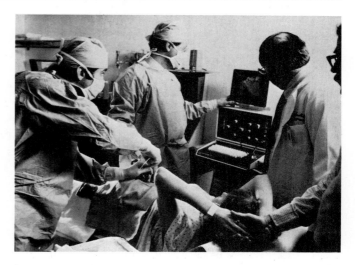

In utero transfusion is just one of several new medical procedures that can be performed directly on the fetus. The advent of such medical breakthroughs raises profound moral and legal questions regarding the rights of the mother-to-be and of her fetus.

As with many other questions of medical ethics and social responsibility, the problem is obvious but the solution is not. The first step toward finding an answer is recognition and discussion of the issue, not only by physicians and other professionals but also by everyone else concerned about the future of the developing person.

Some men react even more destructively by resorting to wife-beating. According to Richard Gelles (1975), there are five likely reasons for this:

1. *Sexual frustration,* if the husband or wife mistakenly thinks intercourse wrong all during pregnancy.

2. *Stress,* especially from anticipated economic burdens.

3. *Biochemical changes in the woman,* that make her harder to live with. She might be unusually tired, or she might cry more easily.

4. *An attempt to get rid of the fetus,* by causing an "accidental" miscarriage.

5. *The increased defenselessness* of the pregnant woman.

For the most part, however, couples enjoy the second trimester of pregnancy. Physically, most women feel better during this period than they did earlier or than they will later. Sexual relationships often improve, not only over what they were during the first trimester but sometimes even over what they were prior to pregnancy (Masters and Johnson, 1966), perhaps because the couple is now better adjusted to their new adventure, and, additionally, the fear of accidental pregnancy is temporarily suspended.

The Third Trimester In the third trimester, the mother is almost constantly aware of her future baby's presence. Not only is she visibly pregnant but she can see fetal movement as the surface of her abdomen ripples and bulges with the movement of the fetus's head, elbows, knees, and feet. When she sits or lies down in a way that causes the fetus to rest against a bone, the fetus squirms in reaction. She can feel the fetus startle at a sudden loud noise; and she can also sense the fetus quieted when she is walking, lulled by the rhythmic rocking movement.

During the last months of pregnancy, everyday life generally becomes difficult and more restricted. Going grocery shopping, tying one's shoes, and even getting to sleep can be major accomplishments. As the due date approaches, most obste-

Figure 4.16 *A little work and a lot of help is the combination that is usually welcomed by most moth-ers-to-be in the last months of pregnancy.*

tricians advise couples to avoid sexual intercourse, since there is a greater risk of newborn jaundice and respiratory problems if the baby is born soon after sex (Naeye, 1979). Some women find that coping with late pregnancy takes so much effort that they have little time for their careers, their social lives, their families, or their housekeeping. They should not blame themselves if these tasks are neglected, for fetal health in the last months may suffer if the mother is overtired. For many parents, the waiting for birth in the final weeks is the hardest aspect of the entire pregnancy. As one expectant father reported:

> Sharon was getting bored with her big belly. She was at the stage where she was getting food stains on her clothing, as if this immense protuberance wasn't really part of her. Her attitude was "Come on Baby, hurry up." But we were both very anxious. Not about the birth itself . . . [but about] the change in our lives. We were beginning to snap at each other. [Quoted in Bing, 1970]

Despite these problems, most women are glad they are having the baby, in contrast to their mixed reactions during the first trimester (Colman and Colman, 1977).

Nutrition

The last trimester is also the time when the nutritional needs of both the woman and the fetus become greatest, as the fetus gains weight rapidly and the mother's body prepares for birth. The importance of nutrition is shown by research that finds that giving malnourished women additional calories and protein in the last half of pregnancy reduces prematurity and other problems dramatically (Habicht et al., 1974; Stein and Susser, 1976). In addition, if the mother is well-nourished, the fetus is able to store extra iron and other nutrients during the last weeks before birth to use during its first postnatal weeks.

This does not mean that a well-nourished woman should overeat. Providing nutritional supplements to women who are already reasonably nourished does not affect the birth weight of their children (Rush et al., 1980). Furthermore, being overweight during birth can be a problem just as it is at other periods of life. But it does mean that ample food is far better than insufficient food: doctors once worried about their pregnant patients who gained more than two pounds a month; they now worry much more about their patients who gain less than two pounds.

Preparation for Birth

Finally, the third trimester is the time when both husband and wife become involved in the practical aspects of preparation for parenthood, from preparing the baby's living space to planning the route to the hospital. They may also join a class for expectant parents, both to learn the teamwork of the breathing and relaxing exercises that will make labor easier and to learn how to care for their newborn.

Many parents also benefit from the emotional discussion that often occurs in childbirth classes (Kitzinger, 1983). Couples can air their fears and get information regarding the birth process as they talk with other parents-to-be. Often the class discussions reveal concerns that might otherwise have remained unspoken. One common fear is that the fetus will be born deformed, seriously ill, or dead. A good counselor will not only make it clear that such outcomes are rare but will also indicate the kind of help that is available if a tragedy does occur. Couples also commonly worry about their ability to "perform" properly when the crucial day finally arrives. Actually, if they have been able to share their concerns and practice their exercises, many couples find themselves immensely proud of each other and of themselves during birth, as we will see in the next chapter.

Figure 4.17 *Couples who do all they can to care for their baby-to-be, and who share their fears and hopes during pregnancy, are likely to have an easier time weathering the stresses of the birth process and early infancy.*

SUMMARY

From Zygote to Newborn

1. The first two weeks of prenatal growth are the germinal period. During this period, the single-celled zygote grows to an organism more than a hundred cells in size, travels down the Fallopian tube, and implants itself in the uterine lining, where it continues to grow.

2. The developing organism is divided into inner and outer cells. The outer cells, the trophoblast, form the membranes that provide nourishment and protection during the prenatal period. The inner cells will become the embryo.

3. The placenta, formed from the cells of the trophoblast, enables fetal nourishment to be provided, and fetal waste products to be removed by the mother's bloodstream. Although the placenta allows substances to pass between the two bloodstreams, it keeps the blood supplies of mother and fetus separate.

4. The period from two to eight weeks after conception is the period of the embryo. The development of the embryo is cephalo-caudal (from the head downward) and proximo-distal (from the inner organs outward).

5. At eight weeks after conception, the future baby is only about an inch long. Yet it already has the organs and features of a human baby, with the exception of the sex organs, which take a few more weeks to develop.

6. From the eighth week after conception until birth is the fetal period. The fetus grows rapidly; muscles develop and bones begin to harden. The sex organs take shape, and the other organs complete their formation. The fetus attains viability when the brain is sufficiently mature, between the twenty-fourth and twenty-sixth week after conception.

7. The average fetus weighs 2 pounds at the beginning of the third trimester and 7½ pounds at the end. The additional pounds, plus maturation of brain, lungs, and heart, ensure survival for more than 99 percent of all full-term babies.

Preventing Complications

8. Teratogens (substances that can cause birth defects) can affect fetal development throughout pregnancy, but are especially likely to do so in the first eight weeks, the critical period. Some babies, because of their sex or genetic predisposition, or because of their mother's health or poor prenatal care, are more vulnerable to teratogens than others.

9. Certain diseases and a large number of drugs are teratogenic. For instance, rubella and thalidomide are teratogenic to almost every fetus exposed to them. Recently, two of the most commonly used drugs,

cigarettes and alcohol, have been shown to be harmful. Radiation and certain pollutants can also prove harmful in large doses.

The Expectant Parents

10. Pregnancy is stressful for both expectant parents, especially in the early months. How they react to that stress affects their baby's future, as well as their relationship to each other.

11. A diet providing adequate protein and calories is especially important during the last trimester. Good nutrition helps to prevent preterm birth and enables the fetus to store nutrients for use during its first weeks of postnatal life.

12. Prospective parents who understand their feelings about their unborn child and are well-informed about prenatal development are more likely to have an alert, healthy baby.

KEY TERMS

germinal period *(99)*	trimester *(102)*
period of the embryo *(99)*	age of viability *(103)*
period of the fetus *(99)*	teratology *(103)*
implantation *(99)*	teratogens *(103)*
trophoblast *(100)*	critical period *(104)*
amniotic fluid *(100)*	anytime malformations *(104)*
placenta *(100)*	
embryonic disc *(101)*	rubella *(104)*
neural tube *(101)*	toxoplasmosis *(105)*
cephalo-caudal development *(101)*	eclampsia *(106)*
proximo-distal development *(101)*	fetal alcohol syndrome (FAS) *(108)*

KEY QUESTIONS

1. What parts of the body develop during the period of the embryo?

2. What parts of the body develop during the period of the fetus?

3. What determines the sex of the fetus?

4. During which trimester of pregnancy is the developing organism most susceptible to damage by teratogens? Why?

5. What are the effects of maternal smoking on the fetus?

6. What factors make a fetus more likely to be harmed by teratogens?

7. How do the attitudes of prospective parents change from the first trimester to the second trimester?

8. How does prenatal nutrition affect development?

9. What are some benefits of classes for expectant parents?

RECOMMENDED READINGS

Cole, K. C. *What only a mother can tell you about having a baby.* New York: Berkley Press, 1981.

This book provides information about all the nonmedical, nontechnical aspects of pregnancy—the emotional quirks, the taste preferences, the private fears and fantasies—that are of special interest to mothers-to-be.

Kitzinger, Sheila. *Birth over thirty.* New York: Penguin, 1985.

Kitzinger examines all aspects of later pregnancies, especially those that occur when the woman is in her late thirties or early forties. Typical topics, such as Down's syndrome and Cesarian sections, are covered, as well as the more unusual topics, such as how to tell adolescent children about pregnancy or how to cope with being the middle-aged mother of an infant.

Heinowitz, Jack. *Pregnant fathers.* Englewood Cliffs, N.J.: Prentice-Hall, 1982.

Fathers, like mothers, exhibit a wide range of normal reactions to pregnancy—from fear to delight, from indifference to intense involvement. Jack Heinowitz, who is a psychologist and a family therapist, as well as a father, is especially adept at helping fathers recognize their less-than-enthusiastic emotions and at making suggestions for building the relationship between themselves, their wives, and their infants.

Shapiro, Howard I. *The pregnancy book for today's woman.* New York: Consumers Union, 1984.

In addition to sound advice about nutrition and exercise, this book includes the best specific information about teratogens; among them various prescription drugs, immunizations, and environmental and occupational hazards.

Jimenez, Sherry Lynn Mims. *The other side of pregnancy.* Englewood Cliffs, N.J.: Prentice-Hall, 1982.

Writing with sensitivity and wisdom, Sherry Jiminez discusses the causes and consequences of miscarriage and stillbirth. As a birth-education instructor, she is particularly aware of the parents' emotions. For instance, she explains why well-intentioned comments such as "It was probably for the best" do more harm than good, for they deny the grief many parents feel. This book is particularly recommended for parents who have experienced fetal death, as well as for health professionals who might serve them.

Guttmacher, Alan F. *Pregnancy, birth, and family planning.* Revised and updated by Irwin H. Kaiser. New York: Signet, 1984.

Written for expectant parents by a famous obstetrician, this book is filled with facts and reassurance. It emphasizes the pregnant woman's physical condition and problems, but includes material on the father, the fetus, the newborn, and the infertile couple as well.

Birth

Chapter 5

Hold a baby to your ear
As you would a shell:
Sounds of centuries you hear
New centuries foretell.

Who can break a baby's code?
And which is the older—
The listener or his small load?
The held or the holder?

E. B. White
Poems and Sketches of E. B. White

The Normal Birth
The Newborn's First Minutes

Variations, Problems, and Solutions
The Low-Birth-Weight Infant

Stressful Birth

The Birth Experience
The Baby's Experience

The Parents' Experience

The Older Sibling's Experience

Bonding Between Baby, Mother, and Father
Animals and Bonding

Bonding in Humans

Adoption

Chapter 5

Although birth is a universal human experience, the circumstances of each birth can vary greatly, with consequences extending far beyond the physical event, affecting child, mother, and father in the days and months ahead. The process of birth, its possible variations, and its significance for participants will be the subject of this chapter.

If birth takes place several weeks early, how will the newborn's health and appearance differ from that of an infant born the usual 40 weeks after conception?

What are some of the factors that may make birth stressful for mother and child?

What are the benefits of prepared childbirth for both the baby and the parents?

Will the bond of affection between mother and child depend on their first meeting just after birth?

The moment of birth marks the most radical transition of the entire life span. No longer insulated from the harsh conditions of the outside world, no longer guaranteed the nourishment and oxygen that have been provided through the umbilical cord, the fetus is thrust into a new environment where needs and desires will only sometimes be satisfied. The fetus thus becomes a newborn, a separate human being who begins worldly existence almost entirely dependent on others.

Birth is also a transforming experience for parents and other family members. For parents having their first child, the event prompts the realization "I am a mother" or "I am a father," and brings a new sense of the responsibilities, worries, sorrows, and joys that go with being a parent. The arrival of a second or third child transforms the family interaction and changes the status of the other children: the only child becomes a brother or sister; the "baby" of the family becomes an older sibling. Such changes in rank may have emotional and intellectual consequences. Children who have siblings, for instance, tend to be less cooperative than only children (Falbo, 1984). Each birth also adds a grandchild, cousin, niece, or nephew to the extended family, sometimes affecting the self-concept of older relatives. As one man newly elevated to the status of grandfather put it, "Now I'm immortal" (Kornhaber and Woodward, 1981).

We will now look more closely at this moment of transition, and at the first days of life for newborns and their families.

The Normal Birth

In the last months of pregnancy, the fetus and the uterus prepare for the birth process. The muscles of the uterus contract and relax at irregular intervals, gaining tone and widening the cervix a centimeter or two. Sometime during the last month, most fetuses change position for the final time, moving so that their heads are in the mother's pelvic cavity. They are now in position to be born in the usual way, headfirst.

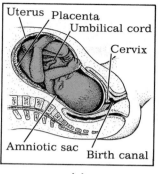

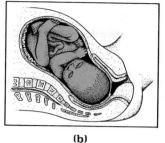

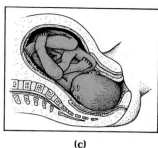

(a)

(b)

(c)

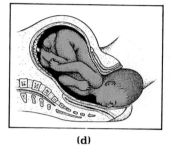

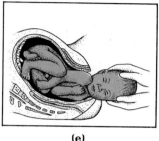

(d)

(e)

Figure 5.1 (a) *The baby's position as the birth process begins.* (b) *During the first stage of labor, the cervix dilates to allow passage of the baby's head.* (c) *Transition. The baby's head moves through the* "birth canal," the vagina. (d) *The second stage of labor. The baby's head moves through the opening of the vagina and* (e) *emerges completely. The head is turned and the rest of the body emerges.*

The birth process itself usually begins with uterine contractions that most women think are just movements of the fetus or the irregular contractions they have recently been experiencing. But when the contractions become strong and regular, or when the amniotic sac (the "bag of waters") breaks, it is clear that the **first stage of labor** has begun. During this stage the uterine muscles tighten and release, gradually pushing the fetus downward until the cervix dilates about 4 inches (10 centimeters), allowing the fetus's head to squeeze through (see Figure 5.1). Although this stage may last from a few minutes to a few days, usually it takes about eight hours in first births and between four to six hours in subsequent births (Danforth, 1977).

When the cervix is almost fully dilated, a process called **transition** begins, as the fetus's head begins to move out of the uterus into the birth canal, or vagina. During this stage, contractions often come very rapidly, and the woman feels nauseated, or chilled, or ready to quit. Luckily, transition usually lasts only a few minutes.

The **second stage of labor** begins when the head first appears at the opening of the vagina. The skin surrounding the vagina stretches with each contraction until the head emerges. Within a few seconds of the next contraction, the baby is fully born. This stage usually lasts less than an hour.

The birth process, however, is not quite finished. Minutes after the baby is born, the **third stage of labor** occurs when contractions expel the placenta.

The Newborn's First Minutes

People who have never witnessed a birth often picture the newborn being held upside-down and spanked by the attending doctor or midwife to make the baby start breathing. Actually, this is seldom necessary, for newborns, or **neonates,** usually breathe and cry on their own as soon as they are born. In fact, sometimes babies cry as soon as their heads emerge from the birth canal. Nevertheless, there is much for those attending the birth to do. Any mucus that might be in the throat is suctioned out, the umbilical cord is cut, and the baby is wiped clean and wrapped to preserve body heat.

TABLE 5.1   **The Apgar Scale**

Characteristic	0	1	2
Heart rate	absent	slow (below 100)	rapid (over 100)
Respiratory effort (breathing)	absent	irregular, slow	good, baby is crying
Muscle tone	flaccid, limp	weak, inactive	strong, active
Color	blue, pale	body pink, extremities blue	entirely pink
Reflex irritability	no response	grimace	coughing, sneezing, crying

Source: Apgar, 1953.

To quickly assess the newborn's physical condition, a measure called the **Apgar scale** is used to assign a score of between 0 and 2 to the baby's heart rate, breathing, muscle tone, color, and reflexes at one minute after birth and again at five minutes (see Table 5.1). If the total score is 7 or better, the newborn is not in danger; if the score is below 7, the infant needs help establishing normal breathing; if the score is below 4, the baby is in critical condition and needs immediate medical attention (Danforth, 1977).

Next the infant is carefully examined for any structural problems, such as a cleft palate, a spinal defect, or a hip dislocation. Silver nitrate or tetracycline drops are put in the newborn's eyes to prevent infection that might result from bacteria picked up in the birth canal. All this can be done as the baby lies next to the mother, allowing her to assure herself that her new child is healthy (Davis, 1983).

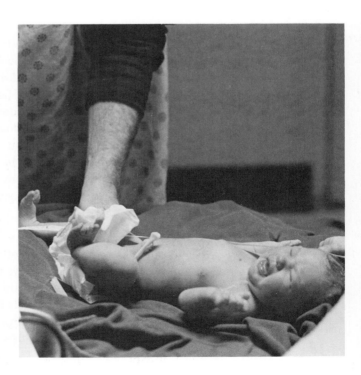

Figure 5.2 *This neonate, still wet from the birth process, seems to be passing the Apgar with flying colors. The doctor will undoubtedly give him two points each for reflex irritability, breathing, and muscle tone. If he's pink and his heart rate is rapid, he will rate a perfect 10.*

The Newborn's Appearance The news that the newborn's health is good is always reassuring, especially since many normal newborns look abnormal to someone who has never seen one before. Newborns' heads, especially the upper head, seem disproportionately large relative to their trunks and short, sometimes quite skinny, limbs. Often their heads are elongated and sometimes even pointy, because the bones of the skull overlap during birth as the head squeezes through the birth canal. This overlapping causes no lasting damage, because the bones of a baby's skull do not fuse together until the *fontanelles* ("soft spots") on the head close several months after birth. Typically, newborns have no hair; but some have hair on their faces and bodies as well as on their heads.

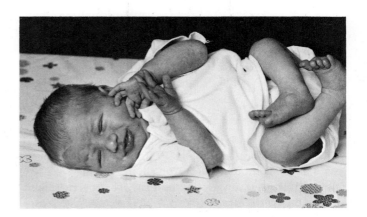

Figure 5.3 *Newborns come by their splotchy skin, misshapen heads and chinlessness naturally. The squinty eyes, however, are the result of the antibiotic drops administered soon after birth to prevent possible damage from bacteria in the birth canal.*

Most newborns have flat noses and virtually no chin, a fact that makes it easier for them to get milk from the mother's breast. Their skin also might look strange: especially if the baby is born a bit early, the skin may be covered with a waxy white substance called vernix; if the baby is a bit late, the skin is often red, splotchy, and wrinkled. All of these characteristics are temporary; an Apgar score of 7 or higher is a much better indication of neonatal health than appearance is.

Variations, Problems, and Solutions

As we have seen, birth is usually a short and natural process that results in a healthy newborn. However, this is not always so. Birth can be long and complicated, or a medical emergency may sometimes result in a lifelong handicap for the newborn. Because the possible physical and psychological consequences of birth complications can be important factors in development, we will review some of the variations in the birth process that can cause difficulties. They fall into two main categories: birth that occurs too early and birth that causes too much stress for the fetus.

The Low-Birth-Weight Infant

Most newborns weigh about 7½ pounds and are born full-term, that is, about forty weeks after conception. However, in the United States, about 7 percent of all newborns weigh less than 5½ pounds (2,500 grams) at birth, and are designated as **low-birth-weight infants** (Miller, 1985).

Most low-birth-weight infants are born more than three weeks early, and hence are called **preterm,** a more accurate designation than *premature.* Others, born close to the due date but weighing less than most full-term neonates, are called **small-for-dates.**

In deciding whether a particular low-birth-weight infant is to be considered preterm, an evaluation of the neonate's physical maturity is more important than an estimate of the number of weeks of gestation. Preterm infants show many signs of immaturity. For example, they often have fine, downy hair (lanugo) and a thick coating of vernix on their faces or bodies. If born more than six weeks before term, their nipples are not yet visible, and, if they are boys, their testicles have not descended into the scrotum. Most of these characteristics pose no serious problem. Vernix and lanugo disappear, and nipples and testicles emerge naturally within a few days or weeks.

There is one characteristic, however, that can be critical: the immaturity of such reflexes as breathing and sucking. Even full-term babies sometimes need a few

RESEARCH REPORT   ## The Problems of the Preterm Infant

Although preterm birth is the leading cause of newborn death, medical breakthroughs within the past twenty years have meant that most preterm infants survive. Indeed, increased survival of preterm infants is the main reason the infant mortality rate in the United States in 1980 (about 9 per 1,000 live births) was less than half what it was in 1960.

However, the survival of increasing numbers of very low-birth-weight infants means that there are an increasing number of children with developmental problems. The same medical interventions that have saved lives over the past two decades have sometimes created lifelong problems, among them blindness (from inhaling high concentrations of oxygen administered to aid breathing) and cerebral palsy (from brain damage that occurred during the emergency birth process) (Davies, 1976; Silverman, 1980). As longitudinal data has revealed the causes of the more extreme developmental problems some preterm infants have experienced, medical procedures have been altered to make obvious damage less common. However, even today preterm infants are likely to develop more subtle problems. For example, during toddlerhood they are slower to put two words together to make a simple sentence and less likely to play in an imaginative way (Ungerer and Sigman, 1983). Indeed, especially in the early years, the average scores of preterm children on many specific measures of cognition are lower than those of full-term children; those with very low birth weights are most likely to show deficits (Field et al., 1981).

What could be the cause of these problems? If maternal malnutrition was the reason for the infant's low birth weight, the infant may continue to be malnourished, and thus be susceptible to later learning problems. The birth process itself may cause damage, for low-birth-weight infants are more vulnerable to any stress during birth than full-term infants are.

In addition, the preterm infant's experiences after birth may be an important part of the answer. During the first weeks of life, the daily care of preterm infants is dictated by precautions; they do not get certain kinds of stimulation, such as the regular handling normally involved in feeding and bathing. Until recently, infants in the intensive care nursery were rarely touched and infrequently seen by their parents. At the same time, these infants are subjected to a number of abrasive experiences that normal infants are not, such as breathing with a respirator, being fed intravenously, and sleeping in bright light.

Recognizing these differences, several researchers have attempted to provide preterm infants with substitutes for the soothing experiences and regular stimulation they miss. In one experiment, infants born six or more weeks early were rocked mechanically while being exposed to the sound of a recorded heartbeat for fifteen-minute sessions many times each day (Barnard and Bee, 1983). These infants showed immediate differences in activity level from that of a control group that received the normal hospital treatment; and, in a follow-up at 2 years, they were significantly ahead of the control group in intellectual ability. The authors speculate that the lulling quality of the stimulation, as well as its regularity, "may have aided in the development of crucial, but subtle, aspects of the central nervous system."

days to coordinate these reflexes to be able to suck and breathe without experiencing such difficulties as spitting up or hiccupping. But preterm babies need more than a few days. They need special equipment and skilled care to sustain life until their reflexes mature. They must be placed in heated isolettes to maintain normal body temperature and to keep them free from infection. If they are more than six weeks early, they must be fed intravenously.

The most critical problem for preterm babies, however, is obtaining oxygen. Babies born more than five weeks prematurely usually do not produce normal levels of **surfactin,** a substance that coats the lungs and aids normal reflexive breathing. An infant with a severe surfactin deficiency often breathes irregularly or may even stop breathing for no apparent reason. This problem is called the **respiratory distress syndrome,** or *hyaline membrane disease,* a problem experienced by 60 percent of the infants born three months early and by 20 percent of those born one month early. Respiratory distress syndrome causes about half of all the newborn deaths in North America (Behrman and Vaughan, 1983).

Also, in recognition of the special problems of preterm infants and their parents, hospitals have changed some traditional procedures to allow more opportunities for contact, even in the first difficult days. The time spent together may help to establish the early bonds between parent and child. ("Bonding" is discussed in more detail on page 142.)

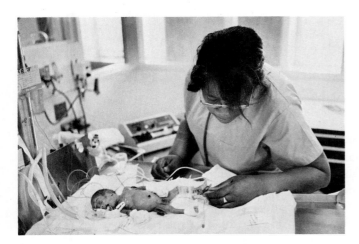

Born weighing only 2 pounds, this infant's heart rate, breathing, temperature, and blood acidity will be monitored continually until he reaches a weight of about 5½ pounds. Although his condition appears to be extremely fragile, current medical technologies give him an excellent chance of survival. However, the medical environment required to meet his most critical physical needs may deprive him of subtle, but important, types of stimulation.

Studies of parent-infant interaction during the first year of life have found other differences in the typical experiences of preterm and full-term infants. Parents of preterm infants tend to be more active with their babies—rubbing, poking, talking, offering the bottle—than parents of full-term babies are. For their part, preterm babies tend to be more passive than full-term babies (Field, 1980; Bakeman and Brown, 1980; Crnic et al., 1983). It is as if the parents, noticing their babies' relative passivity, try to push them into normal behavior, while the infants, reacting to more stimulation than they can comfortably handle, withdraw. Given the nature of this interaction, it is not surprising to find that parents and preterm infants smile at each other less frequently in the first months of life than do parents and full-term infants (Field, 1980).

Research also points to the importance of the preterm child's home environment. For instance, most of the learning problems that middle-class preterm children exhibit in the first months of life disappear by school age. Lower-class preterm children, on the other hand, continue to have learning difficulties (Broman et al., 1975; Sameroff and Seifer, 1983). Apparently, families with little education and low income have fewer resources for coping with the special demands of the preterm child. When families of similar class status are compared, one factor that correlates with better cognitive development of preterm children is the mother's ability to adapt to the child's special needs (Sameroff and Seifer, 1983).

Taken together, these studies suggest that relatively simple changes in the hospital environment and a more adaptive parent interaction may lead to better development in preterm infants.

Causes of Low Birth Weight   Low birth weight can result from many factors. One common cause is multiple pregnancies. Twins usually gain weight normally until eight weeks before the due date, then gain more slowly than the single fetus does. The average twin is born three weeks early, and weighs less than 5½ pounds. Triplets are usually born even earlier and weigh even less.

Often a "small-for-dates" baby is small because the mother was malnourished, or because the placenta and the umbilical cord did not function properly. Prenatal infections and genetic handicaps can also cause small or immature neonates.

The incidence of low-birth-weight babies follows socioeconomic patterns, with lower-class mothers twice as likely as upper-class mothers to give birth to preterm infants, primarily because poor women are more likely to be malnourished, ill, or have inadequate prenatal care. Age is also a factor: teenage mothers are twice as likely to give birth to babies weighing under 1,500 grams (3 pounds, 5 ounces) as are women between the ages of 25 and 30 (Vital Statistics Report, 1984).

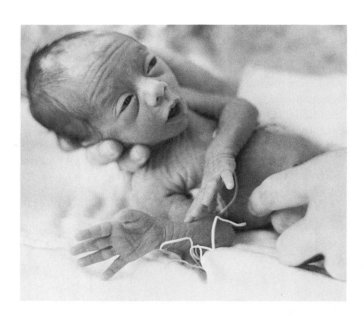

Figure 5.4 *Even though they weigh much less than average neonates, low-birth-weight babies are typically almost as long as their heavier contemporaries. The result is a scrawny, wizened appearance that may not disappear for many weeks, even when, like this infant, they are almost sufficiently developed to be treated like normal babies.*

Consequences of Low Birth Weight   Babies who weigh less than 2,500 grams have more medical problems than full-term babies. One reason is that many of the same conditions that cause low birth weight, such as an ill mother or a genetically handicapped fetus, also cause other complications that impair the health of the newborn. In addition, the birth process itself is more likely to harm a preterm baby than a full-term infant. Medication given to the mother during birth usually causes no serious damage to a full-term baby, nor is the normal newborn harmed by a few moments without oxygen. However, both these factors are more likely to damage preterm infants.

For very small babies, life itself may be uncertain. Since they are less resistant to infection, a mild cold can make them seriously ill. About 95 percent of all babies who weigh between 3 and 5½ pounds survive, but most of the infants who weigh under 3 pounds die. A few hospitals have highly specialized nurseries and are sometimes able to save the lives of some of the newborns who weigh less than 2 pounds (900 grams). For babies this small, physical maturity is more crucial than birth weight (Behrman and Vaughan, 1983).

Stressful Birth

Other complications can arise when the birth process becomes too long and stressful. The causes of a stressful birth can be many. For instance, the fetus's head might be large relative to the woman's pelvis, or contractions might not be strong enough, or the woman might be overtired, overanxious, or overmedicated. The problem can also be in the position of the fetus. For instance, about one labor in four begins with the fetus's back lodged against the mother's back, allowing less flexibility than the more usual back-to-front position. In this case, appropriately called "back labor," the fetus usually rotates spontaneously just at transition. However, if the fetus remains facing in the wrong direction, the second stage of labor becomes longer and more difficult. Another problem occurs when the fetus presents itself for birth buttocksfirst instead of headfirst, the **breech position** that occurs in about 3 percent of all births (Queenan and Hobbins, 1982).

The major problem that can result from any long and stressful birth is **anoxia,** a lack of oxygen. Moments of anoxia occur even in a normal birth, as strong contractions temporarily squeeze the umbilical cord. This is not harmful to the fetus, any more than momentarily holding one's breath is. However, repeated and prolonged anoxia can cause brain damage and even death, especially if the fetus is undernourished or preterm. Fortunately, medical advances in the past twenty years have included fetal monitoring to detect anoxia before it becomes too stressful and to indicate when delivery should be speeded up so serious damage does not occur. Fetal monitoring also allows doctors to know when a labor that appears to be difficult is actually creating no unusual stress on the fetus and therefore can continue without intervention (Sher and Dix, 1983; McCleary, 1974).

The most common type of **fetal monitor** consists of a sensing device that is fitted around the woman's midsection to measure and record the fetus's heart rate as well as the strength and frequency of contractions. Another type of fetal monitor is attached to the scalp of the fetus, and can measure the amount of oxygen in the bloodstream.

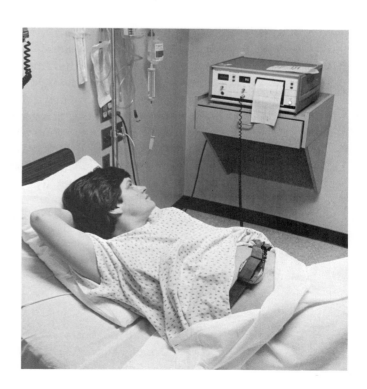

Figure 5.5 *This woman is resting between contractions, as the monitor tracks the regular heartbeat of her fetus. While monitors have been criticized for making women unnecessarily nervous, most women find them reassuring. In addition, the monitor often shows the beginning of a contraction before the woman herself feels it. If she has had training in natural-birth techniques, this signal allows her to begin the special breathing promptly, avoiding some of the pain and tension she would have felt with no forewarning.*

When monitoring reveals a weak or erratic fetal heart rate, or birth is not progressing as rapidly as it should, or the mother becomes exhausted and shows signs of physical stress (e.g., high blood pressure), several ways of hastening birth can be used. The best known is the **Cesarean section,** performed by making a surgical incision in the mother's abdomen to remove the fetus quickly. Cesareans now account for 16 percent of all births (Sher and Dix, 1983), a dramatic increase from 5 percent in 1968 (Donovan, 1977). Many of these Cesareans are performed even before labor begins, when sonograms and stress tests reveal that vaginal birth will probably be too stressful (as is likely to be the case with a breech birth in a relatively young or old first-time mother).

Once labor has reached the second stage, other techniques can hasten delivery. Either **forceps,** a medical instrument shaped to fit around the fetal head, or a special **vacuum extraction tube** can be used to pull the fetus through the birth canal. Once the fetal head begins to emerge, an **episiotomy,** a small surgical incision in the skin surrounding the vagina, is often performed to speed birth by a few minutes. All of these techniques require some form of anesthesia for the mother.

Figure 5.6 *Obstetrical forceps are two large, spoon-shaped blades that are gently placed around the baby's head to help pull it out of the birth canal. Forceps applied relatively late in the birth process, called "low forceps" and illustrated here, are much less hazardous than "high forceps," used before the fetal head has begun to emerge.*

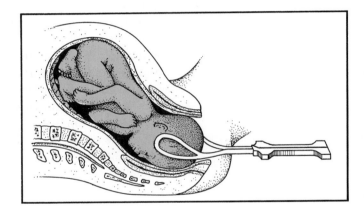

These and other medical techniques have saved lives and prevented brain damage, probably in millions of cases. Nevertheless, many critics, including some doctors, believe that these procedures tend to be overused in a typical hospital setting, resulting in a more expensive and less humane birth process (Davis, 1983). Moreover, recuperation takes longer if surgery and anesthesia are involved. A Cesarean, for instance, is fairly stressless for both mother and child at the moment of birth, but in the days immediately after birth, the mother is much less likely to feel up to cradling, feeding, and bathing her infant than she would have felt if she had delivered vaginally.

The most frequently criticized delivery practice is the use of medication. In North America, more than 90 percent of all deliveries involve the use of drugs to speed up contractions and diminish pain. From a medical perspective, these drugs are usually very helpful, since they reduce some of the stress of the birth process.

As with all medical interventions, however, these drugs carry some risk, especially to the fetus. Virtually all obstetrical medication enters the mother's bloodstream and rapidly crosses the placenta into the baby's blood supply. The dose, the timing, the nature of the drug, and the maturity of the fetus all affect the impact the drug will have. Obviously, smaller doses given late in the birth process are safer for the fetus than larger, earlier doses.

In special circumstances, such as a preterm birth, obstetrical medication can slow down the newborn's breathing reflexes to the point of danger. Physicians are well aware of this risk, and therefore usually give anesthesia sparingly, especially in comparison to a decade ago.

However, even when obstetrical medication causes no apparent harm in the birth process, it may result in negative effects in the hours and days after birth. Even low doses of medication can affect newborn behavior, including making the newborn less alert (Lester et al., 1982), and the greater the dose, the greater the effects tend to be. For example, in one study of forty-four normal newborns, those born to the more heavily medicated mothers were less responsive to their surroundings and harder to cuddle in the first days after birth. Although these particular signs of lessened responsiveness decreased during the first month, at the end of the month, these same babies were smiling least (Alexandrowicz and Alexandrowicz, 1974). Another study found that mothers who had more anesthesia reported more difficulties and fewer rewards from child care than mothers who had had no medication (Murray et al., 1981). In general, the mothers most likely to experience postnatal depression (the "baby blues") are those who receive the most anesthesia (Davis, 1983).

Specific conclusions about medication used in birth are often controversial (Kolata, 1979). For example, the correlations in the studies cited above do not prove that greater use of medication causes greater difficulty in the mother-infant relationship. Alternative explanations are plausible. In some cases mothers who had required more medication may have been less prepared, physically or psychologically, for birth. Certainly medication is sometimes essential to ensure the physical well-being of mother and infant. However, from a developmental viewpoint, birth is much more than a physical event; it is also the beginning of a long relationship between mother and child. Anything that impairs the alertness of either partner during their first meeting needs to be carefully examined.

The Birth Experience

Simply describing the sequence and procedures of birth tells little about how the participants are affected by their experience. The psychological and social effects of birth and the days thereafter may have profound and long-lasting influences on all family members.

The Baby's Experience

How does it feel to be born? Buddha called birth one of the inevitable sufferings of human existence. Otto Rank, a psychoanalyst, thought of birth as a traumatic event that affects all of later life. He reasoned that the experience of being thrust from the comfort and security of the uterus into a harsh world of hunger, cold, and noise causes lifelong fear and anxiety, and a continuing effort—at least symbolically—to return to the womb (Rank, 1929). Although this idea caught the imagination of a good many theorists and brought the term "birth trauma" into common use, there is no scientific evidence to support it. In fact, it seems to be contradicted by a number of observations. For one thing, many medical procedures that are very painful for older children, such as circumcision or the setting of a broken bone, produce very few cries in the newborn. This suggests that newborns may have a reduced sensitivity to pain. In addition, if newborns are held securely next to their mother's body or wrapped snugly in a soft blanket immediately after birth, they quickly become peaceful and curious—not the usual reaction after a traumatic experience.

Gentle Birth   Nevertheless, there are many who feel that the first moments of life are made unnecessarily difficult for most babies. Indeed, the French obstetrician Frederick Leboyer describes many common obstetrical practices as the "torture of the innocents" (Leboyer, 1975). Such rituals as setting newborns on a cold metal scale, putting silver nitrate in their eyes, separating them from their mothers immediately, and startling them with the bright lights and loud noises of the typical delivery room are only some of the procedures he condemns.

Leboyer is particularly critical of the usual habit of cutting the umbilical cord the moment the baby is born. This practice makes newborns instantly dependent on breathing, subjecting them to "the burning sensation of air entering the lungs," rather than allowing them a few minutes to adjust to this new way of obtaining oxygen.

Leboyer believes there are many ways the birth experience can be made joyful for the newborn. The delivery room can be quiet and dimly lit. The baby can be placed, stomach down, on the mother's abdomen immediately after birth, to be caressed until the umbilical cord stops pulsating and whatever mucus may have accumulated in the baby's throat during birth flows out naturally. Then the baby can be placed in a relaxing warm bath. According to Leboyer, newborns who experience such a **gentle birth** cry only once or twice, and then seem blissful. An American obstetrician who practices gentle birth reports that about one baby in ten actually smiles (Grover, cited in Berezin, 1980). There is also some evidence that babies born by means of gentle birth are more alert in the first thirty hours after birth (Salter, 1978).

Although many obstetricians worry that attempts to make the neonate's first moments comfortable might divert attention from the medical needs of the mother and child, Leboyer's concerns have made many parents, obstetricians, and nurses think more carefully about the neonate's initial encounter with the world outside the uterus. And while few hospitals have instituted soft lighting and warm baths in the delivery room, most now permit mothers to hold and comfort their babies moments after birth. Procedures such as weighing the newborns or putting silver nitrate in their eyes are often done later, in the newborn nursery.

Figure 5.7 *This newborn is being held in warm water reminiscent of the amniotic fluid that used to surround him. Leboyer believes that this relaxing moment eases the transition from the uterus to the outside world. Leboyer believes that the blissful smile on this neonate would be much more common if "gentle" birth techniques were used more often.*

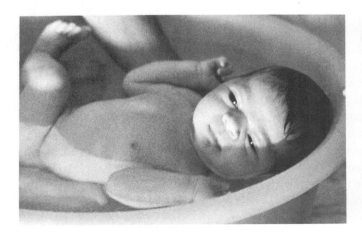

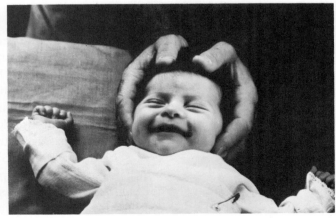

The Parents' Experience

As we have seen, a number of biological and medical factors can interact to determine whether a birth is fairly simple or complicated. However, psychological factors are also important in determining both the mother's and the father's overall experience of the birth. Psychological factors can make a long labor exhilarating, and a short one terrifying. They can make both parents swear "never again" after what physicians would call an easy birth, or can make even an emergency Cesarean so rewarding that the couple are ready to plan a repeat experience. Three psychological factors are especially important: preparation for childbirth, support from other people, and the environment in which labor occurs.

Preparation for Childbirth   First-time parents-to-be often approach childbirth with negative feelings picked up from television dramas or novels. Indeed, a recent study (Leifer, 1980) of women who were pregnant for the first time found that almost all had negative attitudes about giving birth. Some attributed their apprehension to television programs in which, as one woman put it, "whenever they have a woman bearing a child, it seems like she's screaming horribly or she's fainting, she can't control herself." Others had picked up their attitudes from their mothers and older women whose view generally seemed to be "It's horrible at the time but . . . you soon forget it."

Fortunately, this situation is changing as more and more parents-to-be prepare for birth, not only by learning about the natural processes and medical techniques involved in birth (knowledge that, in itself, reduces fear, tension, and therefore pain [Dick-Read, 1972]), but also by practicing specific breathing and concentration techniques known as the **Lamaze method** of childbirth. The Lamaze method has important psychological as well as physical benefits: both parents are often understandably proud of their active involvement in the safe and speedy arrival of their infant (Bing, 1983). Indeed, when both partners attend childbirth classes and when the husband as well as the wife is an active participant in the labor and birth process, the result is less pain, less anesthesia, shorter labor, and more positive feelings about birth and about oneself (Felton and Segelman, 1978; Fisher et al., 1972; Enkin et al., 1972).

Figure 5.8 *A husband's psychological—and physical—support can help to ensure a safe, speedy, and satisfying birth. In addition to keeping his wife in the position that is most comfortable for her, this husband coaches her in breathing and pushing.*

A CLOSER LOOK   **Prepared Childbirth**

Forty years ago in North America and Western Europe, it was common obstetrical practice to administer general anesthesia during delivery, so most women who gave birth in hospitals were unconscious when their babies were born. Today, general anesthesia is rarely used in normal births, partly because women are now being taught to use psychological techniques to relieve pain. The specific methods are based on principles of conditioning interpreted and popularized by a French obstetrician, Fernand Lamaze.

Lamaze began his practice using the conventional procedures of his time, delivering babies for women who were too heavily anesthetized to realize they were giving birth. In 1951, Lamaze traveled to the Soviet Union and saw many women giving birth without medication and without the screams of agony he had assumed were inevitable unless drugs were used. He learned that Soviet doctors had applied Pavlov's theory of classical conditioning (see page 47) to childbirth, teaching women to associate birth with pleasant feelings and mental images, such as a peaceful rural scene, and to lessen discomfort by using specific breathing techniques. These techniques were then practiced so often before birth that they became a conditioned response during birth. In short, women concentrated on the work, rather than the pain, of having a baby.

Lamaze returned to Paris and changed his obstetrical methods, stressing the mother's *active* participation in, and control of, the birth process. By chance, one of his first patients was Marjorie Karmel, an American. Early in pregnancy she "was not interested in natural childbirth—not even if they were giving it away." Later she decided "to string along for a week or two," and joined a class in the Lamaze method. In the end, she felt so "exhilarated and excited" after delivering her first baby through the Lamaze method that she wrote a best-selling book about the experience.

In the past twenty-five years, millions of North Americans have read Karmel's *Thank You, Dr. Lamaze* (1983, originally published 1959) and classes to prepare for a Lamaze childbirth are now common.

One important part of the Lamaze method is that each woman has a "coach," someone who stays with her throughout labor and birth to time her contractions, help her regulate her breathing, massage her back, and help her focus on the work of giving birth. Although originally the coaches were the women who taught the Lamaze classes, within the past twenty years fathers have increasingly taken over this role and done very well at it, as can be inferred from one father's description of his experience:

. . . Hard contractions had developed and Alice was in back labor . . . I became a one-man band, actually breathing and blowing louder than Alice, my right hand pounding out the rhythm on her arm, while my left hand did a wild effleurage [massage] on her back. Her urge [to push] was almost unbearable, and occasionally she gave way, but I put her back on the track by saying firmly, "Go back! Start over! Stay on top!"

. . .

The most exciting moment came for me at the end of transition, when, with my hand against Alice's back, I felt the baby turn—shoulders, elbows, and all. How fantastic to know what it was!

And then we pushed Alice into the delivery room, where it only took 20 minutes before the baby was born, and Alice claimed it was sheer heaven. [Quoted in Bing, 1983]

As the teacher explains the birth process, these husbands learn how to support their wives when it is time to push the fetus through the birth canal. Many couples have found that classes like this one not only make birth easier but also bring them closer together. In addition, the sharing of exercises, anticipations, and anxieties often begins friendships between couples who otherwise would not have met.

Not all parents-to-be prepare for childbirth, however. Middle-class parents are far more likely to attend classes than lower-class parents, especially when the lower-class parents are also relatively young and from minority groups. Partly for this reason, the less education and income women have, the more likely they are to experience pain, loneliness, and confusion during childbirth (Nettlebladt et al., 1976; Davenport-Slack and Boylan, 1974).

How much difference does the woman's experience of childbirth make to her? According to a study that compared the birth experiences of a group of first-time mothers, mostly college-educated and middle class, the difference can be considerable. Those mothers who had had Lamaze training had short labors and positive reactions to birth and their babies. Those who received conduction anesthesia, which blocks sensation in the lower half of the body while allowing the woman to remain awake, had quite normal labors, and generally positive or neutral attitudes about birth and their babies. They complained, however, that they felt detached from the entire experience. Those who went through natural childbirth but had not prepared for it as the Lamaze women had were positive about their babies but quite negative about the birth process itself—not surprisingly so, since their labors tended to be the most difficult. Finally, those who had general anesthesia and were unconscious during birth felt most negative about the whole event and the baby (Leifer, 1980).

Hospital and Home   In addition to preparing for childbirth, a growing number of couples in recent years have reacted against the depersonalization and medicalization of hospital birth by deciding to have their babies at home, convinced that home birth is not only safer but also more humane. According to advocates of home birth, the absence of many standard hospital procedures—from dressing the mother-to-be in the regulation hospital "johnnie" to the almost routine performance of an episiotomy—makes the mother more comfortable, and consequently makes birth more relaxed and natural (Kitzinger, 1983; Romalis, 1981).

Recently, many hospitals have responded to the home-birth trend by setting up their own "birthing rooms," pleasant bedroom environments especially equipped for childbirth. Most large cities also have maternity centers that allow for a relaxed and natural birth in an informal setting while at the same time providing equipment and personnel to meet any emergency that might arise.

Birth Attendants   The sensitivity of doctors, nurses, and midwives to the psychological needs of the mother and father can be essential to making birth a satisfying experience. As one woman said of her nurse: "I don't know what we would have done without her. She talked in a very soft, relaxing voice all during the contraction . . . I just listened to her, relaxed, and the pain disappeared like magic" (Quoted in Bing, 1983).

On the other hand, an insensitive attendant can be a hindrance. One doctor, for example, insisted on having one of his patients give birth lying down with her feet up, despite her objections (many women prefer to give birth squatting, or sitting half upright), and was about to use forceps when the husband intervened saying he would call in another physician. The doctor relented, and the birth proceeded normally. However, the doctor continued to be a source of annoyance. In the words of the father, "He was making jokes about hemorrhoids and in general assuming a stand-up comic stance. It was one of the most important moments of our lives and we didn't want Milton Berle present" (quoted in Bing, 1983).

The Father's Participation The preceding example suggests the potential importance of the father's presence during birth, not only as a help to his wife but as an informed participant in the birth process. Before 1970 fathers were rarely allowed in the delivery room. It was thought that, at best, they would merely be in the way and might even disrupt the birth process by becoming faint or ill.

Fortunately, hospital regulations are changing. Increasingly, fathers are present when their infants are born, even when medical intervention, such as a Cesarean, is needed. In many American hospitals and homes in which the Leboyer bath is included, the father is the one who bathes the baby (Berezin, 1980).

The results of such participation by the father are generally very positive. Consider what this father had to say about his experience:

> I administered oxygen to her [his wife] between contractions and coached her on pushing, holding her around the shoulders as support during each push. She was magnificent. Slowly I began to feel a kind of holiness about all of us there, performing an ageless human drama, a grand ritual of life. The trigger was probably the emergence of the baby's head—coughing, twisting, covered with blood, as purple as error, so eager for life— that set me into such intensities of joy and excitement that I cannot possibly adequately describe them. It was all so powerful I felt as though my head might come off, that I might simply explode with joy and a sense of participation in a profound mystery. I did explode, was literally reborn myself, saw how my birth, all births, the idea of birth, is profoundly right, good, joyous.
>
> Christopher was placed in my wife's arms even before the umbilicus was cut; shortly after it was cut he was wrapped (still dripping and wonderfully new like a chick out of an egg) and given to me to hold while my wife got her strength back.
>
> He was very alert, apparently able to focus his attention on me and on other objects in the room; as I held him he blossomed into pink, the various parts of his body turning from deep purple and almost blue, to pink, to rose. I was fascinated by the colors, time stopped; I thought my friends hooked on LSD should simply take a wife, have a baby, and watch it born! [Quoted by Tanzer and Block, 1976]

Not all husbands are so moved by watching their children born, of course, but the overall reaction is almost always good. For instance, in one early British study of 544 fathers who had been present during the delivery, 542 were glad they had been there, one was not sure, and only one regretted it (Pawson and Morris, 1972). In another study, husbands who were with their wives during delivery were more likely to be "highly pleased and enthusiastic about the birth process than were husbands who saw only the first stages of labor (Henneborn and Cogan, 1975). In addition, their wives used less medication and felt less pain than did the wives of the men who were not present during the delivery.

Research in the past decade has led to the conclusion that the earlier a father becomes involved with his child, the more likely it is that he will become an effec-

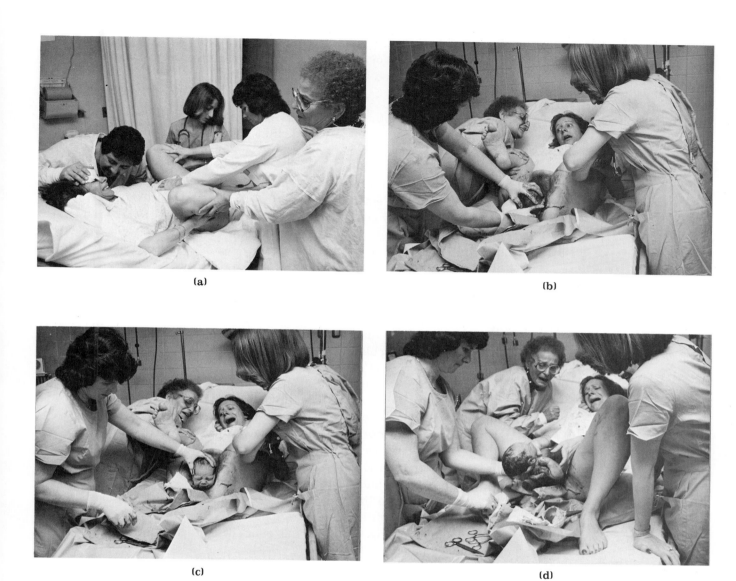

(a)

(b)

(c)

(d)

Figure 5.9 *Many hospitals have tried to make hospital births more homelike, as in this "birthing room." This birth occurs on a bed, not a steel table, and this woman is aided by midwife, husband, and her mother, rather than by unfamiliar doctors and nurses.*

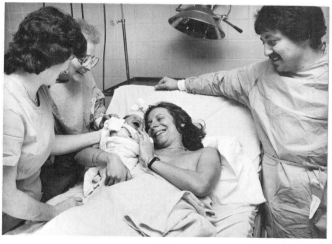

(e)

tive parent (Lamb, 1981). The elimination of barriers to the father's presence at the birth and encouragement of his participation in the birth process are positive steps toward establishing a good father-child relationship.

The Older Sibling's Experience

The birth of a younger brother or sister is not necessarily a happy event. During the period of hospital confinement, a young child at home may feel that Mother has disappeared, especially if this is the first time she has been away for more than a day or so. Further confusion may arise if a stranger is brought in to care for the child. The mother's hospitalization may be especially frightening if the young child associates hospitals with sickness and death.

When mother and baby come home, things often get worse rather than better. The parents are busy tending to the newborn, and may often be tired. They want the older children to be quiet and self-sufficient. Visitors come to admire the newborn, making older children feel slighted. To top it off, the baby is not like a doll or a friend. Instead, it cries and sleeps, and never plays.

No wonder many older siblings are disturbed by the birth of a baby. A child who asks "Isn't it time to take it back to the hospital?" or who is inclined to give the baby a bite instead of a kiss is not unusual. Some children revert to babyish behavior, crawling, whining, talking baby talk, or wetting the bed for the first time in months; sometimes they may direct aggression at the baby or at their parents (Field and Reite, 1984). Children who cope with stress in these ways are neither abnormal nor unhealthy, as long as they are able to return to normal behavior when they become accustomed to the presence of the new member of the family.

The birth of a new sister or brother often brings about permanent changes in the family routine, including less parental attention and encouragement for the older children. In addition to producing some emotional upset and jealousy, which may be inevitable in older siblings (Dunn and Kendrick, 1982), such changes may also have a negative effect on their intellectual performance as well. Robert McCall (1984) found that children's IQ scores dropped 10 points within two years after the arrival of a younger sibling. However, this effect became insignificant by the time the older children became 17.

Figure 5.10 *Older children may adjust more quickly to their new status in the family if they are allowed to visit their mother and new sibling in the hospital. Being able to visit their mother also helps to reassure them about her well-being.*

There are many things parents can do to help an older child adjust to the change in his or her life. For instance, a child can be brought to visit the mother in the hospital,* be given a present when a visitor arrives with a baby gift, and be encouraged to hold and care for the newborn. But more important than such specifics are the parents' recognition of the older sibling's feelings and needs and their continuing efforts to make the older child feel as loved as he or she was before the new arrival.

Bonding Between Baby, Mother, and Father

In recent years, one of the topics in human development that has captured much attention is the concept of bonding between parents and newborn children. The term **parent-infant bond** is used to emphasize the tangible, as well as the metaphorical, fastening of parent to child in the early moments of their relationship together.

Animals and Bonding

Questions about the nature of the parent-infant bond in humans actually arose from animal studies that revealed the formation of a quite specific bond between mother and newborn in virtually every species of mammal. Animal mothers, for instance, nourish and nurture their own young and nearly always ignore, reject, or mistreat the young of others. How, exactly, is this bond formed? Maternal hormones released during and after birth, the smell of the infant, and the timing of the first contact all play a role. In many animals, early contact between mother and infant can be crucial to the establishment of the parent-infant bond. For example, if a baby goat is removed from its mother immediately after birth, and returned a few hours later, the mother sometimes rejects it, kicking and butting it away. However, if the baby remains with her for the critical first five minutes, and then is separated from her, she welcomes it back. Many other animals react in like fashion (Klaus and Kennell, 1976).

Bonding in Humans

Does a similar critical period exist for humans? While researchers recognize that human behavior is much less biologically determined than animal behavior, nevertheless, they have tried to determine whether the amount of time mothers spend with their newborns in the first few days makes any difference in the mother-child bond. In certain cases, early contact does seem to be important (see Research Report). However, for most experienced mothers with healthy babies, immediate mother-infant contact does not seem to make any lasting difference in the relationship (Macfarlane, 1977). Indeed, several reviews express concern that the importance of early contact between mother and child will be overemphasized, resulting in feelings of guilt and blame and sorrow when a woman, for any reason, does not spend much time with her infant in the early days of life (Lamb and Hwang, 1982; Myers, 1984).

---

*Visitation is subject to hospital regulations, of course. Whether or not a hospital allows such visits might be an important factor in choosing where to give birth.

RESEARCH REPORT   **Mother-Infant Contact**

The landmark study of mother-infant bonding (Kennell et al., 1974) examined both early (immediately after birth) and extended contact between mothers and their newborns. Twenty-eight mothers and their full-term, healthy newborns participated in the study. Most of the mothers were poor, uneducated, and unwed; their average age was 18. Half of these women followed the standard routine for that hospital: not much more than a glance at their infants at birth, a short visit within the next twelve hours, and then about thirty minutes with their babies for feeding every four hours, except at night. The other half spent an hour with their naked infants (warmed by a special heat panel) within three hours after birth, and five hours per day for each of the first three days in the hospital.

Many differences developed between these two groups of mothers. Throughout the first year of life, the mothers who had more contact were more likely to soothe their babies, cuddle them, pick them up when they cried, enjoy them when they were present, and worry about them when they were not. The infants thrived under the attention, and scored better on tests of physical and mental development at 1 year than did the babies who did not have the extended contact. Even when the babies were 2 years old, mothers who had had the extra contact spoke to them more often and more warmly, giving them fewer commands and more encouragement, than the mothers who had had only routine contact with their newborns (Klaus and Kennell, 1976).

Extra contact also seems beneficial in the case of preterm infants. Because many preterm infants initially seem forbiddingly frail, and are frequently attached to mechanical support devices, their parents are often uninclined to, or unable to, hold and play with them. A study that compared married, middle-class women who had had premature babies found that the mothers who had had the most contact with their babies felt the most confident of themselves in the hospital (Seashore et al.,

1973) and cuddled and smiled at their babies most at home (Leifer et al., 1972).

Dozens of other studies have been done with many groups of various backgrounds—Canadians (Thompson et al., 1979; Kontos, 1978), lower-class Jamaicans (Ali and Lowry, 1981), urban Guatemalans (Sosa et al., 1976), middle-class Swedes (Carlsson et al., 1978), Britons of various social classes (Whiten, 1977), and white middle-class Americans (Taylor et al., 1979). Most studies have found that early contact and extended contact correlate with more maternal attention and affection later on (Goldberg, 1983).

It should be noted, however, that, despite generally favorable findings, the various studies of extended early contact are mixed in their conclusions, and in their quality (Goldberg, 1983). Some studies find differences with male infants but not with females; others find no effect at all. The methodology of many of the studies is open to criticism: the sample size has often been small; the nurses, testers, and mothers were rarely "blind" to the fact that they were being studied; and "contact" has been variably defined, with the extended-contact groups in some studies actually spending less time with their infants than the normal-contact group in other studies.

In addition, most of the positive results of additional contact have been with first-time mothers, or mothers who were young, poor, or otherwise under special stress. For them, the extra time with their newborns, as well as the implicit message that they were capable of interacting and caring for their new babies, may have made a difference. As one review states:

To give a mother immediate and active contact with her newborn baby in the hospital involves more active contact with hospital staff than for a mother isolated from [her] infant. It may be that, for socially and economically deprived groups, it is this relationship with hospital personnel, accompanied by expressions of interest, encouragement, and reassurance . . . that is important. [Chess and Thomas, 1982]

Relatively little research has been done on the question of fathers and bonding. However, there is some evidence that fathers, too, can be affected by early contact. (Certainly they are capable of a powerful absorption in their newborns, as the Closer Look on engrossment suggests.) In one study of the effects of early contact, some fathers were allowed to hold their infants for 10 minutes immediately after the birth, while others were granted only the usual glimpse of the infant (Rodhölm, 1981). In a second study, fathers were given 4½ hours alone with their infants during the hospital stay (Keller et al., 1981). Three months later, the fathers in both studies who had had extra contact engaged in more face-to-face play with their babies.

A CLOSER LOOK   Engrossment

According to some research, fathers often become fascinated with their newborns to an extent that surprises the men themselves. One particular study of this phenomenon termed the father's fascination *engrossment* (Greenberg and Morris, 1974). Engrossment was manifested in seven typical ways:

1. *Visual awareness of the baby.* The men thought they could recognize their own infants among a crowd of newborns. The men who had been present at delivery thought they could spot their babies with 100 percent accuracy; some of those who had not seen their babies born were not that sure.

2. *Tactile awareness of the baby.* One father wrote, "One hears the expression 'soft as a baby's backside' I suppose, but when I touched it, it seemed incredibly soft, like velvet."

3. *Awareness of the distinctive characteristics of the baby.* Fathers seemed certain that this particular infant, rather than any of the dozens of others in the nursery, was theirs. This was especially true of the fathers present at delivery. One wrote, "The fact that you actually see it born— you *know* it's yours. I'm not suggesting that if you don't go into the delivery room they swap them. But you see your wife actually giving birth. And you know that this is something the two of you have produced."

4. *The infant is perceived as "perfect."* One father wrote, "In the afternoon I walked up and down and looked at all the babies in that room up there and they all looked a bit ugly, a bit rubbery, and then when she came out she looked so beautiful, really, a little gem, so beautiful."

5. *Extreme elation.* From a father who had been present at birth: "I took a look at it and I took a look at the face and I left the ground—I just left the ground. I thought, 'Oh, Jesus Christ! This is marvelous.'"

6. *Strong feeling of attraction.* As one father said, "When she starts moving I go and pick her up and she starts moving in your hands and your arms and you can feel her moving up against you. It's like a magnet."

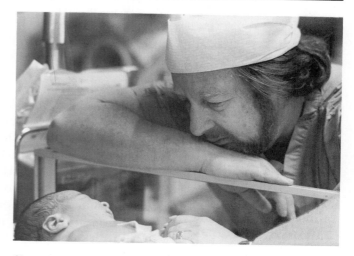

Shortly after birth, the newborn's heightened alertness and his father's excitement result in what seems to be a moment of mutual fascination.

7. *Increased sense of self-esteem.* These fathers were proud of themselves, as well as of their wives and babies.

Among the fathers included in this study were Arabs, Israelis, Irishmen, and West Indians from a broad range of social and economic backgrounds. However, since all the babies in this study were first-borns, and all the deliveries were normal, a conclusion based on the reactions of these fathers must be tentative. Despite this limitation, the authors of the study believe that engrossment is an inborn potential that is activated by a father's contact with his newborn. According to them, since infants are more alert and active in the minutes right after birth than they are in the next several days, engrossment is especially likely to occur if the father is present during the birth. Activity of any kind—grasping, sucking, kicking, looking—is interpreted by both mother and father as a response to them.

Although early contact between father and newborn, just as between mother and newborn, may be beneficial, it is not essential for bonding to occur. Even Klaus and Kennell, the original researchers in human bonding, now emphasize that the events right after birth are just one episode in a long-term process of bonding between parent and child (Klaus and Kennell, 1982). As another review of the literature concludes: "Separation of the mother and child in the neonatal period may have effects on maternal behavior which last a few months but it is unusual for effects to persist longer than that . . . it is clear that both mothers and fathers can, and commonly do, develop strong attachments to their children in the absence of neonatal contact" (Rutter, 1981).

The bond between parent and child is forged at many moments in their life together, not just the first ones. However, as you will see in the next three chapters, it is crucial that this bond between parent and child be formed.

Adoption

Biological ties and early contact are important, but they should not be overemphasized. The crucial factor is that each child has someone, whether a biological parent or an unrelated care-giver, who provides loving, caring, individual attention and stimulation. According to several reports, most adopted children have better childhoods than they would have had if they had not been adopted.

A study that followed the development of all the babies born in Great Britain between March 3 and 8, 1958, found that of those who were born to unwed mothers, the ones who were adopted usually fared better on measures of physical, emotional, and intellectual development than did their contemporaries who stayed with their biological mothers (Pringle, 1974). Another more detailed study followed a small sample of infants institutionalized because their parents, many of whom were unwed mothers, could not properly care for them at the time of their birth. Of these children, some were adopted, some were given foster care, and some were returned to their biological parents. It was found that, in general, the adopted children fared best (Tizard, 1977). (Research like this does not mean that unwed mothers cannot provide good care for their children. Obviously, despite the social prejudice against them, some unwed mothers give their children all the love and stimulation a child needs to thrive. But this research does suggest that many adoptive parents give their children good care, and that many "natural" parents need help in learning how to raise their children.)

Further evidence that early contact is not essential to the parent-infant bond comes from studies showing that children adopted by families whose background is different from their own fare better than similar children who grow up without families, spending time in institutions or a series of foster homes (Kadushin, 1970).

Furthermore, although the persistence of racial discrimination in the United States continues to make *intra*racial adoptions easier for parents and better for children than *inter*racial adoptions, thousands of interracial adoptions have been successful. Black children adopted by white families do well on tests of intelligence,

Figure 5.11 *Although this couple's black adopted daughter and Native American adopted son may miss some of the benefits of growing up in the cultures into which they were born, they will not miss the important pleasures and ordinary problems of family life.*

school achievement, and on measures of social adjustment (Simon and Altstein, 1977). Studies show that both intraracial and interracial adoptive families share many of the same successes and problems as families with biological ties (Simon and Altstein, 1981; McRoy and Zurcher, 1983).

In short, the bond between parent and child grows or atrophies for many reasons; the first days of life are significant, but circumstances and events before birth and throughout childhood are essential as well.

Figure 5.12 *How a child comes into a family is less important than how well the family establishes a sense of closeness and well-being for all its members. If the intimacy communicated by this photograph is a prevailing theme in this family's life together, the newest member will probably acquire the resources required to cope with life's less serene moments.*

SUMMARY

The Normal Birth

1. Birth typically begins with contractions that push the fetus, headfirst, out from the uterus and then through the vagina.

2. The Apgar scale, which rates the neonate's vital signs at one minute after birth, and again at five minutes after birth, provides a quick evaluation of the infant's health. Although neonates may sometimes look misshapen, most are healthy, as revealed by a combined Apgar score of 7 or more.

Variations, Problems, and Solutions

3. Preterm or small-for-dates babies are more likely than full-term babies to suffer from stress during the birth process and to experience medical difficulties, especially breathing problems, in the days after birth. Some long-term developmental difficulties may occur as well.

4. Variations in the birth process—such as breech births, prematurity, and anoxia—can result in a birth that is stressful for mother and child. However, fetal monitoring can provide early warning of these problems, and if necessary, delivery can be hastened by Cesarean section, forceps, or vacuum extraction. None of these procedures

is risk-free, but they may, in some cases, save lives and prevent possible brain damage.

5. In North America, fewer than one woman in ten gives birth without the aid of drugs. Even if obstetric medication causes no apparent harm, it may affect the newborn's behavior, making the infant less alert and responsive in the first days of life.

The Birth Experience

6. Some people believe that the fetus is insensitive to the birth process; others feel that the baby suffers during and after birth. Leboyer advocates "gentle birth," an idea accepted, in part, by many doctors, nurses, and parents today.

7. While biological factors are the primary determinants of birth complications and the length of labor, psychological factors play a large role in the parents' overall experience of birth. Women who are prepared for birth—knowing what to expect and how to make labor easier—and who have the support of their husbands and other sensitive birth attendants are most likely to find the birth experience exhilarating.

8. The extent to which fathers participate in the birth process affects how they feel about it. Fathers who see their babies being born or who care for them in the first days of life are more likely to be thrilled by the birth process and engrossed with their infants. Women whose husbands are present throughout delivery feel less pain and use less medication.

Bonding Between Baby, Mother, and Father

9. Although factors involved in the formation of the parent-infant bond are more specific and critical in animals than in humans, studies show that especially for inexperienced mothers, the amount of early contact between mother and newborn may be influential.

10. Studies of adopted children show that good parent-child relationships can occur even when the physiological and the early psychological factors that promote parent-infant bonding are absent. Biological relationships are not necessary to cement the parent-child bond. Love, care, attention, and stimulation are the crucial factors.

KEY TERMS

first stage of labor (125)

transition (125)

second stage of labor (125)

third stage of labor (125)

neonate (125)

Apgar scale (126)

low-birth-weight infant (127)

preterm (128)

small-for-dates (128)

surfactin (129)

respiratory distress syndrome (129)

breech position (131)

anoxia (131)

fetal monitor (131)

Cesarean section (132)

forceps (132)

vacuum extraction tube (132)

episiotomy (132)

gentle birth (134)

Lamaze method (135)

parent-infant bond (141)

KEY QUESTIONS

1. What vital body signs does the Apgar scale measure? What does the Apgar score tell about the health of the newborn?

2. What are the most serious problems of low-birth-weight infants?

3. What are the causes of low birth weight?

4. What medical techniques can be used to speed up delivery if birth becomes too stressful for the fetus?

5. What are the advantages and disadvantages of medication administered during childbirth?

6. What are the advantages of Lamaze courses for parents-to-be?

7. What alternatives do parents have in choosing where their child will be born?

8. What are the advantages of the father's presence during the delivery?

9. How does the arrival of the newborn affect the older children in a family?

10. How is the formation of the parent-infant bond different in animals than it is in humans?

RECOMMENDED READINGS

Berezin, Nancy. *The gentle birth book: A practical guide to Leboyer family-centered delivery.* New York: Pocket Books, 1983.

Berezin explains the reasons for, and procedures of, gentle birth, as well as other practices, such as Lamaze-training and breast-feeding. While the claim that babies, when gently born, are more alert and responsive in the days and months after birth has not yet been scientifically proven, the procedures Berezin advocates can be done relatively easily in most hospitals, if the staff allows it, and might well be worth trying.

Bing, Elizabeth. *Dear Elizabeth Bing: We've had our baby.* New York: Pocket Books, 1983.

Dozens of new mothers and fathers tell their stories. Included are many examples of the father's role, the use of helpful Lamaze techniques, and the significance of helpful or interfering doctors and nurses. As the personal reports make clear, preparation for birth is important even when unexpected complications require medical intervention, such as a Caesarian section.

Davis, Elizabeth. *A guide to midwifery: Heart and hands.* New York: Bantam, 1983.

Written by a midwife who has helped to deliver hundreds of babies in hospitals and homes, this book provides detailed instructions for potential coaches and midwives. It also presents the underlying philosophy of home birth assisted by midwives.

Nance, Sherri. *Premature babies.* New York: Berkley, 1982.

The national organization of Parents of Prematures provided much of the information and personal reflections in this book, and thus it is filled with practical information as well as emotional support. Issues usually ignored in books about birth, from coping with the guilt at having had a premature baby to adjusting baby clothes and products, are dealt with sympathetically. The book not only assures parents that most "premies" develop normally, it also gives advice on getting early help for the baby who is developmentally delayed or disabled.

Cherry, Sheldon H. *Understanding pregnancy and childbirth.* New York: Bantam Books, 1984.

This book covers much of the same material as the Guttmacher book, recommended in Chapter 4. However, Cherry devotes almost half of his book to birth processes, including various technological advances, as well as alternate birth methods.

Karmel, Marjorie. *Thank you, Dr. Lamaze.* Philadelphia: Lippincott, 1983.

The story of Karmel's birth experiences with Dr. Lamaze in Paris and her subsequent search for a similar obstetrician in New York. A warm, first-person account.

Macfarlane, Aidan. *The psychology of childbirth.* Cambridge, Mass.: Harvard University Press, 1977.

A British pediatrician reviews pregnancy, birth, and the first days of life, with special emphasis on the effects that many common practices have on the health of the infant. Includes discussion of the mother-infant relationship.

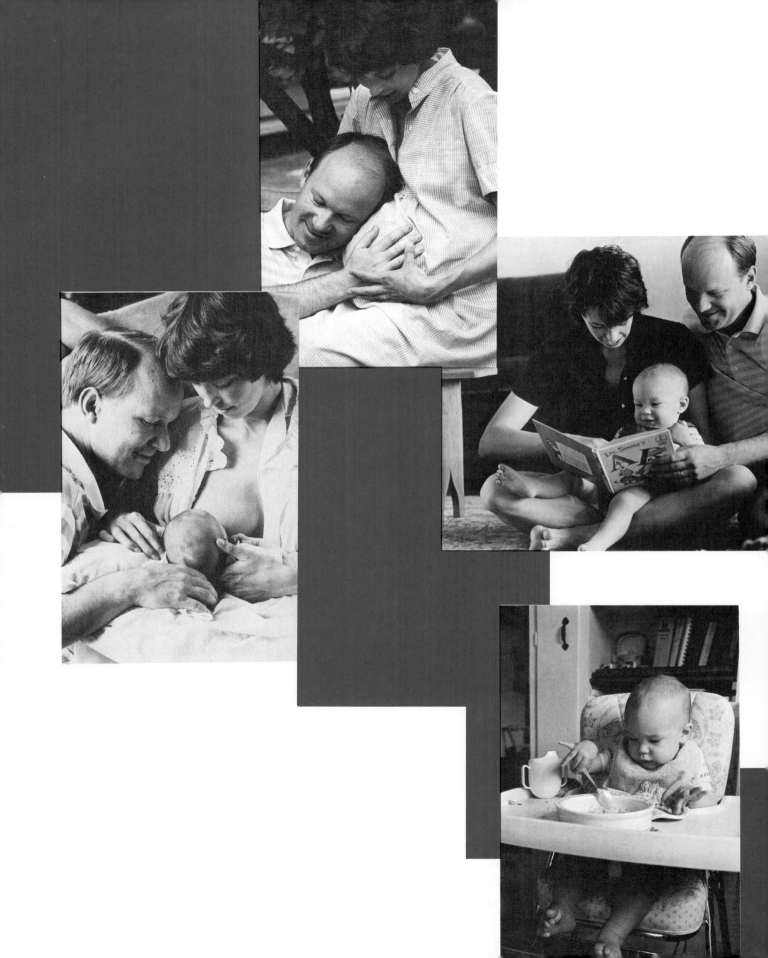

The First Two Years: Infants and Toddlers

Part II

Adults usually don't change much in a year or two. Sometimes their hair gets longer or grows thinner, or they gain or lose a few pounds, or they become a little wiser or more mature. But if you were to be reunited with some friends you hadn't seen for several years, you would recognize them immediately.

If, on the other hand, you were to care for a newborn twenty-four hours a day for the first month, and when next you saw the baby it was a year or two later, the chances of your recognizing that child are similar to those of recognizing a best friend who had quadrupled in weight, grown 14 inches, and sprouted a new head of hair. Nor would you find the toddler's way of thinking, talking, or playing familiar. A hungry newborn just cries; a hungry toddler says "more food" or climbs up on the kitchen counter to reach the cookies.

While two years seem short compared to the more than seventy years of the average life span, children in their first two years reach half their adult height, complete the first of Piaget's four periods of cognitive growth, and have almost finished the second of both Freud's and Erikson's sequence of stages. Two of the most important human abilities, talking and loving, are already apparent. The next three chapters describe these radical and rapid changes.

The First Two Years: Physical Development

Chapter 6

He who would learn to fly one day must first learn to stand and walk and run and climb and dance: one cannot fly into flying.

Nietzsche
"On the Spirit of Gravity"

Size and Shape
Proportions

Brain Growth and Maturation
Development of the Sensory and Motor Areas

Regulating Physiological States

Sensation and Perception
Research on Infant Perception

Vision

Hearing

The Other Senses

The Development of Motor Abilities
Motor Skills

Variations in Timing

Nutrition
The Early Months

Nutrition After Weaning

Serious Malnutrition

Chapter 6

Since her birth, this 8-month-old has grown 10 inches and gained 14 pounds—just two of the most obvious changes that occur in these early months. These facts, impressive as they are, don't even hint at the developing physical abilities that will transform the world for this child (and her family) during her first two years.

What determines when this infant will take her first steps? Do babies all over the world begin to walk at about the same age?

If this baby were placed at the top of this step-stool, she would be more fearful of the height than she would have been two months ago. What might be the reason for this change?

This infant grasps the stairs easily, but she would not find it easy to pick up, say, a coin from the floor. Why not?

At 8 months, this little girl has much greater control over her actions than she did when she was 1 month old. How do maturation and experience interact to bring about these advances?

An infant's physical development happens so rapidly that size, shape, and skills seem to change daily. This is no exaggeration. Pediatricians expect normal neonates to gain an ounce a day for the first few months, and parents who keep a detailed baby diary record new achievements every day, such as taking a first step on Monday, taking two steps on Tuesday, and five steps by the weekend. In infancy, as in every other stage, physical development is affected by the interaction of genes, experience, diet, and the quality of care.

Size and Shape

The average North American newborn measures 20 inches (51 centimeters) and weighs a little more than 7 pounds (Lowrey, 1978). This means that the average neonate is lighter than a gallon of milk, and about as long as the distance from a man's elbow to the tips of his fingers. In the first days of life, most newborns lose about 10 percent of their body weight before their bodies adjust to sucking, swallowing, and digesting on their own.

Once they have made these adjustments, infants grow rapidly, doubling their birth weight by the fourth month, tripling it by the end of the first year, and growing about an inch longer each month for the first twelve months. By age 1, the typical baby weighs about 22 pounds (10 kilograms) and measures almost 30 inches (75 centimeters) (Lowrey, 1978).

Figure 6.1 *These figures show the range of height and weight of American children during the first two years. The lines labeled "50th" (the fiftieth percentile) show the average; the lines labeled "90th" (the ninetieth percentile) show the size of children taller and heavier than 90 percent of their contemporaries; and the lines labeled "10th" (the tenth percentile) show the size of the relatively small children, who are taller or heavier than only 10 percent of their peers. Note that girls (color lines) are slightly shorter and lighter, on the average, than boys (black lines).*

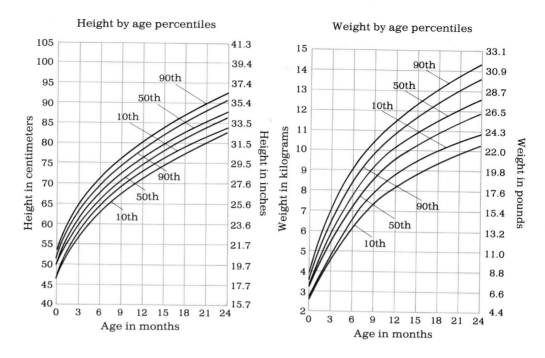

Growth in the second year proceeds at a slower rate. By 24 months, most children weigh almost 30 pounds and measure between 32 and 36 inches (81 to 91 centimeters), with boys being slightly taller and heavier than girls. In other words, typical 2-year-olds are almost a fifth of their adult weight and half their adult height (see Figure 6.1).

Much of the weight gain in the first months of life is fat, providing both insulation and a source of nourishment that can be drawn on should teething or other problems cut down on food intake for a few days. After 8 months or so, weight gain includes more bone and muscle. (Indeed, once they start walking, most children lose fat rather than gain it, and the toddler's pudgy cheeks and potbelly gradually disappear.)

In infants who were born very small, weight gain frequently occurs even more rapidly than it does in other babies. A 4-pound infant might double in weight in two or three months, rather than the usual four, and might weigh five times his or her birth weight by 1 year. This remarkable phase of growth is called the **birth catch-up,** because these tiny babies seem to be racing to catch up to normal size. In contrast, newborns who are heavier and longer than average grow at a somewhat slower than normal pace.

The birth catch-up is particularly common among offspring of small mothers and large fathers. This may be a biological adaptation that allows children who are genetically programmed to become large adults to begin life in a small uterus and be born through a narrow pelvis (Tanner, 1978).

Proportions

The growth that changes the baby's body shape in the first two years follows the head-downward (cephalo-caudal) and center-outward (proximo-distal) direction of development. Most newborns seem top-heavy because their heads comprise about one-fourth of their total length, compared to one-fifth at a year and one-eighth in adulthood. Their legs, in turn, represent only about a quarter of their total body

Figure 6.2 *As shown in this figure, the proportions of the human body change dramatically with maturation, especially in the first years of life. For instance, the percentage of total body length below the belly button is 25 percent at two months past conception, about 45 percent at birth, 50 percent by age 2, and 60 percent by adulthood.*

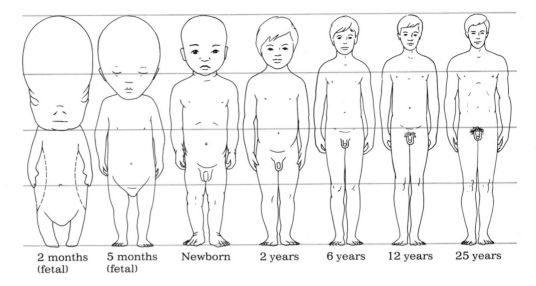

| 2 months (fetal) | 5 months (fetal) | Newborn | 2 years | 6 years | 12 years | 25 years |

length, whereas an adult's legs account for about half. Proportionally, the smallest part of a newborn's body is that part farthest from the head and most distant from the center—namely, the feet. By adulthood, the feet will be about five times as long as they were at birth, while the head will have only doubled in size. Even the head grows more at the bottom than at the top; the newborn's underdeveloped chin will not reach its final proportion relative to the skull until adolescence.

Brain Growth and Maturation

One reason that the newborn's skull is relatively large is that it must accommodate the brain, which at birth has already attained 25 percent of its adult weight. The neonate's body weight, by comparison, is only about 5 percent of its adult weight. By age 2 the brain is about 75 percent of its adult weight, while the 2-year-old's body weight is only about 20 percent of what it will be in adulthood.

Weight, of course, provides only a crude index of brain development. More significant are the changes in the maturing nervous system, which consists of the brain, the spinal cord, and the nerves. The nervous system is made up of long, thin, nerve cells called **neurons.** At birth, it contains virtually all the neurons it will ever have. Further development will consist primarily in the growth and branching of these cells into increasingly dense connective networks that transmit messages—in the form of electrical impulses—between the brain and the rest of the body. Almost every bodily function—from breathing and heartbeat, to seeing and hearing, to sleeping and waking—is regulated by this interchange of information. As the nervous system matures, the neurons become coated with a fatty insulating substance called **myelin,** which helps to transmit neural impulses faster and more efficiently. The myelination process continues until adolescence (Guthrie, 1980; Schwartz, 1978). These changes in the nervous system allow a child to gain increasing control over motor functions and to experience refinements in perceptual abilities.

Development of the Sensory and Motor Areas

Figure 6.3 (a) *Areas of the brain are specialized for the reception and transmission of different types of information.*

Research has shown that both experience and maturation play important roles in brain development. For example, myelination of the nerve fibers in the visual cortex of the brain will not proceed normally unless the infant has had sufficient visual experience in a lighted environment.

The role of maturation is apparent in the growth and development of the neurons that make up the nerve fibers. These cells increase in size and in the number of connections between them as the infant matures, enabling impressive increases in the control and refinement of actions. The cross-sectional drawings in (b) and (c) show the development of nerve fibers in the visual cortex between birth and 1 year. Drawings (d), (e), and (f) illustrate changes in the neurons themselves.

In the first months, brain development is most rapid in the primary sensory areas and the primary motor areas—the areas that control the senses and simple body movements. While development of these areas of the brain is essential to infants' increasing ability to use their senses and move their bodies, it is also true that sensory stimulation and motor activity are essential to the development of these areas. This fact is most clearly shown by research in which animals that were prevented from using their senses or moving their bodies in infancy became permanently handicapped (Parmelee and Sigman, 1983). Chimpanzees who were kept in castlike restraints to prevent them from moving did not climb when they were released. Dogs who were prevented from experiencing pain actually burned their noses by sniffing a lit candle when they were allowed free rein. Frogs whose eyes had been surgically repositioned so that they would see at an unnatural angle were unable to achieve a normal perspective after their eyes had been returned to their natural position: despite months of experience trying to catch flies with their tongues, the frogs' aim was always off (Schwartz, 1978). Not only does the functioning of such animals become impaired; their brains deteriorate as well.

In very simple terms, these abnormalities occur because the deprivation of certain basic sensory experiences prevents the development of the normal neural pathways that transmit sensory information. As researchers explain it metaphorically, the "wiring" of the brain—that is, the basic structures that allow the development of specific capacities—is genetically programmed and present at birth. What is required is the "fine-tuning" that occurs with the development of the connective networks, and it is this fine-tuning process that can be affected by experience, or the lack of it.

As best we know, the brain development that permits seeing and hearing in humans likewise becomes "fine-tuned" through visual and auditory experiences in the first months (Parmelee and Sigman, 1983). This is not to say that an infant would not be able to see colors or understand speech unless he or she had an opportunity to do so in the first days of life. Nor does it mean that intensive exposure to visual, auditory, and motor stimulation is desirable in the first weeks. (Indeed, many newborns would react to such stimulation by shutting it out with tears or sleep.) However, it does mean that, even for such a biologically programmed event as early brain maturation, experience also plays a role.

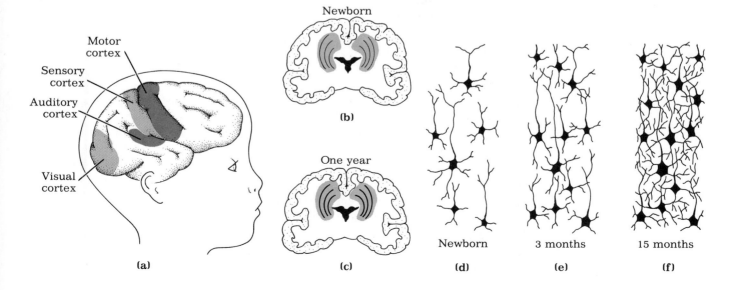

Motor cortex
Sensory cortex
Auditory cortex
Visual cortex

Newborn

(b)

One year

(c)

Newborn

(d)

3 months

(e)

15 months

(f)

(a)

**Regulating
Physiological States**

An important function of the brain in the early months of life is to regulate the infant's physiological conditions, or states. A full-term infant will normally exhibit at least three distinct, regularly occurring states: *quiet sleep*, in which breathing is regular and slow (about thirty-six breaths per minute) and muscles seem relaxed; *active sleep*, in which the facial muscles move and breathing is less regular and more rapid (forty-six or more breaths per minute); and *alert wakefulness*, in which the eyes are bright and breathing is relatively regular and rapid (Thoman, 1975).

Because each state produces a particular pattern of electrical activity in the brain, referred to as **brain waves,** the patterns can be measured and recorded by an electroencephalogram (EEG), a device which picks up electrical impulses from the nerve cells (see Figure 6.4). Brain waves change rapidly from about three months before term to about three months after, reflecting the maturation that is taking place (Parmelee and Sigman, 1983). The infant born three months early has long periods of "electrical silence" on the EEG, a pattern apparent at no other time

---

A CLOSER LOOK   **Sudden Infant Death**

Each year in the United States about 10,000 infants go to sleep and never wake up. They seem to be healthy, normal babies; then suddenly, inexplicably, they stop breathing and die. The phenomenon is called *sudden infant death syndrome (SIDS)*, but the term is merely descriptive, because the actual cause of death is still unknown. This uncertainty makes it especially hard for parents to accept a SIDS death: in the absence of clear-cut symptoms or explanations, they often blame themselves.

Neighbors, relatives, and even the police sometimes blame the parents as well. In one case, for example, a baby died of SIDS while his father was caring for him. Unaware that a healthy infant can die suddenly of an unknown cause, and taking the facial discoloration caused by SIDS to be a sign of foul play, the police arrested the father for murder. He was not released from jail until after his child's funeral, when analysis of the autopsy findings confirmed that the infant had died of SIDS (Raring, 1975).

As the accompanying table indicates, several characteristics are more common among the victims of SIDS than among other infants (Guilleminault et al., 1982). Apparently, part of the cause is genetic, for a baby born to a family that has already lost a baby to SIDS often shows unusual sleep patterns, waking less often than a normal infant (Harper et al., 1981).

Since the characteristics shown in the table provide only a

Factors Correlated with SIDS

	SIDS More Likely	SIDS Less Likely
Characteristics of Mother		
Age	Under 20	Over 30
Blood type	O, B, or AB	A
Personal habits	Smoker	Nonsmoker
Characteristics of Infant		
Sex	Male	Female
Birth order	Later-born	First-born
Birth weight	Under 5½ lbs	Over 5½ lbs
Apgar score at 1 minute	7 or lower	8 or higher
Characteristics of Pregnancy		
Mother's health	Urinary infection	No complication
Length of pregnancy	Less than eight months	Full-term
Mother's nutrition	Anemia (not enough iron)	No anemia
Situation at Time of Death		
Time of year	Winter	Summer
Age of infant	2–4 mos.	Under 1 mo., more than 6 mos.
Infant health	Has a cold, with stuffy nose	Has no cold, nor runny nose
Feeding	Bottle-fed	Breast-fed

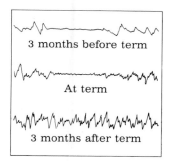

3 months before term

At term

3 months after term

Figure 6.4 *The more mature pattern of brainwave activity shows many more bursts of electrical activity and greater overall intensity as can be seen in this electroencephalogram of quiet sleep.*

except when a person is near death (Thompson, 1982). Infants born closer to term, but still early, show their brain immaturity in many ways. They never seem quite awake or quite asleep, and their breathing and muscle activity are irregular (Thompson, 1982). As the brain develops, brain waves and physiological states become more cyclical and distinct. As the weeks go by, for instance, infants are asleep and awake for longer, more regular periods.

Brain development is also associated with the degree of the infant's responsiveness to the outside world. For example, a sudden loud noise or a moment of pain (as from a pinprick) makes a normal neonate startle and cry. But soon the baby "self-soothes," that is, becomes more relaxed and quiet on its own, as nerve impulses diminish and brain waves display a pattern associated with a calmer state. On the other hand, the less mature nervous system of the preterm infant takes longer, and requires more intense stimuli, to be aroused; and once crying occurs, the preterm infant takes longer to settle down again.

rough profile of infants at risk, researchers are trying to pinpoint the causes of SIDS in order to prevent it completely. The most promising line of research looks at the types of brain waves, sleep cycles, and breathing patterns in early infancy that correlate with SIDS (Schulte et al., 1982; Weissbluth et al., 1982). Relatively minor neurological abnormalities at birth, as reflected in the EEG and in certain types of behavior (e.g., the particular way the neonate cries [Lester and Zeskind, 1982; Zeskind and Lester, 1978]), often indicate an infant who is at risk for SIDS.

Once high-risk babies have been identified, measures can be taken to minimize their susceptibility. For example, since the babies who die of SIDS often have a slight cold at the time, parents whose babies are at risk can take such precautions as preventing contact between the baby and anyone who has a cold and using a humidifier in the baby's room during winter to make breathing easier. The parents can also be trained in artificial respiration and in the use of a special monitor that signals when the baby takes an overlong pause between breaths.

An additional measure comes from an intriguing hypothesis advanced by Lewis Lipsitt. He believes that the learning experiences of the infant may help protect them against SIDS. Lipsitt (1982) points out that "eventual SIDS victims often have generally subdued activity. They suck weakly, move less, respond with higher thresholds to noxious events, and, in general, engage their environment

less. Such infants *may* subject themselves to fewer opportunities for learning than normal infants do." This hypothesis would explain several interesting correlations between a baby's experiences after birth and the incidence of SIDS. For instance, breast-fed babies are less vulnerable to SIDS. In part, this may be because they get more practice breathing through their noses than bottle-fed babies do, since breast-feeding requires more constant sucking. This practice may make it easier for them to breathe when they have a cold.

Similarly, the fact that first-born babies seem less vulnerable to SIDS may be explained by the fact that parents tend to provide more stimulation for the first child than for later babies. This stimulation may help compensate for the passivity of those infants who are at risk of SIDS because "they engage their environment less" (Lipsitt, 1982).

Lipsitt's hypothesis is as yet unproven. However, by the time an infant is 1 year old, the risk of SIDS decreases markedly, a fact that may be attributed in part to physiological maturation, especially brain development, and in part to the infant's experiences, another example of how inborn vulnerabilities may be affected by events after birth.

Sensation and Perception

Psychologists draw a distinction between sensation and perception. **Sensation** occurs when a sensory system responds to a particular stimulus. **Perception** occurs when the brain processes that response so that the individual becomes aware of it. This distinction may be clear to you if you have ever done your homework while playing the stereo and realized that you had worked through an entire album but had actually heard only snatches of it. During the gaps in your "listening," your auditory system was sensing the music—your tympanic membranes, hammers, anvils, stirrups, and the like were vibrating in response to sound waves—but you were not perceiving the music; you were not consciously aware of it.

At birth, both sensation and perception are apparent. Newborns see, hear, smell, and taste, and they respond to pressure, motion, temperature, and pain. Most of these sensory abilities are immature, becoming more acute as the infant develops (Lowrey, 1978).

The perception demonstrated by newborns is very selective. Neonates pay attention to bright lights, loud noises, and objects within a foot of their eyes, and usually screen out almost everything else. Their perceived world is simple—not all the "great, blooming, buzzing confusion" psychologists once believed it to be (James, 1950).

Research on Infant Perception

Over the past twenty years, there has been an explosion of research on infant perception. Technological breakthroughs—from brain scans to computer measurement of the eyes' ability to focus—have enabled researchers to measure the capacities of infants' senses and to gain a greater understanding of the relationship between perception and physiology.

The basis of this research is the fact that the perception of an unfamiliar stimulus elicits a physiological response, for example, slowed heart rate, concentrated gazing, and, in the case of infants who have a pacifier in their mouths, intensified sucking. When the new stimulus becomes so familiar that these responses no

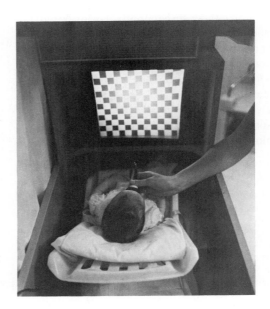

Figure 6.5 *In this experiment in infant perception, the nipple on which the infant is sucking is connected to an element that can focus the image on the screen. Another device records the frequency and strength of the sucking. Typically, infants show their interest by sucking fairly intensely when they see a new image. Then, as they become habituated, their sucking tapers off.*

longer occur, the infant is said to be *habituated* to that stimulus. Employing this phenomenon of **habituation,** researchers have been able to assess infants' ability to perceive by testing their ability to discriminate between very similar stimuli. Typically, they present the infant with a stimulus—say a plain circle—until habituation occurs. Then they present another stimulus similar to the first but different in some detail—say a circle with a dot in the middle. If the infant reacts in some measurable way to the new stimulus (a change of heart rate, a narrowing of the pupils, a refocusing of gaze), the difference in stimulus is taken to have been perceived.

Vision

At birth, vision is the least well developed of the senses. Newborns focus well only on objects that are about 10 inches away. The distance vision of the neonate is about 20/600, which means that the baby can see an object 20 feet (6.1 meters) away no better than an adult with normal 20/20 vision could see the same object 600 feet (183 meters) away. By 4 months, distance vision is 20/150; and by 6 months, visual acuity approaches 20/20 (Salapatek, 1977).

Although we can accurately measure infants' ability to see, it is not easy to tell precisely what they perceive. Do they simply stare at whatever comes into focus? Can they distinguish one object from another? Do they prefer particular things, perhaps a brightly colored rattle or a face?

Some answers to these questions were provided in a now-classic experiment by Robert Fantz (1961), who showed six types of disks to 2-month-old infants and measured the duration of their gaze at each one. He found that babies looked longer at patterned disks than at plain red, white, or yellow ones, and looked longest of all at the disk of a smiling face (see Figure 6.6). This research led some psychologists to conclude that 2-month-olds can not only see patterns but can also recognize the human face as such, a conclusion that occasioned much celebration of the infant's social skills.

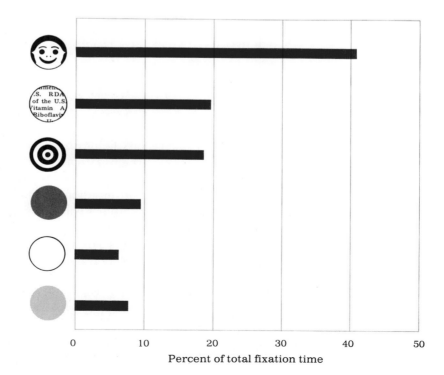

Figure 6.6 *What do 2-month-olds like to look at? Fantz found that they liked faces best of all. He measured how long 2- and 3-month-olds stared at the six types of disks portrayed here, presented one by one. As this graph shows, the infants stared at the face disk more than twice as long as at the disk of newsprint or the bull's eye, and more than four times as long as at the pattern-less disks.*

Percent of total fixation time

The celebration was premature, however. It is true that very young infants pay more attention to faces than to most other objects they encounter. But further research involving human faces has found that infants are intrigued with faces, not because they recognize them as faces, but because faces have an interesting pattern within an outlined circle (the face framed by the hair) (Caron et al., 1973; Haaf et al., 1983).

There is a developmental shift in precisely what part of the face infants find most interesting: 1-month-old babies look more at the hairline than at the eyes (according to one study, 57 percent compared to 30 percent of total fixation time), but 2-month-old babies look more at eyes than at the hairline (49 percent compared to 33 percent) (Haith et al., 1977).

By 3 months some celebration is in order, for at that age infants respond to their mother's facial expressions and show that they recognize their mother's photograph (Barrera 1981a, 1981b). By 6 months, or perhaps earlier, infants who are shown the photo of an unfamiliar individual several times will be able to distinguish it from a stranger's photo that they have not been shown before. They can also differentiate men's faces from women's, and show definite preferences for happy facial expressions over sad and angry ones (Cohen et al., 1979).

Figure 6.7 *Differences in how infants scan the human face become apparent between the ages of 1 and 2 months: (a) 1-month-olds concentrated on the edges of the head; (b) 2-month-olds tended to focus on features of the face, especially the eyes.*

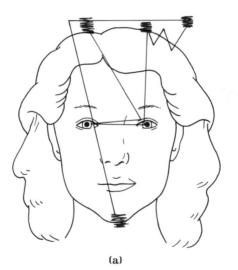

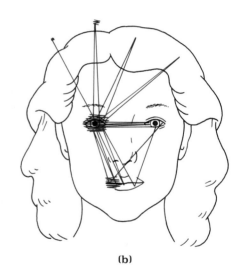

(a)   (b)

Hearing

Relative to his or her vision, the newborn's hearing is quite acute. Sudden noises startle newborns, making them cry; rhythmic sounds, such as a lullabye or a heartbeat, soothe them and put them to sleep. When they are awake, they are quite attentive to the sound of conversation. Indeed, by the end of the first month, the infant can distinguish the mother's voice from, and prefers it to, the voices of other women (DeCasper and Fifer, 1980).

By the age of 1 month, infants can also perceive differences between very similar sounds. In one experiment, 1-month-old babies activated a recording of the "bah" sound whenever they sucked on a nipple. At first, they sucked diligently; but as they became habituated to the sound, their sucking decreased. At this point, the experimenters changed the sound from "bah" to "pah." Immediately the babies sucked harder, indicating by this sign of interest that they had perceived the difference (Eimas et al., 1971). It may even be that newborns have some ability to discriminate between vowels (Clarkson and Berg, 1983).

RESEARCH REPORT   **Depth Perception**

Depth perception, the ability to see that one surface (such as the floor) is lower than another (such as the table) develops early. Eleanor Gibson and Richard Walk (1960) first learned this by experimenting to see if infants would crawl over a visual cliff, an apparent drop of several feet that actually was covered by a protective sheet of transparent glass (see photos). Even when their mothers urged them to crawl onto the glass, babies between the ages of 8 months and 12 months hesitated to go over the "edge."

Joseph Campos and his colleagues (1970) decided to see if depth perception develops in babies too young to crawl. To do this, they used a variant of the visual-cliff experiment, placing the infant not only on the "shallow" side of the visual cliff, as Gibson and Walk did, but also on the "deep" side (actually on the protective glass). They measured the infant's heart rate on both sides, theorizing that if the babies recognized that they were over a "cliff," their heart rates would speed up, but if they could not perceive the depth, their heart rates would be the same on both sides.

As had been suspected, compared to babies older than 8 months, who showed a rapid increase in heart rate on the "deep" side, infants slightly younger than 8 months showed no significant heart-rate differences between the two sides. What the researchers had not foreseen was that very young babies—as young as 2-months-old—would show a *decrease* in heart rate on the "deep" side, indicating that they perceived the difference, and were interested in it but not afraid of it. The younger babies were also much less likely to fuss or cry on the deep side than the older babies were.

Thus, depth perception develops in the first months of life, but fear of falling over an edge does not appear until about 8 months. Why is there this lag between perception and fear? Campos and his colleagues (1978) have several ideas. Perhaps perceptual and cognitive maturation are necessary before the baby realizes what the edge of a drop means. Maybe babies under 6 months are essentially fearless. Or it may be that babies have to fall, or almost fall, once or twice before fear of a drop develops. In fact, probably several of these factors play a role.

These photos show the visual cliff used by Joseph Campos and his colleagues. Normally, babies older than 8 months old crawl happily toward their mothers to play, but when such crawling would take them over the apparent edge of a "cliff," almost all babies stay on the "shallow" side.

By the age of 4 months, many infants can identify the voices of the most familiar people in their lives. For example, in one experiment (Spelke and Owsley, 1979), infants were placed in a baby seat facing both their parents. While the parents sat expressionless and silent, a loudspeaker alternately played a recording of either the mother's or the father's voice. Infants as young as 3½ months consistently looked at the parent whose voice was being played.

The Other Senses

Two of the infant's senses seem poorly developed at birth: taste and pain. Newborns prefer to suck on a bottle of sweet rather than sour milk, and cry for a moment when their heel is pricked to obtain blood for a blood test, but these responses are much weaker than those of an older baby. The newborn's more general sense of touch does appear to be fairly well developed, however: crying newborns can usually be soothed by being wrapped or swaddled in a blanket, or by being held snugly.

Figure 6.8 *As evidenced in cultures throughout the world (the United States, the Ivory Coast, and Ecuador are shown here), infant carriers not only make it easier to hold a baby while working or strolling; they also keep babies happy. In the early months, front carriers allow infants to see the parent's face, hear the heartbeat, and feel the cradling movement of walking. In later months, back carriers allow babies to observe the sights and sounds of the world from a lofty perch. From the infant's perspective, the traditional baby carriage is a much less satisfying mode of transport, because it prevents constant contact with the parent and severely limits the view.*

The sense of smell functions at a very young age. Not only do infants turn away from smells like vinegar or ammonia, but breast-fed babies are more quickly roused from sleep by the smell of a cloth that their mother has worn under her bra than by the smell of a cloth worn by another breast-feeding mother (Russell, 1976).

All told, research on infant perception reveals some senses functioning well in the first weeks of life, with notable maturation at about 2 months and again at about 8 months. For the care-giver, evidence of these sensory developments is most apparent when the infant compares something strange with something familiar. By age 1, for example, the senses are so acute, and preference for familiar people and objects is usually so strong, that some babies scream at the voice or sight of a stranger, require the feel of a special blanket before they sleep, and often refuse food that smells or tastes unfamiliar.

The Development of Motor Abilities

The newborn has several important motor abilities. At first, these abilities are limited to **reflexes,** that is, involuntary physical responses to a given stimulus. Some of these reflexes are essential for life itself, and others disappear in the months after birth.

Three sets of reflexes are critical for survival and become stronger as the baby matures. One set maintains an adequate supply of oxygen. The most obvious reflex in this group is the **breathing reflex.** Normal newborns take their first breath even before the umbilical cord, with its supply of oxygen, is cut. For the first few days, breathing is somewhat irregular, and reflexive *hiccups, sneezes,* and *spit-ups* are common, as the newborn tries to coordinate breathing, sucking, and swallowing.

Another set of reflexes helps to maintain constant body tempera[...] fants are cold, they cry, shiver, and tuck their legs close to their bod[...] helping to keep themselves warm. A third set of reflexes ensures adequ[...] ishment. One of these is the **sucking reflex:** newborns suck anything that [...] their lips—fingers, toes, blankets, and rattles, as well as nipples of various sha[...] Another is the **rooting reflex,** which helps babies find a nipple by causing them [...] turn their heads and start to suck whenever something brushes against their [...] cheek. *Swallowing* is another important reflex that aids feeding, as is *crying* when the stomach is empty.

The following five reflexes are present in normal, full-term newborns. (1) When their feet are stroked, their toes fan upward **(Babinski reflex).** (2) When their feet touch a flat surface, they move as if to walk **(stepping reflex).** (3) When they are held horizontally on their stomachs, their arms and legs stretch out **(swimming reflex).** (4) When something touches their palms, their hands grip tightly **(grasping reflex).** (5) When someone bangs on the table they are lying on, newborns usually fling their arms outward and then bring them together on their chests, as if to hold on to something, and they may cry and open their eyes wide **(Moro reflex).** All these reflexes disappear in the first months of life. (Preterm babies usually develop and lose these reflexes later than full-term babies.) Several of these reflexes are thought to be vestiges of earlier evolutionary development. The grasp reflex, for instance, is crucial for infant monkeys who must hold tight to their mother as she moves from tree to tree. Obviously these reflexes are not necessary in humans today, if they ever were, but they are useful as signs of normal brain and body function.

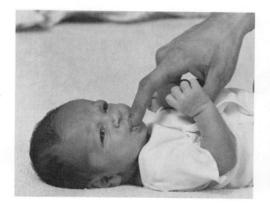
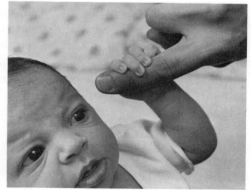
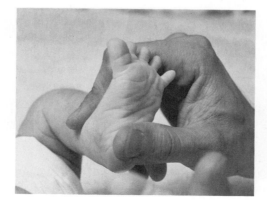
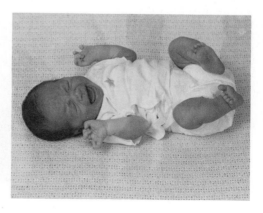

Figure 6.9 *At 3 weeks, Joanna displays some of the many reflexes of the newborn—sucking, grasping, fanning her toes, and raising her arms as she cries.*

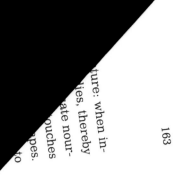

ndeed, tests of reflexes are frequently used to assess the newborn's physical dition. The most notable of these measures is the **Brazelton Neonatal Behav- l Assessment Scale,** which rates twenty-six items of infant behavior, such as tion to cuddling, orientation to the examiner's voice and face, trembling, star- ;, and irritability. The Brazelton scale is a useful diagnostic tool for assessing enital problems and an even more useful research tool for comparing the ical development of infants born in different cultures or under different cir- tances.

Motor Skills

Further evidence of normal brain and body function soon becomes apparent, as the infant gradually masters various **motor skills,** that is, control of movements of various parts of the body.

During the months after birth, development in the primary sensory and primary motor areas of the brain transforms infants from dependent creatures who stay in one spot when laid down to active children who wiggle, turn, sit, crawl, stand, and finally walk on their own.

The Sequence of Motor Skills   The sequence, if not the timing, of motor skills is the same the world over. To begin with, motor abilities follow the same cephalo-caudal and proximo-distal patterns as physical growth does. Infants lift their heads, and then their heads and shoulders, before they can sit up, and can sit up steadily before they can stand, thus following the head-downward direction of control.

The specifics of arm, hand, and finger control follow the proximo-distal pattern. As we have seen, at birth, infants have a reflexive grasp, but they seem to have no control of it. Similarly, newborns may wave their arms and hands and feet when they see dangling objects, but rarely do they succeed in hitting them until about their third month. At this point, however, they are still unable to grab the object because they close their hands too soon or too late.

By 6 months, most babies can reach, grab, and hold onto dangling objects (Bower, 1979). But when they successfully grab an object, they have a new problem: they

Figure 6.10 *At 4 months, identical twins Adam and Ryan have enough strength and coordination to lift their heads and their shoulders; by 8 months, they can pull their bodies forward in a crawl. With each new motor skill come new opportunities for exploration and pleasure, as Adam and Ryan demonstrate at 9, 10, and 18 months. (Monozygotic twins usually sit up, stand, and walk within a few days of each other. Dizygotic twins often vary by weeks or even months.)*

4 months

8 months

Figure 6.11 *If care-givers are sufficiently patient to clean up afterward, infants can develop their motor skills by feeding themselves as soon as they can sit up in their highchairs. A floor covered with crumbs of toast, or a face covered with spaghetti, is a small price to pay for thrice-daily practice in hand skills.*

can't let go. A toy seems stuck in their hands u
hands relax and the object, unnoticed, drops ou
in the next month or so. By 8 or 9 months, they a
catch objects that are tossed toward them, even wi.
fast and from an unusual angle (von Hofsten, 1983). (U.
catch and hold does not develop until the second year.)
tered is picking up small objects with the fingers. At first,
hand, especially the palm and the fourth and fifth fingers to gi
Then they use the middle fingers and center of the palm (pa.   the
index finger and the side of the palm (radial grasp) (Johnston, 1ᵇ   y, they
use thumb and forefinger together (pincer grasp), a skill mastered   ietime between 9 and 14 months (Frankenberg and Dodds, 1967). At this point, infants delight
in picking up every tiny object within sight, including bits of fuzz from the carpet
and bugs from the lawn.

Locomotion   Most babies first learn to move from place to place by lying on their
stomachs and pulling themselves ahead with their arms. **Crawling** on hands and
knees, which involves the coordination of arms and legs, comes later: for some
babies, as early as 5 months; for others, as late as 12. Some babies do not crawl at
all, achieving mobility instead by either scooting along on their buttocks, rolling
over and over, doing the "bear walk" (on all fours, without letting their knees or
elbows touch the ground), or even cruising unsteadily on two feet, moving from
place to place by holding onto tables, chairs, or bystanders.

On average, a child can stand with support at 5 months, can walk while holding a
hand at 9 months, and can walk well unassisted at 12 months (Frankenberg et al.,
1981). In recognition of their accomplishment of walking, babies at this stage are
given the name **toddler,** although, technically, children are *infants* until they begin
to talk. Toddlers are named for the characteristic way they use their legs, toddling
from side to side. Since their heads and stomachs are relatively heavy and large,
they spread out their short little legs for stability, making them seem bowlegged,
flatfooted, and unbalanced.

9 months

10 months

18 months

Figure 6.12 *Once the sense of balance develops, there is no end to its possible applications, especially since the excitement of a new accomplishment is not yet accompanied by any thought about possible consequences.*

In fact, 1-year-olds *are* unbalanced, falling frequently. They trip on the edge of a rug, or slip on the grass, or topple over because their head and trunk get too far ahead of their legs when they try to run. But falling doesn't stop them, for they don't have far to fall and they are too excited by their new mobility to be discouraged by a momentary setback. By age 2, most children can walk and run quite well, although they still place their feet wide apart for balance. They can even walk backward and climb stairs, using the two-footsteps-to-each-stair method.

By age 1, the improvement in hand skills, combined with the ability to walk, allows the child to explore objects and areas that were previously inaccessible. A parent's feeling of pride in the infant's eagerly awaited first steps is often followed immediately by a heightened perception of the fragile or possibly dangerous objects that exist within a few feet of the floor. By age 2, there are few places that cannot be reached by a determined toddler.

Variations in Timing

Although all healthy infants develop the same motor skills in the same sequence, the age at which these skills are acquired can vary greatly from infant to infant and still be considered normal. Table 6.1 shows the age at which half of all infants in the United States master each major motor skill, and the age at which 90 percent master each skill. These averages, or **norms,** are based on a representative sample of more than a thousand white, black, Mexican, and Native American infants. Infants known to be brain-damaged or mentally retarded were excluded.

Norms vary from place to place and from time to time. The average baby in Stockholm walks at 12½ months, more than a month earlier than the average baby in Paris (Hindley et al., 1966). The earliest walkers in the world seem to be from Uganda, in Central Africa, where, on the average, babies walk at 10 months. In addition, norms can change over time. Compared to the mid-1960s norms of the Denver study represented in Table 6.1, for example, the norms of fifty years ago in the United States show babies progressing more slowly then. Shirley (1933) found, for instance, that, on average, babies did not walk alone until 15 months, the same

TABLE 6.1 **Age Norms (in Months) for Motor Skills**

Skill	When 50% of All Babies Master the Skill	When 90% of All Babies Master the Skill
Lifts head 90° when lying on stomach	2.2	3.2
Rolls over	2.8	4.7
Sits propped up (head steady)	2.9	4.2
Sits without support	5.5	7.8
Stands holding on	5.8	10.0
Walks holding on	9.2	12.7
Stands momentarily	9.8	13.0
Stands alone well	11.5	13.9
Walks well	12.1	14.3
Walks backward	14.3	21.5
Walks up steps	17.0	22.0
Kicks ball forward	20.0	24.0

Source: From the revised Denver Developmental Screening Test (Frankenburg et al., 1981).

age reported in the Gesell Developmental Schedules (Gesell and Amatruda, 1947), which are based on babies tested in the 1920s.

Reasons for Variation Why does this variation occur? On the one hand, cultural patterns of infant care are probably responsible for some of the variation among babies. For instance, Ugandan mothers often hold their infants in a standing position on their laps, allowing them to practice stepping movements. Mary Ainsworth (1967) thinks this helps explain the precocious motor development of the Ugandan babies. In Kenya, lower-class rural babies are given daily practice in sitting and walking, so they are more advanced in these skills than middle-class urban Kenyan babies (Super, 1976). Environmental factors may also help to explain the change in American motor norms over the past half century: infants today receive better nourishment and medical care, and spend less time in playpens, than infants did fifty years ago.

But there is other evidence that shows that inherited factors, such as activity level, rate of physical maturation, and body type, are the primary cause of variation in the acquisition of walking and other motor skills. For instance, identical twins are more likely to sit up, and to walk, on the same day than fraternal twins are, a fact suggesting that genes are more important than family encouragement of motor abilities (Wilson and Harpring, 1972).

Genes may also be a factor in the apparent change in norms in the United States. The infants tested by both Shirley and Gesell were almost all descendants of western and northern Europeans. The more recent Denver norms are based on a sample that includes a larger proportion (18 percent) of two ethnic groups known to walk early, blacks and Mexican-Americans.

Given that there is evidence to support both sides, probably most developmentalists would say that the age at which a *particular* baby sits up and walks depends on the interaction between inherited and environmental factors. Each infant has a genetic inner timetable, which can be faster or slower than that of other infants from the same ethnic group and even from the same family; and each infant also has a family and culture that provide varying amounts of encouragement, nutrition, medical care, and opportunity to practice.

Nutrition

Obviously, nutrition is an important topic in the physical development of the infant, for adequate nutrition is a prerequisite for the changes of size and shape, the brain development, and the skill mastery that we have just described.

At first, infants are unable to eat or digest solid food, but their rooting, sucking, swallowing, and breathing reflexes make them well adapted for consuming the quantities of liquid nourishment that they need.

The Early Months

In these early months, breast milk is the ideal infant food (Jelliffe and Jelliffe, 1977; Ogra and Greene, 1982). It is always sterile and at body temperature; it contains more iron, vitamin C, and vitamin A than cow's milk; and it also contains antibodies that provide the infant some protection against any disease that the mother herself has had, or has been inoculated against, from chickenpox to small pox, tetanus to typhoid. In addition, breast milk is more digestible than cow's milk or formula, which means that breast-fed babies have fewer allergies and digestive upsets than bottle-fed babies, even when both groups of babies have similar family backgrounds and excellent medical care (Larsen and Homer, 1978).

Despite the advantages of breast milk, breast-feeding is no longer the most common method of feeding infants. Sterilization, pasturization, the rubber nipple, the plastic bottle, canned milk, powdered milk, and premixed infant formulas available in handy six-packs have meant that millions of modern babies survive and thrive without ever tasting breast milk (see Closer Look).

Nutrition After Weaning

In order to thrive during the first two years, infants need about 50 calories per day per pound of body weight (110 per kilogram) (Lowrey, 1978). By 6 months or so, some of these calories can come from "solid" foods that may gradually be added to the diet. Cereals are needed for iron and B vitamins, fruits for vitamins A and C, and, when these first solids are well-tolerated, vegetables, meat, fish, and eggs can be introduced to provide additional nutrition. By the time the infant is a year old, the diet should include all the nutritious foods that the rest of the family consumes.

In North America, an ample and varied diet is fairly easy to obtain. In fact, a peanut butter sandwich on enriched bread, a pint of fortified milk, one orange, and one egg provide more than the 23 grams of protein, most of the needed vitamins and minerals, and a substantial part of the 1,300 daily calories recommended for 2-year-olds. When problems occur in the nutrition of American toddlers, the cause is not usually inadequate supply but family food practices that allow toddlers to eat when, what, and how much they choose (Eichorn, 1979). One problem that can result from this indulgence is, obviously, obesity. Other, less visible consequences are specific vitamin and mineral deficiencies, such as "milk anemia," so named because the toddler who stays on the bottle for most meals is unlikely to get enough iron. According to the most recent large-scale nutritional survey in the United States, almost half the children between ages 1 and 5 do not get enough vitamin A or C, and 95 percent do not get enough iron in their daily diets. This makes them one of the least well nourished age groups in the nation (National Center for Health Statistics, 1979).

Fortunately, serious forms of malnutrition are uncommon among children in developed countries. Unfortunately, this is not true in many areas of the world; and the consequences for the individual's development are potentially serious.

A CLOSER LOOK   **Breast Versus Bottle**

If breast milk is best, why do many women choose to give their infants formula? The reasons have little to do with nutrition directly, but are greatly influenced by the cultural attitudes and social pressures of our modern world. While breast-feeding is usually the better choice in terms of the infant's health, it is often the more difficult choice to make.

Many women find that, even if they want to breast-feed, it may not be easy to make that choice. Problems may begin in the hospital, if procedures make it impossible for the mother to have her newborn near her day and night, so that she can nurse whenever the infant is hungry. Cultural attitudes may make breast-feeding inconvenient, if not impossible, except in the privacy of one's own home.

Another consideration is that the convenience afforded by bottle-feeding is well-suited to many contemporary women, who feel they do not have the time to devote to breast-feeding. In order for breast-feeding to succeed, especially in the early weeks, nursing should occur every two or three hours or even more often if the baby demands it (Riordan, 1983), with each feeding lasting twenty minutes or more. For many women who work outside the home or whose daily activities require them to be out in public much of the time, meeting this kind of schedule would be difficult if not impossible.

In addition, most women today are aware that traces of whatever drug a breast-feeding mother ingests— cigarettes, alcohol, birth-control pills, and so forth—will show up in her milk. Consequently, many women decide that, rather than feeling guilty about compromising the quality of their milk or being as careful after pregnancy as they had to be before, they would rather feed their baby formula.

Fathers are influential too. Some men are jealous of the close relationship that exists between a nursing mother and her infant, a relationship that seems to exclude them. Many contemporary fathers want to be involved in all aspects of infant care right from the start, and, especially if they are unaware of the advantages of breast-feeding, prefer that their child be bottle-fed so they can sometimes do the feeding.

Nonetheless, while the popularity of bottle-feeding increased dramatically from the beginning of the twentieth century until about 1970, over the past ten years a shift in maternal attitudes, hospital practices, and social approval has resulted in an increase in the number of women who breast-feed.

This trend is applauded and encouraged by virtually all professionals interested in child development, for breast-feeding not only provides good nutrition but also aids in the mother-infant relationship. While breast-feeding does not guarantee a good relationship—any more than bottle-feeding precludes it—the consensus among development-alists is that breast-feeding generally fosters good maternal care.

While convenience is one reason for bottle-feeding, some mothers find breast-feeding more convenient. In addition, breast-fed babies, who have less colic, less diarrhea, and fewer illnesses, are easier to care for. However, while breast-feeding obviously means that an infant must rely on his or her mother for most meals, fathers often like to participate in feeding their infants. Interestingly, many babies will accept a supplementary bottle from their fathers much more readily than from their breast-feeding mothers.

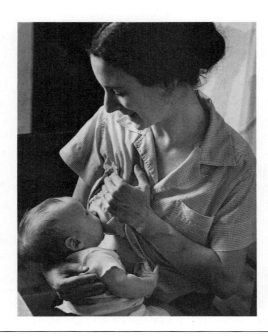

Serious Malnutrition

In the first year of life, severe protein-calorie deficiency can cause **marasmus,** a disease that occurs when infants are severely malnourished. Growth stops, body tissues waste away, and the infant dies. During toddlerhood, protein-calorie deficiency is more likely to cause **kwashiorkor.** The child's face, legs, and abdomen swell with water, sometimes making the child appear well-fed to anyone who doesn't know the real cause of the bloating. Because in this condition the essential organs claim whatever nutrients are available, other parts of the body are degraded, including, characteristically, the child's hair, which usually becomes thin, brittle, and colorless.

The primary cause of marasmus in developing countries is early cessation of breast-feeding. In many of these countries, breast-feeding was usually continued for at least two years, but now is often stopped much earlier in favor of bottle-feeding, usually powdered formulas. Under normal circumstances, such formulas are an adequate and safe source of nutrition. However, if the mother cannot read the instructions on the can, or if the water used to prepare the formula is contaminated, bottle-feeding can be fatal. (Even when the water is known to be contaminated, sterilizing it is difficult when fuel for boiling is scarce.)

A comparison of the survival rates of breast-fed and bottle-fed babies from the same impoverished background reveals that bottle-fed babies have fared much less well: in Chile, for instance, they are four times more likely to die; in Egypt, five times more likely (Grant, 1982). Similar results have been found in many other countries. Unfortunately, commercial formulas are still promoted in these countries as the "modern" way to feed infants.

When not fatal, severe and long-lasting malnutrition can cause intellectual as well as physical deficits. For instance, a longitudinal study of African teenagers

Figure 6.13 *There have been many contributing causes to the recent famine in the countries of Africa, among them, weather conditions, farming practices, and government policies. In each area struck by this disaster, the toll in the health of children has been the same: increases in marasmus and kwashiorkor, and many more deaths from diseases like measles and chicken pox, illnesses that are not often fatal to children who are otherwise in good health.*

Figure 6.14 *Many Third-World countries are emphasizing the importance of early nutrition by providing classes and teaching aids designed for their cultures. Programs such as this one in Nigeria can be successful in changing the focus of medical attention from simply the cure of very ill children to prevention and early treatment.*

who had been chronically malnourished as infants found that their intellectual abilities, especially the ability to reason, were impaired when compared to other teenagers from the same socioeconomic class and tribe who were adequately nourished (Hoorweg, 1976). Similarly, a longitudinal study of children in Guatemala found that those children who were chronically malnourished in early childhood tended to be physically shorter and cognitively slower in middle childhood (Bogin and MacVean, 1983).

Fortunately, even severe short-term malnutrition does not cause serious irreparable damage. In cases of temporary malnutrition, catch-up growth restores the body, just as the birth catch-up remedies small birth weight (Tanner, 1978). A dramatic example of this comes from a study of thousands of adults who as infants had survived months of severe famine in the part of the Netherlands sealed off by the Nazis toward the end of World War II. The evidence from this study indicates that these infants did not experience any lasting physical or intellectual damage, as long as they were well cared for after the war was over. Those who had been seriously malnourished in the first months of infancy were just as tall and smart as those of their contemporaries who were not subjected to the famine (Stein et al., 1975).

Serious Malnutrition in the United States While severe and extensive malnutrition is not common in the United States, neither is it unknown. As is the case with other types of infant maltreatment, the problem frequently begins in the family and in the community (Sherrod et al., 1984), so the solution is more complex than simply providing food.

Consider one example. An 8-month-old girl was admitted to a Boston hospital. She was emaciated; she could not sit up; she did not respond when spoken to. In the hospital, the baby rapidly gained weight, started to smile and play with the nurses, and was discharged. Two months later she was readmitted, "a small, dirty, smelly infant, with restless movements of her hands, and again, underweight" (Newberger et al., 1976). Clearly, her malnutrition could not be cured without paying attention to the environment that caused the problem.

This time the hospital staff took an ecological approach. Treatment focused on the mother, who had four children, no husband, little money, and few friends or relatives. She was given medical treatment for a chronic infection and dental care for aching teeth. A social worker helped place the two older children in a nursery school, and found a homemaker and a public health nurse to give the mother day-to-day support. These measures helped the baby as well as her mother. Four years later the little girl entered kindergarten, normal in her physical and psychological development.

Conclusions As the authors who described this case point out, treating both mother and child was necessary for a solution of this particular problem. For prevention of such problems, a broader ecological approach, combating social ills such as poverty and isolation, would be necessary.

A similar conclusion could be drawn for all aspects of physical development covered in this chapter. For the most part, babies grow and develop skills as rapidly as their genes allow, as long as their family and culture provide the opportunity. At the same time, when things go wrong, the cause is usually complex. Biological, familial, and cultural conditions all interact to affect the growth of the child.

SUMMARY

Size and Shape

1. In their first two years, most babies gain about 20 pounds (9 kilograms) and grow about 15 inches (38 centimeters). The proportions of the body change. The newborn is top-heavy, for the head takes up one-fourth of the body length, partly because the brain, at birth, has attained a high proportion of its adult size in comparison to other parts of the body. In adulthood, the head is about one-eighth of the body length.

Brain Growth and Maturation

2. Although at birth the nervous system has virtually all the nerve cells it will ever have, these neurons grow and form branching networks during infancy and childhood, resulting in increasing efficiency of communication between the brain and the rest of the body.

3. Fetal brain maturation during the last weeks of a normal pregnancy is responsible for the full-term infant's more regular patterns (states) of sleep and wakefulness, and also for changes in the infant's ability to respond to, and to control responses to, the environment.

4. The development of motor control and perceptual abilities depends on an interaction between brain maturation and the infant's experience.

Sensation and Perception

5. Both sensation and perception are present at birth, and both become more developed with time. Some senses—notably hearing—seem very acute within the first months of life; others—notably vision—develop more slowly throughout the first year.

The Development of Motor Abilities

6. At first, the newborn's motor abilities consist of reflexes. Some reflexes are essential for survival; the purpose of other reflexes is not apparent. However, all reflexes are indicative of brain development.

7. Motor skills follow the cephalo-caudal and proximo-distal sequences; the upper part of the body is controlled before the lower part is, and the arms are controlled before the hands and fingers are. Although the sequence of motor-skill development is the same for all healthy infants, babies vary in the ages at which they master specific skills, because the development of these skills depends on the interaction of cultural, environmental, and genetic forces.

Nutrition

8. Breast milk is the ideal food for most babies; however, commercial formulas, properly prepared, are an acceptable substitute. A mother's choice to bre   bottle-feed typically depends on many fa   education, life style, and cultural pressures.

9. By the time a child is 1 year old, a diet that includes all the major food groups will usually provide adequate calories, iron, and vitamins. In the developed countries, serious malnutrition is uncommon. However, specific imbalances and obesity do occur, usually as the result of

The First Two Years: Cognitive Development

. . . he co-operates
With a universe of large and noisy
feeling states
*   Without troubling to place*
Them anywhere special, for, to his eyes,
Funnyface
*   Or Elephant as yet*
Mean nothing. His distinction between
Me and Us
Is a matter of taste; his seasons are Dry
and Wet;
*   He thinks as his mouth does.*

W. H. Auden
"Mundus et Infans"

How Cognitive Development Occurs

Interaction Between Maturation and Learning

Piaget's Theory

Sensorimotor Intelligence

Postscripts to Piaget

"The American Question"

Teaching and Learning in Infancy

Special Programs for High-Risk Infants

Teaching the Privileged Infant

Language Development

Theories of Language Development

Steps in Language Development

Teamwork: Adults and Babies Teach Each Other to Talk

Chapter 7

The pace of cognitive development is dramatic: an infant begins life capable of satisfying his or her curiosity about the world only through such basic activities as sucking, grabbing, staring, and listening, and yet within two years, he or she will be capable of anticipating future events, remembering past ones, imitating the actions of others, and pretending. The development of language is similarly remarkable: for a newborn, crying and smiling are the major modes of expression, yet by age 2, the average toddler will be able to converse simply but effectively with others.

In this chapter, we will discuss how these significant accomplishments occur, including answers to the following questions:

Which physical and cognitive abilities are involved in the infant's increasing knowledge of, and control over, the objects and people in his or her environment?

Infants seem to follow a sequence in the development of their cognitive abilities. Is there any advantage to accelerating their progression through this sequence?

Is infant IQ a good predictor of intelligence in later years?

Are children born with some of the abilities required for using language, or are all language abilities learned?

Adults throughout the world change their speech patterns in special ways when they talk to children. What are the common features of "baby talk" and how do they promote language learning?

Infants begin life knowing nothing about the world around them. But the reflexes, senses, and curiosity that they are born with soon begin to inform them. By age 1 they have already learned about many of the objects in their environment (that some make noise, that others move, that some are fun to play with, that some are not to be touched), about people (that some are familiar and trustworthy, that others are strange and unpredictable), and about experiences (that playing in sandboxes is enjoyable, that visiting the doctor can hurt). Even more impressive, they have learned to communicate quite well. They understand many of the gestures and words of other people, and can make their own needs and emotions known in a variety of ways, including saying a word or two themselves.

By age 2, the simple mental abilities of the 12-month-old baby have developed into the more complex talents of the "demon explorer"—an imaginative, reflective, verbal creature who, being both mobile and purposeful, knows many ways to get what he or she wants and to create new experiences (Spock, 1976).

All these achievements are part of **cognition,** that is, the interaction of all the perceptual, intellectual, and linguistic abilities that comprise thinking and learning. If cognitive development is "how we acquire and use knowledge in adapting to the vicissitudes of the world" (Caron and Caron, 1982), then the infant's cognitive development during the first two years is impressive indeed.

But what are the precise steps involved in this remarkable development? And how much adult help or environmental stimulation is needed for cognitive development to occur? In other words, how much do infants know automatically, how much do they teach themselves, and how much must they be taught?

How Cognitive Development Occurs

Not so many years ago, developmentalists too often found themselves obliged to take sides in the controversy between those who thought that biological forces were the crucial factor in determining cognitive development and those who thought that social forces were more important. This debate took many forms and was given many names ("heredity versus environment," "maturation versus learning," and "nature versus nurture"), but the essential question was the same: Is a child's cognitive growth influenced more by internal forces such as genes and maturation or by external factors such as family, teachers, toys, and neighborhood?

Interaction Between Maturation and Learning

In the last twenty years, research has brought a measure of calm to this controversy. Psychologists recognize that *both* maturation and learning are essential. The development of sensorimotor skills—when the baby can focus well visually, or when the baby walks—seems to depend more on physiological maturity than on anything else. Indeed, maturation seems to be a prerequisite for the development of skills of all kinds, even, as we shall see later, for finding objects that have disappeared from sight and for speaking words.

At the same time, experience has also proven to be indispensable. For example, in Chapter 6 we have seen not only that brain maturation is required for the development of motor, sensory, and perceptual abilities, but also that the infant's experiences and new abilities actually promote the development of the brain's capacities.

Difference in Emphasis Although developmentalists now agree that maturation and learning work together, they continue to debate the relative contributions of each during different periods of development. They are also at odds on the questions of when specific cognitive abilities develop, whether cognitive "milestones" develop all at once or gradually, and how individual experiences affect the pace of learning.

To sort out these controversies, we will start with the observations and ideas of Jean Piaget. While many cognitive psychologists now question certain aspects of Piaget's analysis of cognitive development, Piagetian theory and its description of cognitive stages are so basic to our understanding that it is impossible to discuss infant cognition without taking them as the starting point (Brainerd, 1983).

Piaget's Theory

Remember that Piaget emphasized the total organization of intelligence—the process of understanding—through which the individual interprets his or her world. As we saw in Chapter 2, Piaget proposed that the individual's mode of thinking goes through four distinct periods, the first occurring between birth and age 2, and the others following at about ages 2, 6, and 12. Within each of these four periods, smaller but discernible shifts in thinking occur.

Sensorimotor Intelligence

Piaget called the first period of cognitive development, the period that begins at birth and lasts until age 2, **sensorimotor intelligence.** He did this for a good reason: very young babies, unlike adults, think exclusively with their senses and motor skills. Present a typical adult with a plastic rattle and that person might refer to it by name, classify it according to function, evaluate it esthetically, while at the same time having thoughts ranging from the fascinations of infancy to the fluctuating costs of petrochemicals. Give a rattle to a baby and he or she will stare at it, shake it, suck it, bang it on the floor. As Flavell (1985) puts it, the infant "exhibits a wholly practical, perceiving-and-doing, action-bound kind of intellectual functioning: he does not exhibit the more contemplative, reflective, symbol-manipulating kind we usually think of in connection with cognition."

Thus, the first two years of cognitive development are called the sensorimotor period because the child both learns about the world and expresses this learning chiefly through his or her senses and motor skills. Within this general period of sensorimotor intelligence, there are, according to Piaget, six stages, each characterized by a somewhat different way of understanding the world (see Table 7.1).

TABLE 7.1 **The Six Stages of Sensorimotor Development**

To get an overview of the stages of sensorimotor thought, it helps to group the six stages in pairs. The first two involve the infant's own body *(primary circular reactions).*

I. BIRTH TO 1 MONTH	*Reflexes*—sucking, grabbing, staring, listening.	
II. 1–4 MONTHS	*The first acquired adaptations*—accommodation and coordination of reflexes—sucking a pacifier differently from a nipple; grabbing a bottle to suck it.	

The next two involve objects and people *(secondary circular reactions).*

III. 4–8 MONTHS	*Procedures for making interesting sights last*—responding to people and objects.
IV. 8–12 MONTHS	*New adaptation and anticipation*—becoming more deliberate and purposeful in responding to people and objects.

The last two are the most creative, first with action *(tertiary circular reactions)* and then with ideas.

V. 12–18 MONTHS	*New means through active experimentation*—experimentation and creativity in the actions of "the little scientist."
VI. 18–24 MONTHS	*New means through mental combinations*—thinking before doing makes the child experimental and creative in a new way.

Stage One: Reflexes (Birth to 1 Month)   Sensorimotor intelligence begins with newborns' reflexes, such as sucking, grasping, looking, and listening. In Piaget's terms, these reflexes represent the only *schemas,* or general ways of thinking about and interacting with the environment, that neonates have. Take sucking as an example: neonates suck everything that touches their lips, using the schema that all objects that can be sucked should be sucked. Similarly, infants grasp at everything that touches the center of their palm, stare at everything that comes within focus, and so forth. Through the repeated exercise of these reflexes, newborns gain information about the world, information that will be used to develop the next stage of learning.

Stage Two: The First Acquired Adaptations (1 Month to 4 Months) The second stage of sensorimotor intelligence begins when infants adapt their reflexes to the environment. Again let us take the sucking reflex as an example. By the time infants are 3 months old, they have organized their world into objects to be sucked for nourishment (breasts or bottles), objects to be sucked for pleasure (fingers or pacifiers), and objects not to be sucked at all (fuzzy blankets and large balls). They also learn that efficient breast-sucking requires a squeezing sucking, whereas efficient finger- and pacifier-sucking do not. In addition, once infants learn that some objects satisfy hunger and others do not, they will usually spit out a pacifier if they are hungry, although otherwise they will contentedly suck one.

Even more impressive, between 1 and 4 months infants can begin to coordinate two actions. For instance, while newborns will suck their thumb whenever it happens to come in contact with their mouth, they do not know how to get their thumb into their mouth. When they can do so, thus coordinating the sucking reflex with the motor skill of moving their arm, they are performing a stage-two behavior.

Figure 7.1 *At the sensorimotor stage of development, even Mother's face is a site for active exploration by all the infant's senses and motor skills.*

Between 1 and 4 months infants can also begin to coordinate perceptions and actions. They hear a noise and turn to locate it (though not always in the right direction) (McGurk and Lewis, 1974), or they see an object and try to touch it (rarely successfully) (Bower, 1977). These behaviors are obviously not very well developed but they are clearly more advanced than simple reflexes.

Primary Circular Reactions. Stages one and two also mark the beginning of what Piaget called **circular reactions,** in which a baby's given action triggers a reaction, in the baby or in someone or something else, that in turn makes the baby repeat the action.

Figure 7.2 *This pleasurable primary circular reaction—the coordination of sucking and hand movement—is evidence that this wide-eyed infant has entered the second stage of sensori-motor development.*

Piaget described three types of circular reactions: primary, secondary, and tertiary. In the **primary circular reaction,** typical of stage two, the baby's own body is the source of the response: babies suck their thumbs, kick their legs, or stare at their hands again and again, seemingly for the pleasure of it.

The following selections from Piaget's observations of his son Laurent show the adaptation of the sucking reflex as well as the primary circular reaction:

CIRCULAR REACTION

PRIMARY CIRCULAR REACTION

During the second half of the second month, after having learned to suck his thumb, Laurent continues to play with his tongue and to suck, but intermittently. On the other hand, his skill increases. Thus at 1 month, 20 days, I notice he grimaces while placing his tongue between gums and lips and in bulging his lips, as well as making a clapping sound when quickly closing his mouth after these exercises.

During the third month he adds to the protrusion of his tongue and finger sucking new circular reactions involving the mouth. Thus from 2 months, 18 days Laurent plays with his saliva, letting it accumulate within his half-open lips and then abruptly swallowing it. About the same period he makes sucking-like movements, with or without putting out his tongue, changing in various ways the position of his lips; he bends and contracts his lower lips, etc. [Piaget, 1952a]

Stage Three: Procedures for Making Interesting Sights Last (4 Months to 8 Months)   In the third stage, babies become more aware of objects and other people, and they begin to recognize some of the specific characteristics of the things in their environment.

Secondary Circular Reactions.   Infants show this new perspective when they perform **secondary circular reactions.** Here, the response babies get from someone or something when they perform a specific action causes them to repeat the action in hopes of getting the same response. A baby might accidentally squeeze a rubber

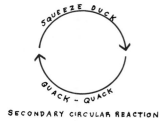

SECONDARY CIRCULAR REACTION

duck, hear a quack, and squeeze the duck again. If the quack is repeated, the infant will probably laugh and give another squeeze, for most babies are delighted to realize that they can control the objects around them.

Piaget called stage three "procedures for making interesting sights last," because babies interact diligently with people and objects to produce exciting experiences. Realizing that rattles make noise, for example, babies at this stage shake their arms and laugh when someone puts a rattle in their hands. Vocalization increases a great deal, for now that babies realize that other people can respond, they love to make a noise, listen for a response, and answer back.

Another interesting reaction that develops at this time is ticklishness. According to Burton White (1975), what causes tickling movements to tickle may well be the awareness that another person is making them, which explains why younger babies do not laugh when they are tickled. (It also explains why you cannot tickle yourself.) Stage-three babies also often chortle or smile gleefully when their stomachs are kissed or blown on.

Figure 7.3 *This baby's obvious show of delight in having his stomach kissed will probably be interpreted by his mother as a request for an encore.*

Stage Four: New Adaptation and Anticipation (8 Months to 12 Months) The major intellectual accomplishment that signals the beginning of stage four is the infant's awakening understanding that objects continue to exist even when they cannot be seen. This recognition is called **object permanence.**

For younger babies, "out of sight" is literally "out of mind": if a 5-month-old drops a rattle out of the crib, for example, the baby will not look down to search for it. It is as though the rattle has completely passed from the infant's awareness. However, toward the end of stage three, babies show tentative signs of realizing that when objects disappear, they have not vanished forever. When a toy falls from the crib, the 7-month-old might look for it for a moment rather than immediately lose interest in it. By stage four, the momentary impulse to look for an object that has disappeared becomes an active effort to search for it (see Closer Look, next page). Piaget interpreted the search for objects as the emergence of the concept of object permanence. It signals the beginning of "goal-directed behavior."

A CLOSER LOOK   **Piaget's Test of Object Permanence**

Piaget developed a simple test for object permanence: show a baby an interesting toy and then cover it up with a cloth or blanket. If the baby tries to uncover it, he or she must suspect that the toy still exists. Here is how Piaget tried this test on his daughter Jacqueline toward the end of her 7th month:

I take the duck . . . and place it near her hand three times. All three times she tries to grasp it, but when she is about to touch it I place it very obviously under the sheet. Jacqueline immediately withdraws her hand and gives up.

Any number of researchers have run some form of this object-permanence test on infants of various ages, and nearly all have had the same results as Piaget: children do not search for the hidden object before their 8th month. In one variation of this research, Ann Bigelow (1983) even gave infants a clue to help them find hidden objects: she used noise-making toys that emitted a continuous sound during the test. Nevertheless, as Piaget would have predicted, infants younger than 8 months did not search for the hidden toy, in spite of the steady noise coming from its hiding place. Because object permanence was not developed in these infants, the clue of the noise was, in fact, no clue at all.

Recently, I had occasion to run Piaget's test myself. When the art director of the present revision of this book asked if we couldn't find a new set of photographs illustrating the concept of object permanence, I volunteered my infant daughter Sarah as the test subject. Sarah was only 7 months old at the time, but because she was

precocious-seeming in many respects, I decided to perform some trial runs of the test to be sure she wasn't ahead of Piaget's predicted schedule. She wasn't. While she watched, I hid various objects under a blanket, and, as soon as they were out of her sight, Sarah completely lost interest in them.

Confident that neither Piaget nor Sarah would let me down, I scheduled the photo session of the test for the following month. Four weeks later, with cameras clicking away, every time I showed Sarah a fascinating object and then covered it with a cloth, she quickly uncovered it—so quickly, in fact, that it was hard to photograph the sequence. Our persistance, however, was rewarded by the sequence on the next page.

Object permanence is more than a curious aspect of infant development. Once infants realize that objects exist even when out of sight, and that they can be found by careful searching, infants become more knowledgeable and purposive, demanding specific people and certain toys to which they have become attached. One infant cries for several minutes after his mother leaves; another refuses to go to sleep without a particular blanket; a third finds the teddy bear that fell out of the crib without screaming for parental assistance; a fourth opens the cupboard to get the cookies. In short, by gaining an understanding of object permanence and acting on this understanding, infants become less malleable, more self-assertive, and consequently, much more characteristically human.

Between 8 and 12 months, as infants become more knowledgeable about the things in their world, they do, indeed, become more deliberate and purposeful in what they do with them. Whereas younger infants are likely to apply the same schema to all objects, either sucking, or dropping, or shaking them, infants in stage four are likely to choose particular schemas to use with particular objects. Here, for example, is Piaget's description of his 9-month-old daughter Jacqueline as she tried out some of her old schemas on a new object:

Jacqueline looks for a long time at a straw table mat, then delicately touches the edge, grows bold enough to touch [the mat], then grasps it, holds it in the air, . . . shakes it, and ends by tapping it with her other hand. This behavior is accompanied by an expression of expectation and then of satisfaction. [Piaget, 1952a]

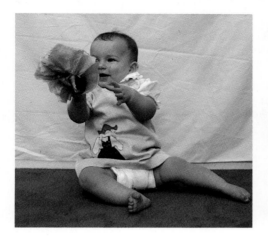
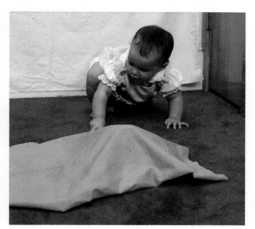
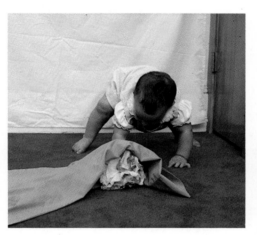
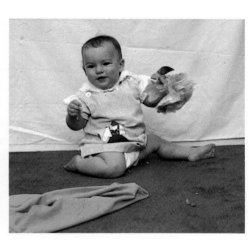

Between 8 and 12 months, finding a toy that has been "hidden" is a cognitive challenge that leads to deliberate action, and to much delight if the challenge is met.

Babies at stage four develop definite ideas about what they want. They might see something clear across the room and crawl toward it, ignoring many interesting distractions along the way. Or they might grab a forbidden object—a box of matches, a thumbtack, a cigarette—and cry with rage when it is taken away, even if they are offered a substitute that they normally find fascinating. If they are placed in a playpen when they do not want to be, they are likely to make their feelings known by throwing all the toys out and then demanding to be put on the floor with them.

Finally, stage-four babies anticipate events. They might cry when they see Mother putting on her coat, and might even hide the hat she usually wears with that coat. If they enjoy splashing in the bathtub, they might squeal with delight when the bath water is turned on. Younger babies often spit out distasteful food after they taste it; 12-month-olds are sufficiently wise to keep their mouths tightly shut when they see spinach on the spoon.

Figure 7.4 *Once infants become goal-oriented, they tend to become much less tractable, and can make very clear what they do and do not want. Although this boy may not speak his first word for several months, he is obviously quite adept at communicating his preferences.*

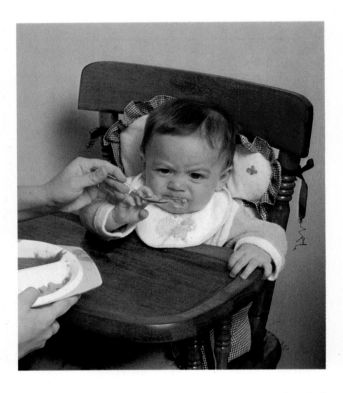

Stage Five: New Means Through Active Experimentation (12 Months to 18 Months)
The toddler's ability to anticipate contributes to the development of the next stage of sensorimotor development, a time of active exploration and experimentation in which the infant often seems bent on discovering all the possibilities in his or her world.

Tertiary Circular Reactions.   Typical of the exploration and experimentation that occur in this stage are **tertiary circular reactions.** Unlike the primary and secondary circular reactions, in which babies repeat the same action again and again, tertiary circular reactions are marked by variations of a given behavior. A toddler might first hit a toy drum with a drumstick, then, in turn, hit it with a pencil, a block, and a hammer. Similarly, the toddler might first pat a lump of clay, then squeeze it, then pound it, then rub it into the carpet.

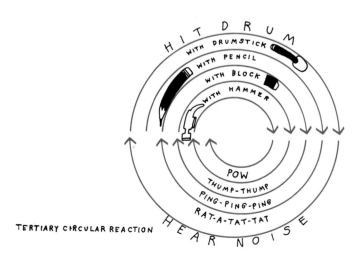

TERTIARY CIRCULAR REACTION

The Little Scientist. Because of the explorations that characterize this stage, Piaget referred to the stage-five toddler as a little scientist who "experiments in order to see." Having discovered some action or set of actions that is possible with a given object, stage-five infants seem to ask, "What else can I do with this? What happens if I take the nipple off the bottle, or turn over the trash basket, or pour water on the cat?" Their "scientific method" is trial and error.

Because of their penchant for experimentation, toddlers find new ways to achieve their goals. Through their trial-and-explorations they learn, for instance, that they can bring a toy closer by pulling on the string tied to the end of it, or that they can "reach" the plate of cookies in the middle of the dinner table by pulling on the tablecloth (Piaget, 1952a). No doubt, parents of toddlers could cite many other examples of the little scientist's experiments, from the delightful to the disastrous.

Figure 7.5 *Do dogs eat flowers? This "little scientist" is out to collect data on this question.*

Stage Six: New Means Through Mental Combinations (18 Months to 24 Months) At this stage, toddlers begin to anticipate and solve simple problems by using **mental combinations** before they act. That is, they are able to try out various actions mentally without having to actually perform them. Thus the child can invent new ways to achieve a goal without resorting to physical trial-and-error experiments. Consider how Jacqueline solved the following problem at 20 months.

> Jacqueline arrives at a closed door with a blade of grass in each hand. She stretches out her right hand toward the knob but sees that she cannot turn it without letting go of the grass. She puts the grass on the floor, opens the door, picks up the grass again and enters. But when she wants to leave the room, things become complicated. She puts the grass on the floor and grasps the doorknob. But then she perceives that in pulling the door toward her she will simultaneously chase away the grass which she placed between the door and the threshold. She therefore picks it up in order to put it outside the door's zone of movement. [Piaget, 1952a]

What makes mental combinations possible at this point is **representation,** the emerging ability to create mental images of actions and things that are not actually in view.

Representation, which is a primitive form of symbolic thought, also allows the child to reproduce behavior seen in the past. For example, one day Jacqueline saw a neighbor's child have a temper tantrum in a playpen: he screamed, shook the playpen, and stamped his feet. She had never seen anything like it. The very next day, Jacqueline had a tantrum of her own, complete with stamping. Piaget refers to this kind of acting-out of a detailed mental image as **deferred imitation.**

Pretending   Perhaps the strongest, and most endearing, sign that children have reached stage six is their ability to pretend. Pretending involves not only deferred imitation (as when a child sings a lullaby to a doll before tucking it into bed) but also mental combinations, as an action from one context (riding in a car) is mentally combined with another (pushing a toy car around a table).

Figure 7.6 *Pretending becomes possible when toddlers reach the stage of mental combinations, at about 18 months. At this point, imagination is expressed primarily through bathing, feeding, or other simple care-giving activities performed with a doll or toy animal; but soon it evolves into the elaborate dramas of the preschool and school-age child. (Judging by the condition of this doll's head, the little girl shown here was an industrious "little scientist" before she became a "little mother.")*

Full Object Permanence   Closely related to the ability to use mental combinations is the full emergence of object permanence. As we have seen, in stage four the infant begins to hunt in earnest for hidden objects. As time passes, the infant's searching for out-of-sight objects becomes longer and more determined. However, the stage-four infant is capable of a fascinating mistake. Suppose a 10-month-old is playing with a ball and it rolls out of sight under a chair. The infant will crawl after it, even if the crawling takes a good deal of effort. But if, after being recovered, the ball rolls out of sight again, this time under a couch, and is not found quickly, the stage-four baby will look for the ball where it was last found—under the chair.

The toddler in stage five will not make that error. As long as the stage-five toddler sees the object disappear, he or she knows where to look. However, the stage-five child cannot imagine "invisible" displacements, that is, hiding places that he or she has not actually *seen* used as such. Whenever Piaget hid a coin in his hand for instance, and then put his hand under a blanket, leaving the coin there, Jacqueline looked in his hand for the coin but didn't think of looking under the blanket for it.

Jacqueline's arrival at stage six was apparent when in a later search for the coin she looked first in her father's hand, and then, without hesitation, under the blanket—still without ever having seen the coin placed there. Her ability to use mental combinations enabled her to imagine where the coin might be, even if she did not actually see it go there. At this point, according to Piaget, object permanence is fully developed.

The Significance of Stage Six Behavior   Stage-six behaviors all share an important characteristic. They are a step beyond the simple motor responses of sensorimotor thought and a step toward "the more contemplative, reflective, symbol-manipulating activity" (Flavell, 1985) that we usually associate with cognition. As you will see in Chapter 10, mental representation, deferred imitation, and pretending all blossom into the symbolic thought typical of the next period of cognitive development.

Postscripts to Piaget

Piaget's description of sensorimotor thought is generally regarded as a valid and useful analysis of infants' mental development (Wachs, 1975; Uzgiris and Hunt, 1975; Kramer et al., 1975). However, a number of researchers who have followed up on Piaget's work caution against applying his cognitive framework too rigidly (Fischer, 1980; Flavell, 1982; Gelman and Baillargeon, 1983). To begin with, Piaget's sensorimotor stages are descriptions of *developmental functions;* that is, they are general statements about the developmental changes peculiar to the human species as a whole. They are based on "typical" behavior and do not reflect *individual differences* (McCall, 1981). Yet individual differences in native ability and environmental experiences can have a significant impact on cognitive development and its timing. Consequently, the ages Piaget assigned to various stages must be regarded as approximate. Piaget's own children, for example, reached some of the stages of sensorimotor intelligence "ahead of schedule," probably because Piaget, in constantly testing their abilities, gave them more practice and experience than most children receive.

In addition, Piaget's delineation of distinct mental stages seems to suggest that the child's cognitive development is discontinuous, moving from one stage to the next all at once. A number of researchers who have enlarged on Piaget's work now believe that the typical child's mental development is much more gradual and continuous than Piaget represented it to be, with the child arriving at each new stage skill by skill, behavior by behavior.

Finally, although most developmentalists accept Piaget's general outline of cognitive growth in infants, several researchers have questioned some of his measures for assessing the infant's development. Object permanence is a case in point (Ruff, 1982; Willatts, 1984). While they agree with Piaget that children gradually develop an understanding of the permanence of objects, and that uncovering a hidden toy is one demonstration of this understanding, they think that Piaget's tests of object permanence can be affected by factors that Piaget didn't take into account, such as knowing how to search and the motivation to search. Even the hiding place can make a difference: infants who would not lift a blanket to search for an object might look behind a screen or under a cup for one (Willatts, 1984). A different critique of object permanence is offered by Jerome Kagan, who thinks that 9-month-old infants show an improved ability to search for hidden objects, not because they "possess a new cognitive structure," but because of "an increase in the ability to retrieve schema of prior events, a growth in what contemporary psychologists would call memory capacity" (Kagan, 1979).

Perception and Cognition   Another group of researchers might be said to believe that Piaget's description of sensorimotor intelligence overemphasizes the motor aspects of cognitive development to the neglect of its sensory aspects. Piaget inferred intellectual development from children's actions, but it is the contention of perception researchers that infants, especially in the early weeks, know more than they are able to demonstrate through their very limited motor abilities.

Foremost among these researchers are James and Eleanor Gibson. On the basis of a lifetime of research, the Gibsons (1979, 1982) believe that babies are born with the motivation and competence to begin setting their perceptual world in order, and that they coordinate their various senses to understand the objects and people of their world as soon as they draw breath. On this point the Gibson's are joined by another prominent researcher, T. G. R. Bower, whose investigations indicate that newborns try to look for sounds, grasp at objects, and respond to human faces. Bower also believes that considerable perceptual learning, particularly aural, occurs even before birth (Bower and Wishart, 1979). Other researchers have also shown that infants have more complex perceptions of the world than their actions would suggest. For example, 2- to 4-month-old infants were shown two lines forming a right angle (Schwartz and Day, 1979). Once they were habituated to this form, half of them were shown the same angle in a different orientation and half were shown a different angle. The infants in the first group stared less at their angle than the infants in the second group stared at their new angle, suggesting that the first group had some understanding that they were looking at the same angle as before, even though it had been rotated.

Similarly, 4-month-old infants demonstrated a recognition of relative size. First they were shown several different instances in which two identical shapes of different size appeared one above the other, the smaller on top. After becoming used to this size ordering, they looked with extra attention when a large shape appeared above a small one (Caron and Caron, 1981). The same general research format has revealed that infants younger than 8 months can distinguish sets that differ in number (two versus three), color, size, density, and shape (Caron and Caron, 1982).

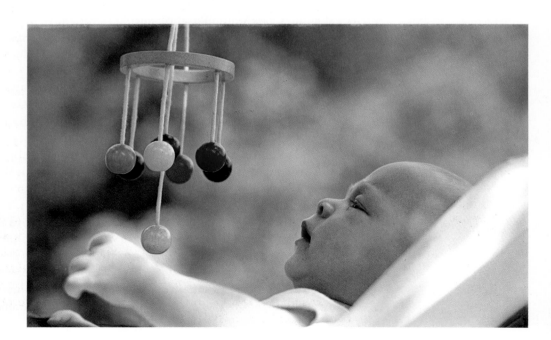

Figure 7.7 *During the first six months of life, infants develop definite ideas about which objects are within reach and the right size for grabbing and pulling. Chances are that this baby will soon stop staring and start yanking.*

Another series of studies demonstrates that infants younger than 4 months are more prone to grasp at objects that are within reach and the right size for holding than at objects that are out of reach or too big. They even know which objects appear squeezable and which do not (Gibson, 1982).

Although these studies of perception were not designed to prove or disprove Piaget's theory, most researchers now agree that Piaget underestimated early perceptual abilities and hence certain aspects of cognitive development during the first six months of life (Caron and Caron, 1982; Gratch, 1979).

It should be noted, however, that this research on perception substantiates one of Piaget's most important ideas—that infants are active learners. As Eleanor Gibson (1979) writes, perceptual learning

> is not a passive absorption but an active process . . . self-regulating, in the sense that modification occurs without the necessity of external reinforcement . . . Discovery of distinctive features and structure in the world is fundamental in the achievement of this goal.

This indeed sounds very much like Piaget's descriptions of the infant's search for knowledge as "a process of equilibrium," an "internal mechanism" of "self-regulation . . . a series of active compensations."

"The American Question"

The fact that Piaget saw infants as self-motivated, active learners brings us to a disagreement between Piaget and many North American psychologists about how optimal cognitive development occurs. As you can see from Piaget's stages, he viewed infants as actively organizing their experiences themselves. He spoke of children adapting their reflexes, making interesting sights last, finding new ways to achieve their goals—and made little mention of the role of parents or specific learning experiences. He did not think development should be accelerated. Many psychologists in the United States and Canada, on the other hand, share the belief that parents should feed an infant's curiosity by providing instruction and an enriched environment, because the infant's powerful desire to learn will benefit from well-organized experiences. In fact, Piaget called "What should we do to foster cognitive development?" the "American question," because it was one of the first questions Americans asked when he lectured to them. Piaget's implication was that something about American society, rather than something about infant development, makes us ask that question.

Teaching and Learning in Infancy

Whatever the reason, Americans not only asked the question, they set about to answer it, demonstrating that infants can learn to do many things, if the learning process is correctly programmed. Learning-theory research has shown, for instance, that with proper reinforcements, such as a pleasant taste or an interesting sight, infants can be taught to turn their heads in a particular sequence, kick their legs at a target, vocalize more often, or perform any number of infant behaviors on cue (Fitzgerald and Brackbill, 1976).

Even newborns can be taught. In a pioneering study, Siqueland and Lipsitt (1966) found that the rooting reflex in the newborn (turning the head toward an object that brushes against the cheek) is normally a weak response, occurring about 25 percent of the time. Setting out to strengthen this response, they brushed babies' cheeks and gave them a bottle of sugar water to suck for 2 seconds every time they displayed the reflex. Within half an hour, the rooting reflex was being exhibited 75 percent of the time.

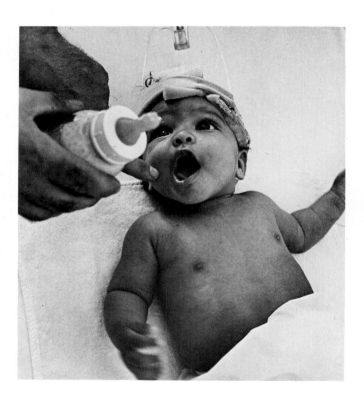

Figure 7.8 *Newborns sometimes reflexively turn their heads toward the side on which their cheek has been stroked. This little girl will exhibit the rooting reflex with much greater frequency than normal because she is being reinforced for doing so with sips of sugar water. In other words, she is being taught that turning her head after a stroke on the cheek produces something pleasurable. The instrument attached to her head records the speed and direction of her head turns, and thus provides an objective measure of her learning rate.*

However, there is an important constraint on infant conditioning: the task that is to be learned must involve behaviors that are already in the infant's repertoire (Sameroff and Cavanaugh, 1979). This means that the experimenter must be mindful of the limitations in the infant's abilities and inabilities, as the Research Report on memory makes clear.

It should also be noted that infants learn best when the tasks are related to their most important biological goals: surviving and thriving. Thus infants can readily be taught skills that help them to get nourishment, attract the attention of their caregivers, and interact with interesting phenomena in their environment (Lipsitt, 1982).

Some learning theorists assert that in addition to learning through conditioning, infants seem to be primed for social learning. In particular, they point to studies showing that even in the first weeks of life, babies try to imitate facial expressions (Meltzoff and Moore, 1983; Field et al., 1982). However, there is some doubt that this is true social learning, for at least one team of researchers thinks it may be a reflex that disappears, as other reflexes do, when the infants are a month old or more (Abravanel and Sigafoos, 1984). Nevertheless, there is no doubt that from the first moments of life, infants pay particular attention to other people.

RESEARCH REPORT   **Infant Memory**

Hundreds of experiments have shown that the memory of young infants is quite weak. There is evidence that memory improves at about 1, 4, and 8 months (Lipsitt, 1982), but even in the second half of the first year, retention of information from one day to the next has been hard to demonstrate. A review of infant memory concludes that "most studies have shown retention for only a matter of seconds or minutes" (Werner and Perlmutter, 1979).

Following the American penchant for accelerating development, several researchers have wondered if infant memory could be improved. For example, Cornell (1980) let 6-month-old infants look at the photograph of a face for 20 seconds, broken into four 5-second viewing periods separated by 3-second intervals. The infants were then shown the same photograph together with the photograph of a second face. When the pair of faces was presented 5 seconds after they had viewed the first photograph, the infants could distinguish the first face from the second. However, when the pair of faces was presented 1 minute after the first, the infants acted as if both faces were new to them.

In a follow-up test, Cornell decided to add an element that might make the task more sensitive to the memory potential of the infant. He applied a well-known rule regarding adult memory, specifically that memory improves if the learning sessions are separated by a period of time, rather than massed together. (This rule of "distributed practice" explains why cramming for a final exam is not as effective as studying on a regular basis throughout the term.) Cornell gave some 6-month-olds breaks that lasted a minute (rather than 3 seconds) between their four learning episodes. Although the total learning time was still 20 seconds, distributed practice helped the infants remember. They could distinguish between the two faces for up to an hour after the training period.

In another experiment, 3-month-old infants were conditioned to make a mobile move by kicking their feet, which were attached to a ribbon. They learned this task quite well, but, two weeks later, when again placed in the crib with the mobile tied to their feet, they showed no

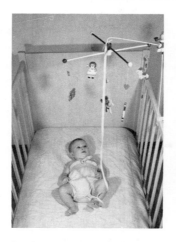

In the photo at left, a 3-month-old infant is learning to kick her foot to make a mobile move. However, after two weeks of being unattached to the mobile and not seeing it move, she will have forgotten what to do when the ribbon is once again tied to *her foot. But if she is given a "reminder session" (photo at right) in which she sees the mobile moving, her "lessons" will likely come back to her, and when the ribbon is attached to her foot she will start kicking.*

evidence of having remembered how to make the mobile move (Sullivan, 1982).

The experiment was then repeated with another group of infants, but this time the infants were allowed a "reminder" session a day before the test. In the reminder session, the infants were able to look at the mobile, but they were not in a position to kick it, nor were they tied to the ribbon that would activate it. The next day, they were positioned correctly and tied to the mobile. At this point, they kicked as they had learned to do two weeks before. This experiment has been repeated with younger infants (8 weeks old) after a longer interval (18 days), with the same result (Davis and Rovee-Collier, 1983).

Evidence such as this clearly suggests that infants can be taught to remember some images and behaviors earlier than had previously been thought. The question is, as we will see in the next section, What is the value, if any, of such learning outside the laboratory?

Special Programs for High-Risk Infants

Because of research showing that infants can be taught many skills, some psychologists have tried to improve infants' cognitive development by providing special programs of enrichment and instruction. For the most part, these efforts have been with infants who have been at risk for cognitive problems, either because of birth complications or because they live in an impoverished environment. In one case, for example, thirty preterm babies from low-income families were randomly assigned to two groups (Scarr-Salapatek and Williams, 1973). The fifteen infants in the control group received the normal hospital and home care for preterm infants, care which generally meets their physiological needs but not necessarily their cognitive ones. The other fifteen preterm infants were given special stimulation in the hospital: bright decorations suspended above their isolettes within a few hours after birth and daily "play" periods with a nurse as soon as the infant could maintain constant body temperature. Mothers of the experimental group were taught special techniques for playing with their babies, and a psychologist visited them regularly in the first year to provide new games and encouragement. After one month, the babies in the experimental group began to surpass the control group in motor and perceptual abilities. By the end of one year, they were advanced in many ways, including scoring an average of 10 points higher on a test of infant intelligence.

Training mothers to stimulate their babies has been done in many large-scale programs. In one of the most famous, the Florida Parent Education Program (Gordon, 1969), instructors visited mothers from low-income families once a week to teach them specific games to play with their infants. Many of the activities were designed to reflect Piaget's stages of infant development. For instance, at about 8 months of age, mothers were encouraged to hide objects and have the baby search for them—taking care to make the play period an enjoyable experience. If the baby didn't search for the object, for example, the mother was to find it, and perhaps hide it again with part of it showing.

Compared to a control group of similar infants, those children who were given such special learning experiences in the first two years of life showed improved cognitive development. Even seven years later, when they were in the third grade, these children scored better on tests of reading and math concepts (Guinagh and Gordon, 1976).

Other programs designed to help infants who are somehow at risk for understimulation have, similarly, shown a measure of success, although the degree of success varies from program to program and infant to infant (Beller, 1979; Halpern, 1984). Even when the gains are not spectacular, developmentalists are, of course, in favor of special training for infants who might need help.

Teaching the Privileged Infant

The success of some of these interventions has spawned a number of accelerated-infant-development programs available to the public. While some of these have captured the attention of the popular press and the money of middle- and upper-class parents, they make most developmentalists wary. Perhaps the most famous program is that of the Better Baby Institute in Philadelphia, which, for $400 a week, teaches parents how to teach their infants to swim and walk and how to get their toddlers to learn to read poetry, speak foreign languages, play musical instruments, and perform other such advanced feats.

The sudden increase in such programs seems to be related to the current trend for couples to have fewer children, particularly two-career couples who begin their families relatively late in marriage. Understandably, but not necessarily wisely, such parents sometimes think that providing "the best" for their one or two children includes giving them an early start in the skills demanded by a competitive world. However, as David Elkind (1981) points out, in supposedly acting in behalf of their children, these parents may be responding to the pressures for achievement that they themselves feel.

Whatever the actual successes of programs like these, most developmentalists would still question the value of such accelerated learning. A theme of Piagetian theory, backed up by research from many disciplines, is that infants are remarkably able to learn from the experiences that are normally present in a good home, and that they do not need, or benefit from, extra stimulation. Indeed, too much stimulation, like too little stimulation, may be detrimental (White, 1975; McCall, 1981).

A related point is raised by Howard Gardner (1983), who investigated the Suzuki method of musical training for infants, which begins almost from birth. Although marveling at the musical skills mastered by Suzuki preschoolers, many of whom were well on their way to playing Vivaldi and Mozart, Gardner notes that there can be personal costs to such intensive undertakings:

> From the point of view of the child, he is devoting many hours each week to a single kind of pursuit and to the development of a single intelligence—at the cost of stimulating and developing other intellectual streams. More dramatically, this regimen makes great demands upon the mother: she is expected to devote herself unstintingly to the development in her child of a certain capacity. If she succeeds, plaudits are likely to come to the child; if she fails, she will probably be blamed.

Figure 7.9 *One of the basic tenets of the Suzuki method—the close connection between a child's musical performance and the mother's involvement—is apparent at this concert for budding violinists.*

The major question is, Why *should* an infant be taught to swim, or a toddler be taught to read? If the intention is to give the child an advantage later on, the approach is mistaken, for children who develop early in one area or another do not necessarily maintain their headstart. This fact is clear from research on infant intelligence scores, which has shown that, except in cases involving cognitive problems, intelligence levels in infancy do not predict intelligence in later years. In fact, the child who is above average in infant IQ is just as likely to be somewhat below average as somewhat above average in later years. As Kagan and Klein (1973) observe, "There is no reason to assume that the caterpillar who metamorphoses a bit earlier than his kin is a better adapted, more efficient butterfly."

Most developmentalists would advise parents who want to help their infant's cognitive growth to play with their baby at the level appropriate to the baby's stage of development. Just like an active toddler, the parent should "experiment in order to see" what produces a fascinated stare or a happy grin in the baby, and what produces overexcitement, boredom, fear, or frustration. The active baby will show the sensitive parent how and when to teach, and when to sit back and allow the infant to explore and discover independently.

Figure 7.10 *Facial expression is often the best key to a child's receptivity to cognitive experiences. It's easy to tell that this little girl is enjoying her lesson.*

Language Development

Everywhere in the world, in every language, children are talking by age 2, with a grasp of basic grammar and a vocabulary that is frequently surprising in scope. Consider, for example, these sentences uttered by 24-month-old Sarah:

> Uh, oh. Kitty jumping down.
> What drawing? Numbers? [said when her mother was
>   transcribing her words]
>
> Want it, paper.
> Wipe it, pencil.
> What time it is? [said upon seeing a watch]

These sentences show that Sarah has a varied vocabulary and a basic understanding of word order (for example, Sarah said "Kitty jumping down," rather than "down jumping kitty," or "jumping kitty down," or "kitty down jumping"). They also show that she has much to learn, for she incorrectly uses the pronoun "it" and its referent together, omits personal pronoun subjects, and puts the predicate nominative before the predicate in the interrogative. Sarah's impressive but imperfect language is quite similar to that uttered by 2-year-olds in many families and cultures. On the basis of detailed studies of thousands of babies, we know quite a bit about the sequence of verbal skills in the first two years of life, and Sarah, both in her early days and now at age two, is typical.

Theories of Language Development

What accounts for the rapid development of language between birth and age 2? Are infants dependent on the example and instruction of adults to gain an understanding of language? Or are they born with a powerful desire to communicate and a subtle grasp of the underlying principles of language? Each of these positions has been taken by an opposing group of scholars.

Learning Theory: Skinner Some researchers, following the lead of B. F. Skinner (1957), maintain that children learn to talk through conditioning. As Skinner explains it, when a baby babbles "ma-ma-ma" and Mommy comes running with the physiological reinforcers of food or clean diapers, or the social reinforcers of a smile or a hug, the baby is likely to say "ma-ma-ma" again. In addition, since Mother is usually delighted to think that the baby is actually addressing her, she is likely to repeat "mama" whenever the infant babbles it.

As time goes on, the infant becomes conditioned to associate "mama" with the presence of Mother and learns to call "mama" whenever Mother is needed. In a similar fashion, the infant learns to associate various other vocalizations with specific events and things. According to learning theorists, the words and phrases children learn depend on the nature, frequency, and timing of the conditioning process. Some families reinforce almost every utterance: when the child says

Figure 7.11 *Learning the word "nose" is easy when it becomes a mutual game of show-and-tell accompanied by parents' delighted approval.*

"juh," for example, the child is given juice; when the child says "ca," someone responds "Yes, cat." Other families withhold rewards until the child gets a word "right" or scold and lecture when the child gets it "wrong"; and still others tend to ignore the toddler's efforts to communicate. Following the general principles of conditioning, it would be likely that a child in the first instance would develop extensive language skills; a child in the second might tend to be reluctant to use much speech; a child in the third might be very limited in language skills.

At the same time, learning theorists emphasize that learning by association, without specific reinforcement, is also part of the process. Many parents, for instance, habitually name the articles of clothing they put on their infants, the food they put in their mouths, the objects they put in their hands. The infant naturally makes the link between the name and the thing. A more striking example of unreinforced language learning can be seen in the case of toddlers' uttering profanities that their parents never intended them to hear, much less learn and repeat.

A Structural View: Chomsky   Coming at language learning from a very different perspective, Noam Chomsky (1968) and David McNeill (1970) hold that children have an innate predisposition to learn language at a certain age, much like the innate disposition to stand up as soon as their bodies are sufficiently mature.

Chomsky believes that babies have an inborn understanding of the basic structure of language, which he calls the **deep structure.** For instance, infants seem to be born knowing that one important way to communicate is by making noises. They also soon demonstrate a recognition that small differences in pronunciation and inflection can change the meaning of a word, and that some sentences are statements and others are questions. These are things that do not have to be *learned*. What does require learning is the particular vocabulary and grammar, or **surface structure,** of a language. Chomsky believes that children learn the surface structure as rapidly as they do because they already understand the deep structure, which helps them grasp the underlying rules of grammar that govern the flawed and incomplete sentences that most adults speak.

To emphasize the inborn, automatic nature of the infant's linguistic ability, Chomsky devised a figure of speech, the **language acquisition device (LAD),** to refer to the human predisposition to learn language. According to Chomsky, in-

Figure 7.12 According to Chomsky, this infant was born with the rudiments of language and the will to talk. What remains to be acquired is knowledge of the particular combination of sounds that comprise the surface structure of her own language.

fants' innate language-learning ability causes them to listen attentively to speech sounds in the early weeks of life and to imitate speech sounds and patterns throughout infancy. LAD also triggers babbling at about 6 months, the first word at about 1 year, and the first sentences at about 2 years, no matter what the child's language, nationality, race, or socioeconomic background.

Later Research Skinner's and Chomsky's views of language learning represent opposite extremes, which both theorists continue to maintain (Skinner, 1983; Chomsky, 1980). However, since the initial descriptions of their theories, substantial research on early language development has shown that neither position tells the whole story. Rather, actual language learning is an interactional process that occurs between nature and nurture—that is, between the maturation that propels cognitive growth generally and the communication that occurs in the parent-child relationship. This will be increasingly clear as we look, first at the steps in language learning, and then at the family context that makes such learning possible.

Steps in Language Development

Children the world over follow the same sequence and approximately the same timetable for early language development (see Table 7.2). The first area in which they become competent is *language function*—that is, the communication of ideas and emotions. Indeed, speaking of language solely in terms of its function, it can be said that infants are born using language, a language of noises and gestures. As you will see, within the first two years of life, this rudimentary ability to communicate evolves into an impressive command of *language structure*, that is, the particular words and rules of the infant's native tongue.

TABLE 7.2 **Language Development**

NEWBORN	Reflexive communication—cries, movements, facial expressions.
2 MONTHS	A range of meaningful noises—cooing, fussing, crying.
6 MONTHS	Babbling, including both consonant and vowel sounds.
10 MONTHS	Comprehension of simple words; intonation of language; specific vocalizations that have meaning to those who know the infant well. Deaf babies express their first sign.
12 MONTHS	First spoken words that are recognizably part of the native language.
12–18 MONTHS	Slow growth of vocabulary, up to 50 words. Holophrases.
21 MONTHS	First combination of words into two-word sentences.
24 MONTHS	Vocabulary of more than 200 words. Grammar apparent in word order, suffixes, prefixes, pronouns (specifics depend partly on the particular native language).

First Communications Normal babies are born able to cry in several ways, as researchers have discovered by analyzing recorded cries (Wolff, 1969). The usual "hunger," or "rhythmic," cry follows this pattern: short cry (about .6 second), brief pause (about .2 second), intake of breath (.2 second), pause, and another short cry. The "mad" cry follows the same pattern, but with more force. The "pain" cry is louder and longer; a cry lasting 4 seconds, a pause and deep breath lasting 7 seconds, and another 4-second cry.

These early cries are reflexes rather than deliberate attempts to communicate. But just as other reflexes are, according to Piaget, the starting point for the acquisition of differentiated responses, the newborn's first cries develop into communication skills. As care-givers learn to respond to the needs the infant expresses through various cries, the infant becomes more adept at expressing those needs.

Very young babies communicate in other ways as well. In the first months of life, facial expressions and body movements provide clues about infant emotions. The **pleasure smile**, a relaxation of the facial muscles that indicates contentment (Oster, 1978), and the arm-waving that means excitement, are two examples that are apparent even in the first days of life. With responsive parents, infants soon learn that these gestures are meaningful.

Figure 7.13 *By responding quickly to her infant's cry of distress, this mother is helping the infant to communicate verbally. Her older child is also conveying his feelings effectively. Ideally she will respond sympathetically to him too.*

Cooing   As early as 5 weeks of age, babies make noncrying sounds when they see faces or hear voices. The utterance of these sounds is called **cooing**, because the infant repeats the same vowel sounds again and again, varying the pitch slightly, the way a pigeon does when it coos (Lenneberg, 1967). Also in the early weeks, the infant uses a variety of other sounds to indicate mild distress, surprise, or pleasure.

Babbling   By 5 months, babies have added several consonant sounds to the vowels of cooing, and by 6 months, utterances include several distinct sounds and combinations of sounds. Continual repetition of the same sound, called **babbling** (partly because "ba-ba-ba" is one of the first repetitions), primes babies for uttering their first words, which are usually made up of the sounds they babble most. Infants everywhere babble the same sounds at almost exactly the same age, no matter what language their parents speak. Even babies who are deaf or mentally retarded babble in the familiar way at about 6 months.

A CLOSER LOOK   Babbling and Language Development in Deaf Babies

Babies with normal hearing, enjoying the sounds they make, babble to themselves, to mirrors, to toys, to animals, and especially to older people who babble back. Deaf babies babble the same sounds at 6 months as other babies, but since they cannot hear themselves or others' responses, they receive no reinforcement for their babbling. Consequently, they communicate with gestures rather than sounds, and their early babbling disappears rather than turning into speech.

Since they do not understand or develop speech, most deaf or hard-of-hearing babies are severely handicapped in language development, usually experiencing difficulties with written vocabulary and grammar all their lives (Meadow, 1975). However, research on infants whose parents communicated with them using American sign language (Ameslan), just as other parents would have used words, has found that deaf babies develop sign language as fast as hearing babies develop spoken language. One bright little girl, Ann, signed her first two words ("pretty" and "wrong") at 10 months and used 142 signs and 14 letters of the manual alphabet at 19½ months (Schlesinger and Meadow, 1972).

In Ann's case, her parents had her hearing tested in the first days of life because they themselves were congenitally deaf. However, most parents simply take it for granted that their baby hears normally, and many hearing problems are not suspected until secondary speech problems become obvious. For example, a profoundly deaf 2-year-old may not have begun to talk, and the speech of a moderately deaf 5-year-old may be unusually limited in clarity and scope. By this time the hearing problem may have become a lifelong language handicap, because the first years of language development may be crucial. (The idea of a critical period in language development is discussed in Chapter 10.)

This deaf toddler is learning to express himself in American sign language. If he is given adequate opportunities for learning, *chances are good that his language ability will develop at a rate that will match or exceed that of a hearing 2-year-old.*

When a hearing impairment is diagnosed within the first two years, hearing aids, surgery, or special education can usually prevent the difficulty from becoming a major handicap (Bolton, 1976). As Ann's progress demonstrated, the impoverished language that is typical of many deaf children need not occur if sign language is substituted for spoken language early in life. Indeed, sign language may be easier to learn and use than spoken language. One study followed eleven infants with normal hearing who received early exposure to Ameslan because one or both of their parents were deaf (Bonvillian et al., 1983). These infants signed their first word at about 8 months, and had an average vocabulary of fifty words at 18 months—the upper limits of vocabulary for normal children at this age.

At first, babies probably babble for the pure physical pleasure of making movements and noises with the mouth, tongue, lips, and throat, in much the same way they enjoy kicking their legs or moving their fingers. The infant babbles when alone and is also likely to vocalize while someone else is talking, as if to join in the general noise-making. But by 8 months or so, babies begin to babble conversationally rather than simply for the delight in practicing a new motor skill. The typical infant is still while someone talks, and then responds with babbling, and then is still again. It seems as if the baby has learned the first rules of conversation: Don't talk when someone else is talking, and respond when it's your turn.

Figure 7.14 *Although these two women probably could not communicate verbally with each other, they are speaking the same language—Motherese—in conversing with their infants.*

Meaningful Sounds   Even before infants utter their first words, they begin to learn the intonation of language. Using a single sound, they express happiness, distress, a command, or a question. A psychologist from the Soviet Union, Tonkova-Yampol'skaya (1973), recorded the rise and fall of voice tones for babies and adults expressing each of these four types of communication and found that the infant pattern closely follows the adult pattern (see Figure 7.15).

Figure 7.15 *Intonation patterns of infants younger than 12 months are surprisingly similar to those of adults, both in sound intensity and fundamental tone frequency, as shown from vocal responses recorded on magnetic tape. The pattern for distress or discomfort (a) is apparent in the first month of life; for happiness (b), by 3 months; for a command (c), by 10 months; and for a question (d), by 12 months.*

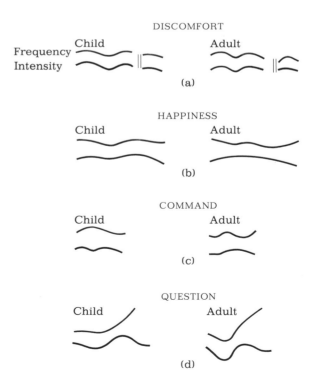

Attentive parents can discern definite meaning from the intonation and sounds a baby makes at this point: one linguist reports that his 10-month-old son had a "repertoire" of twelve sounds that had distinct meaning. For instance, "ennn," said in a pitch falling from high to low, was interpreted as "Nice to see you, at last," while "nn," beginning in midrange and dropping to low, was "That tastes nice" (Halliday, 1979).

Comprehension At every stage of development, including the preverbal stage, children understand much more than they express. When asked "Where's Mommy?" for instance, many 10-month-olds will look in her direction; or when asked "Do you want Daddy to pick you up?" will reach out their arms. In addition, as the infant learns to anticipate events (stage four of sensorimotor development), words such as "hot!" "no!" or "bye-bye" take on meaning. Of course, context and tone help significantly to supply that meaning. For example, when parents see their crawling infant about to touch the electrical outlet, they say "No" sufficiently sharply to startle and thus halt the infant in his or her tracks. Typically, they then move the child away, pointing to the danger and repeating "No. No." Given the frequency with which the mobile infant's behavior produces similar situations, it is no wonder that infants seem to understand "No" at an early age.

First Spoken Words Finally, at about 1 year, the average baby speaks one or two words, not pronounced very clearly or used very precisely. Usually caregivers hear, and understand, the first word before strangers do, which makes it hard to pinpoint, scientifically, exactly what a 12-month-old can say. In fact, when the criterion for regarding an utterance as speech is that it be recognizable to a stranger, many normal 12-month-olds cannot be said to have started speaking at all. Even the most precocious usually have less than a dozen words in their vocabulary.

The first words a child speaks are usually the words that are most important to the child. Many are associated with some movement or action the child can do, as might be expected, since the child is at the sensorimotor stage of development. For instance, Katherine Nelson (1973) followed the language development of eighteen children for a year beginning at about their first birthdays. In their vocabularies, eleven children had "shoe," seven had "clock" (meaning "watch" as well), and six had "key"—all objects that move or that can be held by a 1-year-old—while none had "diaper" or "crib," words referring to objects that are common in infants' lives but that are not normally part of their sensorimotor schema. Other research has also found that early words often express, and, in fact, typically accompany action, for example, "bye-bye" and waving, and "bang" and hitting (Corrigan, 1978).

You might think that once a child could say a few words, additional words would come easily. But this is not the case. Vocabulary increases gradually, perhaps a few words a month. By 18 months, the average baby knows somewhere between three and fifty words (Lenneberg, 1967).

Piaget's research suggests that the child must reach stage six of sensorimotor development, the stage of mental representation, before language learning can become rapid. Piaget's explanation seems plausible, for in order to really grasp the connection between words and referents, a toddler must be able to think about an object or action without using sensorimotor skills. A firm sense of object permanence is also necessary to enable the child to connect the word "ball," for instance, with an actual ball, whether the child is playing with it or is about to get it out of the toy box. Many of the toddler's first sentences seem to show that mental representa-

Strategies for Learning Language: Referential and Expressive

Katherine Nelson (1973, 1981) has noted an interesting distinction in children's language learning. Some children seem to take a "referential" approach, using language primarily to label the objects in their world. Others adopt an "expressive" strategy, using words primarily to engage in social interaction. These preferences are apparent in a child's early vocabulary. For example, excluding personal names, 14-month-old Jane's vocabulary included twice as many referential words as expressive words:

Referential words		Expressive words	
girl	cake	up	bye
baby	water	all gone	hi
ball	bottle	hot	row-row
walker	key	more	school*
doggie	drawer		
kitty	clock		
cracker	top		
cookie	that		

On the other hand, 17-month-old Lisa also had a twenty-four-word vocabulary, but she used nearly twice as many expressive words as referential words:

Referential words		Expressive words	
puppy	doll	see	please
dog	fork	outside	thank you
car	water	go	yes
keys	that	eat	not now
ball		drink	want
		tickle-tickle	woof-woof
		hi	where

*School is considered expressive rather than referential, because Jane used it as the place where Daddy goes.

Nelson found similar patterns of referential and expressive orientation in all the children she studied, and these patterns persisted into the preschool years.

What makes a child lean toward one learning style rather than another? Part of the answer may be that some children are naturally more absorbed with the things in their world while others are more interested in self and other people. In addition, the mother's teaching strategy plays an important role: some mothers seem to favor a referential style, setting out to teach their toddlers the names of animals, foods, parts of the body, etc. Others are more expressive, wanting their children to learn "please" and "thank you," or "hi there" and "bye-bye."

Another factor appears to be birth order. Referential learning is more common among first-borns, especially those with college-educated mothers who read to their children and usually respond to their questions about what this or that is. Expressive learning is more common among later-borns, whose mothers typically spend more time controlling and guiding the interpersonal behavior of their children and much less time teaching vocabulary (White, 1979). In addition, later-borns' older siblings typically issue far more social directives (e.g., "Stop it," "Put it down," "Sit over here") than referential questions (Nelson, 1981). Thus it makes sense that later-borns often consider language a social tool rather than a naming device.

It is Nelson's contention that one style is not necessarily better than the other. While Nelson's referential children usually had larger vocabularies than expressive children who were the same age, the complexity of language (as measured by the number of words in their sentences at

tion ("See dis," "Wha dat?") and object permanence ("Where dis," "Allgone dat") are ideas of such significance that they are often put into words.

At first, infants apply the few words they know to a variety of contexts. This characteristic, known as **overextension,** or overgeneralization, might lead one child to call anything round "ball," and another to call every four-legged creature "doggie." But once vocabulary begins to expand, toddlers seem to "experiment in order to see" with words just as they do with objects. The "little scientist" becomes the "little linguist," exploring hypotheses and reaching conclusions. It is not unusual for 18-month-olds to walk down the street pointing to every animal, asking "doggie?" or "horsey?" or "kitty?"—perhaps to test their hypotheses about which words go with which animals.

age 2) was similar for both groups. Nelson also points out that while a referential teaching style may generally seem best for increasing vocabulary, it may not necessarily be so, particularly if there is a mismatch between the child's learning style and the parent's teaching patterns.

Nelson found that the most crucial factor in the speed of language learning is the mother's overall acceptance or rejection of the child's early language attempts. To illustrate this, Nelson cites two examples, in both cases a referential child and a referential mother.

Mother: Jane. Here's a bottle. Where's the bottle? Here's a bottle.
Jane: Wah wah.
Mother: Bottle.
Jane: Bah bah.
Mother: Bah bah.
Jane: Bah bah.
Mother: Oh, bah bah. Here's a ball.
Jane: Baw.
Mother: Ball. Yes.
Jane: Uh. Uh boo?
Mother: Ball.

Paul: Go.
Mother: What? Feel.
Paul: Fe.
Mother: What's that? A dog. What does the dog say? One page at a time. Oh, that one over there. What's that one there?
Paul: Boah.
Mother: What? You know that.
Paul: Bah.
Mother: What?

Paul: Ah wah.
Mother: What?
Paul: Caw.
Mother: Car?
Paul: Caw, awh.
Mother: Little kitty, you know that. [Nelson, 1973]

Not surprisingly, Jane was one of the youngest children to speak 50 words, reaching this milestone at 15 months, while Paul was one of the slowest, not speaking 50 words until he was 20 months old.

Nelson found that another important factor affecting the speed of language learning was whether the mother was more inclined to give commands or to ask questions that encouraged a response. Even a preponderance of benign directives, such as "Here, play with the baby" or "Make the truck go over here" had a strong negative correlation with the child's verbal fluency. By contrast, questions that invite a response ("What do you want to eat?" "Is the sun out today?") were positively correlated with fluency.

Nelson found that when the maternal teaching style was more rejecting than accepting, and when the mother's referential strategy was not in keeping with her child's inclinations, language development suffered a great deal. This is shown by one boy who, being the first-born child of college-educated parents, might have been expected to learn language quickly. Typically, however, when he wanted to play, his mother wanted him to sit still so she could read him a book. Some of the effects of this mismatch were many temper tantrums and the slowest language development of the group. The boy did not reach the 50-word stage until 23 months.

Even when the toddler's vocabulary is larger, some words seem to be used idiosyncratically. Take the simple word "daddy," for example. For many 2-year-olds, "daddy" can refer to any man, or to any man with a moustache, or only to their own father, depending on their understanding of the word's meaning (Thompson and Chapman, 1977). One toddler whose parents took turns taking care of her and leaving the house for work demonstrated a consistent but unconventional understanding of parental titles: she called whichever parent stayed home "mommy" and whichever one left "daddy" (Cowan, 1978).

As children learn their first words, they usually become adept at expressing intention. Even a single word, amplified by intonation and gestures, can express a whole thought. When a toddler pushes at a closed door and says "bye-bye" in a demanding tone, it is clear that the toddler wishes to go out. When a toddler holds on to Mother's legs and plaintively says ''bye-bye'' as soon as the babysitter arrives, it is equally clear that the child is asking Mommy not to leave. Single words that express a complete thought in this manner are called *holophrases*.

It is important to note that vocabulary size is not the only, nor the best, measure of early language learning. Rather, the crux of early language is communication, not vocabulary. If parents are concerned about their nonverbal 1-year-old son, they should look at his ability and willingness to make his needs known and to understand what others say. If those skills seem to be normal, and if the child hears enough simple language addressed to him every day (through someone's reading to him, singing to him, talking about the food he is eating and the sights he sees), he will probably be speaking in sentences before age 2.

Combining Words Within about six months of speaking his or her first words, a child begins to put words together. As a general rule, the first two-word sentence appears between 18 and 21 months (Slobin, 1971). Combining words demands considerable linguistic understanding because, in English and in most other languages, word order affects the meaning of the sentence. However, even in their first sentences, toddlers demonstrate that they have figured out the basics of subject-predicate order, declaring ''Baby cry'' or asking ''Rain stop?'' rather than the reverse.

Toddlers also indicate that they are aware of other grammatical conventions. The words ''no'' and ''more,'' for example, are among the first words most children learn. Once children reach the two-word sentence stage, they use these words correctly—''No spinach,'' ''More cake''—and creatively—''No sleep,'' ''More bath.'' They also learn pronouns and adjectives, especially the first-person singular and possessive: ''I want it,'' ''Mine,'' ''My toy.'' By age 2, many children use ''s'' to form plurals and the ''-ing'' ending to distinguish imperatives—''Run!'' ''Jump!'' ''Dance!''—from declaratives—''Mommy running,'' ''Kitty jumping,'' ''Daddy dancing.'' A detailed discussion of the young child's grammar—mastery and mistakes—appears in Chapter 10, pages 302–305.

Teamwork: Adults and Babies Teach Each Other to Talk

Early research in language development tended to concentrate primarily on either the infant as learner or on the parents as teachers. In recent years, however, researchers have focused on the parent-child interaction, recording and analyzing what each half of the partnership says and does in their communications with each other. This led to the discovery that infants are primed to listen and respond to speech and that care-givers are often quite skilled at facilitating the infant's language learning.

As detailed in Chapter 6, even in the first weeks of life, infants turn their heads and open their eyes wide when they hear voices, and show excitement when someone talks to them, and have preferences for certain voices. Even babies under a month old have demonstrated in laboratory experiments that they can hear the difference between very similar speech sounds, suggesting that this ability is inborn (Clarkson and Berg, 1983).

For their part, adults talk to infants even in the first days of life, using a special form of language called **baby talk.** The term ''baby talk,'' as used by researchers, does not refer to the way people think babies talk—the ''goo-goo-ga-ga'' that few infants actually say. Rather, it refers to the particular way people talk to infants, a distinct form of language that some psychologists have nicknamed *Motherese*. Baby talk differs from adult talk in a number of features that are consistent throughout all language communities (Ferguson, 1977): it is distinct in its pitch (higher), intonation (especially low-to-high fluctuations), vocabulary (simpler and more concrete), and sentence length (shorter). It also employs more questions, commands, and repetitions, and fewer past tenses, pronouns, and complex sentences, than adult talk does. People of all ages, parents and nonparents alike, speak baby talk with infants (Jacobson et al., 1983).

The function of baby talk is clearly to facilitate early language learning, for the sounds and words of baby talk are those that infants attend to, and speak, most readily. In addition, difficult sounds are avoided: consonants like "l" and "r" are regularly missing, and hard-to-say words are given simple forms, often with a "-y" ending. Thus, a father becomes "daddy," stomachs become "tummies," and rabbits become "bunnies," because if they didn't, infants and parents wouldn't be able to talk about them. One example of the parents' readiness to adapt language to fit the needs of the infant was shown in an experiment in which mothers and their 13-month-old infants were observed while they played with a variety of toys representing the more ferocious members of the cat family—including a cougar, a leopard, and a lion. Eighty percent of the mothers reduced this variety to "kitty," some even saying "meow" and urging the infant to pet the "nice kitty-cat." Other categories of toys were similarly simplified with inaccurate but familiar labels (Mervis and Mervis, 1982).

In the earliest stages of baby talk, the conversation is, of course, rather one-sided. However, as the child grows more responsive and communicative, the general interaction between parent and child becomes more like a conversation in its give and take. For instance, the games that parents and babies often play in the last half of the first year, such as peek-a-boo and patty-cake, typically involve a turn-taking ritual. Bruner (1974–1975) believes this mutual game-playing is the first step in language learning.

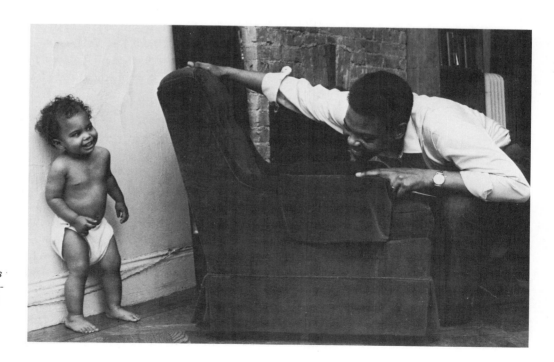

Figure 7.16 *Even a simple parent-infant game like hide-and-seek incorporates some elements of conversation, including turn-taking between players and mutual attention to facial expressions.*

A CLOSER LOOK   **Berger Learns the Rules of Baby Talk**

In the weeks just before the Berlin wall was put up in 1961, I went to work in a day-care center at a refugee camp in West Berlin. The children, aged 4 and younger, spoke several languages, none of which I knew, and as I prepared for my first day, I worried that I would not be able to communicate with them. After a few minutes on the job, however, I realized that communication would be no problem when a 2-year-old tugged my hand and said a two-syllable word I immediately understood, even though I had never heard it before. He wanted me to take him to the bathroom.

I was soon to discover that my young friend's message takes a similar form in any number of languages: a repeated single syllable generally beginning with a hard consonant. Indeed, researchers have discovered a number of commonalities and implicit rules of baby talk that exist across nearly all languages. To begin with, baby talk is made up of a small vocabulary of simple words that are amplified with gestures and vocal expression. Many of these words consist of single repeated syllables (such as "no-no," "bye-bye") and often tend toward onomatopoeia, mimicking a sound or quality associated with the object or action being named ("choo-choo," "bow-wow," "pooh-pooh").

One of the most striking commonalities arises from the fact that the early words of baby talk are made up of the sounds characteristic of babbling—"m," "p," "b," "t," and "d" plus a vowel sound. Consequently, two of the first and most important words in babies' vocabularies—"mother" and "father"—take a nearly universal form (see table).

	Mother	Father
English	mama, mommy	dada, daddy
Spanish	mama	papa
French	maman, mama	papa
Italian	mamma	babbo, papa
Latvian	mama	tēte
Syrian Arabic	mama	baba
Bantu	ba-mama	taata
Swahili	mama	baba
Sanskrit	nana	tata
Hebrew	ema	abba
Korean	oma	apa

The "conversational" aspect of the parent-child interaction is strengthened between 5 and 7 months, as parents begin to treat burps, smiles, yawns, gestures, and babbling as part of a dialogue (Snow and Ferguson, 1977). For instance, in the following "exchange," the mother asks and answers several questions, as if the baby's smile and burp were significant communications:

Child: (Smiles)
Mother: Oh, what a nice little smile! Yes, isn't that nice?
(Pause)
There. There's a nice little smile.
Child: (Burps)
Mother: What a nice wind as well! Yes, that's better, isn't it?

Even when the baby seems to do nothing, the parent is likely to carry on the conversation as though it were actively two-way. A mother might say, "Don't you want to take a nap now?", pause a second or two as though allowing the baby to answer, and then say, "Of course you do," in agreement with the imagined response (Stern, 1977). In fact, the response is not all in the mind of the mother. Babies show with facial expressions that they listen to maternal speech, and they indicate when they are ready to hear more.

Once the child begins to talk, many conversations between parent and child show the parent interpreting the child's imperfect speech and then responding with short clear sentences the child can understand, often with special emphasis on important words. Naturalistic observation is the best way to study this interaction, for facial expression and intonation are as much a part of baby talk as the words spoken. However, recorded dialogues like the following (Halliday, 1979) help give the flavor:

> Nigel's mother is putting him to bed.
>
> Mother: And when you get up in the morning, you'll go for a walk.
> Nigel: *Tik.*
> And you'll see some sticks, yes.
> *Hoo.*
> And some holes, yes.
> *Da.*
> Yes, now it's getting dark.
> *I wa [repeated thirteen times].*
> What?
> *I wa [seven times]. Peaz.*
> What do you want in bed? Jamie? [his doll]
> *No!*
> You want your eiderdown? [quilt]
> *(grins) Yeahh!*
> Why didn't you say so? Your eiderdown.
> *Ella [three times].*

In most episodes of baby talk, the child is an active participant, responding to the speaker and making his or her needs known. In this one, Nigel asked for his quilt a total of twenty times, persisting until his seemingly foolish mother finally got the point.

A Social Interaction In many interchanges between adult and toddler, the child starts the conversation with no apparent motive in mind. An 18-month-old might say "Hi" over and over until he or she gets a response, and then point out and name various things within sight, such as a book, a doll, a table, a chair, expecting to be listened to and to have a reply. Perhaps these toddlers are reviewing what they have learned, or it may be that they are teaching adults just as they themselves were taught. Often, however, it seems that the specifics of such a conversation have no particular significance in themselves. As we have seen repeatedly, infants are motivated to understand the world: the same motivation that makes toddlers resemble little scientists makes infants seek to understand the noises, gestures, words and grammatical systems that describe the world in which they live. Central to the achievement of understanding language is the verbal interaction of parents and child. As one researcher writes:

> language . . . could not emerge in any species, and would not develop in any individual, without a special kind of fit between adult behavior and infant behavior. That fit is pre-adapted: It comes to each child as a birthright, both as a result of biological propensities and as a result of social processes learned and transmitted by each new generation. [Kaye, 1982]

Thus parent and baby together accomplish what neither could do alone: teach a person to talk. As we will see in the next chapter, the same parent-infant relationship is at the core of the psychosocial development of the child.

SUMMARY

1. Impressive changes in the infant's capacity to understand and communicate with the world are the result of developments in cognition, the interaction of the perceptual, intellectual, and linguistic abilities that result in thinking and learning.

How Cognitive Development Occurs

2. Although most developmental researchers agree that both maturation and learning contribute to cognitive development, questions remain about their relative contributions during different periods of development.

Piaget's Theory

3. From birth to age 2, the period of sensorimotor intelligence, infants use their senses and motor skills to understand their environment. They begin by adapting their reflexes, coordinating their actions, and interacting with people and things. By the end of the first year, they know what they want and have the knowledge and ability to achieve their simple goals.

4. Infants younger than 8 months believe that when an object disappears from their sight, it no longer exists. But by the age of 1½, when the concept of object permanence is fully developed, toddlers can imagine where to search for an object hidden in their presence, even though the object itself may have been covered from their sight as it was being hidden.

5. In the second year, toddlers find new ways to achieve their goals, first by actively experimenting with physical objects, and then, toward the end of the second year, by manipulating mental images of objects and actions that are not in view.

6. Although recent research confirms Piaget's general description of the stages of human development, some researchers tend to place more emphasis on individual differences and a gradual, rather than sudden, progression from one stage to another. With regard to the sensorimotor stage of development, Piaget's emphasis on skills requiring motor abilities may not have revealed the full extent of the infant's sensory capacities.

"The American Question"

7. Experiments in learning have proven that infants can be taught tasks that involve abilities they already have. Enriched environments and activities can improve the cognitive skills of deprived infants. For normal infants, the learning experiences available in the home are usually sufficient, and too much stimulation may be detrimental. Accomplishments achieved at an earlier than average age are no guarantee that performance will continue to be above average in later years.

Language Development

8. According to Skinner, children learn language through reinforcement and association. Chomsky believes children have an inborn ability to understand and use the basic structure of language. Each culture teaches its children the particular structures, such as vocabulary and grammar, of its own language.

9. Language skills begin to develop at birth, as babies communicate with noises and gestures, and practice babbling. Infants say a few words by the end of the first year, and they understand more words than they speak. By age two, most toddlers can combine two words to make a simple sentence.

10. Children vary in how rapidly they learn vocabulary, as well as in the way they use words. In the first two years, the child's comprehension of simple words and gestures, and willingness and ability to communicate are more significant than the size of the child's vocabulary.

11. Language learning is the result of the interaction between parent and child. The child is primed to learn language, and adults all over the world communicate with children using a simplified form of language called baby talk, which suits the child's abilities to understand and repeat.

KEY TERMS

cognition *(176)*

sensorimotor intelligence *(178)*

circular reaction *(179)*

primary circular reaction *(180)*

secondary circular reaction *(180)*

object permanence *(181)*

tertiary circular reaction *(184)*

mental combinations *(185)*

representation *(186)*

deferred imitation *(186)*

deep structure *(196)*

surface structure *(196)*

language acquisition device (LAD) *(196)*

pleasure smile *(198)*

cooing *(198)*

babbling *(198)*

overextension *(202)*

baby talk *(204)*

KEY QUESTIONS

1. What is the major controversy about cognitive development in infancy?

2. According to Piaget, what is the basic characteristic of infant thought?

3. Give an example of a circular reaction.

4. Between the ages of 6 and 18 months, what changes occur in the infant's understanding of objects that are out of sight?

5. Why did Piaget refer to the 1-year-old as "the little scientist"?

6. What cognitive developments make it possible for the toddler to pretend?

7. What have recent researchers, following Piaget, contributed to our understanding of the infant's perceptual and cognitive abilities?

8. What kinds of behaviors can be conditioned during infancy?

9. Which babies benefit most from cognitive enrichment programs?

10. What are the differences between Skinner's and Chomsky's theories of language development?

11. In what way do children's first words reflect their stage of cognitive development?

12. How would one evaluate the language development of a child under the age of two?

13. How do the special features of baby talk make it possible for parents and children to communicate with each other?

RECOMMENDED READINGS

Kaye, Kenneth. *The mental and social life of babies: How parents create persons.* Chicago: University of Chicago Press, 1984.

A leading researcher in infant cognition puts infant cognitive development into perspective. He explains that parents create the framework that allows infants to construct their knowledge of their world, pointing out that the parents are not only the senior partners, but also the ones who may cast the deciding vote about how a child will develop.

Piaget, Jean. *The origins of intelligence in children.* New York: International Universities Press, 1966.

Piaget is never easy to read, not even for psychologists who specialize in cognition. But his ideas provide the context for most contemporary notions of cognitive development in childhood, so the effort to understand him may be worth it. This book of 419 pages is entirely about the six stages of sensorimotor intelligence. It includes many examples taken from Piaget's experiences with his three children.

White, Burton. *The first three years of life.* 2nd ed. Englewood Cliffs, N.J.: Prentice-Hall, 1985.

White tries to apply research on infant cognitive development to the practical business of raising an infant. He gives suggestions for toys and games that babies like in the first three years of life. This book tends to be repetitive, but has many useful suggestions nonetheless.

Beck, Joan. *How to raise a brighter child.* New York: Pocket Books, 1984.

Ilg, Francis L. and Ames, Louise B. *Child behavior.* Revised ed. New York: Harper and Row, 1982.

These two books should be read together, for they provide quite different viewpoints about the parents' role in infant and child development. The Beck book gives dozens of suggestions for accelerating a young child's intellectual development, promising to increase IQ 20 points or more. By contrast, Ilg and Ames, who worked closely with Arnold Gesell and the Gesell Institute, advise letting infants and children develop at their own pace, and speak out in favor of letting older children repeat a grade, especially if they had been pushed too rapidly in early childhood. Together, these books present both sides of the debate about whether parents are more likely to overstimulate or understimulate their children.

The First Two Years: Psychosocial Development

Chapter 8

Babies control and bring up their families as much as they are controlled by them; in fact, we may say that the family brings up a baby by being brought up by him.

Erik Erikson
Childhood and Society

I waited so long to have my baby, and when she came, she never did anything for me.

Mother of severely abused 4-year-old girl
The Battered Child

Emotional Development
The First Half Year
8 Months to 2 Years

Personality Development
Traditional Views: The Omnipotent Mother
Freud: Oral and Anal Stages
Erikson: Trust and Autonomy
Mahler: Symbiosis and Separation-Individuation
Temperament

Parent-Infant Interaction
The Beginning of the First Year: Synchrony
The End of the First Year: Attachment
The Second Year: Caring for Toddlers

Child Abuse and Neglect
Causes of Child Abuse and Neglect
Treatment and Prevention

Chapter 8

The emotional life of the developing person begins very early, earlier even than many researchers had believed. In the first month, in fact, infants can express a number of emotions and can, in turn, respond to the moods, emotions, and attentions of others. One reason these communications are so readily exchanged is that we seem to be born with a capacity for a universal language of emotional expression—a basic understanding of the meaning of each other's smiles, tears, and quizzical glances. Which other aspects of our personalities are we born with and which develop as we mature and interact with others? This question and the ones that follow reflect some of the topics that will be examined in Chapter 8.

How does the infant's increasing sense of self-awareness affect his or her relationships with others?

What factors are important in helping a child to develop a sense of trust?

What are the implications of an infant's attachment, or lack of attachment, to his or her mother?

What are the differences in ways mothers and fathers play with their infants, and what is the effect of these differences?

What are the characteristics of the child, the parents, and society that lead to an increased risk of child abuse?

As you remember from Chapter 1, psychosocial development includes not only factors that are usually considered characteristic of the individual's psyche, such as emotional expression, self-awareness, and temperament, but also factors that are clearly social, such as the parents' relationship to their offspring, or the culture's impact on the child. Although each of these factors is, of necessity, examined separately, it is in actuality impossible to separate the development and workings of the individual psyche from the social world in which it operates. Thus, as you make your way through this initial chapter on psychosocial development, keep in mind that the development is interactive and holistic, even while we study it topic by topic.

Emotional Development

It was once thought that young infants did not have real emotions. True, they cry when they are hungry and, beginning at about 6 weeks, smile when they see a face peering at them, but these reactions were thought to be simple reflexes or primitive urges not truly related to the emotions felt by older children or adults.

Recently, however, researchers, inspired in part by the surprising discoveries (described in chapters 6 and 7) concerning infant perception and cognition, have taken a new look at infant emotions. They have discovered that even very young infants may well express, and respond to, many emotions—including joy, surprise, anger, fear, disgust, interest, and sadness (Campos et al., 1983). Indeed, it seems as if there is a developmental "schedule" by which infants acquire the capacity for specific emotions.

The First Half Year

One of the first emotions that can be discerned in infants is fear. When infants a few days or even a few hours old hear a loud noise or feel a sudden loss of support, or see an object looming toward them, they often cry and look surprised and afraid (Sroufe, 1979; Izard, 1978). Slightly older babies have more pronounced fear reactions, and also seem angry at times, as when, for instance, they are forcibly prevented from moving (Stenberg and Campos, 1983).

Sadness, or at least a sensitivity to it, is also apparent early in infancy. In an experiment in which mothers of infants between 1 month and 3 months old were told to look sad and act depressed, their infants responded by looking away and fussing (Tronick et al., 1978; Cohn and Tronick, 1983). More explicit findings were provided by an experiment in which the facial expressions of a 3-month-old girl who had been severely abused were filmed and later shown to "blind" judges for assessment: without knowing anything about her condition, the judges rated her as undeniably sad (Gaensbauer, 1980).

Infants express their emotions vocally as well as physically. At least two emotional cries can be distinguished from the basic hunger cry, which consists of a repeating pattern of a short cry, a brief pause, an intake of breath, and then another short cry. One of these cries, longer and louder than the hunger cry, with a longer pause between sounds, signifies pain; another, similar to the hunger cry in timing, but noticeably louder, signifies anger (Wolff, 1969). When new mothers of various cultural backgrounds listened to prerecorded infant cries, they were quite able to distinguish among them (Zeskind, 1983). Fathers also can hear the differences in infants' cries (Boukydis and Burgess, 1982), as can nonparents of both sexes (Zeskind et al., 1985).

What about the more positive emotions in early infancy? Newborns show the wide-eyed look of interest and surprise, and the accompanying slow-down of heart rate, when something catches their attention (Field, 1982). Smiles also begin early: a half-smile at a pleasant noise or a full stomach appears in the first days of life; a **social smile**—a smile in response to someone else—begins to appear at about 6 weeks (Emde and Harmon, 1972). By 3 or 4 months, smiles become broader, and babies laugh rather than grin if something is particularly pleasing.

This research corroborates reports from the people who perhaps should know young infants best: their mothers. When mothers were asked if their 1-month-old babies expressed any emotions, they said yes, and listed them: 99 percent said their 1-month-olds expressed interest, 95 percent said joy, 84 percent anger, 74 percent surprise, 58 percent fear, and 34 percent sadness (Johnson et al., 1982).

Since infants cannot tell us what they are feeling, however, you may be wondering whether parents and researchers are possibly fooling themselves, seeing emotions that are not actually there. At least one leading investigator believes that parents generally read more into a baby's actions and expressions than the baby actually feels (Kaye, 1982), and several researchers think that, while precursors of some emotions may be present at birth, a certain amount of experience and cognitive development is required before true emotions, including fear and happiness, can be expressed (Izard, 1978; Sroufe, 1979).

However, scientists who, with the help of videotapes, have systematically studied infant facial expressions have been struck by the similarity between certain infant expressions and those that signal specific emotions in adults (see Research Report). When clear, validated signs of an emotion accompany a situation in which that emotion would be appropriate—when a newborn looks fearful at a sudden loud noise, or when a 4-month-old looks angry when prevented from moving—it

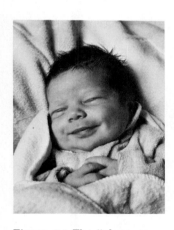

Figure 8.1 *The "pleasure smile" of this sleeping infant is probably an inborn response to the satisfactions of a full stomach and a smoothly functioning digestive system, just as most of the early cries are automatic responses to hunger or indigestion.*

RESEARCH REPORT   **Measuring Emotion**

The measurement of emotions in infants is, obviously, a difficult task. Since babies can't say what it is they are feeling, researchers have had to rely on their own subjective interpretations of infants' behaviors and expressions—a task equivalent to your deciding whether the infant in the picture below is expressing anger, fear, sadness, or some other emotion. However, researchers

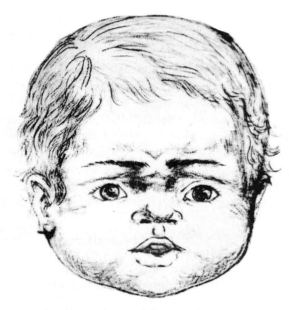

Can you tell which emotion this infant is expressing?

have discovered that, in fact, many facial expressions are universally understood: people from one society are able to look at photographs of people from quite distinct and distant societies and recognize expressions of anger, joy, sadness, disgust, surprise, and fear (Ekman et al., 1969; Izard, 1971). Further, there is a strong tendency for facial expressions to be significantly correlated with physiological, situational, and verbal signs of emotion. Despite obvious cultural differences, the facial clues of the common basic emotions are similar throughout the world.

This implies that basic emotional expression is, at least in part, innate: there is "a prewired communication process, a process now known to require no social learning either for the reception . . . or production . . . of at least some facial and gestural signals (Campos et al., 1983).

The discovery of the universality of many facial expressions led scientists to search for ways to achieve an objective analysis of emotional expressions, free of

cultural biases. One approach led to the systematic categorization of facial positions that signal specific emotions. For example, in one system called MAX (Izard, 1980), twenty-seven distinct positions of the facial features are described. Some of these are listed in the table that follows.

Maximally Discriminative Facial Movements (MAX) Codes

Brows (B); (Forehead [F]; Nasal root [N])
20. *B:* Raised in arched or normal shape. (*F:* Long transverse furrows or thickening; *N:* Narrowed.)
21. *B:* One brow raised higher than other (other one may be slightly lowered).
22. *B:* Raised; drawn together, straight or normal shape. (*F:* Short transverse furrows or thickening in mid-region; *N:* Narrowed.)
23. *B:* Inner corners raised; shape under inner corner. (*F:* Bulge or furrows in center above brow corners; *N:* Narrowed.)

Eyes/Nose/Cheeks
30. Enlarged, roundish appearance of eye region owing to tissue between upper lid and brow being stretched (upper eye furrow may be visible); upper eyelids not raised.
31. Eye fissure widened, upper lid raised (white shows more than normal).
33. Narrowed or squinted (by action of eye sphincters or brow depressors).
36. Gaze downward, askance.
38. Cheeks raised.

Mouth/Lips
50. Opened, roundish or oval.
51. Opened, relaxed.
52. Corners pulled back and slightly up (open or closed).
53. Opened, tense, corners retracted straight back.
54. Angular, squarish (open).

Looking at a videotape, advanced frame by frame, or examining a photograph, the scientist can note which of the twenty-seven positions are present and compare them to a numbered list of facial positions. Various combinations of these positions reveal specific emotions. Thus 20 + 30 + 50 is surprise; 21 + 31 + 53 is fear; 38 + 52 is happiness, and so on. An even more comprehensive system, called FACS, scores fifty-eight possible facial and head movements (Eckman and Frieson, 1976, 1978) and has been adopted for the special facial characteristics (e.g., the sucking lip) of the very young infant (Oster, 1982).

These research tools have advanced the study of infant emotion in the past decade, for researchers now have an objective way to determine what a particular infant expresses. They would know, for instance, that the infant in the picture here is actually experiencing interest and excitement.

seems reasonable to conclude that the emotion is, in fact, being expressed. In addition, although the primary focus of this research has been on facial expressions, it has also involved the study of other emotional indicators such as gestures, vocal expressions, changes in heart rate. It now seems clear that, while exact ages for the appearance of specific emotions are still a matter of debate, infants have a richer emotional life, at younger ages, than anyone suspected a decade ago.

8 Months to 2 Years

At about 8 months, infants' emotions become much stronger, more varied, and distinct. For example, many new experiences produce fear. In fact, if you were to graph the fears of infancy, the shape of the graph would be an upside-down U (Kagan, 1983). Fears are low in early infancy, begin to rise sharply toward the end of the first year, and then decline as the second birthday approaches.

One fear, **fear of strangers** (also called stranger anxiety), is universal. This emotion is first noticeable at about 6 months and becomes full-blown by 12 months, when every normal infant is at least wary of strangers, and many quite normal infants seem terrified, hiding and crying, when an unfamiliar person comes too close. A related emotion is **separation anxiety,** the fear of being left by mother or other care-giver. Like other fears, separation anxiety emerges at about 8 or 9 months, peaks at about 14 months, and then gradually subsides (Weinraub and Lewis, 1979).

Figure 8.2 *This mother may, at first, be puzzled, or even embarrassed by her child's response to the kind stranger. However, at this stage, this infant's behavior is simply a sign that she understands the difference between the familiar and the unusual.*

As at any age, specific conditions affect the intensity of an infant's emotion (Smith, 1979). Thus, fear of strangers is weak if the infant is in a familiar place and with a familiar person; absent if the stranger is a child; and strong if the stranger behaves strangely (by making scary noises, for example, or by suddenly moving within inches of the baby's face). The stranger's appearance is important, too: babies are less wary of midgets than of taller adults (Brooks and Lewis, 1976), and more wary of strangers with thick glasses or large, unusual hats.

As every parent knows, anger is another emotion that becomes much more common in toddlerhood. When videotapes of infants being inoculated between 2 and 19 months were categorized by "blind" raters who could see only the children's faces, ratings of anger increased dramatically between 8 and 19 months. In addition, the duration of anger increased, from a fleeting expression in early infancy to a lengthy demonstration at 19 months (Izard et al., 1983).

Finally, as infants become older, they smile and laugh more quickly, and more selectively (Lewis and Michalson, 1983). For instance, the sight of almost any human face produces a stare and then a smile in the typical 3-month-old, but the typical 9-month-old may grin immediately at the sight of certain faces—and might remain impassive or burst into tears at the sight of certain others.

Despite this increased selectivity of older infants, their happy expressions are more frequent than those of younger infants, because more things make them happy. For instance, toddlers smile at unusual sights, such as Daddy crawling on the floor or Mommy wearing a funny hat. These experiences are funny because they are somewhat familiar as well as somewhat surprising; if the experience becomes too different (Daddy making loud scary noises and threatening gestures while he is crawling, for instance), the laughter might turn to tears.

At about 8 months, babies become likely to laugh in anticipation of an enjoyable experience (Sroufe and Waters, 1976), as well as in reaction to one. Thus, while younger babies laugh when their stomachs are being kissed or when they are splashing in the bath, older babies begin to squeal in delight as their mother's lips approach their naked bellies, or as the water begins to fill the bath.

Finally, when infants play with other infants, their play is likelier to be more emotional—with more joy as well as more anger—as they mature (Hartup, 1983).

Emotion and Cognition What might explain this intensification of emotional development that causes the infant under 6 months to be quite a different creature from the toddler at 12 months or more? Since several emotional shifts occur at about 8 months, which is the same time that a new cognitive stage and new memory abilities appear (see Chapter 7), the emotional changes may be the result of a "cognitive metamorphosis" (Zelazo, 1979). In other words, being able to think and remember in a much more mature way, the infant can recognize more reasons to be happy or afraid, and be quicker to anger or sorrow (Sroufe, 1979).

Self-Awareness In addition, one of the most important cognitive features of later infancy is the development of a certain measure of **self-awareness.** The emerging sense of "me and mine" makes possible many new emotions, including shame, guilt, jealousy, and pride (Campos et al., 1983). At the same time, a sense of self allows a new awareness of others, and hence allows defiance and true affection (Sroufe, 1979).

The sense of self emerges gradually over the first two years. In the first month, infants have no awareness of their bodies as theirs. To them, for example, their hands are interesting objects that appear and disappear: 2-month-olds, in effect, "discover" their hands each time they catch sight of them, become fascinated with their movements, then "lose" them as they slip out of view. Even 8-month-olds often don't seem to know where their bodies end and someone else's body begins, as can be seen when a child at this age grabs a toy in another child's hand and reacts with surprise when the toy "resists." By age 1, however, most infants would be quite aware that the other child is a distinct person, whom they might well hit if the coveted toy is not immediately forthcoming.

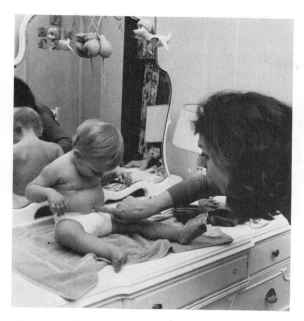 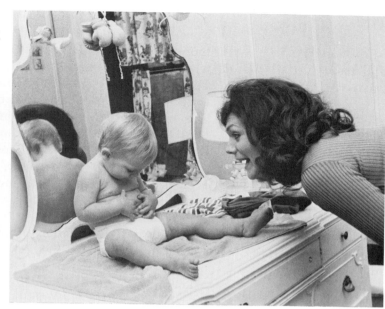

Figure 8.3 *Fingers and toes may already be old hat for this infant; however, increasing self-awareness allows him to make a surprising new discovery—his "belly button."*

Evidence of the emerging sense of self was shown in an experiment in which babies looked in a mirror after a dot of rouge had been surreptitiously put on their noses (Lewis and Brooks, 1978). If the babies reacted to the mirror image by touching their noses, it was clear that they knew they were seeing their own faces. After trying this experiment with ninety-six babies between the ages of 9 and 24 months, the experimenters found a distinct developmental shift. None of the babies under a year reacted to the mark, whereas most of those between 12 and 24 months did.

Figure 8.4 *Mirror images make young infants smile and try to touch "the baby." It is not until about 18 months that children realize that they are looking at themselves.*

This increased self-awareness is also apparent in looking at the toddler's emotions. The infamous toddler temper develops partly because, as children become more aware of themselves, they become more conscious of being thwarted or hurt, as well as more aware of their ability to thwart others. For instance, one observational study found that conflict between mothers and their toddlers increased over the second year from an average of three per hour at 14 months to six per hour at 24 months. Moreover, many of these conflicts were provoked by the child; and, as the toddlers grew older, their reaction was more self-assertive: in comparison to when they were 14 months old, toddlers at 18 months were four times as likely to express anger, and three times as likely to laugh, when their mothers attempted to remonstrate with them. By 24 months, they were eight times more likely to get angry and four times more likely to laugh (Dunn and Munn, 1985).

Likewise, the emotions of pride and shame depend on self-concept, which is probably why these emotions do not appear until toddlerhood (Campos et al., 1983). Once they emerge, these emotions are more apparent than they are later in life, because toddlers have not yet learned to hide their feelings. Consider these two examples. One toddler in nursery school learns how to put on his snow jacket by laying it open on the floor, putting his arms through the sleeves, and then flipping it over his head. He is so proud that he insists on donning his jacket every time he leaves the house, even when winter is long over. Another toddler enjoys picking up the phone whenever it rings, but is forbidden to because, instead of speaking, she merely listens while the caller keeps repeating "Hello?" The prohibition stops her—except when she thinks she is alone. Then she picks the receiver up, listens, and slams it down shamefacedly when someone enters the room!

As these examples show, self-awareness and self-concept are related to the reactions of others to oneself, an important insight in understanding personality development. In fact, infants at about 1 year become much more attentive to the emotions of others, using them as a guide to their own self-expression, as is clearly shown in the Closer Look on the following page.

Personality Development

Now that we have seen how emotional capacities develop during infancy, the next question is, How do the infant's emotional responses begin to take on the various patterns that form personality. What happens to evoke or create emotions, personality traits, and social skills during infancy, so that, by age 2 (if not before), the child is a distinct individual?

Traditional Views: The Omnipotent Mother

In the first half of the twentieth century, when psychologists first turned their attention to childhood, they stressed the crucial importance of the mother, who, they believed, created the child's personality through her manner of child-rearing. In their view, the infant was a passive, particularly vulnerable recipient of the mother's ministrations, shaped almost entirely by the mother's powerful influence.

This view was popularized by a host of child-advice books, one of which was, in typical fashion, "Dedicated to all Mothers in Whom lies the power to Create a Healthier and Happier World" (Schick and Rosenson, 1932). Another, written by the

A CLOSER LOOK   **Overcoming Fears and Hiding Tears**

The importance of parental reactions is illustrated by one research example. As you know, at about 8 months of age, infants become afraid of a visual cliff, refusing to crawl over the precipice even when their mothers urge them on. This is an example of an innate fear that manifests itself after a certain amount of maturation—no matter what the infant's particular experiences, or temperament, or parental reaction.

However, recently a team of researchers (Sorce et al., 1985) decided to test the importance of the parent's reaction in an ambiguous situation, specifically when the visual cliff was only 30 centimeters deep (about 12 inches) and the allure of a musical toy made crawling over the cliff quite attractive. Typically, 12-month-old infants would crawl near the edge of the cliff and hesitate, looking at their mothers. At this point, the mothers were instructed to give one of the following facial signals—happiness, fear, interest, anger, or sadness. With the most relevant of these cues, the results were quite striking: most of the infants who saw joy or interest on their mother's face crossed over the visual cliff to the toy, while none of the infants who saw fear did. Obviously, these 12-month-old infants could and did learn how to react by observing their mother's reactions.

An experiment with a similar purpose showed that whether unfamiliar toys became scary or interesting to infants depended on their mother's apparent reaction to them (Gunnar and Stone, 1984).

As infants become more experienced with the reactions of others, they learn to modify their own expressions of emotions. This is most clearly seen with regard to crying. While every newborn cries in pain, some toddlers virtually always cry, some seldom cry, and some cry only when they see blood or a sympathetic adult. An amusing example of this is 20-month-old Lucy, who was playing quietly in her backyard, while her mother watched from inside.

Lucy runs to get a toy at the far end of the yard. She falls on her knees and starts to cry. Immediately, she looks up and sees that no one is paying any attention. She stops crying and walks to the back door of the house. As she approaches the door, she starts to cry again. [Lewis and Michalson, 1983]

Similarly, as children grow older, they learn when to modify their expression of all the various emotions, hiding their fear in one situation and their sadness in another, with boys particularly being taught to be brave and tearless. It is probably not too much of an exaggeration to say that whereas researchers once thought that parents taught their children how to express emotions, they now think it is more likely that parents teach infants how not to express them.

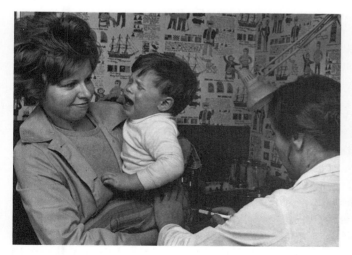

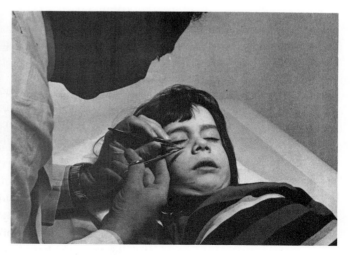

Despite his mother's reassuring smile, the toddler on the left registers a definitive protest upon receiving a "shot" in the buttocks. However, by the time he reaches middle childhood, it is likely that he will have internalized his parents' and his culture's message that good children don't cry. The boy on the right doesn't flinch as stitches are removed from the sensitive area beneath his eye.

director of the Bureau of Child Health of New York, explained that "Father and mother must realize it is largely within their power to determine whether or not a child will be nervous or calm and well poised" (Baker, 1923).

The idea of the "created" personality was endorsed by the leading behaviorist of the times, John Watson, who trumpeted:

> Give me a dozen healthy infants, well-formed, and my own specific world to bring them up in, and I'll guarantee to take any one at random and train him to become any type of specialist I might select—doctor, lawyer, artist, merchant-chief and, yes, even beggar-man and thief . . . [Watson, 1925].

So certain was Watson of the parents' central influence in shaping the child that he cautioned:

> failure to bring up a happy child, a well-adjusted child—assuming bodily health—falls squarely upon the parents' shoulders. [By the time the child is 3] parents have already determined . . . whether . . . [the child] is to grow into a happy person, wholesome and good-natured, whether he is to be a whining, complaining, neurotic, an anger-driven, vindictive, over-bearing slave driver, or one whose every move in life is definitely controlled by fear. [Watson, 1928]

Like Watson, Sigmund Freud stressed the early years, and the influence of the mother (Kagan, 1979). He felt that the experiences of the first four years of life "play a decisive part in determining whether and at what point the individual shall fail to master the real problems of life" (Freud, 1963, originally published in 1918). He also thought that the child's relationship with the mother was "unique, without parallel, established unalterably for a whole lifetime as the first and strongest love-object and as the prototype of all later love-relations" (Freud, 1947, 1964).

While Watson's pronouncements had substantial influence at the time, Freud's psychoanalytic view of the mother's role had a far longer lasting impact, in part because it was a central feature of his comprehensive view of personality development. Even today, to understand most theories of infancy, one must be familiar with Freud's basic ideas.

Freud: Oral and Anal Stages

As we noted in Chapter 2, Freud viewed human development in terms of psychosexual stages that occur at specific ages. According to Freud (1935, 1960), development begins with the **oral stage**, so named because in the first year of life the mouth is the infant's prime source of gratification. Not only is the mouth the instrument for attaining nourishment, it is also the main source of pleasure: sucking, especially at the mother's breast, is a joyous, sensual activity for babies. Thus Freud viewed the mother's attitudes and actions in feeding her infant, and the timing of weaning, as a crucial part of the infant's psychological development.

In the second year, Freud maintained, the infant's prime focus of gratification becomes the anus, particularly the pleasure taken in stimulation of the bowels. Accordingly, Freud referred to this period as the **anal stage**. This change is more than a simple shift of locus; it is a shift in the mode of interaction, from the passive, dependent mode of orality to the expulsive mode of anality in which the child has some control, and hence some power.

According to Freud, both these stages are frought with potential conflict for the infant, conflict that can have long-term consequences. If mothers frustrate their infants' urge to suck—by making nursing a hurried, tense event, or by weaning the infant from the nipple too early, or by continually preventing the child from sucking on fingers, toes, and other objects—those infants will become adults who are "fixated," or stuck, at the oral stage, excessively eating, drinking, chewing, biting, smoking, or talking in quest of the oral satisfaction denied them in infancy. Further, in adulthood, oral types may tend to be generous, disorganized, and habitually late; that is, they act "babyish" so someone will "mother" them. Or they may deny these tendencies by adopting an overly tough, independent stance with others, gratifying their oral tendencies by sarcastically biting people's heads off.

Similarly, if toilet training is overly strict or premature (occurring before the age of 1½ or 2, when children are physiologically ready, as well as psychologically mature enough to participate in the toilet-training process), it will produce adults who have "anal" personalities. They will be either anally retentive—overemphasizing neatness, cleanliness, precision, and punctuality—or they will be anally expulsive, exhibiting messiness and disorganization in nearly all matters. People with anal retentive personality structures are said to have difficulty relaxing and are overcautious about meeting new people or participating in new experiences. Often, when they do abandon their caution, they overreact, becoming excessively emotional, perhaps in an explosive temper. Further, in certain cases Freud traced severe psychological disturbances to the infant's early oral and anal experiences (Freud, 1963, originally published in 1918).

Although Freud's ideas concerning orality and anality have been extremely influential, research has failed to support the linking of specific conflicts during these stages to later personality traits. Rather, it has shown that the parents' overall pattern of warmth and attention is much more important to the child's emotional development than the particulars of either feeding and weaning or toilet training (Caldwell, 1964; Martin, 1975). This broader perspective is reflected in the theories of Erik Erikson and Margaret Mahler, two contemporary psychoanalytic theorists who have studied infancy.

Erikson: Trust and Autonomy

As you will remember from Chapter 2, Erik Erikson is one of the best known of the neo-Freudians, that is, theorists who have modified many of Freud's insights to create their own version of psychoanalytic theory. Rather than emphasizing the specific events of the oral and anal stages, Erikson focuses on the overall patterns of child-rearing during this period.

According to Erikson, development occurs through a series of basic conflicts throughout the life span (see Chapter 2). The basic conflict of infancy centers not on experiences related to oral gratification per se but on the larger pattern of interaction of which these experiences are a part (Erikson, 1963). In Erikson's terms, the conflict of infancy is one of **trust versus mistrust.** Babies learn to trust their world if they are kept well-fed, warm, and dry significantly more often than they are left hungry, cold, and wet.

In taking this broader perspective, Erikson contends that babies begin to develop a secure sense of self when their mothers provide a "consistency, continuity, and sameness of experience," so they learn to know that their needs will be met along predictable and benevolent lines. Like Freud, Erikson believes that the mother should usually be the primary care-giver. However, he notes that mothers from different cultures raise children differently, and therefore he shies away from any specific rules of what the mother should or should not do. He explains that "the amount of trust derived from earliest infantile experience does not seem to depend on absolute quantities of food or demonstrations of love, but rather on the quality of the maternal relationship."

Similarly, Erikson's view of toddlerhood places the idea of anality in the broad context of the conflict of **autonomy versus shame and doubt.** Toddlers want to rule their own actions and bodies. If they fail in their efforts to do so, because their care-givers are too restrictive and forbidding, they come to feel shame and to doubt their abilities.

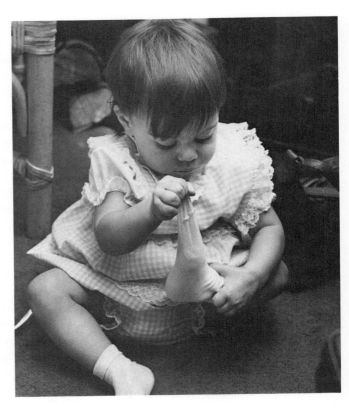

Figure 8.5 *The toddler's growing independence can be a mixed blessing. The girl in this photo may be starting to get herself ready for bed. On the other hand, it is equally likely that her mother has just finished dressing her.*

For many toddlers, the struggle for autonomy does, in fact, center around toilet training, and Erikson believes that some mothers instill shame and self-doubt in the child who defecates at the wrong time and place. But Erikson notes that as toddlers' increasing mobility allows them to move from safe, boring experiences toward more exciting and potentially dangerous ones, they encounter many other kinds of conflict that lead to the development of self-confidence or doubt. In all the conflicts of toddlerhood, Erikson (1963) agrees with Freud that parents should not be too strict, but he also warns against permissiveness:

> Firmness must protect him [the toddler] against the potential anarchy of his as yet untrained sense of discrimination, his inability to hold on and let go with discretion. As his environment encourages him to "stand on his own feet," it must protect him against meaningless and arbitrary experiences of shame and of early doubt. [Erikson, 1963]

Like Freud, Erikson believes that problems arising in early infancy can last a lifetime. The adult who is suspicious and pessimistic, or who always seems burdened by self-doubt, was an infant who did not develop sufficient trust, or a toddler who did not achieve sufficient autonomy.

Mahler: Symbiosis and Separation-Individuation

The most influential recent re-formation of psychoanalytic theory comes from Margaret Mahler (Mahler, 1968, Mahler et al., 1975). She focuses explicitly on the relationship between the infant and the mother, a relationship that changes as the infant matures.

In Mahler's view, the first weeks of a baby's life are so dominated by primitive needs for food and sleep that most other experiences are filtered out. "The infant spends most of his day in a half-sleeping, half-waking state . . . protected against extremes of stimulation, in a situation approximating the prenatal state . . ." This stage is called "normal autism," because infants are so self-absorbed that they are unaware that anyone else exists in the world, caring for them.

Then, from about 2 months on, the infant enters a period of **symbiosis,** during which dependence on the mother is so strong, and motor skills and intellectual abilities so immature, that the infant feels literally part of the mother. This fusion with the mother is a prerequisite for the later development of the sense of self, according to Mahler. The infant's dependence on the mother forms a secure foundation for later exploration and independence.

Obviously, then, the mother's responses to the infant are crucial to the development of a secure symbiotic stage. Following Freud's lead, Mahler believes that the feeding process is significant during this period, especially the way the mother holds the baby. The infant who is cradled and comforted while sucking on the breast or bottle will have a much more satisfying symbiotic stage than the infant who is held rigidly, or worse, not held at all (Mahler et al., 1975).

Separation-Individuation   At about 5 months, a new period begins that lasts until about age 3. This is **separation-individuation,** when the infant gradually develops a sense of self, apart from the mother. Mahler refers to this as the time of "psychological birth," when babies break out of the "protective membrane" that had enclosed them and "hatch" by crawling or walking away from mother.

During this period, according to Mahler, infants show that they are very much dependent on their mothers even as they show their desire for independence. In the early phases, "all infants like to venture and stay just a bit of a distance away from the enveloping arms of the mother; as soon as they are motorically able to, they like to slide down from mother's lap, but they tend to remain or to crawl back and play as close as possible to mother's feet" (Mahler et al., 1975). Even when they are literally out of touch with their mothers, they repeatedly look back. Thus eye contact replaces the physical contact sought by the younger infant.

Between 15 and 22 months, toddlers attempt greater psychological separation from their mothers, and then become frightened at how independent they have become, perhaps regressing to a period of babyish clinging. Because they are caught between two opposite needs, toddlers can be moody, showing sorrow and dependence, or anger and aggression. Even well-adjusted toddlers show their ambivalence by darting away hoping to be chased, or following their mother around, hoping to be noticed. Ideally, the mother will recognize the toddler's need for both independence and dependence, allowing a measure of freedom as well as comforting reassurance when it is needed.

Figure 8.6 *One difficult question that parents of toddlers must face is how to encourage exploration while setting reasonable limits.*

Like Freud and Erikson, Mahler (1968) believes that each stage of development is important for later psychological health. Indeed, Mahler thinks severe mental illness results directly from maladaptive mothering in the first six months of life. The resolution of the separation-individuation stage also has lasting implications: adults who avoid intimacy, or fear independence, may still be trying to resolve the tension of separation-individuation and achieve a proper sense of self.

Thus, as you have seen, instead of an exclusive emphasis on feeding and toilet training, Erikson and Mahler recognize the need for a much broader view of parental behavior than Freud did. They also note that the older infant has a role in his or her own development, seeking autonomy or separation-individuation.

However, many researchers (e.g., Kagan, 1978; Campos et al., 1983; Snyder, 1978; Horner, 1985) believe that, like Freud, contemporary psychoanalysts overemphasize the mother's exclusive relationship with her baby, particularly with regard to her power to shape the infant's development. According to these critics, Freud's followers portray young infants as far more passive and susceptible to the mother's influence than they actually are. This view of infants runs counter to the evidence for early perception and cognition, and, as you soon will see, to evidence that newborns come into the world already possessing strong personality traits that will endure no matter what their parents do.

Temperament

As psychologists use the term, **temperament** refers to a person's characteristic emotions, moods, and responses. As we have just seen, the underlying assumption of many early child-care specialists was that temperament develops as a result of the parents' attitudes toward, and behavior with, the child. This led, quite logically, to a readiness to blame the mother for any personality problem or character fault a child might have. An alternative explanation has been sought by researchers who have looked for temperamental characteristics that are inherited, and consequently present at birth.

The most famous and extensive longitudinal study of innate temperament is called the New York Longitudinal Study (NYLS), conducted by Alexander Thomas, Stella Chess, and Herbert Birch. According to their initial findings (1963), babies in the first days and months of life differ in nine personality characteristics:

1. *Activity level.* Some babies are active. They kick a lot in the uterus before they are born, they move around in their basinettes, and as toddlers, they always run. Other babies are much less active.

2. *Rhythmicity.* Some babies have regular cycles of activity. They eat, sleep, and defecate on schedule almost from birth. Other babies are much less predictable.

3. *Approach-withdrawal.* Some babies delight in everything new; others withdraw from every new situation. The first bath makes some babies laugh and others cry; the first spoonful of cereal is gobbled up by one baby and spit out by the next.

4. *Adaptability.* Some babies adjust quickly to change; others are unhappy at every disruption of their normal routine.

5. *Intensity of reaction.* Some babies chortle when they laugh and howl when they cry. Others are much calmer, responding with a smile or a whimper.

6. *Threshold of responsiveness.* Some babies seem to sense every sight, sound, and touch. For instance, they waken at a slight noise, or turn away from a distant light. Others seem unaware even of bright lights, loud street noises, or wet diapers.

7. *Quality of mood.* Some babies seem constantly happy, smiling at almost everything. Others seem chronically unhappy: they are ready to complain at any moment.

8. *Distractibility.* All babies fuss when they are hungry, but some will stop fussing if someone gives them a pacifier or sings them a song, while others keep complaining until they are fed. Similarly, when babies spot an attractive but dangerous object and reach for it, some of them can be distracted by another, safer object while others are more single-minded.

9. *Attention span.* Some babies play happily with one toy for a long time. Others quickly drop one activity for another.

Thomas and Chess (1977) believe that "temperamental individuality is well established by the time the infant is two to three months old," before the parents could affect personality much. In terms of various combinations of personality traits, most young infants can be described as one of three types: *easy* (about 40 percent), *slow-to-warm-up* (about 15 percent), and *difficult* (about 10 percent).

In a series of follow-up studies carried into adolescence (Thomas et al., 1968; Thomas and Chess, 1977; Carey and McDevitt, 1978), temperamental characteristics showed some stability. Thus, the easy baby remains a relatively easy child, while the difficult one is more likely to give his or her parents problems. Similarly, the slow-to-warm-up infant who cried on seeing strangers at 8 months may well hide behind mother's skirt on arriving at nursery school and avoid the crowd in the halls of junior high.

This does not mean that temperament remains exactly the same throughout life. Indeed, some of the NYLS characteristics are not particularly stable. Rhythmicity and quality of mood, for instance, are quite variable, meaning that the infant who has been taking naps on schedule might not do so a few months later, and the baby who has seemed consistently happy might become a malcontent if life circumstances change. The age of the child is also important. In the first few years, stability is more evident from month to month than from year to year (Peters-Martin and Wachs, 1984; Bronson, 1985).

Other Research   However, other researchers using a variety of measures, settings, and statistical tests agree that certain temperamental characteristics are apparent in the first months of life, and remain quite stable as the child gets older (Rothbart

Figure 8.7 *At any age, differences in temperament can make one person's treat another person's trauma.*

and Derryberry, 1981; St. Clair, 1978; Hubert et al., 1982). Evidence is particularly convincing for three characteristics: activity level (Goldsmith and Gottesman, 1981); sociability or shyness (Matheny, 1980; Daniels and Plomin, 1985); and fearfulness (Goldsmith and Campos, 1982). This means that the infant who is active, friendly, and fearless will probably become a busy, brave, and outgoing child, while the relatively quiet, shy, and timid infant will remain so. Taken together, this evidence appears to confirm the idea that some children are indeed "easy," while others are "slow to warm up."

The "difficult" pattern of temperament shows some stability as well, according to studies of children who display behavior problems. Many of these children have a poor ability to concentrate and a quick temper, traits that appear early in infancy and tend to continue throughout childhood and adolescence. These cases may be the result of normal heredity, or of prenatal damage, or of brain damage at birth. No matter which of these explanations about origin is correct, however, the result is an infant with a distinct, and in this case difficult, pattern of interaction with the world (Ross and Ross, 1982).

The research on temperament has powerful implications for parents. It means that parents need not necessarily feel responsible for all the personality traits and characteristics of their developing children. Some children are, because of their inborn characteristics, difficult to direct and hard to live with, while others are, by nature, easy-going and seemingly unaffected by turbulent or unresponsive parenting (Rutter, 1979).

The authors of the NYLS have expressed the belief that the recognition of the impact of temperament has a most salutary impact on the "blame the mother" ideology which had previously been so pervasive among mental health professions. Child-care experts from various disciplines could reassure mothers that a child's problems could stem from many causes. Unnecessary and destructive maternal guilt was relieved, with positive effects for both mother and child. [Chess and Thomas, 1982]

The Parents' Role   The message from research on temperament and research on emotions is quite clear: infants have emotions and the beginnings of personality from birth, and these develop with maturation. Consequently, psychologists no longer hold parents responsible as the sole creators of the child's personality. However, this does not mean that temperament works in social isolation. For example, the parents' role is clearly shown in a study of 152 infants reared by adoptive parents and 120 infants reared by their biological parents (Daniels and Plomin, 1985). At 12 and 24 months, the infants and their parents were rated on a variety of measures of sociability. As you would expect, a correlation was found between the adopted infants' temperament and that of their biological parents, even when the biological parents had had no contact with their infants since birth. Significantly, however, there was a stronger correlation between the adopted infants' sociability and that of their adoptive parents, suggesting that parental influence in this instance was greater environmentally than genetically. The strongest correlations of all, of course, were found where nature and nurture coincided: when raising their biological children, social parents had very outgoing toddlers and shy parents had shy children.

The outcome of the early temperamental patterns is influenced by the culture as well as by the family. For example, research finds that shy girls are likely to continue to be shy, but that timid boys often outgrow their timidity. Research also finds that the opposite pattern occurs with aggressiveness: girls, but not boys, become less aggressive as they mature. These patterns can be explained by the fact that our culture (and, in turn, parents) tend to value and encourage reservedness in females and assertiveness in males (Kagan, 1983).

Finally, the modifying influence of the child's ecological niche is further demonstrated by longitudinal research suggesting that even a very difficult infant can become a reasonably well-adjusted toddler or teenager if the family situation is supportive, and that constructive influences from the neighborhood or the school can help a child overcome a difficult first few years (Murphy and Moriarty, 1976; Thomas and Chess, 1977; Werner and Smith, 1982).

Parent-Infant Interaction

As we have now seen, neither the parents' method of handling the child nor the infant's innate characteristics are sole determinants of infant psychosocial development. A third factor—the interaction between the parent and the child—is now seen as crucial. This interaction is affected by the personality of the parent and the temperament of the child, as well as by the child's stage of development. Essentially these stages, and the nature of the parent-child interaction, can be described by three words: synchrony, attachment, and exploration.

The Beginning of the First Year: Synchrony

State-of-the-art methodology enables researchers to investigate early parent-infant interaction at a level of detail that was previously impossible. Scientists can videotape a parent-infant pair with three cameras; one focused on the baby, one on the parent, and the third on both of them. The resulting tapes are then viewed frame-by-frame and analyzed by carefully trained observers and cleverly programmed computers, producing a wealth of detail about the nature of parent-infant interaction (Touliatos and Compton, 1983; Lester et al., 1985).

Such analysis has revealed that the parent-child interaction is often characterized by a particular type of coordination, called **synchrony,** which leads those who describe it to turn to metaphors. According to various analysts, synchrony is the intricate "meshing" of a finely tuned machine (Snow, 1977), a patterned "dialogue" of exquisite precision (Schaffer, 1984), and the interplay of musicians improvising a "duet" or of dance partners executing a piece of skilled "choreography" (Stern, 1977).

To be sure, the specific behaviors of care-givers playing with their babies are not impressive in themselves: mothers and fathers open their eyes and mouths wide in expressions of mock surprise, make rapid clucking noises or repeated one-syllable sounds ("ba-ba-ba-ba-ba," "di-di-di-di," "bo-bo-bo-bo," etc.), raise and lower the pitch of their voice, change the pace of their movements (gradually speeding up or slowing down), tickle, pat, lift, and rock the baby, and do many other simple things. Nor are the infant's behaviors very complex: babies stare at their parent partner or look away, vocalize, widen their eyes, smile and laugh, move forward or back, or turn aside.

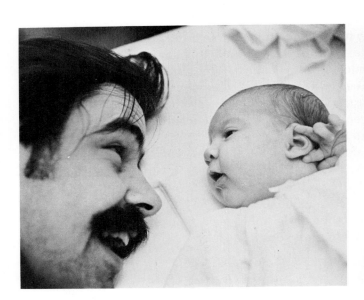 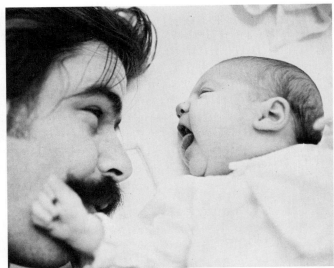

Figure 8.8 *A moment of synchrony!*

But what is fascinating to observers is the coordination of parts in the unwritten script that the parent and infant seem to follow, a coordination that becomes more impressive the more carefully one examines it. Seasoned veterans who have observed and analyzed hundreds of reels of videotaped infants and parents explain: "We have become more and more aware of the . . . balances between attention and nonattention, excitement and recovery, and of reciprocity in both togetherness and separateness" (Brazelton et al., 1979).

A Typical Interaction   Consider the following account of a mother and her 3-month-old, which, in actuality, only begins to hint at the split-second complexity that can be seen in videotapes of mother-child synchrony. The researcher's description starts with the mother nursing her infant.

> Until this point, a normal feeding, not a social interaction, was underway. Then a change began. While talking and looking at me, the mother turned her head and gazed at the infant's face. He was gazing at the ceiling, but out of the corner of his eye he saw her head turn toward him and turned to gaze back at her. This had happened before, but now he broke rhythm and stopped sucking. He let go of the nipple and the suction around it broke as he eased into the faintest suggestion of a smile. The mother abruptly stopped talking and, as she watched his face begin to transform, her eyes opened a little wider and her eyebrows raised a bit. His eyes locked on to hers, and together they held motionless for an instant. The infant did not return to sucking and his mother held frozen her slight expression of anticipation. This silent and almost motionless instant continued . . . until the mother suddenly shattered it by saying, "Hey!" and simultaneously opened her eyes wider, raising her eyebrows further, and throwing her head up and toward the infant. Almost simultaneously, the baby's eyes widened. His head tilted up and, as his smile broadened, the nipple fell out of his mouth. Now she said, "Well, hello! . . . hello! . . . Heello . . . Heeelloo!" so that her pitch rose and the "hellos" became longer and more stressed on each successive repetition. With each phrase the baby expressed more pleasure, and his body resonated almost like a balloon being pumped up, filling a little more with each breath. The mother then paused and her face relaxed. They watched each other expectantly for a moment. The shared excitement between them ebbed, but before it faded completely, the baby suddenly took an initiative and intervened to rescue it. His head lurched forward, his hands jerked up, and a fuller smile blossomed. His mother was jolted into motion. She moved forward, mouth open and eyes alight, and said, "Ooooooh . . . ya wanna play do ya . . . yeah? . . . I didn't know if you were still hungry . . . no . . . noooo . . . no I didn't . . . " And off they went. [Stern, 1977]

A seemingly more difficult task than knowing how to amuse and excite a baby is knowing when to stop the game. Some infants need less stimulation than others, and all need to break off from the excitement of play after a few minutes. The following account shows how the same mother-infant pair stopped their game, with the baby first suggesting, then insisting, that the play end.

> During the next four cycles of the renewed and slightly varied game, the mother did pretty much the same, except that on each successive cycle she escalated the level of suspense with her face and voice and timing. It went something like: "I'm gonna get ya . . . I'mmmmm

gonna get ya . . . I'mmmmmmmmmm goooonaa getcha . . . I'mmmm gooooooonaaa getcha!!" The baby became progressively more aroused, and the mounting excitement of both of them contained elements of both glee and danger . . . As the excitement mounted he seemed to run that narrow path between explosive glee and fright. As the path got narrower, he finally broke gaze with mother, appearing thereby to recompose himself for a second, to deescalate his own level of excitement. Having done so successfully, he returned his gaze to mother and exploded into a big grin. On that cue she began, with gusto, her fourth and most suspenseful cycle, but this one proved too much for him and pushed him across to the other side of the narrow path. He broke gaze immediately, turned away, face averted, and frowned. The mother picked it up immediately. She stopped the game dead in its tracks and said softly, "Oh honey, maybe you're still hungry, hun . . . let's try some milk again." He returned her gaze. His faced eased and he took the nipple again. The "moment" of social interaction was over. [Stern, 1977]

Although the baby's initial breaking of his gaze as a sign that he had had enough of the game did not get his message across, his turning away and frowning did. Researchers studying videotapes have discovered that even very young infants have many ways to indicate that they have had enough: they look blank or look away; fuss or frown; yawn or close their eyes; turn their bodies away or fold their arms and legs closer to themselves; or punch or kick someone or something away (Brazelton et al., 1974). If none of this works, babies cry loudly or even let their bodies go limp.

While virtually all infants and care-givers synchronize their interaction to some extent (Kaye, 1982), some seem better at it than others. There are "missteps in the dance," which are more likely to occur if the care-givers are preoccupied with their own problems. A depressed mother "may be able to go through all the practical activities of caregiving, but she will not be able to light up her face or voice or movements" (Stern, 1977). Or a mother may be overcontrolling to the point where she ignores the infant's attempt to break off the dialogue, as one mother did:

Whenever a moment of mutual gaze occurred, the mother went immediately into high-gear stimulating behaviors, producing a profusion of fully displayed, high-intensity, facial and vocal . . . social behavior. Jenny invariably broke gaze rapidly. Her mother never interpreted this temporary face and gaze aversion as a cue to lower her level of behavior, nor would she let Jenny self-control the level by gaining distance. Instead she would swing her head around following Jenny's to reestablish the full-face position. Jenny again turned away, pushing her face further into the pillow to try to break all visual contact. Again, instead of holding back, the mother continued to chase Jenny. . . . She also escalated the level of her stimulation more by adding touching and tickling to the unabated flow of vocal and facial behavior . . . Jenny closed her eyes to avoid any mutual visual contact and only reopened them after [she had moved her head to the other side]. All of these behaviors on Jenny's part were performed with a sober face or at times a grimace. [Stern, 1977]

While this example clearly shows the effects of the mother's personality, it should be noted that the infant's personality and predispositions also affect the ease of synchrony. For example, some infants are constitutionally more sensitive to stimulation than others, and these would have particular problems with an intrusive mother like Jenny's. Further, many early problems with synchrony are overcome as the infant grows older. For example, 5-month-old infants are better able to lead the interaction than 3-month-olds (Lester et al., 1985), so they have a better chance of regulating their parents' behavior. Jenny, the baby in the example above, eventually became more able to adjust to the mother's sudden overstimulation, and the mother, finding her infant more responsive, no longer felt the need to bombard her with stimulation as she had earlier. With time, Jenny and her mother established a mutually rewarding relationship.

The End of the First Year: Attachment

Just as the moment-by-moment harmony between parents and young infants has captured scientific attention, so has the **attachment** between parents and slightly older infants been the subject of extensive research. "Attachment," according to Mary Ainsworth (1973), "may be defined as an affectional tie that one person or animal forms between himself and another specific one—a tie that binds them together in space and endures over time." Not surprisingly, when people are attached to each other, they try to be near one another, and they interact with each other often. Thus infants show attachment by "proximity-seeking" behaviors, such as approaching, following, and clinging, and "contact-seeking" behaviors, such as crying, smiling, and calling (Ainsworth and Bell, 1970). Parents show their attachment by keeping a watchful eye on their infant, even when safety does not require it, and by responding to the infant's vocalizations, expressions, and gestures. (As we shall presently see, attachment is a reliable indicator of the quality of the parent-child relationship and a good predictor of the future competence of the child.)

Measuring Attachment Attachment can be measured in many ways. In a naturalistic study of mother-infant pairs in Central Africa, Ainsworth (1973) noted when infants cried, smiled, or vocalized differently with their mothers than with other people; whether babies cried or tried to follow their mothers when they left to go somewhere; if babies used their mothers as a base for exploration (going away from mother to explore and then coming back to reestablish contact with her); and how often infants clung to, or scrambled up on, the mother. She also studied how the mothers fed, comforted, and showed affection to their babies. No single behavior signified attachment. For example, Ainsworth particularly noted up to what age the mothers breast-fed their babies, but found that the duration of breast-feeding did not necessarily predict strength of attachment. Instead, Ainsworth determined that the overall pattern of infant-mother interaction, with responsiveness and alertness in both partners, indicated a secure relationship.

To assess attachment in a laboratory setting, Ainsworth developed a laboratory procedure (see Table 8.1) in which infants are observed in a well-equipped playroom in seven successive episodes, with their mother, with a friendly stranger, and by themselves. On the basis of her field observations, Ainsworth felt that the in-

TABLE 8.1   **Summary of Episodes of the Strange Situation**

Number of episode	Persons present	Duration	Brief Description of Action
1	Mother, baby, and observer	30 seconds	Observer introduces mother and baby to experimental room, then leaves.
2	Mother and baby	3 minutes	Mother is nonparticipant while baby explores; if necessary, play is stimulated after 2 minutes.
3	Stranger, mother, and baby	3 minutes	Stranger enters. Minute 1: stranger silent. Minute 2: stranger converses with mother. Minute 3: stranger approaches baby. After 3 minutes, mother leaves unobtrusively.
4	Stranger and baby	3 minutes* or less	First separation episode. Stranger's behavior is geared to that of baby.
5	Mother and baby	3 minutes† or more	First reunion episode. Mother greets and comforts baby, then tries to settle him again in play. Mother then leaves, saying "bye-bye."
6	Baby alone	3 minutes* or less	Second separation episode.
7	Stranger and baby	3 minutes* or less	Continuation of second separation. Stranger enters and gears her behavior to that of baby.
8	Mother and baby	3 minutes	Second reunion episode. Mother enters, greets baby, then picks him up. Meanwhile stranger leaves unobtrusively.

*Episode is curtailed if the baby is unduly distressed.
†Episode is prolonged if more time is required for the baby to become reinvolved in play.

fant's reactions to the comings and goings of the mother and the stranger would indicate the security of attachment.

In this laboratory test about two-thirds of all American infants demonstrate **secure attachment.** Their mother's presence in the playroom is enough to give them courage to explore the room and investigate the toys; her departure causes some distress (usually expressed through verbal protest and a pause in playing); and her return is a signal to reestablish contact (with a smile or by climbing into the mother's arms) and then resume playing. Securely attached infants also show a clear preference for their mothers over the stranger.

Other infants, however, show one of two types of **insecure attachment.** Some are anxiously resistant: they cling nervously to their mother even before her initial departure and thus are unwilling to explore the playroom; they cry loudly each time she leaves; they refuse to be comforted when she returns, perhaps continuing to sob angrily even when back in her arms. Others are avoidant: they engage in no interaction with their mothers and show no apparent stress when she leaves, and, on her return, they avoid reestablishing contact, sometimes even turning their backs. Insecurely attached infants tend to respond to the stranger no more negatively than they respond to their mothers. In some cases, they even react more positively toward the stranger.

Attachment and Care-Giving   Ainsworth's procedure for measuring attachment has been used in hundreds of studies. From these we have learned that attachment is one indication of the quality of care in early infancy (Ainsworth et al., 1978; Sroufe, 1985; Bretherton and Waters, 1985). Researchers have found that mothers who provide excellent care in the early months are much more likely to have infants who, at 12 months and 18 months, are securely attached than are mothers

Figure 8.9 *This little girl clinging to her mother's "apron strings" exemplifies the most literal form of attachment. However, the best indication of secure attachment involves no contact at all: it is the child's readiness to allow some distance between him- or herself and the mother, using the mother's presence as a reassuring base for exploration.*

who are neglectful of their i
understanding of their i
tures of "excellent c
infant's need for sti
specific signals s
infant in ways
(Egeland and S
giving in the ea

Furthermore,
forms of insecu
tend to have fus
have anxiously a

The security of
environment. Am
tal discord, loss of
attachment; corre
(Vaughn et al., 1979)
in attachment in mid
provide a buffer that
gree), but middle-class
mothers have returned
This is not to say that

infants who acquired a new care-giver between 12 and 18 months, 23 percent changed from secure to insecure attachment, while 21 percent changed from insecure to secure attachment (Thompson et al., 1982). Thus, in this sample at least, the relationship between mother and child was just about as likely to improve as to worsen when the mother no longer provided full-time care.

RESEARCH REPORT   **Fathers and Infants**

While traditional views of infant development typically focused on mothers, the past decade of research on fathers and infants has led to the following conclusion:

With the exception of lactation, there is no evidence that women are biologically predisposed to be better parents than men are. Social conventions, not biological imperatives, underlie the traditional division of parental responsibilities. [Lamb, 1981]

To be specific, fathers are just as capable of sensitively caring for young infants—bottle-feeding, changing, bathing, and soothing them—as mothers are (Parke and Tinsley, 1981). Fathers also show synchrony in play and speak Motherese just as well as mothers. Further, father-infant attachments appear at the same age, and function the way, as mother-infant attachments do (Lamb,

acting quite
ences

are away from the house more than mothers are. But even when both parents are home, such as during the evenings or weekends, the difference holds. While fathers sometimes feed, diaper, and cradle their new babies when both parents are present, mothers do it more frequently (Belsky et al., 1984b).

In addition, the father's involvement seems to be more affected by certain circumstances than the mother's is. Fathers are significantly more involved with first-borns than with later-borns (Belsky et al., 1984b), with sons (Parke, 1979), and when their relationship with the child's mother is strong. This holds true for both adolescent and adult fathers (Belsky et al., 1984b; Lamb and Elster, 1985).

Fathers' play is also different from mother's play. Fathers typically are noisier, make bigger gestures, and are more inclined to use the element of surprise in their play. According to slow-motion examination of tapes of parent-infant interaction, mothers' play is much more modulated and contained than fathers', providing "an envelope for verbal interaction," whereas fathers' play is more physical exciting (Brazelton et al., 1979). Even in the first hs of the baby's life, fathers are more likely to play ing the baby's legs and arms in imitation of r kicking, or climbing, or by zooming the baby air ("airplane"), or by tapping and tickling the ach; mothers, on the other hand, are more or sing soothingly, or to combine play with routines such as diapering and bathing Tinsley, 1981).

erences between mothers' and fathers' play are n infants. Even 3-month-olds typically react with ible excitement when approached by their fathers en approached by their mothers. In the first of life infants are more likely to laugh—and more to cry—in episodes of play with Daddy.

nfants grow older, fathers generally increase the time y spend with them, and their tendency to engage in ysical play becomes more pronounced. Fathers are kely to swing their toddlers around, or "wrestle" with hem on the floor, or crawl after them in a "chase."

Other research has shown that fathers and other care-givers can, and often do, provide the same secure attachment and base for exploration that mothers, in Ainsworth's classic research, do. Again, sensitivity to the child's needs is key. Fathers who are responsive to their infants tend to have infants who are securely attached to them (Lamb, 1981). Similarly, toddlers become securely attached to

Mothers, on the other hand, are more likely to read to their toddlers or help them play with toys (Parke and Tinsley, 1981). These differences continue to be reflected in infants' reactions. According to one study (Clarke-Stewart, 1978), 20-month-olds are more responsive during play with their fathers than with their mothers. By 30 months, differences are even more apparent: 2-year-olds are generally more cooperative, involved, and interested in their fathers' games than in their mothers' play, and judging by their smiles and laughter, they have more fun.

The father-infant relationship varies with the sex of the child: fathers and sons play together more, and show greater attachments, than fathers and daughters do. It also varies with the culture. Compared to American toddlers, for instance, Swedish toddlers seem notably more attached to and affectionate with their mothers than with their fathers (Lamb et al., 1983), possibly because, although typically more involved in day-to-day infant care, Swedish fathers are less likely to play with their toddlers than American fathers are.

Of course, it would be a mistake to assess a parent's impact on a child merely by looking at time spent in care-giving, security of attachment, or laughter during play. Indeed, in some cases, a parent's most powerful influence on a child may be an indirect one, as he or she encourages, or sabotages, the mothering or fathering of the spouse (Pederson, 1981). For example, as we will see later in the discussion of child abuse, two parents are generally better than one in ensuring good care for the child. However, in some cases, mothers provide better care for their infants when their spouse is gone, because the father was so critical and demanding when he was part of the household. As a leading research team explains:

In our experience, single parents are rather less abusive than couples, which is surprising because one would think that a spouse would provide support in the face of crisis. In fact a spouse who is not supportive is worse than no spouse at all when it comes to childrearing. [Kempe and Kempe, 1978]

Further, the influence of any particular father is affected not only by his individual characteristics, but also by the attitude of his wife and the influence of the culture. Recent changes in our own society—particularly the increase in the number of mothers in the work force—have meant that today's fathers are much more involved with their infants than they once were. From the perspective of the developmentalist, this is a welcome change: infants thrive under their fathers' care and attention (Lamb, 1981).

Babies obviously love a good game of catch—but have you ever seen a mother playing one with her infant?

their nursery-school teachers who are responsive to them (Anderson et al., 1981). It should also be noted that an attachment between an infant and his or her father, grandparent, teacher, or other care-giver in no way prevents a secure mother-infant relationship (Ainsworth et al., 1978; Lamb, 1981). This finding has important implications, since 40 percent of the mothers of infants under age 1 are employed. In approximately two-thirds of these cases, the care-givers are relatives (primarily fathers and grandparents) with nonrelatives caring for the remaining third (including 5 percent in infant day-care centers) (Klein, 1985). The crucial factor in attachment as well as in a great many other measures of infant development seems to be not who provides the care but how responsive the care provided is (Clarke-Stewart and Fein, 1983).

The Importance of Attachment Why is attachment considered so important? Part of the reason stems from the psychoanalytic emphasis on the developmental importance of the early relationship between mother and child (Bowlby, 1973, 1980). But much more influential is longitudinal research that documents the results of secure and insecure attachment. It clearly shows that secure attachment at age 1 sets the stage for exploration and mature personality development during the preschool years.

For example, observations in nursery school show that 3-year-olds who were rated securely attached at age 1 are significantly more competent in certain social and cognitive skills: they are more curious, outgoing, and self-directed than those who were insecurely attached. The 3-year-olds who are securely attached are also more likely to be sought out as friends and to be chosen as leaders (Sroufe, 1978). Furthermore, securely attached infants become children who interact with teachers in friendly and appropriate ways, seeking their help when needed. By contrast,

Figure 8.10 *Children's behavior in nursery school is often related to their attachment history. If this little girl typically stations herself in the teacher's lap, unwilling to play with the other children, there is reason to suspect that she may not have been securely attached to her mother two years earlier.*

anxiously attached infants become preschoolers who are overly dependent on teachers, demanding their attention unnecessarily and clinging to them instead of playing with other children or exploring the environment (Sroufe et al., 1983). Even at ages 5 and 6, differences are apparent between children who were securely and insecurely attached as infants (Arend et al., 1979; Main and George, 1985).

The Second Year: Caring for Toddlers

The synchrony of the early months, and the developing attachment as the first birthday approaches, set the stage for the next challenge to parent-infant interaction, one that even parents who have managed the dependency needs of the infant fairly easily may find difficult (White, 1975; Greenspan and Greenspan, 1985; Mahler et al., 1975). As infants become more secure as well as more mobile, they explore the environment in ever greater scope. Whether this exploration is regarded as a process of separation-individuation, or the crisis of autonomy, or the experimentation carried out by the curious "little scientist," the fact is that this exploration is sometimes disconcerting to the parents and dangerous to the child. Partly because the challenges of toddlerhood are difficult for many parents to meet, a good deal of research has been devoted to discovering which specific parental characteristics and actions encourage or discourage healthy toddler development.

HOME One answer to that question is summarized by **HOME** (an acronym for Home Observation for the Measurement of the Environment), which is a list of forty-five family and household characteristics that have been shown to correlate with children's development (Caldwell and Bradley, 1984). These characteristics, divided into six subscales, are rated by a trained observer while visiting an infant and care-giver at home.

The Six Subscales of HOME

1. *Emotional and verbal responsiveness of mother.* Example: Mother responds to child's vocalizations with vocal or verbal response.

2. *Avoidance of restriction and punishment.* Example: Mother does not interfere with the child's actions or restrict child's movements more than three times during the visit.

3. *Organization of the physical environment.* Example: Child's play environment appears safe and free of hazards.

4. *Provision of appropriate play materials.* Example: Child has one or more toys or pieces of equipment that promote muscle activity.

5. *Maternal involvement with child.* Example: Mother tends to keep child within visual range and to look at the child often.

6. *Opportunities for variety in daily stimulation.* Example: Mother reads stories to child at least three times weekly.

HOME has been used to evaluate the environment of young children from many racial, cultural, and socioeconomic groups, with better success in predicting children's later cognitive development than either conventional intelligence tests or measures of social class (Elardo et al., 1975; Bradley and Caldwell, 1976; Elardo et al., 1977). Thus, contrary to the traditional methods of predicting an infant's competence, HOME would suggest that a lower-class toddler who is of average IQ but who has a responsive, involved mother and a safe, stimulating play environment is likely to become a more competent preschooler than a middle-class infant who seems more advanced, but whose HOME scores are low.

Each of the six subscales of HOME are important. However, analysis of which aspects of HOME correlate best with later development reveals that, particularly for boys, the best predictor of future competence is Provision of Appropriate Play Materials (Bradley and Caldwell, 1980, 1984). Since "appropriate" is meant to indicate toys that encourage the child's motor and cognitive development, play materials do not need to be expensive "educational" toys; large cardboard boxes, pots and pans, and a collection of stones (too big to swallow) and plastic bottles can be great toys for toddlers. The next most important predictors of future achievement are Variety of Stimulation and Maternal Involvement.

Figure 8.11 *Several studies, including HOME, have found that toddlers who are read to every day are more likely to be verbal, intelligent schoolchildren than are toddlers who are rarely read to.*

Especially for boys, availability of appropriate playthings during toddlerhood predicts later intellectual competence. Many simple objects fit this description— for example, pots and pans stack, make noise, and don't break.

Similar findings have been reported by Burton White and Jean Carew-Watts (1973). Having discovered significant differences in social and cognitive competence among kindergartners, White and Carew-Watts attempted to determine when and how these differences emerged. They found that, by age 3, the children who would become competent kindergartners were already ahead of their peers. But when they studied infants, they found no clues (except in cases involving serious abuse, neglect, or mental retardation) to indicate which infants would or would not become competent kindergartners. On the basis of these findings, they concluded that, for North American children, toddlerhood is the most critical period for the development of competence in early childhood (White, 1975).

The next step was to find out what factors during toddlerhood turn 1-year-olds into "competent" or "incompetent" 3-year-olds. Focusing on maternal behavior, White and Carew-Watts identified the characteristics of mothers (whom they called "A" mothers) who fostered competent children and those (whom they called "C" mothers) who did not.

Characteristics of Competent Children

SOCIAL SKILLS
1. Seeking adult attention in socially acceptable ways.
2. Using adults as sources of help.
3. Expressing hostility and affection to adults.
4. Leading and following peers.
5. Expressing hostility and affection to peers.
6. Competing with peers.
7. Praising oneself and showing pride in one's accomplishments.
8. Involving oneself in adult role-playing, or otherwise showing a desire to grow up.

COGNITIVE SKILLS
1. Linguistic competence—ability to understand and communicate.
2. Intellectual competence, including ability to deal with numbers and rules and to understand other points of view.
3. Executive abilities, such as planning complex activities.
4. Attentional ability, specifically, the ability to work on one's own project while being aware of other people.

"A" mothers all showed several characteristics in common. They enjoyed their toddlers and talked to them at a level the children could understand. The child's learning and happiness were more important to them than the appearance of the house, so they organized the environment to be safe and interesting. They permitted their children to take minor risks and, at the same time, set reasonable limits—allowing a 1-year-old to, say, jump on the bed but not on the staircase. Finally, "A" mothers were generally busy and happy.

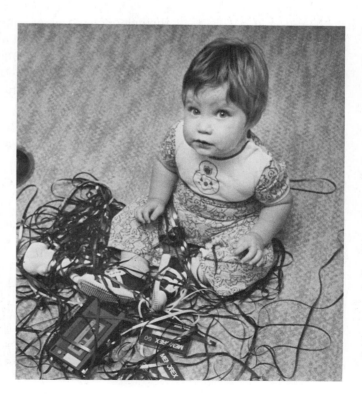

Figure 8.12 *An "A" mother coming upon this scene would probably tell herself that she should have put the tapes out of reach. A "C" mother would wish she had left her baby in the playpen.*

"C" mothers were more varied than "A" mothers. Some were depressed, disorganized, and listless. They seemed to have stopped trying to provide adequate stimulation for their children. Others were overprotective, constantly interfering with their children's natural curiosity and independence. Still others were more interested in the housekeeping than in their children's activities, and consequently ignored their toddlers most of the time.

The original White and Carew-Watts study was limited in that it studied the younger siblings of children who had already demonstrated their level of competence, and it focused on the mother's behavior rather than on the interaction between care-givers and infants. To confirm and extend the original research, Jean Carew undertook a longitudinal study (Carew, 1980). She observed forty-five toddlers in their daily activities at 1, 1½, 2, and 2½ years, noting the nature of their experiences. The experiences, which were rated for the intellectual stimulation they provided, included solitary ones (in which the child played alone), passive experiences (as when watching television), and social experiences. Those children who spent a relatively large proportion of their day in intellectually stimulating experiences during toddlerhood were the children who scored relatively high on several tests of cognitive development at age 3. Particularly important for later development were the intellectually stimulating experiences that the care-giver provided at ages 1 and 1½. Apparently, although toddlers can generate their own intellectual experiences, the most potent experiences for later competence are those initiated by someone else. (One interesting feature of this study is that about half of the children were cared for primarily at home by their mothers, while the other half attended a day-care center. The general conclusions were the same whether the care-givers were mothers or day-care teachers.)

You will note that we seem to have come back to the idea that the care-giver's behavior is crucial. In fact, there is no denying the importance of the care-giver's role in fostering synchrony, or attachment, or exploration. The difference between the evidence of recent studies and the thrust of traditional theory, however, is the current emphasis on the infant's active participation in the process and ways it can affect the care-giver's behavior. This is clear in two examples from the Carew-Watts study of mother-toddler interaction.

The first example is a mother and her 24-month-old daughter Sonja, who has just begun the interaction by saying that she went to a circus.

Mother: No, you didn't go to the circus—you went to the parade.
Sonja: *I went to the parade.*
What did you see?
I saw . . .
What?
Big girls.
Mother smiles. *Big girls* and what else?
Drums.
Mother chuckles.
Sonja laughs, as if remembering the parade.
Mother blows up a balloon.
What made all the loud noise at the end?
Trumpets.
Yes and fire engines. Do you remember the fire engines?
You hold my ears a little bit.
Mother smiles: Yes, I did, just like this. (Puts her hands on Sonja's ears.)
Sonja laughs.

In this case Sonja begins the interaction and the mother helps her remember and recount her experiences. Indeed, each partner escalates their mutual enjoyment, as when Sonja says, "You hold my ears a little bit" and then the mother playfully holds her ears again. Thus both mother and daughter are creators in this interchange and, judging by their laughter, each enjoys the interaction they are developing together.

The other example comes from 18-month-old Terry, who begins the interaction by his active exploration.

> Terry sits in front of the bookshelf, pulling books out. He pulls out a book and picks up a piece of paper (his sister's school worksheet) and looks at it. Terry pulls out another book. Mother comes over and says "Terry, No" and removes him saying "Don't touch again," and slaps his hand. Terry babbles something back.
>
> Terry goes back and touches the books. Mother "No." Terry throws himself on the floor and whines. He gets up and picks up a doll and throws it on the floor. He throws it again. Terry marches back to the shelf and pulls at the books again. Mother yells "No," and goes to remove him. Terry marches around and then picks up a framed picture from the shelf. Mother: "Terry!" and comes to remove him. "Don't touch." Terry laughs. Mother: "I am not playing with you!" He goes and picks up another picture. Mother tells his sister to get it from him and she does so. Terry tries to get it back. Mother goes and pulls him away from the shelf. Mother: "Don't touch it again, you know it. Don't laugh, fresh kid." Terry laughs and walks to the TV. [Carew, 1980]

One way to analyze this episode is to take the traditional stance and criticize the mother. Terry gave clear signals that he wanted his mother's attention (taking the books down, throwing the doll, and taking the pictures) and his mother's reaction was, at best, ineffectual, and at worst, destructive. For instance, she created a conflict between Terry and his sister, and then intervened on behalf of the sister—an episode that may well lead to greater sibling rivalry. Ideally, Terry's mother should have seen that he needed distraction and attention as well as restriction and prohibition. She should have moved him, not only away from the books, but also toward something he would like—perhaps reading to him from one of his own books, or looking at a family photo album with him.

However, instead of simply blaming the mother, as traditional approaches would do, consider Terry's contribution to this interaction, as well as the overall context. Terry stubbornly persists in doing what his mother doesn't want him to do, and laughs at his mother's rebuke. As you remember from the description of infant emotions, Terry's reaction is not unusual for a toddler, but that doesn't necessarily make it easier to handle. Further, Terry's temperament may not be particularly easy. At least in this incident, he is difficult to distract, quick to complain, and easy to anger. Finally, the situation is not an easy one: for obvious reasons, many mothers are less patient and creative with their second child than with their first, especially if the first is still relatively young (White, 1979). The recognition that caregivers, children, and the overall context are important in understanding a child's development will help us with the last topic of this chapter.

Child Abuse and Neglect

Of all the developmental problems discussed in this text, child maltreatment is the most destructive to the child who experiences it, to the care-giver who commits it, and to the society that allows it. Yet child abuse and neglect are a serious problem in every nation of the world (Leavitt, 1983).

The actual prevalence is hard to estimate, since maltreatment often goes unreported (Brown, 1983). Even the reported cases, however, show that abuse is all too common. In the United States, one out of every forty-three American children under age 14 was reported as abused or neglected in 1982 (National Center for Child Abuse, 1983). That is more than a million reported cases a year. Most experts believe that the actual incidence, as well as the rate of reporting, has been rising over the last decade (Brown, 1983).

The problems of estimating the true incidence of abuse reveal some of the difficulties in treatment and prevention, for maltreated children cannot be helped unless someone recognizes their need for help. The difficulty begins with definitions. What, exactly, is **child abuse?** In fact, it is a cluster of different behaviors, each of which results in harm to the child's development.

The most obvious form of abuse is severe physical abuse, the "battered child syndrome" first described in 1962. Since then, pediatricians and emergency room staff have been trained to examine cases of "accidental" injury and required to report suspected abuse (Solnit, 1980). They look for hidden bleeding from bruises

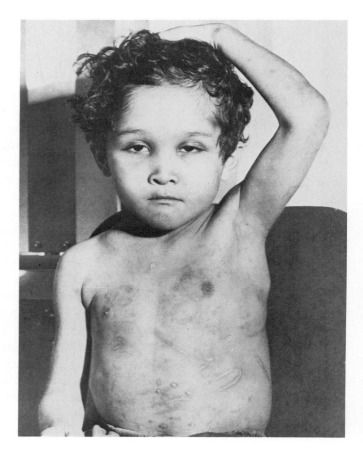

Figure 8.13 *While the severe battering of a child may be the most disturbing kind of abuse to witness, long-term and repeated physical and psychological abuse is much more common and more damaging. When asked about his injuries, which included cigarette burns, welts, and bite marks, this 5-year-old explained: "My stepfather sometimes says, 'I'm a lion. You're a piece of meat.' I guess he doesn't like me."*

under the skull; burn marks that are round (from cigarettes), or lattice-like (from hot radiators), or that stop suddenly part-way up the child's body (from scalding bathwater); partially healed fractures; and many other signs that indicate that a particular injury was not an accident at all. Such severe abuse comprises only about 4 percent of all reported cases.

However, less extreme physical abuse, producing cuts, welts, bruises, or no marks at all can sometimes be as destructive as extreme abuse. Vigorously shaking an infant, for example, is a common reason for the brain damage too often found in abused children (Martin, 1980).

Emotional maltreatment and sexual abuse can be more destructive, in the long term, than physical abuse. Unfortunately, they often go unrecognized and unreported, and therefore do not get treated until years after the damage is done. Particularly for sexual abuse, one reason for underreporting is that people simply had not believed that the sexual abuse of young children could occur. In recent years, increased public awareness of the problem, and the establishment of agencies to deal with sexual abuse, have resulted in a doubling in the sexual-abuse reporting (Brown, 1983). (These two types of abuse are discussed later in this book, at the stages of development when they become more common, emotional maltreatment in Chapter 14 and sexual abuse in Chapter 17.)

Finally, **neglect** is actually the most common form of maltreatment as well as the most destructive, causing more deaths, injuries, and long-term problems than abuse (Cantwell, 1980; Wolock and Horowitz, 1984). Some instances of neglect are blatant and horrifying: infants who are allowed to starve or freeze to death are examples. Others are less obvious, involving infants who are debilitatingly undernourished, or whose parents rarely cradle, talk, or play with them. Furthermore, many childhood accidents (by far the greatest cause of childhood death and serious injury) can be traced to neglect, although they are rarely reported as such.

Figure 8.14 *Neglect is more common than abuse, and more destructive. It is a factor in most of the accidental deaths that occur to children through age 10 in the United States each year. Neglected children are also more likely to be stunted physically, cognitively, and emotionally, than abused children.*

Causes of Child Abuse and Neglect

Traditionally, the cause of abuse was seen as residing solely in the "disturbed" abuser who lost control. Parents were blamed and sometimes punished, and often the child was removed from the home. However, as the ecological approach has become more widely used to understand child abuse, the focus in searching for causes has moved from the idea of the "pathological parent" to the interaction among parent, child, and society, and the emphasis has shifted from placing blame to early diagnosis and prevention (Thompson, 1983; Cohn, 1983). Let us look first at the overall social and cultural milieu in which maltreatment occurs.

The Social Context   Some cultures have a much lower rate of deliberate parental maltreatment than others. Such cultures have three characteristics:

1. Children are highly valued, as a psychological joy and fulfillment. They also tend to be more of an economic asset than a liability.

2. Child care is shared by many people. If the mother is unwilling or unable to care for her child, other relatives are ready to take over, sometimes for a few moments, other times for years.

3. Young children are not expected to be responsible for their actions. In some cultures, almost any punishment of children younger than age 3, or even age 7, is considered abusive and unnecessary.

The importance of social values and conditions is exemplified by the different rates of child abuse among the Polynesian people who live in their traditional home, the Pacific Islands, and those who have emigrated to New Zealand (Ritchie and Ritchie, 1981). Among the former, abuse is virtually nonexistent. Their society fully meets the three criteria listed above, for children are highly valued, cared for by many adults (in fact, in Polynesian, the same word is used for "adult" and "parent"), and children are considered unteachable until they are at least 2 years old.

However, when Polynesians move to New Zealand, the rate of child abuse skyrockets, surpassing the rate of the Caucasian New Zealanders many times over. The demands of the new life style make it impossible for the parents to continue their old parenting habits of relaxed permissiveness and informal and extensively shared child care. Meanwhile, it takes time to develop viable new patterns (such as learning how to enforce new guidelines for children's behavior without resorting to physical punishment, finding ways to replace the freely available care-givers of the past, and limiting family size so that the children are not an overwhelming financial burden).

Cultural Factors Affecting Abuse in America.   Comparing the three characteristics of nonabusive societies with the patterns common in the United States reveals why abuse is so prevalent in this country. First, children are often considered to be both a financial and personal burden. Not surprisingly, the incidence of abuse and neglect rises as income falls; very poor parents (family income under $5,000 per year) are the most likely to abuse their children (Pelton, 1978), especially if the living conditions are crowded and available friends and helpers are few.

Second, in the United States, social support for mothers of young children is scarce. If she is lucky, a mother has relatives and friends who willingly help her, but many mothers, especially teenage mothers, are not so fortunate. Grandmothers, for instance, once the mainstay of practical help, are now much more likely to live a distance away and to be involved with careers and social worlds of their own.

Social isolation allows child abuse in two ways. First, compared to parents who have an active network of friends and family members, isolated parents are more likely to take out their problems (such as the crisis of divorce or unemployment) on their children. Second, when abuse begins, others are reluctant to intervene until the pattern is well established and considerable harm has been done. It is not surprising, then, that study after study finds a correlation between social isolation and child abuse (Thompson, 1983; Kempe and Kempe, 1984; Cohn, 1983).

Finally, our culture's attitude about young children may add to the problem. The emphasis on the infant's and preschooler's ability to learn may cause some parents to forget that young children are also immature, self-absorbed, and dependent on others. For example, many abusing parents consider irritating but normal infant behavior to be deliberate and therefore amenable to correction: they punish infants for "crying too much" or punish toddlers for being unable to control urination or defecation. Complicating this aspect all the more is the fact that physical force—from an occasional slap to frequent batterings—is a common form of punishment in most American homes (Gelles, 1978).

Problems in the Parents According to Ruth and Henry Kempe (1978), of every ten parents who severely abuse their children, one is so mentally ill as to be untreatable. Such persons have delusions ("God is telling me to kill this child") or they communicate only by bashing. They are cruel or fanatical, and completely closed to reason. With these parents, the only solution is removing the child from the home.

But most abusive parents are not very different from average parents. They love their children, and want the best for them. In fact, it may be a sense of failure as a parent that triggers their abusiveness. When the infant cries, for instance, they may interpret the crying as a form of accusation. As the Kempes write:

> An average mother will regard a crying or fussy baby as hungry or wet or full of gas. She will proceed to feed, change, burp him, and then put him down in the crib and say, "Baby, you're tired," close the door, then turn on the radio or talk to a friend. The abusive parent is unable to leave the crying child, and tries harder and harder to pacify him until in a moment of utter frustration she is overwhelmed by the thought that the baby, even at two weeks of age, is saying, "If you were a good mother I wouldn't be crying like this." It is precisely because the parent tries to be extra good, to be loved and earn the love of the child, that intractable crying is seen as total rejection and leads to sudden rage. The abuse is clearly not a rational act. It is not premeditated, and it is often followed by deep grief and great guilt. Such parents are seen by doctors and nurses as being very solicitous. Third parties find it hard to believe that so loving a parent could have inflicted such serious injury. [Kempe and Kempe, 1978]

For some abusive parents, the seeds of the problem were sown early in their development, for they themselves were abused or neglected as children. Researchers believe that this type of childhood experience might make abusers out of the abused in two ways: it hinders the development of self-esteem, patience, and social skills and it provides a negative, destructive model of parenting.

An additional factor that increases the likelihood of maltreatment is drug dependency. One study of addicts found virtually all of the parents were neglectful to

Factors Associated with Child Abuse

According to several studies (Kempe and Helfer, 1980; Cohn, 1983; Kempe and Kempe, 1984; Thompson, 1983), adults are more likely to be child abusers if

Background Variables

they were abused or neglected as children

they grew up in a culture markedly different from that in which they are now living

they have little education

they are under age 20

Social-Setting Variables

they have few friends or nearby relatives

they are drug abusers, especially alcoholics

they are victims or perpetrators of spouse abuse

they have recently experienced family stress (e.g., death of a parent, loss of a job, new pregnancy, divorce)

they have several children, especially several under age 6

their living space is crowded, with no privacy

they are responsible for the care of a child who is not their biological offspring (such as a step-child, or cousin)

Personality Variables

they have difficulty coping with anger

they have low self-esteem

they have inconsistent and/or unrealistic expectations of children

Bear in mind that no one of these factors by itself is an inevitable signal of potential abuse. However, the more of these conditions that occur in combination, the greater the likelihood that abuse will occur.

---

some degree. In addition, 27 percent of the alcoholics and 19 percent of the heroin addicts physically or sexually abused their children (Black and Mayer, 1980).

Problems in the Child   The systems approach to child development has made researchers look more closely at the other partner in the abusive parent-child relationship. Sometimes something in the infant triggers, or encourages, a destructive pattern (Friedrich and Boriskin, 1983).

Babies who are unwanted, who are born too early, who were the product of an unhappy love affair or a difficult pregnancy, who are the "wrong" sex, or who have physical problems, can become victims of their parents' disappointment. Even the baby's appearance, as in the case, say, of the little boy who looks just like the father who left the mother early in pregnancy, or the little girl who reminds her father of his abusive mother, can trigger rejection instead of love. Parents may also be unhappy and frustrated over their baby's temperament, wanting a more quiet one, or a more active one, or a less difficult one (Steele, 1980). All these disappointments may lead to unresponsive and rejecting parenting, which as we have seen, is likely to make a child much more difficult than he or she otherwise would have been. Note, however, that maltreatment, then, is more likely to create a hard-to-manage child than vice versa. In short, abused children are not to be blamed for their fate.

Figure 8.15 *A mismatch between a parent's idea of what infants are like and the individual infant's actual temperament leads to problems for both: round babies do not fit into square holes.*

All children—particularly those who have special problems—deserve love and attention. Parents who have difficulty providing these basics may well need special help in understanding and caring for their children.

Treatment and Prevention

Even when abuse has already occurred, intervention can halt the process. A four-year British study of severely abused infants whose families had participated in an intensive therapy program found that about two-thirds were doing fairly well—with normal cognitive and psychological development in the children and better family development generally. The other third showed notable retardation and disturbance, but even in these cases the family had typically managed to provide better care for the other children in the family (Lynch and Roberts, 1983). An American team of child-abuse researchers (Kempe and Kempe, 1978) believe that 80 percent of abusing parents can be helped so that they no longer physically punish their children. Both short-term help (a hotline for parents when they find themselves losing control and an around-the-clock crisis nursery where parents in need of a few hours' peace can drop off their children), and long-term help (individual and family therapy) are needed.* One of the most important forms of help may be provision of good medical care for parents, since parental health problems often accompany abuse.

---

*An organization called Parents Anonymous, with chapters in every major city, helps abusing parents in much the same way that Alcoholics Anonymous helps alcoholics.

Most experts agree that early warning is essential to prevention and that the child's first weeks and months should be the focus of particular concern (Schwartzbeck, 1983). Among the warning signs are an absence of synchrony (an infant or parent might repeatedly avoid eye contact), the failure of the infant to gain weight from one pediatric checkup to the next, the failure of a parent to bring the infant in for checkups, and signs of insecure attachment. If such signs are noted, a supportive network—either of friends and relatives or of professionals—can be activated before destructive parent-infant interactions become habitual.

How early can babies "at risk" be spotted and helped? According to one study, the process can begin at birth. The Kempes (1978) studied 350 families (with their consent) in the labor and delivery room, looking for worrisome signs such as an apparent lack of love between the parents, a failure on the part of parents to look their newborns in the eye or touch them, or parental disappointment over the baby's sex or appearance. They found a hundred "high-risk" families and divided them into two groups: a control group who received routine services and an experimental group who received the routine services and, in addition, were assigned a pediatrician who saw the baby for regular checkups. The doctor also called the family at least once a week to provide encouragement and answer questions.

This personal intervention did not prevent all forms of abuse and neglect. In fact, twenty of the fifty families showed signs of "abnormal parenting practices," and three of the babies were so below height and weight for their age that they were treated for "failure to thrive." But the pediatrician's attention did stop physical abuse: whereas by age 2 five of the fifty control-group babies needed hospital treatment—for, among other injuries, a fractured femur, a fractured skull, barbiturate poisoning, a subdural hematoma (hemorrhage on the surface of the brain), and third-degree burns—none of the fifty experimental-group babies was hospitalized for abuse.

This study clearly demonstrates the importance of support networks for families at risk. And, in fact, hospitals and community agencies are increasingly offering support programs, not only to help high-risk parents but to help all parents, recognizing that every parent can benefit from this kind of guidance (Gray and Kaplan, 1980; Shay, 1980). Further, a look at the broader context of abuse suggests that since poverty, youth, and ignorance correlate with poor parenting, measures that raise the lowest incomes, discourage teenage parenthood, and increase the level of education will probably lower the rate of abuse. And since social isolation and unrealistic expectations make it harder to provide good care for young children, any program that fosters friendly contact with others and an accurate understanding of the needs of children should be encouraged. With a little experienced guidance, most parents can become better at appreciating their children and learning how to relate to them with greater respect and with mutual delight.

CHAPTER SUMMARY

Emotional Development

1. In the first days and weeks of life, infants are capable of expressing many emotions, including fear, anger, sadness, happiness, and surprise. Toward the end of the first year, the typical infant expresses emotions more readily, more frequently, and most distinctly.

2. In the second year, cognitive advances cause infants to become more conscious of the distinction between themselves and others. This realization leads to the expression of new emotions, among them jealousy, affection, pride, and shame.

Personality Development

3. In the traditional view of personality development, mothers are the almost omnipotent creators and shapers of infant character. In the first half of the 20th century, this view was put forth in child-rearing manuals, in the pronouncements of the leading behaviorist, John Watson, and, from a different perspective, in the theoretical assumptions of Sigmund Freud.

4. Freud argued that the child-rearing practices encountered in the oral and the anal psychosexual stages, had a lasting impact on the person's personality and mental health. Further, he believed that the child's early relationship with his or her mother was the prototype for all future relationships.

5. Erikson and Mahler built on Freud's ideas, broadening his concept of the first two stages. According to Erikson, the infant experiences the crises of trust versus mistrust, and then autonomy versus shame and doubt. Mahler envisions three phases of infant development: normal autism, symbiosis, and then separation-individuation. Like Freud, both of these psychoanalytic thinkers stress the lifelong impact of the care-giver's actions during the first two years.

6. Contemporary developmentalists generally do not accept Freud's stages of infant development. Erikson and Mahler are more influential on current thought. However, many critics contend that the psychoanalytic theorists overemphasize the impact of the mother's role in the first two years.

7. An alternative view is that infants are born with definite personality characteristics. The New York Longitudinal Study (NYLS) found that nine temperamental traits are apparent in the early weeks of life and show some stability as children mature. Other research confirms a genetic component for some traits.

Parent-Infant Interaction

8. In addition to the parents' actions and the infants' temperament, developmentalists now stress the interaction between parent and child.

9. The early parent-child interaction is characterized by synchrony, a harmony of gesture, expression, and timing which can make early nonverbal play a fascinating interchange. Attachment between parent and child becomes apparent toward the end of the first year. Secure attachment tends to predict curiosity, social competence, and self-assurance later in childhood; insecure attachment tends to correlate with less successful adaptation in these areas.

10. Father-infant interaction is characterized by synchrony and attachment, just as mother-infant interaction is. However, while fathers are as capable care-givers as mothers are, they tend to spend less time with their infants and to engage in more stimulating physical play than mothers do.

11. During toddlerhood, an important aspect of parent-infant interaction is how the parent encourages, or restricts, the child's exploration of the environment. Developmental researchers agree that the mother's responsiveness to her child and the stimulation of the play materials and setting are significant determinants of infant development.

Child Abuse and Neglect

12. Child maltreatment can take many forms—physical abuse, emotional maltreatment, sexual abuse, and neglect.

13. The causes of abuse are many, including problems in the society (such as cultural attitudes about children), in the parent (such as drug addiction), and in the child (such as being sickly or difficult). The most effective strategies emphasize prevention and treatment rather than blame. In addition, measures that reduce the stresses and increase the social support for families with young children would help make child maltreatment less likely.

KEY TERMS

social smile *(213)*
fear of strangers *(215)*
separation anxiety *(215)*
self-awareness *(216)*
oral stage *(220)*
anal stage *(220)*
trust versus mistrust *(221)*
autonomy versus shame and doubt *(222)*
symbiosis *(223)*

separation-individuation *(223)*
temperament *(224)*
synchrony *(228)*
attachment *(231)*
secure attachment *(232)*
insecure attachment *(232)*
HOME *(237)*
child abuse *(242)*
neglect *(243)*

KEY QUESTIONS

1. Which emotions develop in the first year?

2. Which factors influence whether a baby will be afraid of a stranger?

3. What are some consequences of the toddler's growing sense of self?

4. What are the similarities among the theories of Freud, Erikson, and Mahler?

5. What are some enduring temperamental characteristics that seem to be present from the first months of life?

6. How do maturation and culture affect emotional development?

7. What are the possible causes for sex differences in infant emotional development?

8. What are the similarities and differences between mother-infant and father-infant interaction?

9. How does attachment affect cognitive development, and vice versa?

10. What are some of the important factors in a child's development of social and cognitive competence?

11. How might parents adjust their care-giving routines in response to their infants' particular characteristics?

12. What are some of the reasons parent-infant interaction does not always go well?

13. How common is child abuse and neglect?

14. What can be done to help abused children and their parents?

RECOMMENDED READINGS

Scarr, Sandra. *Mother care/Other care.* New York: Warner Books, 1985.

A very well-informed and realistic book, which not only discusses the advantages and disadvantages of the various forms of day care but also examines historical and contemporary views of motherhood. Herself a prominent scholar in developmental psychology, as well as a mother of four, Scarr knows full well how hard it is to meet our culture's demand to be both Superwoman and Supermom. Scarr clearly explains the developmental needs of babies and young children, which, she believes, must be the determining factor in deciding the type of care a child should receive.

Erikson, Erik. *Childhood and society.* 2nd ed. New York: Norton, 1985.

Erikson's classic work describing each of his eight stages. Particularly relevant to this chapter is Erikson's explanation of the effect of infancy on later development. This is shown in the case history of an emotionally disturbed girl and in his discussion of childhood among the Sioux and Yurok Indians.

Stern, Daniel. *The first relationship.* 4th ed. Cambridge, Mass.: Harvard University Press, 1985.

Describes research in mother-infant interaction, as well as practical application of this research. Includes what can go wrong ("missteps in the dance") and an honest appraisal of what psychologists know and do not know about parent-child relationships.

Kempe, Ruth S., and **Kempe, C. Henry.** *Child abuse.* 8th ed. Cambridge, Mass.: Harvard University Press, 1985.

The best book to date on child abuse, written by two authors who are famous for their work on the detection and care of abuse victims in Denver, Colorado. The book includes discussions of child neglect and sexual abuse, but the focus is on the treatment and prevention of physical abuse.

Part II

The Developing Person So Far: The First Two Years

Physical Development

Brain and Nervous System

The brain triples in weight. Neurons branch and grow into increasingly dense connective networks between the brain and the rest of the body. As neurons become coated with an insulating layer of myelin, they send messages faster and more efficiently. The infant's experiences help to "fine-tune" the brain's responses to stimulation.

Motor Abilities

Brain maturation allows the development of motor skills from reflexes to coordinated motor abilities, including grasping and walking. At birth, the infant's senses of smell and hearing are quite acute, and although vision at first is sharp only for objects that are about 10 inches away, by 6 months, acuity approaches 20/20.

Cognitive Development

Cognitive Skills

The infant progresses from knowing his or her world only through immediate sensorimotor experiences to being able to "experiment" on that world mentally, through the use of mental combinations and an understanding of object permanence.

Language

Babies' cries are their first communication; they then progress through cooing and babbling. Interaction with adults through "baby talk" teaches them the surface structure of language. By age 1, an infant can usually speak a word or two, and by age 2 is talking in short sentences.

Psychosocial Development

Personality Development

The major psychosocial development during the first two years is the infant's transition from total dependence to increasing independence. This transition is explained by Freud in terms of the oral and anal stages, by Erikson in terms of the crises of trust versus mistrust and autonomy versus shame and doubt, and by Mahler in terms of separation–individuation.

Understanding Self and Others

In the first months, infants have very little understanding of themselves and others as separate persons. Between the ages of 1 and 2, they begin to develop self-awareness and, consequently, become much more attentive to the reactions of others.

Parent–Infant Interaction

Parents and infants respond to each other first by synchronizing their behavior. Toward the end of the first year, secure attachment between child and parent sets the stage for the child's increasingly independent exploration of the world.

The Play Years

Part III

The period from age 2 to 6 is usually called early childhood, or the preschool period. Here, however, these years are called the play years to underscore the importance of play. Play occurs at every age, of course. But the years of early childhood are the most playful of all, for children spend most of their waking hours at play, acquiring the skills, ideas, and values that are crucial for growing up. They chase each other and dare themselves to attempt new tasks, developing their bodies; they play with words and ideas, developing their minds; they play games and dramatize fantasies, learning social skills and moral rules.

The playfulness of young children can cause them to be delightful or exasperating. To them, growing up is a game, and their enthusiasm for it seems unlimited, whether they are quietly tracking a beetle through the grass or riotously turning their play area into a shambles. Their minds seem playful too, for the immaturity of their thinking enables them to explain that "a bald man has a barefoot head," or that "the sun shines so children can go outside to play."

If you expect them to sit quietly, think logically, or act realistically, you are bound to be disappointed. But if you enjoy playfulness, you might enjoy caring for, listening to, and even reading about children between 2 and 6 years old.

The Play Years: Physical Development

Chapter 9

*The lost child cries,
  but still he catches fireflies.*

Ryusui Yoshida
The Lost Child

Physical Play
Sensorimotor Play
Mastery Play
Rough-and-Tumble Play
The Importance of Play

Size and Shape
Height and Weight
Growth Problems

Brain, Eyes, and Other Organs
Brain Maturation
The Two Halves of the Brain
Eye Maturation
Body Changes

Mastering Motor Skills
Gross Motor Skills
Fine Motor Skills
Children's Art

Activity Level
Accident Rates

Sex Differences and Similarities
Implications

Chapter 9

Between the ages of 2 and 6, increases in children's strength and motor skills, along with their more adultlike body proportions, allow the exploration and mastery of their world to proceed by leaps and bounds, both literally and figuratively. In this chapter we will examine not only the physical changes that occur in the play years but also the implications these changes have for behavior and learning, including topics such as the following:

What is the importance of children's play in the development of physical and social skills?

What are the hereditary and environmental factors that affect growth?

What are some of the growth problems that may occur in early childhood?

Which aspects of physical development have a bearing on a child's readiness for school?

Which activities are important in helping children refine their motor skills?

In which physical abilities are boys and girls of this age similarly skillful? In which abilities does one sex have an advantage over the other?

The primary topic of this chapter is the development of the body and brain that occurs during early childhood, making the average 6-year-old very different from the average 2-year-old in size, shape, and acquired skills. But before describing the changes involved in this development, let us look at children at play. Once we can picture how children use their bodies as they grow, the significance of the changes in height, weight, and motor skills will be easier to understand.

Physical Play

Developmentalists look at children's play in several ways. One important way—in terms of the social interaction that occurs in play—is explained in Chapter 11. In this chapter, we will describe three types of play involving physical activity.

Sensorimotor Play

Play that captures the pleasures of using the senses and motor abilities is called **sensorimotor play.** We have already seen that infants regularly engage in this kind of play, delighting in such things as watching a turning mobile or kicking the side of the basinette. This pleasure in sensory experiences and motor skills continues throughout childhood. For example, given the chance, preschool children will happily explore the many sensory experiences that can be extracted from their food,

Figure 9.1 *Given that children enjoy the feel of paint as much as the sight of it, this young artist couldn't have picked a more appropriate place to practice her craft.*

feeling various textures as they mix noodles and meat together with their hands, watching peas float after they put them in their milk, listening to the slurping sound they make as they suck in spaghetti, tasting unusual combinations such as cocoa sprinkled on lemonade. Children find similar opportunities for sensorimotor play in almost any context, in the sandbox, the bathtub, or a mud hole.

In addition to play that engages their primary senses, children enjoy exploring their sense of motion and balance. For example, preschoolers love to roll down a hill, thrilling to the careening of their bodies, the topsy-turvy whirl of sky, trees, and grass, and the overpowering dizziness they experience when they try to get up. All the sensory joys contribute to each child's understanding of the physical world and his or her connection to it.

Mastery Play

Much of the physical play of childhood is **mastery play,** a term used to describe the play that leads to the mastery of new skills. Children waste no opportunity to develop and practice their physical skills. A simple walk to the grocery store can become episode after episode of mastery play, as the child walks on top of a wall, then jumps over every crack in the sidewalk (so as not to "step on a crack and break your mother's back"), then skips, or walks backward, or races to the store. Along the way, there may be ice patches to slide across, or wind to run against, or puddles to jump over, or into. Similarly, making a snack, getting dressed, or listening to music all are occasions for mastery play. Hand skills are also developed in mastery play, as when children tie knots in their shoelaces, put pegs in pegboards, or use a pair of scissors to make snippets of paper out of a single sheet.

Figure 9.2 *Balancing is a skill learned gradually throughout childhood. These girls have already mastered the fundamentals, and they are learning the significance of the design of a particular balance board, and whether it is better to stand with feet apart or together.*

Children may even master skills their parents would rather they not: 4-year-olds climb to the top of a jungle gym and fearlessly hang upside down by their legs, or pump themselves high on swings and then leap off, or pry open a camera that is loaded with film. Almost anything can be a challenge, especially if an older sibling can do it, and does it with an "I dare you."

Mastery play is most obvious when physical skills are involved, but it includes almost any skill the child feels motivated to learn. For instance, as children grow older, mastery play increasingly includes activities that are clearly intellectual, such as play with words or ideas.

Rough-and-Tumble Play

The third type of physical play we will describe here is called **rough-and-tumble play.** The aptness of its name is made clear by the following example:

> Jimmy, a preschooler, stands observing three of his male classmates building a sand castle. After a few moments he climbs on a tricycle and, smiling, makes a beeline for the same area, ravaging the structure in a single sweep. The builders immediately take off in hot pursuit of the hit-and-run phantom, yelling menacing threats of "come back here, you." Soon the tricycle halts and they pounce on him. The four of them tumble about in the grass amid shouts of glee, wrestling and punching until a teacher intervenes. The four wander off together toward the swings. [cited in Maccoby, 1980]

One distinguishing characteristic of rough-and-tumble play is its mimicry of aggression, a fact first noted in observations of young monkeys' wrestling, chasing, and pummeling of each other (Jones, 1976). The observers discovered that the key to the true nature of this seemingly hostile behavior was the monkeys' **play face,** that is, a facial expression that seemed to suggest that the monkeys were having fun. The play face was an accurate clue, for only rarely, and apparently acciden-

Figure 9.3 *Time to intervene to protect the victim from the three attackers? Not as long as the "victim" is smiling. This is rough-and-tumble play.*

tally, did the monkeys actually hurt each other. (The same behaviors accompanied by a frown usually meant a serious conflict was taking place.)

In human children, too, rough-and-tumble play is quite different from aggression, even though at first glance it may look the same. This distinction is important, for rough-and-tumble play is a significant part of the daily activities of many children in preschool, especially after they have had to sit quietly for a period of time (Jones, 1976). Adults who wonder when to break up a "fight" may be helped by knowing that facial expression is as telltale in children as it is in monkeys: children almost always smile, and often laugh, in rough-and-tumble play, whereas they frown and scowl in real fighting (Aldis, 1975).

Rough-and-tumble play is a social activity that usually occurs among children who have had considerable social experience, often with each other. Not surprisingly, then, among children in nursery schools, newcomers, younger children, and only children take longer to join in rough-and-tumble play than to participate in any other form of play (Shea, 1981; Garvey, 1976). Rough-and-tumble play is also more likely to occur among boys than among girls—three times more likely according to one carefully controlled study (DiPietro, 1981). (The implications of this and other sex differences in the physical development of preschool children are discussed at the end of this chapter.)

The Importance of Play

Although for children, play is something done simply for fun, developmentalists view children's play as work, a major means through which physical and social skills are strengthened and honed.

The first evidence of the importance of play came from ethology, which is the scientific study of the behavior of animals, usually observed in their natural habitat. Through studies like the ones done of monkeys at play, ethologists have discovered that healthy animals of all species, and both sexes, play when they are young. Even animals whose nourishment is inadequate, causing them to spend a great deal of time searching for food, still spend some of their time and their energy in play (Muller-Schwarze et al., 1982). Researchers have also been struck by the similarity between the play of young animals and the skills needed by the full-grown animals of that species. Consider the play of kittens (Egan, 1976). They will sniff and pat any mouse-sized object. If it moves, they crouch and pounce. If it is furry, they will also bite it, carry it around, shake it, and toss it. If the object is alive, and the kitten is hungry, the furry creature is then killed and eaten. But when the kitten is not hungry, the object is played with for a long time, especially if it continues to move. Well-fed kittens play as much as hungry kittens; they just don't eat their prey when they are done. Obviously, kittens who become skilled at kitten's play will become cats who are skilled at catching prey.

Similarly, juvenile animals of all species playfully practice the motor skills that adult animals will need. They race around (often in circles!); they pretend to fight (with apparent surprise when the game stops if someone is hurt); they build simple beds, or nests, or lairs that will never be used.

While they are engaged in physical play, young animals of many species, including all the primates, also playfully practice social skills that may be critically important for survival. For example, most kinds of monkeys live in fairly large groups: in order to live together peacefully, all the adults must know how to assert their rights without antagonizing other adults to the point of a serious fight. So, by pretending to fight with each other, baby monkeys learn complicated behaviors of dominance and submission, using facial expressions, body language, and mock chase and retreat to regulate their interaction. Without the opportunity to play with their peers, young monkeys become adults who are socially isolated, or who start fights they cannot handle, becoming seriously wounded or even getting killed (Harlow and Harlow, 1962).

Nurturant behaviors are learned through play as well. Primates in early adolescence seem particularly interested in infants, playing with them and caring for them whenever the infants' mothers allow it. Such play is evident in juveniles of both sexes, although male monkeys tend to play more actively, and less gently, with younger monkeys than female juveniles do (Mitchell and Shively, 1984).

Looking again at human children, it becomes clear that sensorimotor play, mastery play, and rough-and-tumble play, all help develop various skills that children will need later in life. And as we shall see at the end of this chapter, some researchers believe that sex-related differences in children's play patterns may have telling implications for later development. Thus, while play and work are often considered opposites, and parents sometimes complain that their children play too much (sometimes even punishing them for "playing around"), developmentalists are convinced that even the most care-free, spontaneous play is related to serious productive work (Garvey, 1977; Vandenberg, 1978; Smith, 1984). For children, playing is clearly a productive part of growing up (Rubin et al., 1983).

Size and Shape

The increasingly vigorous and masterful physical play of the preschooler is aided by the changing shape and increasing strength of the child's body. During the preschool years, the child becomes slimmer as the lower body lengthens. The kindergarten child no longer has the protruding stomach, round face, and disproportionately short limbs and large head that are characteristic of the toddler. By age 6, the proportions of the child's body are not very different from those of the adult (Sinclair, 1978).

Height and Weight

Of course, while their body proportions change, children grow steadily taller and heavier as well. From age 2 through 6, children add almost 3 inches (7 centimeters) and gain about 4½ pounds (2 kilograms) per year. By age 5, the average North American child weighs about 40 pounds (18 kilograms) and measures 43 inches (109 centimeters).

Many children are taller or shorter than these averages (see Figure 9.4). Weight is especially variable: about 10 percent of American 5-year-olds weigh less than 35 pounds and another 10 percent weigh almost 50 pounds (National Center for Health Statistics, 1976).

Figure 9.4 *As these charts show, boys (black line) and girls (color line) grow more slowly and steadily than they did in the first two years of life. Consequently, weight gain is particularly slow, with most children losing body fat during these years. The weight that is gained is usually bone and muscle.*

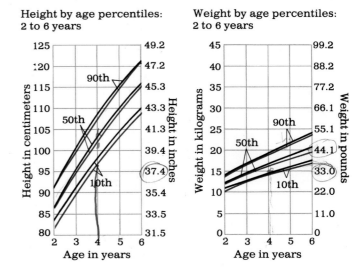

Of the many factors that influence height (see Table 9.1), the two most influential are genetic background and nutrition (Meredith, 1978). In general, children from northern Europe have the tallest average height, and children from southern Asia, the shortest. For instance, 3-year-olds from The Netherlands average 38 inches (97 centimeters), almost 6 inches (15 centimeters) taller than their contemporaries from Bangladesh. In fact, 3-year-old Dutch children are taller, on average, than 5-year-olds from several other countries.

TABLE 9.1 **Factors Affecting the Height of Preschoolers**

Taller than average if	Shorter than average if
well nourished	malnourished
rarely sick	frequently or chronically sick
northern European or African ancestors	Asian ancestors
mother is nonsmoker	mother smoked during pregnancy
upper class	lower class
lives in urban area	lives in rural area
lives at sea level	lives high above sea level
first born in small family	third or later born, large family
male	female

Sources: Eveleth and Tanner, 1976; Meredith, 1978; Lowrey, 1978; Vaughan, 1983.

Figure 9.5 *Since preschoolers tend to equate size with age, and age with wisdom and power, the question of "who is taller" often leads to some stretching of the facts.*

Health care is also an important factor in that children who are repeatedly or chronically sick tend to become malnourished, and this, in turn, affects their growth. Upper-class children, urban children, and first-born children are all somewhat taller than average, largely because their diet and medical care are better (Eveleth and Tanner, 1976).

Generally, boys are slightly taller and heavier than girls, although this varies depending on the culture. Even in the early years, boys in India are markedly taller and heavier than their sisters because boys are much preferred and therefore are given better care (Poffenberger, 1981). In North America, the heaviest children tend to be female because girls are more likely than boys to eat too much and exercise too little (Lowrey, 1978). (The problem of childhood obesity is discussed in Chapter 12, p. 360.)

Eating Habits   Whether a child is short or tall, his or her annual height and weight increase much more slowly from age 2 to 6 than during the first two years of life. (In fact, between ages 2 and 3, an average child adds fewer pounds than during any other twelve-month period until age 17.) Since growth is slower during the preschool years, children need fewer calories per pound during this period than they did from birth through toddlerhood. Consequently, their appetites are smaller, a fact that causes many parents to worry. Indeed, in the view of their parents, 42 percent of the boys and 31 percent of the girls between the ages of 4 and 5 do not "eat well." In most cases, this decline in appetite does not represent a serious problem, for it rarely indicates a serious behavioral disorder and it usually improves markedly by age 8 (Achenbach and Edelbrock, 1981). Serious malnutrition is much more likely to occur in infancy and in adolescence than in early childhood (Abraham et al., 1974).

Of course, as at any age, the diet during the preschool years should be a healthy one. The most common nutritional problem during the preschool years is iron deficiency anemia, the chief symptom of which is chronic fatigue. This problem, which stems from an insufficiency of quality meats and dark-green vegetables, affects mostly the poor (including 34 percent of all black, 13 percent of all white, and 9 percent of all Hispanic preschoolers [Eichorn, 1979]). In addition, too much fat, salt, or cholesterol in childhood can produce health problems later on. Although most nutritional problems during the preschool years are related to low family income, it should be noted that too many "sweets" can be a contributing factor. Candy, soda, and sweetened cereals can spoil a small appetite faster than they can a large one, and they therefore should be limited to make sure the child consumes enough of the foods that contain essential vitamins, minerals, and protein.

Figure 9.6 *Prevention, not punishment, is the best approach if a child doesn't want to finish his or her food. If junk food is eliminated from the diet, and if meals are not stressful times when people argue about eating, the child's appetite will assure that enough nourishment is consumed.*

There is another reason sweets should be limited. Tooth decay is a chronic disease that is directly correlated with sugar consumption. While other factors, such as quality of dental care, frequency of brushing and flossing, and fluoridation of the water are also important, a summary of various kinds of research—cross-sectional and longitudinal, national and international—makes it clear that snacking, especially snacking on sugary foods, is likely to result in tooth decay a few years later (Newbrun, 1982). While this may seem a minor problem in the preschool years, the long-term consequences can include tooth loss and gum disease.

Growth Problems

In any given group of nursery-school children, one or two are usually noticeably bigger or smaller than their classmates. In all likelihood, they are perfectly normal and in the best of health; they are simply genetically destined to be tall or short at this stage of development.

However, about one child in a thousand suffers from a growth disorder, either **dwarfism,** which results in abnormal shortness, or **giantism,** that results in abnormal tallness. Because there is substantial normal variation in height, simply comparing a young child's height to that of the average child usually does not distinguish normal from abnormal growth. A much better way to spot problems is to examine bone growth (Lowrey, 1978).

As a child grows, the soft cartilage of the skeleton hardens into bone, becoming fully hardened only when growth stops in late adolescence. This hardening process, called **ossification,** can be measured with x-rays. By comparing x-rays of a child's hand or foot (in which ossification of the many small bones is easy to measure) with x-rays showing average skeletal maturity at that age, **bone age** can be calculated.

If actual bone age is much different from expected bone age, growth problems are to be suspected. For example, an unusually tall 4-year-old's height is just right if the bone age is 5; too tall if the bone age is 3 (height in this case is outdistancing skeletal maturation); and too short if the bone age is 7 (height here is progressing more slowly than skeletal maturation) (Sinclair, 1978).

Treatment of Growth Problems If a growth problem is discovered, treatment depends on the cause. Giantism has several causes, all in the physical domain and each requiring specific medical treatment, usually drug therapy and surgery (DiGeorge, 1983). Dwarfism, however, can involve psychosocial as well as physical causes. When a growth deficiency is the result of a genetic condition or a prenatal abnormality, children can usually be given hormones to regulate their growth. The earlier the problem is detected and treated, the better the chance of normal height (Tanner, 1978).

The second general cause of dwarfism is physical problems that appear during childhood. Chronic infections (such as hookworm or dysentery), untreated diabetes, kidney disease, and prolonged malnutrition all stunt growth. If these problems are remedied in time, a growth catch-up often allows the child to reach normal height (Lowrey, 1978).

Figure 9.7 *Gary Coleman, born with a serious kidney abnormality, has been able to live a relatively normal and very successful life as a television star, thanks to advances in kidney transplant technique. However, the combination of the effects of his disease and the drugs necessary to treat it have stunted his growth: at age 15, he was 4 feet 2 inches tall, about as tall as the average 8-year-old. Doctors hope that he may be able to add another 12 inches to his stature before growth ends.*

Finally, psychological factors can be the cause of growth problems. Too much stress or not enough attention can prevent normal production of growth hormones, even if genes, medical care, and nutrition are adequate. This problem is called **deprivation dwarfism.**

Of course, it is not always possible to separate the effects of malnutrition from those of maltreatment because the two often occur together. However, some abnormally short children are overweight rather than underweight, which is a sign that the problem may be deprivation dwarfism. While children suffering from deprivation dwarfism sometimes do not eat at all, at other times many such children overeat, stealing from the refrigerator at night and even gobbling up food set out for the cat or the dog (Tanner, 1978). Apparently, a pattern of erratic eating, coupled with the physiological effects of psychological stress, interferes with normal growth processes.

A related factor is abnormal sleep patterns. Since peak production of growth hormones occurs during the hours of deep sleep, a child who is deprived of sleep (perhaps because of poor sleeping conditions, nightmares, or late bedtimes) may also be deprived of these hormones (Wolff and Money, 1980).

Most children suffering from deprivation dwarfism grow rapidly if they are admitted to the hospital, but stop growing and even lose weight when they return home (Gardner, 1972). Since the cause of the disorder is neither physical abuse nor apparent malnutrition, it is difficult to require counseling for the parents, and even more difficult to remove the child from the home. James Tanner suggests that consent for the child's removal is more likely to be obtained if, rather than blaming the parents for being inadequate, clinicians try to keep family morale intact by telling the parents that their child needs the special care required by "delicate children" (Tanner, 1978). If children suffering from deprivation dwarfism are removed from their homes and then given good foster care, they often demonstrate a "spectacular" recovery, undergoing a period of catch-up growth and then developing normally (Tanner, 1978).

Brain, Eyes, and Other Organs

Changes in size and shape are the most visible signs of physical development between ages 2 and 6. However, changes in the central nervous system and in various organs are probably even more important to the child's development, for they underlie many emerging abilities. They make it possible, for example, for most 6-year-olds to tie a shoelace, ride a bicycle, and to sit and learn in a first-grade classroom for hours at a time, things that even the biggest and brightest 2-year-old cannot do.

Brain Maturation

The most important development is brain maturation. As indicated in Chapter 6, during childhood the brain develops faster than any other part of the body. One simple indication of this is weight: by age 5, the brain has attained about 90 percent of its adult weight, even though the average 5-year-old's body weight is less than one-third the average adult's (Tanner, 1978). Part of this increase in brain size is due to the ongoing process of myelination, which provides the nerves with an insulating sheathing that speeds up the transmission of neural impulses. The pattern of

A CLOSER LOOK　　**The Left-Handed Child**

While adults usually don't notice a child's hand preference until preschool years, evidence suggests that it begins to develop early in life. Even newborns show some signs that presage handedness. Sixty-five percent of all infants prefer to turn their heads to the right when they are lying on their stomachs in their cribs, and fifteen percent prefer to face left, preferences that correlate with later handedness (Michel, 1981). By 7 months, many infants prefer grabbing with one hand or the other (Ramsay, 1980), and those that are prone to thumb- or finger-sucking tend to favor one hand over the other for this activity. Typically, the preferred hand in these cases becomes the preferred hand for throwing, writing, and the like.

By age 2, about one child in ten favors the left hand, although many are inconsistent in their preference (Hardyck and Petrinovich, 1977). Indeed, about half of all toddlers and preschoolers sometimes use the nonpreferred hand for drawing or other tasks (Gottfried and Bathurst, 1983).

Recent evidence points toward genes as the origin of hand preference (Corballis, 1983). For instance, one study found that the handedness of adopted children shows little correlation with that of their adoptive parents, but significant correlation with the handedness of their biological parents (Carter-Saltzman, 1980). Another study found that while left-handed mothers are equally likely to pass along their hand-preference to their daughters as to their sons, left-handed fathers are particularly likely to pass the trait on to their sons—which is one reason why boys are more often left-handed than are girls (Longstreth, 1980).

Whether a child is right- or left-handed would be a matter of only passing interest if it were not for the cultural connotation of left-handedness. Throughout history, left-handedness was considered wrong, and right-handedness, right. Indeed, according to the Bible, it is the blessed who are at God's right hand; the cursed are at his left. The English words "sinister," meaning evil, and "dextrous," meaning skilled, come directly from the Latin words *sinister* ("left") and *dexter* ("right"). Indeed, the words for "left" in almost every language connote something negative:

Mancino means "deceitful" in Italian; *linkisch,* "awkward" in German; *na levo,* "sneaky" in Russian. In Spanish *zurdo* also means "malicious," and *no ser zurdo,* "to be not left-handed," in addition means "to be very clever." . . . moreover, the French word for left, *gauche,* is applied to those social misfits who make a habit of putting their foot in their mouth. [Fincher, 1977]

Because of this view, many left-handed children have been forced by parents and teachers to become right-handed. Those who refused were considered stubborn and disobedient, or even a child of the devil.

Given this background, it is worth noting the advantages and disadvantages that lefties experience, if only to defend the left-handed child against the lingering prejudice that he or she might encounter. To begin with, except for the minority whose left-handedness can be attributed to brain damage, left-handed children and adults are as intelligent and as capable in most skills as right-handed people (Kinsbourne and Hiscock, 1983; Tan, 1985). Sometimes they even have an advantage in that

the myelination process bears significantly on the child's developing abilities: the areas of the brain associated with hand-eye coordination, for example, do not become fully myelinated until around age 4; those associated with the ability to maintain focused attention, not until the end of childhood; those associated with language and intelligence, not until age 15 or so (Tanner, 1978).

Brain maturation of this sort is especially important when one considers the abilities that are required for formal education. Unless the child is neurologically able to concentrate, merely sitting in one place and keeping one's eyes on the teacher can be a difficult task. In fact, it appears that concentration, especially the ability to screen out distractions, does improve markedly between ages 4 and 7 (Higgins and Turnure, 1984). Similarly dependent on a certain level of brain maturation are school skills such as reading, which involves controlled and attentive coordination between the eye muscles and several areas of the brain; and writing, which is not only a motor skill but also involves coordination of sounds, letters, words, and small movements of the fingers.

they show a greater tendency toward ambidexterity than do right-handed people (Fincher, 1977). Interestingly, lefties become famous artists more frequently than their proportion in the general population would predict. It may be that the genetic tendency toward left-handedness is associated with other talents, particularly those involving spatial perception (Corballis, 1983).

However, left-handed children are handicapped in mastering one basic skill, handwriting. For one thing, it is hard to use the left hand to write languages that read from left to right, such as English, without covering the words and smudging the paper as the writing hand moves along the line just written. Some languages are easier for the left-handed because they are written from top to bottom, like Chinese, or from right to left, like Hebrew. However, no matter where they are placed on the page, letters or characters in almost every language are usually formed from left to right and counterclockwise. This presents a difficulty for lefties, who naturally draw from right to left and clockwise (Linksz, 1973). They would rather write this way: Left ← than this way: **Left** →.

Thus, left-handed children may need extra encouragement and patience when it comes to learning penmanship. In fact, one researcher (Linksz, 1973) feels that left-handed children should be taught to write with their right hand, and allowed to use their left hand for everything else. However, most psychologists believe that because a child who shows a clear preference for the left hand is obeying genetic instructions, the child should not be switched. Some educators suspect that forcing a left-handed child to switch creates other problems, such as

Lefties often use one of two basic strategies to avoid smears and smudges as they proceed across the page—they may either hook their arm and wrist or they may turn the paper. The latter solution seems to correlate with more efficient brain development.

stuttering or reading difficulties, although research has not confirmed this (Spache, 1976).

It is confirmed however, that hand preference is apparent in the early days of life, and that it is linked to the organization of the brain. Therefore, efforts to switch a leftie run counter to the child's nature. Instead, when a preschool child seems to be left-handed, it is time to find another leftie to teach such basic skills as shoe-tying and pencil-holding, and to buy scissors designed for the left hand or a baseball mitt for the right.

The Two Halves of the Brain

One of the most important aspects of the development of the brain has to do with its being organized into left and right hemispheres, each controlling one half of the body. Oddly enough, the left hemisphere of the brain controls the right side of the body, while the right hemisphere controls the left half of the body. Thus the right hand, foot, eye, ear, and so on, are "wired" to the left side of the brain; and the left hand, foot, and so on are wired to the right.

As the brain matures, it becomes more specialized; that is, particular parts of the brain tend to be used for certain abilities. In 95 percent of right-handed adults as well as 70 percent of left-handed adults, the left side of the brain is the location of many areas that deal with aspects of logical analysis and language development, including speech, while the right side contains many areas for various visual and artistic skills, including recognizing faces, responding to music, and spatial perception (Kinsbourne and Hiscock, 1983).

Obviously, for a person to be fully functioning, both sides of the brain need to work together smoothly. (Despite reports from the popular press to the contrary, no normal person is solely a right-brain or left-brain thinker [Gardner, 1982; Bradshaw, 1983]). Therefore the development of the network of nerves that connect the two sides, in the corpus callosum, is particularly important. As the corpus callosum becomes increasingly myelinated between ages 2 and 8 (Yakovlev and Lecours, 1967), the functioning of the two halves of the brain becomes more closely integrated. Interestingly, the corpus callosum is significantly larger in left-handed individuals, which suggests that left-handed children may develop stronger communication networks between the two halves of the brain, and thus develop greater bihemispheric functioning, than right-handed children.

Brain specialization obviously increases the capacity of the person to perform a variety of intellectual and motor tasks. At the same time, however, such specialization makes it harder for the brain to compensate for loss of function of particular areas due to injury. This is seen most dramatically in the case of language loss in people who have suffered damage to the language area of the brain. If the victim is a young child, language function may be taken up by another area of the brain, and the child may learn to speak normally again. If the victim is past adolescence, when language specialization is completed, he or she is likely to be forever mute (Gardner, 1982).

Another indication of brain specialization in early childhood is the clear emergence of hand preference during these years (see Closer Look). Interestingly, as children begin to become more skilled at manipulating objects with one hand (usually their right), they also become more skilled at sensitively touching objects with the other. A study of fourteen right-handed blind children, for instance, found that they could read Braille more quickly and accurately with the fingers of their left hand than with the fingers of their right (Hermelin and O'Connor, 1971). (This study was prompted by a blind child who had injured his left hand and said he could not do his schoolwork because his "reading hand" was hurt.) Like hand preference for manipulation, hand preference for sensitive touching develops during early childhood, another indication that the brain specialization occurs during these years (Rose, 1984).

Figure 9.8 *Sometimes preschoolers use their left hand to paint or write simply because their right hand is busy doing something else. (One of the author's former undergraduate students had learned to write with his left hand because he usually kept his right thumb in his mouth. As an adult, he is right-handed for everything except writing, the opposite pattern of many left-handed persons.)*

Eye Maturation

Brain maturation probably underlies the improvement of vision that occurs during the preschool years. Children younger than 6 do not usually have sufficiently developed eye muscles to allow them to move their eyes slowly and deliberately across a series of small letters (Vurpillot, 1968). As a result, preschoolers are likely to guess at a word on the basis of the first letter rather than looking at the entire word.

Because preschoolers have not achieved visual maturity does not mean that they cannot see small details: even 3-year-olds can, momentarily, focus on a tiny image (Hillerich, 1983). It is sustained and systematic focusing that is particularly hard. Until age 5 or 6 many children have an additional visual limitation: they are often farsighted; that is, they can see better at a distance than they can up close.

By age 6, most children can focus and scan reasonably well, although they are still much less skilled at scanning than adults are (Mackworth and Bruner, 1970; van Oeffelen and Vos, 1984). By age 8, most children are able to follow a line of small print. Of course, as with all aspects of physical maturation, individual differences are common. To make sure a particular child can see well enough to do schoolwork, educators recommend a thorough visual examination before the first grade, including tests of near and far vision, eye strain, and binocular vision (the ability of both eyes to work together) (Bond et al., 1979).

Body Changes

Many parents find that by age 6 their "sickly" child is ill less often, the allergic child is less sensitive to particular foods and dust, and the bed-wetting child is usually able to stay dry. Physiological factors underlie each of these changes.

For instance, 5-year-olds have fewer colds and intestinal upsets than they did when they were younger (Bayer and Snyder, 1971), partly because their immune system becomes more highly developed, and partly because they have already been exposed to, and therefore produced antibodies to, the more common viruses. Stomachaches become less common as the functioning of the digestive system becomes more regular; ear infections become rarer as the distance from the inner ear to the outer ear increases; respiratory illnesses become less severe as the trachea (windpipe) grows longer; and fevers tend to be lower as the normal body temperature becomes lower and more stable (the average temperature of a 1-year-old is 99.7 F, or 37.6 C; by age 5, it is 98.6 F, or 37.0 C [Lowrey, 1978]).

Further, as children's bodies grow, their patterns of sleeping, eating, and elimination begin to approximate adult patterns, because their brain waves become more adultlike and their stomachs and bladders become larger and more stable. This means that 5-year-olds can go for longer periods without a nap, a snack, or a trip to the bathroom. These are some of the maturational changes that contribute to a child's readiness for school (see Closer Look, next page).

As is true in almost all cases of maturation, these changes are gradual, and individual differences are common. For example, about 21 percent of all 6-year-olds sometimes or always wet their beds, and one child in eight still has this problem at age 10 (National Center for Health Statistics, 1971). Part of the reason some children are slower to develop nighttime bladder control is physiological: some children have smaller bladders or sounder sleep patterns than other children the same age. Emotional factors are often involved as well, as shown by a rise in bed-wetting when children sleep away from home. Thus, punishing a child for wetting the bed or for daytime accidents may compound the problem, for emotional stress makes bladder control more difficult.

Readiness for School

The discussion of the preschooler's physical maturation, particularly that of the brain and eyes, raises an important question: When is a child ready for formal education? Until the middle of the twentieth century, the answer to this question was definitive: at age 6. Indeed, according to the laws of the land, 6-year-olds must attend school, but younger children need not.

Before the 1960s, even preschoolers who did attend some sort of school were not usually taught academic skills. Most kindergartens, for instance, avoided teaching children to read and discouraged parents from doing so (Hillerich, 1983). By first grade, however, in virtually every school district, children were assumed ready for formal education and the three R's were taught to all.

Using age 6 as an indicator of readiness for academic subjects worked well for the average child, but children who matured early became bored and those who matured late became frustrated. In the 1960s educators decided that some children were ready to start learning some basic skills, particularly reading, at age 5 and that others were not ready until age 8. In order to distinguish the two, they developed readiness tests (e.g., Ilg and Ames, 1965; de Hirsch et al., 1966) that asked 5-year-olds to demonstrate gross motor skills, such as hopping on one foot, or fine motor skills, such as drawing a person or copying a rectangle, or intellectual skills such as telling a story or counting to ten. To varying degrees, scores on each of these tests correlated with school achievement later on (Telegdy, 1975; Flynn and Flynn, 1978; Lindquist, 1982). Depending on their scores, some kindergarteners were taught to read and write, while other children were kept at playing with blocks and dolls until age 7 or 8 (Cicourel et al., 1974).

Many parents objected to this solution, for children who were "unready" in kindergarten were likely to be at the bottom of the academic heap throughout their school career (Satz et al., 1978). Indeed, some parents and educators began teaching 4-year-olds to read and add, hoping that an academic headstart would boost their later school achievement (see Chapter 10 for a discussion of preschool education). On the other hand, many teachers thought it was a mistake to begin formal education with children who seemed unready, for they had seen too many first-graders crying in despair because they could not master the printed page, or could not write without tearing the paper or breaking the pencil point.

The controversy about when children should be taught academic skills is still not settled. As you would expect from the "better baby" movement described in Chapter 7, some experts (e.g., Doman, 1980; Emery, 1975) advise parents to begin teaching reading and math during the preschool years, partly because early reading at home will supposedly make a child smarter and less frustrated than children who learn to read in school.

Others take the opposite viewpoint. Dorothy and Raymond Moore (1975) contend that many children, especially boys, are not ready for any kind of formal education until age 8, 9, or even 10. According to them, late starters are better achievers and less frustrated than children who are forced to begin first grade too early. Similarly, the Gesell Institute, the center for the study of child development founded at Yale, maintains that two-thirds of all American children begin formal education before they are really ready and it suggests that repeating one of the early grades is the best solution for many unhappy "overplaced" children (Ilg et al., 1981).

Mastering Motor Skills

Between ages 2 and 6, as the child's body becomes slimmer, stronger, and less top-heavy, **gross motor skills** (as large body movements such as running, climbing, jumping, and throwing are called) improve dramatically.

The improvement is apparent to anyone who watches a group of children at play. Two-year-olds are quite clumsy, falling down frequently and sometimes bumping into stationary objects. But by age 5, many children are both skilled and graceful. Most North American 5-year-olds can ride a tricycle, climb a ladder, pump a swing, and throw, catch, and kick a ball. Some of them can even skate, ski, and ride a two-wheeled bicycle, activities that require balance as well as coordination. In fact, almost any gross motor skill that does not require much strength or judgment can

Which point of view is right? Probably most developmentalists would agree with David Elkind (1978), a cognitive psychologist who stresses that "reading English, far from being a simple matter of discriminating letters and associating sounds, involves complex mental processes from the very start." The child has to be able to regulate the many perceptions, both visual and auditory, involved in word recognition.

Elkind thinks that formal reading instruction probably should be delayed until the child is about 6 or 7. At the same time, he thinks that those 4-year-olds (about 1 in 100) who are eager and able to learn reading should be allowed to, without pressure from parents to master the skill. In fact, one study found that many very gifted children taught themselves to read by age 2 or 3, sometimes despite their parents' efforts to discourage them—including such occasional extremes as removing all children's books from the house (Robinson, 1981). At least until elementary school, then, readiness to read seems to depend largely on the individual child's maturation, interests, and experiences, not on any preset chronological age.

Picture books can be very useful for developing a number of skills that are basic to reading, including the importance of looking carefully and of turning pages in sequence. The most important lesson being taught here, however, is that books are fun.

Psychologists Eleanor Gibson and Harry Levin (1975) assert that the essential experiences a child should have before beginning academic instruction include scribbling, looking at books, and playing rhyming games. At the same time, they caution:

Reading, word games, printing, and so on, should not be forced on a child or formalized. They should be fun, not work. . . . "Home learning" kits of various kinds are advertised like patent medicines, and the consumer would do well to be equally wary of them. The only magic in learning to read is the magic that the child supplies himself when a rich and responsive environment gives him the chance.

For reasonably normal children, factors such as chronological age, motor skills, social development, and intelligence are not directly linked to the readiness to do elementary-school work (Hillerich, 1983). Reading to preschool children, listening to them, and helping them learn the vocabulary and concepts that describe their world are far better for developing "readiness" for reading and other academic activities than trying to teach them to recite the alphabet, write their names, or recognize letters and numbers.

muscle

be learned by most healthy 5-year-olds, if they have a patient teacher and plenty of time and space to practice (Sinclair, 1973).

Gross Motor Skills

Most young children practice their motor skills wherever they are, whether in a well-equipped nursery school with climbing ladders, balance boards, and sand-boxes, or on their own, with furniture for climbing, fences for balancing, and gardens or empty lots for digging up (Whiting and Whiting, 1975). On the whole, pre-school children learn basic motor skills by teaching themselves and learning from other children, rather than by specific adult instruction. So as long as a child has the opportunity to play with other children in an adequate space, motor skills will develop as rapidly as maturation and body size allow.

Figure 9.9 *The materials and equipment required for the development of gross motor skills are minimal: someone to play with and something to play on. Unfortunately, not all children are fortunate in having a large, safe, inviting area in which to run and climb. Each year, many children are injured playing in such dangerous areas as debris-filled lots or condemned buildings.*

However, neither opportunity to play nor adequate space are to be taken for granted in today's society. A study by Murphy and Moriarty (1976) describes playing conditions in one ideal city:

> . . . little traffic and practically no danger from marauders. Ways of life of neighboring families were sufficiently similar so that most mothers permitted the preschool and school-age children to explore freely and to develop friendships with the children in the neighborhood. This meant that it was possible for the child to get outdoors much of the time through his own efforts, even before the age of two, and roam a wide area. . . . Even the homes of most of the poor . . . at that time . . . still had yards up to 50 feet wide and 100 feet deep. [Murphy and Moriarty, 1976]

The authors were writing about Topeka, Kansas, in the 1950s, a city they regarded as unique in its accommodation of children. Few urban children today are as fortunate as the Topeka children were, especially lower-class children in large cities. Play space inside urban apartments is scarce; halls, elevators, and sidewalks are dangerous. Ecological studies have shown that children younger than 9 use public parks infrequently, because the parks are usually too distant, too crowded, or too dangerous for the small child (Gump, 1975). Suburban children are not necessarily better off, especially if the nearest neighborhood playmates are too far away for easy access.

Fine Motor Skills

Fine motor skills, which are the skills that involve small body movements, are much harder for preschoolers to master than gross motor skills. Such things as pouring juice from a pitcher into a glass without spilling, cutting food with a knife and fork, and achieving anything more artful than a scribble with a pencil are difficult even with great concentration and effort. Preschoolers can spend hours trying to tie a bow with their shoelaces, often producing knot upon knot instead.

The chief reason many children experience these difficulties is simply that they have not developed the muscular control or judgment needed for the exercise of fine motor skills, in part because the myelination of the necessary parts of the central nervous system is not complete. For many preschoolers, this liability is compounded by their still having short, fat fingers. If utensils, toys, and clothes for the preschool child are not selected with these limitations in mind, frustration and destruction can result: preschool children may burst into tears when they cannot button their sweaters, or mash a puzzle piece in their attempt to make it fit into the wrong position.

Figure 9.10 Activities such as doing puzzles and weaving not only teach fine motor skills, they also help the child understand spatial relationships and discriminate small differences in size and shape; skills such as these may foster reading readiness.

The Value of Fine Motor Skills Many educators consider the development of fine motor skills to be an important goal of the preschool curriculum. One of the first and most influential of these was Maria Montessori, who nearly a century ago designed a series of puzzles, peg boards, and small motor tasks that encourage coordination between the eye, the hand, and the brain. Her approach gave rise to Montessori schools, which continue to emphasize development of fine motor skills, and comparison studies suggest that such schools prepare children well for formal learning (Miller and Dyer, 1975; Miller and Bizzell, 1983). Happily, the fine motor skill that seems most directly linked to later development is one that is easy for parents and teachers to encourage—the skill of making marks on paper.

A CLOSER LOOK   **Very Nice! What Is It?**

As with most other motor skills, limited skill in "artistic" endeavors does not keep preschoolers from trying. When young children see a pencil, pen, crayon, or magic marker, their first impulse is to draw—on paper, books, walls, or themselves. Their early markings look haphazard to most adults, but psychologists who study them find an amazing sense of order and design (Goodnow, 1976; Allard, 1983).

For example, Kellogg (1970) has identified four loosely age-related stages of artistic development:

1. *Placement stage (up to age 3):*   The child experiments with placing marks on paper, using various scribbles to cover all or part of the page.
2. *Shapes stage (age 3):*   The child tries to make basic shapes, a circle, an "X," a square.
3. *Design stage (age 3½):*   The child uses basic shapes and scribbles to make designs—a circle within a circle, or a series of crosses.
4. *Pictorial stage (ages 4 to 5):*   At this stage the child tries to form pictures of people, animals, and buildings. The older the child, the more detailed the drawings tend to be.

Note that the first drawings are not necessarily intended to be representational. Many children prefer drawing shapes and designs to drawing pictures of real things, and they are mystified at the typical adult question "What is it?"

Once children begin drawing people and things, they expect everyone else to understand exactly what they have created. To them, two vertical lines topped by a circle with two dots inside is obviously Mommy (see Mommy at right). Why would anyone need to ask "What is it?"

It is interesting to speculate why children's drawings at the pictorial stage include, or omit, the particular features that they do. Why, for instance, do early drawings of people begin with the "tadpole stage," (Gardner, 1980) often including head, eyes, legs, arms, hair, and often even hands and feet before they begin to include the trunk? That children simply do not perceive the torso would seem a very unlikely explanation, especially since children know something is missing when they see a doctored photograph that shows a person with a "missing" midsection.

A cognitive explanation is more plausible: children draw body parts in order of their importance to them, and the torso is probably less important to them, perhaps because it seems not to do anything, as hands and feet do. It is also possible that children consider the trunk to be included in their circle-and-line figures. When Goodnow (1977) asked children to add a stomach or belly button to their stick figures, for instance, the children did not act as if they had omitted the midsection from their drawing, they simply added a dot or a circle in the appropriate place.

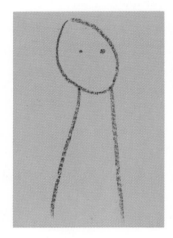

Mommy.

Children's Art

Developmentalists agree that children use art as a form of mastery play. On the simplest level "the child who first wields a marker is learning in many areas of his young life about tool use" (Gardner, 1980). This is not mere speculation. One classic longitudinal study found a link between fine motor skills, such as drawing a rectangle, and later reading, writing, and spelling abilities (de Hirsch et al., 1966). One test of children's intelligence asks the child to draw a person, and then measures the complexity of the drawing to obtain an indication of intellectual ability. Scores on the Goodinough-Harris Drawing Test correlate reasonably well with other intelligence scales and are often used to supplement them (Anastasia, 1982).

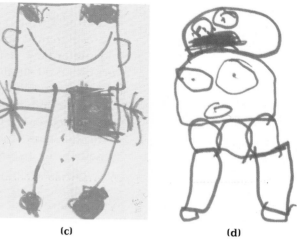

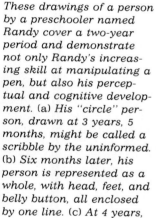

(a)

(b)

(c)

(d)

These drawings of a person by a preschooler named Randy cover a two-year period and demonstrate not only Randy's increasing skill at manipulating a pen, but also his perceptual and cognitive development. (a) His "circle" person, drawn at 3 years, 5 months, might be called a scribble by the uninformed. (b) Six months later, his person is represented as a whole, with head, feet, and belly button, all enclosed by one line. (c) At 4 years, 4 months, Randy attaches the legs to the head and the arms to the legs, a typical pattern followed by preschoolers throughout the world. (d) At 5 years, 2 months, Randy's drawing of "Daddy" shows recognition of the torso, but evidences Randy's difficulty in attaching it to the legs. (e) Finally, at 5 years, 5 months, Randy draws a person complete with hat, teeth, and even the correct number of fingers.

(e)

The scribbling of the young child can be compared to the babbling of the infant (Gardner, 1980). Both are a way to master certain raw materials that at some later date will lead to communication. With time, scribbles become the first representational drawings; the written prose, poetry, and sketches of the adult can be seen as a logical outgrowth of these first attempts to express concepts in a visual way. From this perspective, providing a child with pencils, markers, paint, and paper is as important to the development of communications skills as providing the other tools for early physical development, such as things to climb, things to throw, and places to run.

Activity Level

Children during the early preschool years, at about age 2 or 3, have a higher activity level than at any other time in the entire life span (Eaton, 1983). This seems true no matter how "activity level" is measured. In one cross-sectional study, researchers observed children between the ages of 3 and 9 to measure both how frequently they changed activities and how often they moved from place to place (Routh et al., 1974). For both measures, activity decreased markedly from age 3 to 6, and continued to decrease at a slower rate from 6 to 9.

In the same study, parents were asked about their child's activity at home—whether, for instance, the child wriggled when watching television, fidgeted when eating, or moved a lot during sleep. Again, scores decreased with age, with one exception. Age 6 saw a small increase, perhaps because the children were temporarily more restless at home in response to the new restrictions of school.

Figure 9.11 *If a preschooler is in the vicinity of someone or something that moves, it is unlikely that the person or object will be allowed to be stationary for long.*

Accident Rates

The child's gradual decrease in activity, as well as the development of motor skills and cognitive maturity, helps explain why a child's likelihood of being seriously injured in an accident decreases with each passing year after age 3. (Of the childhood accidents that result in death, fatal poisoning occurs most often at age 1; drowning is most frequent at age 2; and death resulting from being struck by a motor vehicle is highest at age 3 [National Center for Health Statistics, 1984a].) Older children have more freedom of movement and are exposed to danger more often than are younger children, but they are more able to regulate their behavior. A 3-year-old, for instance, is more likely to run in front of a moving car than an 8-year-old is; indeed, 8-year-olds are sufficiently cautious that they play ball on many less-trafficked streets in relative safety.

This gradual development of caution should not give the wrong impression, however. Throughout childhood, from ages 1 to 11, accidents are by far the leading cause of death, killing more young people than the next five causes combined (National Center for Health Statistics, 1984b). A child has about 1 chance in 1,000 of dying before he or she reaches age 16, and most children need stitches or a cast sometime before they are 10 years old.

A child's chances of having an accident depend primarily on three factors: the amount of adult supervision, the safety of the play space, and the child's activity level. Because these three factors differ, some groups of children have many more accidents than others. For instance, boys are more active than girls, and, as we saw in Chapter 1, take more risks; consequently, they have more accidents than girls, about one-third more at age 1, and twice as many at age 5. Asian-American children have fewer accidents than any other American ethnic group, probably because their parents traditionally keep them nearby; this makes the children safer, although more dependent (Kurokawa, 1969). Impoverished children have more accidents than wealthier children, probably because their play areas are more hazardous. All these factors become more salient as children grow older, so that for every ten white girls between the ages of 5 and 9 who die in accidents, seventeen black girls, nineteen white boys, and thirty-five black boys die (National Center for Health Statistics, 1984a).

Figure 9.12 *Eating even a few flakes of lead-based paint from the walls of an old building can cause brain damage. Such paint is now illegal for toys or interior walls, but many old, poorly maintained buildings have many layers of lead paint. (As soon as the photographer shot this picture, he made sure this little girl played in a safer place.)*

The fact that parents are, obviously, primarily responsible for their children's safety should not blind us to the responsibility of the larger society for protecting all young children (Margolis and Runyon, 1983). Our failure to do this is revealed by comparing accidental deaths and fatalities from disease in childhood: while the latter have steadily declined over the past twenty years, thanks to the efforts of preventive medicine and laws requiring immunization, the accident rate has remained virtually the same (Butler et al., 1984). Such obvious measures as requiring car seats for young children, getting drunk drivers off the road, and providing safe spaces for preschoolers to play in could make a marked difference. Unfortunately, relatively little is known about the specific impact of various preventative steps because research on prevention of accidents lags far behind research on other causes of death. For example, although 4.1 million years of life (computed from age at death to age of retirement) are lost annually in the United States through accidents, only $112 million dollars is spent each year on research in prevention. Meanwhile, expenditures for cancer research amount to $998 million dollars each year for the 1.7 million years of life lost annually (Foege, 1985).

Sex Differences and Similarities

The sex difference in accident rates raises the larger question of sex differences in physical development. Before looking at these differences, however, it is important to stress the many similarities that exist. Boys and girls follow almost identical paths of physical development during early childhood (Tanner, 1978). They are about the same size, and can do the same things at the same age. Knowing a preschool child's sex provides few clues concerning that child's physical development (Pissanos, 1983).

It is also important to stress that the advantage of one sex over the other in most skills is very slight. One researcher studying children's running and jumping skills found that, while the average boy was ahead of the average girl at every age, there was a great deal of overlap (Milne et al., 1976). For instance, while half of the kindergarten boys could jump 35 inches in the standing long jump and could run 400 feet in 50 seconds, so could about 45 percent of the girls. Similarly, the range of ability in running was as great for the girls as for the boys and the overlap was substantial. This means that most boys know several girls their age who can jump farther and run faster than they can. Most of the variation in strength and skill among children is caused by individual differences rather than by any differences that are related to gender.

Figure 9.13 *As with all other areas of development, knowing what is average for a particular group tells us nothing about the abilities of particular individuals within the group or how these individuals will compare with individuals from another group. It is likely that some of the girls pictured here will be better runners than some of the boys. Many boys and girls will simply perform equally well.*

Drawings by Charles Schulz; © 1972 United Feature Syndicate, Inc.

Figure 9.14 Batting a ball is one skill that boys generally perform better than girls, partly because, except for a year or two during early adolescence, the average male has stronger hands and arms than the average female of the same age. Another reason is that boys receive more encouragement for ball playing—for instance, most Little League teams are still all male. Until girls have an equal opportunity to accept or reject the rewards for athletic skill, we will not know how high their batting averages could be.

Nevertheless, when averages based on groups of boys are compared with those of groups of girls, several interesting differences appear. Boys are slightly taller and more muscular. Their forearm strength is notably greater than that of girls (Tanner, 1978). They also lose their "baby fat" sooner and have somewhat less body fat throughout childhood. Girls, on the other hand, mature more rapidly in several ways. For instance, their bone age is usually a year or more ahead of the bone age of boys the same chronological age and they lose their "baby" teeth earlier (Lowrey, 1978).

Some of these physical differences may underlie differences in particular motor skills between girls and boys. By age 4, boys are usually superior in activities that require gross motor skills, especially those like throwing and hitting that involve arm strength. At the same time, girls are more coordinated in skipping and galloping (Sinclair, 1973). Some studies have found girls to be better than boys in certain fine motor skills, especially when speed is involved (Laosa and Brophy, 1972; Ilg and Ames, 1965). A 6-year-old who cannot print legibly is more likely to be male than female.

Of course, male-female skill differences could be caused by varying amounts of practice rather than by basic body or brain differences. For instance, preschool boys spend more time playing outside, engaging in energetic activities like running, climbing, and rough-and-tumble play, than girls do. Girls, on the other hand, spend more time at arts and crafts, and in cooperative and turn-taking games such as jump-rope, jacks, and playing on swings (Harper and Sanders, 1975; Rubin, 1977; di Pietro, 1981).

Further, preschoolers show the same preference as older children for playing with someone of the same sex (see Research Report, next page). This strengthens whatever sex differences in play patterns there are. If a child wanted to spend a great deal of time in a particular activity favored by the opposite sex, he or she would probably hesitate, since his or her favorite playmates would be doing something else. Meanwhile, the children of the opposite sex might not welcome the lone boy who wants to play hopscotch or the girl who wants to play cops and robbers.

RESEARCH REPORT   **Girls and Boys Together**

Historical and cross-cultural studies have long noted that, while children of both sexes sometimes play together, generally girls play with girls, and boys with boys. Indeed, even in the 1980s, the typical elementary-school playground during recess reveals sex segregation in play activities—until late childhood, when games that pit boys against girls begin to be played. In recent years, as the more rigid restrictions on sex roles have lifted, developmentalists have wondered how much of the children's continuing preference for the same sex is learned through family, school, and media influences and how much of it is inborn. Two studies shed some light on this topic.

In one, preschool teachers made a deliberate attempt to encourage cross-sex playmates, reinforcing children with praise whenever they played with the opposite sex (Serbin et al., 1977). Over a ten-day period, the incidence of cross-sex play increased markedly. However, when the reinforcements were removed, children quickly reverted to their old habits, the girls playing with the girls, and the boys playing with the boys.

Another study (Jacklin and Maccoby, 1978) explored the extent to which differences in playmate preference would emerge if the children playing together did not know their playmate's sex, and if adults took care not to influence the children's play. Pairs of 2½-year-olds, dressed in T-shirts and jeans with no adornment that would reveal sex, played in a laboratory with a series of toys that would foster either competition or sharing. The children did not know each other, and the adult observers agreed that the sex of the children was not apparent. (When they guessed who was male or female, they often guessed wrong.) Nevertheless, in spite of not knowing if their playmate was a boy or a girl, children played differently with children of the same sex than with those of opposite sex. The most notable difference was that mixed-sex pairs interacted less. Furthermore, in boy-girl pairs, the girls were likely to stand aside and watch while the boys were active. In contrast, same-sex pairs interacted much more, smiling, talking, and pushing, with boys being particularly likely to engage in a tug-of-war over attractive toys.

Finally, a naturalistic study (La Freniere et al., 1984) of 142 children attending preschools in Quebec found that, as children grew older, more of their friendly approaches to

Even though boys and girls are engaged in very similar activities very close by, *they tend to gravitate to same-sex groups.*

other children were made to children of the same sex, rising steadily from 51 percent at age 1½ to 72 percent at age 5. In this Canadian study, sex differences appeared even in these same-sex trends. While the 2-year-old boys were equally likely to approach children of either sex, the 2-year-old girls directed their affiliative acts toward other girls 69 percent of the time, a preference that held fairly constant through age 5. As time went on, however, the boys grew more likely to prefer each other, and by age 5, they directed 75 percent of their affiliative acts toward other boys.

While these studies suggest that children choose same-sex playmates because of some innate biological affinity, other explanations are possible. Perhaps parents in early infancy shape their sons and daughters' styles of interaction, so that by age 2, boys have already learned boyish behaviors while girls have learned girlish ones, and each sex may then prefer to play with playmates who have the same patterns. At the moment there is no way of knowing which explanation is the more accurate. Nevertheless, it is quite clear from the research that for one reason or the other, or possibly a combination of both, sex preferences in play partners are formed by early childhood.

Figure 9.15 *Notice the sex differences in this K-1 classroom. The girls seem more attentive and sit closer to the teacher, who is, like more than 90 percent of all elementary-school teachers, female. Are these differences cultural or biological or both?*

Thus, we do not know to what extent sex differences in play occur because girls are encouraged to do some things while boys are encouraged to do others, and to what extent natural preferences caused by hormonal or brain differences make boys chase each other across the playground while girls sit down and play jacks. But there is no doubt that boys get more experience with gross motor skills, and less with fine motor skills, than girls do, and that boys practice their skills in playful aggression while girls tend to practice their skills in more peaceful contexts.

Implications

What are the implications of these sex differences in children's play patterns? Some psychologists (e.g., Gilligan, 1982) have speculated that the play activities of boys prepare them for the largely masculine business world, where self-assertion and competition lead to success. Meanwhile, the play activities of girls teach them to be cooperative, patient, and relatively passive, as they play in smaller groups and gain skills that might help them raise a family but handicap them in the larger work world.

This raises the question: What should happen in the future? Given the fact that women are increasingly employed outside the home, and that men are taking more active roles in family life, should preschool girls be encouraged to play rougher, more active games, while their male contemporaries are encouraged to spend more time in quiet and cooperative play? Or should we let nature and tradition alone, at least as far as sex differences in early childhood are concerned?

In Chapter 11, where sex-role development is examined in greater detail, these questions will be raised again, and an attempt will be made to answer them. Next, however, let us look at cognitive development during the play years, a type of development that virtually no developmentalist is willing to leave to chance or tradition.

SUMMARY

Physical Play

1. Play is the work of early childhood. Through sensorimotor play, mastery play, and rough-and-tumble play, children develop their bodies and skills.

Size and Shape

2. During early childhood, children grow about 3 inches (7 centimeters) a year. Normal variation in growth is caused primarily by genes and nutrition, although physical and emotional health can also affect height.

Brain, Eyes, and Inner Organs

3. The child's brain and eyes become more mature during these years. This maturation is probably necessary before the child can do typical first-grade work, although the precise relationship between brain, eyes, and learning is not clear. Reading is a complex perceptual and conceptual task, which demands much more than left-right distinctions and visual maturity.

Mastering Motor Skills

4. Gross motor skills improve dramatically during this period, making it possible for the average 6-year-old to do many things with grace and skill.

5. Fine motor skills, such as holding a pencil or tying a shoelace, also improve, but more gradually. Many 6-year-olds, especially left-handed ones, find writing difficult.

Activity Level

6. At about the age of 2 or 3, children have a higher activity level than at any other time in the life span.

7. Because the activity level tends to decline after age 3, children's chances of injuring themselves decrease as age increases. Supervision, play space, and the sex of the child also correlate with the frequency of accidents.

Sex Differences and Similarities

8. The average boy plays more active games and is taller and more muscular than the average girl. He is usually better at gross motor skills, such as throwing a ball, than she is, but she is usually better at fine motor skills, such as drawing a person. During these years, however, the similarities between the sexes are much more apparent than the differences. However, the extent to which these differences are influenced by either biological or social factors is not known.

KEY TERMS

sensorimotor play *(256)*
mastery play *(257)*
rough-and-tumble
  play *(258)*
play face *(258)*
dwarfism *(263)*
giantism *(263)*
ossification *(264)*
bone age *(264)*
deprivation
  dwarfism *(265)*
gross motor skills *(270)*
fine motor skills *(273)*

KEY QUESTIONS

1. What are some of the physical and social skills that are learned, in part, through play?

2. What causes variations among children in height and weight during early childhood?

3. How does the shape of the child's body change during early childhood?

4. What are some of the important brain developments during early childhood?

5. What visual developments occur in early childhood?

6. Why is there a controversy about when children should learn to read?

7. In what motor skills have average 5-year-olds developed competence?

8. How do gross motor skills develop?

9. What difficulties do children experience in mastering fine motor skills?

10. What conclusions can be drawn from statistics on accident rates among children?

11. What are the main similarities and differences in the physical development of boys and girls in early childhood?

RECOMMENDED READINGS

Gardner, Howard. *Art, mind and brain: A cognitive approach to creativity.* New York: Basic Books, 1982.

A series of essays by a leading developmental psychologist, this book links theory, research, and informed speculation to stimulate one's thinking about creativity. Two of the five parts are particularly relevant to this chapter, specifically "Artistic Development in Children," which includes discussions of music and metaphor as well as of drawing, and "The Breakdown of the Mind," which discusses brain development and damage. A third section, "On Education and the Media," includes insightful comments about toys and television.

Bissex, Glenda L. *Gnys at wrk: A child learns to write and read.* Cambridge, Mass.: Harvard University Press, 1980.

This book is one of the best examples of the synergy between parenthood and research in developmental psychology. Glenda Bissex records her son's writing and reading development, beginning at age 5, when, to get her attention, he gave her a note asking "RUDF" (are you deaf?). Surrounded by the models and materials that promote literacy (books, a typewriter, and reading parents), but without formal education, young Paul discovered the written symbols of our culture. The title of the book is derived from the sign he posted on his door: DO NAT DSTRB GNYS AT WRK (Do not disturb: Genius at work). Based on research and theory as well as on the data provided by Paul, Bissex concludes that literacy obviously requires adult and cultural input, but that the motivated child often seems able to "discover" many of the rudiments without formal instruction.

National Research Council, *Injury in America: A continuing public health problem.* Washington D.C.: National Academy Press, 1985.

This book makes clear the important point that accidents don't just happen: circumstances that are very much under human control set the stage for injuries that kill far more children than all diseases combined. Among the specific recommendations are ways to make automobiles safer, and ways to lower the homicide rate among adolescents. (Teenagers are killed by other teenagers far more frequently than they kill themselves.)

Elkind, David. *The hurried child: Growing up too fast too soon.* Reading, Mass.: Addison-Wesley, 1981.

Noting that clinical psychologists rarely see an overprotected "spoiled" child today, Elkind says that the spoiled children of yesteryear have been replaced by the "hurried" children of today. In our rush to help children grow up—pushing preschoolers to read, requiring school-age children to supervise themselves while their parents are working, and encouraging preteens to adopt the clothes and manners of young adults—we are, says Elkind, robbing our children of a precious period of their lives—childhood.

The Play Years: Cognitive Development

Chapter 10

"Mommy, I'm so sorry for the baby horses—they cannot pick their noses."

"I'm barefoot all over."

"Why do they put a pit in every cherry? We just have to throw the pit away."

Preschool children quoted in Chukovsky, 1968

How Preschoolers Think

Symbolic Thought

Preoperational Thought

Revising Piaget

Language Development

Language and Thought

Vocabulary

Grammar

Pragmatics

Differences in Language Development

Teaching and Learning

Headstart

Parent Involvement

Chapter 10

An adult who asks a preschool child "What is it?" or "How does it work?" is likely to hear some surprising answers. Although children at this age are never at a loss for an explanation, they seem to formulate their ideas according to entirely different rules of logic than those used by adults. What are the characteristics of children's thinking at this stage and how do mature patterns of logical thinking develop? These and the following questions will be among the topics discussed in this chapter.

How do children progress from understanding the world through actions and perceptions to using symbols such as words?

Why do preschoolers tend to understand everything from their own point of view?

Why do children at this stage almost always judge by appearances, insisting, for example, that long, narrow containers always hold more than short, wide ones?

How do children use language to adjust their behavior?

What factors limit a preschooler's ability to communicate?

What factors are conducive to language learning?

The thoughts and verbal expressions of children between the ages of 2 and 6 have always amused, delighted, and surprised adults. A child who wonders where the sun sleeps, or who calls a naked baby "barefoot all over," or who writes a letter to God about the thunder (see Figure 10.1) is bound to make us smile. Recently, however, researchers studying the intellectual underpinnings of preschool thought have found that they involve much more than charming nonsense. As you will soon learn, early childhood is an impressive period for the development of imagination and language, and even of the basic structures of logic.

Figure 10.1 *The ambitious project of writing a letter to God is a touching and amusing testament to this 4-year-old's faith in the written word and in God's readiness to consider every petition.*

How Preschoolers Think

In explaining the cognitive changes of early childhood, we will begin with Piaget's depiction of them. This is not to say that Piaget's descriptions of the preschooler's cognitive development are universally accepted—in fact, much of the recent research activity in this area centers on modifying and qualifying Piaget's views (Gelman and Baillargeon, 1983; Flavell, 1982). Nevertheless, Piaget remains the most influential theorist in the area of childhood cognition, and although some aspects of his delineation of cognitive development in early childhood appear to need amending, the overall picture Piaget drew provides a firm foundation for understanding the preschooler's thought processes.

Symbolic Thought

The most significant cognitive gain in early childhood is, according to Piaget (1962), the emergence of symbolic thought. As you remember, in the last stage of sensorimotor intelligence, toddlers' thinking is no longer tied to their actions and perceptions; they can begin to "figure things out" mentally. Mental representation, deferred imitation, and pretending all begin at about age 1½ or 2. These budding mental abilities come to full flower between ages 2 and 6, as imagination and language open up new ways of thinking and playing.

To understand how liberating symbolic thought can be, think for a moment about what symbols are. A **symbol** is something that stands for, or signifies, something else. A flag symbolizes a country, a handshake symbolizes friendship, a skull and crossbones symbolizes poison. Each symbol encapsulates a host of emotions and ideas, "packaging" them in a way that allows a person to think quickly and concisely and to move about mentally in the past and the future, as well as in the present. Thus the mind is no longer bound by the limits of immediate sensory and motor experience. Words are the most common symbols, and, whether spoken or written, they are the most liberating. For instance, in English, the sound "dawg" symbolizes a four-legged animal that barks, as do the three written letters "dog." Other languages obviously have quite different sounds, and quite different spellings, but all languages have spoken and written symbols for the general concept of dogness. Knowing the symbols that stand for dog makes it easier to remember dogs, to think about them, and to talk about them. Eventually the verbal symbol for dog will become linked with dozens of other symbols associated with dogs and dogness—literal and figurative—and the word itself will call forth a chain of images, ideas, and information. Thus the capacity for symbolic thought opens up much broader and deeper powers of the mind than existed when thought was limited to senses and motor skills (Gardner, 1982).

Pretend Play One of the most fascinating consequences of symbolic thought is the imaginative play that it makes possible. Indeed, pretending is a favorite activity during the preschool years, when children are old enough to think symbolically but too young to distinguish reality from fantasy very well.

Between ages 1 and 6, pretend play becomes more frequent and more complex with each passing year (Rubin et al., 1983). Whereas the 1-year-old might play with a cup and saucer independently, using them strictly as noisemakers by banging them on the floor, and whereas the 2-year-old is likely to put the cup on the saucer and pretend to drink, and nothing else, the 4-year-old can transform the cup and

Figure 10.2 *During the pre-school years, children become increasingly adept at using props to symbolize their ideas and fantasies. At the same time, the limitedness of their cognitive ability is often reflected in the logical inconsistencies of their pretending. For example, Superman does not need a hardhat and few brides bring their babies to their weddings.*

saucer into almost anything (Lowe, 1975). The child might begin by pretending to pour tea and eat an imaginary cookie, and then, at a moment's notice, turn the cup and saucer into a space ship, a hat, or a domed dwelling. By the end of early childhood, at age 5 or 6, the objects of pretend play can be invisible, existing solely in the child's mind (Rubin et al., 1983).

This growth in the use of symbols occurs as the child gradually develops, and becomes able to mentally coordinate, an increasing number of schemas for the objects in his or her world. This progression is particularly clear when children play with something that could represent a person, such as a doll or stuffed animal. When children first play with such toys, at about age 2, the doll or animal is used to represent one fairly simple action at a time. For example, a doll might be put to bed and left there, ending that particular episode of pretend play. With time, the child will put the doll through a sequence of related behaviors—making her wash her hands, cook the dinner, and eat it. Finally, at age 3 or 4, the child has the doll taking on more complex roles, talking and interacting with other dolls and toys, forming a family, or a school group, or a group of friends and foes. Each of these levels of symbolic play develops in sequence, and is seen as evidence of increasing cognitive development (Case, 1985; Watson, 1981; Corrigan, 1983). By age 4 or 5, much of the symbolic play of children involves other children, as a group acts out "hospital," "store," or "family." (Such social play is discussed in the next chapter.)

Preoperational Thought

Although children's capacity to relate symbols to each in a meaningful way increases dramatically during the preschool years, it does not include the ability to relate them in a consistently logical way. According to Piaget, preschoolers cannot perform "operations," which are the "schemes of connected relational reasoning"

(Isaacs, 1974). In other words, they cannot regularly apply the rule "If this, then that . . ." One example is the idea of **reversibility**—that is, the idea that reversing a process will bring about the original conditions from which the process began. This sounds much more complicated than it actually is, for what it means in practical terms is that the child may know that 3 + 2 = 5 but not realize that the reverse is true, that 5 − 2 = 3. It also means that a preschooler who walks to school every day but gets a ride home would, if asked to walk home one afternoon, probably reply, "But I've never walked home before. I don't know the way." To emphasize the preschooler's inability to understand such logical operations, Piaget refers to the cognitive period from age 2 to 7 as the period of **preoperational thought.**

Centration The most notable characteristic of preoperational thought, as described by Piaget, is **centration,** the tendency to think about one idea at a time—that is, to "center" on it—to the exclusion of other ideas.

Preoperational children are particularly likely to center on their perceptions, especially on the more obvious aspects of their visual perceptions, rather than consider a broader view of a situation or experience. Thus, in the preschooler's mind, the tallest child or adult is probably the oldest and the best as well (Kuczaj, 1977). Similarly, in the preschooler's view, a cut "hurts" because it bleeds, so covering it with a bandage will make it feel better. Likewise, if the morning sun is streaming through the bedroom window, that means it is time to get up and have breakfast—never mind that it is 5 A.M. on a June morning and Mommy and Daddy are sound asleep.

Because they are so inclined to center on what they perceive, children have trouble remembering and understanding transitions and transformations: rather, they think in terms of either/or, making their reasoning static rather than dynamic (Flavell, 1977). For example, they think of themselves as a "good" child or a "bad" one, not as a child who is sometimes good in some ways and sometimes bad in others (Harter, 1983). A related problem is preschoolers' difficulty in understand-

Figure 10.3 *Centration often leads preschoolers to reason that a son must be a little boy, not a grown man, and that Grandma is too old to be a mommy.*

ing cause and effect, partly because they center on one aspect of an event rather than on the relationship between events (Cowan, 1978). This difficulty is particularly apparent when a child has caused some mishap. Children who fall down might blame the sidewalk or another child several feet away. Or a 3-year-old might say, and believe, that a vase fell and broke because it wanted to, or even that it fell *because* it now lies in dozens of pieces on the floor.

The characteristics of preoperational thought are demonstrated most clearly in Piaget's experiments. Let us look closely at experiments in conservation, the most famous of the concepts that Piaget considered impossible for preoperational children.

The Problem of Conservation   As you read in Chapter 2, **conservation** (the idea that amount is unaffected by changes in shape or placement) is not at all obvious to young children. Rather, when comparing the amount of liquid in two glasses, they are impressed solely by the relative height of the fluids. If they are shown two identical glasses containing equal amounts of lemonade, and then watch while the lemonade from one glass is poured into a taller, narrower glass, they will insist that the taller, narrower glass has more lemonade than the remaining original.

Preschool children usually have the same problem with regard to conservation of many other sorts (see chart on p. 291). Consider **conservation of matter.** Make two balls of clay of equal amount, and then ask a 4-year-old child to roll one of them into a long skinny rope. When this is done, ask the child whether both pieces still have the same amount of clay. Almost always, 4-year-olds will say that the long piece has more.

Similarly, **conservation of number** is beyond preschoolers. In one Piagetian test (Piaget, 1952b), an experimenter lines up pairs of checkers in two rows and asks the child if both rows have the same number of checkers. The child will almost always say yes. With the child watching, the experimenter next elongates one of the rows by spacing the checkers farther apart, and then asks the child if the rows now have the same number or if one has more. The preoperational child almost always says that the longer row has more.

In such conservation problems, according to Piaget, the problem is that the preschooler centers on appearances and thus ignores or discounts the transformation that has occurred. Older children, usually at around age 7 or 8, understand the

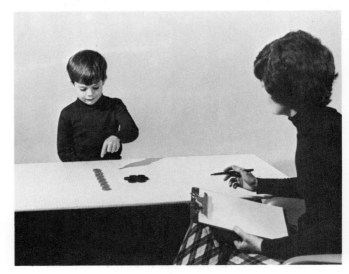

Figure 10.4 *At age 6, Jed judges the row of checkers to contain more than the cluster, even though a moment earlier he had counted both groups when they were in rows and found seven in each. Such a response is typical of a preoperational child who does not yet understand the concept of conservation of number.*

Tests of Various Types of Conservation

	Start with:	Then:	Ask the child:	Preoperational children usually answer:
CONSERVATION OF LIQUIDS	Two equal glasses of liquid.	Pour one into a taller, thinner glass.	Which glass contains more?	The taller one.
CONSERVATION OF NUMBER	Two equal lines of checkers.	Lengthen the spaces between one line.	Which line has more checkers?	The longer one.
CONSERVATION OF MATTER	Two equal balls of clay.	Squeeze one ball into a long, thin shape.	Which piece has more clay?	The long one.
CONSERVATION OF LENGTH	Two sticks of equal length.	Move one stick.	Which stick is longer?	The one that is farther to the right.
CONSERVATION OF VOLUME	Two glasses of water with equal balls of clay inside.	Change the shape of one ball.	Which piece of clay will displace more water?	The long one.
CONSERVATION OF AREA	Two identical pieces of cardboard on which are placed the same number of equally-sized blocks.	Rearrange blocks on one piece of cardboard.	Which has more cardboard covered up?	The one with the blocks not touching.

logical operation of reversibility, and realize that pouring the lemonade back into the shorter and wider glass, or rolling the clay back into a ball, would return things to their original state. Older children would also be able to arrive at these conclusions by applying the logical operation of **identity**—the idea that the content of an object remains the same despite changes in its shape. However, because of their tendency toward centration, and their resulting immature reasoning, Piaget contends that it is impossible for preoperational children to grasp the concept of conservation, no matter how carefully it is explained.

Egocentrism One of the things preschoolers center on most is themselves, producing a type of thinking referred to as egocentrism. **Egocentrism** means that thinking centers on the ego, or self. Thus the egocentric child's ideas about the world are limited by the child's own narrow point of view: the child does not take into account

Figure 10.5 *These recipes (from* Smashed Potatoes, *edited by Jane Martel) show many characteristics of preschool thought, among them literal interpretation of words ("Sometimes you can call it a bird, but it's not") and an uncertain idea of time ("Cook them for plenty of time") and quantity ("A giant lump of stuffin'").*

A whole turkey

1 big bag full of a whole turkey
   (Get the kind with no feathers on,
   not the kind the Pilgrims ate.)
A giant lump of stuffin'
1 squash pie
1 mint pie
1 little fancy dish of sour berries
1 big fancy dish of a vegetable mix
20 dishes of all different candies; chocolate balls,
   cherry balls, good'n plenties and peanuts

Get up when the alarm says to and get busy fast. Unfold the turkey and open up the holes. Push in the stuffin' for a couple hours. I think you get stuffin' from that Farm that makes it.

I know you have to pin the stuffin' to the turkey or I suppose it would get out. And get special pins or use big long nails.

Get the kitchen real hot, and from there on you just cook turkey. Sometimes you can call it a bird, but it's not.

Then you put the vegetables in the cooker — and first put one on top, and next put one on the bottom, and then one in the middle. That makes a vegetable mix. Put 2 red things of salt all in it and 2 red things of water also. Cook them to just ½ of warm.

Put candies all around the place and Linda will bring over the pies.

When the company comes put on your red apron.

Chops

Some chops that are enough to fill up your pan
Fresh salt and pepper
Fresh flour
1 ball of salad lettuce
1 sponge cake with ice cream

Put the chops in the bag and shake them for 5 hours — and the flour too.

Put them in a skillet pan on the biggest black circle on the roof of your stove. Cook them for plenty of time.

Fringe up the lettuce in little heaps in all the bowls.

Go on the porch and bring the high chair and have your supper everybody!

Note: But stoves really is dangerous — and you shouldn't go near one till you get married.

that other people may have thoughts and feelings different from the ones he or she is having at the moment.

To say that preoperational children are egocentric means only that because of their cognitive immaturity, they are naturally self-centered, not that they are selfish (Piaget, 1959). A 3-year-old boy hearing his father crying, for instance, might try to comfort his daddy by bringing him a teddy bear or a lollipop. Obviously, this child is not being selfish: he is willing to give up something of his own. But he is egocentric: he assumes that his father will be consoled by the same things he himself finds consoling.

Egocentrism is also apparent in **animism,** the idea held by many young children that everything in the world is alive, just as they are. When thinking animistically, children whose play is interrupted by nightfall might get angry at the sun for "going to bed" too early, or they might begin to cry when they drop a stuffed animal because they think they have hurt it. Animism, as well as egocentrism, is what allows children to accept many of the mythical explanations that adults offer them—that Santa Claus, with his one small sled, brings toys to all children, including a large number for the child in question; that Jack Frost paints on the windows and makes snow so the child can make snowmen; that Mother Nature brings spring so the child can smell the flowers. Children create their own animistic, egocentric explanations as well: they say that the moon follows them when they walk outside at night; or that the thunder comes because they have been bad.

Piaget's Three Mountains   According to Piaget, children are, because of their egocentrism, unable to take another's point of view until at least age 7. The basis for this assertion is Piaget's classic experiment (Piaget and Inhelder, 1963) in which children between the ages of 4 and 11 were shown a large three-dimensional exhibit of three mountains of different shapes, sizes, and colors (see Figure 10.6). First,

Figure 10.6 (a) *Replications of Piaget's three-mountains experiment are used to measure the ability to imagine a different point of view. The child is first shown a display model of three mountains, and then is shown ten drawings of various views of the mountains. The child is asked to select the drawing that most accurately portrays the point of view of a doll seated at various positions around the table. For instance, if a child were sitting in position 1 looking at the three-mountain display (here shown in an overhead view) and asked how the display would look from sitting-position 4, which picture—(a), (b), or (c)—should the child select? Preoperational children often wrongly select their own view (b) rather than correctly choosing (a).*

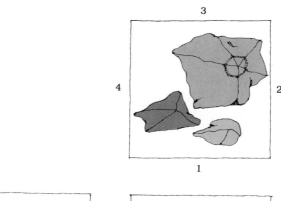

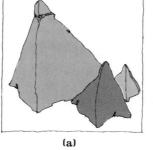

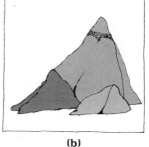

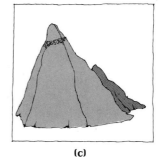

(a)   (b)   (c)

the children would walk around the exhibit and view it from all sides, and then they were seated on one side of the table that held the exhibit, with a doll seated on another side. Then each child was asked to choose which one of a series of photos showed the scene that the doll was viewing.

No matter where the doll was seated, children younger than 6 mistakenly chose the photo that showed the mountains as they themselves were viewing them. By age 6 or 7, most children realized that the doll's view would be somewhat different from their own, but they often failed to pick the correct photo. Between 7 and 9, children generally chose correctly, with occasional errors and, finally, at ages 9, 10, and 11, most of the children performed this task perfectly. From these results, Piaget concluded that children under 7 were too egocentric to take the perspective of another, a conclusion many researchers now question.

Revising Piaget

The standard Piagetian experiments have been replicated hundreds of times with children from various cultures, and the results have nearly always been the same: preoperational children make many mistakes with the three-mountains experiment, just as they make mistakes with the conservation experiments using glasses of lemonade, or lumps of clay, or rows of checkers (Dasen, 1977; Donaldson et al., 1983).

Perspective-Taking in Preschoolers   However, most developmentalists now believe that the three-mountains task was too complex to be a valid test of the child's ability to take someone else's perspective. Simpler experiments have shown that even preschool children can begin to understand another's view point, at least in an elementary way. According to one study, 4-year-olds can choose how Grover, the Sesame Street character, would view a country scene (a farmhouse with animals beside a lake with a sailboat) from different positions (Borke, 1975). In another experiment, even 3-year-olds were 90 percent correct in specifying when a camera placed in three different positions would take a picture of the "front," "back," or "side" of an object (Ives, 1980).

Figure 10.7 Although the problem of hiding the little boy behind "walls" where the policemen will not be able to see him becomes increasingly complex in the sequence from (a) to (d), even very young children performed surprisingly well.

Finally, when perspective-taking becomes part of a game, children between the ages of 3½ and 5 show themselves to be quite capable. This was the general conclusion of one series of experiments in which children were asked to hide a little boy behind a series of "walls," so that policemen who were looking for him could not find him (Hughes and Donaldson, 1979). When the walls made four quadrants (Figure 10.7b) and the policemen were placed so that they could see into three of them,

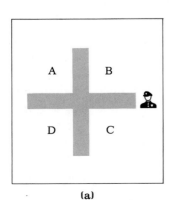

(a)

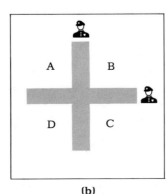

(b)

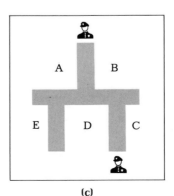

(c)

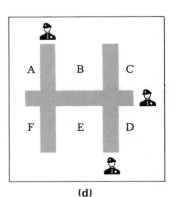

(d)

73 percent of the children correctly picked the fourth quadrant as the hiding place in each of four trials, and 17 percent made only one error in the four trials. In a more complicated set-up (Figure 10.7d), eight out of ten 4-year-olds made no errors, and seven out of ten 3-year-olds made no errors or only one error. (Two of the 3-year-olds who were counted among the failures actually did very well—one by hiding the boy under the table and one by hiding him in her hand—despite the experimenter's best efforts to explain that this was not the way to play the game.)

The researchers ask the key question:

> Why do children find these tasks so easy to grasp, compared with problems like the three mountains task? We believe it is because the policemen tasks make human sense in a way that the mountain task does not. The motives and intentions of the characters (hiding and seeking) are entirely comprehensible, even to a child of three, and he is being asked to identify with—and indeed do something about—the plight of a boy in an entirely comprehensible situation. This ability to understand and identify with another's feelings and intentions is in many ways the exact opposite of egocentrism, and yet it now appears to be well developed in three-year-olds. [Hughes and Donaldson, 1979]

Instruction in Conservation A number of researchers have attempted to teach children the concept of conservation. Their results have depended, apparently, on how that teaching was done. If an adult merely explained that, for instance, the amount of lemonade in both the tall and the shorter glasses has to be the same because the amounts were identical when the lemonade was in identical glasses, such an attempt at correcting the illogic of the child would generally fail, unless the child was relatively old (about age 6 or 7) and presumably almost ready to figure out conservation on his or her own (Inhelder et al., 1974). The experience of one psychologist, the father of a 5-year-old, is probably typical:

> The father had apparently made repeated attempts to drill the child on the conservation of water problem. One day the father proudly demonstrated the child's skill . . . [but] on the first two trials, the boy said, "There's more water in this glass; it's higher." The father's face fell. Given a third try, his son said, "Oh, it's the same, it's still the same amount of water." The father beamed proudly, while the son added in a tiny whisper, "But it really isn't." [Cowan, 1978]

However, some researchers who have attempted to teach various types of conservation—including conservation of liquids, matter, and number—have achieved greater success by altering the basic format of the experiment. As in the case of the hide-the-boy-from-the-policemen experiment, simplifying the task, encouraging the child's active participation, and making the experiment seem like a game rather than a test were principles that seemed to help children grasp the concept of conservation at least a little bit. In one study, 4-year-olds learned to conserve after careful instruction, including demonstrations, descriptions of what was occurring, and an opportunity for the children themselves to perform the experiments while the experimenter told them how well they were doing (Denney et al.,

21/68

Preoperational Conceptions of Death, Illness, and Divorce

The limitations of preoperational thought often make it hard for children to understand death, illness, or divorce. In fact, their egocentric thinking often causes children to blame themselves for these events. A 4-year-old boy might think that he killed Grandma by saying something mean to her, or that God made his tonsils infected because he did something bad, or that Mommy and Daddy are separating because he got dirt on the carpet.

Explanations to relieve the child's anxiety should be phrased in terms the preoperational child can understand. When my daughter Bethany was 4, she was told that her grandmother had died because she was very old. Three weeks later she refused to eat any cake at her own birthday party, crying, "I don't want to be 5. I don't want to die." Although I am not at all sure what happens after death, I have found that it is much easier for a preoperational child to believe that Grandma died because she was ready for heaven, where she will be peaceful and happy, than to understand the biological consequences of aging.

Preschool children who are told that their parents are divorcing because they are angry at each other and no longer love each other often center on the idea that anger means separation. They wonder if their parents will stop loving them as well, especially if they do something to make their parents angry. It is important to reassure children in these circumstances that they are not to blame for what is happening between their parents, and that no matter how Mommy and Daddy feel about each other, their love for the child is forever.

The need for providing children with specific, clear information when their parents are breaking up was

These two children, Josh and Lila, lived with their grandmother while she was dying and have now been brought to visit her

coffin. Adding a flower to the array, as Lila is doing, is a tangible way to say "goodbye" to a much-loved relative.

shown to be crucial in several ways in an extensive longitudinal study of children's reactions to divorce (Wallerstein and Kelly, 1980). This study found that, in particular, children between 3 and 5 years old resisted dealing with the realities of the divorce and were susceptible to unfounded worries. They fantasized that their parents still lived together, or would reunite soon; they worried that the absent parent was dead, or had nowhere to sleep; they were concerned that they themselves would soon be left hungry or alone. As the following case demonstrates, clear explanation, along with regular contact with the noncustodial parent, is one of the

1977). Another study (Field, 1981) found that such training need not be temporary: 79 percent of a group of eighty-five 4-year-olds still understood conservation several months after training, demonstrating this on simple tests of number, length, liquid, and matter. Three year-olds, however, had difficulty learning conservation no matter how good the training process (Field, 1981).

Conservation of Number. Similarly, the crucial role of the human context is revealed by a series of experiments in which preschool children seemed to know much more about number than Piaget would have predicted. Several researchers followed the standard conservation-of-number procedures with one telling exception. Rather than having the rearrangement of one row of checkers be a deliberate move on the experimenter's part, they made the change in arrangement seem

correlates of a more realistic and healthy adjustment:

John, a sturdy, handsome youngster of three, was brought to us by his young father. His mother had left suddenly, after a bitter quarrel. The child was described as tearful, frightened, and very confused. He was sleeping fitfully, wetting his bed nightly, and hitting his baby sister. This behavior began after the mother's departure. John had been offered no explanation, in part because the father had himself been overwhelmed by grief, and in part because he considered the child too young to understand.

At our suggestion the father undertook to explain to the child that his parents had separated because of their unhappiness. He recalled the many quarrels which the child had witnessed, and assured him that these would not continue and that the father was better able to care for John and would continue, reliably, to do so. John responded with many urgent questions which had preoccupied and worried him and which were the basis for his regressive behavior and changes of mood. One highly significant concern that John revealed was that he had been afraid that his mother "burned up in a fire." (There had been a relatively minor fire in the household the week before the mother left.) John asked urgently whether his mother was well and begged to see her. After the visit was arranged and mother and child visited over cocoa and cookies, John returned home with his father and began to sob. His father took him in his arms and said, "I understand, son, that it is hard when Mommy isn't coming back to live with us." John responded, tearfully, "Daddy, can we have another talk?" Gradually, within the next few weeks, as the father's care and assurances continued, the child's regressions disappeared and his mood began to stabilize.

While such explanations are important, it must be realized that the child's egocentric understanding of an event such as death or divorce is not usually transformed by a single simple explanation, however logical. Wallerstein and Kelly (1980) report:

Preschool children were often given to self-blame. Kay told us that her father had left because her play was too noisy. Jennifer said her father objected to her messily trained dog and left for that reason. Max savagely beat the "naughty baby doll" [presumably a representative of himself]. These self-accusations, which severely troubled these children, were highly resistant to change by educational measures or by explanations undertaken by parents or teachers. These children clung to their self-accusations with great tenacity.

This study of children who had experienced divorce is useful for understanding children who experience other traumas as well. In particular, it shows the need for sensitivity to children's questions and unexpressed fears; for repeated reassurances that the child's basic needs will be met; and for specific experiences that help put fearful fantasies to rest (just as contact with the absent parent can be reassuring, visiting the hospital and meeting the doctor and nurses before the child has surgery, for instance, or attending the funeral of a loved grandparent, can be helpful). For a child who tends to center on one idea and cling to it, reversals and ambiguity are particularly hard to comprehend, so custody fights, temporary reconciliation, or threats from one parent to the other are very troubling for young children. Similarly, the idea of death, however figurative, should not be associated with disciplinary measures ("I'm going to kill you if you ever do that again") or masked in lies ("Grandpa went on a long trip"). As explained in the next chapter, it is hard enough for the preschool child to differentiate reality and fantasy, without adults adding to the problem in times of emotional turmoil.

accidental by having a naughty teddy bear carry it out. Under these circumstances, preschool children were more likely to correctly say that both rows still contained the same number (McGarrigle and Donaldson, 1974; Light et al., 1979; Dockrell et al., 1980).

Another series of experiments was designed to discover if children between 3 and 5 years old could recognize when a small group of identical toys was surreptitiously rearranged to make a longer or shorter line, or when one or two toys were taken away from a group of five (these transformations were done "magically," while the display was hidden under a cup). Virtually every child tested showed that he or she noticed the change. Moreover, many of the children gave evidence that they were counting the display—often with idiosyncratic number sequences (instead of 1-2-3, some used 1-2-6 and others A-B-C). Despite their use of these irregular designations, however, the children knew what they were doing: when one toy was missing, they would say something like "Look, it used to be 1-2-6 but now it's only 1-2." Evidence of counting was apparent even among the 2-year-olds who participated: fourteen out of sixteen counted in some fashion or other.

The experimenters did not conclude that preschool children are at ease with the number system. Not only did they use their own sequence of numbers, but many of them miscounted, especially when the number of toys was five or more. But it is clear that some understanding of number is present even among very young children (Gelman and Gallistel, 1978).

If preschoolers do have some understanding of conservation of number, then why do they fail Piaget's test of conservation? One explanation is that the array in Piaget's experiment is too large for children to use counting, so they have to rely on misleading appearance. The other explanation is that the testing situation itself may encourage a wrong answer. The child may assume that the experimenter, who took such care to rearrange the row of checkers, intended to ask which line is longer rather than which line has more, and the child may therefore answer the question he or she thought was asked.

In looking to these experiments as qualifications of Piaget's findings, it should be remembered that they were *designed* to evoke whatever rudiments of perspective, number, and so forth the young child might possess. Real life is not so designed. Even though preschoolers show some understanding of these concepts in certain conditions, it takes years of maturation and experience before children show mastery of the underlying logical structures.

As Rochel Gelman, a leading researcher in cognitive development, points out:

> Despite the many competencies of the young, they nevertheless fail or err on a wide range of tasks that do not seem to be that difficult. . . . The young child, to be sure, has many pieces of competence. However, they are exceedingly fragile. The older child can show that competence across a wide range of tasks. Hence, the idea is that development involves going from the fragile (and probably rigid) application of capacity to a widely based use of these. [Gelman et al., 1982]

A similar pattern of competency and fragility is apparent in the other notable intellectual accomplishment that occurs during early childhood—the development of language.

Language Development

As we saw in Chapter 6, babies normally begin talking at about a year. Language develops slowly at first, as toddlers typically add only a few new words to their vocabulary each month, speak in one-word sentences, and have trouble communicating many simple ideas, sometimes frustrating themselves as well as the most patient care-giver who tries to understand what the child wants. However, during the preschool years, as cognitive powers increase, an "explosion" of language occurs, with vocabulary, grammar, and the practical uses of language showing marked and rapid improvement.

Figure 10.8 *The language development that occurs during the preschool years gives the child the ability to express the wide range of his or her feelings and in a variety of new ways, from friendly tête-à-têtes and whispered asides to full-tilt shouting matches.*

Language and Thought

Virtually all developmentalists agree that the symbolic thinking that characterizes the cognitive development of preschoolers is what makes this language development possible. They are in less agreement, however, about the precise relationship between thought and language. Piaget believed that cognitive development comes first: a child must first understand a concept before he or she is capable of using the words that describe it (1976). Thus words that refer to the appearance and disappearance of things and people ("bye-bye," "all gone," "where," "no more") emerge after full object permanence has been demonstrated.

Jerome Bruner disagrees with Piaget. He thinks that by kindergarten, language ability affects almost every aspect of a child's thought and behavior, and that language becomes a "means, not only for representing experience, but also for transforming it" (Bruner, 1964, 1983). Once a child learns different words referring to anger, for instance, the child becomes better able to differentiate among various gradations of this emotion, explaining that he or she is "mad," or "upset," or "hurt." In turn, this refined description helps both the child and others to better understand the child's feelings and, perhaps, deal with them more effectively. In stressing the impact of language, Bruner is echoing an idea expressed fifty years ago by the Russian psychologist Lev Vygotsky (English edition, 1962). Vygotsky thought that beginning with symbolic thinking, at about age 2, cognitive development and language development become interrelated, the progress of one thereafter affecting the progress of the other.

Most developmentalists agree with Piaget that infants form concepts first and then learn the words to express them. But most also believe that, at some point during early childhood, language helps form ideas, as suggested by Bruner and Vygotsky. In Lois Bloom's (1975) words: "There is a developmental shift between learning to talk and talking to learn." Furthermore, most believe that language helps children regulate their social behavior, and, at the same time, that the give and take of everyday social experience is essential to children's language learning (Genishi and Dyson, 1984; Schiefelbusch and Pickar, 1984). Older children and adults are able to learn words and grammatical rules in abstraction, but preschool children depend on practical experience with them. Thus language is at the heart of many aspects of development during early childhood, and for this reason, it is particularly important to understand how language develops.

Vocabulary

The language explosion that occurs during the preschool years is most obvious in the growth of vocabulary—from about 50 words at 18 months, to 200 words at age 2, to between 8,000 and 14,000 words at age 6 (Lenneberg, 1967; Carey, 1978). This means that, from age 2 to age 6, the average child learns between six and ten words a day!

The learning of new words follows a predictable sequence according to parts of speech. Nouns are generally learned more readily than verbs, which are learned more readily than adjectives, adverbs, conjunctions, or interrogatives. Within parts of speech, the order is predictable as well. For instance, the first interrogatives children learn are "where?" and "what?" then "who?" followed by "how?" and "why?" (Bloom et al., 1982). Basic nouns, such as "dog," are learned before specific nouns, such as "collie," or more general nouns such as "animal" (Anglin, 1977; Blewitt, 1982).

RESEARCH REPORT   **The Critical Period for Language Development**

In the 1960s many researchers believed that the years from 2 to 5 were the critical years for intellectual development, especially for language learning (Bloom, 1964; Hunt, 1961; Lenneberg, 1967). One reason for this belief came from extensive experimental research with lower animals, which proved that early experience can make the difference between a cognitively advanced or retarded animal. This was notably true in language development. For example, an adult male finch sings an elaborate song to attract a female finch and to tell other finches that a particular territory is his. In order to produce the song correctly, he must hear other finches sing it before he reaches puberty. If he is experimentally prevented from doing so, the song he instinctively develops in adulthood will be only a rough approximation of the finch's song, lacking the necessary characteristics to help him find a mate or stake out his territory.

According to Eric Lenneberg (1967), humans experience a similar critical period during the years before puberty, especially the preschool years, when the ear, brain, and voice are primed for learning language. Support for this hypothesis came from children who had lost their language capacity due to brain damage but in time were able to relearn language. Adults who had lost their language capacity through the same type of damage appeared unable to regain it. Also supporting this idea was the fact that on moving to a new country, children usually learned a second language with much less effort than their parents.

Later research raised some doubts concerning the critical-period hypothesis, however. For instance, some children who have had very limited cognitive stimulation and little exposure to language in early childhood develop normally when they are placed in a supportive and stimulating environment (Clarke and Clarke, 1976). In addition, some adult victims of brain damage do learn to speak again, and adults do learn new languages, occasionally mastering half a dozen or more distinct tongues (Gardner, 1983). In general, carefully controlled research suggests that older children and adults learn a new language at least as well as younger children (McLaughlin, 1984). But the real test of the critical-period hypothesis is not the ability to recover from brain damage or master a second language. The crucial question is whether a person can learn a first language after puberty. There is no way to answer this question experimentally, for we cannot temporarily deafen children as ethologists did with baby finches.

But a girl named Genie, who was born in California in 1957, has provided some answers. Genie's childhood consisted almost exclusively of abuse and isolation. Her father hated children; her mother was unable to help her daughter because she was terrified of her husband and virtually blind herself. For the first twenty months of her life, Genie was underfed and ignored most of the time. Then the real abuse began. As Susan Curtiss (1977) describes it:

Genie was confined to a small bedroom, harnessed to an infant's potty seat . . . Unclad, except for the harness, Genie was left . . . to sit, tied up, hour after hour, often into the night, day after day, month after month, year after year. At night, when Genie was not forgotten, she was removed from her harness only to be placed in another restraining garment—a sleeping bag which her father fashioned to hold Genie's arms stationary. . . . Therein constrained, Genie was put into an infant's crib with wire mesh sides and a wire mesh cover overhead. Caged by night, harnessed by day, Genie was left to somehow endure the hours and years of her life.

The vocabulary-building process happens so quickly that, by age 5, some children seem to understand and use almost any specific term they hear. In fact, 5 year-olds can learn almost any word or phrase, as long as it is explained to them with specific examples and used in context. One 5-year-old surprised his kindergarten teacher by explaining that he was ambidextrous. When queried, he said, "That means I can use my left or my right hand just the same."

In fact, preschoolers are able to soak up language like a sponge, an ability that causes most researchers to regard early childhood as a crucial period for language learning (see Research Report). This ability is shown in another, less charming kind of "advanced" language usage, when children come home spouting profanity picked up on the street. Any words that seem to shock adults are exciting to a child, so an angelic 3-year-old who has seen the look this new vocabulary produces in Mom may run off to try it on Grandma too.

This drawing of a person, similar to what a 3-year-old might do, was drawn by Genie when she was almost 15. It is clear that her isolation had pervasive effects on many types of communication abilities.

Genie's isolation lasted for over eleven years. During this time she was totally cut off from all language. She overheard no conversation and was never spoken to. Her father "communicated" with her by behaving as though he were a wild dog, baring his teeth, barking and growling, and scratching her with his nails. Whenever she herself made a sound, she was beaten.

When she was rescued, Genie could not talk, and had no understanding of how to relate to people. Since she was long past the age when children learn to talk and develop social skills, most psychologists would have predicted a grim future for her, devoid of language and normal social interaction.

But Genie surprised the psychological community. After six years, first in a hospital and then with a foster family, Genie could talk in sentences and attend school. She expressed normal emotions, including affection for her new care-givers, and was able to communicate some of her memories of her terrible childhood. One interesting part of her language production was that she followed many of the same sequences, and made some of the same errors, that preschool children do. She dropped the "s" before words like "spoon" and "stop," and used the word "no" at the beginning of a sentence to make positive statements negative, as in "No take me home" and "No want to eat breakfast."

Genie's progress proves that language can develop after puberty. However, her speech is still far from normal. She does not use personal pronouns or the words "this" and "that"; she rarely uses auxiliary verbs (as in "I have eaten," or "I was jumping"); and she has problems with articulation. The fact that these errors persist implies that her early language deprivation, coupled with abuse and malnutrition, has permanently restricted her language-learning capacity. It may be that certain parts of the brain that allow children to learn language must be activated in early childhood, while other parts permit learning throughout life (Gardner, 1983).

What has current research on Genie and other children taught us about critical periods? Most developmentalists now believe that cognitive development is quite flexible or "plastic," in that new learning can occur at many points in the life span. Strictly speaking, critical periods in human cognition probably do not exist. However, there may well be "sensitive periods," when development is particularly vulnerable to environmental stress, or responsive to environmental stimulation. Early childhood is probably a sensitive period for language development, and probably for other forms of cognition as well. Although not the only time a person can learn a first language, all evidence suggests that it is the best time.

The world is so
you have something
to stand on

Little stones are for little children
to gather up and put in little piles

A hole is to dig

Difficulties with Vocabulary Despite the child's ability to learn new words more rapidly in early childhood than at any other age, vocabulary during this period is limited in several ways by the child's preoperational thought processes.

Because their thinking is concrete, emphasizing appearances and specifics, preschoolers' vocabulary consists mainly of concrete nouns and adjectives, with very few abstract nouns such as "justice," "economy," "government." For the same reason, when preschool children define words, they usually think about actions a child could do, and come up with egocentric definitions such as "A hole is to dig."

Another limitation results from the fact that young children, through a kind of verbal centering, tend to take everything literally. This means preschoolers have trouble understanding metaphorical speech. When a mother, exasperated by her son's continual inability to find his belongings, told him that someday he would lose his head, he calmly replied: "I'll never lose my head. I'll find it and pick it up." Another child laughed when his grandmother said winter was coming soon. "Do you mean that winter has legs, and is walking here?" (Chukovsky, 1968).

Many common figurative uses of words also give preschool children trouble. Before age 6, most children do not understand what is meant when an intelligent child is called "bright," a stern grandparent, "hard," or an unfriendly neighbor, "cold" (Asch and Nerlove, 1960).

Also, because children center on one specific concept and have difficulty with transformations, words expressing a comparison, such as "tall" and "short," "near" and "far," and "deep" and "shallow," are difficult (de Villiers and de Villiers, 1978). Once they know which end of the swimming pool is the deep one, they might obey instructions to stay out of deep puddles by splashing through every puddle they see, insisting that none of them are deep.

Other words expressing relationships are difficult as well. Many children think that all other children are brothers or sisters, and have trouble understanding what makes a person an aunt, or a cousin, or a nephew. Many also confuse "here" and "there," and "yesterday" with "today" and "tomorrow." More than one excited child has awakened on Christmas morning and asked "Is it tomorrow yet?"

Grammar

Grammar includes the structures, techniques, and rules that languages use to communicate meaning. Word order and word form, prefixes and suffixes, intonation and pronunciation, all are part of grammar. Grammar is apparent even in children's two-word sentences, since they almost always put the subject before the verb.

The child's use of various grammatical forms is a far better indicator of the child's verbal sophistication than vocabulary is. For this reason, an indicator called **MLU,** for **mean length of utterance** of each of the child's sentences, is often used to measure a child's language development (Brown, 1973). (An utterance is a meaningful unit of sound. For the most part, each word is one utterance, although some words count as more than one because each part has a distinct meaning. The word "jumping," for example, counts as two utterances, because the "ing" is a meaningful addition to the word "jump.") As measured by MLU, the 2-year-old who speaks in sentences that average four utterances in length ("Put coat on me," "Mommy take red ball") actually shows a far better mastery of language than the child who has a larger vocabulary but still uses only one or two utterances per sentence.

By age 3, children typically demonstrate extensive grammatical knowledge. They not only put the subject before the verb, but also put the verb before the object, explaining "I eat apple" rather than using any of the other possible combinations of those three words. They can form the plural of nouns, the past, present, and future tense of verbs, the subjective, objective, and possessive forms of pronouns. They are well on their way to mastering the negative, progressing past the simple "no" of the 2-year-old ("No sleepy," "I no want it," "I drink juice no"). Preschoolers can use the more complex negatives of "not," "nobody," "nothing," and even "never," and they are progressing toward the impressive negations of the school-age child, such as "I'll come with you, won't I?" or "He hurts no one because he doesn't want to hurt anyone."

Children's understanding of grammar is revealed when they create words that they have never heard, like those in the chart below. Each of the words in the chart

Children's Knowledge of Grammar in Creating Words

Rule followed	Word	Context
Add "un" to show reversal.	"unstraightening"	Child asked if a pliars is used for unstraightening wire.
	"unhate"	Child tells mother: "I hate you. And I'll never unhate you."
Add characteristic adjective before a noun to distinguish particular example.	"plate-egg," "cup-egg"	Fried eggs, boiled eggs.
	"sliverest seat"	A wooden bench.
Add "er" to form comparative.	"salter"	Food needs to be more salty.
Create noun by saying what it does.	"tell-wind"	Child pointing to a weathervane.
Add "er" to mean something or someone who does something.	"lessoner"	A teacher, who gives lessons.
	"shorthander"	Someone who writes shorthand.
Add "ed" to make a past verb out of a noun (as in punched, dressed).	"nippled"	"Mommy nippled Anna," reporting that Mother nursed the baby.
	"needled"	"Is it all needled yet?" asking if Mother has finished mending the pants.
Add "s" to make a noun out of an adjective.	plumps	buttocks
Add "ator" to mean a something that does something.	heaterator	"I have a good heaterator," explains a child who feels warm without a sweater.

Sources: Examples come from Bowerman, 1982; Clark, 1982; and the Berger children.

shows not only the child's mastery of grammatical rules but the presence of egocentrism as well, in that the children all expected others to understand their linguistic creations.

Children learning the same language usually master grammatical forms in the same sequence. For example, when Roger Brown (1973) followed the language development of three children, Adam, Eve, and Sarah, in great detail, he found that they all could add "ing" to verbs and "s" to nouns to make the plural before they could form the present or past tense. Jill and Peter de Villiers (1973) found the same sequence when they studied speech progression in a large cross-section of English-speaking children. The sequence of grammar development varies, however, depending on the particular language the child is trying to master, since certain grammatical distinctions are easier to make in some languages than others (Slobin, 1982; Akiyama, 1984).

Difficulties with Grammar   Children tend to apply the rules of grammar even when they should not. This tendency, called **overregularization,** can create trouble when their language is one that has many exceptions to the rules, as English does. For example, one of the first rules of grammar that children use is adding "s" to form the plural. Thus many preschoolers, applying this rule, talk about foots, snows, sheeps, and mouses. They may even put the "s" on adjectives, when the adjectives are acting as nouns, as in this dinner-table exchange between a 3-year-old and her father:

> Sarah: I want somes.
> *Father: You want some what?*
> I want some mores.
> *Some more what?*
> I want some more chickens.

Overregularization can be amusing, but it also can illustrate progress in grammar. For example, many 2-year-olds, who are still learning new words one by one, use irregular verbs correctly: "came" for the past tense of "come," "went" for the past tense of "go." They are simply repeating what they have heard. But when they are older and wiser about the rules of forming the past tense, they talk about people who "comed" and "goed" (Ervin, 1964).

Once preschool children learn a rule, they can be surprisingly stubborn in applying it. Jean Berko Gleason reports the following conversation between herself and a 4-year-old:

> She said: "My teacher *holded* the baby rabbits and we *patted* them." I asked: "Did you say your teacher *held* the baby rabbits?" She answered: "Yes." I then asked: "What did you say she did?" She answered again: "She *holded* the baby rabbits and we *patted* them." "Did you say she *held* them tightly?" I asked. "No," she answered, "she *holded* them loosely." [Gleason, 1967]

Although technically wrong, such overregularization is actually a sign of verbal sophistication, since children are, clearly, applying rules of grammar. After children hear the correct form often enough, they spontaneously correct their own speech, so parents can probably best help development of grammar by example rather than explanation or criticism.

Figure 10.9 *This mother has obviously become accustomed to her son's use of overregularization.*

No, Timmy, not "I sawed the chair." It's "I saw the chair" or "I have seen the chair."
Drawing by Glenn Bernhardt

Overregularization sometimes limits a child's understanding of language. In English, the normal word order is subject-verb-object, and children regularly follow this order in their earliest sentences as they say "Mommy give juice" or "I want ball." But when preschool children are confronted with the reversed word order of the passive voice, they generally become confused. For instance, when they hear "The truck was bumped by the car," they often think the truck did the bumping (de Villiers, 1980).

They also think sentence order is a clue to time sequence (de Villiers and de Villiers, 1979). When they are told "You can go outside after you pick up your toys," they think they can play first and pick up later; similarly, if they are told "Before you eat your cookie, you must wash your hands," they are likely to comply by eating the cookie first.

Finally, some grammatical forms demand more logic than most preoperational children are capable of. The conjunction "and" is very simple (though many young children use "and" to string together sentences that have no logical connection). But conjunctions that express conditionality, such as "unless," "although," and "nevertheless," are beyond most 5-year-olds.

Pragmatics

In addition to studying the growth of children's grasp of the meanings and forms of language, developmentalists have recently undertaken the study of **pragmatics,** the practical communication between one person and another in terms of the overall context in which language is used (Rice, 1982). The major emphasis of this study is that a person's communicative competence depends on that person's knowing how to adjust vocabulary and grammar to reflect the social situation.

Children learn these practical aspects of language very early. Evidence of such pragmatic understanding of language can be seen in 2- or 3-year-olds' use of "baby talk" when talking with younger children or with dolls and in their using a deeper voice to give commands to dogs and cats. Similarly, preschoolers become more

A CLOSER LOOK   **Articulation**

In some ways, the preschooler's ability to pronounce words is far better than that of adults. Certainly when learning a second language, developing the correct accent is impossible for most adults but seems to come easily to children (Asher and Garcia, 1969; Oyama, 1976). However, for many preschoolers, the ability to articulate certain words clearly and correctly lags behind their vocabulary and grammar. For the most part, this is because they have not yet gained the ability to coordinate tongue, jaw, and breath to correctly produce certain sounds. This fine motor skill will come in time, and no special training is needed.

Meanwhile, in order to understand what preschool children are trying to say, it is helpful to know that pronunciation during these years follows common patterns. One such pattern is to simplify words beginning with a double consonant. Some children do this by dropping the first consonant. "Spoon" becomes "poon"; "smack" becomes "mack"; and a girl might say that she's afraid that if she "pills" something on her "kirt" it will "tain." Others prefer to replace both consonants with another sound, so "truck" and "train" become "guck" and "gain." Another way children simplify pronunciation is to make all the consonants in a word the same, so "doggie" becomes "goggy" or "doddie."

Children also prefer to have voiced consonants such as "b," "d," and "g," which are formed without expelling much breath, at the beginning of words, and unvoiced consonants, such as "p," "t," and "k," at the end of words. Thus, they may turn "toe" into "doe," "pop" into "bop," and "dog" into "dok" (de Villiers and de Villiers, 1979). This helps explain why preschoolers change the order of the consonants in many polysyllabic words. "Magazine" is best pronounced "mazagine," for instance, if one strives to keep the "g" at the beginning rather than at the end of a syllable. These preferences do not necessarily mean the child cannot form certain sounds. One linguist's son always replaced "th" with "f," so "thick" became "fick." At the same stage, he replaced "s" with "th," so "sick" became "thick" (Smith, 1973).

Once parents and teachers understand a child's preferences, they can figure out what the child is saying, despite the odd pronunciation. Correcting or teasing the child, or withholding something the child is asking for until the child uses the right pronunciation, not only is unhelpful but might make the problem worse. This is certainly the case with stuttering, a difficulty many preschoolers have to some extent.

While adults should not criticize the child's mispronunciation, neither should they adopt it, for the child may come to believe that the mispronunciation is correct. Children can actually hear the difference, even though they cannot say it. For instance, on seeing a display of candy in a store, one girl asked her daddy for a "yeh-yo yah-yi-pop." Her father, smiling, said "You want a yeh-yo yah-yi-pop?" The girl's response: "Daddy, sometimes you talk funny."

Most children with articulation problems outgrow them by elementary school, although some sounds (especially "l" and "th") still give many 7-year-olds difficulty. However, if the problem with pronunciation is sufficiently great that, even at age 4 or 5, a child still has trouble making himself or herself understood, a speech therapist should be consulted. At this age many children are able to do exercises and practice sound combinations that will help their speech. Preschoolers with noticeable and uncorrected speech problems often develop other problems during elementary school if teachers and other children cannot understand them (Murphy and Moriarty, 1976).

---

formal when playing the role of doctor of teacher or train conductor, and they use "please" more often when addressing someone of higher status (Rice, 1984).

Another pragmatic development is shown in children's developing ability to relate an event sequentially, as they become more aware of the usual "scripts" for various everyday events. By age 3 or 4, children can follow the usual script in telling what happened at, say, a restaurant (order food, eat it, and pay for it), or a birthday party (give presents, play games, have cake and ice cream), and they can also relate specific details of these experiences that are different from the usual sequence (Nelson and Gruendel, 1981). From a practical language perspective, the ability to make meaningful conversation about events that happened some time before is even more important than the breadth of one's vocabulary or the correctness of one's grammar.

Figure 10.10 *It is obvious from their body language that these two children have different points of view—perhaps about who might like to ride the bike next. Their ability to communicate their opinions and come to an agreement is an indication of their pragmatic skills.*

Inner Speech   There is another practical use of language that develops during early childhood. Language can be a way of formulating ideas to oneself. This private use of language is called **inner speech.** The development of inner speech begins when preschoolers talk out loud to themselves; next they whisper; and then they silently mouth the words they are thinking. Finally, they form the words in their heads as adults often do, without giving any visible or audible clues that they are talking to themselves (Kohlberg et al., 1968). Thus, 3-year-olds usually talk aloud as they manipulate their dolls or trucks; 8-year-olds are much quieter, or even soundless, as they take their toys from one imagined experience to another. Even 8-year-olds, however, are likely to talk aloud or whisper when they are confronted with difficult cognitive tasks. For example, a child who is trying to add 169 and 58 without pencil and paper is likely to whisper "Put down 7, carry 1, . . . ," and a child who is trying to spell "receive" may recite "*i* before *e* except after *c*." Indeed, the use of inner speech to help memory and cognition seems to increase between the preschool and school-age years (Flavell, 1970; Berk and Garvin, 1984).

Finally, during the preschool years children grow to understand a great deal about the practical functions of language as it is addressed to them. They are able to comprehend more complex grammar, and more difficult vocabulary, than they can produce. This is one reason adults should not use baby talk with a child who has already mastered the basics of language.

Indeed, one of the impressive characteristics of preschoolers is their attempt to understand and respond to language that they cannot really grasp. This was shown experimentally when a group of 5-year-olds were asked to answer questions such as "Is milk bigger than water?" "Is red heavier than yellow?" Virtually all of them gave definitive answers, such as "Yes, because it's more thicker" or "Yes, yellow's not bright and red is" (Hughes and Grieve, 1980). It is also shown in children's gradual mastery of proper listening behavior, such as nodding the head and saying things like "Uh huh" and "Really?" to indicate that the speaker is heard and understood, even when this is not the case (Garvey, 1984).

Difficulties with Pragmatics Piaget (1959) found that about half the statements made by preschool children were instances of egocentric speech, in that the children did not even try to consider the viewpoint of anyone else. Some egocentric speech is a simple **monologue,** in which children talk to themselves or to other people without waiting for a response. Another form of egocentric speech, called the **collective monologue,** occurs when two children have a conversation but neither one listens or responds to what the other says. Here is a collective monologue between two 4-year-olds:

> Jenny: They wiggle sideways when they kiss.
> Chris: *(Vaguely) What?*
>   My bunny slippers. They are brown and red and sort of yellow and white. And they have eyes and ears and these noses that wiggle sideways when they kiss.
>   *I have a piece of sugar in a red piece of paper. I'm gonna eat it but maybe it's for a horse.*
>   We bought them. My mommy did. We couldn't find the old ones. These are like the old ones. They were not in the trunk.
>   *Can't eat the piece of sugar, not unless you take the paper off.*
>   And we found Mother Lamb. Oh, she was in Poughkeepsie in the trunk in the house in the woods where Mrs. Tiddywinkle lives.
>   *Do you like sugar? I do, and so do horses.*
>   I play with my bunnies. They are real. We play in the woods. They have eyes. We all go in the woods. My teddy bear and the bunnies and the duck, to visit Mrs. Tiddywinkle. We play and play.
>   *I guess I'll eat my sugar at lunch time. I can get more for the horses. Besides, I don't have no horses now.*

According to the nursery-school teacher who reported this conversation, neither child seemed even aware, let alone upset, that the other child was not responding to the same topic (Stone and Church, 1973).

Probably because they are egocentric, preschool children tend to overestimate the clarity of their communications and also overestimate how well they understand others (Beal and Flavell, 1983). A child might say "I want my toy" without specifying which toy. That the child does not realize the incompleteness of the request is indicated by the child's becoming upset if someone fetches the wrong toy. Or a child might begin talking in detail about someone the listener has never met.

A further example of egocentrism can be seen in children's thinking they understand more than they do. Young children are well known for jumping to conclusions based on poorly comprehended material and then insisting that they are right. They are particularly likely to do this when statements are open to more than one interpretation. One kindergarten boy resolved never to go back to school because, after being told to sit and wait "for the present," he didn't receive a gift (Donaldson, 1978). As in this case, ambiguous communications, either spoken by children or heard by them, are often not recognized as such, with a resulting breakdown in the communication process (Flavell et al., 1981; Beal and Flavell, 1982).

Figure 10.11 *Adults can help children develop communication skills by creating situations that support learning naturally and enjoyably, such as in word games that involve songs, touch, and body movement.*

According to one study of 5-year-olds, even children who are trained in recognizing ambiguous statements uttered by someone else are not necessarily very good at recognizing their own ambiguous speech (Sonnenschein, 1984). Specific feedback and suggestions about the clarity of their speech help preschoolers become better at communicating. Rarely, in the normal course of events, do they get such feedback, and for this reason many preschoolers are less adept at pragmatics than they might be. In one study (Robinson and Robinson, 1981), those children who were the most precise in describing the clothes on one doll so that a partner could dress another doll in identical garb were also those whose mothers were, in the home, quite specific in helping the children explain exactly what they meant.

Differences in Language Development

By the time children enter kindergarten, differences in language skill are great. While one child seems to know the name of almost every object and action within that child's experience, and can converse in complex sentences, another child has only a basic vocabulary using a few words at a time.

To some extent, one can predict which groups of children are likely to be more advanced in language. On most measures of language production, girls are more proficient than boys; middle-class children, more proficient than lower-class children; first-borns, more proficient than later-borns; single-born children, more proficient than twins, who, in turn, tend to be ahead of triplets (Rebelsky et al., 1967). Note, however, that these group variations are small compared to the differences among individual children from the same group. Thus some lower-class twin boys know far more words than other lower-class twin boys. Similarly, a linguistically advanced lower-class twin boy will have a far better grasp of language than the average middle-class, single-born, girl.

It is also important to note that some of the differences between one child and another, as measured by language tests, may be the result of a child's comfort with the testing situation. Edward Zigler and his colleagues (1973) showed that economically disadvantaged children scored much better on a vocabulary test when they were familiar with the examiner and the format of the test, and when they felt relaxed. Courtney Cazden (1976) reports that the language of lower-class children becomes much more elaborate when they are personally involved with the topic.

The importance of context is further highlighted by a study (Genishi and Dyson, 1984) that showed children exhibiting much greater language competence when playing with friends than when being questioned by a language researcher.

Nevertheless, even when such factors are considered, there are significant differences among groups of children, and, even more, among individual children (Slaughter, 1983; Snyder, 1984). Researchers who try to explain these differences usually look at the nature and the amount of the language children hear. In general, they have found that mothers talk more to daughters than to sons (Goldberg and Lewis, 1969; Cherry and Lewis, 1976); that middle-class parents provide their children with more elaborate explanations, more responsive comments, and fewer commands than lower-class parents do (Hess and Shipman, 1965; Zegiob and Forehand, 1975); and that parents talk more to first-borns and single-borns than to later-borns or twins (Jacobs and Moss, 1976; Lytton et al., 1977; White, 1979). Particularly important is the parents' attitude about children's language: in cultures where it is thought that children should be seen and not heard, where "idle talk" is frowned on, and where "talking fresh" is punished, children's language production is not encouraged, and, not surprisingly, children do quite poorly on tests of language development (Ward, 1971; Schieffelin and Eisenberg, 1984).

Looking more closely at individual differences, it seems that general parent-child factors, such as strength of attachment or the amount of time spent together, are not particularly good predictors of a child's language competence. However, the amount and quality of conversation between adults and children are relevant. Children become more linguistically competent if the significant adults in their lives encourage them to talk, and reply to their comments with specific and contingent responses (Snow, 1984). (If, for instance, a child says, "I saw a fire engine," a response like "Was it a long red fire engine?" is much more helpful than something like "That's nice.") Adults can also provide experiences that act as a "scaffold" on which to build language skills (Schiefelbusch, 1984; Genishi and Dyson, 1984). Such activities might include looking at picture books together; going on excursions that

Figure 10.12 *These city children visiting a farm for the first time will probably come away with more complex ideas—and feelings—about words such as "cow," "milk," and "barn" than they have gotten from picture books alone.*

provide opportunities for new vocabulary and topics of discussion; and pretending together (pragmatic skills are evoked in an imaginary tea party or classroom or trip to the moon). Such measures work as well for learning a second language as for learning a first (McLaughlin, 1984).

The importance of language encouragement and social opportunities is one reason many early-childhood experts have stressed the quality of the learning environment for the young child. As we will now see, that environment can make a difference not only for the child's language development but for his or her attitudes about future education.

Teaching and Learning

As we have learned, during early childhood, egocentricity declines, elements of logic begin to emerge, vocabulary multiplies, and sentences lengthen. Part of the reason for these developments is the maturation of the child's cognitive capacity, but, as is increasingly clear, the child's experiences also play an important role. In experiments in which young children demonstrate competencies beyond those predicted by a strict interpretation of Piaget, as well as in the development of the practical skills of language, the context of learning appears increasingly crucial. We have already seen that specific attempts to teach a particular skill, such as the conservation-training experiments, have some success. The question then arises, What might be the effects of more global attempts to foster cognitive development during the preschool years?

Headstart

The most comprehensive research on the power of preschool education has focused on a massive experiment in social change called Headstart (Zigler and Berman, 1983). In the early 1960s in the United States, social scientists and social reformers were particularly concerned that few health or educational services were available to impoverished children during the preschool years, years that were thought to be critical for the child's later achievements. They advocated giving children who might be disadvantaged by their home environment or culturally deprived by their community some form of compensatory education, a "headstart" that would remedy the deficiencies of their early upbringing.

Beginning in 1965, hundreds of thousands of "disadvantaged" children, from many racial and ethnic backgrounds, living in many communities, attended a variety of Headstart programs: some full-time, some part-time, some concentrating on classroom activity, some teaching parents how to educate their children in the home. One reason for the diversity of the Headstart program was its rapid, unstructured development, which saw 20,000 children attend programs in about 2,000 different communities in the program's first full year.

The first results from Project Headstart were encouraging. Children learned a variety of intellectual and social skills between September and June of their Headstart year, averaging a gain of five points on intelligence tests. This is a significant gain, and was considered especially important because intelligence tests focus on the language and reasoning skills that are needed for later school achievement. In addition, Headstart children had fewer behavioral problems and greater motivation at the end of their Headstart year than they had had at the

Figure 10.13 *It is likely that intensive, individualized attention to the many skills involved in learning a second language will help this Spanish-speaking preschooler perform well in, and enjoy, his first-grade classes.*

beginning of it. Even children who attended only for a summer showed some gains (Horowitz and Paden, 1973). More recent preschool programs designed to improve cognitive development of disadvantaged children replicate these early results: in fact, IQ gains of 10 or more points are not unusual after intensive, well-designed day care (Zigler et al., 1982; Ramey and Haskins, 1981).

Long-Term Benefits Unfortunately, initial research on the long-term effects of Headstart was disappointing. Many of the social and cognitive gains that children received from Headstart seemed to fade after a few years (Westinghouse Learning Corporation, 1969; Bronfenbrenner, 1975). By second or third grade, the accomplishments and IQ gains of Headstart children were generally indistinguishable from those of their peers, in part because the IQ advances of Headstart children faded, and in part because non-Headstart children gained somewhat in cognitive abilities after they were in school.

However, more recent research suggests that Headstart indeed made a difference (Lazar and Darlington, 1982; Schweinhart and Weikart, 1983). Rather than a fade-out, there was merely a **sleeper effect,** in which the changes were not apparent for a few years, and then reemerged. Overall, the original Headstart children, who are now young adults, are more successful than their non-Headstart contemporaries from the same neighborhoods.

As they make their way through elementary school, Headstart graduates score higher on achievement tests and have more positive school report cards than non-Headstart children from the same backgrounds and neighborhoods. By junior high, they are significantly less likely to be placed in special classes or made to repeat a year. In adolescence, Headstart graduates have higher aspirations and a greater sense of achievement. When asked to tell about "something you've done that made you feel proud of yourself," the Headstart graduates were more likely to mention an accomplishment at school or on the job, or significant helpfulness to their families. A far higher proportion of non-Headstart than Headstart young people responded that they couldn't think of anything to be proud of.

Since the Headstart programs began, other comparisons of children with and without preschool education have been done. According to several thorough reviews, good preschool education advances the cognitive as well as the social development of children from disadvantaged homes, and probably helps those from more advantaged homes as well (Rutter, 1982; Belsky et al., 1982; Clarke-Stewart, 1984; Scarr, 1984). All reviewers take care to point out, however, that virtually all studies have been done on relatively high-quality schools and day-care centers. Such centers are characterized by a low teacher-child ratio, a well-trained staff, a curriculum geared toward cognitive development rather than behavioral control, and space and groupings organized to facilitate creative and constructive play. They also tend to be expensive, subsidized by a university, an employer, or the government.

Unfortunately, scientifically rigorous studies of preschool education are virtually impossible to do (Clarke-Stewart and Fein, 1983). We cannot arbitrarily assign some children to one type of family interaction and some to another; nor can we randomly make some families send their children to nursery school and others care for them at home. The many variables that might affect a child's learning during the preschool years—such as the child's age, sex, family background, family interaction, neighborhood, and the size, curriculum, and values of the preschool education received—are difficult to untangle.

Nevertheless, the importance of quality seems clear from a number of studies. One was a large comparison done in Bermuda (McCartney, 1984), where 84 percent of the children between 2 and 4 years old spend their days in some sort of preschool. When factors such as parents' socioeconomic status and values were controlled, quality of care in the day-care centers, particularly the amount of adult-child conversation, had a noticeable effect on the children's verbal skills and on their overall intellectual development.

The best centers were the ones where teachers spent more time teaching the children (usually in small groups) and less time controlling the children (usually done one child at a time). The best centers also engaged the children in a variety of activities designed to foster creative, motor, social, and language skills.

In another comparison study, this one of four different preschool programs for disadvantaged children in Kentucky, two showed most long-term gains: a Montessori program, which emphasizes individual work with materials especially designed for self-education, and a Darcee program, which emphasizes language skills. Both programs stressed good work habits and attitudes, including persistence, concentration, and the desire to achieve (Miller and Bizzell, 1983).

Parent Involvement

One other aspect of most successful programs is that they directly involve the parents (Palmer, 1978; Gray and Wandersman, 1980; Seitz et al., 1985). In some cases, this involvement is center-based, with parents serving as volunteers in the classroom and as members of the board. In other cases, teachers or social workers visit homes, teaching mothers specific patterns of play and conversation that would foster intellectual skills and providing other forms of support as well.

One successful visiting program was amazingly simple. Mothers were visited at home twice a week for two years, when their children were between 24 and 28 months old (Levenstein, 1970). The visitors were called "toy demonstrators," because they brought a toy or book as a gift each time. They encouraged the mothers to use the toys to develop their children's imaginations, verbal skills, and self-direction.

In the first years of this program, the visitors were professionals (social workers or psychologists). In later years, people from the community were trained to visit other families, and some of the original mothers joined the project as toy demonstrators themselves. Follow-up studies show that many of the programs using nonprofessionals were as successful as the ones conducted by professionals had been, with the children showing benefits as much as ten years later (Levenstein et al., 1973; Madden et al., 1976).

Another program also was quite simple (Slaughter, 1983). In this one, mothers living in housing projects in Chicago were assigned to one of three groups: a group who participated in a toy-demonstrators' project, a group who met for discussions related to child development, and a control group who were tested periodically and who received the toys without any "demonstration." All three groups benefited, mothers and children alike, but the discussion group was the most successful overall when the mother's self-confidence and interaction with her children, and the child's verbal expressiveness and overall IQ, were measured. The reason, according to the project directors, was that "the mothers' discussion program assumed that, though of similar backgrounds, mothers had something to offer each other. Their basic competencies and resiliencies were reinforced even as they learned different parenting approaches."

It is noteworthy that a variety of strategies seems to foster the development of intellectual skills during the play years, and no one treatment has been found that, if given in a prescribed dose at some critical period, guarantees optimal development. It may well be that any program that respects the role of the parents, and focuses on conceptual and language skills, will foster cognitive development. Programs and experiments that consider the entire context of the child's cognitive development as we have examined them in this chapter—that foster imagination, self-motivation, language, and social awareness—seem to work well whether they occur at home or at school.

SUMMARY

How Preschoolers Think

1. When children become capable of symbolic thought—that is, of using words, objects, and actions as symbols—their ability to understand, imagine, and communicate increases rapidly.

2. According to Piaget, preoperational thought is essentially prelogical. For instance, preoperational children cannot figure out the logical principles of conservation, classification, chance, or gradual change. They center on one feature of an experience rather than looking at the relationship among several features.

3. The preoperational child believes that other people and even objects think and act the same way he or she does. This general characteristic is called egocentrism, which is quite different from selfishness. One consequence of

egocentrism is that preoperational children have difficulty understanding a point of view other than their own.

4. A number of Piaget's critics have shown that preschoolers may have some of the cognitive capacities Piaget's standard tests suggest they don't have until the school years. However, it is also true that although young children may demonstrate some rudiments of perspective, number, and so forth, they cannot yet apply them to a wide range of real-life situations.

Language Development

5. Most developmentalists agree that infants form concepts first and then learn the words to express them. At some point in early childhood, language becomes a tool for forming ideas and regulating action.

6. Language accomplishments during early childhood include learning 10,000 or so words, and understanding

almost all basic grammatical forms. However, as you might expect with children who are basically prelogical, they often misunderstand grammatical rules, metaphors, and abstractions. For many children, articulation lags behind other aspects of language development.

7. Children learn many aspects of language, including pronunciation, so rapidly during early childhood that psychologists wondered if this was a critical period for language development. However, while these are the best years for learning to talk, language skills can develop at a later age.

8. Children's language learning can be evaluated from the perspective of pragmatics—the use of practical communication in a variety of contexts.

9. Children who are at the egocentric stage of development have difficulty with conversational skills. They are as likely to talk in monologues or collective monologues as they are to engage in socialized speech.

Teaching and Learning

10. There are many similarities in the nature and sequence of cognitive development in all children. However, there are differences as well, especially in how rapidly children pass each milestone of intellectual growth.

11. One source of these differences is the child's home, particularly with regard to how the parents interact with their children.

12. Children who have attended preschool programs like Headstart, which are designed to improve their intellectual abilities, tend to show improvements in social and cognitive skills through adolescence and young adulthood. In addition, Headstart graduates often experience a greater sense of achievement than their peers.

KEY QUESTIONS

1. How does symbolic thinking expand the cognitive potential of the young child?

2. What are the characteristics of preoperational thought?

3. What are several examples of the concept of conservation?

4. Why doesn't the young child understand conservation?

5. How well can young children understand another point of view?

6. How does the increasing capacity to use language affect thought in early childhood?

7. What are the impressive language accomplishments of the young child?

8. What are the limitations of language ability of the young child?

9. What are some examples of ways in which children adjust their communication to the social situation?

10. What are some of the factors responsible for individual differences in language learning?

11. What benefits have Headstart graduates experienced?

KEY TERMS

symbol *(287)*	egocentrism *(291)*
reversibility *(289)*	animism *(293)*
preoperational thought *(289)*	mean length of utterance (MLU) *(303)*
centration *(289)*	overregularization *(304)*
conservation *(290)*	pragmatics *(305)*
conservation of matter *(290)*	inner speech *(307)*
conservation of number *(290)*	monologue *(308)*
identity *(291)*	collective monologue *(308)*
	sleeper effect *(312)*

RECOMMENDED READINGS

Clarke-Stewart, Alison. *Daycare.* Cambridge, Mass.: Harvard University Press, 1982.

This book summarizes the research on day care and concludes that good day care comes in many forms, including day-care centers, informal care in someone's home, and full-time mother-surrogate care in the child's own home. Each form has advantages as well as possible problems: no one kind of care is necessarily best. The crucial factors for cognitive as well as psychosocial development include sufficient individual attention and sufficient concern for the curriculum of language and self-expression.

de Villiers, Peter A., and **de Villiers, Jill G.** *Early language.* Cambridge, Mass.: Harvard University Press, 1979.

The de Villierses are a husband-wife team who are experts in child language. In this book, they explain the process of learning a language between birth and age 6. The book is filled with charming examples from the children of linguists, and also includes references to the early language of deaf, retarded, and autistic children, to shed light on the normal process.

Singer, Dorothy G., and **Revenson, Tracey A.** *How a child thinks: A Piaget primer.* New York: New American Library, 1978.

This is a readable summary of Piaget's ideas, including many examples from Piaget and from other sources. Thinking during early childhood is presented with particular care. The last chapter, "Beyond Piaget," includes some thoughts about the ways teachers, parents, and television influence the learning of preschool children.

The Play Years: Psychosocial Development

Chapter 11

Lady . . . lady, I do not make up things, that is lies. Lies is not true. But the truth could be made up if you know how. And that's the truth.

Lily Tomlin, as Edith Ann

The Self and the Social World
The Development of Self-Concept

Social Skills and Self-Understanding

Play
Categories of Social Play

Dramatic Play

Sibling Interaction

The Importance of Social Play

Parenting
Hostility and Affection

Patterns of Parenting

Punishment

Possible Problems
Aggression

Fantasy and Fear

Serious Psychological Disturbances

Sex Roles and Stereotypes
Three Theories of Sex-Role Development

A New Theory: Androgyny

Chapter 11

In the preschool years, children become more capable of seeing "eye to eye" with others and are more influenced by others' perceptions of themselves. Their growing capacity for communication, imagination, and social understanding allows them to participate in ever-more-elaborate play scenarios with other children and to explore various social roles. In this chapter we will consider the ways in which preschoolers develop their ideas about themselves and their relationship to the social world, including topics such as those that follow.

How does the development of a child's self-concept influence his or her ability to form relationships with others?

How do children benefit from the increasingly complex interactions of social play?

What are the various types of disciplinary patterns that parents adopt and how do these patterns affect children's behavior?

What do young children know about sex differences?

How do children learn sex roles?

Picture a typical 2-year-old and a typical 6-year-old, and consider the psychosocial differences between them. Chances are the 2-year-old still has many moments of clinging, of tantrums, and of stubbornness, vacillating between dependence and self-determination. Further, many 2-year-olds cannot be trusted alone, even for a few moments, in any place where their relentless curiosity might lead them into destructive or dangerous behavior.

Six-year-olds, by contrast, have the confidence and competence to be relatively independent. They can be trusted to do many things by themselves, perhaps getting their own breakfast before school and even going to the store to buy some more cereal. They also can show affection with parents and friends without the obvious clinging or exaggerated self-assertion of the younger child. Six-year-olds are able to say goodbye to their parents at the door of the first-grade classroom, where they go about their business, befriending certain classmates and ignoring others, playing cooperatively with their peers, and respecting and learning from their teachers.

It is apparent that in terms of self-confidence, social skills, and social roles, much develops during early childhood. This chapter examines that development, looking precisely at what occurs and exploring how it occurs.

The Self and the Social World

Self-concept, self-confidence, and self-understanding, as well as social attitudes, social skills, and social roles, are familiar topics for scientists who study adult personality. Until recently, however, relatively little attention was paid to the development of these aspects of the human character in childhood (Harter, 1983). Now that researchers in child development have begun to investigate these areas, they have found that early childhood is a seminal period for their formation and growth.

The Development of Self-Concept

As we saw in Chapter 8, the idea of self emerges gradually during the latter stages of infancy. By early childhood, children begin to have clearly defined (although not necessarily accurate) concepts of self (Harter, 1983). They assiduously note which possessions are theirs, claiming everything from "my teacher" to "my mudpie"; they repeatedly explain who they are and who they are not ("I am a big girl"; "I am not a baby"); and they relish many forms of mastery play that allow them to show that "I can do it."

Typically, they form quite general, and quite positive, impressions of themselves. Indeed, much research, as well as anecdotal evidence, shows that preschool children regularly overestimate their own abilities. As every parent knows, the typical 3-year-old believes that he or she can win any race, do perfect cartwheels, count accurately, and make up beautiful songs. In a laboratory test, even when preschoolers had just scored rather low on a game, they confidently predicted that they would do very well the next time (Stipek and Hoffman, 1980). Only when it is specifically pointed out to them how poorly they have done will they revise their estimates downward (Stipek et al., 1984).

In addition, most preschoolers think of themselves as able in all areas—competent at physical skills as well as at intellectual ones (Harter and Pike, 1984). This is greatly different from children older than age 8, who make clear distinctions between domains of competence, asserting that they are rather good in intellectual skills but poor in athletic ones, for example (Harter, 1983).

Theories of Self and Others   Each of the three major theories of development recognizes the emerging self-concept of the preschool child. The most encompassing psychoanalytic view is that of Erik Erikson (1963), who notes that the child comes into "free possession of a surplus of energy which permits him to forget failures quickly and to approach what seems desirable . . . the child appears 'more himself,' more loving, relaxed, and brighter in his judgment, more activated and activating." The child initiates new activities with boldness and exuberance.

Indeed, the crisis of this stage, according to Erikson, is **initiative versus guilt.** In this crisis, which is closely tied to the child's developing sense of self and the

Figure 11.1 *While preschoolers' confidence frequently surpasses their abilities, nonetheless, their increasingly refined motor and cognitive skills and developing social awareness enable them to undertake complex cooperative tasks, such as building this intricate cityscape.*

awareness of the larger society, preschoolers eagerly take on new tasks and play activities and feel guilty when their efforts result in failure or criticism. Their readiness to take initiative reflects preschoolers' desire to accomplish things, not simply to assert their autonomy as they did when toddlers. Thus, in a nursery-school classroom the older preschoolers take the initiative to build impressive block towers, whereas the younger child in the autonomy stage is more likely to be interested in knocking them down.

One result of the child's growing self-concept is a turning away "from an exclusive attachment" to parents and moving toward becoming a member of the larger culture. Erikson sees children at this stage as filled with enthusiasm to learn many things, including the social roles of mother or father, as well as citizen, neighbor, and worker, following the customs of whatever culture the child experiences.

When initiative fails, according to Erikson,—when the eager exploration leads to a broken toy, a crying playmate, or a criticizing adult—the result is guilt, an emotion that is beyond the scope of the infant because it depends on an internalized conscience and a sense of self (Campos et al., 1983).

As we saw in Chapter 10, cognitive theory also shows preschool children developing a sense of themselves and then, from that, a sense of others. As children's new symbolic thinking expands their control over the world, they develop the capacity to imagine all kinds of possibilities and can talk about virtually anything in their experience. As their cognitive processes mature and their social experiences accumulate, their egocentric sense of self becomes less narrow, and social understanding increases.

Finally, learning theory notes that toward the end of early childhood, praise and blame, as reinforcements and punishments, become powerful as they could not be earlier, because now children are aware of themselves, and of how others perceive them (White, 1965).

The differing emphases of the psychoanalytic, cognitive, and learning theories are particularly noteworthy, and intriguing, with regard to the development of sex roles in children, a topic we will take up toward the end of this chapter. For the moment, it should be borne in mind that all three perspectives acknowledge the emerging importance of self-knowledge and self-confidence to interaction with others and to a growing understanding of the wider social world.

Social Skills and Self-Understanding

The close relationship between the child's sense of self and his or her interactions with the social world has been shown empirically as well as theoretically. The first step in social interaction between two preschoolers is often a matter of establishing the individuality of each of them, as they tell each other their names and ages and show off any interesting toy or garment they may have. What might look to adults like bragging and self-preoccupation may actually be a social overture.

One aspect of this relationship between self-awareness and social awareness was shown in a study in which seventy-eight 2-year-old boys were tested for their self-understanding (Levine, 1983). Their comprehension of possessive pronouns was assessed by seeing if they could correctly follow commands such as "Tickle your stomach," "Touch my nose," and "Touch your toes." The accuracy of their use of "I" and "me" was also tested. In addition, their self-recognition was measured by means of the mirror-and-a-dot-of-rouge experiment described in Chapter 8 (page 217). Then they were paired off, and put in a playroom together. Typically, the first step of interaction was asserting selfhood, usually in terms of ownership, as shown in the following dialogue between two boys who are relatively high in their development of self-concept. (Each boy is sitting on a toy car, and holding his own nerf ball.)

John: My ball.
Jim: *Mine ball.*
My ball. [I] have this. No. [the warning came in spite of the fact that Jim has made no move toward the toy]
My ball.
No.
No ball.
No ball ball. Two ball ball.
Mine.
No.
My ball. Boon ball. [smiles]
Bump!
Yup!
Car's going bump.

This particular play session began with ten statements of self-assertion before a joke ("boon ball") was used to initiate actual play. Finding this pattern repeated again and again in their study, the authors conclude:

> a child's increased interest in claiming toys may not be a negative sign of selfishness but a positive sign of increased self-awareness. . . . With development a toddler's interactions take on a different character, marked by possessiveness and an attempt to make sense of the other child as a separate social being. [Levine, 1983]

In this study, those who had the more firmly established self-understanding as measured by the pretests were also those who engaged in more interactive play. Similar results have been found in a number of contexts: the children who are most social are those who have a better-developed sense of self, as well as a more secure feeling of self-assurance in a given setting (Hartup, 1983). Further, children who are skilled at social interaction tend to be those who are quite confident of their own ability. For example, they are less dependent on teachers in a nursery school or parents at a playground than children who are more awkward at the skills of friendship (Rubin, 1980).

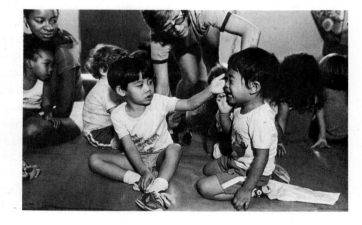

Figure 11.2 *While even infants show their awareness of another's distress by crying along, children do not develop the ability to empathize with others until they develop a better sense of themselves.*

Indeed, self-understanding is closely related to social understanding at many stages of life (Gardner, 1983). This raises an important question: How does personal knowledge—both intrapersonal and interpersonal—develop? In all likelihood, it begins in a social context, through the child's interactions, with peers, siblings, parents, and strangers. One of the most important of these interactions in early childhood is play.

Play

As we saw in Chapter 9, play is the work of preschoolers: through it they develop physical skills and expand their cognitive grasp of their world. Play is also important to preschoolers' psychosocial development, as children develop social skills and roles through social play and dramatic play.

Categories of Social Play

Half a century ago Mildred Parten (1932) studied preschool children and observed five ways children play when other children are around:

1. **Solitary play**   A child plays alone, seemingly unaware of any other children playing nearby.

2. **Onlooker play**   A child watches other children play.

3. **Parallel play**   Children play in similar ways with similar toys, but they don't interact.

4. **Associative play**   Children interact, including sharing materials, but they don't seem to be playing the same game.

5. **Cooperative play**   Children play together, helping each other or taking turns.

Originally, Parten's classification was used as a measure of a child's maturity, since onlooker play is most common at age 2 and associative and cooperative play become common at 5. In fact, these categories devised fifty years ago are still relevant today. Many recent studies have confirmed that the advanced forms of social play are characteristic of the older, more experienced, children in a nursery-school setting (Holmberg, 1980; Harper and Huie, 1985).

However, it would be a mistake to apply the developmental progression of social play too rigidly as an indicator of social maturity, erroneously predicting that 2-year-olds are incapable of the more advanced forms of play, or that 5-year-olds who engage in solitary or onlooker play are immature. In fact, quite young children who have had experience with other children are likely to chase each other (rough-and-tumble play), chatter together (language play), and simply enjoy each other's company, all elements of associative play. And children aged 5 and more usually spend some part of their schoolday in solitary play—a sign not of immaturity but of the ability to concentrate on a task (Roper and Hinde, 1978; Smith, 1978). Further, children of any age who are new to a group often begin their attempts at interaction by being onlookers, standing near the play activity and watching, waiting for an appropriate moment to say something like "What are you doing?" or, more bravely, "Can I play?"

Nevertheless, Parten's categories are useful for evaluating both the various kinds of play that children engage in and the types of settings that promote these

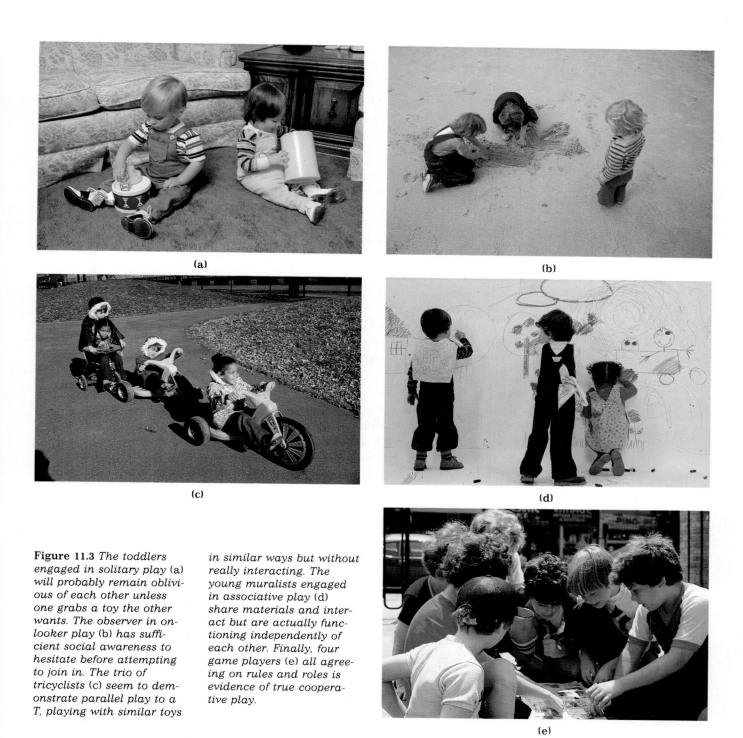

Figure 11.3 *The toddlers engaged in solitary play (a) will probably remain oblivious of each other unless one grabs a toy the other wants. The observer in onlooker play (b) has sufficient social awareness to hesitate before attempting to join in. The trio of tricyclists (c) seem to demonstrate parallel play to a T, playing with similar toys in similar ways but without really interacting. The young muralists engaged in associative play (d) share materials and interact but are actually functioning independently of each other. Finally, four game players (e) all agreeing on rules and roles is evidence of true cooperative play.*

different kinds of play. Such evaluation can be important, for, as we will see later in the chapter, children who are old enough to regularly engage in associative or cooperative play, but do not, are a cause for concern. Further, some contexts—such as nursery schools in which there are a relatively large group of acquainted children and ample toys and space—foster a larger percentage of associative and cooperative play than others and thus are probably better for children's social development (Rubin, 1980).

In general, developmentalists agree that the higher forms of social play are very important in the life of the preschooler, for through the social interaction that is central to such play children learn the skills, and gain the self-knowledge they need to become competent in the larger social world. The intellectual and social sophistication of cooperative play is shown in the most complicated form of social play of all, dramatic play.

Dramatic Play

The beginnings of **dramatic play** coincide with the achievement of symbolic thinking and can be clearly seen, for example, in a child's "feeding," cuddling, and punishing a doll or stuffed animal. As children get older, they can create elaborate scenarios for these inanimate creatures. However, the aspect of dramatic play that is of interest to us here is the social development that occurs when two or more children cooperate in creating their own drama. Numerous studies have found that such mutual fantasy play becomes more common and more complex between the ages of 2 and 6 (Rubin, et al., 1983).

For instance, Catherine Garvey (1977) found many examples of dramatic play when she studied forty-eight preschool children ranging in age from 2 years and 10 months to 5 years and 7 months. Each child was paired with a playmate the same age; then both children were placed in a well-equipped playroom to do whatever they wanted.

Many of these pairs, even some of the youngest, chose to engage in dramatic play. The 2- and 3-year-olds often played a simple mother-and-baby game; older children sometimes played a parent-child game or, if they were of the opposite sex, a husband-wife game (which tended to be a somewhat more complicated interaction, since it usually involved making some compromises about who does what).

Older children created many other roles, including Hansel and Gretel, Dr. Jeckel and Dr. Hines (sic), and St. George and the dragon. The children's creativity was shown not only in their choice of roles but also in their willingness to change their dramatic play to suit each other's whims.

Figure 11.4 *Bows and bracelets, hats and high heels, feathers and fancy baby carriages—all the trappings of future motherhood, or simply the stuff of fantasy? Dramatic play can be seen as preparation for adulthood, or as an expression of childish imagination, or both.*

Garvey found that most dramatic play employs certain standard plots, often centering around simple domestic scenes. Others involve such things as one player announcing that a child or pet is sick or dead and the other player automatically becoming the healer, administering food or medicine, or performing surgery, to restore life and health. In a third standard type of drama, one child announces a "sudden threat" (the appearance of a monster, for instance), then both children take the role of victim or defender, attacking or fleeing. The episode can end happily ("I got him!") or unhappily ("He ate me. I'm dead."), unfolding naturally yet without prearrangement.

Interesting age and sex differences appeared in Garvey's research on sudden-threat dramas. For instance, 2- and 3-year-olds were usually victims; 4- and 5-year-olds were usually defenders. When an older pair of children were of the opposite sex, the boy was more likely to be a defender, and the girl, an observer or victim.

One episode between two 5-year-olds illustrates this pattern. A boy and girl were playing that they were a husband and wife at home. Suddenly the girl announced a fire. The boy immediately quenched it with a toy snake (transformed to a fire hose), making water noises as he did so. The girl then declared that the fire had started up again, so the boy put it out once more. When fire appeared yet again, this time in heaven and threatening to burn God, the boy declared the snake-hose magical and destroyed the fire once and for all!

Dramatic play such as this is not only fun; it also helps children try out social roles, express their fears and fantasies, and learn to cooperate.

Sibling Interaction

Figure 11.5 *Older brothers and sisters are an important learning resource for younger siblings. At the same time, older siblings learn from the interaction, too—in this case, how to maintain a sense of humor in the face of a small catastrophe.*

One aspect of interaction among children that has been studied recently is how siblings get along with siblings. Much, of course, has already been said about sibling rivalry, and it is true that siblings are more likely to quarrel with each other than they are with nonrelated children. However, researchers have found that the flip side of sibling rivalry has been understressed: siblings are also more likely to have positive interactions with each other, showing more nurturance and cooperation than they would be likely to show with an unrelated child. This is true for siblings who are preschoolers or even younger, as well as for older siblings, and it is true for brother-sister pairs as well as for same-sex pairs (Dunn and Kendrick, 1982).

In most families, parents greatly influence the nature of sibling interactions, setting the stage in any number of ways for rivalry—by, say, comparing one sibling unfavorably with another—or for cooperation (Dunn and Kendrick, 1982). Indeed, the mere presence of the parents affects the sibling interaction. In general, siblings are less likely to fight, and more likely to play with each other, when their mother is absent than when she is present (Corter et al., 1983). When both parents are present, sibling interaction becomes even less frequent than it is when only the mother is present (Lamb, 1978). Apparently, parental attention is a powerful magnet, sufficient to pull a child away from a normal play pattern with a brother or sister.

It should be noted that, contrary to popular wisdom, having a sibling is not necessarily better for one's development than being an only child. In most ways, only children fare as well or better than children with siblings, partly because, today, most parents of only children provide social interaction by arranging for play dates, nursery-school classes, and so forth (Falbo, 1984).

The Importance of Social Play

That social play is enjoyable and interesting proves nothing about its importance. Would there, in fact, be any harm done if a preschool child never played with other children? Say, for instance, that an isolated farm family has only one child, or that a

---

RESEARCH REPORT   ## Self and the Social World of Primates

Extensive evidence about the relationship between development of the individual and development of social skills has come from experiments with thousands of rhesus monkeys at the Wisconsin Primate Laboratories. In early research, Harry and Margaret Harlow raised monkeys in social isolation, with no contact with their mothers or their peers (Harlow and Harlow, 1962). When these monkeys were put in with a normal monkey troop in adulthood, they were unable to adjust. Sometimes they hid in a corner, burying their head in their arms. If they tried to mate, they were unable to position themselves correctly. Sometimes they attacked older and larger monkeys, or mothers with infants, and were seriously injured. If the monkeys had been in isolation six months or more (the equivalent of 5 years in human terms), these maladaptive behaviors persisted throughout adulthood, no matter how much time the monkeys were given to adjust to the normal interaction of the troop. If they became mothers (through artificial insemination), these monkeys often attacked and killed their own babies.

The Harlows next set out to learn which aspect of social isolation was the crucial one, isolation from mother or isolation from peers. Some monkeys were raised with their mothers, but without peers; others were raised without their mothers, but were given daily play periods with normal age-mates. Both groups fared better in adulthood than did the monkeys who had been completely isolated, but monkeys who were raised by their mothers

The behavior of the monkey on the left in the first photo is typical of monkeys raised in isolation: they *initially cringe from the other monkeys but will attack if approached too closely. Monkeys raised*

but without any playmates usually seemed more disturbed, as adults, than monkeys who were raised without their mothers but with peers.

For instance, if rhesus monkeys did not have playmates when they were young, they became socially withdrawn and unusually aggressive during adolescence, sometimes picking a fight with a much larger male monkey or a female monkey with an infant (Harlow and Mears, 1979; Suomi and Harlow, 1976). Such aggression led to quick,

city mother wants to keep her child at home, away from the dangers of the street. Couldn't the child in either case learn social skills from adults, or from other children later on?

To some extent the answer is yes. Children are adaptable, and they can learn most essential skills in many ways and at many ages. But there is evidence suggesting that social play in early childhood provides crucial experiences that would be hard for adults to provide or for children to acquire at a later stage of life. For example, learning to play with friends teaches reciprocity, nurturance, and cooperation much more readily than interaction with adults does (Eisenberg et al., 1985; Youniss, 1980). It is also true that as preschool children become more experienced in social play, and more familiar with their playmates, their play becomes more complex and their friendships more selective (Howes, 1983; Hartup, 1983). Clinically, the importance of dramatic play is evidenced by the fact that when children have difficulty with social skills, educators and therapists typically use role-playing to help them learn what they apparently did not learn in normal dramatic play. Finally, suggestive evidence on the importance of preschool interaction comes from research on social deprivation in lower primates (see Research Report).

together without their mothers often cling to each other for security, as the monkeys on the right are doing. If placed with normal monkeys, they will gradually develop normal monkey behavior.

and sometimes fatal, counterattack. If these "unsocialized" monkeys survived adolescence, they sometimes became adults who seemed normal, although they remained overly aggressive and relatively unaffectionate. By contrast, orphaned monkeys who had played with peers were much closer to normal in their interactions with other monkeys.

Could socially isolated monkeys be rehabilitated? Harlow and Suomi (1971) tried reinforcing (with food, for example)

normal social contact and punishing (with painful shocks) inappropriate behavior, but without success. They then tried social play, putting monkeys raised in isolation for six months together with normal monkeys the same age, but the maladjusted newcomers were attacked and rejected. Finally, the psychologists tried putting an isolated monkey with a younger monkey. Success! The smaller monkey did not intimidate the maladjusted older monkey. The two learned to play together, and by age 1, the disturbed monkey had totally recovered from the early deprivation. Even monkeys who had been isolated for over a year have been rehabilitated by playing with younger "therapist" monkeys (Novak and Harlow, 1975).

Of course, conclusions from such primate research cannot be applied wholesale to people. For instance, humans have far greater intellectual skills, including a measure of self-analysis and direction, that help them adjust to other people if they do not learn social skills from direct early childhood experiences. However, studies of humans who have severe problems with social skills (such as being severely shy or uncontrollably aggressive) reveal that many such people grew up with hostile parents, no siblings, and little interaction with friends and relatives (Gilmartin, 1985). Thus, experimental research with nonhuman primates, as well as retrospective data from human adults, suggests that social play in childhood may teach the skills and concepts that help children become mature, fully functioning human beings.

Parenting

How does the parents' behavior affect the child? What kinds of parenting foster children who are pleased with themselves and friendly with others, and what kinds are associated with children who are unhappy, insecure, and hostile? The answers to these questions are elusive, because there is no simple relationship between child-rearing patterns and how a child turns out. As the systems approach makes clear, the outcome of any given child-rearing pattern on any given child depends on many factors that interact with each other, including the child's age, sex, and temperament; the parents' personality characteristics, personal history, economic circumstances, and the like; the needs of all the family members; and the values of the culture.

Hostility and Affection

However, while there is no single path that good parenting follows, researchers have pinpointed several pitfalls to avoid and goals to strive for (Martin, 1975; Maccoby and Martin, 1983). They have shown, for example, that parents who are hostile and rejecting toward their children are likely to have hostile and antisocial children. Thus, if parents are critical, derogatory, and dissatisfied with their children, their children are likely to become dissatisfied with themselves. If parents are insensitive to the child's point of view, the child will be less able to understand the viewpoints of others. The opposite is also true. Warm parents who are understanding and accepting of their children generally raise children who are happy and friendly.

Although parents' attitudes toward their children are important throughout childhood, they are especially so during the preschool years, partly because the child's self-concept is in the early stages of formation at this time, and partly because most preschool children think of their parents as all-powerful and all-knowing and take their judgments as definitive. Nevertheless, the generality that parents' hostility or warmth forms a child who is antisocial or loving should not blind us to the fact that, in some cases, the antisocial behavior in a child may be the cause of parental hostility rather than the result of it (Bell and Harper, 1977). (This is an important point that will come up again in the following section of patterns of parenting and in the discussion of severe disturbances in young children.)

Patterns of Parenting

That parents should be loving and understanding with their children is, of course, not news. The question is, What is the best way to communicate that love and understanding? What types of child-rearing might most contribute to happy and productive children? Seeking an answer to these questions, Diana Baumrind (1967) set out to determine general patterns of parenting style and the nature of their effects. She began by observing 110 children in their nursery-school activities, and on the basis of their actions, rated their self-control, independence, self-confidence, and the like. She then interviewed both parents of each child, and observed parent-child interaction in two settings, at home and in the laboratory, in order to see if there was any relationship between the parents' behavior with the child and the child's behavior at school.

On the basis of her research findings, Baumrind has delineated three basic patterns of parenting:

1. **Authoritarian** The parents' word is law, not to be questioned, and misconduct is punished. Authoritarian parents seem aloof from their children, afraid to show affection or give praise.

2. **Permissive** The parents make few demands on their children, hiding any impatience they feel. Discipline is lax, and anarchy, common.

3. **Authoritative** The parents in this category are similar in some ways to authoritarian parents, in that they set limits and enforce rules, but they are also willing to listen receptively to the child's requests and questions. Family rule is more democratic than dictatorial.

Figure 11.6 *The authoritarian parent gives the child almost no freedom, and the permissive parent allows too much leeway. The authoritative parent, on the other hand, finds a balance between these two extremes, providing firm guidelines as well as a sympathetic ear.*

An Example To see the differences among these three patterns more clearly, imagine that it is five minutes before bedtime for a 4-year-old girl. In the authoritarian family, the child would probably already be getting ready, brushing her teeth and putting on her pajamas. If she were to ask "Can I please stay up another half hour?" the parents would probably say, "You know the rule. Get to bed now, right this minute."

In the permissive family, the parents would probably say "Don't you think it's time for bed?" to which the child would likely respond "I want to watch one more TV program." The parents might then suggest that the show is not worth watching, but the girl would probably stay up anyway, finally falling asleep in front of the television.

In the authoritative family, the child might ask to stay up later, explaining that she wants to watch one more program. The parents would probably listen to the request, ask what the program is, and, if there is school the next day, refuse with an explanation. If the program is particularly worthwhile, they might let the child see it—after she has brushed her teeth, put on her pajamas, and promised to get up on time in the morning without complaint.

According to Baumrind (1967, 1971), the following generalizations tend to be true. The sons of authoritarian parents tend to be distrustful, unhappy, and hostile; and neither the sons nor daughters of such parents are high-achievers. The children of permissive parents are the least self-reliant, the least self-controlled, and the most unhappy. (The boys are low-achievers, although the girls do quite well in school.) The children of authoritative parents are the most self-reliant, self-controlled, and content and are friendly, cooperative, high-achievers.

The basic conclusions of this study have been confirmed by other research. Children who grow up in families that give them both love and limits are most likely to become successful, happy with themselves, and generous with others. Children whose parents are overly strict are likely to be obedient but unhappy; those whose parents are overly lenient are likely to be aggressive and lack self-control.

Generalizations such as these must be cautiously interpreted, however (Martin, 1975). Remember, children affect parents just as much as they are affected by them. Hostile, unfriendly children may produce authoritarian parents rather than the reverse being the case. Likewise, children who have some measure of self-reliance and self-control may produce relaxed, flexible parents (Bell and Harper, 1977). Further, the overall family situation affects the way parents deal with their children, for example, families with many children and little money tend to be more authoritarian, for obvious reasons (Belsky, 1984).

Be that as it may, parents are the adults, and presumably more capable of patience and understanding than children, so they have a greater responsibility for the nature of the family interaction. It is also true that parents, early in childhood, set the stage for later parent-child interactions. For example, mothers who are responsive to their children's demands at 10 months tend to have children who are compliant with their mother's wishes at 3 years (Martin, 1981); by contrast, parents who are relatively indifferent to their children at 3 years have children who have poor self-control and difficulty with normal social interaction in adolescence (Block, 1971).

Punishment

The task of setting and enforcing limits without resorting to the hostile tactics of the authoritarian parent is not easy. One problem is that, at first, physical punishment seems to be effective. It usually stops the child from misbehaving at that moment, and it provides an immediate outlet for parental anger. Unfortunately, parents who are quick to use physical force in punishing their children rarely realize the long-term effects that almost every research study of physical punishment has found.

Effects of Physical Punishment   When Barclay Martin (1975) reviewed the literature on punishment, he cited twenty-seven different studies on the effect of harsh punishment. The precise definition of "harsh" varied from study to study, but, generally, it referred to punishment that was more severe than that used by other parents in the same community.

As already suggested, because harshly punished children might be temporarily obedient, their parents sometimes conclude that harsh punishment is good. However, it seems that children store up frustration at this punishment, and when they finally vent it—at school, or against their parents in later years—they are likely to use the mode of expression they have become accustomed to: violence. In twenty-five of the studies reviewed by Martin, harsh punishment at home correlated with

A CLOSER LOOK   **It Sounds Easy But . . .**

When I teach my students about the three styles of parenting described by Baumrind, most of them readily agree with her conclusions. Some of them even see the authoritarian parents' methods as coming close to child abuse, or the permissive parents' as approaching child neglect. Most of them readily accept the authoritative style as the best, although a few students think the permissive approach is not as bad as the research suggests it is, and that the 4-year-old boy who isn't made to go to bed will soon learn for himself that late bedtimes make difficult mornings. Students who champion the permissive approach may have a point, for one longitudinal study found that although loving, permissive families tend to produce difficult children, most of these children eventually become cooperative, caring adults (McClelland et al., 1978).

However, the most vocal objections to Baumrind's findings come from students who are parents themselves. They say that Baumrind makes maintaining a consistently authoritative pattern sound much simpler than it actually is. Suppose you tell the 4-year-old that she should go to bed because the particular program she wants to stay up for is not worth watching, and suppose she insists that it is. As one student said, "You know you shouldn't hit her, and you know you shouldn't let her watch, but what else can you do?" "Simple. Pull the plug," a nonparent

answered. The parent replied: "I tried that. My children put the plug back in, and we almost played tug-of-war with the cord. I ended up yelling at them to get upstairs to bed before I counted to ten or else . . ." The problem is that without the child's cooperation, push often comes to shove, and the authoritative parent feels obliged to become authoritarian or permissive. Good parenting demands patience, creativity, and skill.

It also demands involvement. Indeed, a review of parent-child relationships suggests that the crucial element in good parenting is often not the type of punishment or the nature of the rules, but the involvement of the parents with the children (Maccoby and Martin, 1983). Even authoritarian and permissive parents can do a fairly good job if the children realize that the parents truly care and are concerned for the children's well-being. The problem is that many children interpret both authoritarian and permissive parenting as a sign that they are not really loved. Consequently, parents must not only care about their children; they must also show the children that they care. For instance, yelling at children to "go to bed or else" is not so bad if the parent also explains that children need their sleep and comes upstairs later to give a goodnight kiss. Much worse is making the children afraid to ever ask for exceptions to the rules, or letting children do whatever they want because it is easier that way.

---

aggression against other children, against teachers, and against society. Children who were harshly punished in childhood were more likely to become antisocial delinquents in adolescence. This relationship is especially clear for boys, who, significantly more often than girls, are harshly punished in childhood, are considered "problem children" in elementary school, and are arrested for violent crimes in adolescence. (Apparently the connection between harsh punishment and misbehavior is not immediately apparent during the preschool years, since the only two studies in Martin's review that did not show such a link were based on interviews with mothers of preschoolers.)

The Effects of Criticism   Parents who do not use physical punishment can be hostile in other ways, especially by being critical and derogatory. Such treatment is more likely to make children become withdrawn and anxious than violent—especially if the child is a boy and the hostile parent is the father (Martin, 1975). Since, again, these consequences are not clear until middle childhood, the man who, for instance, continually tells his shy 4-year-old son to stop acting like a sissy does not realize that he is likely to succeed only in making the boy more frightened and withdrawn.

Figure 11.7 *While physical punishment is temporarily more effective in calling a halt to unwanted behavior, in the long run, verbal remonstrances have a greater impact. The boy may remember the pain and be especially careful not to get caught again, but the girl is more likely to feel sorry for what she did and try not to do it again.*

In much the same way, parents trying to make preschool children less dependent sometimes merely worsen the problem. Many mothers report that after a scolding for being too dependent, their children are even more likely to whine, cling, and make demands (Yarrow et al., 1968). Punishing dependence probably leads to increased dependent behavior because the child, feeling rejected, tries to get reassurance, and one way young children get reassurance is by acting babyish. Usually the parent of a crying, clinging child gets tired of pushing the child away before the child gets tired of crying.

Children sometimes ask for more attention precisely when their parents are least able or willing to give it. This was briskly demonstrated in an experiment that compared the reactions of nursery-school children when their mothers were busy filling out a questionnaire and then when their mothers were ready to help them. As any experienced mother might have guessed, the children asked the most questions when the mothers were the most busy (Sears et al., 1965).

As with physical punishment, one of the problems with deciding how to control a child verbally (whether to command or cajole, criticize or praise) is that the effects are not immediately apparent. This was shown experimentally when mothers were asked to get their preschoolers to perform a task that would earn money for handicapped or poor children (Chapman, 1979). Some of the mothers chose to command their children to do it; others tried to persuade them to. The children worked under two conditions: with the mother present and with the mother absent. When the mother was present, the children who had been commanded to do the work worked harder than those who had been persuaded. But when the mother was absent, the children who had been persuaded to work worked harder. This experiment, and many other studies, suggest that immediate but transitory obedience from children occurs if the parents are strict and demanding, but that long-term and long-lasting good behavior results from a more authoritative approach.

Suggestions Obviously, how to reprimand a child effectively without doing physical or emotional harm is a complicated problem. Nevertheless, developmentalists, no matter what their theoretical orientation, almost all agree with the following suggestions (Parke, 1977):

1. Positive reinforcement for good behavior is more effective, in the long run, than punishment for bad behavior. Parents who want their children to be more independent, for instance, should encourage them to do things on their own rather than yelling at them when they cling.

2. Expected behavior should be within the child's physical, cognitive, and psychological capacities. Since preschool children have trouble understanding situations involving cause and effect or accident and intention, parents should carefully consider whether the child could foresee the consequences of a particular undesirable action before meting out a punishment. The preschooler who is punished for ripping his pants while playing may well be unfairly treated.

3. Rules and expectations should be explained in advance, including the reasons behind them and the consequences for violating them. While preschool children will not always understand the reasons, explaining them emphasizes the necessity of the rule or expectation and gives the child the sense that punishments are not arbitrary.

4. Punishment for breaking an understood rule should be consistent and immediate. Putting a little girl in her room for three minutes the moment she begins to bite her sister is more effective than yelling "Stop fighting—and just wait until your father hears how you've been acting!"

5. Children follow the example set by others. If parents find their children misbehaving, they should make sure they themselves are not providing the wrong behavior model.

6. If the child breaks rules frequently, parents should consider the possibility that the problem lies in some aspect of the home situation rather than in the child. For instance, the rules may be too vague or too difficult, or the child may not get enough attention for good behavior and therefore may misbehave to attract notice, or the child may be tired or hungry or sick.

A number of developmentalists call particular attention to the final item of this list, pointing out that parents should give more attention to the prevention of discipline problems through organization of the environment and through establishment of good parent-child relationships than to the specifics of what to do when the child-rearing system breaks down (Patterson, 1980; Holden, 1983). This is especially important during early childhood, when parents have a great deal of control over the child's environment and when the parent-child relationships are quite intense. A good relationship is like "money in the bank" (Maccoby and Martin, 1983), ready for use in later childhood. As one review explains, "If parents can do what is necessary early in the child's life to bring about a cooperative, trusting attitude in the child, that parent has earned the opportunity to become a nonauthoritarian parent" (Maccoby, 1984).

Of course, the temperament of the child as well as the impact of the larger systems of the society can make it easier or harder to raise a cooperative and competent child. This is readily apparent in the following Research Report on one of the most powerful cultural influences in our society, television.

RESEARCH REPORT   ## Television: A Dilemma for Parents

Virtually every child in the United States watches television (it is estimated that 99 percent of all households have one or more TV sets). According to the Nielsen survey of preschoolers' TV viewing, in 1984 children between the ages of 2 and 5 watched an average of 27 hours and 9 minutes of television each week (Re:act, 1984).

With so much of children's attention being focused on the TV screen, decisions about children's television viewing can be a frequent source of parent-child conflict. Compounding the difficulties parents may have making these decisions is the controversy over the potential effects of television viewing on the young. Many critics feel that the possible benefits of TV may be purchased at too high a price, and they cite three major problems: the effect of commercials; the content of programs; and the time that could be better spent.

Preschool children usually accept commercial messages uncritically, because, being preoperational and egocentric, they have great difficulty understanding when the truth is bent, or fantasy exploited, in order to sell a product. At times the gullibility of preschool children can be dangerous. One 4-year-old spent two days in intensive care in the hospital after swallowing forty children's vitamins: he had gotten the idea from TV commercials that the vitamins would make him "big and strong real fast" (Liebert et al., 1973). Because young children believe almost everything they see in commercials, they want almost everything they see in them. The parents are therefore placed in the position of resisting the constant demands of their children, or succumbing, buying everything from expensive toys that soon become boring or broken to sugared cereals and drinks that promote tooth decay.

An additional complaint about commercials is that they tend to reinforce certain social stereotypes. For one thing, a disproportionate number of children in commercials are blond males. When girls do appear, they are usually shown in passive roles (Feldstein and Feldstein, 1982). Similarly, minority children are typically among the cast of supporting characters—virtually never the leading characters.

The second major criticism of children's television has to do with the amount of violence it portrays. Many psychologists maintain that TV violence promotes violence in children, primarily through example. Albert Bandura has found that a child who sees an example of violence is not only likely to copy that example immediately but is also likely to refer to that example for future behavior

The one-eyed monster can be addictive, not only for children who never seem to get their fill of cartoons, but also for the parents who find they can spend Saturday morning in bed if the television is on.

(Bandura, 1977). The effect is interactive and cumulative: children who watch a lot of television are more likely to be aggressive than children who do not, and children who are aggressive are likely to watch a lot of TV violence.

Preschool children may be even more likely to be influenced by violence on television than older children are, because they have an especially hard time differentiating reality from fantasy. In television cartoons, which are beamed primarily at young children, physical violence occurs an average of seventeen times per hour. The good guys (Popeye, Underdog, Road Runner) do as much hitting, shooting, and kicking as the bad guys, yet the consequences of their violence are sanitized, never being portrayed as bloody or evil. In cartoon land, demolition, whether of people or things, is just plain fun.

Parents, of course, assume, or hope, that young children know that the cartoons are "just pretend." But after a careful review of the literature, Stein and Friedrich (1975) concluded that, if anything, the mayhem in cartoons has a stronger impact on preschoolers than similar violent drama with real people would have, perhaps because cartoons are, at one and the same time, gross simplifications and gross exaggerations of real life.

Even the unrealistic tempo of "action" television may have an effect. One study found that television shows with high action and rapid changes of scene (as in cartoons) increase children's aggression, no matter what the content of the program, presumably because the sensory excitement predisposed the children to act without reflection (Greer et al., 1982).

A related concern over the cumulative effects of watching repeated violence on television is that children will become inured to the fact and consequences of violence, a hypothesis that has experimental research to support it (Parke and Slaby, 1983). Children who see a lot of violence on television may thus become more passive when viewing actual violence in real life and may be more inclined to be passive victims themselves when they think they cannot respond in kind.

Many educators and parents have tried to reform children's television, their most successful efforts being through Action for Children's Television (ACT), begun in Boston in 1968. By 1972 they had helped to ban children's vitamin commercials and advertisements with a TV hero directly promoting a product. They have also helped reduce the total advertisement time on children's programs from a total of sixteen minutes per hour to about twelve minutes.

At the same time, public television has developed special educational programs such as "Sesame Street" and "Mister Rogers." Although these two programs differ in method and content, research has shown that both succeed in their teaching efforts, especially when parents watch with their children (Cook et al., 1975; Tower et al., 1979). In many other countries, notably Japan, Great Britain, and Sweden, the government requires that at least an eighth of the total viewing time be allotted to children's programs, whose content is intended to be educational (Lesser, 1984).

Nevertheless, a growing group of critics is concerned that even the best television does more harm than good because it robs children of play time, making them less creative, less verbal, less social, and less independent (Singer and Singer, 1977; Winn, 1977). Some support for this idea has come from experiments with certain families who voluntarily gave up television viewing. The parents of these families reported that their children played and read more, that siblings fought less, that family activities became more common, that mealtimes were longer, and that bedtimes were earlier (Winn, 1977; Chira, 1984). Unfortunately, these experiments lasted only a month, and the families were volunteers. Thus, these results, though provocative, were certainly not the outcome of a carefully controlled, scientific experiment. The families knew that the experimenters expected to see

improvements in family life and no doubt hoped that these expectations would be borne out.

A controlled scientific experiment on the effects of television is almost impossible, because families that do not have television are so rare. It is virtually impossible to find two groups of children who are similar in every way except that some watch television and some do not. However, studies have shown that children who watch a lot of television tend to be lower achievers than children who watch a little (Stein and Friedrich, 1975; Gadverry, 1980).

One reason for this correlation may be that language skills cannot be mastered in the early years without individualized communication between adult and child. Among the evidence for this hypothesis is the case of Jim, a normal child born to deaf parents. The parents hoped their son would learn to talk by watching television, which he was doing for hours each day. However, Jim did not begin to talk at all until age 2½; and by 3 years, 9 months, his language was immature and abnormal—in fact, his grammatical structures, such as "Be down go" and "Big two crayon," would have been unusual for a 2-year-old. At that point, with intensive, personal language therapy, Jim learned in five months what he hadn't learned in forty-five months of television viewing. At 4 years, 2 months, his language was normal for his age (Bard and Sachs, 1977).

Another reason is that television tends to cut off social communication, which, as we have seen, is essential for enhancing the social skills that children must develop. A child who enters first grade without the interactive abilities that come from playing with other children may not be able to learn as well from the teacher or from the other students.

What can a parent do? Some professionals recommend no television at all, especially for preschoolers. Others suggest that parents watch with their children, so that they can personalize the learning on educational programs and criticize or censor the content of noneducational television. Many parents have found it easier to impose a simple rule—only an hour a day, or only before dinner, or only on Saturday—than to try to prohibit television completely or censor each program. Although there is no clear consensus on how parents should control television viewing, one thing is certain: no psychologist who has studied the effects of children's television thinks parents should let their preschoolers watch whatever and whenever they want.

Possible Problems

No matter how careful and judicious parents are, preschool children sometimes do and say things that cause worry. They seem too ready to strike out at others, or they retreat into their own imaginary world, or they refuse to play. At what point does normal social immaturity become abnormal psychological development? Of course, there is no simple answer to such a question, because there is no one "point" or dividing line between normal and abnormal behavior. However, developmentalists have learned a great deal about usual and unusual behavior during early childhood, and about how to help those children who have special problems.

Aggression

When children first start playing with other children, in toddlerhood, they are rarely deliberately aggressive. They might pull a toy away from another child or even push someone over, but they do so to get an object, or remove an obstacle, rather than to hurt. As children grow older, the frequency of deliberate physical aggression increases, normally reaching a peak sometime during the preschool years, and then declining (Parke and Slaby, 1983).

Developmental Trends   For example, one researcher observed 102 children between the ages of 4 and 7 in six nursery-school classes (Hartup, 1974). Each time a child was physically or verbally abusive to another child, the observer recorded the activities that preceded and followed the incident, as well as the age and sex of the aggressor. As the children grew older, aggression decreased markedly. The decline was particularly apparent for **instrumental aggression,** which is aggression that involves quarreling over an object, territory, or privilege. That is to say, younger children were much more likely than older children to fight over who was to be at the front of the line, or who had a particular toy first. **Hostile aggression,** which is aggression that is an attack against someone rather than a fight about some thing, did not decline as rapidly, but it also gradually became less frequent as children grew older.

Figure 11.8 *Young preschoolers show instrumental aggression at its simplest. The goal in the first photo is possession of the toy, and any method of getting it is permissible. If the tears and tugging do not work, the next step is likely to be getting help from a grown-up or hitting or kicking the other child—an effective, but immature, way to win. Hostile aggression, as shown in the second photo, can involve both name-calling and physical force. The goal is not simply to gain an object, but to hurt someone.*

Another interesting age difference appeared. When they were the target of a derogatory comment from a peer ("dumb-dumb," "fatso," or the like), younger children were almost as likely to respond physically as verbally (48 percent to 52 percent, respectively). Older children were much more likely to react with a threat or another insult (78 percent) than with a push or punch (22 percent).

Similar results have been found in other research. Brothers and sisters typically engage in physical fights more during preschool years than later, and usually these quarrels involve toys that they don't want to share. As time goes on, fighting between siblings becomes less frequent, and when it does occur is more verbal than physical and is likely to involve such things as invasion of one another's privacy or the division of household duties and rights (Strauss et al., 1980; Steinmetz, 1977).

The developmental trend toward less aggression as children grow older is equally apparent in both sexes, although boys are involved in more aggressive instances than girls at every age. This boy-girl difference has been found in many cultures (Whiting and Whiting, 1975). It even occurs in nonhuman primates, including those in the Harlows' studies who had had no experience with older monkeys. This makes it seem that at least some of the sex differences in aggression are biologically based, though to what extent is still a matter of debate (Tieger, 1980; Maccoby and Jacklin, 1980). (Specific theories about male-female differences are discussed at the end of this chapter.)

It should be noted that a certain amount of aggression in preschoolers is normal. If a pair of 3-year-olds are playing with a toy and a sudden argument about whose toy it is results in a hit on the head or a slap on the face, that is not unusual. Indeed, a certain amount of aggression is not only normal, it is a healthy sign of self-assertion as well as an occasion for social learning, for the reaction of other children and adults may well help children learn about certain of the dynamics of social relations (Hay and Ross, 1982).

Adult Intervention   However, while a show of force is a normal response to provocation in a 3-year-old, this does not mean that adults should simply ignore preschool aggression entirely. During early childhood, children need to learn how and when to modify their aggressive impulses, partly because, by school age, aggressive children are decidedly unpopular with peers as well as with teachers (Patterson, 1982). In addition, if a pattern of aggression continues into the later years of school, it may be a precursor of delinquency and adult criminality (Rutter and Garmezy, 1983).

Furthermore, if a preschool child is unusually aggressive, this may well indicate that something is wrong in the child's life. We know that influences from the various ecosystems affect the incidence and the extent of a child's aggression. For example, children whose parents use physical punishment, who watch violent television, and who play with aggressive children are likely to be more aggressive than children without such examples (Berkowitz, 1973; Parke and Slaby, 1983). Patterson (1982) found that parents of very aggressive preschoolers either overuse physical aggression themselves or have given up trying to control the child's aggression. Both overcontrol and undercontrol are more likely to be a parental approach to sons than to daughters, which may be one of the reasons boys are more aggressive than girls.

The most frightening evidence that unusual aggression during early childhood may indicate problems at home comes from children known to be physically abused. Even at age 2, such children typically are not only more aggressive than other children, but they are also aggressive in contexts in which other children would not be. Simply hearing another child cry—a stimulus that normally makes other pre-schoolers nurturant—can make an abused child lash out (Main and George, 1985).

Two chilling examples come from a study in which observers in four preschools wrote down everything each child did for half an hour. Some of the children had been abused at home, but the observers were not specifically looking for signs of aggression in them. In one case, when a child started crying for no apparent reason

> Martin (an abused boy of 32 months) tried to take the hand of the crying other child, and, when she resisted, he slapped her on the arm with his open hand. He then turned away from her to look to the ground and began vocalizing very strongly, "Cut it out. CUT IT OUT!" each time saying it a little faster and louder. He patted her, but when she became disturbed by his patting, he retreated, hissing at her and bearing his teeth. He then began patting her on the back again, his patting became beating, and he continued beating her despite her screams.

> Another distress incident . . . began when Kate, 28 months, deliberately swung into the infant Joey, knocking him over with her feet. When Joey lay prone on the ground in front of her, she looked "tenderly down on him" and patted him "gently on the back" a few times. Her patting, however, became very rough and she began hitting very hard. After this, she returned to her swinging while the infant lay prone and still in front of her. Kate stopped swinging to lean forward and hit him hard six or seven times further until he finally crawled away. [Main and George, 1985]

Incidents such as these did not occur among other children who had not been abused themselves. It is obvious from these examples, then, that when a pre-schooler consistently acts with inappropriate and excessive violence, immediate intervention is needed to help the parents as well as the child.

Fantasy and Fear

Another characteristic of preschool children is that they sometimes have vivid nightmares, elaborate daydreams, and imaginary friends and enemies. These flights of fancy can worry their parents, but in fact this active fantasy life is normal and healthy. Children at the preoperational stage of thinking have difficulty distinguishing reality from fantasy; for them, dreams are believable. A child waking up from a nightmare might insist that there is a rhinoceros under the bed and refuse to be comforted by assurances that rhinoceroses are confined to zoos and, in any case, cannot fit under beds. Instead of trying logic, parents should use actions—perhaps turning on the light, looking under the bed, and announcing that there is nothing there except, of course, dirty socks, broken crayons, and cookie crumbs.

In addition, because young children center on physical appearance, many of them are genuinely frightened at the sight of a friend wearing a Halloween costume or of a parent pretending to be a lion. They worry about bodily wholeness and can be quite troubled when they see a person who has an obvious physical abnor-mality. In addition, everyday objects that make things disappear—the toilet bowl, vacuum cleaner, or bathtub drain—seem ominous to many small children, because they egocentrically wonder if these devices might make them disappear too.

Figure 11.9 *For many pre-school children, night-mares don't stop when they wake up. After all, when you have trouble distinguishing fantasy from reality, and cannot think logically about relative sizes, almost anything could be hiding under your bed.*

Because their thinking is so centered, young children can imagine something and then act as though what they have imagined is real. For instance, many children, especially those with few real playmates, create imaginary playmates, who serve as companions for games, reassurance in scary situations, and sometimes as scapegoats for mischief or accidents. Children usually take these imaginary playmates quite seriously, and anyone who denies their existence (say, by sitting down on a chair said to be occupied by one) is likely to be confronted by an angry child. Selma Fraiberg (1968) was well aware of this when she encountered her niece's imaginary playmate Laughing Tiger (so named because he always laughed and never bit):

> At dinner that evening my niece did not take notice of me until I was about to sit down. "Watch out," she cried. I rose quickly, suspecting a tack. "You were sitting on Laughing Tiger!" she said sternly. "I'm sorry. Now will you please ask him to get out of my chair." "You can go now, Laughing Tiger," said Jan. And this docile and obedient beast got up from the table and left the company without a murmur. [Fraiberg, 1968]

Preschool children with such creative imaginations are neither liars nor disturbed; they are simply showing a normal characteristic of preoperational thought. In fact, they may be smarter, more creative, and better adjusted than children who do not have such vivid fantasies (Pines, 1978).

Sometimes an irrational fear, or **phobia,** becomes so strong that it interferes with the child's normal functioning. In this case, psychologists recommend two techniques (Alexander and Malouf, 1983). The first is **modeling,** through which the phobic child observes another child happily experiencing the feared object (Kornhaber and Schroeder, 1975). For instance, a child who is afraid of the ocean may gain courage by seeing another child playing in the water. The second technique is **gradual desensitization,** in which the child slowly becomes accustomed to the feared object or experience (Wolpe, 1969). In this type of therapy, a child who is afraid of dogs might first be led to sit near a friendly small dog who is docile, quiet, and passive; then to pet the dog; then to become accustomed to larger and more active dogs. These two measures, used together, are much more effective than ridicule of the child or forced exposure to what is feared. A child who is terrified of dogs should never be told that only babies are afraid of dogs; nor should a child who is afraid of the water be thrown into it so that he or she will "get over" the fear.

Serious Psychological Disturbances

Although a measure of aggression and of withdrawal are usually nothing to be concerned about in early childhood, severe psychological problems can appear during these years. Generally they are signaled by abnormal interpersonal relationships (Rutter and Garmezy, 1983). Just as the infant who does not establish an attachment to his or her mother is a source of concern, so the preschool child who is unable or unwilling to play with other children may have a serious problem.

The most severe disturbance of early childhood is called **autism,** from the word element "auto-," meaning self. Autistic children are so self-involved that they hardly recognize that other people exist, and prefer self-stimulation to stimulation from others. They are given to performing the same behavior again and again, and can spend hours on end turning a toy around and around in their hands or even banging their heads against the wall. The least change in their world can produce pathological terror.

The first signs appear in infancy. Autistic babies do not cuddle when held but become rigid or limp, and they cry and avert their eyes, rather than smile, when familiar people greet them. The diagnosis is confirmed if at age 2 or 3 the child still does not play with others or try to converse (Ornitz and Ritvo, 1976).

Autistic children are usually mute, but sometimes they engage in a type of speech called **echolalia,** echoing, word for word, such things as singing advertisements or the questions put to them. If an autistic child is asked "Are you hungry?" the most usual response, if any, is "Are you hungry?"

Other children seem normal in infancy, but show evidence of withdrawal during childhood. Some children reportedly talk normally at home, but are mute when with other children or adults (Kratochwill, 1981). In most cases, this **elective mutism** gradually disappears as the child has experience in a good preschool or some other social setting that allows the child's fear of others to gradually subside (Brown and Lloyd, 1975). However, in some cases elective mutism is a precursor of serious problems with speech and behavior, as well as a sign of problems in the home.

Figure 11.10 *Autistic children are so involved in their own world that even getting them to make eye contact or smile requires intensive, one-to-one interaction with others. In some cases, physical restraints, such as the special chairs shown here, may be necessary to prevent them from retreating from a social situation.*

In other children, thought processes and social skills seem to deteriorate. Their speech becomes disorganized, their nightmares more terrifying, and their emotions less predictable. The usual diagnosis in these cases is **childhood schizophrenia,** a disorder which is symptomatically similar to schizophrenia in adults (Achenbach, 1982).

Causes At first, psychiatrists and psychologists were convinced that difficulties in the early parent-infant relationship were the probable cause of most of the emotional problems that children exhibit, so they blamed the parents in cases of autistic or schizophrenic children (Achenbach, 1982). Apparent confirmation for this view came from analysis of the typical personality structure of these parents: the parents of an autistic child often seemed cold, aloof, and unusually intellectual; the parents of schizophrenic children often seemed to have a love-hate relationship with their child, showering affection one moment and rejecting the child the next.

However, more recent evidence suggests that both autism and schizophrenia are strongly influenced by congenital factors. Autistic children often have a history of prenatal rubella, postnatal seizures, or other early signs of possible brain damage. Further, the first symptoms of autism itself appear so early that it is highly unlikely that the parents' behavior could be the cause of the condition. A 4-week-old baby with seemingly normal parents who prefers to look away from faces, for instance, is so abnormal at such a tender age that the cause must be inborn. In addition, it is exceedingly rare for parents to have more than one autistic child, which suggests that something in the child, rather than the nature of the parents' behavior, causes the disorder. It is probably safe to conclude that if parents of autistic children seem aloof and cold, this parental response is more likely a reaction to, rather than the cause of, the children's condition (Bender, 1973).

The evidence that parent-child relationships do not contribute to elective mutism or childhood schizophrenia is less clear. We know that shyness and schizophrenia in children and in adults are partly genetic, but we also know that identical twins do not always have the same patterns of emotional disturbance or health, so genes are not the sole cause of either of these disorders. However, as with other types of severe disturbance in childhood, it is generally agreed that abnormal parenting is not usually the sole cause (Achenbach, 1982; Rutter and Garmezy, 1983).

Cures Fortunately, severe psychological problems in childhood are rare: only 6 children in 10,000 are diagnosed as autistic or schizophrenic (Werry, 1972). Unfortunately, most children with either problem never recover completely. For autistic children, the chances of recovery improve if the child develops useful speech before age 5; for schizophrenic children, the chances of recovery improve if the first symptoms appear relatively late in childhood.

For both disorders, the most successful treatment methods usually combine behavior therapy with individual attention: autistic children can sometimes learn to talk, and schizophrenic children, to control their anxiety, if a step-by-step conditioning process is set up and reinforcement is carefully delivered.

Furthermore, while parental behavior is probably not the sole cause of severe psychological problems, it can be an influential factor, part of the problem or part of the cure. Parental participation in the child's treatment is often the most important factor affecting the future of the child. Ideally, parents should provide the stability, reassurance, and learning environment that disturbed children need.

But it is much easier to state that parents of disturbed children need to provide stable and consistent support than it is to suggest just how they might do so, given the stresses of their situation, and the fact that since psychologists and psychiatrists themselves do not always agree on what factors make a particular child emotionally disturbed or what measures will foster long-term improvement (Alexander and Malouf, 1983). Consider Noah, the son of Josh and Fuomi Greenfeld, who was diagnosed as autistic. His parents spent years finding special therapy and providing patient education for him, but by the time Noah was 10, they became depressed and discouraged. Noah's father says he feels guilty

for all the things I no longer do for Noah. Such as run after doctors or seek out miracle cures. I just try to take him for granted . . . I take for granted that I have to live in a house with blankets chewed, pillows strewn about, chairs upturned. I take for granted that I have to be constantly wary of his bowel movements . . . I take for granted that I have to sit with him as he eats and that I have to brush his teeth twice a day and that he has to be coached in the acts of dressing and undressing . . . I take for granted that I must walk with him in the evenings, that I must drive him to school each day, that I must pick him up in the late afternoons. I take for granted that I constantly have a baby to care for.

I also take for granted that what I do is so little, that what Fuomi does is so much more. [Greenfeld, 1978]

Sex Roles and Stereotypes

One final, and very important, topic has occupied the attention of many developmental theorists and researchers. This topic is gender identification and sex-role development.

Children learn about gender very early. Most 2-year-olds know whether they are boys or girls, identify strangers as mommies or daddies, and know that Daddy has a penis and that Mommy has breasts. By age 3, children can consistently apply gender labels (Thompson, 1975). They refer to boys, brothers, and policemen as "he" and to girls, sisters, and policewomen as "she." Further, children's behavior acknowledges traditional distinctions between boys and girls at a very early age. By age 3, if not before, children prefer to play with sex-typed toys (dolls versus trucks) and enact sex-typed roles (nurses versus soldiers) (Eisenberg-Berg et al., 1979; O'Brien et al., 1983; Huston, 1983, 1985). As the following Research Report shows, children also have definite ideas of typical male and female behavior and misbehavior.

This does not mean that children understand that gender is biological. Until age 4 or 5, they are likely to think sexual differences depend on clothes, hair, or maturation, rather than on biology, believing that a girl would be a boy if she cut her hair short or that a boy might become a girl if he wore a dress. One preschool girl visited the neighbor's new baby, who was having a bath. Later, her parents asked if the baby was a boy or a girl. "I don't know," she replied, "it's so hard to tell at that age, especially when it's not wearing clothes" (Stone and Church, 1973).

RESEARCH REPORT   **Sexual Stereotypes in 3-Year-Olds**

We all are aware of the changes in traditional sex roles over the past decade or so. More women are serving in public office, or working as lawyers, or training as engineers than ever before; and more men are sharing in the care of their children and in the housework. These trends are particularly apparent among younger, better-educated people, although changes in sex roles have occurred in every community.

We would expect these changes to reach little children, especially children of college students and faculty. However, this turns out to be only partially the case, according to Deanna Kuhn and her colleagues (1978), who found that 2- and 3-year-olds at the Stanford University nursery school already believed many traditional sex-role concepts.

The research design of this study was simple. Each child was shown two paper dolls, one named Lisa and one named Michael, and then was asked which doll would do or say certain things. For some of the actions and statements, the children were equally likely to pick Lisa or Michael. But on the whole, Lisa was more likely to be picked for traditional female behaviors, and Michael, for traditional male behaviors.

Both boys and girls held the following stereotypes:

Girls are more likely to

play with dolls	clean the house
help mother	become a nurse
talk a lot	
never hit	
say "I need some help"	

Boys are more likely to

help father	become a boss
say "I can hit you"	mow the grass

The following stereotypes were held by boys but not girls:

Girls are more likely to

cry

be slow

cook the dinner

Boys are more likely to

be loud

be naughty

grow up to be a doctor or a governor

These stereotypes were held by girls but not boys:

Girls are more likely to

look nice	say "I can do it best"
give kisses	take care of babies

Boys like to

fight

be mean

This study found evidence that some sexual stereotypes are declining. The children held no sexual stereotypes for

playing ball	being the leader
playing house	being kind
running fast	being neat
being smart	saying "I can do it"
being messy	washing the car
being dirty	washing the dishes

Best of all, no sexual stereotype was shown when the children had to choose whether Lisa or Michael was more likely to say "I love you."

Children at 4 and 5 often exaggerate sexual stereotypes of behavior, as is apparent in their play. Garvey (1977) found that preschoolers are usually quite willing to let a play partner change the plot in dramatic play but they are not willing to let the daddy cook while the mother goes off to work. Many children even adopt the role of Super Mommy or Super Daddy. One little girl busily cared for all of her twenty-six children, one for each letter of the alphabet. One boy, playing a husband-wife game with a girl, walked through the door and announced, "Okay, I'm all through with work, honey. I brought home a thousand dollars."

In this day of greater equality for women, many parents are astonished to hear their 5-year-old daughters ask for hair ribbons and organdy dresses or express hopes of becoming stewardesses and nurses, despite the parents' suggestions that they become pilots or doctors. Five-year-old boys have stereotyped ideas of the male role as well. One told his father, a professor who lived a sedentary academic life, "Oh, Daddy, how old will I be when I can go hunting with you? We'll go in the

Figure 11.11 *This girl's pleasure at her newly acquired figure is typical of children aged 4 to 6, who usually believe the appearance of femininity or masculinity equals the fact, and that more is better. At this age, boys are given to sticking objects in their pants to exaggerate the size of their penis, and children of both sexes (not yet sure of the internal anatomical differences between male and female) like to stuff the front of their shirts with a pillow "baby."*

woods, you with your gun, me with my bow and arrow. Daddy, wouldn't it be neat if we could lasso a wild horse? Do you think I could ride a horse backward if someone's leading me like you?" (Kohlberg, 1966).

By age 6, these preferences become full-blown prejudices, when most children (even those from liberated homes) express stereotypic ideas of what each sex should do, wear, or feel (Huston, 1983). Indeed, by age 4, preschool girls and boys react approvingly or disapprovingly toward each other, according to their choice of sex-appropriate toys and play patterns (Roopnarine, 1984). The boy who wants to help the girls dress the dolls or the girl who wants to be one of the space warriors is likely to be soundly criticized by his or her friends.

Three Theories of Sex-Role Development

We have already discussed the nature-nurture issue several times, and you are well aware that developmentalists disagree about what proportion of observed sex differences is biological—perhaps a matter of hormones, of brain structures, or of genes carried by the sex chromosomes—and what proportion is environmental. However, even for differences that seem most closely related to nurture, theorists hypothesize various reasons for their existence; specifically, they ask, What is the origin of sex-role preferences and stereotypes that children develop during the preschool years? Each of the three major psychological theories has a somewhat different answer.

Psychoanalytic Theory   Freud (1938) called the period from about age 3 to 7 the **phallic stage,** because he believed its center of focus is the penis. At about age 3 or 4, said Freud, a boy becomes aware of his penis, begins to masturbate, and develops sexual feelings about his mother who has always been an important love object for him. These feelings make him jealous of his father—so jealous, in fact, that, according to Freud, every son secretly wants to kill his father. Freud called this phenomenon the **Oedipus complex,** after Oedipus, son of a king in ancient Greek mythology. Abandoned as an infant and raised in a distant kingdom, Oedipus later returned to his birthplace, and, not realizing his relationship to them, killed his father and married his mother. When he discovered what he had done, he blinded himself in a spasm of guilt.

According to Freud, little boys feel horribly guilty for having the lustful and murderous thoughts that characterize the Oedipus complex and imagine that their fathers will inflict terrible punishments on them, among them blindness and castration, if they ever find out about these thoughts. They cope with this guilt by means of **identification,** a defense mechanism through which people imagine themselves to be like a person more powerful than themselves.

As part of their identification with their fathers, boys copy their fathers' masculine behavior and adopt their moral standards. Through this process, they develop their superegos, or conscience, to control the forbidden impulses of the id (see page 40). Freud believed that if a boy does not experience the Oedipus complex—because, say, there is no father in the household—he is likely to identify with his mother too much, thereby increasing his chances of eventually becoming homosexual. (Although there is some evidence that a son raised without a father will have some difficulty with sex-role development, there is no hard evidence for the link between the absence of the father and homosexuality, and few psychologists support this aspect of Freud's theory.)

Freud offered two overlapping descriptions of the phallic stage as it occurs in little girls. One form, the **Electra complex,** follows the same pattern as the Oedipus complex: the little girl wants to get rid of her mother and become intimate with her father. In the other version, the little girl becomes jealous of boys because they have a penis, an emotion called **penis envy.** Somehow the girl decides that her mother is to blame for this state of affairs, so she becomes angry at her and decides the next best thing to having a penis of her own is to become sexually attractive so that someone with a penis, preferably her father, will love her (Freud, 1965; originally published in 1933).

In both versions, the consequences of this stage are the same for girls as for boys: guilt and fear, and then adoption of sex-appropriate behavior and the father's moral code. By the time this stage is over, children of both sexes have acquired their superego (although, according to Freud, a girl's is not as well developed as a boy's). This strict conscience makes it difficult for people of any age to break the moral codes or transcend the sex roles they learned in childhood.

Learning Theory Learning theorists take another view about sexual attitudes during early childhood. They believe that virtually all sexual patterns are learned, rather than inborn, and that parents, teachers, and society are responsible for whatever sex-role ideas and behaviors the child demonstrates.

Preschool children, according to learning theory, are reinforced for behaving in the ways deemed appropriate for their sex and punished for behaving inappropriately. In some ways, research bears this out. Parents, peers, and teachers are all more likely to reward sex-appropriate behavior than inappropriate behavior (Langlois and Downs, 1980; Harter, 1983).

Interestingly, boys are criticized more often for wanting to play with traditional girls' toys than girls are for wanting to play with boys' toys. Even in toddlerhood, boys are criticized for wanting to play with dolls (Fagot, 1978). Furthermore, fathers

A CLOSER LOOK   **Berger and Freud**

As a woman, and as a mother of four daughters, I have always regarded Freud's theory of female sexual development as ridiculous, not to mention antifemale. I am not alone in this opinion. Psychologists generally agree that Freud's explanation of female sexual and moral development is one of the weaker parts of his theory, reflecting the values of middle-class Viennese society at the turn of the century more than any universal pattern. Many female psychoanalysts (e.g., Horney, 1967; Klein, 1957; Lerner, 1978) are particularly critical of Freud's idea of penis envy. They believe that girls envy, not the male's sexual organs, but the higher status the male is generally accorded. They also suggest that boys may experience a corresponding emotion in the form of womb and breast envy, wishing that they could have babies and suckle them.

However, my own view of Freud's theory as complete nonsense has been modified somewhat by the following experiences with my three oldest daughters when each was in the age range of Freud's phallic stage. The first "Electra episode" occurred in a conversation with my oldest daughter, Bethany, when she was 4 or so.

Bethany: When I grow up, I'm going to marry Daddy.

Me: But Daddy's married to me.

Bethany: That's all right. When I grow up you'll probably be dead.

Me: (Determined to stick up for myself) Daddy's older than me, so when I'm dead, he'll probably be dead too.

Bethany: That's O.K. I'll marry him when he gets born again. (Our family's religious beliefs, incidentally, do not include reincarnation.)

At this point, I couldn't think of a good reply. Bethany must have seen my face fall and taken pity on me.

Bethany: Don't worry Mommy. After you get born again, you can be our baby.

The second episode was also in a conversation, this time with my daughter Rachel.

Rachel: When I get married, I'm going to marry Daddy.

Me: Daddy's already married to me.

Rachel: (With the joy of having discovered a wonderful solution) Then we can have a double wedding!

The third episode was considerably more graphic. It took the form of a "valentine" left on my husband's pillow by my daughter Elissa, who was about 8 at the time. It is reproduced below.

Obviously, these bits of "evidence" do not prove that Freud was correct. But Freud's description of the phallic stage seems not to be as bizarre as it first appears to be.

Theodore Lidz (1976), a respected developmental psychiatrist, offers a plausible explanation of the process evident in my daughters and in many other children. Lidz believes that all children must go through an Oedipal "transition," overcoming "the intense bonds to their mothers that were essential to their satisfactory pre-Oedipal development." As part of this process, children imagine becoming an adult and, quite logically, taking the place of the adult of their own sex whom they know best, their father or mother. This idea must be dispelled before the sexual awakening of early adolescence, otherwise an "incestuous bond" will threaten the nuclear family, prevent the child's extrafamilial socialization, and block his or her emergence as an adult. According to Lidz, the details of the Oedipal transition vary from family to family, but successful desexualization of parent-child love is essential for healthy maturity.

Figure 11.12 *This father is gratified, as most fathers would be, to find that his son wants to be "just like Dad," and has rewarded the youngster with a toy motorcycle, a positive reinforcement for a particular type of masculine sex role. The girls on the right, in the swimsuit phase of a beauty contest, are being initiated into the kinds of "female" behavior and appearance that society rewards with trophies and applause.*

are more likely to expect their girls to be "feminine" and their boys to be "masculine" than mothers are. Fathers are more gentle with their daughters and are more likely to engage in rough-and-tumble play with their sons (Maccoby and Jacklin, 1974). Thus, in our society at least, sex-role conformity seems to be especially important for males.

Influences from the macrosystems, including everything from who runs for president to who does what in television commercials, also teach children sex-appropriate behavior (Huston, 1983). Indeed, children expect to be punished by the adult community in general if they stray too far from traditional sex roles. In one study, a 5-year-old girl decided to be the father and told a 5-year-old boy to be the mother (Greif, 1976). The boy was clearly upset, saying he *had* to be the father. The girl ignored his complaints until he appealed to authority, threatening to "tell" on her if she didn't let him be the father. At this threat, she gave in, apparently believing that adults would not have let her get away with her game of role reversal.

Modeling. Social-learning theorists (Sears et al., 1965; Mischel, 1970, 1979; Bandura, 1977) combine the psychoanalytic emphasis on parents and the behavioristic emphasis on learning. They say that children learn much of their sexual and moral behavior by observing other people, especially people whom they perceive as nurturing, powerful, or similar to themselves. For all these reasons, parents are important models during childhood.

Whether children see their parents acting with compassion or indifference, with honesty or deception, in typically feminine or masculine ways, they try to follow their example. Children also imitate attractive or powerful people they see in the neighborhood, or on television, especially if they see them reinforced for what they do.

Social-learning theorists are not surprised when preschool children seem precociously and dogmatically conscious of sex roles, even when the parents espouse less traditional views. In this case, actions speak louder than words, and most adults are more sex-stereotyped, in their behaviors as well as self-concept, during the years when their children are young than at any other time in the life span (Gutmann, 1975; Feldman et al., 1981). Imagine a typical modern child-free couple who try to avoid traditional sex roles, both of them being employed and both sharing the housework. Then the wife becomes pregnant. The most likely sequel is that she will take a maternity leave, quit her job, or work part-time. This traditional pattern is reinforced by the biological fact that only the woman can breast-feed, the sociological fact that relatives and friends generally expect the woman to provide most infant care, and the economic fact that the husband's salary is usually higher than the woman's. If the wife stays home, it is likely that she will do more than half the housework. If she does go back to work full-time, typically she will find another woman to care for her child, either at home or in a day-care center. Further, while most two-career families without children share the housework, once the employed wife becomes an employed mother, and the quantity of housework mounts, she typically does the major portion (Haas, 1981; Condron and Bode, 1982). Thus, at home as well as in the larger society, most preschoolers have many models for sex-stereotyped behavior.

Cognitive Theory In explaining gender identification and sex-role development, cognitive theorists (Kohlberg, 1966, 1969; Cowan, 1978) focus on the effects of the child's cognitive limitations and misperceptions which make it difficult for them to understand and apply male-female distinctions. A child may decide one day that all girls have long hair and cannot become firefighters, and the next that girls can be short-haired firefighters but cannot wear cowboy boots. Because of their cognitive immaturity, until they are at least 4 or 5, children do not realize that they are permanently male or female. Once they understand this, they try to adopt appropriate sex-role behavior, at first with the rigidity typical of the initial stages of comprehension of an idea, and then with more flexibility.

That an orderly progression of attitudes toward sex roles parallels the child's passages through the stages of cognitive development was demonstrated in a study by Lawrence Kohlberg and Dorothy Ullian (1974), who interviewed boys and girls between the ages of 3 and 18. They found that, at age 3, children know what sex they are, but do not realize that maleness and femaleness are permanent characteristics based on genital differences. Boys think they could become mommies; girls think they could become daddies; and both sexes think boys would be girls if they wore dresses and girls would be boys if they had their hair cut very short. In other words, 3-year-olds tend to be confused about the relationship between appearances and reality in connection with sex roles, the same confusion they experience in connection with conservation experiments.

By contrast, most 6-year-olds realize that sex is a permanent characteristic. Usually they are pleased to be whatever sex they are, for they believe that their own sex is the "better" one. For example, 6-year-old boys think males are stronger, smarter, and more powerful than females. In addition, children of both sexes believe sex identity is defined by observable physical signs, such as strength, depth of voice, clothes. One boy, asked why he thought men were smarter than women, said they had bigger brains. This emphasis on physical differences is true for 6-year-olds in many cultures and in many types of families, including fatherless ones.

Similar results were found in the Goldmans' study of children's comprehension of sex information mentioned in Chapter 2 (page 58) (Goldman and Goldman, 1982). The children's cognitive stage was related to their understanding of sex differences and sex roles, with younger children being quite stereotyped and inflexible. In both studies, older children had a broader, more balanced understanding of masculinity and femininity.

A New Theory: Androgyny

Each theoretical position on gender identification and sex-role development has merit. Obviously, sex differences are both inborn and learned, and cognitive maturity as well as considerable observation of others is needed before one can grasp the complexity of modern sex differences and similarities. Current evidence suggests that the first signs of sex differences in behavior and sex preferences in toys occur at age 1 or 2, before the child has a cognitive grasp of male-female distinctions, and before much social learning can occur (O'Brien and Huston, 1985). However, once children have a more intellectual understanding and more exposure to peers and the larger society, by about ages 4 and 5, their grasp of sex differences becomes much firmer, and, consequently, their own behavior becomes more stereotyped (Ruble et al., 1981; Huston, 1983).

But the existence of these developmental patterns is of little help to a parent or teacher trying to decide which qualities to encourage or discourage in a child. Although almost everyone recognizes that traditional sex roles are too restrictive, many parents hesitate to treat their daughters and sons in the same way, because they worry that their girls might become too "masculine" or their boys too "feminine."

Parents, as well as developmentalists, might be helped by a new concept, androgyny. This concept has been developed to counter the misconception that masculinity and femininity are exact opposites—an assumption that leads a great many people to believe that the more one follows the masculine role, the less feminine one becomes, and vice versa. **Androgyny**—strictly speaking, the state of having both male and female sexual characteristics—has come to be used in connection with a person's defining himself or herself primarily as a human being rather than as a male or female.

Several measures of androgyny have been developed in which a person chooses which adjectives are closest to describing one's own personality (Bem, 1974; Spence and Helmreich, 1978). For instance, someone who is rated as high in aggression, dominance, competitiveness, and activity, and low in gentleness, kindness, emotionality, and warmth, would be typically masculine; someone who was the opposite would be typically feminine. A person who was high in both sets of characteristics would be androgynous.

Thus androgynous men and women share many of the same personality characteristics, instead of following the traditional sex-role patterns. For instance, traditional males rate significantly higher than traditional females on a personality trait labeled "dominant-ambitious," but androgynous males and females score about the same, because the men see themselves as less dominant than the traditional male does while the females see themselves as more dominant than the traditional female does (Wiggins and Holzmuller, 1978). Androgynous people are nurturing as well as independent and try to be neither unemotional nor passive.

Because they are flexible in their sex roles, and able to display the best qualities of both traditional stereotypes, androgynous people are generally more competent

Figure 11.13 *During childhood, at least, our culture allows greater sex-role latitude to girls than to boys. For example, while most parents would encourage their daughter's budding interest in woodworking, not all parents would be so pleased to find that their son is tenderly caring for a doll.*

and have a higher sense of self-esteem than people who follow traditional sex-role behavior (Spence and Helmreich, 1978).

This suggests that it is good to encourage children to develop all their potential characteristics, encouraging them to engage in rough-and-tumble play outside as well as quiet play in the doll corner. Instead of saying such things as "Boys don't cry" and "Girls don't fight," we should apply the same standards to both sexes, teaching children that both crying and fighting are sometimes appropriate behaviors. In fact, it may be particularly important to encourage girls to assert themselves and boys to be nurturant, thus counteracting the pull of nature and nurture.

The concept of androgyny is not without its critics, however (Locksley and Colten, 1979). For example, parents who follow relatively traditional male and female roles may do a better job of child-rearing than androgynous parents, according to Diana Baumrind (1982), because they tend to be more child-centered. Certainly in the "chronic state of emergency" that the myriad and never-ending tasks of parenting entail, it may well be more efficient for fathers and mothers to play the traditional complementary parental roles (Gutmann, 1975). Further, the fact that the concept of gender differences comes naturally to children suggests that parents should not be too stringent in trying to deny it.

In fact, Sandra Bem (1981), one of the designers of the androgyny scale, recognizes that the idea of gender differences is useful to help young children organize their perceptions of the adult world. The problem comes, if at all, when children and their parents remain rigid in applying this schema, causing the rigid stereotyping to stifle the full development of the child or the adult. Thus the child's sex-role concepts, like the child's definition of selfhood, mode of play, use of aggression, and all the other themes of this chapter, should change with exposure and maturity. This development, rather than any one "correct" view of behavior, is what makes the preschool child gradually become ready for the next stage of life, the school years, which are presented in the next trio of chapters.

SUMMARY

The Self and the Social World

1. As children develop a more clearly defined idea of self, they become more confident and eager to take on new activities and to try new ones. According to Erikson, the accomplishments of this age help to resolve the crisis of initiative versus guilt.

2. An increasing sense of self-recognition helps children to increase their social understanding and to become more skilled in their relationships with others.

Play

3. Playing with other children prepares preschoolers for the demands of school and the social relationships they will later develop. As children grow older, they spend more time in associative and cooperative play than in the more simple onlooker or parallel play that is characteristic of the younger child.

Parenting

4. Parent-child interaction is complex, with no simple answers about the best way to raise a child. However, in general, authoritative parents, who are warm and loving but willing to set and enforce reasonable limits, have children who are happy, self-confident, and successful. Authoritarian families, in which punishment is strict, tend to produce aggressive children. Children from permissive families often lack self-control.

5. Preschool children need to know clear and consistent rules, and what the consequences are for breaking them. The most effective punishments are consistent and immediate.

Possible Problems

6. Normal preschool children sometimes use physical force to get what they want and sometimes have vivid fantasies that they think are real. These behaviors are to be expected in a child who is trying to cope with the many ideas and problems of social interaction but is without the thought processes available to older children and adults.

7. Some children show signs of serious psychological problems, such as autism or schizophrenia. The causes of these disturbances are multifactorial. The best chances for improvement lie in a structural treatment program in which parents participate.

Sex Roles and Stereotypes

8. While all psychologists agree that children begin to learn sex roles and moral values during early childhood, they disagree about how this occurs.

9. Freud believed that the guilt and fear that children feel because of the fantasies of the Oedipal complex result in the development of their superegos. Erikson stresses the child's initiative and exuberance, noting that the child sometimes feels guilty when this energy gets out of bounds.

10. Learning theorists think children learn their values from the reinforcement they receive for acting appropriately, and from the punishment they get for behaving inappropriately. The example set by their parents, as well as the role models they see in their community or on television, is also important.

11. Cognitive theorists remind us that young children are illogical and egocentric. We should not expect them to understand moral values, or the nature of sex roles. For example, the typical preschool child thinks maleness and femaleness are the result of clothes and hair style rather than biology.

KEY TERMS

initiative versus guilt *(319)*	phobia *(339)*
solitary play *(322)*	modeling *(339)*
onlooker play *(322)*	gradual desensitization *(339)*
parallel play *(322)*	autism *(340)*
associative play *(322)*	echolalia *(340)*
cooperative play *(322)*	elective mutism *(340)*
dramatic play *(324)*	childhood schizophrenia *(341)*
authoritarian parenting *(329)*	phallic stage *(344)*
permissive parenting *(329)*	Oedipus complex *(345)*
authoritative parenting *(329)*	identification *(345)*
instrumental aggression *(336)*	Electra complex *(345)*
hostile aggression *(336)*	penis envy *(345)*
	androgyny *(349)*

KEY QUESTIONS

1. How does children's increasing self-knowledge affect their relationship with others?

2. Why is social play important?

3. As children grow older, how does their dramatic play change?

4. What are the three basic patterns of parenting?

5. What kinds of punishment are worst for young children and why?

6. What are some ways of preventing or correcting discipline problems?

7. How does the preschooler's stage of cognitive development affect the fantasies and fears that may occur at this stage of development?

8. What are the essential disagreements between Freud and learning theorists about the origin of sex roles during early childhood?

9. According to cognitive theorists, why do 5-year-olds have particularly stereotyped ideas of sex roles?

RECOMMENDED READINGS

Garvey, Catherine. *Play*. Cambridge, Mass.: Harvard University Press, 1977.

This is a scholarly and lively presentation of the many forms of play and the many things children learn while playing. Garvey includes many quotations from children engaged in dramatic play, showing how children develop their social ideas and skills.

Greenfeld, Josh. *A place for Noah*. New York: Washington Square Press, 1980.

This book tells about Noah Greenfeld, a child diagnosed as autistic and later considered brain-damaged, and about his parents and older brother as they try to live with him. This book helps to create an understanding of some of the hope, despair, and anger of the parents of severely disturbed chil-dren. You will also get an idea of the kinds of help psycholo-gists and educators can provide, and of the many ways the entire community—professionals and lay people alike—fail to offer the support that the Greenfelds, and thousands of other families like them, need.

Bettelheim, Bruno. *The uses of enchantment: The meaning and importance of fairy tales*. New York: Vintage Books, 1977.

Bruno Bettelheim, a famous child psychologist from the Freudian tradition, has worked with emotionally disturbed children. In this book he analyzes children's fairy tales and shows how they express and explain the child's fantasies, especially those of the phallic stage.

Reit, Seymour. *Sibling rivalry*. New York: Ballantine Books, 1985.

This reassuring book emphasizes not only that sibling rivalry is normal but also that it can help to foster social skills and close relationships. The authors subscribe to the popular wisdom that birth order influences children in specific ways (middle children are manipulative, last-borns are babyish) and discusses ways to cope with these tendencies. (As you read this book, keep in mind that recent research does not necessarily corroborate these birth-order effects.)

Part III

The Developing Person So Far: Ages 2 Through 6

Physical Development

Brain and Nervous System

The brain continues to develop faster than any other part of the body, attaining 90 percent of its adult weight by the time the child is 5 years old. Myelination proceeds at different rates in various areas of the brain. This differential neurological development has some bearing on the child's readiness for certain types of activity.

Motor Abilities and Perception

The child becomes stronger, and body proportions become more adultlike. Large body movements, such as running and jumping, improve dramatically. Fine motor skills, such as writing and drawing, develop more slowly.

Between the ages of 2 and 3, the activity level is higher than at any point in the life span.

Cognitive Development

Cognitive Skills

The child becomes increasingly able to use mental representation and symbols, such as words, to "figure things out." However, the child's ideas about the world are often illogical and much limited by the inability to understand other points of view.

Language

Language abilities develop rapidly; by the age of 6, the average child knows 14,000 words and demonstrates extensive grammatical knowledge. Children also learn to adjust their communication to their audience.

Psychosocial Development

Personality Development

According to Erikson, increased levels of energy at this stage enable the child to boldly and exuberantly initiate new activities. The outcome of the crisis of this stage of life—initiative versus guilt—will depend on whether the child often succeeds and is praised for his or her endeavors or whether efforts fail and the child is unrewarded, or worse, blamed.

Understanding Self and Others

The child's ability to interact with others depends on a well-developed sense of self. As children's social and cognitive skills develop, they engage in increasingly complex and imaginative types of play, sometimes by themselves and, increasingly, with others.

Parent-Child Interaction

As children become more independent and try to exercise more control over their environment, the parents' role in supervising the child's activities becomes more difficult. Some parenting styles and some forms of discipline are more effective than others in encouraging the child to develop both autonomy and self-control.

The School Years

Part IV

If someone asked you to pick the best years of the entire life span, you might choose the years from 7 to 11 and defend your choice persuasively. To begin with, physical development is usually almost problem-free, making it easy to master dozens of new skills.

With regard to cognitive development, most children are able to learn quickly and think logically, providing the topic is not too abstract. Moral reasoning has reached that state where right seems clearly distinguished from wrong, with none of the ambiguities that complicate moral issues for adolescents and adults.

Finally, the social world of middle childhood seems perfect, for most school-age children think their parents are helpful, their teachers fair, and their friends loyal. Their future seems filled with promise— at least most of the time it does.

However, school and friendships are so important at this age that two common events can seem crushing: failure in school and rejection by peers. Some lucky children escape these problems; others have sufficient self-confidence or family support to weather them when they arise; and some leave middle childhood with painful memories, feeling inadequate, incompetent, and inferior for the rest of their lives.

The next three chapters celebrate the joys, and commemorate the occasional tragedies, of middle childhood.

The School Years: Physical Development

Chapter 12

Growth itself contains the germ of happiness.

Pearl S. Buck, 1967
To My Daughters, With Love

The doctor says I'll be okay when I'm 14. Well, I'm only 9.

David, diagnosed as having minimal brain dysfunction
Dorthea M. Ross and Shelia A. Ross, 1982
Hyperactivity: Current issues, research, and theory

Size and Shape
Variations in Physique
Childhood Obesity

Motor Skills
Differences in Motor Skills

Children with Handicaps
Separate Education
Mainstreaming
Learning Disabilities
Hyperactive Children

Chapter 12

For most children, the school years are a time of stable growth and notable improvement in physical skills. For some, unfortunately, it is a time when certain types of disabilities become more pronounced in their consequences. In this chapter, we will examine the physical changes and variations, and also the problems, that are characteristic of middle childhood. The following questions are among the topics we will consider in this chapter.

How is a child's physical development affected by genetic and cultural patterns?

What are the effects of being overweight on a school-age child?

Which games and sports are best suited to the skills of children in middle childhood?

Should children with physical, emotional, or cognitive handicaps be educated in the regular classroom setting?

What are the true symptoms of hyperactivity, and what are some of the methods used to treat this disorder?

In general, physical development in middle childhood seems relatively smooth and uneventful, compared to the rapid growth of early childhood or the transformations of puberty. This is apparent in a number of ways. For one, disease and death are rarer during these years than during any other period. For another, most children master new physical skills (everything from tree climbing to break-dancing) without much adult instruction, provided their bodies are sufficiently mature and they have an opportunity to practice these skills. In addition, sex differences in physical development and ability are minimal, and sexual urges seem to be submerged, so the task of understanding sexual identity remains simplified for the time being. Certainly when physical development during these years is compared to the rapid and dramatic changes that occur during adolescence, middle childhood seems a period of relative tranquility. Now let us look at some of the specifics.

Size and Shape

Children grow more slowly during middle childhood than they did earlier or than they will in adolescence. Gaining about 5 pounds (2¼ kilograms) and 2½ inches (6 centimeters) per year, the average child by age 10 weighs about 70 pounds (32 kilograms) and measures 54 inches (137 centimeters) (Lowrey, 1978).

During these years children become proportionally thinner as they grow taller. In addition, muscles become stronger, enabling the average 10-year-old, for instance, to throw a ball twice as far as the average 6-year-old. The capacity of the lungs increases and the heart grows stronger, so with each passing year children are able to run faster and exercise longer than before.

These changes can be affected by experience as well as maturation, as shown by studies of girls who train for serious competitive swimming, often beginning at age 8 or earlier to swim three or four hours a day. By adolescence, their lung and heart capacity is significantly greater than that of their peers who were comparable in body type and strength before the training (Eriksson, 1976).

Variations in Physique

Many healthy children are noticeably larger or smaller than average. The range is so great that, for example, if the 8-year-olds who are among the tallest and heaviest 10 percent of their age group were to stop growing for one year while their classmates grew normally, they would still be taller than half their contemporaries and heavier than three-quarters of them (National Center for Health Statistics, 1976).

In some regions of the world, most of the variation in size is caused by malnutrition, with wealthier children being several inches taller than their contemporaries from the other side of town—whether the town is Hong Kong, Rio de Janeiro, or New Delhi. But as we saw in Chapter 9, most children in North America get enough food during middle childhood to grow as tall as their genes allow. So heredity, rather than diet, causes most of the variation we see (Eveleth and Tanner, 1976).

Not only does size vary, but the rate of maturation also varies from child to child. For instance, a relatively tall 7-year-old might have the muscle maturity and coordination more typical of a 5-year-old. At the other end of middle childhood, some 10- and 11-year-olds begin to undergo the changes of puberty, and may find that they are superior to their peers not only in height but in strength and endurance as well. Thus, various rates of development are quite normal.

Figure 12.1 *Normal, healthy 10-year-olds come in many sizes, as illustrated by these fifth-grade Californians. Typically, black children tend to be ahead of their classmates in height, while children of Asian descent tend to be shorter than members of other ethnic groups.*

These variations follow genetic, and perhaps cultural, patterns. French-speaking Canadian children, for example, tend to be smaller, stronger, and to have greater heart and lung capacity than their English-speaking Canadian peers (Shephard, 1976). Black American children tend to mature somewhat more quickly (as measured by bone growth and loss of baby teeth) and to have longer legs than white American children.

While it may be comforting for parents and teachers to know that healthy children come in all shapes and sizes, it is not always comforting to the children themselves. As we saw in Chapter 10, toward the end of the preschool period, children's capacity to take others' points of view increases and they become more aware of the opinions of others. This trend continues in middle childhood. However, school-age children are not very adept at anticipating how their own comments might affect someone else, so they are very likely to tell each other "You're so short, you look like a first-grader" or "Your long legs remind me of a spider"—without realizing that such comments can make a child feel abnormal and ashamed. Deliberate insults that refer to physical characteristics related to race or ethnicity can cut even deeper.

In addition, in elementary school, children compare themselves to one another, and those who are "behind" their classmates in areas related to physical maturation may feel deficient. Physical development during this period even affects friendships, for, in part, they become based on physical appearance and competence (Hartup, 1983). Consequently, children who look "different," or who are noticeably lacking in physical skills, often become lonely and unhappy.

Childhood Obesity

The hardest size difference to bear in middle childhood is **obesity.** Although the point at which an overweight child qualifies as "obese" depends partly on the child's body type, partly on the proportion of fat to muscle, and partly on the culture's standards on this question, most experts contend that at least 10 percent of American children are sufficiently overweight to need slimming down (Grinker, 1981; Lamb, 1984). There is no doubt that the North American elementary-school children who are the heaviest 5 percent for their height can be classified as obese. Compared to the average child who weighs about 66 pounds at 53 inches, children in this group weigh 85 pounds or more at the same height (National Center for Health Statistics, 1976). These children are obese by almost everyone's standards.

Obesity is a serious physical and medical problem at any stage of life, for the obese person runs a greater risk of serious illness (Lamb, 1984). It is often a psychological problem as well. Children begin developing negative beliefs about obesity even as preschoolers (Fritz and Wetherbee, 1982), but it is not known if being fat affects their self-concept. In middle childhood, however, fat children are teased, picked on, and rejected. They know they are overweight, and they often hate themselves for it (Grinker, 1981). Obese children have fewer friends than other children (Staffieri, 1967); and when they are accepted in a peer group, it is often at a high price, such as answering to nicknames like "Tubby," "Blubber," or "Fat Albert," and having to constantly suffer jokes about their shape.

Help for Overweight Children   Clearly, an overweight child needs emotional support for a bruised self-concept, as well as help in losing weight. But reducing is difficult, and psychological encouragement is often scarce, partly because obesity is usually fostered by family attitudes and habits that are hard to break (see Closer

Look, next page). Obese children sometimes try crash diets, which make them irritable, listless, and even sick—adding to their psychological problems without accomplishing much long-term weight loss. To make matters worse, strenuous dieting during childhood can be physically harmful, since cutting down on protein or calcium could hinder important bone and brain growth (Winick, 1975). Unless a child is seriously obese, in which case careful weight reduction is in order, nutritionists generally recommend stabilizing the weight of overweight children to allow them to "grow out" of their fat.

The best way to get children to lose weight is to increase their physical activity. Indeed, inactivity may be as much a cause of childhood obesity as overeating. Overweight children tend to be less active than their peers, burning fewer calories and adding pounds even when they eat less than other children (Mayer, 1968). However, exercise is hard for overweight children, for they are not often chosen to play on the team, and they are likely to be teased and rebuffed when they try to join in group activities.

Parents and teachers can help overweight children to do the kinds of exercise in which their size is not much of a disadvantage—walking to school rather than taking the bus, or doing sit-ups at home—or even an advantage, as it might be in swimming. Parents can also exercise with their children, not only making activity easier and providing a good model, but bolstering the child's self-confidence as well. The importance of changing the child's eating and exercising patterns is apparent when one realizes that if the childhood weight problem reaches the point that the child is obese, and continues at that level throughout the childhood years, it is likely to last a lifetime (Grinker, 1981; Lamb, 1984). Thus, parents of the obese child who do nothing about it are jeopardizing the health as well as the happiness of their child in later years.

Figure 12.2 *Even if they join in physical activities and are accepted by their peers, overweight children often feel painfully self-conscious, especially when the activity requires donning a costume that calls more attention to one's appearance.*

Causes of Childhood Obesity

Typically, no one explanation suffices for a particular instance of obesity; rather, the problem is generally created through the interaction of a number of influences (Lowrey, 1978; Weil, 1975; Wolff and Lipe, 1978; Grinker, 1981). These influences begin in infancy, continue through childhood, and are still significant in adulthood.

1. *Heredity.* Body type, including the distribution of fat, as well as height and bone structure, is inherited. Therefore, not everyone can be "average" in the ratio of height to weight. However, no child should be 20 percent or more heavier than average. The saying that "fatness runs in the family" is more often a rationalization for poor eating and exercise habits than a valid genetic explanation.

2. *Activity level.* Inactive people burn fewer calories and are more likely to be overweight than active people. This is even more true in infancy and childhood than in the rest of life.

3. *Quantity of food eaten.* In some families, parents take satisfaction in watching their children eat, always urging them to have another helping. The implication is that a father's love is measured by how much food he can provide, a mother's love, by how well she can cook, and a child's love, by how much he or she can eat. This is especially true when the parents or grandparents grew up in places where starvation was a real possibility. Not surprisingly, in the United States, children and grandchildren of immigrants from developing countries are more likely to be overweight.

4. *Types of food eaten.* Besides the obvious culprits, many common foods, from cornflakes to ketchup, have sugar as a major ingredient. Children who eat too much of these foods become overweight. On other diets—those emphasizing fruits and vegetables—it is hard to become fat. Unfortunately, but understandably, the diet of North American families who are below the poverty line tends to be high in fat, consisting of pork more than other meats and of fried foods more than broiled or steamed (Eichorn, 1979). In addition, research shows that animals and people develop tastes for certain types of foods depending on what they have become accustomed to eating, as well as on what their body needs (Grinker, 1981). Thus the "treats" and "junk food" that some parents regularly give their children may be creating dietary cravings that will lead directly to weight problems.

5. *Attitude toward food.* Some people consider food a symbol of love and comfort, and eat whenever they are upset. This pattern may begin in infancy, if parents feed their babies whenever they cry rather than first figuring out if the baby is lonely or uncomfortable rather than hungry (Heald, 1975). It may then continue through childhood, as parents, teachers, and even pediatricians use sweets as a reward or consolation, or as compensation for lack of emotional warmth (Lowrey, 1978).

6. *Overfeeding in infancy and late childhood.* For most of life, the number of fat cells in a person's body remains relatively constant, no matter what that person eats. Adults become fatter because each fat cell becomes fuller, or thinner because each cell gets emptier; but new cells are not formed. However, in the first two years of life and during early adolescence, when total body fat increases in anticipation of the rapid growth that follows, the number of fat cells is particularly likely to increase. The actual number of cells is related to nourishment, for malnutrition slows down the rate of cell multiplication, and overfeeding speeds it up (Grinker, 1981). This is one more reason why fat babies and adolescents become adults who want more food and gain weight more easily than people who were not overfed as children. Even when these adults diet and lose weight, their bodies still contain those extra cells, just waiting to fill up with fat again, like sponges ready to soak up water.

Motor Skills

The fact that children grow more slowly during middle childhood may be part of the reason they become so much more skilled at controlling their bodies during these years. (Compare this control, for instance, with the clumsiness that typically accompanies sudden changes in body shape and size during puberty.) School-age children can perform almost any motor skill, as long as it doesn't require very

This would explain why chubby babies are more likely than average-weight babies to become overweight children and obese adults. However, scientists do not believe that there is a direct path from overfeeding to extra fat cells to adult obesity, for fat babies do not always become fat children or adults, and even those who follow this path may be directed by genes rather than childhood diet (Roche, 1981).

Recent research points the finger at another culprit in childhood obesity, one that exacerbates several of the influences already cited: television-watching. According to a large longitudinal study (Dietz and Gortmaker, 1985), excessive television-watching (more than twenty-five hours a week) is directly correlated with being overweight. In addition, those children who watch several hours of TV a day during middle childhood are more likely to become obese adolescents. The researchers suggested three

factors that make TV fattening: while watching television, children burn few calories, consume many snacks, and are bombarded with, and swayed by, commercials for junk foods.

One more explanation of obesity should be mentioned, even though it is not one of the common reasons. In a few instances of obesity in children, an abnormality in the growth process is the cause (Lowrey, 1978). In these cases, obesity is only one sign of a complex physiological problem which usually involves retardation of normal physical and mental growth. It must be stressed, however, that disorders of this type account for less than 1 percent of all cases of childhood obesity. Therefore, parents of the fat school-age child should, in all likelihood, be much more concerned about the effects of diet and exercise, than about physiological disturbances.

When Father's role is to "bring home the bacon," and Mother's role is to prepare home-baked goodies, Junior is often expected to do his part by eating and enjoying everything he is offered.

much power or judgment of speed and distance. The skills of typical North American 8- and 9-year-olds may include swinging a hammer well, sawing, using garden tools, sewing, knitting, drawing in good proportion, writing or printing accurately and neatly, cutting fingernails (Gesell et al., 1977), riding bicycles, scaling fences, swimming, diving, roller skating, ice skating, jumping rope, and playing baseball, football, and jacks. Of course, which particular skills a child masters depends, in part, on opportunity and encouragement.

**Differences in
Motor Skills**

Boys and girls are just about equal in physical abilities during these years, except that boys have greater forearm strength (Tanner, 1970) and girls have greater overall flexibility. Consequently, boys have an advantage in sports like baseball, whereas girls have the edge in sports like gymnastics. But for most physical activities during middle childhood, neither body size nor sex is as important as age and experience. Short children can become fast runners, boys can do cartwheels, and girls can hit home runs.

However, the maxim "Practice makes perfect" does not necessarily hold (Astrand, 1976). Every motor skill is related to several other abilities, some depending on body size, others on brain maturation, others on genetic talent, and others on practice.

Figure 12.3 Sex differences in motor skills make boys slightly better at pulling themselves up with their arms, and girls slightly better at twisting and leaping.

For example, brain maturation is a key factor in **reaction time,** which is the length of time it takes a person to respond to a particular stimulus. One study of reaction time in people between the ages of 7 and 75, found that the 7-year-olds took about twice as long as the typical adult to press a button in response to flash of light (.75 seconds as opposed to .37 seconds). The 9-year-olds were notably better than the 7-year-olds, and the 11-year-olds were better still, but none of these three age groups did as well as any adult group, even the 75-year-olds (Stern et al., 1980). Thus in any sport in which reaction time is crucial, the average older child has a decided advantage over a younger one, and the average adult is quicker than the average child.

Other individual and age differences also come into play. Some are obvious, such as the advantage of height in basketball and of upper body strength and size for tackle football. Other differences may not be so obvious to the teacher or parent. For example, the ability to coordinate one's body movements is no more equal in children than in adults, so that some children are not able to aim a kick in soccer, or execute a leap in ballet, nearly as well as others.

Looking closely at the sports that adults value reveals that few are well-suited for children, because they demand precisely those skills that are hardest for them to master. Even softball is much harder than one might think. Throwing with accuracy and catching both involve more distance judgment and eye-hand coordination than many elementary-school children possess. In addition, catching and batting depend on reaction time. Younger children are therefore apt to drop a ball even if it lands in their mitt, because they are slow to enclose it, or to strike out by swinging too late. Thus a large measure of judgment, physical maturity, and experience is required for good ball playing.

Figure 12.4 *Most sports that adults organize for children are scaled-down imitations of professional sports. Unfortunately, many coaches and parents do not scale down their expectations of children's abilities to perform. As a result, many children are excluded from participating, and those that make the team are often subjected to criticism and haranguing that spoil the fun.*

Games Children Play Ideally, the physical activities of elementary-school children should center around skills that most children can perform reasonably well: kick ball and dodge ball more than softball and football; relay races with equally matched teams rather than individual running races. Interestingly, the games that children organize themselves (tag, hide-and-seek, kick-the-can, king of the mountain, ring-a-lievio) often include children of varying ages and abilities, and involve relatively simple skills. The pressure on any individual child to perform adequately in these types of games is obviously much less than in games emphasizing one-on-one competition.

The fact that many sports that adults value are not ideal for children does not mean that physical activity should be deemphasized. In fact, regular exercise, in moderation, is as physically beneficial for children as for adults (Lamb, 1984). In addition, according to a study that compared the school achievement of two similar groups of children, one with a daily program of physical activity and the other without one, spending an hour or more in regular physical activity may well benefit a child's academic work (Bailey, 1977).

Children with Handicaps

Thus far we have been discussing the needs of essentially normal children, who require physical activity as well as social acceptance to function happily and well during middle childhood. But what about atypical children, for whom physical activity or social interaction poses special problems, particularly in a school setting? Can a blind 6-year-old be expected to learn in a classroom with children of normal vision? Can a child in a wheelchair play with other third-graders? What about the child who does not look abnormal, but who has cognitive problems that become painfully apparent in the classroom, such as the child who is mentally retarded, or has a learning disability, or is hyperactive? As we saw in the case of David in Chapter 1, social interaction between "special" children and their classmates is often problematic.

Traditionally, the education of children with special needs was accomplished in one of two opposite ways. When the handicaps were not very obvious, children were placed with normal children, to do the best they could. When children could not "pass" as normal, they were educated separately with as little contact as possible with normal children. Let us look more closely at both alternatives.

Separate Education

Because teachers did not feel prepared to handle them, and parents wanted to protect them from loneliness and mockery, many handicapped children were kept at home, educated by their parents or a tutor or not taught at all. Others spent their entire childhoods in schools for special children. From the point of view of the special child, such segregation seemed warranted, since in regular schools, children tend to be intensely compared with the rest of their class, and the children themselves often become openly critical of their classmates.

However, in the 1960s educators and parents began to question whether separate education was always best for children with special problems—either obvious problems like blindness or less apparent difficulties such as moderate mental retardation. For one thing, handicapped children need to learn many cognitive skills that are best learned in a regular classroom. In addition, three other arguments against the separate education of special children seemed compelling:

1. *Social skills.* Most children, handicapped or not, learn social and survival skills by playing and learning with other children. Therefore, many specialists reasoned, normal children and special children should benefit from sharing a classroom.

2. *The effect of labeling.* Children who are labeled as "different," and put in a special environment because of it, learn to see themselves as different and inferior. The child who is deaf will consider deafness his or her most important characteristic, rather than simply one attribute. The retarded child will feel unable to do anything, and, even as an adult, will be plagued with shame and self-doubt. Moreover, once children have become labeled as handicapped and are segregated, their adjustment to special treatment within a self-contained classroom may make it difficult for them to outgrow the stereotype or the special educational milieu. The deaf child who learns with other hearing-impaired children might never learn to lipread; the child who seemed mentally retarded at age 7 because of a temporary family problem (such as frequent moves and, consequently, frequent changes of school, or a bitter divorce that undermined the child's ability to cope with school) might, if placed in a special classroom, remain classified as retarded at age 11. Unfortunately, once a child is labeled as needing special education, the label tends to stick.

3. *Discrimination.* The isolation that was claimed to be for the good of the special child appeared to many observers to be a form of segregation intended to benefit teachers and normal children who would rather not deal with the disabled child. Many also saw another form of discrimination at work, since a relatively high proportion of children in special classes were nonwhite, non-English-speaking, and of low socioeconomic status.

The weight of all the arguments against separate education led to a new movement called mainstreaming.

Mainstreaming

By the end of the 1960s many educators were calling for the integration of handicapped children with normal children as much as possible and as early as possible (Nix, 1976; Dunn, 1973; Gardner, 1977; Deno, 1973). This practice is called **mainstreaming,** because the handicapped children join the main group of normal children. In the United States, mainstreaming occurred gradually, school by school, state by state, until federal law in 1975 mandated that all children, no matter what their handicaps, receive public education in the "least restrictive" environment that is educationally sound. This means that handicapped children are mainstreamed unless it can be proven that mainstreaming is deleterious to them.

To help meet the needs of mainstreamed children, many schools adopted the idea of the **resource room,** a facility in the regular school run by specially trained teachers and equipped with special learning materials. A child with learning problems can be assigned to the resource room for particular help for several hours a day, even in midyear, without disrupting friendship patterns or the child's sense of being part of a regular class. In addition, communication between regular and special teachers, which is essential to the child's optimal learning, is facilitated when both types of teachers have classrooms within the same school.

Figure 12.5 (a) *This photo of a class at the Lexington School for the Deaf shows several of the advantages of special education. The curriculum is designed to accommodate the students' disability; the class size is small, and because the students all have the same problem and all are wearing a hearing aid, no one feels "different." (b) Individual therapy sessions provide the special help required for this hearing-impaired boy to derive the most benefit from his classes at a regular public school.*

(a)

(b)

Despite the many advantages it seems to offer—not the least of which is that teachers and children become more aware of the special needs of handicapped people—mainstreaming for every "special" child has not proven to be the simple solution that some hoped it would be (Carlberg and Kavale, 1980). One problem is that many special children need extensive and expensive supportive services to help them learn in the regular classroom. Especially in recent times, when money for education has been in short supply, many school systems have had to cut back on, or forego, such services, including even resource rooms, and some schools have simply added the special child to the regular teacher's workload, often leaving the special child to "sink or swim." Not surprisingly, few school professionals are currently enthusiastic about mainstreaming (Baker and Gottlieb, 1980).

Another problem is that social skills are not necessarily furthered simply by mixing children together in the same room (Gresham, 1982; Strain and Shores, 1983). Special children tend to be socially isolated, in part because they look and act different; in part because some cannot participate as equals in gym or recess activities while others are obviously not equal in academic work; and in part because the social skills of many have been limited by their handicap.

Figure 12.6 *Mainstreaming works particularly well for children who are physically disabled but who have no social or academic deficits.*

Finally, as we saw with David in Chapter 1, some handicapped children who could manage in a regular school, may, at various times, derive greater benefit from special education. This holds true for emotionally disturbed children as well (Forness et al., 1984).

It seems clear, then, that the promise of mainstreaming has to be balanced against the realities of each individual case of special needs. Ideally, decisions about a disabled child's education should be made by special and regular teachers, as well as by the parents, so that each child benefits from the right combination of special and mainstream learning. Given the current state of affairs, each child needs a wide range of educational alternatives.

Learning Disabilities

Most of the problems we have discussed so far in this chapter are evident to some degree before the school years. However, it is not until middle childhood that a more subtle form of handicap becomes apparent, as a child seems to be unable to master one or another skill as readily as other children. If a child of average or better-than-average intelligence is about two years behind the usual school achievement in some specific area, and there is no obvious explanation (such as a problem with hearing or vision), that child may well have a **specific learning disability.** For example, a child might have **dyslexia,** which is a disability in reading. Dyslexic children may seem bright and happy in the early years of school, volunteering answers to some difficult questions, diligently completing their work sheets, sitting quietly looking at their books. However, as time goes on, it becomes clear that the child is not really reading: the child might guess at simple words (occasionally making surprising mistakes) or try to explain what he or she just "read" by telling about the pictures.

The specific reading problems of dyslexic children can be many and varied. Sometimes words are read backward ("was" becomes "saw"), although true "mirror reading" is rare. Sometimes the child has difficulty associating the sound of a word with its written form, or cannot readily distinguish between letters that are similar in shape. In fact, the precise problem underlying a particular instance of dyslexia is often hard to specify, which is why the disorder is such a stumbling block for teachers as well as children. Whatever the exact nature of the problem, however, dyslexia usually is apparent—though often undiagnosed—by the second grade, when a child is still trying to master primers, and becomes more and more pronounced as the child grows older.

Figure 12.7 *The classroom behavior of children with learning disabilities is usually normal until they are faced with a situation beyond their capacities.* (a) *This boy listens to his teacher's question,* (b) *thinks and gets part of the answer, then* (c) *temporarily despairs at getting the rest. Whether this stressful moment becomes a productive pause, the prelude to an angry outburst, or the beginning of a despondent day depends, in part, on how this child's teacher and classmates respond to his faltering.*

(a)

(b)

(c)

Another common disability is **dyscalcula,** that is, great difficulty in math. This problem usually becomes apparent somewhat later in childhood, at about age 8, when it is clear that even simple number facts, such as 3 + 3 = 6, are memorized one day and forgotten the next. Soon it becomes clear that the child is guessing at whether two numbers should be added or subtracted, and that everything the child knows about math is a question of rote memory rather than understanding.

A third problem is **dysgraphia,** a difficulty in printing and handwriting that produces the large, uneven letters characteristic of a much younger child. A dysgraphic child might take three times longer than any other classmate to write out an assignment, and still produce a paper that is messy and hard to read.

While the number of children suffering from learning disabilities is hard to estimate, since relatively few are officially diagnosed and counted, a conservative estimate is 10 percent.

What Causes a Learning Disability? None of the learning problems just described is caused by a lack of effort on the child's part, although, unfortunately, parents and teachers sometimes tell learning-disabled children that they are not trying hard enough. In fact, the precise cause or causes of learning disabilities are hard to pinpoint, although many professionals believe that the origin is often organic. It seems as if some parts of the learning-disabled child's brain do not function as well as they might: there seems to be a **minimal brain dysfunction** that impairs some cognitive skill.

One reason for thinking that brain dysfunction is the cause of learning disabilities is that people with these disabilities often think like people who have suffered brain damage. For instance, a woman with a brain tumor was presented with the following problem: "A boy is eight years old. His father is thirty years older, and his mother is ten years younger than the father. How old is she?" The woman tried three times—first adding 8, 30, and 10 to get 48 and then dividing by 3; then subtracting 10 from 30; then subtracting 10 from 30 again—finally she added 8 and 30, subtracted 10, and got the correct answer, 28. Her difficulty sounds familiar to anyone who has taught people with dyscalcula. The fact is, however, that this woman's disability disappeared when the tumor was removed (Farnham-Diggory, 1978). Other victims of brain damage sometimes lose their ability to read, write, spell, or speak normally, even though other aspects of their functioning are normal. This fact led early researchers to think that minimal brain damage (perhaps sustained during prenatal development or in the birth process) was the cause of childhood learning problems too.

However, a growing number of professionals now believe that, although learning disabilities are sometimes attributable to brain damage, they are more often the result of an inherited difficulty in brain functioning—perhaps involving faulty connections between the left and right hemispheres or between the sensory areas, such as those having to do with vision and hearing (Farnham-Diggory, 1978). The theory that these difficulties are inherited seems plausible because siblings and other relatives of children with learning disabilities often have some learning difficulties themselves.

For at least two reasons, however, we must be cautious in citing organic or genetic causes for learning disabilities. First, it is difficult to prove that a particular form of brain damage or a particular pattern of inheritance causes a particular learning problem. In fact, sometimes, but not always, many specific prenatal and postnatal factors can be linked to learning disabilities; at the same time, many disabilities appear even when nothing untoward in the genetic or prenatal history is apparent.

More important, sometimes people mistakenly conclude that it is impossible to ameloriate an organic problem. In fact, no matter what the cause of learning disabilities, the way teachers and parents respond to a child who displays difficulties in learning can make an enormous difference to the child's chances of overcoming the problem. If teachers and parents recognize that a child with a learning disability is neither lazy nor stupid, they can help the child become a competent adult.

That might seem to be an overly optimistic statement about a 9-year-old who is dyslexic, unable to read even the simplest words, or a 13-year-old who spells brother "brith" and helicopter "throccatei" (Farnham-Diggory, 1978). But many such children learn basic skills eventually, especially if they are given patient, individual tutoring. In general, the earlier a disabled child gets special help, and the more that help is tied to the particular problem (not just help in reading, for instance, but help in recognizing shapes for one child, in phonics for another), the better (Achenbach, 1982). One reason for early intervention is that children who have great difficulty with schoolwork that others find easy often become social outcasts as well as learning-disabled (Cunningham and Barkley, 1978; Hartup, 1983).

Finally, the experiences and problems of learning-disabled children contain a lesson for adults who are evaluating children. No child should be expected to be average or better than average in everything. Recognizing this, we need to teach children ways to overcome some of their specific disabilities, to be patient until they grow out of others, and to compensate for those disabilities that remain. Each of us is less proficient in some skills than most other people are, and each of us has found ways to keep these deficiencies from becoming serious handicaps.

Figure 12.8 *There can be many reasons why a child's attention may wander from schoolwork. If a serious learning problem can be ruled out, and there are no disturbing problems at home, then the child may simply have stayed up too late the night before. In any case, discovering the cause of the problem is more beneficial than simply urging the child back to work.*

The Learning-Disabled Child in School

Learning-disabled children never have an easy time at school. However, their difficulties can be significantly lightened if everyone involved knows why a particular child does not learn what other children seem to master quickly. Consider the experiences of two boys, Teddy and Pat.

Teddy is learning-disabled "in almost all modalities" (Osman, 1979), a fact that practically guarantees academic difficulties, and, eventually, behavior problems, if special help is not forthcoming from the home as well as from the school. Happily, Teddy never became disruptive or withdrawn, largely because he and his parents learned early how to cope with his disabilities.

His parents thought something was wrong as soon as Teddy began school, when he changed from a happy, cheerful preschooler to a cranky kindergartener who frequently complained that the "mean teacher" was giving him too much "hard work." He began having nightmares and wetting his bed almost every night. In first grade, he was shamed before the whole class when he was asked to read aloud and couldn't, and again when the teacher made everyone miss recess while they waited for him to copy his sentence from the board.

Soon after that, the school psychologist tested Teddy and diagnosed him as learning-disabled. Teddy remained in regular classes, but his teachers attempted to help him by structuring his assignments in ways that would make them easier for him to handle. Teddy also spent time each day in a resource room (his "haven"), where a special teacher gave him individual help. Finally, his parents became his support team, explaining Teddy's special needs to teachers and administrators before he became frustrated, embarrassed, or punished for not doing what he could not do.

Although this special help cushioned the psychological impact of Teddy's learning disabilities, he fell well behind his classmates. Consequently, at age 9, he was put in a special class for learning-disabled children. He finally began to read, and, after three years, was considered ready for placement in a regular sixth-grade class in a middle school.

Although sympathetic, Teddy's regular teachers were not always prepared to help him, however. For example, his math teacher "wanted to help" but had no time, and, besides, felt that it would not be fair to give him individual attention, or to allow him to study from the test itself or to use a calculator to avoid computational errors. Even the resource-room teacher had no time to help, but she let Teddy use the tape library, which included cassettes of most of the textbooks. With special help from his parents, his tape recorder, and a tutor, Teddy managed to get through junior high.

Pat's first eight years of school were far more problematic—not because his learning problems were worse (in fact, he was dyslexic but not impaired in other areas)—but because no one recognized his problems as disabilities (Lamm and Fisch, 1982). Pat explains it well:

I wasn't good at reading. I was failing, but I was also one of the biggest kids in the class so no one called me stupid or dummy . . . [The teachers] knew I couldn't do the work so they would send me on errands in the school. Pat, get this! Pat, get that! I felt dumb. I thought that I must have been absent the day they taught us how to read. I used to hate it. I didn't want to go to school but my mother said, "You have to go!" I'd say "I'm sick," and I came close to staying out.

The worst part was when I'd fail, and I'd have to bring a paper home to have my mother sign it. . . . my mother would yell at me, that really hurt. My brothers who were in high school and my sisters would yell at me and say "What's wrong with you?" They had all gone to the same parochial school, and I was the only one having this trouble. My mother just couldn't take the school calling up all the time, and so she finally just left my sisters there and took me out and put me into public school . . .

It was a school in which we did everything verbally at first. I felt good that I was finally coming home with good marks and my mother was happy . . . Then after a while we sat down and started with the pencil and paper and books again, and that's when I started to fail all over again.

Hyperactive Children

The same note of optimism, and awareness of individual differences, will help us attempt to understand one of the most puzzling problems that sometimes occurs in childhood—**hyperactivity**. A hyperactive child is one who is overly active, impulsive, distractible, and excitable, especially at the wrong times and places (Ross and Ross, 1982). About 5 percent of all school-age children are considered hyperactive

That's when they said that something was the matter. I'd just be sitting in class and they'd say, "Pat, go down to the office!" Well, I was used to that from the other school. I went down, took a test, and came back. The guidance counselor . . . told my mother that he would continue to test me but said I was being lazy. I asked my mother why I was being tested and she said, "Maybe you need glasses." . . . I thought that everyone was like me and had trouble reading . . .

I stayed in that school for the fourth and fifth grade. They decided that junior high school was out and that they were going to have to find another program for me. Then fall came around and . . . they said, "How would you like to repeat the fifth grade?" . . . I ended up doing fifth-grade work for another year.

Then around came fall again and . . . I was put in another school which had a special program . . . for the neurologically impaired. . . . The math was addition and the reading was words like "cat" that I had memorized years ago when I was a little kid. I never got in trouble. I never talked. . . . The other kids in the class made noise; some were retarded, some had emotional problems, and some were tough guys—behavior problems . . . I was absent a lot, but I would go in when they said that I had to pass a test for my report card . . . I hated that school . . . it was a total waste of time.

Fortunately, Pat's social isolation, withdrawal, and wasted learning time came to an end at this point, because he was tested and found to be dyslexic. Knowing this helped Pat with the difficult school years ahead:

I was dyslexic. I wasn't mentally disturbed, and I wasn't mentally retarded . . . since I had been messed around with for three years they promoted me, but to the eighth grade and that was tough . . . School would be out at two-thirty, and I would stay there and work until four. Then I'd go home to work and I would do sixth and seventh grade work to catch up . . . One teacher gave me a lot of help; she was there when I needed her. Last year I went to high school as a freshman in a regular class. . . .

For both Teddy and Pat, high school was difficult. However, Pat found that once he understood what his problem was, he had the confidence to cope with it:

I'm relaxed now, and I'm not shy. When a teacher asks me to stand up and read page 101–103 during the class, I can say to her that I have trouble reading and I can't do that. I never used to be able to say that. The teacher then says that she'll talk to me after class, and I explain it to her. I know what is wrong with me, and the people know what is wrong, so I don't have to worry. I know what I have to do to get around it and how to help myself.

Since Teddy had more problems than Pat, he found high school more difficult, but as his mother puts it, he "wages his own battles now" (Osman, 1985). For example, he tells each teacher at the beginning of the term that he is learning-disabled and asks not to be called on unless his hand is raised. He became particularly good in social studies, because the teachers let him tape their lectures. By his senior year, he had worked with the head of the department to create courses in American history, world history, and African and Asian history that were specially designed to provide learning-disabled students the same depth of coverage available in the regular courses.

What is to be learned from these two examples? First, many teachers and parents find it hard to accommodate a learning-disabled child. Second, even with special help, the problems do not go away. The task is to find ways to by-pass some of them and to overcome others with special work. Finally, once the problem is recognized, and the learning-disabled child understands it, the child can gradually learn to compensate on his or her own. Both Teddy and Pat are making it through high school and can contemplate college and employment only "slightly more terrified than other kids" (as Teddy's mother put it). At this point they have the knowledge that they have overcome a difficult period of their lives, and their sense of self-esteem and self-understanding seems sufficient to allow the prediction that they will be reasonably well-adjusted, normally functioning adults. In fact, they might do much better than average. Among the famous people who were learning-disabled as children are Hans Christian Anderson, Woodrow Wilson, Nelson Rockefeller, and Winston Churchill. In each case, overcoming and compensating for their difficult experiences as children helped them become the strong achievers they turned out to be.

by their parents, teachers, or pediatricians, and about 1 percent are considered hyperactive by all three (Lambert et al., 1978).

Hyperactivity appears early in life: many a hyperactive child, as an infant, managed to destroy the hand-me-down crib that older siblings had used without damaging, or seemed much more accident-prone as a toddler than his or her age-

Figure 12.9 *Many children have moments when they seem out of control—too active, too aggressive, and too inattentive for adults to manage. While these behaviors are symptoms of hyperactivity, or attention deficit syndrome, a child is not considered to be truly hyperactive unless these symptoms are apparent over a long period of time and in many different settings.*

mates. However, children are not usually labeled "hyperactive" until elementary school, when it becomes apparent that they cannot sit quietly in one spot and concentrate on schoolwork. Many hyperactive children also have a specific learning disability, which compounds the problem. In fact, according to some professionals, hyperactivity is itself a form of learning disability, whether or not it is accompanied by specific difficulties in learning particular skills. To emphasize this view, these professionals prefer to call the problem **attention deficit disorder** rather than hyperactivity (Rutter and Garmezy, 1983).

Most hyperactive children (at least 80 percent) are boys, and the majority, boys and girls, come from families of low socioeconomic status (Cantwell, 1975). Whether this is so because school life is more difficult for boys and lower-class children or because these children are more vulnerable to the problem is not certain. Both factors are probably involved.

In most people's minds, it is the parents and teachers who most suffer the consequences of hyperactivity. But hyperactive children suffer too, as is clear from the following remarks:

> *Boy, 6 years, 11 months:* I am very tired of everything always being wrong and having to go for tests and my mom and dad look awful worried and soon I might have to go to another school. And what I would like a lot would be if I could just sit still and be the way the other kids are and not have all these things happen. And most of all I wish I did not break that mirror at Teddy Work's birthday party.

> *Boy, 8 years, 4 months:* I just wish I could be just an *ordinary boy*, like I mean OK in school but not all A's and have the other kids ask me to play ball, and most of all I wish I would not cry when I get mad. It's really terrible when you can't stop crying and everyone's looking.

Causes of Hyperactivity When confronted with a child who is considerably more active than other children and cannot concentrate very well, it is not easy to explain that child's behavior. However, we do know at least five reasons why some children are much more active than the normal child.

1. *Genetic differences.* As we saw in Chapter 8, activity level is one of the genetic characteristics that clearly vary from person to person. Some children naturally kick a lot in the uterus, run around as soon as they can walk, and want to keep active every minute of the day.

2. *Prenatal damage.* One of the most common precursors of hyperactivity is prenatal damage of some sort (Hartsough and Lambert, 1985). Thus, a person who was prenatally exposed to a teratogen may have escaped major harm but show minor problems in physical development and learning ability. According to one study, for example, 4-year-olds whose mothers drank moderately during pregnancy (averaging five drinks a week) had more difficulties with concentration than children whose mothers did not drink (Streissguth et al., 1984). On a more general level, children who have a higher-than-average number of minor physical anomalies, such as low-seated ears or widely spaced eyes or a third toe that is longer than the second toe, also tend to be more active and more aggressive than other children (Waldrop and Halverson, 1971; Bell and Waldrop, 1982). Presumably, prenatal difficulties led to both the physical characteristics and the social difficulties.

3. *Lead poisoning.* Lead poisoning in its early stages leads to impaired concentration and hyperactivity. (If left undetected and untreated, it can lead to severe illness and death.) One of the prime causes of lead-poisoning in children is the ingestion of lead-based paint. Although the interior use of lead-based paint is now illegal, many older buildings, particularly those in run-down areas, are still coated with this potentially harmful paint, which is usually peeling off the walls. If a child were to eat a few chips of this paint each day, the child would suffer lead poisoning within a few months. A second source of lead poisoning is air that is heavily polluted by automobile and truck emissions. For example, the area around Newark, New Jersey, notorious for its heavy-traffic tie-ups, is an "acknowledged lead belt" (Ross and Ross, 1982). Doctors recommend that all young children who have had prolonged exposure to either of these lead sources be tested for the early signs of lead poisoning. If the initial blood test is positive, further testing and treatment can prevent serious damage.

4. *Diet.* Severe vitamin deficiencies, especially of the B vitamins, impair concentration. In addition, certain foods, such as milk, chocolate, sugar, and cola, and some chemical additives, seem to make some children restless (Connors, 1980).

5. *Family influences.* Compared to other children, hyperactive children come from families who move often, have fewer children, and are less concerned about the child's academic performance than about controlling the child's behavior. Obviously, each of these factors may be the result, rather than the cause, of the child's behavior. However, after elaborate study, some researchers are convinced that these family differences contribute as much to a child's hyperactivity as genetic or temperamental variables (Lambert and Hartsough, 1984).

6. *Environment.* The ecological niche in which some children find themselves may exacerbate hyperactivity. The hyperactive child is especially likely to "misbehave" in an exciting but unstructured situation (such as the typical birthday party) or in a situation with many behavioral demands (such as a long church service, or dinner in a fancy restaurant). Children with no place to play, or who watch television hour after hour, may become restless, irritable, and aggressive. In one study of Puerto Rican children living in the crowded tenements of New York City (Thomas et al.,

1974), the parents' concern for their children's safety led them to keep their children in school or at home virtually all the time. Not surprisingly, 53 percent of these children were considered hyperactive by their parents. In one case, a family with a son described as a "whirling dervish" moved to a new house, which had a small yard. To his parents' delight, the boy quickly "outgrew" his hyperactivity.

Help for Hyperactive Children   What should be done to help hyperactive children? Before 1970, most professionals believed that children grew out of hyperactivity, so they suggested that nothing should be done except to help the parents cope with their temporary problem. However, we now know that many hyperactive children continue to have problems in adolescence and adulthood, not only with hyperactivity but with academic demands and social skills as well. Many become disruptive and angry: indeed, in England, where hyperactivity is a less commonly applied diagnostic label, most children who would be diagnosed as hyperactive in the United States are diagnosed as suffering from a conduct disturbance (Rutter and Garmezy, 1983). While hyperactivity and conduct disorder are not synonymous, many children who manifest one of these problems also have the other. Since ignoring the problem in middle childhood not only makes a child and his family miserable but may set the stage for worse problems later on, professionals now agree that the hyperactive child needs help (Ross and Ross, 1982).

However, the kind of help needed is controversial, especially the two forms of help most widely and readily given, the Feingold diet and psychoactive-drug therapy.

The Feingold Diet.   According to a very popular hypothesis, hyperactivity is actually a toxic reaction to certain foods, and eliminating those foods from the hyperactive child's diet will work miracles (Feingold, 1974). According to Benjamin Feingold, the physician who originated this idea, hyperactive children should be put on a diet completely free of artificial colors and flavoring, the preservatives BHT and BHA, and aspirin—no easy task since virtually all commercially available baked goods, cereals, luncheon meats, frozen dinners, ketchups, mustards, and toothpastes, and almost all medicines prescribed for children, contain one or more of the forbidden additives. For some children, Feingold also recommended that certain foods containing natural salicylates, such as apples, oranges, cucumbers, strawberries, tomatoes, and tea, also be avoided.

His suggestion was enthusiastically received. By 1979 grateful mothers had formed the National Feingold Association with 30,000 members and 120 branches (Ross and Ross, 1982) to promote the diet as well as to lobby for more accurate food labeling. The cure rate from his diet was said to be at least 30 percent.

However, scientific research finds that only a small group of hyperactive children are significantly helped by a change in their diet (Weiss et al., 1980; Swanson and Kinsbourne, 1980). Even this modest success rate is questioned by some scientists. As one review concludes, "On the basis of all the evidence available at this time, in answer to the question "Is there anything to Dr. Feingold's hypothesis?" one might answer, "Yes, something—but not much and not consistently" (Conners, 1980).

What accounts for the difference between scientists' view of the Feingold diet and that of the mothers? To begin with, the typical "proof" for the effectiveness of the diet comes from parents who so desperately want their child to quiet down that they are willing to go to the extraordinary lengths that are required to change the child's entire diet. Given this, it is easy to suggest other reasons for the seeming success of Feingold's plan: first, some children benefit from the extra attention and sympathy, and become less difficult; second, some children improve with time, and this improvement is misinterpreted as proof that the diet works; and finally, some parents simply imagine improvements, perhaps to justify their efforts.

At the moment, we can say that some children are helped in some way by removing additives from their diet (Weiss, 1982), but we do not know which children will benefit nor precisely which additives in what quantities might be harmful.

Drugs. For reasons not yet determined, certain drugs that stimulate adults, such as amphetamines and methylphenidate (Ritalin), have a reverse effect on hyperactive children. Approximately 350,000 children take such drugs each day (Ross and Ross, 1982). For many hyperactive children, the results are remarkable, allowing them to sit still and concentrate for the first time in their lives (Sprague and Ullman, 1981). Indeed, some physicians think that an overactive child who does not respond to such drugs is not really hyperactive.

Drug therapy is not a panacea, however. Unfortunately, drugs are sometimes prescribed for children without proper diagnoses or without follow-up examinations—an abuse that can harm the child. For instance, children are sometimes prescribed an overly large dosage and become lethargic, or they sometimes continue to be given the psychoactive drug even after the basic hyperactivity has abated.

In any case, by the time a child has become a candidate for psychoactive drugs, the child's behavior has usually created school, home, and personal problems that no drug can remedy. Psychoactive drugs should never be given as a one-step solution; instead they should be part of an ongoing treatment program that involves the child's cognitive and psychosocial worlds (Werry, 1977).

Psychological Therapy. Usually the hyperactive child needs help overcoming a confused perception of the social world, and a bruised ego, while the family needs help with their own management techniques and interaction. As noted in Chapter 2, many families with difficult children unwittingly get caught in a vicious cycle of aggression and anger, in which the parents' and siblings' responses to the problem child act to perpetuate that child's problem behavior (Patterson, 1982). Generally, the most effective types of therapy have been those developed from learning theory, such as teaching the parents how to use behavior-modification techniques with their hyperactive child, and helping the child see the effect of his or her own behavior, although other forms of therapy may be better for some children (Ross and Ross, 1982; Dubey et al., 1983).

Teacher Response. Teachers are often the first professionals to suggest that a particular child might be hyperactive, for they are able to compare these children with their peers in a relatively structured setting. However, teachers, like parents, are often not aware that they may be contributing to the child's difficulties. One study showed that some classroom environments, labeled **provocation ecologies,** made the problem worse, while others, called **rarefaction ecologies,** ameliorated the problem. In the former, structure was either unusually rigid or completely absent, and noise was either completely forbidden or tolerated to a distracting degree. Teachers who managed to diminish hyperactivity were flexible in terms of minor disruptions (for example, allowing children to ask questions of their neighbors so long as they did so quietly), but also provided sufficient structure so that the children knew what they should be doing and when (Whalen et al., 1979).

This is not to say that, with proper teaching, hyperactive children suddenly quiet down and concentrate on their work. On the contrary, as with all physical handicaps and disabilities, no school, family, or neighborhood, no matter how structured or flexible, can make the problem disappear. However, like all "special" children, hyperactive children can be greatly helped or harmed by the particular ecosystem of which they are a part.

Conclusion. It should be clear from our discussion of hyperactive children, as well as of the physically handicapped and the learning-disabled, that physiological, educational, and social influences can interact to produce problems, and that all these influences must be understood before the impact of these problems can be reduced. However, our focus on the more apparent physical problems must not blind us to the reality that the same interactional approach should characterize attempts to understand and meet the needs of all school-age children. Further, we must remember that each child has some of the strengths and liabilities typical of children in middle childhood, as well as capabilities and problems that few others share. This is, of course, true whether we are looking at physical development, as in this chapter, or at the cognitive, cultural, and social aspects of development, which we shall investigate in the next two chapters.

SUMMARY

Size and Shape

1. Children grow more slowly during middle childhood than at any time until the end of adolescence. There is much variation in the size and rate of maturation of healthy North American children, primarily as a result of genetic, rather than nutritional differences.

2. Overweight children suffer from peer rejection and poor self-concept. More exercise, rather than severe dieting, is the best solution.

Motor Skills

3. School-age children can perform almost any motor skill, as long as adult strength or judgment is not a prerequisite. Physical exercise is beneficial for strength, growth, and coordination. The activities that are best for children are those that demand only those skills that most children of this age can master.

Children with Handicaps

4. Children with obvious physical handicaps often were excluded from regular schools, assigned to special classes, limited to home tutoring, or given no education at all. Now the law requires that these children must be provided public education, in the regular classroom if possible.

5. Children with learning disabilities such as dyslexia (severe reading problems) or hyperactivity (high activity levels with low concentration ability) have generally been part of the regular classroom, but they need special attention and help to learn to cope with their problems.

6. Learning disabilities may originate in a brain dysfunction of some sort, but whether the cause is organic or not, many educational and psychological measures can help children with these disabilities. Psychoactive drugs also help some children, but these should be used carefully and cautiously.

KEY TERMS

obesity *(360)*
reaction time *(364)*
mainstreaming *(367)*
resource room *(367)*
specific learning
  disability *(369)*
dyslexia *(369)*
dyscalcula *(370)*
dysgraphia *(370)*

minimal brain
  dysfunction *(370)*
hyperactivity *(372)*
attention deficit
  disorder *(374)*
provocation
  ecologies *(377)*
rarefaction
  ecologies *(377)*

KEY QUESTIONS

1. What causes the variation in physical growth and skill in middle childhood?

2. How does obesity affect a child's development?

3. What are the advantages of mainstreaming?

4. What are the disadvantages of mainstreaming?

5. What are the symptoms of learning disability?

6. What are the possible causes of hyperactivity?

7. What are the arguments for and against use of psychoactive drugs to control hyperactivity?

8. What other types of treatment are helpful in controlling hyperactivity?

RECOMMENDED READINGS

Farnham-Diggory, Sylvia. *Learning disabilities.* Cambridge, Mass.: Harvard University Press, 1978.

A readable and scholarly discussion of learning disabilities, including hyperactivity, as well as the disabilities that affect specific academic skills. The discussion of the definitions, causes, and treatments of learning disabilities makes clear how much we have yet to learn on this subject.

Wolff, Jurgen M., and **Lipe, Dewey.** *Help for the overweight child.* New York: Penguin Books, 1980.

A practical, balanced view of the world of the overweight child and how to change it. The book reflects the authors' good sense, as well as their knowledge of specific weight-control techniques developed by behaviorists.

Featherstone, Helen. *A difference in the family: Living with a disabled child.* New York: Penguin, 1981.

While many books discuss the problems of handicapped children, few reveal the difficulties a child's handicap raises for other members of the family. Written from her own experience, as well as from that of other parents, Featherstone honestly describes the emotional and practical strains of having a seriously disabled child. This book is recommended for everyone who would like more insight into the day-to-day lives of all families, not just "families with a difference."

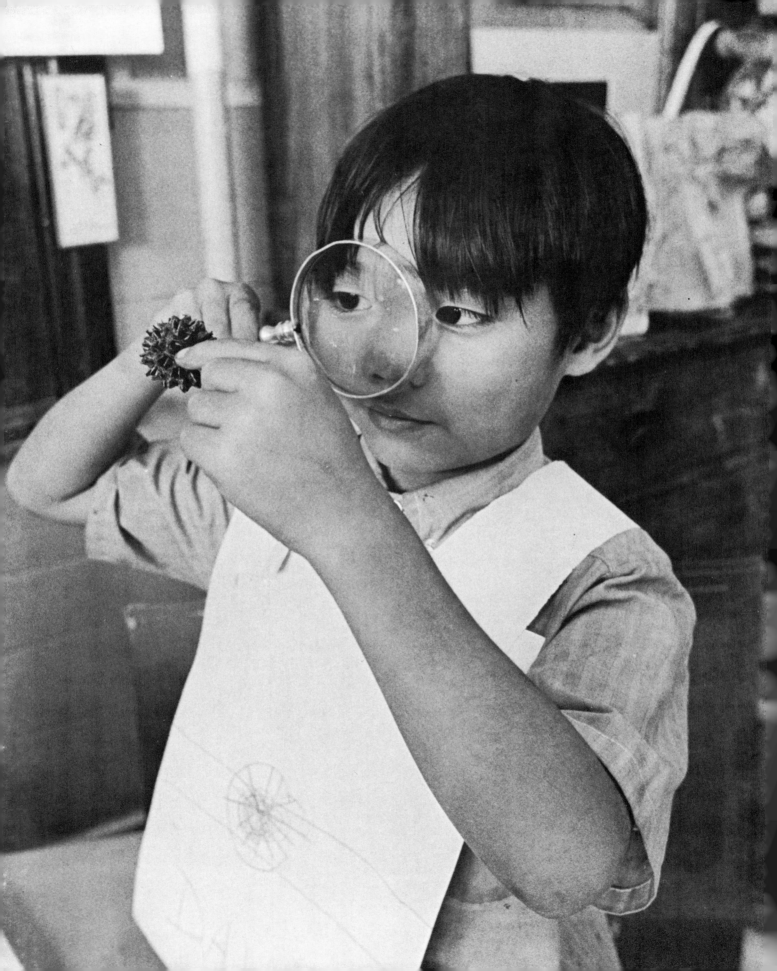

The School Years: Cognitive Development

Chapter 13

I hear, and I forget.
I see, and I remember.
I do, and I understand.

Ancient Chinese proverb

Ten years from now I will be 19, and
    probably in college, and live away
    from home . . .
But if I don't go to college, I will romp
    and roam.

Ten years from now I will be quite pretty,
    and have lots of dough . . .
and if I don't, Oh No!

Ten years from now everything will be
    fine, and I WILL BE MINE.

Rachel, age 9
"Ten Years from Now"

Concrete Operational Thought
The 5-to-7 Shift
Logical Ideas
Application of Concrete Concepts
Modifying Piaget

An Information-Processing View
Memory
Metamemory
Learning How to Learn

Language
Vocabulary
Grammar
Pragmatics
Nonstandard English
Learning a Second Language

Measuring Cognitive Development
Achievement Tests
Aptitude Tests

Chapter 13

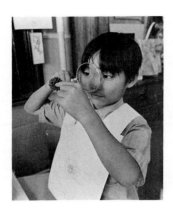

During the school years, children's cognitive development enables them to focus their thinking less egocentrically and more accurately on the facts and relationships that they experience in the world. They become astute observers who can organize objects according to their particular characteristics and understand ideas of time and distance. These new abilities to investigate the world more objectively will be among the topics of this chapter, as will the questions that follow:

How does the ability to recognize that people and objects can simultaneously belong to a number of different categories affect the child's understanding of subjects as diverse as mathematics, family relationships, and geography?

What cognitive developments account for the child's new grasp of concepts such as conservation of number and conservation of liquids?

What are some of the factors that affect how much children remember and how well they remember it?

What factors may influence a child's success in learning a second language?

What are some of the ways of measuring children's intellectual potential and achievement?

The thinking and learning of the typical 11-year-old is radically different from that of the typical 6-year-old. For example, most sixth-graders can figure out which brand and size of popcorn is the best buy, can be taught to multiply proper and improper fractions, can memorize a list of fifty new spelling words, and can use irony appropriately—accomplishments beyond virtually every first-grader.

Even their approach to learning is different. Take the first day of school, for example. Six-year-olds enter school filled with excitement and fear, often dressed in their Sunday best and clinging tightly to their mother's or father's hand. By age 11, children arrive at school with new notebooks and sharpened pencils, ready for the serious business of learning. They appear casual and confident, even when they aren't, and they would angrily balk if their parents offered to walk them to the classroom. While first-graders worry about getting lost or wetting their pants, sixth-graders worry about finishing homework or failing a test.

Not surprisingly, there is a vast difference as well in what teachers expect of students over this five-year period. If first-graders can learn to stay quiet when they are supposed to, read simple words, and add simple numbers, that's considered accomplishment enough. Sixth-graders are expected to know their multiplication tables and spelling rules; they are supposed to understand the morals of the stories they read and the general principles underlying the mathematical formulas they use. They are urged to plan ahead and to hand in work that is neat and correct.

These changes in behavior, attitudes, and expectations reflect, in part, the growth of children's cognitive abilities as their thinking becomes less egocentric and more logical. These abilities can be seen in the reasoning strategies children use, the school-related skills they master, and, as we shall see later, even in the jokes they tell. This chapter describes the cognitive processes that produce these skills, the language development that expresses them, as well as the rating systems, such as IQ and achievement tests, that are used to measure them.

Concrete Operational Thought

What underlies the differences we have just described is, according to Piaget, the attainment of **concrete operational thought,** through which children can reason about almost anything specific they perceive. Between ages 7 and 11, children usually come to understand logical principles, as long as the principles can be applied to concrete, or specific, cases. As they become increasingly able to decenter, they are able to think more objectively and are less likely to be misled by mere appearances or to peg their judgments on a single feature of an object or situation. They can watch water being poured from a narrow glass into a wide one and explain why the quantity of liquid remains the same. They can sort dogs into breeds or flowers into species without confusion. They are quick to say that 8 is greater than 5, and just as quick to confirm that 11,108 is greater than 11,105. Moreover, according to Piaget, their reasoning can be generalized across tasks and situations: thus if they can apply a logical principle in one context, they can apply it in other analogous contexts. However, they can reason only about the concrete, tangible things in their world: they are not yet able to reason about abstractions, as can the adolescent who has reached formal operational thought.

The 5-to-7 Shift

In Piaget's theory of the sequence of cognitive development, true concrete operational thinking is preceded by a transitional period between the ages of 5 and 7—sometimes called the **5-to-7 shift**—in which the child has not quite outgrown preoperational thought nor firmly reached concrete operational thought. Piaget notes that although children sometimes intuitively grasp the right answer on tests of concrete operational logic, they frequently do not understand the underlying principles that led them to their conclusion (Cowan, 1978).

For instance, many 6-year-olds may answer correctly on the conservation-of-liquids test (page 55), saying that the taller, narrower glass contains the same amount as the shorter wider glass, but when asked to explain their answer might act as if reasons are unnecessary because the answer is so obvious and the reasons too difficult to formulate. (The adult's "Why?" is typically answered with "Because.") They also might fail to arrive at the correct answer to another problem that depends on the same underlying principle. In the conservation-of-liquids experiment, for instance, a child might correctly answer that both glasses contain the same amount, but then, if the liquid from one of the glasses is poured into six smaller glasses, insist that the amount of liquid has increased. Piaget (1967) concludes: "Experimentation has shown decisively that until the age of seven, the child remains prelogical."

Logical Ideas

Beginning at about age 7 or 8, children become true concrete operational thinkers. The hallmark of concrete operational thought is the ability to understand certain logical principles—such as identity and reversibility—when these principles are applied to specific, or concrete, cases. (Identity, you will remember, is the idea that an object's content remains the same despite changes in its shape, and reversibility is the idea that a transformation process can be reversed to restore the original form.) A grasp of both identity and reversibility enables the child to realize, among other things, that rolling a ball of clay into a long, thin rope of clay does not alter the amount of clay.

Further, according to Piaget, once these principles are mastered, they can be applied in many contexts. Once children have a firm grasp of identity, for instance, they know that the number 24 is always 24, whether it is arrived at by adding 14 and 10 or 23 and 1; they also know that their mother was the same person when she was a child.

What seems to lie behind the child's understanding of concrete operational principles is the decline in egocentrism and the newly acquired ability to simultaneously hold in mind and relate various characteristics of objects, or persons, or situations (Biggs and Collis, 1982). This is particularly clear with the principle of **reciprocity,** the idea that a change in one dimension of an object effects a change in another dimension. Thus in the conservation-of-liquids test, the concrete operational thinker can mentally relate the differences between the height and width of the two glasses (realizing "It's taller but it's narrower" or "It's shorter but it's wider") and can therefore explain why the different-sized glasses contain the same amount of liquid.

Two other concepts become part of the child's way of thinking during middle childhood: *classification* and *seriation*. Mastery of both concepts reveals the child as a logical thinker rather than a thinker heavily influenced by superficial appearances or egocentric perceptions.

Classification and Class Inclusion   **Classification** is the concept that objects can be thought of in terms of categories, or classes. For example, a child's parents and siblings belong to the class called *family. Toys, animals, people,* and *food* are other everyday classes. According to Piaget, most preschool children understand these labels, but many do not understand that they refer to systematic categories (Inhelder and Piaget, 1970). Thus a preschool child might tell a sibling "If you hit me, you can't be in my family," and at the same time consider that family to include the pet dog and a litter of gerbils.

A related but more complicated concept is **class inclusion,** the idea that a particular object or person may belong to more than one class. Even when children younger than 8 have learned who is in their family and who is not, they are usually unable to think of a particular family member in terms of more than one category. Thus children who have brothers or sisters might assume that brothers and sisters belong to the category *child,* and that adults, therefore, cannot be brothers and sisters (Piaget, 1962). This confusion was illustrated in an interview between Piaget and a 7-year-old boy:

> Child: All boys are brothers.
> *Piaget: Is your father a brother?*
> Yes, when he was little.
> *Why was your father a brother?*
> Because he was a boy.
> *Do you know your father's brother?*
> He doesn't have a brother.

Children at this stage have a great deal of trouble not only with family categories and subcategories but with every type of classification. Consider the following experiment, modeled on a series of experiments conducted by Piaget. An examiner shows children seven toy dogs. Four of them are collies, and the other three are a poodle, an Irish setter, and a German shepherd. First the examiner questions the children to make sure that they know that all the toys are dogs and that they can name each breed. Then comes the crucial question: "Are there more collies or more dogs?" Until the concept of classification is firmly established, usually not until age 7 or 8, most children say "More collies." They cannot simultaneously keep in mind the general category *dog* and the subcategory *collie,* mentally shifting from one to the other.

Another experiment involves several levels of classification, with multicolored shapes that can be subdivided by color, or by shape, or by both color and shape. Inhelder and Piaget (1970) found that most children between 2½ and 5 were unable to sort multicolored shapes into categories consistently. Typically, when asked to put together the ones that belonged together, a 4-year-old would first put a circle next to a circle, but then, noticing that the second circle was blue, would put a blue square next to it. In all Piaget's classification experiments, children younger than 7 rarely show full comprehension of categories and subcategories. By contrast, school-age children sort such objects into shape and subdivide by color, or vice-versa, without a moment's hesitation, suggesting to Piaget that classification and class inclusion are well understood during the concrete operational period.

Seriation **Seriation** refers to the arrangement of items in a series, as in the laying out of sticks from shortest to longest, or of crayons from lightest to darkest. Like other logical operations, seriation begins to be understood toward the end of the preoperational period, but the concept is usually not firmly established until age 7 or 8. Thus, during the 5-to-7 shift, if a typical 6-year-old is asked to arrange a series of ten sticks according to length, the child might first put together three sticks—a short, medium, and long—and then insert the others, rearranging several of the sticks before getting the correct order. A typical 8-year-old, in contrast, would look at the whole jumble of sticks, pick out the shortest, then the next shortest, and so on, systematically and quickly arranging the series.

Figure 13.1 *Sorting these eggs may involve complex classification and seriation concepts, since the attributes of size, color, and species might all be relevant. It is a challenging task for a school-age child.*

Application of Concrete Concepts

Mathematics   Many of the concepts of concrete operational thought are said to underlie the basic ideas of elementary-school math. For instance, the concept of seriation may be necessary for a firm understanding of the number system. This would explain why 5-year-olds, who often can recite numbers correctly in sequence, are nevertheless often puzzled by simple questions such as "Which is greater, 6 or 8?" or "What number is one less than 5?" (Piaget and Szeminska, 1965). These concepts take a long time to develop; many first-graders need to do much finger-counting and hard thinking in order to add simple sums. In fact, in most cases, if you add one item (another apple, another penny) to a series of items that a 5-year-old has already counted, the child will have to count the series all over again to find out how many there are.

Figure 13.2 *Fractions are one of the most difficult concepts in elementary-school math. Children who have previously learned that each number in the sequence of whole numbers is larger than the one that came before have difficulty understanding that with fractions, this order is reversed:* $\frac{1}{8}$ *is smaller than* $\frac{1}{4}$, *which is smaller than* $\frac{1}{2}$. *As at earlier ages, children can come to understand such concepts more easily by using learning materials they can manipulate.*

Other math difficulties may occur because an understanding of classification is needed to comprehend place value. Thus many elementary-school children have trouble understanding the difference between, say, 501, 51, and 15. Similarly, without an understanding of reversibility, the child may not realize that if 6 + 5 equals 11, 11 minus 5 must equal 6; and without a grasp of reciprocity, the child will have trouble understanding that the area of a rectangle that is 1 inch by 30 inches is the same as the area of a rectangle that is 6 inches by 5 inches.

According to Piaget, until the child understands these ideas, math must be learned problem by problem—mostly by rote—rather than really understood. He says, "The indefinite series of numbers and, above all, the operations of addition (plus its inverse, subtraction) and multiplication (plus the inverse, division) are, on the average, accessible only after the age of seven" (Piaget, 1968).

Time and Distance Partly because children under 7 do not understand seriation, they have trouble understanding measurements of time and distance. Even telling time by looking at a clock is difficult, for the relationships between the minute and hour hands, and between A.M. and P.M. are hard to grasp. Similarly, decades and centuries are open to misinterpretation. Told the date of the first automobile, or of Emancipation, a 6-year-old might ask his or her parents if they were alive before cars were invented, or if they saw the slaves being given their freedom. Such mistakes are rare by age 8, when the basic thought processes of concrete operational thought enable children to have a better understanding of the passage of time (Piaget, 1970a).

Likewise, distance concepts are so poorly understood before middle childhood that, after looking at a map, a 6-year-old might talk about taking a walk from California to New York or, even more telling, from Toronto to Canada. This lack of a sense of distance, plus a lack of classification skills, lead to frustration for those who try to teach first-grade children the geographical distinctions between cities, states, and countries.

Figure 13.3 *When they were a few years younger, at the preoperational stage, these children might have thought that a walk around the actual continental United States would not take much longer than a walk around this one.*

However, once children attain concrete operational thought, they understand that some places are at a distance much farther than they can see or walk to, and that one geographical area may be part of other geographically defined areas. Sometimes they delight in their new understanding so much that, in giving their addresses, they include not only their names, streets, cities, and states but also their country, continent, and hemisphere, and then "the Earth, the Solar System, the Milky Way Galaxy, the Universe."

Combining the concepts of time, speed, and distance is even harder than understanding any one of these ideas separately. When shown two toy trains that move along a track, one of them stopping farther along than the other, preoperational children always say that the one in front is the faster—regardless of when or where the trains started or how fast they were actually traveling (Piaget, 1970b). The ability to judge the relationship of time, speed, and distance develops gradually throughout concrete operational thought.

Modifying Piaget

As noted at several points in earlier discussions of Piagetian theory, a number of cognitive researchers have attempted to modify certain of Piaget's ideas by emphasizing the individual differences in, and the unevenness of, children's progress through the cognitive stages described by Piaget. Whereas Piaget tended to describe the child's movement from one stage to the next as occurring fairly quickly once begun, and also as occurring across the board, in all domains, these researchers maintain that the child enters a new stage gradually in certain domains—say, math or science—but not in others, like social understanding.

Particularly in the case of concrete operational thought, these researchers believe that cognitive development is considerably more heterogeneous, or inconsistent, than Piaget's descriptions would suggest. According to Flavell (1982), two of the factors that account for this heterogeneity are the hereditary differences among individuals in terms of abilities and aptitudes and the environmental differences in terms of "cultural, educational, and other task-related experiential background." The sum of these differences, says Flavell, might well produce a great deal of cognitive heterogeneity:

> Imagine, for example, a child or adolescent who is particularly well-endowed with the abilities needed to do computer science, has an all-consuming interest in it, has ample time and opportunity to learn about it, and has an encouraging parent who is a computer scientist (whence much of the aptitude, interest, and opportunity, perhaps). The quality and sophistication of the child's thinking in this area might well be higher than that of most adults in any area. It would also likely be much higher in this area than in most other areas of the child's cognitive life. His level of moral reasoning or skill in making inferences about other people might be considerably less developed, for instance. The heterogeneity could be a matter of time constraints as well as a matter of differential aptitudes and interests; that is, time spent at the computer terminal is time not spent interacting with and learning about people.

As we saw in Chapter 10, some researchers have also suggested that many children demonstrate signs of at least partial entrance into concrete operational thought earlier than Piaget would have predicted. This contention is bolstered by studies (Anglin, 1977; Winer, 1980; Koslowski, 1980) showing that on simplified versions of Piagetian tests for classification and seriation, preschoolers sometimes reveal the same kind of "fragile" grasp of these concepts that we saw them reveal for conservation and perspective-taking in Chapter 10.

The Legacy of Piaget   Despite these revisions and criticisms, Piaget's comprehensive view of children's cognitive development is considered correct in most aspects. Regarding school-age children, three of Piaget's ideas in particular have been supported time and time again as further research has been performed. First, compared to the thinking of the preschool child, the thought of the school-age child is characterized by a more comprehensive logic, and markedly broader grasp of the underlying assumptions and ideas of rational thought. While the specific concepts of conservation, classification, and so forth, may not distinguish the thinking of the 8-year-old from that of the 4-year-old as definitively as Piaget believed they do, the typical overall thinking of the 8-year-old on almost any issue is less egocentric and more logical than the 4-year-old's.

Second, children are active learners. They learn best by questioning, exploring, and doing. In fact, Piaget's theories provided the theoretical framework for making American classrooms in the 1970s and 1980s quite different places from those in the 1950s (Ravitch, 1983) (see Closer Look on the next page).

Figure 13.4 *These shelves are evidence that the schoolteacher in charge here applies two of Piaget's ideas—that children learn by doing and that children learn in a variety of ways.*

Finally, how children think is as important as what they know. Piaget's interest in the underlying structures of thought has led to a realization that what distinguishes the thinking of school-age children from that of preschoolers is not new information but new cognitive organizations. What children need to learn, then, is not so much new facts as new ways to assemble facts (Flavell, 1985).

Piaget in the Classroom

My own grade-school education began in a traditional American public school in the late 1940s, before Piaget's ideas had become known to American educators. I remember that the children sat at assigned desks that were bolted to the floor, all doing the same work at the same time. The teacher sat at a desk in the front. Her job, in addition to instructing, was to announce, according to a fixed schedule, the task of the moment (such as doing a math worksheet on the 4× table, or taking turns reading out loud beginning on a certain page), and to make sure everyone did it, with no interaction among the students (whispering and passing notes were forbidden). Work was graded, and students who got everything correct had gold stars attached to their papers, and their neatly printed work might be displayed on the wall. These students might also be appointed "line leader" for the class's single-file march to the lunchroom. For those who were quick and eager learners, it was a pretty boring routine.

This approach had changed dramatically by the time my oldest children began public school in the mid 1970s, partly because educators had begun to hear of Piaget. Many regarded his understanding of children and children's minds as being much more perceptive and benevolent than the assumptions that lay behind traditional education, which, some felt, fostered prejudice, passive learning, and competition while discouraging creativity, social skills, and emotional development (Silberman, 1970; Featherstone, 1971; Howes, 1974). The growing acceptance of Piagetian theory provided the foundation for a new form of education, called open education. In the setting of the open classroom—in which many learning areas were open to the child at once—children of various abilities, and often of various ages, learned together, finding the curriculum topic and level that suited them. For instance, my eldest daughter began to teach herself to read as a kindergartener because she enjoyed the phonics cards that were intended primarily for her second-grade classmates. However, in the first grade she avoided math because she spent most of her time making a book of "poetry," and that was fine with her teacher.

Because Piagetians believe that children grasp the underlying concepts of typical elementary schoolwork more readily if they are actively involved with educational experiences, the emphasis in the classroom is on learning by doing. Counting blocks, or adding nickels and dimes, or measuring the length and width of the classroom is thought to be far more instructive than watching the teacher solve arithmetic problems on the blackboard. Likewise, building a grass house, molding a clay pot, and stringing a fishnet, and then writing about the process, are regarded as more enlightening and memorable than merely reading about these activities in a social studies book. Similarly, class discussion of how and why one society is different from another is considered more intellectually stimulating than simply having the teacher point out various cultural differences. Interaction among children should be welcomed rather than discouraged, for learning is active and social, not passive and solitary. Especially in elementary school, the classroom should be a place where children can experiment and explore, discovering ideas and relationships between ideas for themselves.

Another crucial idea is that the rate of development is different for each child and, "from the Piagetian perspective, there are 'optimal periods' for the growth of particular mental structures which cannot be rushed" (Elkind, 1969). As Eleanor Duckworth (1972) explains:

It is almost impossible for an adult to know exactly the right time for a given question for a given child—especially for a teacher who is concerned with thirty or more children. Children can raise the right question for themselves when the setting is right.

[Schools] can help to uncover parts of the world which children would not otherwise know how to tackle . . . . Schools and teachers can provide materials and ask questions in ways that suggest things being done with them; and children, in the doing, cannot help being inventive. [This means] providing a setting which suggests wonderful ideas to children—different ideas to different children—as they get caught up in intellectual problems that are real to them.

The Piagetian view of school learning was not accepted by all educational theorists. It ran counter to the advice from learning theorists, who believed that Piaget grossly underestimated the role of specific teaching and external reinforcement. According to learning theory, each skill and each acquisition of a concept is the result of a chain of learned responses. Consequently, rather than waiting until a child's internal self-regulation makes possible an understanding of subtraction, for instance, a teacher should give the child math lessons, beginning with simple

The differences in these two classrooms are so striking that it is hard to imagine that both photos depict the same event: an attempt to teach math and language arts to third-graders. In the top photo, the teacher uses the traditional "talk and chalk" technique, and the children either quietly try to absorb the material or search for distraction. In the open classroom in the second photo, the teacher does not preside at the front of the room, but, instead, works among the children as they pursue projects that are particularly suited to their needs.

counting exercises, then adding, then subtracting. If the process is carefully planned, and the child is reinforced at each step, the child will learn math concepts and facts earlier and better than children who are left to discover these ideas on their own.

Whereas Piagetians are chiefly interested in the process of learning, learning theorists look more at the product; their focus is on ways of getting children to arrive at the right answers with increasing frequency. Learning theorists therefore emphasize the importance of correcting children's mistakes as well as rewarding their accomplishments. Behaviorists also believe that facts are best learned if they are overlearned, and that repeated practice in penmanship, spelling, and math skills is the best way to ensure that they will be retained years later.

Learning theorists do agree with Piaget on at least this point: the steps in the learning process, and the rate at which they are taken, should be geared to the individual. However, when students do not learn, say the learning theorists, it is not because they have yet to reach some stage of cognitive development. Rather, the teacher might be too punitive, or might inadvertently reward poor performance with special attention, or might try to teach too much too fast rather than dividing the curriculum into carefully programmed steps.

Obviously, disagreements about the best form of elementary education are far from settled, in the classrooms of the country or the halls of government. For example, the Piagetian emphasis on the child's "discovery" of the principles of learning has recently been criticized by the "back to basics" movement, which emphasizes teaching specific basic facts, as well as the use of standardized tests that mark progress and indicate whether or not a child should fail (Ravitch, 1983).

Further, the correctness of any particular educational theory does not necessarily determine what happens in the classroom. Indeed, economic realities, political philosophy, and value questions (such as whether children should learn facts or concepts, a body of knowledge or a way of thinking) are at least as influential on school policy as educational theory. However, whether a child is in an open or highly structured classroom, there is no doubt that Piaget's ideas have made learning a much more active and individualized process than it was. For that today's children and their teachers should be grateful.

An Information-Processing View

Piaget's emphasis on the structures of cognition, as well as the learning theorists' stress on reinforced learning of specific skills and facts, has guided a new group of cognitive researchers who have synthesized many Piagetian and learning theory ideas (Brown et al., 1983). This group takes what is called an **information-processing** view of human learning, so named because it uses the functioning of the computer as a rough model for the workings of the human mind. These researchers do not suggest that the mind processes information exactly like a computer: obviously we have intuition, creativity, and a capacity to change over time that no computer can match. However, the information-processing view has led to a more precise understanding of the way the mind functions, and has had important educational implications.

Figure 13.5 *According to information-processing theory, the output of the human mind depends not only on the input but also on the capacity of the brain to store, organize, and retrieve what it has received.*

In applying the information-processing model to children's learning, developmentalists emphasize that the output of a computer depends not only on the input, that is, the information fed into it, but also on the program and capacity of the computer. Unless the computer is programmed to understand the input, and has the memory capacity to hold it, the computer cannot process the input correctly. Consequently, say the proponents of this view, instead of simply looking at the general educational milieu of the child, we must also look closely at the capacity and program of the child's mind.

Memory

The topic most studied by those using the information-processing model has been memory. Developmentalists have suggested that there are two aspects of memory that should be considered separately. One is **memory capacity**—how much information the brain can hold and how well it can be processed and stored. The other, **metamemory,** involves the understanding and use of various memory techniques that can be used to keep things in mind.

Memory Capacity Memory capacity involves three levels of storage. The first is called the **sensory register,** which temporarily stores sensory information as it is received (as in the afterimage that occurs like an instant photo when you close your eyes). The sensory register holds material very briefly, for less than a second. As best we can tell, the capacity of the sensory register is about the same in children of all ages and in adults (Hoving et al., 1978).

Once in the sensory register, material fades unless it is processed and stored in **short-term memory,** where it stays for up to a minute. From short-term memory, material may be further processed into **long-term memory,** where it can remain for days, months, or years. A simplified version of this processing and storage sequence can be seen in the following example. Say you are listening to a radio show and hear a call-in phone number announced for a contest. If you have no interest in calling, and therefore are paying no attention to the number, the number will get no further than your sensory register: you will not recall it. If you do want to call, and mentally note the number, it will move to short-term memory, probably staying there long enough for you to dial the call. However, unless you have repeated the number to yourself several times, or have noted some memorable peculiarity in the sequence of numbers, the phone number will not have moved into long-term memory. If you get a busy signal and try to dial again, you may find yourself unable to do so.

Although it is impossible to equate exactly the various memory tests given to children and those given to adults, as well as to measure precisely short-term memory and long-term memory for both age groups, a careful review of memory research concludes that, by school age at least, the basic memory capacity of children is quite similar to that of adults (Stern, 1985). That is, children can store about as many items of information, for about as long, as adults can. Thus differences in capacity are not the primary reason memory improves notably between ages 6 and 11, and continues to improve thereafter.

Metamemory

The main reason adults remember better than children, and older children remember better than younger children, is the difference in their respective metamemories (Ross and Kerst, 1978; Brown and De Loache, 1978; Liben, 1982; Stern, 1985). Let us look at metamemory in more detail.

Selective Attention One key to being able to remember well is knowing that one should pay attention to certain items and ignore others. A review of the research on **selective attention** (Pick et al., 1975) found that the ability to screen out distractions and to concentrate improves steadily during middle childhood.

One classic experiment showed this development (Maccoby and Hagen, 1965). Children between the ages of 6 and 12 were asked to remember the background colors of a series of pictures—an elephant, a scooter, a water bucket, and so forth. They were not asked to remember the subjects of the pictures. As expected, memory for background colors improved steadily with age: 12-year-olds remembered almost twice as accurately as 6-year-olds. Then the children were asked to name the subjects of the pictures. Ability to remember in this case improved only slightly with age, and then declined. In fact, 12-year-olds apparently had learned to focus their attention and ignore unnecessary information so well that they were actually worse than 6-year-olds at remembering which subjects were on which backgrounds!

Figure 13.6 *What's wrong with this picture? If the boy here is really trying to do his homework, there are several sources of distraction that do not belong in this scene.*

Memory Techniques Beyond improved ability to concentrate selectively, what else do older children do to help them remember? Apparently, older children are better able, and much more likely, to use **mnemonic,** or memory-aiding, devices (Fabricius and Wellman, 1983). For example, they use **rehearsal,** the repetition of the items to be remembered; or they group items to be remembered into categories, a technique called **chunking.** One way to memorize the fifty states by chunking, for instance, would be to learn them by region, or to learn the eight states that begin with "M," the eight that begin with "N," the three that begin with "A," and so forth. A third technique is memorizing general rules rather than specific cases, especially exceptional cases. For instance, if children try to learn irregular spellings simply by trying to memorize them, they will not do very well. They will do much better if, instead, they memorize rules for such irregularities, such as "'i' before 'e' except after 'c,'" "'full' has a double 'l' only when it stands alone, so be careful," and dozens more.

Older children's ability to use strategies to help them remember was shown in one experiment in which preschool, first-grade, and fifth-grade children were shown a series of pictures (Appel et al., 1972). Half of them were simply told to "look" at the pictures, and the other half were told to "try to remember" the names of the pictures.

Under either instruction, the preschool children usually just stared at the pictures and, on average, correctly remembered the nine pictures they were shown about as well when they were told simply to look (48 percent) as when they were told to remember (46 percent). In first grade, children remembered an average of

66 percent of twelve pictures when told to remember, and 63 percent when told to look—again, an insignificant difference. However, when fifth-graders were told to remember, they were much more likely to repeat the names of the pictures to themselves, and to organize the pictures into clusters to make remembering easier. Even though they had fifteen pictures to study, they remembered 81 percent when told to remember compared to 62 percent when told to look.

The conclusions one can draw from this experiment are similar to those from other research: by age 11, most children have learned how to use mnemonic devices, and are ready to apply them when faced with a memory task. Is this learning the spontaneous result of cognitive maturity, or is it the result of specific teaching? While some of it may be self-taught, there is no doubt that metamemory techniques can be taught to children (Stern, 1985). Experimenters have found that even a short practice session with instruction in rehearsal or chunking usually results in improved memory performance in school-age children (Hagen et al., 1975). Similar findings come from naturalistic studies which compare children who have radically different educational experiences. For instance, one study found that children from Liberia who had been trained in memorizing the Koran performed significantly better on a similar memorizing task than Liberian children who had not been trained, even though the actual material to be remembered was equally familiar to both groups (Scribner and Cole, 1981).

Learning How to Learn

The investigation into metamemory led information-processing researchers to look more closely at the steps of learning in general. The study of **metacognition**, or techniques of thinking, is now underway in many laboratories and classrooms.

One general principle has been recognized. It is that children and adults learn new material best when they can link it to some schema or cognitive framework, either one they already have in their possession or one they are currently learning. A simple example of this is learning to spell (Henderson, 1985). Children's first attempts at spelling are rife with phonetic fallacies, as they try to link the sounds they hear to the letters they think make those sounds. Typically, they write "likt" for "liked" and "kaek" for "cake." Rather than memorizing correct spellings word by word, they need to recognize the general rules that they already sometimes use, such as that "ed," not "t," makes the past tense, or that the "k" sound at the beginning of words is much more often a "c" than a "k." Later on, difficult new words with the same root are better learned together than one by one, as are special cases that are similar, such as silent-"p" spellings like "pneumatic," "pneumonia," and "pneumonic."

The importance of a cognitive framework as an aid to memory was shown by an experiment that compared the ability of second-graders, sixth-graders, and adults to use the sequence of a story to remember the story's details (Buss et al., 1983). All three groups were quite able to remember details of a story that was correctly sequenced, but when faced with the task of remembering details from a story that was out of sequence, only the older children and the adults performed well, because both these groups spontaneously unscrambled the story to aid recall. However, after minimal instruction in how sequence could help, second-graders also were able to create a coherent structure to aid their memories. Research such as this suggests to developmentalists that part of the education process should be helping children create structures, strategies, and links arising from their past experiences to help them integrate the knowledge they are receiving.

Figure 13.7 *In a few years, the barefoot Pilgrim woman on the left will be able to memorize all her lines. Meanwhile, the technique of linking abstract historical information to concrete experiences improves both memory and understanding. Mnemonic devices are useful too: When did Columbus sail the ocean blue?*

In fact, if children are not helped to relate new information to their existing knowledge, they will create their own, often misleading, relationships between facts. As one scientist explains:

> Learners try to link new information to what they already know in order to interpret the new material in terms of established schemata. This is why students interpret science demonstrations in terms of their naive theories and why they hold onto their naive theories for so long. The scientific theories that children are being taught in school often cannot compete as reference points for new learning because they are presented quickly and abstractly and so remain unorganized and unconnected to past experience. [Resnick, 1983]

Information processing also emphasizes the importance of the sequence in which material to be learned is presented. For example, in one experiment (Hawkins et al., 1984), children were tested on their ability to follow the logic of paired statements. The children were to pretend that each statement was entirely true and then answer the question that followed. Some of the paired statements were about real things that fit into what the children already knew. For example:

> Rabbits never bite. Cuddly is a rabbit. Does Cuddly bite?

Others were pure fantasy. For example:

> Merds laugh when they're happy. Animals that laugh don't like mushrooms. Do merds like mushrooms?

Finally, some statements went against what the children knew. For example:

> Glasses bounce when they fall. Everything that bounces is made of rubber. Are glasses made of rubber?

Not surprisingly, the nature of the statements influenced the children's ability to answer correctly. Statements that were consistent with the children's existing knowledge were generally answered logically; those that contradicted the child's knowledge were generally answered illogically, with the fantasy examples midway between the two. But the most interesting influence was the specific order of presentation of the examples. Those children who heard the fantasy examples first were much more likely to get problems of all kinds correct than were those who heard the incongruent problems first. Apparently, the fantasy problems helped the children learn how to do these logical problems, preparing them for the apparent nonsense to follow.

This example, and many others like it, emphasize the information-processing point that input should be geared to the program; that is, that the teaching material and sequence of instruction should be adapted to fit the child's cognitive structures. This point, in turn, serves to remind cognitive psychologists and educators that various theories or methods of education may be good for some children some of the time, but not necessarily for most children most of the time (Bennett, 1976; Rotberg, 1981; Minuchin and Shapiro, 1983).

Figure 13.8 *Information-processing theory emphasizes the importance of teaching children the techniques of learning, rather than encouraging them to learn by rote. These sixth-grade students who are becoming acquainted with the use of the dictionary will be better equipped for the vocabulary and spelling demands of later life than those children who have learned to rely mainly on memorized letter sequences and definitions.*

Another lesson from information processing, as well as from other perspectives, is that children's mental structures may vary, depending on age, learning style, and prior experience, and therefore one step in planning education is to design it for the particular child's "program." This does not mean, however, that educators need wait until a particular child is ready for a certain bit of knowledge. In fact, the information-processing view suggests that the idea of "readiness" may have been overemphasized; at least by middle childhood, most children are ready to learn almost any concrete skill or concept, including learning how to learn through metamemory and metacognition techniques. Postponing such learning may be a mistake, according to information-processing theory, for trying to teach facts without linking them to concepts, and expecting children to remember without showing them how to do so, will result in children who forget much of what they have

Figure 13.9 *Although computers are no substitute for talented teachers, they make good partners, capable of providing instruction and practice that can be tailored to the child's cognitive development. Another plus is that computers provide immediate, nonthreatening feedback that helps children identify and correct their own mistakes.*

been taught and cannot apply what they do remember (Resnick, 1983). As you will soon see, these insights about the structures of knowledge apply to language learning just as they do to learning the concepts of math or science. In the next chapter, we will see how they apply to the knowledge that children gain as their social world expands.

Language

As you saw in Chapter 10, the preschool years are the time of a language explosion, in which children's vocabulary, grammar, and pragmatic language skills develop with marked rapidity. Language development during the years from age 6 to 11 is also remarkable, though much more subtle, as children consciously come to understand language *as language*. This understanding gives them greater control in their comprehension and use of language, and, in turn, enlarges the range of their cognitive powers generally. Their understanding of language is a powerful key to new understandings of themselves and their world.

Vocabulary

During middle childhood, children begin to really enjoy words. This is demonstrated in the poems they write (Koch, 1970; Lewis, 1977, 1978), the secret languages they create, and the jokes they tell (see Closer Look on page 400). This makes middle childhood a good time to explicitly help children expand their vocabularies, thus providing a foundation for more elaborate self-expression.

One of the most important language developments during middle childhood is a shift in the way children think about words. Gradually during middle childhood they become more analytic and logical in their processing of vocabulary, and less restricted to the actions and perceptual features directly associated with particular words (Holzman, 1983). When a child is asked to say the first word that comes to mind on hearing, say, "apple," the preschooler is likely to be bound to the immediate context of an apple, responding with a word that refers to its appearance ("red," "round") or to an action associated with it ("eat," "cook"). The older child or adult, on the other hand, is likely to respond to "apple" by referring to an appropriate category ("fruit," "snack") or to other objects that logically extend the context ("banana," "pie," "tree").

Similarly, when they define words, preschoolers tend to use examples, especially examples that are action-bound. For instance, while preschoolers understand that "under," "below," and "above" refer to relative position, they define these words with examples such as "Rover sleeps under the bed," or "Below is to go down under something." Older children tend to define words by analyzing their relationship to other words: they would be more likely to say, for instance, that "under" is the same as "below," or the opposite of "above" (Holzman, 1983).

Figure 13.10 *Language-skill development is probably the most important part of the elementary-school curriculum. It can be fostered in many ways, one of which is to help children describe the characteristics and relationships of everyday objects. For example, this is the best age to teach comparatives, such as small, smaller, smallest.*

Older children's more analytic understanding of words is particularly useful as children are increasingly exposed to words that may have no direct referent in their own personal experience. This understanding makes it possible for them to add to their conceptual framework abstract terms such as "mammal" (extracting the commonalities of, say, whales and mice) or foreign terms such as *yen* (relating this unit of currency to the dollar), and to differentiate among similar words such as "big," "huge," and "gigantic," or "running," "jogging," and "sprinting." Thus, the cognitive maturation of middle childhood, coupled with the school experiences that children have, encourages children to link words with other words. The combination of maturation and experience leads to more rapid intellectual processing, as well as continued vocabulary development.

A CLOSER LOOK   **Thinking and Joking**

In recent years several developmental psychologists have looked at children's humor, finding that cognitive growth in a number of areas, including language, is clearly reflected in the things that children in middle childhood find funny. One of these researchers, Daniel Yalisove (1975, 1978), analyzed children's jokes in considerable detail. He found three types of humor that flourish during middle childhood, each one reflecting different aspects of cognitive development, including the ability to manipulate language playfully.

Language-Ambiguity Jokes

Yalisove calls many of the favorite jokes during middle childhood *language-ambiguity jokes,* for they center on a play on words. Here are four examples:

Why didn't the woman leave the house even when a bear was chasing her?
(Because she didn't want to be seen with a bare behind.)

What is the difference between a jeweler and a jailer?
(One sells watches and the other watches cells.)

Order, order in the court!
(Ham and cheese on rye, your honor.)

If April showers bring May flowers, what do May flowers bring?
(Pilgrims.)

In order to understand jokes like these, the child must not only know that words can have two meanings, and that certain words that sound the same have different meanings, but must also be mentally flexible enough to switch quickly from one meaning to the other. Jokes involving language play become increasingly popular as the child progresses through elementary school. Yalisove (1978) found that two out of every three riddles asked by fourth- and fifth-graders involved puns or some other

form of language ambiguity. Neither younger nor older children used these devices as often as the 9- and 10-year-olds did.

Reality Riddles

Other aspects of cognitive growth are reflected in the riddles children prefer. Consider these two favorites of first- and second-grade children.

How many balls of string does it take to reach around the world?
(One, but it had better be a big one.)

What is even worse than biting into an apple and finding a worm?
(Finding half a worm.)

Yalisove calls riddles like these *reality riddles,* because the child must have a notion of the way things really are in order to perceive the humor in the riddles. To appreciate the first riddle, the child must have a sense of relative size and distance; to appreciate the second, a sense of cause and effect. These ideas are beyond most preschool children, who are in the period of preoperational thought. But school-age children are able to reason about specific events and observable objects, and take delight in using their growing mental powers. Their new way of thinking enables them to realize how big a ball of string would have to be to reach around the world and to know where the other half of the worm must be (McGhee, 1971).

Absurdity Riddles

A third type of joke becomes more common toward the end of middle childhood. Yalisove calls these *absurdity riddles.* For example:

Grammar   Similar progress occurs in grammar. Although most grammatical constructions of the child's mother tongue are mastered before age 6, knowledge of syntax continues to develop throughout elementary school (Chomsky, 1969; Romaine, 1984). Children are increasingly able to use grammar to understand the implied connections between words, even if the usual clues, such as word order, are misleading.

For instance, children younger than age 6 often have trouble understanding the passive voice, because they know that the agency of action in a sentence usually precedes the object acted upon. By middle childhood, however, most children realize that "The truck was bumped by the car" does not mean that the truck did the bumping (de Villiers and de Villiers, 1978). The increasing understanding of the

During middle childhood, children come into their own as joketellers, punsters, and comic raconteurs. No matter what kind of funny business children share, their relating it in secret adds to the hilarity. However, chances are that if the words this girl is whispering were written here, few readers of this book would find them funny. Humor depends not only on context but also on the cognitive stage of the listener.

How do you fit six elephants into a VW?
(Three in the front and three in the back.)

What did the wild-game hunter do when a herd of elephants wearing sunglasses stampeded toward him?
(Nothing. He didn't recognize them.)

What's the easiest way to sink a submarine?
(Knock on the door.)

In order to find these riddles funny, a person has to be able to understand that once the absurd premise of the riddle is accepted, the absurd answers are actually logical. Assuming that elephants can be fitted into a VW, that sunglasses thoroughly disguise appearance, or that sailors in submarines open the door when someone knocks, the answer in each case is sensible. A grasp of the logic within the absurdity is what makes these jokes funny rather than stupid, and requires an understanding of hypothetical ideas and logical consequences which begins to emerge at about age 11 and is characteristic of adolescent thought (which we will explore in Chapter 16).

passive voice is reflected in children's spontaneous speech as well as in research studies: compared to 6-year-olds, 8-year-olds use the passive voice two-and-a-half times as frequently, and 10-year-olds, three-and-a-half times as often (Romaine, 1984).

Similarly, Carol Chomsky (1969) found that upon hearing "John promised Mary to shovel the driveway," children younger than 8 were likely to be misled by the adjacency of "Mary" and the verb infinitive and conclude that Mary is going to do the shoveling. Older children, on the other hand, were not distracted by the fact that "to shovel" followed immediately after "Mary": they knew that Mary was the promisee, which meant John had to be the shoveler.

Chomsky (1969) also demonstrated that with every passing year of middle childhood, children's grasp of syntactical structure is less likely to get confused by detail that is irrelevant to the meaning of the structure. When Chomsky first presented children with a large doll and asked, "Is this doll easy to see or hard to see?" even preschool children answered correctly. But when Chomsky put a blindfold on the doll, most of the sixteen 5- and 6-year-olds answered the same question by saying the doll was hard to see. Only three of the fifteen 7- and 8-year-olds made this mistake, and none of the nine 9- and 10-year-olds were misled by the blindfold.

TABLE 13.1   **Age-Related Adherence to Syntax**

Age of Child	Wrong (Percentage Answering "Hard to see")	Correct (Percentage Answering "Easy to see")
5	78%	22%
6	57%	43%
7	14%	86%
8	25%	75%
9	0%	100%
10	0%	100%

The school-age child's gradual understanding of logical relations helps in the understanding of other constructions such as the correct use of comparatives ("longer," "deeper," "wider"), of the subjunctive ("If you were a millionaire . . ."), and of metaphors (that is, of how someone could be a dirty dog or a rotten egg). The ability to use these constructions depends on a certain level of cognitive development that typically occurs during elementary school. This is true even with languages in which the particular construction is relatively simple. For instance, the subjunctive form is much less complicated in Russian than in English, but Russian-speaking children master the subjunctive only slightly earlier than English-speaking children, because the concept if-things-were-other-than-they-are must be understood before the form can be (de Villiers and de Villiers, 1978).

School-age children have another decided advantage over younger children when it comes to mastering the more difficult forms of grammar. Whereas preschool children are quite stubborn in clinging to their grammatical mistakes (remember the child in Chapter 10 who "holded" the baby bunnies?), school-age children are more teachable. They no longer judge correctness solely on the basis of their egocentric version of the rules, or on their own speech patterns. Assuming that they have had ample opportunity to learn the correct grammar, by the end of middle childhood, children are able to apply the rules of proper grammar when asked to, even if they don't use them in their own everyday speech. Thus, even if they themselves say "Me and Suzy quarreled," they are able to understand that "Suzy and I quarreled" is considered correct.

Pragmatics

You have already seen that preschoolers have a grasp of some of the pragmatic aspects of language: they change the tone of their voice when talking to a doll, for instance, or when pretending to be a doctor. However, preschoolers are not very skilled at modifying vocabulary, sentence length, and nonverbal cues to fit particular situations. The many skills of communicating improve markedly throughout middle childhood, as children become less egocentric.

One of the clearest demonstrations of schoolchildren's improved pragmatic skills is to be found in their joke-telling, which, in addition to the abilities mentioned in the Closer Look on page 400, demands several skills not usually apparent in younger children—the ability to listen carefully; the ability to know what someone else will think is funny; and, hardest of all, the ability to remember the right way to tell the joke. Telling a joke is beyond most preschool children. If asked to do so, they usually just say a word (such as "pooh-pooh") or describe an action ("shooting someone with a water gun") that they think is funny. Even if they actually use a joke form, they usually miss the point. As one child said after listening to her older sisters tell jokes on a long car trip, "What happens when a car goes into a tunnel?" "What?" her sisters asked. "It gets dark" came the "punch line." By contrast, almost every 7-year-old can tell a favorite joke upon request (Yalisove, 1978).

The process of asking a riddle shows another pragmatic skill that develops during middle childhood—teasing or tricking someone, especially an adult, verbally. Whereas a 7-year-old is likely to deliver the punch line as soon as the listener says "I don't know," or even before, a 10-year-old is more likely to demand several guesses before giving the correct answer with a self-satisfied grin.

Further evidence of increased pragmatic skill is shown in children's learning the various forms of polite speech. School-age children realize that a teacher's saying "I would like you to put away your books now" is not a simple statement of preference but a command in polite form (Holzman, 1983). Similarly, compared to 5-year-olds, 7- and 9-year-olds are quicker to realize that when making requests of persons of higher status—particularly persons who seem somewhat unwilling to grant the request—they should use more polite phrases ("Could I please . . . ?") and more indirect requests ("It would be nice if . . . ") than when they are negotiating with their peers (Axia and Baroni, 1985).

Code-Switching   Changing from one form of speech to another is called **code-switching.** As we will see, children in middle childhood can engage in many forms of code-switching, from the relatively simple process of censoring profanity when they talk to their parents to the complete switch from one language to another.

One of the most obvious examples of code-switching is children's use of one form of speech when they are in the classroom and another when they are with friends after school. In general, the former code, called *elaborated,* is associated with middle-class norms for correct language, while the latter, called *restricted,* is closer to the lower-class norms for pronunciation and vocabulary, as well as for grammar (Bernstein, 1971, 1973). The **elaborated code** is characterized by extensive vocabulary, complex syntax, and lengthy sentences; the **restricted code** by comparison has a much more limited use of vocabulary and syntax and relies more on gestures and intonation to convey meaning. The elaborated code is relatively context-free: the meaning of its statements is explicit. The restricted code tends to be context-bound, relying on the shared understandings and experience of speaker and listener to provide some of the meaning. Switching from one code to another, a disspirited student might tell a teacher, "I am depressed today and don't feel like doing anything," and later confide to a friend, "I'm down, ya know, really down." Research has shown that children of all social strata engage in this type of code-switching, and that pronunciation, grammar, and slang all change in the process (Rogers, 1976; Holzman, 1983; Romaine, 1984).

It seems clear that both elaborated and restricted codes have their place. It is good to be able to explain one's ideas in elaborate and formal terms when necessary. In fact, two of the basic three skills taught during these years, reading and

Figure 13.11 *Not only does rope-jumping call on physical skills and social cooperation, but the rhymes that accompany it have exercised the language and memory skills of generations of children.*

writing, depend on the comprehension of language in a situation devoid of gestures and intonations. At the same time, it is good to be able to express oneself informally with one's peers, using more emotive, colloquial, and inventive modes of communication than those of the standard, accepted code. While many adults rightly stress the importance of children's mastery of the elaborated code ("Say precisely what you mean in complete sentences, and no slang"), the code that is used with peers is also evidence of the child's pragmatic skill.

Nonstandard English

The importance of allowing children more than one code becomes clear with forms of nonstandard English that are a source of group identification and pride. This has been studied with regard to various group dialects in Scotland (Romaine, 1984), the dialect and grammar used by Americans living in Appalachia (Wolfram and Christian, 1976), British Black English (Sutcliffe, 1982), and is apparent in many other English-speaking communities as well (Wells, 1982; Hughes and Trudgill, 1979). Let us look in detail at **Black English,** a form of English spoken by many of this country's 26 million blacks, especially those who live in large urban areas.

Black English used to be considered simply poor English until linguists realized that the so-called errors were actually consistent alternative grammatical forms, some of which originated in African linguistic patterns. For example, the word "be" in standard English is primarily used as part of the infinitive "to be." But in Black English, "be" can also be used to indicate a repeated action or existential state (Labov, 1972). Thus, in Black English, one can say, "I am sick" or "I be sick." The first means "I am sick at this present moment"; the second includes the recent past as well as the present. To express the second concept in standard English, one might say, "I have been sick for a while."

Another difference between Black English and standard English occurs in the expression of negation. Almost all children spontaneously use the double or even triple negative, saying "I don't want to see no doctor" or "Nobody never gives me nothing." But since these forms are wrong in standard English, middle-class children are usually corrected by their parents and older peers, and use only single-negative forms by middle childhood. However, consciously or unconsciously, speakers of Black English tend to resist such correction, perhaps because in Black English (as well as in many languages and dialects other than standard English) the double negative can be correct.

Many black Americans can switch easily from Black English to standard English, depending on the context, just as many other Americans or Britons modify their regional accents and colloquial expressions to fit their intended audience. However, many others, especially children, speak only Black English because that is the form of English spoken almost exclusively by their peers, and often by their parents as well. This can lead to both academic and emotional problems in school. Writing a composition becomes very difficult when one's grammar and pronunciation, constantly reinforced in daily nonschool life, make it hard to formulate a sentence in correct standard English or even to learn correct spelling or punctuation. In addition, if the teacher takes the stance that all nonstandard English is incorrect, the effect on children who speak nonstandard English can be quite destructive. As Dorothy Seymour (1971) writes:

> A child is quick to grasp the feeling that while school speech is "good," his own speech is "bad," and that by extension he himself is somehow inadequate and without value. Some children react to this feeling by withdrawing; they stop talking entirely. Others develop the attitude of "F' get you, honky." In either case, the psychological results are devastating and lead straight to the dropout route.

The opposite approach is not necessarily the solution: if the teacher accepts Black English as a legitimate means of expression in all contexts, the children may be penalized when they enter the larger world where proficiency in standard English is expected. Therefore, the best solution seems to be to help children with the pragmatics of code-switching, so that they will become competent in standard English while not being cut off from their original code.

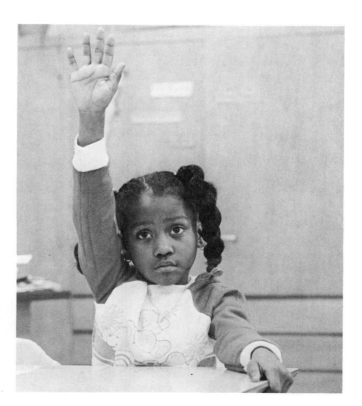

Figure 13.12 *In addition to knowing the right answer, this child also realizes that her teacher may pay as much attention to the "correctness" of her phrasing as to the correctness of her facts.*

The same basic tactic can be used for children who speak with marked regional accents and colloquialisms, or whose first language is not the one spoken in the school. As we have seen, school-age children are able to analyze and apply language rules, so they can be systematically taught a new code, a new dialect, or even a new language.

Learning a Second Language

No country is without a minority who speak a different language, and a majority of the citizens of the world are bilingual (Grosjean, 1982). Linguistically and culturally, and probably cognitively as well, it is an advantage for children to learn more than one language (Diaz, 1985). (Although some critics of bilingualism have correctly noted that one language sometimes interferes with another, such interference seems to be the result of poor teaching or a temporary condition that ends when both languages are separated in the child's mind [McLaughlin, 1984].)

Thus the question for many school systems is how to help children become bilingual. In Canada, the issue is how best to teach all Canadians English and French; in the United States the question is how to teach English to the approximately 3.6 million schoolchildren who have another mother tongue, as well as how to help the English-speaking children learn at least one other language before adulthood (Rotberg, 1982).

Unfortunately, although this question has been one of intense inquiry, no clear answer is apparent. Almost every approach has been tried—from total immersion, in which the child's entire school life occurs in the second language, to teaching the child in his or her mother tongue until childhood is over and then formally instructing the child in the "foreign" language. For all of these methods, results have been mixed (Paulston, 1978). In some cases, near-total immersion has produced second-language fluency without compromising academic achievement (Lambert and Tucker, 1972); in other cases it has resulted in a prohibitively high failure rate (Cárdenas, 1977). And in still other cases, bilingual education—teaching children first in their mother tongue and then gradually increasing their exposure to the majority language—seems to have been the best approach (Dutcher, 1981).

Figure 13.13 *Bilingual education has a good chance of succeeding in this classroom if the wall chart is an indication of the kinds of teaching techniques that are being used. Explaining words in three ways—in Spanish, in English, and with pictures—and choosing words that are similar in both languages helps students to bridge the gap from one language to another.*

In trying to sort out why early and intense learning of the second language works well in some instances, while slower exposure to the new language works better in others, researchers have looked at characteristics of the children and the learning environment. In general, children can successfully take on a second language in the early grades if (1) the program is specifically designed for language learning; (2) the child already has a good mastery of the mother tongue; (3) the parents are supportive of the program; and (4) the language to be learned, as well as the native language, are both of relatively high status in the community (Rotberg, 1982).

When these conditions do not exist, children may have great difficulty learning a new language in the first years of school. For such children, education that first reinforces their native language and culture may well be best, so they are able to master at least one language, and to feel proud of themselves and their heritage, before having to cope with using a second language to communicate.

An alternative strategy is to change the ecosystem somewhat, educating parents, teachers, and the community about the equal merit of both languages (Laosa, 1984). Then the child who arrives at kindergarten speaking Spanish, for instance, will be proud of his or her mother tongue as well as eager to learn a new language. In such a situation, children become their own best teachers.

In fact, even children who do not speak the language they are to learn arrive at school already knowing such basics of communication as expressive gestures and turn-taking, as well as relevent social and cognitive strategies for "getting along" in a new language (Wong Fillmore, 1976; Saville-Troike, 1984). For example, in a study of Spanish-speaking children, aged 5 to 7, in a largely English-speaking setting, Lily Wong Fillmore found that children relied on three social and five cognitive strategies for breaking themselves into English.

Social Stategies

1. Join a group and act as if you know what is going on, even if you don't.

2. Give the impression, with a few well-chosen words, that you can speak the language.

3. Count on your friends to help.

Cognitive Strategies

1. Assume that what people are saying is directly relevant to the situation at hand. GUESS.

2. Use some expressions you understand, and start talking.

3. Look for recurring parts in the formulas you know.

4. Make the most of what you've got.

5. Work on the big things first; save the details for later.

It was interesting to note some of the first stock phases, or formulas, the children used:

Lookit

Shaddup your mouth.

Whose turn is it?

All right you guys

I don't wanna

I wanna

How do you do these (little torillas/ flowers/ in English)?

Obviously, children need to feel relatively self-confident, and their peers need to be relatively receptive, before these strategies can be used effectively.

It seems that the specific method of achieving bilingualism depends on the psychological and cognitive needs of the child and the child's family background, and the majority and minority culture. The success of any program of bilingual education depends heavily on the commitment of the various ecosystems, most particularly that of the mesosystem of home and school.

Measuring Cognitive Development

Especially in our society, where the skills taught in school are considered crucial for success in later life, parents and teachers want to know how well the process of education is going. Is the child learning as quickly, and as much, as possible? Would another class, another teacher, another curriculum be better? Part of the answer depends on the intellectual characteristics of the child. Is a particular child unusually slow, or extraordinarily gifted, and therefore in need of some special help? In our culture, these questions are sufficiently important that thousands of educators and psychologists have designed tests to answer them.

Achievement Tests

Achievement tests are designed to measure how much a child has accomplished or learned in a specific subject area. In middle childhood, reading and math tests are the most commonly given, although, especially in the higher grades, many schools give tests in science, spelling, and social studies as well. The best-known, and most

Figure 13.14 *The achievement test this fourth-grade boy is taking will measure many skills besides those related to math, among them his ability to concentrate, to put his answers on the correct spot on the sheet, and to make his marks large and dark enough for the computer to read.*

A CLOSER LOOK　　　　Test Construction

Creating an accurate test is a complex process. First of all, the test must be valid—that is, it must measure what it is supposed to measure—and it must also be reliable, so that the same findings would be arrived at over several testings. To take an example from physical measurement, if you wanted to measure weight gain, the most valid way would be to use a scale—not a tape measure. And you would want the scale to be reliable, not susceptible to changes in humidity or position on the floor.

To see how these criteria would be developed in a nationwide achievement test, let us look at the Metropolitan, which was revised in 1978. The first step in ensuring validity was to determine what was being taught in the major content areas in schools throughout the country, as revealed by textbooks, state guidelines, and various syllabi; the next step was to be sure the test reflected this curriculum. For the test to be reliable, the questions had to be clearly written and not require any special knowledge that might be more accessible to one social or ethnic group than to another. The questions were written with this in mind and given to a panel of minority educators for the elimination of any bias. Enough questions were provided at every level so that the test would spot not only children achieving at grade level but also children doing far better or far worse than expected. The directions and administration of the test were designed to be simple and unambiguous, so that the test did not inadvertently test ability to read and follow directions, or the test-giver's personal style.

Once the questions were written, they were field-tested—that is, tried out with hundreds of children of different ages, grades, races, and family incomes. Some of the children were tested and retested to make sure the test was not subject to much unexpected variation from one test date to the next, or from one version of the test to the next. On the basis of this field-testing, some questions were eliminated and others rewritten, until the test seemed sufficiently valid, reliable, and sensitive.

Then the test was standardized by giving it to more than 550,000 children typical of the overall population who would take the test, including a representative sample from public, private, and parochial schools, cities and rural areas, all geographical regions, and so forth. From the performance of this sample group, statisticians determined what score should be considered average for each month of school. For example, twenty correct answers in math might be the average score in the second month of the third grade (3.2); twenty-one correct might be the score of the fourth month of the third grade (3.4); and so forth.

Unfortunately, no matter how many steps are taken, no achievement test can be regarded as completely valid and reliable. In recognition of this, the examiners' manual for the Metropolitan reports how the test was constructed, validated, and standardized. Testers can use this information to interpret test results in a way that is appropriate to the individuals who are being tested (Prescott et al., 1978).

widely used, achievement tests are the Metropolitan Achievement Tests, the California Achievement Tests, and the Iowa Tests of Basic Skills (Anastasi, 1982).

Achievement tests reveal not only what children have learned, but also their weaknesses in specific skills or subject areas. In several states, achievement tests are used to determine whether students will be promoted, especially at certain crucial grades, such as from elementary school to junior high. Within each grade level, they are sometimes used to group students so that the poorest achievers are in one class and the better achievers in another.

In addition, achievement-test scores of groups of children are used by administrators to evaluate how individual teachers, or schools, or school systems are doing. (A recent study even used achievement-test scores to compare schoolchildren in the United States, Taiwan, and Japan [Stevenson et al., 1985]. A carefully selected sample, designed to be representative and comparable between countries, took culturally fair tests of reading and math at the first and fifth grades. Interestingly, the results in reading were quite similar across nations, but in math, the American children were by far the lowest at both grade levels.)

Aptitude Tests

Whereas achievement tests are intended to measure how much a child has accomplished, **aptitude tests** are designed to measure potential, that is, how much a child could accomplish if given the necessary education and encouragement.

Intelligence Tests In middle childhood, the most commonly used aptitude tests are **intelligence tests,** often called IQ (intelligence quotient) tests. The most widely used are the Stanford-Binet and the Wechsler tests (one for preschoolers, one for schoolchildren, and one for adults—WPPSI, WISC-R, and WAIS-R, respectively), all of which test general knowledge, reasoning ability, mathematical skill, memory, vocabulary, and spatial perception.*

To help you understand what the standard IQ tests actually measure, let us look more closely at the WISC-R—the revised edition of the Wechsler Intelligence Scale for Children. All the Wechsler tests are divided into two halves, one containing "verbal" items and one containing "performance" items. Each half has five subtests. The following pairs of questions, which are similar to actual test items, are indicative of the easiest and hardest of the many questions in the verbal half of the WISC-R. The range of difficulty covers kindergarten through high school; as long as a child continues to answer most items correctly, the examiner asks questions of increasing difficulty.

General knowledge: How many thumbs do you have?/Who wrote *The Divine Comedy?*

Reasoning ability: How are a child and an adult alike?/How are an elephant and a whale alike? (Two points are given for the category both belong to: "humans" for the first question, "mammals" for the second; one point for less sophisticated, albeit correct, answers.)

Mathematical skill: What is 4 + 1?/If a train traveling at 32 miles per hour takes three days to get from one place to another, how fast must a train go to travel the same distance in half a day?

Comprehension: What should you do if you arrive at school an hour too early?/What does the saying "You can't make an omelette without breaking some eggs" mean?

Vocabulary: What is a spoon?/What is a mortgage?

The performance half of the WISC-R measures nonverbal skills, such as putting a puzzle together, arranging a series of pictures into a sequence that tells a story, and creating designs with colored blocks to match those shown in sample pictures. After comparing a given child's answers with norms for children who are the same age, the examiner calculates three IQ scores: a verbal IQ, a performance IQ, and a full scale (overall) IQ.

What IQ Scores Mean. Originally, the intelligence quotient was truly a quotient, arrived at by dividing mental age by chronological age and multiplying by 100. Thus, a 10-year-old who scored at the 12-year-old level would have an IQ of 120; and a 15-year-old who scored at the 12-year-old level would have an IQ of 80. Today the system for determining actual score is more refined, but the scores are still roughly equivalent to the old system. Specific labels are sometimes used to designate children who score substantially above or below the expected score at their age.

*Several less popular aptitude tests attempt to avoid reliance on language achievement, among them the Peabody Picture Vocabulary Test (children answer questions by pointing to pictures); the Goodenough-Harris Draw-a-Person test, which measures the detailedness of the drawing; and a test battery that uses Piagetian problems such as conservation and class inclusion (Humphreys et al., 1985).

Figure 13.15 *Although many of the WISC subtests are designed to be culture-free, other kinds of differences between children may be reflected in the test results. For example, in this task, which requires a child to arrange a group of blocks to match a picture, it is likely that boys, as a group, will do better than girls, who are generally less adept at spatial representation.*

Above 130	Gifted
115–130	Superior
85–115	Average
70–85	Slow learner
Below 70	Mentally retarded
50–69	Educable (can learn to read and write)
25–49	Trainable (can learn to care for self)
0–24	Custodial (will need to be cared for)

As you can see from this listing, the range of average scores is from 85 to 115 (100 is considered exactly average). About two-thirds of all people score within this range, and only about 2 percent score above 130 and another 2 percent below 70. (The labels applying to the three lowest score ranges must be considered rough predictions: many people labeled "retarded" learn more than their IQs would predict [Robinson and Robinson, 1976].)

Although IQ tests are supposed to measure the potential of the individual's "pure" genetic intelligence, it is actually impossible to measure potential without measuring a sample of present achievement. As Jencks writes:

> In principle, achievement tests tell whether students have mastered some body of material that the tester deems important. Aptitude tests (such as IQ tests) theoretically tell whether students are capable of mastering a body of material that the tester deems important. In practice, however, all tests measure both aptitude and achievement. [Jencks et al., 1972]

A CLOSER LOOK   **The Gifted Child**

One use of aptitude tests is determining whether a particular child is "gifted" and therefore should have special education of some sort. Giftedness comes in many forms and can be accompanied by a variety of problems.

One type of giftedness is unusual ability in a particular skill, such as music, or dance, or athletics. If the child's ability is spotted and encouraged with special teachers, coaches, and performance opportunities, this enhanced education may well lead to professional proficiency by the teen years. From a developmental point of view, the most likely problem is the possible neglect of basic social and academic skills in the process of fostering the talent.

Another type is intellectual giftedness. About 2 percent of all children are significantly brighter than their peers, perhaps scoring 130 on an IQ test and doing second-grade work in kindergarten. These children are usually given extra class-room enrichment, and typically become leaders in school and in later life, with no special problems because of their ability (Terman and Oden, 1959; Sears, 1977). About one child in every thousand is extremely gifted, reading at the college level while still in elementary school and scoring above 180 on IQ tests. These children tend to have emotional as well as social problems, especially if they are simply given an enriched education with their age-mates. In general, accelerated programs that allow them to learn with older gifted children seem more effective (Robinson, 1981).

A final type of giftedness is extreme creativity. For example, when asked "What can you do with a brick?" most elementary-school children think of less than ten uses, almost always incorporating the brick as building material or using it as a weapon. But a few children think of many more uses, and some of their suggestions are highly imaginative: for instance, tying the brick to a raft and using it for an anchor; or grinding it up to make paint; or putting it next to a water fountain so small children can stand on it to drink. Children who give these kinds of responses are considered highly creative. Their thinking processes can be described as divergent, for they lead to many solutions to every problem, in contrast to those of the convergent thinker, whose mind searches for *the* correct answer for any question.

Of all gifted children, creative children are the ones most likely to get into trouble at school, for their ideas may seem directly opposed to the typical elementary-school's emphasis on conforming and knowing the "right" answers. Creative children are often an exasperating experience for teachers, especially when they come up with a new way to do long division which they consider better, or when they refuse to eat the school lunch because they conjure up images of what certain ingredients might do to their digestive system, or when they daydream or doodle instead of memorizing their spelling words, or when they ask complicated "What would have happened if . . . ?" questions about the history lesson. Creative children often develop a reputation for having "wild and silly ideas," and they are frequently excluded from group activities (Torrence, 1972).

Unfortunately, while it is apparent that some children are much more creative than others, and clear that creativity should not be stifled, it is not obvious how creativity should be measured or precisely what should be done once it is spotted (Tannenbaum, 1983). We do know, however, that classrooms and other situations in which everyone is expected to perform in a certain way to

---

Furthermore, as you remember from Chapter 3, even for questions of aptitude, there is considerable controversy over how much is innate, or genetic, and how much is the result of environment. The one thing we can say for certain is that the major intelligence tests that are designed to measure intellectual aptitude in middle childhood correlate fairly well with other measures of aptitude and with later learning in school.

The Purpose of Aptitude Tests.   Today aptitude tests serve two main purposes. The first is predicting school achievement and diagnosing learning problems. For example, they help teachers know how able a child is, allowing them to give more challenging work to the faster student and easier work to the slower student. They also help spot the very bright child, who might need a special class for the gifted or an opportunity to skip a grade (see Closer Look), and to spot the mentally retarded

produce a certain product thwart and frustrate the creative individual (Amabile, 1983).

One classic study found that school is particularly hard for children who score relatively high on tests of creativity but low on tests of intelligence, for they often lose confidence in themselves and retreat from classroom interaction (Wallach and Kogan, 1965). Children high in both creativity and intelligence may be bored, but usually are able to do well on school assignments and tests. Finally, the child high in intelligence and low in creativity is likely to become addicted to school achievement.

In general, educators and psychologists who study gifted children believe that they need special encouragement, enrichment, and acceleration beginning in the early grades in order to develop their self-esteem and social skills, as well as their talents (Tannenbaum, 1983). Otherwise, they might drop out or fail in their grades. In fact, in their study of famous people from all over the world, most of whom had been gifted children, Victor and Mildred Goertzel (1962, 1978) found that most hated their years in school. Many of them—including Winston Churchill, Thomas Edison, Albert Einstein, Pablo Picasso (who refused to do anything but paint), and Émile Zola (who got a zero in literature and went on to become one of France's most famous writers)—misbehaved, played hooky, failed, or dropped out. Such responses to education were likely to occur in all types of schools (public, private, and parochial) and in every culture.

While it is reassuring to realize that such extraordinary people overcame their early educational experiences, the biographies of such people lead us to wonder how many future inventors, artists, and world leaders are now

Thomas Alva Edison received only three months of schooling before his schoolmaster expelled him, judging him to be retarded. This premature evaluation was disproved by a lifetime of inventing—1,093 patents originating from the world's first industrial research laboratory.

suffering through boring classes with unsympathetic teachers and peers. Another question is even more disturbing: How many other gifted young people, who may have had a little less persistence, talent, or luck, never learned to appreciate their talents or develop their skills?

child who might need a special class for slow learners. As a diagnostic tool, aptitude tests are particularly useful because they help counselors discover why a child is having difficulty learning. If a hard-working, healthy child is failing and scores 70 on an IQ test, the child is probably not intellectually up to doing the regular work. On the other hand, a failing child who has an IQ of 95 or 115 must have some problem other than an impaired intellect—perhaps a poor teacher, a discouraging home environment, or a reading difficulty. As one part of a battery of tests, IQ tests also help diagnose minimal brain damage and emotional disturbances.

The second major use of aptitude tests is in research to compare groups of children, for instance, to compare children in a special educational setting with children in a control group, or children from one area with those of another. For instance, the same study that compared achievement of children in the United

States, Japan, and Taiwan also used a battery of tests to detect any aptitude differences among children from the three countries, in part because an earlier report had suggested that Japanese children are intellectually superior to American children on the WISC-R (Lynn, 1982). The results of the aptitude tests indicated that there was no overall superiority of any of the groups of children in basic cognitive ability; thus the achievement discrepancies were caused by home, school, or cultural values, rather than by different innate learning potentials (Stevenson et al., 1985).

Validity of Aptitude Tests.   For many reasons, IQ tests are a more valid measure of ability than achievement tests are. Not only are they designed to measure aptitude, they are administered in a testing situation that is as conducive as possible to accurate assessment. For example, the Binet and the Wechsler IQ tests can be given only by a psychologist or counselor trained in test administration as well as in establishing rapport with children. The tester reads the test to the child, so poor readers are not handicapped, and each child is tested individually, so the examiner can try to make sure that the child is not anxious, sick, or upset, and that the child understands each question. If the examiner feels that the child could have done better, that is noted on the report of the results.

However, it is impossible to construct a completely fair test of aptitude in a society where educational opportunities are not equal and cultural differences are salient. For instance, some questions on IQ tests—say, "Why is it better to give to an organized charity rather than to a street beggar?" or "Where does the sun set?"— would be more difficult for children who are poor and live in the inner city. Even attempts to develop culture-free tests, such as asking a child to draw a person and

Figure 13.16 *While great expense and effort go into creating standardized tests that are valid and reliable, one of the obstacles to achieving fairness is the diversity of students' educational backgrounds. This fifth-grader engaged in a science project is privileged. His school, unlike many others, can afford expensive equipment, like this microscope, and the special programs and instruction that can encourage learning and help with test-taking.*

then noting how detailed the drawing is, are hindered by cultural variations: some families and schools provide their children much more practice at drawing than others.

In addition, test-taking is more problematic for some children than others. Many children, for example, have been told not to talk to strangers, especially strange men of a different race. Thus, a black 8-year-old girl might say to a white male psychologist "I don't know," rather than guess at an answer.

Finally, most IQ tests are standardized primarily on normal, white, American-born, English-speaking children, even though they are often used to decide the educational future of handicapped, immigrant, nonwhite, or non-English-speaking children. Precisely for this reason, a California court ruled that the standard intelligence tests could no longer be used as the major criterion of "special class" placement, a practice that had resulted in a disproportionate number of children born in other countries being put in classes for the mentally retarded.

In an attempt to modify and refine the scores of minority children on standard IQ tests, Jane Mercer developed the SOMPA (System of Multicultural Pluralistic Assessment). The SOMPA adjusts the WISC-R scores of low-scoring children from minority groups to reflect the California norms for children of that family size, family structure, socioeconomic status, and acculturation. For example, if a child scored 70 on the WISC but came from a large single-parent family living on welfare and speaking a language other than English, the child's SOMPA score would be raised to counterbalance the effects of family background. In addition, the child's ability to function at home and at school is considered (Does the child make his or her own breakfast, walk alone to school, know the names of his or her classmates?). In this way, children scoring low on standard IQ tests but high on SOMPA would remain in regular classes instead of being placed in classes for the retarded. In that it takes culture into account, the SOMPA is a step in the right direction (Messick, 1983), although no one test is as flexible or comprehensive as a thorough, personal, clinical case study (Anastasi, 1982), and there is always the possibility that a child who needs special education will not get it because his or her SOMPA score is too high (Clarizio, 1979).

Figure 13.17 Many psychologists are looking for alternatives to the standard IQ tests, which give the child points for each correct answer. In these photos, Gilbert Voyat, a psychologist who studied with Piaget, gives classification problems to two pre-school girls and a conservation task to a school-age boy. Rather than trying to compare one child with another, as is done in most standard intelligence tests, Voyat is more interested in each child's approach to the problem. He looks at the process of thinking more than the product.

Experts agree that the perfect ability test is not yet available, and that current scores need to be cautiously interpreted. Indeed, professionals who are trained in writing and using IQ tests are often among the most cautious in interpreting them, for they are aware of their shortcomings as well as their strengths (Anastasi, 1982; Helton et al., 1982; Sattler, 1982; Cronbach, 1984). They know that many factors, including racial prejudice, family size, community, and particularly social class, affect IQ scores. Moreover, they know that teachers and parents sometimes misinterpret test scores, reading more into them than is warranted.

Caution in Testing.   Similar problems appear with virtually every kind of test given to children. Consequently, some psychologists believe that tests should be used only to diagnose problems, not to predict future accomplishment, nor to sort and label children and place them into special classes, nor to determine graduation or failure (Clark, 1965; Duffey et al., 1981). Indeed, some psychologists reject IQ tests totally, maintaining that intelligence tests are biased and misleading and have no valid place in the educational system (Jackson, 1975; Williams and Mitchell, 1977). Others think that the tests themselves are accurate, and that blaming them for the larger social ills that they measure is equivalent to the ancient Greek custom of killing the messenger who brings bad news. It is their contention that schools and teachers are sometimes far more biased than tests are and that social action, not revising or abandoning testing, is the solution (Rosenbach and Mowder, 1981).

All are agreed that tests should be used cautiously, if at all, and that influences of the family, peer group, and society can aid or impede every aspect of cognitive achievement in middle childhood. These influences are discussed in more detail in the next chapter, on psychosocial development.

SUMMARY

Concrete Operational Thought

1. According to some developmental psychologists, the years from ages 5 to 7 are a time of transition, when new memory skills, reasoning abilities, and willingness to learn appear. During this period, children sometimes intuit the right answers to logical questions without knowing how they got them.

2. According to Piaget, beginning at about age 7 or 8, children are able to think using the logical structures of concrete operational thought. They can apply their logic to problems involving conservation, classification, and seriation and can distinguish cause and effect. The relationship between time, space, and distance is also better understood, as are others' points of view.

3. While Piaget's ideas about the sequence of cognitive development have been generally acknowledged to be correct, a number of cognitive researchers believe that cognitive changes occur more gradually and more heterogeneously than Piaget's theory suggests.

An Information-Processing View

4. According to information-processing research, cognitive growth during middle childhood is a result of how much information children are given, how efficiently they learn to process it, and how motivated they are to understand and reproduce it. During middle childhood, children learn new strategies for concentrating and remembering, which makes them much more able to master academic skills.

5. Information-processing research has also shown the importance of adjusting the teaching material and sequence of instruction to the child's cognitive structures.

Language

6. Language abilities continue to improve during middle childhood, partly because schools and families encourage this learning, and partly because increased cognitive development makes it easier to grasp difficult grammatical distinctions.

7. The ability to understand that language is a tool for communication makes the school-age child more able to use different forms of language in different contexts, as

does, for example, the child who uses Black English on the playground and standard English in the classroom.

8. Teaching children a second language can be accomplished by a number of different methods—from total immersion in the new language to gradually increasing exposure. However, the most important factors seem to be the commitment of home and school.

Measuring Cognitive Development

9. Achievement tests and aptitude tests can help spot children who are not learning as well as they should, and can diagnose the problem. However, these tests must be carefully prepared and cautiously interpreted.

10. Intelligence tests were originally developed to identify children who could not learn in normal classes, and they are still used to diagnose which children should have special education. However, IQ scores fluctuate much more than was formerly realized, so they are not as good predictive instruments as they were once thought to be.

KEY TERMS

concrete operational thought *(383)*	selective attention *(393)*
5-to-7 shift *(383)*	mnemonic devices *(394)*
reciprocity *(384)*	rehearsal *(394)*
classification *(384)*	chunking *(394)*
class inclusion *(384)*	metacognition *(395)*
seriation *(385)*	code-switching *(403)*
information-processing *(392)*	elaborated code *(403)*
memory capacity *(393)*	restricted code *(403)*
metamemory *(393)*	Black English *(404)*
sensory register *(393)*	achievement tests *(408)*
short-term memory *(393)*	aptitude tests *(410)*
long-term memory *(393)*	intelligence tests *(410)*

KEY QUESTIONS

1. What are some of the cognitive characteristics of the 5-to-7 shift?

2. What are some of the cognitive changes that enable children at 7 or 8 to solve conservation problems?

3. What are some of the concepts that children must be able to apply in order to perform mathematical operations?

4. What are some of the factors responsible for the improvement in memory during middle childhood?

5. What are some of the language skills that develop in middle childhood?

6. What are some of the factors that encourage learning of a second language?

7. What is the difference between an achievement test and an aptitude test?

8. What are the uses of intelligence tests?

9. What are some of the reasons for caution in the interpretation of intelligence tests?

RECOMMENDED READINGS

Edgerton, Robert B. *Mental retardation.* Cambridge, Mass.: Harvard University Press, 1979.

This is an accurate and readable book about the forms, causes, prevention, and treatment of mental retardation. It emphasizes the crucial role of the family in helping a child learn and points out what schools can and cannot be expected to do.

Zimbardo, Philip G., and **Radl, Shirley L.** *The shy child.* Garden City, N.Y.: Doubleday, 1982.

Zimbardo is a psychologist whose research and insights have changed the way developmentalists conceptualize the problem of shyness. In this book, he explains how the child's thinking processes can be used to help the shy child become more outgoing.

Gardner, Howard. *Frames of mind: The theory of multiple intelligences.* New York: Basic Books, 1985.

In this fascinating, seminal book, Howard Gardner argues that the human mind comprises several types of intelligence. Every normal person exhibits some measure of musical ability, kinesthetic sense, language facility, and interpersonal skill, for example, but some individuals have special gifts in one or another of these areas, while other individuals are severely lacking in some capacities. Whether such a lack becomes a problem depends in part on the nature of a particular family, and in part, on cultural values. Thus, language and logic are highly prized in "advanced" cultures, so an individual who is proficient in these areas may be quite successful, even if he or she is clumsy and tone deaf. In other societies, however (Bali is one example), the reverse might be true. Thus, this book reveals the relativity of our school curriculum and our intelligence and achievement tests.

The School Years: Psychosocial Development

CHAPTER 14

The child does not know that men are not only bad from good motives, but also often good from bad motives. Therefore the child has a hearty, healthy, unspoiled, and insatiable appetite for mere morality, for the mere difference between a good little girl and a bad little girl.

G. K. Chesterton

The Three Theories and Middle Childhood
Psychoanalytic Theory
Learning Theory
Cognitive Theory

Social Cognition
Understanding Others
Self-Understanding
The Peer Group

Moral Development
Thinking about Right and Wrong
Moral Behavior

Problems and Challenges
The Expanding Social World
Socioeconomic Status
Problems in the Family
Coping with Stress

Chapter 14

One of the most important social accomplishments of the school years is becoming a valued member of one's peer group, an achievement that requires much more than simply being of the same age as one's peers. Among the skills required are an understanding of self and others and an increasing independence from adults. It also usually involves the adoption of certain codes of dress, behavior, and language. The details of peer-group membership, as well as the topics that follow, will be discussed in this chapter.

What are some of the factors that contribute to the development of a child's self-esteem?

What are some of the personality traits that tend to cause children to be rejected by their peer group?

What factors encourage children to behave cooperatively and generously toward others?

What are the stages of children's thinking about moral issues?

What types of social support are most helpful to children who are experiencing serious stress?

As children between the ages of 6 and 11 become physically stronger and more capable, and cognitively more logical and articulate, their growing abilities serve as the foundation for remarkable psychological and social accomplishments. Children become less dependent on their parents, and more responsible for making their own decisions and governing their own behavior, including everything from choosing which clothes to wear to deciding whether or not to lie or steal. Further, as the parents' role seems to diminish, the influence of other children and the community as a whole grows. We will begin our study of psychosocial development during middle childhood with insights about the nature of the child, and then show how the child's expanding social world provides new challenges for the child to master.

The Three Theories and Middle Childhood

In previous chapters, the three theories often had quite different perspectives on the nature of children and the impact of the social world on them. Addressing the school years, however, all three theories note the increasing competence of children as their horizons expand from the narrow one of family and home to the wider one of school, peer group, and the community. Let us briefly look at the details of these changes, as the three theories portray them.

Psychoanalytic Theory

According to Freud, middle childhood is the period of **latency**, during which the jealousy, passion, and guilt of the phallic stage are submerged, and children's emotional drives are much quieter and steadier. This relative calm frees up children's psychic energy, allowing them to put their effort into understanding their social world and developing their many skills.

Erikson (1963) agrees that middle childhood is a quiet period emotionally and that it is a productive period as well. Once the Oedipal wish to establish a sexual future with the mother or father is over by age 7 or so, "violent drives are normally dormant," giving children new independence from their parents. After the child realizes that "there is no workable future within the womb of his family," says Erikson, the child "becomes ready to apply himself to given skills and tasks." The specific crisis that Erikson sees for this developmental period is **industry versus inferiority.** According to Erikson, as children busily try to master whatever skills are valued in their culture, they develop views of themselves as either competent or incompetent, or, in Erikson's words, as either industrious and productive or inferior and inadequate.

Figure 14.1 The need to be industrious can be fulfilled by almost any activity the child can do well and enjoys—from cake-baking to ice-skating, from chess-playing to music-making. Having successfully built a model rocket, this boy turns his attention to a new construction project— an African village.

Learning Theory

Like Erikson, learning theorists also emphasize the development of skills during middle childhood. They note that school-age children are particularly easy to teach through the use of the laws of learning theory, if those laws are properly applied.

To start with, the use of reinforcers in operant conditioning procedures takes on added power when children are better able to understand the relationship between cause and effect. This is true both in the short term ("Be home by 6 o'clock or you can't watch television") and in the long term ("If you earn an A in math, you can have a bike for Christmas"). Of course, some children are better at remembering consequences and waiting for rewards than others, but almost all 9-year-olds have a firmer grasp of cause and effect than they did at age 6.

Furthermore, school-age children become receptive to a wider variety of reinforcements. Like younger children, they still respond to tangible rewards, such as a cookie, a new toy, or a hug. However, school-age children also respond readily to more subtle reinforcements, such as a word of praise or a moment of special attention, as well as to intrinsic rewards, such as pride in work well done (Bandura, 1977).

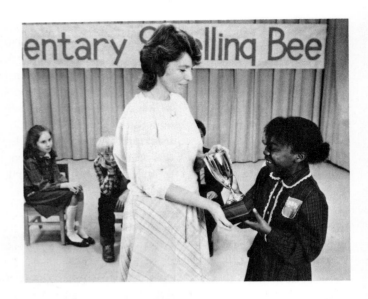

Figure 14.2 *The continuing popularity of the spelling bee, which goes back 200 years in this country, reflects the school-age child's drive for competence (and improved memory capacity). Winners of local spelling bees spend five hours or more each week studying such words as "mansuetude," "eleemosynary," and "syzygy" in preparation for the national contest.*

Indeed, the drive for competence becomes such a potent force in school-age children that it may override the appeal of tangible rewards. As children become better able to evaluate their own performance, at about age 7, they become much more eager to work to master various skills (White, 1959; Bandura, 1981; Harter, 1983). The pride of the child who gets a 100 on a spelling test or hits a home run is almost palpable, making additional "childish" rewards unnecessary. Indeed, whereas the promise of a candy bar might make a 4-year-old work diligently at a task, it might make an 8-year-old lose enthusiasm for a task that he or she might have performed with delight for less overt rewards (Lepper and Greene, 1978).

Social Learning Theory   As contemporary social learning theorists stress, it is crucial to look at the overall context of the learning process rather than solely at the specific details of reinforcement (Zimmerman, 1983). Thus, while praise or tangible rewards may help a child learn to do a specific thing, such as make his or her own bed, the child's overall sense of responsibility is also related to the example set by parents and older siblings, the consistency of the parents' expectations, and the child's own sense of being able to meet those expectations. Taken together, such factors are much more influential than tangible reinforcements. Indeed, according to a review of effective parenting, if parents overload their children with either rewards or punishments, promises and threats lose their effectiveness (Maccoby and Martin, 1983). Likewise, if parents' response to their children's behavior is inconsistent or unclear, the children's behavior can get out of control (Patterson, 1982).

Finally, school-age children are very receptive to modeling techniques. They seem to be much more aware of the actions and attitudes of others than younger children are, and can be remarkably adept at imitating other people. In addition, because they notice other people's good and bad qualities, they have more potential "models" available to them: children between 6 and 11 model themselves after not only their parents but also their teachers and friends, choosing people they see as successful (Bandura, 1977). Of course, the specific behaviors that are chosen to be modeled are not always the ones adults might prefer. When one 8-year-old was reprimanded for being mean to her friends, she explained that she was "practicing to be a teenager"—and using her older sister as a model.

Cognitive Theory

Cognitive theory, like psychoanalytic and learning theory, emphasizes the importance of school-age children's enhanced learning abilities. As we saw in Chapter 13, there is no doubt that school-age children are more logical, less egocentric, and more concrete in their thinking than younger children are. These advances affect not only their math and language ability but also their ability to understand themselves and others (Gelman and Spelke, 1981).

Cognitive psychologists were particularly struck by the change in the child's social awareness when they traced children's growing ability to identify and take into account another person's point of view. John Flavell (1975, 1981) examined this development in a number of experiments, such as asking children to describe an object to someone who can't see it, to tell a story to someone who has never heard it, or to persuade someone to do something that person would rather not do. Skill at all these tasks develops markedly during the school years. Compare the strategies adopted by third-graders (about age 8) and seventh-graders (about age 12) when they were asked to pretend that they were asking their fathers to buy them a television. Here are two of the third-graders:

> Come on, I want a television for my own room. Come on. Please. Daddy, come on. Buy me a television. I want one for my room. Come on. Come on, Daddy. I want you to. There!

> Daddy, would you buy me a TV set? . . . If you don't I'm gonna make the money, and go selling things. And I . . . I know it looks nice in my room, and I think I should have it . . . And if you don't get it for me, I won't bring you any birthday or Christmas present . . . And if you don't I won't—I won't like you and . . . if you don't get me a TV set . . . I'll get . . . If you don't get me a TV set I'll just say you just better.

And here are two of the seventh-graders:

> Oh Father—er, wait a minute—oh, Dad, I just was down shopping and I saw this most lovely, most beautiful TV I ever saw and it's a portable too. And I was wondering—it didn't cost very much, and you could put it on your charge account down there, and I was just wondering if you could kinda buy it for me, for my birthday or Christmas present to have in my own room. Ah—I'm sure you'd like it, and well, if you want it, you buy one for your room too. They're kinda cheap, I mean, well, what you can get out of a TV, they're pretty nice, and oh, it'd just match all the furniture in my room. And I promise I wouldn't let any of my friends come in and watch it, or any of my sisters and brothers to wreck it.

> Oh, hello, Dad. How are you today? Do you want your slippers changed or something? Here, have a cigarette? Oh, you don't want one? Oh, okay. Do you want me to do anything for you? Ah—let's see—hey Christmas is coming. I'll review my list for you. Now there's only one thing I want and that is a television set. Ah—if you get me that you don't have to get me anything else, unless you want to, of course. But you know I need one real much, and ah—

and if I don't feel good I have to come into the living room and watch the TV. I can stay right in my room and be very rested. And ah—you know I can use it a lot. And ah—and when my friends come over they don't have to pack in front of the television. They could stay right in my room and be very quiet. Um, yeah, yeah. And they're real pretty and they make a room look real nice, and they're real small ones too, that you can use if you want—wanted. They wouldn't take up any room and—well, you could get a pretty cheap one. Maybe a used one, a second-hand one. They'd only be used a few times. Anything you want to get me, as long as it's a television set. Okay?

The most striking difference in the seventh-graders' approach was their ability to take into account the needs and values of the person they were trying to persuade. This enabled them to use reasoning rather than brute insistence or threats; to anticipate and attempt to deflect possible objections to their request; and to try to diminish the apparent self-interest of their efforts by referring to the interests of the beseeched. Examples such as these highlight the development that cognitive theorists find most impressive in looking at the child's psychosocial development during middle childhood: children are able to understand the laws and processes of their social world as well as, or better than, they are able to understand the laws of conservation, classification, and so forth (Hoffman, 1981).

Social Cognition

It is clear that all three major theories lead in the same direction when describing the school-age child. They portray a young person who is much more able to leave the confines of the family (as Freud and Erikson explain); much more open to conditioning from the outside world (learning theory); and much better able to understand the social milieu in which they find themselves (cognitive theory). Not surprisingly, then, developmental researchers from a variety of theoretical perspectives have come together in a new research area called social cognition.

Social cognition refers to an individual's understanding of the dynamics of human interaction. Since the study of social cognition has emerged from all three major developmental perspectives, it includes emotion, behavior, and thinking processes (Flavell and Ross, 1981). We will survey the findings in this new area of study by looking first at children's understanding of other people, and then at their understanding of themselves, their peers, and the rules of their society.

Understanding Others

Children's social awareness improves in many ways between ages 6 and 11. For one thing, they become more aware of the multiplicity of social roles an individual can have: 8-year-olds, unlike 6-year-olds, understand that a person can be a father, grandfather, and son, all at the same time (Watson and Amgott-Kwan, 1983; Watson, 1984). Eight-year-olds also realize that a person can have a professional role and a set of personal ones as well. (That kindergartners don't realize this is clearly revealed by their bafflement when they run into their teachers or pediatricians pushing a cart down the aisle of the supermarket or playing with their own children in the park.) Older children are also less likely to cling to sex stereotypes, associating fewer occupations, leisure-time activities, household tasks, or modes of dress exclusively with one sex or the other (Goldman and Goldman, 1982; Archer, 1984; Stoddart and Turiel, 1985). Another advance, for which adults may be grateful, is that older children are better able to recognize and rephrase or avoid potentially offensive statements (Johnson et al., 1984). Thus the 11-year-old is much less likely than the 6-year-old to tell you that your stomach is too fat.

Further, as children grow older, they understand that people have personality traits (Shantz, 1983). Compare the following two descriptions from an extensive study (Livesley and Bromley, 1973) in which children aged 7 and older described other children: the first, from a 7-year-old, focuses exclusively on physical traits, while the second, from a child of 10, emphasizes personality traits and behaviors.

> 7-year-old: Max sits next to me, his eyes are hazel and he is tall. He hasn't got a very big head, he's got a big pointed nose.

> 10-year-old: He smells very much and is very nasty. He has no sense of humor and is very dull. He is always fighting and he is cruel. He does silly things and is very stupid. He has brown hair and cruel eyes. He is sulky and 11 years old and has lots of sisters. I think he is the most horrible boy in the class. He has a croaky voice and always chews his pencil and picks his teeth and I think he is disgusting.

As children become more aware of personality traits, they realize that people who have traits that are different from their own may respond differently than they themselves would in various social situations. For example, in a study comparing 5-, 8-, and 11-year-olds, children at the two older ages predicted that a fearless boy would not run away from a large growling dog, even if they themselves would flee. The 5-year-olds were much more likely to think that any child would do just what they themselves would do (Ross, 1981). In general, at around age 8, there seems to be "a major shift" from a highly concrete evaluation of others to an increasingly abstract understanding that infers motives, beliefs, and personality characteristics from behavior (Shantz, 1983).

The child's increasing ability to recognize others' personality characteristics, and to anticipate how these characteristics might affect their behavior, helps the child in getting along with other people. In one detailed study (Gottman, 1983) in which children between the ages of 2 and 11 were told to play with an unfamiliar peer, the younger children (up to about age 5) tended to just start playing at whatever came to mind. The older children were more likely to introduce themselves and search for some common ground between them to provide a basis for their play. In addition, the older children had a better sense of the proper pacing of personal communication: they first discussed the similarities between them before discussing the differences. Unlike the younger children, they also knew whether and when to reveal private information. For example, one 5-year-old told her new playmate that her mother didn't love her anymore—because, she said, her mother wanted to be left alone with Jimmy (her new boyfriend), instead. Older children never shared such personal information on first meeting. Finally, the older children were better at resolving conflict, using humor, for example, rather than confrontation when disagreements occurred. For all these reasons, the older children were more likely than the younger children to be on friendly terms when the play session was over.

Self-Understanding

Closely related to children's understanding of others is their **self-theory,** or understanding of themselves. According to many psychologists, as people grow older, they develop more complexly differentiated theories of who they are—*theories* in the sense that as it evolves, a person's concept of him- or herself comes to be based on a combination of the evidence of past experiences, the opinion of others, and the person's untested assumptions about himself or herself. Just like other theories, a person's self-theory is subject to change when new evidence or new assumptions emerge, and, again like other theories, it is used to govern future behavior and interpret past experiences (Brim, 1976).

Preschoolers have little, if any, stability in their specific ideas of self, at least in the sense of having a theory about themselves that they can verbalize and use to guide their actions (Harter, 1982). However, children's thoughts about themselves develop rapidly during middle childhood, as their cognitive abilities mature and their social experience widens. In the beginning of the school years, for example, children tend to explain their actions by referring solely to the events of the immediate situation; a few years later they more readily relate their actions to their personality traits and feelings (Higgins, 1981). Thus, whereas the 6-year-old typically says that she hit him because he hit her, the 11-year-old might also explain that she was already upset because she had lost her bookbag and that, besides, he is always hitting people and getting away with it. Further, children's self-theory becomes more differentiated (Harter, 1983), enabling schoolchildren to view themselves in terms of several areas at once. They might see themselves as smart in math but dumb in spelling, with an ability to master geography if they were to put their minds to the task. Similarly, they might feel that they are basically good at making friends, and are considerate of others, but that they have a quick temper that sometimes makes them do things that jeopardize their friendships. Being able to understand various aspects of their personality *sometimes* helps children to modify their behavior. For example, they might apologize for an outburst of anger by referring to their hot temper, or they might even take steps to protect a friend from such an outburst by, say, going for a walk to "cool off."

As their self-theory sharpens, then, children gradually become more self-critical, and their self-esteem dips. Unlike younger children, for example, fourth-, fifth-, and sixth-graders have markedly lower self-esteem if they are aware of their shortcomings in any area (Harter and Ward, 1978). Further, as they mature, children are more likely to feel personally to blame for their shortcomings, and less likely to believe, as younger children often do, that it is bad luck that makes them do poorly (Powers and Wagner, 1984). Girls are especially likely to blame themselves for their difficulties (Stipek, 1984), a tendency apparent throughout childhood. Thus, while children are better able to recognize the diverse areas in which they succeed and fail as they grow older, they are more likely to take failures seriously, and thus their overall self-esteem tends to fall as they understand themselves better. In general, self-esteem, which is usually quite high in early childhood, decreases throughout middle childhood, reaching a low at about age 12 before it gradually rises again (Simmons et al., 1973; Harter, 1983; Savin-Williams and Demo, 1984; Wallace et al., 1984).

Learned Helplessness   These developmental changes affect children's willingness to try to master new skills and learn new material. As one review explains, "developmental change can be a risky business. Greater cognitive capacity for self-reflection can provide the tools for new levels of mastery but can also result in greater inhibition of mastery attempts" (Dweck and Elliott, 1983).

Put another way, compared to younger children, older children are more vulnerable to **learned helplessness;** that is, their past failures in a particular area have taught them to believe that they are unable to do anything to improve their performance or situation. Consequently, whereas a 6-year-old who has failed to master a school lesson several days running is likely to still be eager to try again, an 11-year-old who has failed repeatedly will be likely to quit trying. This has been shown experimentally as well as in naturalistic observation. For example, in an experiment in which children between the ages of 5 and 11 thought they were doing poorly in finding "hidden pictures" in four drawings, the older children were more negatively affected by their alleged failures. They became discouraged and, on the fifth drawing, found fewer pictures and spent less time looking than the younger children (Rholes et al., 1980).

Correspondingly, children who have had several experiences in which their specific performance was judged inadequate—by teachers, peers, parents, or themselves—might well decide "I'm stupid in math" or "I can't play ball" or "Nobody likes me," without giving new math lessons or new ball games or new social interactions a try. As Erikson predicted when he described industry versus inferiority, a child with few successes will develop a sense of inferiority that may lead to anticipation of continued failure and a lower self-esteem for the rest of his or her life.

Developing Positive Self-Esteem The crucial factor in gaining positive self-esteem seems to be feeling that one is competent at varying tasks. Obviously, developing this feeling depends partly on a child's ability: for example, children who are intellectually able at age 7 tend to develop relatively high self-esteem by age 12 (Joreskog, 1973). However, a great deal also depends on the microsystems of family and school, which can make it easier or more difficult for children to develop feelings of competence. Children whose parents are supportive tend to feel more confident and competent than children whose parents tend to criticize and punish (Coopersmith, 1967; Abraham and Christopherson, 1984). Further, children feel better about themselves when their school offers a variety of ways for them to succeed (with arts, dramatics, and sports programs, for example, in addition to regular classes) and when their teachers make a point of praising each child for what he

Figure 14.3 *Whether learning to keep a beat on the bongos or to identify a scarlet tanager, children gain skills and self-esteem when parents share their enjoyment of their own favorite leisure activities.*

(a)   (b)   (c)

Figure 14.4 *In developing countries the work done by school-age children is essential to their families and thus helps to build the children's sense of competence. These industrious children are at work in (a) Colombia, (b) Nepal, (c) the Ivory Coast, (d) Iran, and (e) Mexico.*

or she does well. Children's self-esteem may also be affected by the structure of the classroom and the school, depending on whether the stress is on competition and comparison, or on cooperation and diversity. The school, in effect, is a "social frontier" (Minuchin and Shapiro, 1983), in which children confront unfamiliar adults and children, as well as values and codes of behavior that may be quite different from those of the home. Whether the school attempts to acknowledge and respect these differences, or promotes the idea that there is only one correct way to think and act, can have a profound effect on the child's self-esteem.

The macrosystem also affects the likelihood of a child's developing a feeling of competence and worth. In earlier historical periods, children probably had a better opportunity to develop their self-esteem because they regularly performed useful work. (This opportunity is still readily available in some twentieth-century cultures, in which the families depend on the children and encourage them to develop a sense of their own value [Whiting and Whiting, 1975].) In a society such as ours, where many children perform little useful work, and where competition and comparison are an integral part of most classrooms and sports, many school-age children decide that they are stupid, clumsy, and worthless. Their sense of industry gives way to feelings of abiding inferiority.

The Peer Group

Perhaps the most influential system in which the school-age child can develop his or her self-esteem is the peer group. Acceptance in one's group, and confidence in one's best friend, can go a long way toward building a sense of competence.

Indeed, for many children, emerging independence from parents during middle childhood is linked to growing dependence on peers. A nationwide American survey found that school-age children spend several hours each day playing with friends—more time than they spend watching television, and more time than they spend reading, playing alone, and working combined (Roberts and Baird, 1972). At the same time, an international study of parents in twelve Western countries, including the United States, found that parents and school-age children spend rela-

(d)

(e)

tively little time together. The average employed father spends a mere 2 hours per week directly involved with his children (although he spends about 20 hours in their presence, watching television or eating dinner with them), and the average employed mother spends only 5½ hours in direct involvement with them. Even the mother who is not working outside the home spends an average of only 12 hours a week playing, working, or talking with her school-age children (Szalai et al., 1972).

Not surprisingly, then, during middle childhood, children become increasingly dependent on their peers. For example, in one study, children between the ages of 6 and 10 were asked whom they would turn to for help in various academic and social situations. As they grew older, they were less likely to turn to their parents, and more likely to turn to their peers, partly because they considered their peers more capable of helping them than their parents were (Nelson-Le Gall and Gumerman, 1984).

Figure 14.5 *A snowball fight is an example of a complex peer-group event: choosing teammates and targets, building forts, and agreeing on rules (no iceballs, rock centers, or aiming at the face) calls for lots of cooperation and trust.*

Figure 14.6 *Children's dress codes during school years vary from subculture to subculture and can be quite rigid. The first picture shows two girls in identically "preppie" attire, including hair barrettes, artfully draped cardigans, and crisp designer jeans. The dress of the public-school children is more action-oriented but no less uniform, from the running shoes and athletic tops to the well-worn knees of the boys' jeans.*

The Society of Children When groups of children play together, they develop particular patterns of interaction that regulate their play, distinguishing it from the activities of the adult-organized society. Some social scientists call the peer groups' subculture the **society of children**, highlighting the distinctions between children's groups and the general culture (Opie and Opie, 1959; Knapp and Knapp, 1976). The society of children typically has a special vocabulary, dress codes, and rules of behavior that flourish without the approval, or even the knowledge, of adults. Its slang words and nicknames, for instance, are often ones adults would frown on, and its dress codes become known to adults only when they try to get a child to wear something that violates those codes—as when a perfectly fine pair of hand-me-down jeans is rejected because, by the standards of the dress code, they are an "unfashionable" color, or do or don't have a designer label, or have bottoms that are too loose, or too tight, or too short, or too long. If parents find a certain brand and style of children's shoes on sale, they can bet that they are the very ones that their children would not be caught dead wearing.

The children's subculture also involves codes of behavior, many of which demand independence from adults. By age 10, if not before, children whose parents walk them to school or kiss them in public are pitied; "cry babies" and "teachers' pets" are criticized; children who tattle or "rat" to adults are despised.

The importance of the peer group to school-age children is perhaps most obvious in their organization of clubs or gangs, in which much attention is given to details concerned with rules, officers, dress, and establishing a clubhouse, often deliberately distant from adult activity. Sometimes the club has no announced purpose, its only apparent function being the exclusion of adults and children of the opposite sex (Minuchin, 1977). From a developmental perspective, however, such clubs serve many functions, including building self-esteem, sharpening social skills, and teaching social cooperation. As one researcher describes his club:

> I was a charter member of a second-grade club called the Penguins, whose two major activities were acquiring extensive information about penguins and standing outside in the freezing weather without a coat for as long

Figure 14.7 *A clubhouse is often the place for developing social skills, since questions concerning membership, officers, and activities must be settled without the intervention of adults. Unfortunately, at the same time that most children's clubs enhance the esteem of those who belong, they can also wound the egos of those who are excluded.*

as we could. Like most other groups of this sort, the Penguins did not last very long, but in the making and unmaking of such groups, children are conducting what may be informative experiences in social organization. [Rubin, 1980]

Friendship As children grow older, friendships become increasingly important, and children's understanding of friendship becomes increasingly complex. These changes are reflected in a study of hundreds of Canadian and Scottish children, from first grade through the eighth, who were asked what made their best friends different from other acquaintances. Children of all ages tended to say that friends did things together and could be counted on for help, but the older children were more likely to cite mutual help, whereas younger children simply said that their friends helped *them*. Further, the older children considered mutual loyalty, intimacy, and interests, as well as activities, to be part of friendship (Bigelow and LaGaipa, 1975; Bigelow, 1977).

Similarly, in a United States study (Berndt, 1981) children were asked "How do you know someone is your best friend?" A typical kindergartner answered:

> I sleep over at his house sometimes. When he's playing ball with his friends he'll let me play. When I sleep over, he lets me get in front of him in 4-squares [a playground game]. He likes me.

By contrast, a typical sixth-grader said:

> If you can tell each other things that you don't like about each other. If you get in a fight with someone else, they'd stick up for you. If you can tell them your phone number and they don't give you crank calls. If they don't act mean to you when other kids are around.

Partly because friendships become more intense and more intimate as children grow older, older children demand more of their friends, change friends less often, find it harder to make new friends, and are more upset when a friendship breaks up. They also are more picky: throughout childhood, children increasingly tend to choose best friends who are of the same sex, race, and economic background as they themselves are (Hartup, 1983).

As children become more choosey about their friends, their friendship groups become smaller. Whereas most 4-year-olds say that they have many friends (perhaps everyone in their nursery-school class, with one or two notable exceptions), most 8-year-olds have a small circle of friends, and by age 10, children often have one "best" friend to whom they are quite loyal. Although this trend toward an increasingly smaller friendship network is followed by both sexes, it tends to be more apparent among girls. By the end of middle childhood, many girls have one and only one best friend on whom they depend (Lever, 1976).

Figure 14.8 *While both boys and girls form friendship groups during the school years, girls' friendships tend to be more intimate and the emphasis on conformity more apparent. The sex differences in friendship patterns are especially obvious if one tries to imagine girls posturing like the boys in the first photo, or boys hugging like the girls in the second.*

Thus, as children grow older, friendship patterns become more rigidly set, so that by age 9 or so everyone knows who hangs out with whom, and few dare to try to break into an established group or pair of friends. With the changes of early puberty (at about age 10), some children come to be more advanced than others, disrupting former social patterns and wrecking many friendships. As one girl named Rachel put it:

> Oh, I feel so horrible about friends. Everybody is deserting their best friend and everybody hates someone else and Paula Davis has been stranded with nobody—except me and Sarah. Christine has run off with Liz and Joan has moved up from being an eleven-year old . . . and, oh well, I suppose it happens every year.

Meanwhile, her friend Sarah wrote a sad note to her teacher:

> Rachel is spending all her time with Paula Davis and deserting me. Rachel is conversing very loudly with two idiots in her cubby and I can't concentrate. Rachel is changing, she is not Rachel any more. [Quoted in Rubin, 1980]

The Rejected Child   An estimated 5 to 10 percent of all schoolchildren are unpopular and friendless (Asher and Renshaw, 1981). These children have many problems: not only are they lonely but they have low self-esteem, which affects their learning in school and their happiness at home. Their problems become increasingly serious as they and their classmates grow older, because, as we have just seen, children become more critical of their own and their classmates' failings.

Children also become more aware of clusters of personality traits and behaviors, rejecting those children who are bullies or unusually withdrawn. For example, in one study children were asked which of their classmates fit certain behavior descriptions. Even the 6-year-olds described their aggressive classmates with certain typical behaviors, such as "starts fights," and "bothers others." By ages 9 and 12, children cited many more characteristics as typical of aggressive children (including "mean and cruel" and "show-off") and had definite clusters for withdrawn children ("chosen last," "too shy," and "feelings easily hurt") and popular ones ("understanding," "helpful") (Younger et al., 1985).

Several studies have shown that children who are isolated or rejected by their peers tend to be those who are immature in their social cognition about themselves or others. Compared to popular or average children, for instance, isolated and rejected children tend to misinterpret social situations, considering a friendly act to be hostile, for example (Dodge et al., 1984). Typically, they might interpret good-natured teasing as an insult or regard a request for a bite of their candy bar as a demand. They also have difficulty sharing and cooperating (Markell and Asher,

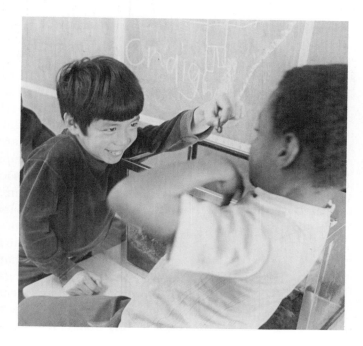

Figure 14.9 *Knowing how to tease without going too far is an important social skill—one noticeably lacking in rejected and isolated children. The glee on the worm-holder's face suggests that he has found an acceptable way to tease his classmate, who will probably react by finding a worm of his own, rather than insulting, punching, or escaping.*

1984), and in understanding what other children's needs might be in various situations (Goetz and Dweck, 1980). If, for example, a new child joins the class and seems reluctant to speak to the other children, a socially skilled child would break the ice, perhaps asking the child if he or she wanted to join in a game. The rejected child, however, might decide that the new child is stuck-up and therefore make no attempt to be friendly. Unfortunately, since the way most children learn social skills is from the normal give-and-take of their play with other children (Youniss, 1980; Rubin, 1980), socially isolated children are excluded from the very learning situation they need the most.

Helping the Rejected Child.   What can be done to help children who are rejected? To some extent, the particular ecological milieu encourages or discourages constructive interaction among children, and a number of influential factors should be acknowledged. For example, parents who are themselves friendly and have a wide social circle tend to have children who are also quite social: the reverse is true as well (Krantz et al., 1984). Another influential area is the school. On the whole, more open and informal classroom settings foster more mutual respect and friendship among the children (Minuchin and Shapiro, 1983). Further, children are likely to have difficulty if placed with dissimilar children, so it is probably unwise to assign a child to a class with very few children of the same sex or intellectual abilities, especially if none of the class has much else in common with the new arrival. Social-class differences may be significant as well. One study found that in a predominantly middle-class school, boys who were verbally outgoing tended to be well liked, while those who were physically outgoing were unpopular; the reverse was true in a lower-class school in which verbally outgoing boys were even less popular than boys who were not outgoing at all (Gottman et al., 1975). In general, then, the first thing adults should look for in helping children develop their friendships is the overall setting (Rubin and Sloman, 1984): Are the examples children see, the peers they meet, and the places where they interact conducive to the development of friendships?

Direct attempts to teach isolated and rejected children social skills have been successful in some cases, when the skills taught were quite specific, such as how to listen and how to respond in a positive way to other children's behavior (Asher and Renshaw, 1981; Bierman and Furman, 1984). We know that one factor in a child's being accepted or rejected by peers is the child's appearance and intellectual achievement (Kleck et al., 1974; Ollendick et al., 1985; Zahr, 1985). Here too, direct remediation may help—perhaps assisting a child with personal grooming, or arranging placement in a different class, or providing academic tutoring. For instance, in one study (Coie and Krehbiel, 1984), socially rejected, low-achieving boys were divided into four groups. One group learned social skills, one academic skills, one both academic and social skills, and one was a control group. Those who learned academic skills improved overall, in reading and math as well as in social acceptance. The boys who learned social skills improved only in one area, reading comprehension. The authors of this study suggest that children who improve their academic skills are likely to feel better about themselves and to concentrate better in class, and that these changes are more crucial to improved social status than simply learning how to engage in social interaction.

However, while many measures may help isolated and rejected children, there is also a danger that too much emphasis may be placed on the need for children to "fit in." As Robert White (1979) cautions:

Historically we have clamored too loud for social adjustment. We have not been sensitive to the dangers of throwing children together regardless of their anxieties and their own social needs. We have been enchanted with peer groups, as if the highest form of social behavior were getting along with age-equals . . .

When children are rejected by the peer group, they need help and sympathy, but they also need to be encouraged to develop their own interests, strengths, and confidence apart from the social scene.

Moral Development

A topic closely related to social cognition has attracted the attention of many developmentalists. That topic is **moral development,** which has been taken to be the ability to understand, and act upon, codes of conduct, including everything from the specific rules of a game to universal ethics that should govern all human behavior. As developmentalists have discovered, between the ages of 6 and 11, children's moral thinking, as well as their moral behavior, becomes more mature. We will look at each of these.

Thinking about Right and Wrong

Research has clearly shown that preoperational children believe that rules of any kind are unchangeable, yet they change them whenever it suits their needs. Piaget (1932/1965) began studying moral development by examining children's understanding of the rules of playing marbles, and he found that even when preoperational children thought that the rules for marbles came from God, they regularly disregarded them. According to Piaget, it is not that preoperational children are wilfully "breaking" the rules when they do, in fact, break them. Rather, their egocentric thinking allows them to improvise new rules as the game progresses—blithely unaware that they are altering the rules to benefit themselves or accommodate their whim.

During the years of middle childhood, Piaget found, children think of rules as codes that must be respected and obeyed, but they also begin to realize that rules can be changed, if all the participants agree to the change. For instance, if older children know that a game must soon be interrupted because they all have to go home for dinner, they usually find a way to bend the rules in order to speed the game along. By age 11, if not before, children reject the preschoolers' idea that rules are absolutes. This cognitive flexibility opens the way to the development of moral reasoning.

Kohlberg's Stages of Moral Development Building on Piaget's theories and research, Lawrence Kohlberg (1963, 1981) studied moral reasoning by telling children and adults a set of hypothetical stories that pose ethical dilemmas. The most famous of these is the story of Heinz:

A woman was near death from cancer. One drug might save her, a form of radium that a druggist in the same town had recently discovered. The druggist was charging $2,000, ten times what the drug cost him to make. The sick woman's husband, Heinz, went to everyone he knew to borrow the money, but he could only get together about half of what it cost. He told the druggist that his wife was dying and asked him to sell it cheaper or let him pay later. But the druggist said "no." The husband got desperate and broke into the man's store to steal the drug for his wife. Should the husband have done that? Why?

Kohlberg examined the responses to such dilemmas and found three levels of moral reasoning: preconventional, conventional, and postconventional—with two stages at each level.

I. **Preconventional** *(emphasis on avoiding punishments and getting rewards).*

> *Stage 1 Might makes right (punishment and obedience orientation).* At this stage the most important value is obedience to authority in order to avoid punishment.

> *Stage 2 Look out for number one (instrumental and relativist orientation).* Each person tries to take care of his or her own needs. The reason to be nice to other people is so they will be nice to you. In other words, you scratch my back and I'll scratch yours.

II. **Conventional** *(emphasis on social rules).*

> *Stage 3 "Good girl" and "nice boy."* Good behavior is considered behavior that pleases other people and wins their praise. Approval is more important than any specific reward.

> *Stage 4 "Law and order."* Right behavior means obeying the laws set down by those in power, being a dutiful citizen.

III. **Postconventional** *(emphasis on moral principles).*

> *Stage 5 Social contract.* The rules of society exist for the benefit of all, and are established by mutual agreement. If the rules become destructive, or if one party doesn't live up to the agreement, the contract is no longer binding.

> *Stage 6 Universal ethical principles.* General universal principles determine right and wrong. These values (such as "Do unto others as you would have others do unto you," or "Life is sacred") are established by individual reflection and meditation, and may contradict the egocentric or legal principles of earlier reasoning.

According to Kohlberg's longitudinal research, people advance up this moral hierarchy as they become more mature. For example, 10-year-old Tommy argued that Heinz should not steal the medicine because he could be put in jail, a stage-1 answer. Three years later, Tommy reasoned at stage 2, saying that Heinz should steal the medicine because he needed his wife to help care for him (Kohlberg, 1971).

At every age, *how* people reason morally, rather than what specific moral conclusions they reach, determines their stage of moral development. For example, someone whose moral reasoning is at stage 3 might argue either that the husband should steal the drug (because people will blame him for not saving his wife) or that he should not steal it (because he had already done everything he could legally and people would call him a thief if he stole).

According to Kohlberg, most 10-year-olds reason morally at stage 1 or 2, and many adults never reach stage 5 or 6 (Kohlberg and Elfenbein, 1975; Colby et al., 1983). In fact, in a recent reformulation of Kohlberg's scoring procedures for rating stages of moral judgment, stage 6 was dropped because so few people were in it (Colby et al., 1983). Kohlberg thinks that a child must be at least at the cognitive level of early formal operations (not usually reached until early adolescence) before he or she can reach stage 3, and that a certain amount of life experience and responsibility is a prerequisite for reaching stage 5. For these reasons, Kohlberg generally sees relatively little progress in moral development during middle childhood.

Note however, that Kohlberg's stages are based on hypothetical situations that are far removed from the realities of most children's daily lives. Other research, using test cases similar to those children typically experience, has found that children are more advanced in their moral thinking than Kohlberg believed them to be. Damon (1984) found that the principle of equality is fairly well understood by age 10, including not only the concept that each person deserves an equal share but also that past deprivations and future opportunities should be taken into account to determine what an equal share is. Piaget also found that, while children under age 8 tended to think that to be unfair was to break some kind of rule, older children equated unfairness with inequality or a breech of social justice. For instance, when asked to give an example of unfair behavior, most children older than 8 thought of situations in which two people are deserving of the same reward but do not get it, or in which someone is treated badly because of their social class. Few younger children thought of such examples. Further, by age 11, most of Piaget's marble players had some understanding of the game of marbles in terms of social-contract agreements, realizing, for example, that all players should decide in advance which of the rules are to be followed.

It is noteworthy that moral reasoning about games is so much more advanced than reasoning about social dilemmas like those in Kohlberg's Heinz story. There are two reasons for this: not only do children reason better about issues in their own experience, they also reason better about issues they have discussed with each other. Many studies have shown that giving children a chance to discuss moral issues helps them develop more complex ethical thinking (Turiel, 1974; Rest, 1983).

Customs and Principles Further proof that moral development occurs during middle childhood comes from a series of studies by Elliot Turiel (1983), who found that school-age children do, in fact, distinguish between social conventions and ethical principles. Thus, at least in practical experience, they know the difference between conventional and postconventional thinking.

For example, Turiel asked one typical 8-year-old what rules he knew. The boy cited a rule that the children in his house must clean up the mess that their guests make, and he explained that this rule could be easily changed if his parents decided to do so. He also knew another rule, that children should not hurt each other, and he explained that this rule should not be changed because hurting is wrong whenever and wherever it occurs. Similarly, he felt that the rule against stealing should not be changed because "people would go crazy." He added, with an impressive sense of social justice, "People that don't have anything should be able to have something, but they shouldn't get it by stealing."

Older children also understand that people sometimes obey customs more readily than they follow principles. For example, Turiel (1983) found that 10-year-olds, but not 6-year-olds, were convinced that it is a more serious transgression for a child to steal an eraser than to wear pajamas to school, because stealing is wrong while the question of appropriate clothing is simply a custom. At the same time, however, the 10-year-olds admitted that they personally would be more likely to commit a minor theft than to dress inappropriately.

Moral Behavior

The various findings of the research on moral development raise a crucial and very practical question. What is the relationship between moral thinking and moral behavior? A classic series of studies found that although most children can explain why honesty is right and cheating is wrong, most children cheat under certain circumstances, such as when their friends put pressure on them to do so, or when the chance of being caught is slim (Hartshorne et al., 1929). Obviously, then, the translation of the intellectual understanding of rules into moral behavior is far from automatic.

On the other hand, while few children live by absolute moral rules no matter what, most studies have shown that moral thought can have a decided influence on action and vice versa (Rest, 1983). Beginning in middle childhood, children begin to apply their moral standards to their own behavior. They try to figure out what the "right" thing to do is, and feel guilty when they do the "wrong" thing.

The reason that children do not always act in accord with their principles, or with the dictates of authority, is that they are faced with several conflicting sets of values, including their own self-interest, the morality of the peer group, the morality of their parents and teachers, and the principles of the culture (Liebert, 1984; Turiel and Smetana, 1984). It takes substantial maturity to be able to coordinate all these conflicting values.

Prosocial Behavior   Conflicting values are particularly apparent in **prosocial behaviors,** which are defined as actions performed to benefit someone else without expectation of reward for oneself. While one might expect children to become more sharing, comforting, and self-sacrificing as they become cognitively more mature, such age trends are not clearcut. In fact, some developmental trends go in the reverse direction: nursery-school children are more likely to share generously and indiscriminately than school-age children are (Radke-Yarrow et al., 1983). Similarly, younger children are more likely than older children to respond if a classmate is in distress (Gottman and Parkhurst, 1980; Ekholm, 1984).

To understand this, researchers have looked closely at the many factors that influence prosocial behavior (Mussen and Eisenberg-Berg, 1977; Eisenberg, 1982). One important factor is the example set by adults: children are more likely to cooperate if they have been rewarded for cooperating, or if they have seen someone else cooperating. Within the typical elementary school, however, teachers of older children are more likely to stress individual achievement than cooperation.

Another important factor is who the potential recipient of the prosocial behavior is. As children's social awareness increases, they become more selective in their interactions, and are more likely to cooperate and share only with someone they like or admire, or with someone who they know needs their help, or with younger children (Burelson, 1982; French, 1984). Children also look out for the interests of their friends because they believe their friends would do the same for them (Rubin, 1980). They are also more likely to share if they are pleased with themselves, and therefore do not feel the need to be self-protective.

Finally, as children become more aware of the larger culture around them, they become more responsive to its values. In some cultures, cooperation increases throughout childhood; in others, it decreases because competition is the preferred mode of interaction.

In general, cooperative behavior is most likely to occur in societies with the following five characteristics (Mussen and Eisenberg-Berg, 1977):

1. stress on consideration of others, sharing, and orientation toward group;

2. simple social organization;

3. assignment of women to important economic functions;

4. members of the extended family (grandparents, aunts and uncles, cousins) living together;

5. early assignment of tasks and responsibilities to children; these tasks are recognized as important to the entire household.

Figure 14.10 *The cooperation required to build this hut for the Holi festival is part of the daily lives of these children in Imphal, India.*

We should not be surprised, then, that in contemporary American society, with complex social organization and small nuclear families where children have few responsibilities, children become less likely to cooperate as they grow older (Mussen and Eisenberg-Berg, 1977; Bryan, 1975; Radke-Yarrow et al., 1983). An intriguing index to the cultural influences in this process is provided by the fact that rural Mexican children are more cooperative than urban Mexican, who are more cooperative than first-generation Mexican-Americans, who are more cooperative than second-generation Mexican-Americans, who are more cooperative than Anglos (Knight and Kagan, 1977; Madsen and Shapira, 1977).

This suggests an interesting conclusion. If children at the end of middle childhood act in ways that adults think are immoral, it is not because they are too young to think or act in moral ways, nor that they do not understand the social situations in which they operate. Rather, it is because their specific experiences at home, in school, with their peers, and in the larger society do not foster the ethical behavior that adults hope to see.

Problems and Challenges

As we have seen, during middle childhood children become actors on a wider stage, taking on school and community roles as well as family ones. Their expanded social world is full of challenges and opportunities for personal growth. It is also full of potential problems as well. Some of these, related to their adjustment to the learning environment at school, are discussed in the previous two chapters. Here we will look at two kinds of problems: those resulting from the larger social systems that children become increasingly involved in, and those originating in the family microsystem.

The Expanding Social World

The macrosystem, or overarching political and economic conditions and cultural values, affects school-age children profoundly, because they are increasingly aware of, and involved in, the world beyond the home. Various psychologists have pointed out particular aspects of the macrosystem that may harm the development of children. For example, many psychologists are concerned that the idea of the possibility of global nuclear war may affect how children think about their own lives. We know that American and Soviet children rate themselves as more worried about the prospect of nuclear war than about any other personal or world problem, with the possible exception of the death of their own parents (Chivian et al., 1985). Children from other countries have also expressed a high level of concern. For example, a Canadian survey found 63 percent of children between the ages of 7 and 11 admitting to having had fears and anxieties about nuclear war at least once in the preceding month, and 10 percent said that they thought about nuclear war almost every day (Goldberg et al., 1985).

However, psychologists are not agreed on what the impact of this concern may be (Bower, 1985). Some argue that the fear of a nuclear holocaust makes children hopeless about their own future (Mack, 1981; Smith, 1983); others contend that this fear may make children more concerned about looking for peaceful methods of resolving international conflicts (Chivian et al., 1985). Indeed, the Canadian study found that those children who thought most about nuclear war were also those who were most likely to think that they personally could do something to prevent it (Goldberg et al., 1985).

Another influence from the culture that may adversely affect children is television. As already discussed in Chapter 11, the excess of violence in current television programming may significantly affect children who watch it hour after hour: it not only presents a heavy dose of role models of both vicious and "heroic" aggressors and of helpless victims, but also shows few positive examples of people who control their own anger or who successfully defuse the anger of others (Parke and Slaby, 1983).

The influence of television may be particularly strong during the school years. In fact, one longitudinal study of children's aggression suggests that "there is a sensitive period at around age 8 to 9 years during which the effects of television can be especially influential in affecting a child's behavior" (Eron et al., 1983). Among the possible explanations for the particular impact of television during these years is that children's increased social cognition makes them better able to understand and follow the examples they see.

Socioeconomic Status

One aspect of the microsystem that has been studied extensively is the impact of the individual's socioeconomic status, which research has revealed to be one of the most powerful influences on a person's life. **Socioeconomic status (SES)** is generally measured in one or more of three ways: family income, parents' education, and father's employment status. Using any of these measures, a child's socioeconomic status correlates with virtually every measure of achievement and adjustment in middle childhood.

In countries in which the gap between rich and poor is very large, low SES means no formal education, no medical care, chronic malnutrition, and a life of hard work beginning in middle childhood. In developed countries, virtually all children get some medical care, attend some school, and have time for play as well as work in middle childhood. Nevertheless, even in the United States 14 million persons under age 18—22 percent of that age group—were living below the official poverty line in 1985. This makes children (not the elderly, as is often assumed) the age group with the greatest number of impoverished members (Malcom, 1985).

Low socioeconomic status affects almost every aspect of children's lives, from the amount of energy they have to face the challenges of school to the future opportunities they are able to envision for themselves. Poverty is especially crippling in middle childhood, since, as the last two chapters have shown, children during these years tend to think in concrete terms and base their self-concept partly on how they compare with other children in terms of possessions, skills, and achievements.

Figure 14.11 *For the 14 million American children who live below the poverty line, the pervasiveness of images of affluence in our society makes poverty particularly difficult to endure. School-age children are keenly aware of the contrast between the exciting lives, large comfortable homes, and fancy clothes of television families and their own deprived conditions. Such comparisons are damaging to their self-esteem and motivation.*

Children who are poor not only lack various necessities for themselves; they are also more likely to lack the attention they should get from their parents. This is true when poverty is part of a chronic family problem, such as a large family's being headed by a single mother, or having a father who is too ill, or too unskilled, to find work. It is also true when the poverty is a consequence of temporary fluctuations in the economy. For example, periods of high unemployment correlate with increases in psychotic disorders, alcoholism, and family violence (Brown, 1983). Thus, children whose parents are in economic difficulty are less likely to find the emotional support they need at home (Garbarino, 1976; Siegel, 1984).

Further, low-income children have fewer opportunities to develop their abilities. As Erikson (1963) describes it, they often settle for inferiority rather than industry, which may hinder them all their lives. The world that many of these children live in makes the mastery of the normal skills of middle childhood extremely difficult. In the words of Kenneth Keniston, it is a

> dangerous world—an urban world of broken stair railings, of busy streets serving as playgrounds, of lead paint, rats and rat poisons, or a rural world where families do not enjoy the minimal levels of public health . . . It is a world where even a small child learns to be ashamed of the way he or she lives. And it is frequently a world of intense social dangers, where many adults, driven by poverty and desperation, seem untrustworthy and unpredictable. Children who learn the skills for survival in that world, suppressing curiosity and cultivating a defensive guardedness toward novelty or a constant readiness to attack, may not be able to acquire the basic skills and values that are needed, for better or worse, to thrive in mainstream society. [Keniston, 1977]

Keniston's statement is corroborated by considerable research. Lower-class school-age children are more likely than their better-off peers to be poor achievers, and to get worse each year.

Partly because their present status seems more dependent on factors over which they have no control, such as their parents' employment and their landlord's decency, lower-class children are more likely to believe that they have little control over their future, and that luck or other people have much more power over their destiny than they themselves have. As a result, they try less hard and accomplish less (Bartel, 1971; Maehr, 1974; Maqsud, 1983). Further, in their schoolwork and in their aspirations for the future, lower-class children are less likely to set realistic goals for themselves, aiming too high or too low (Jencks et al., 1972).

As we will see later, these problems are not inevitable. Many children of low SES become high achievers, partly because their families are supportive of their accomplishments. Before looking at how families can help school-age children, however, let us look at the ways families sometimes impede their development.

Problems in the Family

On the basis of two massive longitudinal studies which looked at many possible correlates and predictors of children's functioning in middle childhood, Michael Rutter (1975, 1979, 1982) found that the nature of family interaction was a much more powerful predictor of problems than family characteristics bearing labels such as "broken home" or "father-absent household" or "step-family" or "working mother." As Rutter and many others have pointed out, when looking at the effect of the family on children, we should look at the functioning, not the structure, of the family (Rutter, 1982; Emery et al., 1984; Hetherington and Camara, 1984). This perspective is helpful in evaluating four circumstances that are often blamed for children's problems: divorce, single parenthood, blended families, and maternal employment.

Divorce In the United States in the 1980s, married couples are divorcing at a rate of nearly 50 percent—two and a half times as often as in the 1960s and four times as often as in the first half of the twentieth century. This means that, for today's school-age children, having divorced parents is a common experience: an estimated one-third have already experienced their parents' divorce, or will do so before they reach 18 years of age (Glick, 1979).

What effect, then, does divorce have on children? In general, children whose parents have divorced achieve less in school, are less happy at home, and are more disruptive in the community than children from intact families. The negative impact of divorce is particularly apparent in the first year or two after the separation, and then gradually declines (Emery et al., 1984). In the first year, especially, many children become more "aggressive, noncompliant, whining, nagging, dependent, and unaffectionate" (Hetherington and Camara, 1984). However, these generalities gloss over the many differences between one child's experience of divorce and another's, differences that permit some children to come through their parents' divorce unscathed, or even benefitted.

Which children will be most negatively affected by a divorce and which will be most likely to make a relatively easy adjustment? While the many variables make prediction difficult, two quite comprehensive, longitudinal studies, one in Virginia (Hetherington et al., 1982) and one in California (Wallerstein and Kelly, 1980; Wallerstein, 1984) have come to similar conclusions, and have been corroborated by a series of studies in the Midwest (Santrock et al., 1982). Thus we are fairly sure that the following five factors affect the adjustment of the child.

1. *Bitterness and hostility.* Much research has shown that the crucial factor in the adjustment of children to their family, no matter whether the parents are married, separated, or divorced, is the amount of family discord, especially the frequency and severity of the disputes the child witnesses (Rutter, 1982; Hershorn and Rosenbaum, 1985). Typically, the decision to divorce and the stressful consequences over the next few months exacerbate anger and open hostility between the parents (Emery et al., 1984). In addition, the legal system tends to fan the flames of anger, encouraging parents to argue over custody and child support. When the children are drawn into the parents' disputes, their specific reactions are hard to predict (a child might withdraw from a parent who formerly seemed a favorite, for instance), but almost always they show emotional strain.

2. *Changes in the child's life.* In most cases, children's lives change for the worse during the period of separation and divorce. For one thing, divorced parents usually have much less money to spend on their children, and this makes a difference in life style, sometimes requiring a change of residence and school, and thereby increasing stress. In addition, parents themselves often change in ways that may upset their children. Typically, the mother is initially overwhelmed with the burden of having to run the household and care for the children while worrying about financial problems and trying to repair her damaged self-esteem. Many women become depressed and withdrawn or, alternatively, try to find jobs, develop new skills, and expand their social lives, just when their children need and demand even more attention than before. Correspondingly, mothers frequently become

more strict, less playful, and more inconsistent in their disciplining (Hetherington et al., 1982). Fathers also change, especially in the first year. Typically, if they are the noncustodial parent, they become more indulgent with their children. Many fathers also adopt a more "youthful" life style, including dating a variety of women. Many change their appearance, adopting a new hair style or growing a beard, or taking on a new look in their wardrobe. All such changes, especially in combination, can greatly increase the child's sense of instability in his or her life.

3. *The age of the child.* There is no "good" age for a child to experience divorce, but children do seem more vulnerable at some ages than at others. Divorce during transitional periods, such as the beginning of first grade or the onset of adolescence, may be particularly hard for a child. While younger children are often more disturbed by the immediate changes brought about by divorce, older children tend to feel the effects longer (Wallerstein and Kelly, 1980; Wallerstein, 1984).

4. *The sex of the child.* Boys generally have a more difficult time adjusting to their parents' divorce than girls do, at least as evidenced by their overtly disruptive behavior at home and school. In fact, conflicts between mothers and sons are still common even six years after divorce, while most mothers and daughters have adjusted fairly well by this time (Hetherington et al., 1982). That boys seem to be more negatively affected by divorce may be simply one more example of the greater vulnerability of boys to various stresses throughout childhood, or it may be specific to the fact that most boys typically live with their mothers after the separation, and thus do not have an adult male role model to help them in everyday life (Rutter, 1982). Suggestive evidence for the later hypothesis comes from studies that suggest that boys tend to adjust better when the father is the custodial parent than when the mother is (Santrock et al., 1982).

5. *Long-term involvement of both parents.* As time goes by, the extent to which continued contact with both parents is maintained is a powerful predictor of the child's well-being. For the 90 percent of children who are in their mother's custody, continued contact with the father is often problematic (see Closer Look). While most fathers see their children often in the months immediately after the divorce, only a minority of noncustodial fathers continue to visit frequently and maintain close relationships with their children (Furstenberg et al., 1982). This is particularly unfortunate, for there is now a substantial body of research that shows that a father's attention to his children (whatever his relationship might be to their mother) correlates with their achievement at school, particularly in math, and their happiness at school and at home (Shinn, 1978; Hetherington et al., 1982; Biller, 1981; Radin, 1982; Lamb, 1982).

Overall, then, divorce is difficult for children. However, the specific circumstances and the general passage of time can limit the negative effects. For example, in some cases, divorce removes the child from a parent who has lost control of his or her anger, or life, and consequently brings an improvement for the child (Emery et al., 1984). In these circumstances, even academic achievement rises significantly in the year after the divorce compared to the year before (Santrock, 1972; Wallerstein and Kelly, 1980). In most other cases, the problems diminish over the years. Most adults adjust to their new status within a year or two, and consequently their children function better as well. Further, the children themselves often find ways to cope with the divorce, developing new friendships and activities. However, even when children are back to functioning normally in school and with their friends, it takes the teachers and the other children time to treat the child normally. In fact, some teachers expect children of divorced parents to be difficult no matter how long ago the divorce occurred (Minuchin and Shapiro, 1983). In many cases, this assumption is unwarranted. If children of divorced parents are still troubled years

A CLOSER LOOK   Custody and Visitation

Divorcing parents, representatives of the courts, and mental health professionals have debated for years over which custody and visitation arrangements are best for children. It is clear by now that no one structure works best for all children. Maternal custody is not necessarily better than paternal custody; joint custody solves some problems but creates others; visitation is a right that parents (and, increasingly, grandparents) can claim, but its exercise is not always in the child's best interest. In general, the best solution is the one that encourages a continued relationship between the children and both parents, while diminishing the hostility that the child observes between the parents.

Unfortunately, these two goals often work at cross purposes. Whatever custody and visitation arrangements are made to foster contact with the noncustodial parent often result in further feuding between the ex-spouses. As Wallerstein and Kelly (1980) report on their observations of various visitation arrangements:

The visit itself became an arena which readily evoked in both parents the ghost of the failed marriage and the fantasies of what might have been . . . The visit is an event continually available to the reply of anger, jealousy, love, mutual rejection and longing between the divorcing adults . . . The fighting between parents occasionally reached pathological, even bizarre, intensity. One gently bred matron, for example, smeared dog feces on the face of her husband when he arrived to see his children. One father sought a court order requiring his wife to make herself invisible when he came to the door.

Obviously, both parents need to do whatever they can to make the visiting process as smooth as possible, for the child's sake. However, there are often problems related to custody that cannot be easily resolved. Many noncustodial parents feel that they are no longer real parents to their children but rather "tour guides" (Weiss, 1975): they feel obliged to do something special with their children whenever they see them (another trip to the circus!), since they do not have the time and continued contact that would foster a more natural relationship. The problems associated with visitation make many noncustodial fathers do two things that are destructive to their children: visit less often and cut back on child support.

Meanwhile, the custodial parent often feels that he or she does all the work of raising the children while the other

parent has all the fun with them. Further, few noncustodial parents contribute as much to the cost of child-rearing as the children need, partly because divorce settlements generally result in inadequate child-support arrangements and partly because few noncustodial parents keep up full support payments year after year (Espenshade, 1979). Obviously, this creates resentment in the custodial parent, who may then complain to the children that the other parent is irresponsible and to blame for whatever financial difficulties the family may be experiencing.

The visiting schedule itself is often a problem (Wallerstein and Kelly, 1980). For instance, the frequency and duration of visits may need to change as children grow older, a fact that few lawyers or divorcing couples think of. While visits of a day or less may be appropriate for very small children, older children and their parents may need more time together to build their relationship. At the same time, for older children and adolescents, a fixed visitation schedule such as every other weekend can wreak havoc with their social life.

Joint custody has been proposed as an ideal solution (Clingempeel and Reppucci, 1982; Roman and Haddad, 1978). Theoretically, both parents share equal responsibility for their children and make joint decisions in matters ranging from the choice of a school to the choice of a dentist. They are kept directly involved with the children, and share the work as well as the expense of child-rearing. However, this solution demands a fair amount of flexibility in the parents, who must cooperate in working out the details of daily care, yet many divorced parents are too bitter and overwhelmed to interact constructively. Consequently, joint custody is not always as beneficial to the children as it is intended to be (Steinman, 1981; Derdeyn and Scott, 1984). As one review concludes:

. . . joint custody seems to be a reasonable and probably beneficial option in cases where neither parent insists on sole custody, where interparental conflict is low, and where the practicalities of everyday living will be minimally disrupted in the child's life. Thus, joint custody seems to be a good option for parents who agree that this is what they want . . . [however] those litigated cases in which a judge is forced to make a difficult custody decision may be exactly the ones for whom joint custody will not work. [Emery et al., 1984]

after the event, it usually is not because of the divorce itself but because of other, related problems such as financial difficulties, continued feuding between the parents, or the lack of a father's interest and support. Divorce is never easy on a child, but to a great degree the parents can determine whether it is a serious and continuing disturbance or a temporary disruption.

Children in Single-Parent Households Households headed by a single parent are increasingly common, either as a result of divorce or separation, or of the death of a parent, or of a mother's never marrying. (Unwed mothers represent the fastest-growing group of single parents, the number of children born out of wedlock having increased nearly threefold between 1973 and 1983 [U.S. Department of the Census, 1985].) In the United States, about one child in five lives in a household headed by a single parent, as does about one child in nine in Canada. Ninety percent of these heads of households are mothers; the other ten percent are fathers.

Studies of the factors that foster competent or inadequate parenting find that the more stresses parents experience, the harder it is for them to be responsive and supportive of their children (Belsky et al., 1984c). Thus, our efforts to help children in single-parent households should begin with efforts to understand the stresses their parents experience. And certainly single parents have many sources of stress in their lives.

To begin with, most single parents suffer from "role overload" as they try to provide nurturance, discipline, and financial support all at the same time (Zill, 1983). Having a job and a family is not easy no matter what one's marital status, but the single parent is particularly likely to have difficulty when a child is sick, or when the job demands overtime, or when school holidays conflict with work obligations. The problems of the single parent increase markedly as family size increases: one child does not put nearly as much strain on the parent as two or more children do (Polit, 1984).

Financial difficulties often seem hardest to overcome. The income of single-parent households is substantially lower than that of two-parent households, even when only one of the parents in those households is employed. About a third of all single parents are forced to rely on welfare at some point, a solution that does not provide adequate support or self-respect. More than half of all households headed by women have incomes below the poverty line (Malcom, 1985).

While single-parent households headed by a man fare somewhat better financially, men as single parents may experience complications that women do not. An extensive study found that many men are less prepared than women to handle the simultaneous demands of child-rearing and career (George and Wilding, 1972). Single fathers also are less willing to ask for outside help, financial as well as psychological, when problems become too difficult to handle alone. Further, single fathers are likely to have problems with their daughters (Santrock et al., 1982), perhaps because fathers tend to rely on their daughters to take over some of the housework and caring for younger children that their wife formerly did (Gasser and Taylor, 1976).

Another problem that many children in single-parent households experience is difficulty with sex-role development (Biller, 1981). Boys without fathers at home often become stereotypically "manly"—fighting and generally getting into trouble at quite a young age. It is sometimes thought that this behavior arises because of the absence of a father's discipline, but, in fact, if the father were present, his more moderate example of male behavior might make stern discipline unnecessary (Biller, 1981). Girls without fathers at home also are affected, although the specific effects may depend largely on the reason for the father's absence. According to one study, girls may become prematurely interested in sexual relationships if their mothers are divorced, and unusually shy and withdrawn if their mothers are widows (Hetherington, 1972).

Figure 14.12 *Single-parent households take many forms, from the affluent, white, father-headed family on the left to the lower-class, Hispanic, mother-headed family on the right. No matter what the form, however, the crucial factor seems to be a strong and loving head of the household—something all four daughters in these photos seem to share.*

Children of single parents are also more likely to be prone to academic difficulties. Both their attendance and their achievement are lower, with a greater number being left back or placed in special classes. Further, growing up in a father-absent house is particularly detrimental to a child's functioning in math. However, some studies find that children in mother-headed families do well verbally (Shinn, 1978; Hetherington et al., 1981). This may be a direct result of having more maternal attention than other children, or it may be indirect, resulting from the greater need to express one's ideas and emotions.

Are the children of single parents headed for hard times, then? Not necessarily. If their parents can find ways to cope with the financial and role overloads placed on them, many children do quite well. Children of widows and widowers, overall, achieve as well as their peers from two-parent families, which shows that it is not single parenthood per se that puts children at risk (Rutter, 1982).

In fact, ecological factors probably make the difference between children who function well in single-parent households and those who do not (Feiring and Lewis, 1984). The crucial factor is usually a network of social support. Friends and relatives can relieve some of the parent's role overload by helping with child care or financial difficulties. Grandfathers and uncles often become significant role models for children without fathers. Since social support is generally much more readily available to the widow than to the divorced woman or unwed mother, this may well explain many of the differences observed in the children of various types of single parents.

Blended Families Especially if they are relatively young at the time of the divorce, most divorced adults marry again. How does this affect the children who become part of a new "blended" family with a step-parent and perhaps step-siblings as well? Obviously, there is no pat answer to this question. The change may bring a marked improvement in the child's life or it may create new problems. Much de-

Figure 14.13 *On the left, adolescent boys from a first marriage; on the right, their father and step-mother; in the future, a half brother or sister who might cause increased stability or increased bitter-ness—or moments of both.*

pends on the particular individuals involved, as well as on the kind of family inter-action that develops. In addition, the benefits of remarriage for a child depend partly on which parent is remarried, and partly on the age and sex of the child.

Remarriage of the Custodial Parent. Typically, if the children are relatively young and living with their mother at the time she remarries, their life improves. This is shown by their achievement in school as well by their subjective reports (Hetherington et al., 1982). Part of the reason for the improvement is that remar-riage usually leads to enhanced financial security for the family and higher self-esteem for the mother, both of which benefit the children. The other major factor, of course, is the presence of the step-father: boys, particularly, are helped when their step-fathers develop an active and helpful relationship with them.

This is not to say that the arrival of a step-father is always good for the children. If he has children of his own, their introduction on the scene may create added diffi-culties for the child who is trying to adjust to the absence of one parent and the presence of a new one (Visher and Visher, 1982). Further, a minority of step-fathers are cruel and abusive to their step-children. While only 10 percent of all children have step-fathers, step-fathers are implicated in 15 percent of cases of physical abuse and 30 percent of cases of sexual abuse (Giles-Sims and Finkelhor, 1984).

When a father who has custody of his children remarries, the results are also usually beneficial. Typically, the step-mother helps considerably with child care and housework, relieving the father and his children of some of the stress of their lives together (Ambert, 1982). The presence of the step-mother seems particularly helpful to girls, who often open up to the new woman in the house. Sons, however, tend to withdraw from the family (Santrock et al., 1982).

Remarriage of the Noncustodial Parent. When the noncustodial parent remarries, difficulties often arise for the custodial parent as well as for the children. Remar-riage of a former spouse is often a further blow to self-esteem of the divorced par-ent and often a threat as well. It is not uncommon for the new spouse to cause alterations in the noncustodial parent's relationship to his or her children—either by reraising custody questions that had been settled, or by insisting that the non-custodial parent see his or her offspring less often than before (Hetherington et al., 1982; Furstenberg et al., 1982).

Overall, the same factors that were relevant to divorce adjustment are relevant to remarriage adjustment. If remarriage means happier parents, more money, and less stress, it benefits the children as well as the adult. Two cautions are in order, however. First, it takes time for children to adjust to a "new" family situation: many react with hostility or withdrawal at first. Second, since the divorce rate of remarriages is even higher than that of first marriages, parents thinking of remarriage "for the sake of the children" should think hard before taking such a step. As you will see at the end of the chapter, most children can adjust to one or two stresses in their lives, especially if the stresses are limited in time, but repeated family disruptions are much more likely to have long-term consequences (Hetherington and Camara, 1984).

Maternal Employment Most mothers of school-age children are in the job market. To be specific, of the mothers who have school-age children but no children under 6, 63 percent who are married, and 75 percent who are single, are employed. Further, of those who have children under age 6, about half are employed.

While it is often suggested that a mother's working is harmful to her children, in fact, it seems that in many ways it may be beneficial to them (Hoffman, 1984; Lamb, 1982). In most cases, the mother's employment relieves some of the financial pressure on the family, and this obviously benefits the children. Further, employed women generally are more satisfied with their lives than full-time housewives are (Newberry et al., 1979; Baruch et al., 1983), and, as a review of the research on maternal working status concludes, "satisfied mothers—working or not—have the best-adjusted children" (Etaugh, 1974).

The evidence that employed women are more satisfied with their lives holds true not only for career women but also for working-class women with relatively unexciting jobs (Ferree, 1976). The reasons are obvious once one thinks about it: employment provides social status, financial control, friendship, standards for job performance, and involvement in the larger world (Jahoda, 1981).

Interestingly, the benefits of maternal employment are even suggested by a study of mothers who were *dissatisfied* with their work status, either because they wished they were home but had to work or because they wished they were employed but were not. This study found that unhappy employed mothers tended to have children who were as well adjusted in school as children of happy women, whatever their job status. However, children of unhappy women who remained at home showed lower school achievement (Farel, 1980).

Daughters are particularly likely to benefit psychologically from their mother's employment. When their mothers are employed, girls tend to think of females as competent, effective, and active, and they look forward to becoming a woman themselves. By contrast, daughters of housewives are more likely to associate femininity with restrictions on physical, social, and economic possibilities (Hoffman and Nye, 1974).

It has also been suggested that in two-parent families, children of working mothers benefit in some ways because their fathers tend to be more directly involved in the household, which benefits the children of both sexes (Hoffman, 1984; Carlson, 1984). Furthermore, children of employed mothers learn responsibility as well as household skills, which enhances their competence and self-esteem. Girls are particularly likely to benefit from their increased responsibilities and independence (Smokler, 1975; Lamb, 1982).

However, some boys may be adversely affected by their mother's employment (Hoffman, 1977; Lamb, 1982). According to one influential Canadian study, boys of lower-class employed mothers are more shy and nervous, dislike school, have lower grades, and are described more negatively by their fathers than are boys whose mothers stay home (Gold and Andres, 1978). The father's attitudes may be crucial to the son's adjustment to maternal employment, for problems are particularly likely to arise when the father is unhappy that his wife is working, and is unwilling to help out at home (Hoffman, 1977).

Figure 14.14 *The effect that a mother's employment has on her son may, in many cases, depend largely on her husband's understanding and help. It is likely that this boy will benefit from the father-son comradery of sharing some daily chores.*

One final concern is often raised with regard to maternal employment, that of the millions of ''latchkey'' children who let themselves into an empty house after school because neither parent is home (Turkington, 1983). However, two careful comparison studies of children aged 9 and older who cared for themselves after school found that their self-esteem, social adjustment, and school achievement were just as good as that of children who had some form of after-school adult care (Galambos and Garbarino, 1983; Rodman et al., 1985). The likely reason is that children who care for themselves after school are not simply left to their own devices. They are taught how to manage on their own, what dangers to avoid, and are in telephone contact with their parents.

Obviously, some families would benefit if their employed mothers had more time and energy to devote to them, and measures such as an increase in flextime, greater benefits for part-time workers, and equality of pay for women would facilitate this. However, the increasing rates of maternal employment under current arrangements should not be seen as a detriment to school-age children. The evidence clearly shows that the opposite is more likely the case.

Coping with Stress

As we have seen, the development of many school-age children is hindered by problems with their peers, their parents, or the larger society. However, particularly in middle childhood, many children cope quite well with a variety of problems. This is apparent statistically: serious problems between children and their parents, and severe emotional disturbance in children, are less common during middle childhood than earlier or later. It is also apparent in longitudinal studies of child development: before age 12, most children encounter some unexpected and potentially handicapping stress, and most develop normally (Murphy and Moriarty, 1976; Garmezy, 1976; Werner and Smith, 1982; Rutter, 1975).

In his study of stresses that lead to severe psychological problems in childhood, Michael Rutter (1979) identified six variables that are strongly and significantly associated with psychiatric disorders:

1. severe marital discord;

2. low social status;

3. overcrowding or large family size;

4. paternal criminality;

5. maternal psychiatric disorder;

6. admission of the child into the care of the local authority.

Rutter found that children with one, and only one, of the six risk factors were no more likely to have psychiatric problems than children with no risk factors. When two of the risk factors occurred together, the incidence of problems more than doubled. When four or more of the risk factors were present, psychiatric problems were four times as likely as when there were two. As Rutter writes, "the stresses potentiated each other so that the combination of chronic stresses provided very much more than a summation of the effects of the separate stresses considered singly" (Rutter, 1979).

Yet, as Rutter and others have found, some children are able to overcome several serious problems. These children, often referred to as "invulnerable" or "stress-resistant," have been studied extensively to see what it is that helps them cope. Two factors seem especially important. The first is competence in any one area. The second is social support.

Figure 14.15 *Rutter found that children who had to cope with one serious problem ran virtually as low a risk of suffering a psychiatric disorder as did children who faced no serious problems. However, when the child had two problems, the chances more than doubled. Four or more problems produced about ten times the likelihood of psychiatric disorders as one. About one child in five who experienced four or more serious stresses actually became emotionally disturbed.*

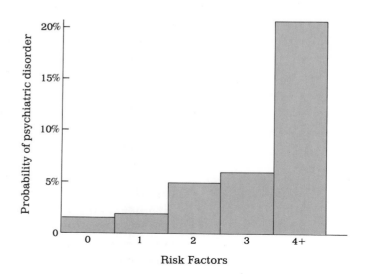

Competence   A theme throughout this chapter has been the importance of competence for school-age children. Several studies have shown that children who have well-developed social, academic, or creative skills—or better yet, all three—are much more able to surmount whatever problems they encounter at home or in their community (Murphy and Moriarty, 1976; Garmezy, 1976; Block and Block, 1980; Werner and Smith, 1982). During middle childhood, intellectual competence is particularly important. Children who are intellectually able, or whose schools encourage them to develop their strengths, are often able to overcome many handicaps. School achievement allows the young slum dweller, for instance, to have aspirations that transcend the circumstances of his or her present living conditions.

Further, school-age children's increasing cognitive competence enables them to achieve some perspective on their own problems, and then use their analysis constructively. Often they decide to change their behavior, as did a tomboy who "decided to be a girl when I was seven"; another girl "decided to stop being shy" at age 10; and a boy whose parents' separation had made him very unhappy during his preschool years decided to begin another life, forgetting the first one (Murphy and Moriarty, 1976).

Children of divorced parents can sometimes become quite insightful about their parents' problems. As Wallerstein and Kelly (1980) report, many of the older school-age children "perceived the realities of their family's disruption and the parent's turbulence with a soberness and clarity we first found startling, particularly when compared with the younger children who so frequently appeared disorganized and immobilized by their worry and grief." Similarly, older children of a schizophrenic are sometimes able to understand that the afflicted parent is not always in touch with reality, and the children make the necessary adjustments (Garmezy et al., 1979). This does not mean that insight comes automatically with maturity, of course. Many children in troubled families need time, as well as counseling, to help them understand their situation.

The School   Especially in middle childhood, schools and teachers can help children develop their competencies and overcome their problems, becoming a buffer between the child and the stresses of home or community (Minuchin and Shapiro, 1983).

Of course, much depends on the nature of the particular school the child attends. Even more important than the academic quality of the curriculum or the size of the classes is the overall emotional tone of the school. This was found in a study of twelve London schools that served lower-class children, many of whom came from crowded families that were headed by single parents or that had parents with serious psychological problems (Rutter et al., 1979). Some of these schools had markedly more students who passed higher-level exams, fewer students who dropped out, and lower rates of juvenile delinquency than would be expected based on the students' backgrounds. One crucial factor that distinguished the more successful schools was that they cared about the children, as evidenced by such simple things as the student's work being displayed on the walls and the frequency of praise from the teachers. Another was that the administration of these schools had definite and high expectations of their teachers, who, in turn, had high expectations of their students. Apparently, in environments that expect and encourage competence, children tend to meet the challenge, overcoming home and community handicaps to do so.

Social Support At virtually every point in the life span, the developing person's social network is crucial to overcoming problems and developing his or her potential. The social network includes all the people who could offer assistance of any sort, from a shoulder to cry on to financial aid. Friends and family members are the main sources of social support, and this is true in middle childhood as well as in the rest of life. Neighbors, clergy, and teachers also can be very influential, especially when the child's problems originate in the family (Garmezy et al., 1979). Among many instances of such support, Murphy and Moriarty (1976) describe a next-door neighbor who filled-in as a "second mother" to a girl whose actual mother was chronically ill and therefore generally unavailable as a parent. Werner and Smith (1982) found that grandparents and siblings often compensated for the neglect or absence of one or even both parents. During middle childhood and later, a stable and supportive adult sibling can be particularly crucial (Bank and Kahn, 1982).

Figure 14.16 *Parents are usually the most important family members, and schools are usually the most important institutions, in the life of school-age children. However, especially for children who experience extraordinary stress, essential support systems may come from a bit further afield. This boy, leaning on his grandfather while they listen to the pastor of a country church, may be getting the special support he needs.*

The role of social support has been highlighted in ethnic groups in which high-risk conditions are almost the norm (Harrison et al., 1984). For example, 49 percent of all black American children are in single-parent households, and 47 percent of all black American children are living below the poverty line (Malcom, 1985). These problems are never easy to live with, but study after study shows that many black families have extensive networks of family support, with grandparents, aunts and uncles, older siblings, and neighbors frequently providing many forms of help—including taking complete care of the child for days, months, or years when it seems in the child's best interest (McAdoo, 1979; Malson, 1983; Lindblad-Goldberg and Dukes, 1985). While the adults in such families sometimes feel overburdened by advice and requests for assistance from their relatives, children benefit from having several possible sources of comfort and support.

RESEARCH REPORT   **The Children of Kauai**

A longitudinal study of children at risk of developing learning or behavior problems began with all the babies born in 1955 on the island of Kauai, Hawaii (Werner et al., 1971). Most of these children were from large, lower-class families, and from ethnic groups (Filipino, Hawaiian, mixed race, and Portuguese) that experience considerable prejudice. In addition to these specific strikes against them, as they grew up, the island itself experienced many stresses, among them economic depression, political upheaval over the question of statehood, and the arrival of hundreds of unemployed, drug-using mainland youth whose example influenced many local young people.

However, despite all these sources of stress, 81 percent of the girls and 70 percent of the boys managed to reach age 10 without serious learning or behavior problems (Werner and Smith, 1982). Those who developed such problems typically had four or more strikes against them: for example, congenital birth problems, birth of a younger sibling before age 2, low maternal education, IQ below 80 at age 2 or below 90 at age 10, or a physical handicap. However, even some children with four or more of these risk factors did quite well. The authors of this study, like other researchers who have followed "high risk" children, believe that in predicting which children are likely to develop problems, it is even more important to look at the factors that cushion children against stress than to examine the number or the severity of the stress factors.

In many instances, the authors found that social support, whether it came from parents, grandparents, siblings, or nonfamily members, was crucial in enabling children to overcome the many risk factors they were born with. Grandparents, for example, often provided "continuity and support," buffering "the effects of family strife."

The authors also report some interesting sex differences that can be explained in terms of social support: maternal employment and having older siblings seemed to help the girls but not the boys, who did better if they were first-born and if their mothers did not work. The father's presence in the home helped the boys, but not the girls. Given some of the research we have discussed in this chapter, the reason for these differences seems clear. Since girls are expected to help more around the house when their mothers are working, their opportunity to develop their competence is enhanced by the mother's employment, whereas the boys' would be less likely to be so. Being the oldest daughter, however, might be difficult, because the amount of work may interfere with academic or social skills. By contrast, being an oldest boy might be better than being a middle-born or last-born son, who would need to compete with older brothers for a secure place in the family constellation. Finally, given what we know about the importance of the father-son relationship, it is not surprising that the father's presence is much more of an asset for boys than for girls.

The importance of the social network is apparent in looking at one eldest son, Martin, who was born with visual difficulties, had an IQ of only 68 at age 2, and had seven younger siblings by age 10. The family was of mixed racial background, their income was low, and neither parent had graduated from high school.

Despite all these risk factors, Martin had one crucial strength: he was surrounded by a supportive family from the time he was born. As a first-born child, his parents and grandparents not only played with him during infancy but also encouraged his intellectual competence. They read to him during the preschool years and regularly attended every parent-teacher conference in elementary school. Martin's father regularly took him along on various expeditions, and made it clear that his first-born son was a special person. The arrival of Martin's seven younger brothers and sisters did not seem to overwhelm Martin or his parents, because the family was close and well-organized, with regular chores for everyone and frequent family outings. At age 10, Martin's IQ was close to normal, his school performance adequate, and his parents were delighted with his behavior.

Two conclusions from this study are noteworthy. First, among the families studied, "support from an informal network of kin and neighbors and the advice of ministers and teachers were more often sought and more highly valued than the services of mental health professionals. Second, "even under adverse circumstances, change is possible if the older child or adolescent encounters new experiences and people who give meaning to one's life, and a reason for commitment and caring." On the basis of these findings the authors of this study suggest that mental health professionals recognize that while intervention can indeed help the school-age child at risk, the best intervention may not be of the traditional type. In their words, "it may make better sense to strengthen informal ties to kin and community than to introduce additional layers of bureaucracy."

As a child approaches adolescence, then, the crucial question is not whether the child has any serious problems but whether the child has a store of strengths, such as supportive parents, cognitive competence, social skills, or personality assets that will help him or her through to adulthood. As you will see in the next three chapters, while adolescence almost always presents problems and challenges, most young people cope very well, using the same resources that helped them overcome whatever stresses childhood contained.

SUMMARY

The Three Theories and Middle Childhood

1. Freud believed that most of the child's emotions are latent during middle childhood, especially sexual and aggressive urges. This enables the child to become less dependent on parents, and more interested in friends of the same sex.

2. Erikson calls middle childhood the industry-versus-inferiority stage, because children like to be busy learning new skills. If they don't develop the competencies their society values, they don't develop their self-esteem and thus feel inferior.

3. Learning theorists stress the school-age child's increasing ability to learn as well as the growing importance of intrinsic reinforcements, social influences, and ability to control oneself.

4. Cognitive theory notes that children become less egocentric during these years. They become more vulnerable to others' opinions, and more able to understand another point of view.

Social Cognition

5. School-age children develop a greater awareness of the many social roles that individuals can have. They also become increasingly aware that others have preferences and characteristics that are different from their own; at the same time, they become better able to adjust their behavior to interact appropriately with others.

6. Children also develop complex theories about themselves and their behavior. These ideas are based on their past experiences, the opinion of others, and untested assumptions about themselves. As children become more knowledgeable about their own abilities and shortcomings, they become more self-critical and their self-esteem dips.

7. Children develop a healthy sense of self-esteem if they become competent at a variety of tasks and if home and school values encourage cooperation.

8. School-age children develop their own subculture, with language, values, and codes of behavior. The child who is not included in this society often feels deeply hurt, for social dependence on peers is strong at this age, even as independence from adults is valued.

Moral Development

9. Children become able to reason about moral dilemmas during middle childhood. According to Piaget and Kohlberg, they move through stages of moral reasoning, from the self-centeredness of the younger child to an emphasis on moral principles.

10. Moral behavior is affected by reasoning ability, and also by culture, family influences, and the particular situation. Prosocial behavior, such as cooperation, can be encouraged or discouraged depending on the child's social world.

Problems and Challenges

11. School-age children's growing awareness and independence make them more susceptible to the influence of the larger society and the effects of socioeconomic class. SES influences all aspects of children's lives, from educational achievement to self-esteem.

12. Whether or not factors such as low SES, divorce, and single-parent households affect children negatively depends on the functioning of family and school support systems.

KEY TERMS

latency *(420)*

industry versus inferiority *(421)*

social cognition *(424)*

self-theory *(426)*

learned helplessness *(427)*

society of children *(430)*

moral development *(435)*

preconventional moral reasoning *(436)*

conventional moral reasoning *(436)*

postconventional moral reasoning *(436)*

prosocial behavior *(438)*

socioeconomic status (SES) *(441)*

KEY QUESTIONS

1. What are the effects of latency on the development of school-age children?

2. How does a child's response to various types of reinforcement change as he or she grows older?

3. How does children's self-theory change from the preschool years through middle childhood?

4. What factors help a child to develop positive self-esteem?

5. What is the role of the peer group during the school years?

6. What evidence is there that the society of children is a powerful force in middle childhood?

7. What are some of the factors that may cause a child to be rejected from the peer group?

8. What are Kohlberg's views on the development of moral judgment?

9. What affects whether children will follow their moral beliefs?

10. How does socioeconomic class affect the development of skills in middle childhood?

11. What are some of the factors that influence the effects of parental divorce on a child?

12. What are some of the problems experienced by single-parent households?

13. What factors tend to make maternal employment beneficial or harmful to a child's development?

14. What are some of the stresses associated with a high risk of serious problems in a child's life?

15. What can help a child cope with stress?

RECOMMENDED READINGS

Osman, Betty, and Blinder, Henriette. *No one to play with.* New York: Warner Books, 1986.

A sympathetic view of the problems with friendship and social skills experienced by many learning-disabled children. Included are practical suggestions of ways in which teachers and parents can help children overcome difficulties.

Rubin, Zick. *Children's friendships.* Cambridge, Mass.: Harvard University Press, 1980.

Friendship is described as a very important, but not always easy or natural, phenomenon. With quotes, anecdotes, and research, Rubin explains the many forms of friendship between children and the skills and problems they entail.

Piaget, Jean. *The moral judgment of the child.* New York: The Free Press, 1965.

Piaget's careful research on the rules of marbles and ideas of justice is illustrated with many quotations from the children themselves. It also includes discussion of adult morality and ethical theory that makes for provocative but heavy reading.

Lickona, Thomas. *Raising good children.* New York: Bantam, 1985.

Writing for parents and teachers, Thomas Lickona explains the insights into moral development gained from the current research and gives practical suggestions as to how children can be taught to act in moral ways. The importance of helping the child to understand moral behavior rather than simply to fear punishment and the crucial impact of the parents' example are underscored. Includes age-appropriate suggestions for raising children from infancy through adolescence.

Coles, Robert. *Children of crisis: A study of courage and fear.* New York: Dell, 1976.

In this sensitive study of the first black children to attend the newly integrated schools of the South, the psychiatrist Robert Coles reveals the strength and resilience of many of those children. The book illustrates the concept of "invulnerables," while describing some of the family and community resources that allowed the children to survive psychologically in a stressful environment.

Paris, Erna. *Stepfamilies: Making them work.* New York: Avon, 1984.

An informed and readable account of the problems stepfamilies face. Written primarily to help parents, this book includes honest discussion of the many possible difficulties these families may face—among them school failure, sexual attraction among step-siblings, and overt rebellion at home.

457

Part IV

The Developing Person So Far: The School Years, Ages 7 through 11

Physical Development

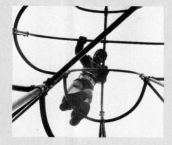

Growth

During middle childhood, children grow more slowly than they did during infancy and toddlerhood or than they will during adolescence. Increased strength and heart and lung capacity give children the endurance to improve their performance in skills such as swimming and running.

Motor Skills

Slower growth contributes to children's increasing control over their bodies. However, since brain maturation is not yet completed, the average 7-year-old may take twice as long as an adult to respond to a stimulus.

Cognitive Development

Concrete Operational Thought

Beginning at about age 7 or 8, children develop the ability to understand logical principles. Once acquired, the concepts of reciprocity, classification, class inclusion, seriation, and number help children to develop a more complete understanding of mathematics and of measurement.

An Information-Processing View

Children's expanded ability to understand and learn can be attributed, in part, to enlarging memory capacity and an increasing ability to use metamemory techniques. At the same time, metacognition techniques enable children to organize their knowledge.

Language

Children's increasing ability to understand the structures and possibilities of language enables them to extend the range of their cognitive powers, to become more analytical in their use of vocabulary, and to enjoy the word-play involved in puns, jokes, and riddles.

Psychosocial Development

Personality Development

According to Freud, middle childhood is the period of latency, during which the intense drives of the phallic stage are submerged, freeing children to learn and be productive. Erikson describes the conflict of this stage as the crisis of industry versus inferiority. Learning theorists suggest that children's greater understanding of cause and effect and their awareness of the actions and attitudes of others make them more susceptible to reinforcement and modeling techniques.

The Peer Group

The peer group becomes increasingly important to children as they become less dependent on their parents and more dependent on friends for help, loyalty, and mutual interests.

Social Systems and the Child

Children are increasingly aware of, and involved in, the world outside the home, and therefore are more likely to feel the effects of political, economic, and family conditions. Whether or not particular situations will be stressful for a child will depend, at least in part, on the child's temperament, his or her competence, and the social support provided by home and school.

Adolescence

Part V

Adolescence is probably the most challenging and complicated period of life to describe, study, or experience. Between the ages of 10 and 20, more changes occur, and greater individual variation is evident, than during any other period. Children's bodies suddenly show the signs of sexual maturing and childish faces become less round and more angular. These biological changes of puberty are universal, but in their particular expression, timing, and extent, the variety shown is enormous and depends, of course, on sex, genes, and nutrition. There is great diversity in cognitive development as well: many adolescents are as egocentric in some respects as preschool children, while others reach the stage of abstract thinking that characterizes adult cognition at its best. Psychosocial development shows even greater diversity, as adolescents develop their own identity, choosing from a vast number of sexual, moral, political, and vocational paths.

Yet such differences should not mask the commonality of the adolescent experience, for all adolescents are confronted with the same developmental tasks: they must adjust to their new body size and shape and to their awakening sexuality, think in new ways, and strive for the emotional maturity and economic independence that characterize adulthood. As we will see in the next three chapters, the adolescent's efforts to come to grips with these tasks are often touched with confusion and poignancy.

Adolescence: Physical Development

Lots of kids I know, they feel all of a sudden they can't be kids anymore. They call themselves kids but they don't feel the same way about it. . . . Their parents may tell them how they act irresponsibly, like kids, but in their minds they aren't thinking irresponsible thoughts . . . their bodies aren't kids' bodies either. It's hard to guess people's age nowadays because everybody looks older; even if they don't, they act older. . . . You think, Hey, I know I'm not old, but it's fun to try, because if I want, I can fail miserably at it. You can pull off this big mask of yours and say "Hi, everybody, it's really me and I'm really a kid. . . ." You hate to admit it, but there are lots of times you wish you still were a little kid, nodding at all the questions people ask.

Jeannie Melchione, age 16
quoted in Cottle, 1979

The Stormy Decade?
Psychoanalytic Theory
A More Balanced View

Puberty
Physical Growth
Sexual Growth
The Timing of Puberty
Gender Differences in Sex Drive

Storm and Stress: Who, When, and Why?
Early and Late Puberty
Boys' Problems, Girls' Problems

Chapter 15

In the teenage years, adolescents are caught up in a torrent of physical, emotional, and cognitive changes. In addition to growing taller, heavier, and stronger at a rate more rapid than at any time since early childhood, the changes associated with sexual growth contribute a new dimension to the way their bodies function and the ways they think about themselves and others. In this chapter we will focus on the nature and consequences of the physical changes that occur in adolescence, including topics such as those that follow.

Is adolescence always a time of stress for teenagers, and consequently for their parents?

In which ways are the patterns of physical and sexual growth similar for both sexes?

What are some of the factors that affect the timing of puberty for a particular individual?

Are there significant differences in sex drive between adolescent boys and girls?

Why do early-maturing girls and late-maturing boys tend to have more problems than their peers?

Adolescence, the years from 11 or 12 through the teens, is a period of many changes, from the quite noticeable physical changes that are the subject of this chapter to the broadening cognitive growth and deepening emotional development that are described in the final two chapters. Since we view these changes, in sum, as changing children into young adults, we seldom fail to take note of them as they occur in individuals we know. Often, however, we are unaware of the ways in which society and culture impinge on these changes, shaping them, delaying or accelerating them, and in all cases influencing how we and those in whom they are occurring regard them. Let us begin our survey of adolescence, then, with a comparison of historical and current views of adolescence.

The Stormy Decade?

What should we expect from young people during the decade from about age 10 to 20? As we saw in Chapter 1, in the United States, hard work and obedience to authority would have been the answer up until a century or so ago. However, once adolescence was "created" by changing cultural and socioeconomic conditions, and then "discovered" and studied as a distinct stage by social scientists, most psychologists came to believe that this period is inevitably characterized by storm and stress. They maintained that emotional turbulence and psychological strain were inherent components of adolescence, as young people try to cope with their rapid physical development, their emerging sexuality, and the problems of identity and independence that they must face as they approach adulthood.

This view was set forth at the turn of the century by the founder of American developmental psychology, G. Stanley Hall (1904), in an influential two-volume treatise titled *Adolescence*. (It was this work that introduced the term "adoles-

Figure 15.1 *Seated front and center is G. Stanley Hall, the leading American proponent of the storm-and-stress view of adolescence. Surrounding him, and lending support to his theory, particularly with regard to adolescent sexuality, are the prime movers of the psychoanalytic movement: left to right, Sigmund Freud, A. A. Brill, Ernest Jones, S. Ferenzi, and Carl Jung. (This photo was taken in 1909 in Worcester, Mass.)*

cence"—coined by Hall from the Latin word for growth—into the English language.) Hall persuasively explained that erratic physical growth coincides with erratic emotional and moral development. According to Hall, adolescence is a time of rebirth: physical maturation changes not only the adolescent's size and physiology; it also changes the young person's way of seeing the world. Consequently, stated Hall, each new generation is capable of surpassing previous generations in moral and intellectual leadership, because the young are idealistic, altruistic, and self-sacrificing. In Hall's view, this "great revolution" is not easily achieved, however, for the young person's development

> often seems insufficient to enable the child to come to complete maturity . . . every step of the upward way is strewn with wreckage of body, mind, and morals. . . . Modern life is hard, and in many respects increasingly so, on youth. . . . Normal children often pass through stages of passionate cruelty, laziness, lying and thievery. [Hall, 1904]

As we will see in this chapter and in the next two, Hall's views have been echoed by theorists and researchers from many perspectives looking at adolescence from many points of view—from physical development to practical and moral reasoning about drug use and sexual activity, from one's sense of individual identity to one's relationships with family and peers.

Psychoanalytic Theory

Hall's views were particularly consistent with those of most psychoanalytic theorists, who believed that the stresses of adolescence are inescapable, since the adolescent's rapid sexual maturation and powerful sexual drives would inevitably conflict with the culture's traditional prohibitions against their free expression. As Peter Blos (1962) put it, "No one is exempt—no matter how warm and understanding the family background. The comfort and security of having been loved may help sustain the adolescent in this moment of terror, but no parent, however devoted and well intentioned, can spare the child this frenzied conflict."

One reason psychoanalytic theorists believed parents cannot prevent the "frenzied conflict" of adolescence is that the parents themselves are part of it. According to Sigmund Freud (1960, originally published in 1935), the impulses and fantasies of the Oedipal complex (see pages 344–345), which have been repressed during the latency period of middle childhood, reemerge at puberty as part of the flood of sexual urges of adolescence. Before young people can reach the **genital stage,** in which sexuality is expressed with contemporaries, they must free themselves of their sexual feelings toward their mother or father. Often this is done by temporarily replacing their respect and love for their opposite-sex parent with contempt and hate, a defense mechanism called **reaction formation** because the person's overt behavior and attitudes represent the opposite of his or her true feelings. As we will see in Chapter 17, adolescents' struggle with this aspect of their emerging sexuality is, in the view of some theorists, part of their struggle to establish a sense of self that is independent of, yet related to, their parents.

Thus, given the sexual drives and conflicts of adolescence and the many stresses associated with gaining independence, teenage turbulence seemed only natural to psychoanalysts. Indeed, Freud's daughter Anna, a distinguished psychoanalyst, believed that we should be more worried about the psychological health of the adolescent who does not seem to be emotionally upset than about the one who does. As she explained it:

> We all know individual children who as late as the ages of 14, 15, or 16 show no such outer evidence of inner unrest. They remain, as they have been during the latency period, "good" children, wrapped up in their family relationships, considerate of their mothers, submissive to their fathers, in accord with the atmosphere, ideas, and ideals of their childhood background. Convenient as this may be, it signifies a delay of normal development, and is, as such, a sign to be taken seriously . . . These are children who have built up excessive defenses against their drive activities and are now crippled by the results, which act as barriers against a normal maturational process . . . They are, perhaps, more than any others, in need of therapeutic help to remove the inner restrictions and clear the path for normal development, however upsetting the latter may prove to be. [A. Freud, 1968]

Since both Hall's scientific research and psychoanalysts' clinical experience have supported the idea that adolescence is destined to be difficult, it is not surprising that this view has dominated developmental psychology for most of this century, and that in the Western world, at least, adolescence is typically expected to be a time of moodiness, depression, and disobedience. Certainly it is a period that contemporary parents are rarely eager for. As Ellen Galinsky writes:

> The teenage years, in American culture today, have an awesome reputation. Some parents . . . picture the worst—their children transformed, surly, turning their backs on their parents, ungrateful, speeding dangerously down highways, hot-rodding, hitchhiking, drinking, metamorphosed by drugs, enmeshed in sex. They imagine that the remaining umbilical cords tying their children to them will be severed—not gently, but chopped off, leaving wounds. [Galinsky, 1981]

A More Balanced View

The "storm and stress" version of adolescence is not without some support from recent research. Contemporary studies have found that a host of problems, from law-breaking to depression, do, in fact, occur more often in adolescence than earlier (Rutter, 1980). However, as we will see in this chapter and the final two, deep and sustained problems such as these are the exception rather than the rule. Careful research on large samples of young people over the past two decades (Douvan and Adelson, 1966; Offer and Offer, 1975; Rutter et al., 1979; Thomas and Chess, 1980) has led to the conclusion that most adolescents, most of the time, are calm, predictable, and purposeful rather than storm-tossed, erratic, and "lost."

How, then, had psychologists arrived at such a firm view of adolescence as a time of trouble? One reason was that they had looked mostly at troubled adolescents. As Joseph Adelson (1979) explains,

> Our concentration on atypical factions of the total body of the young—on addicted, delinquent, and disturbed youngsters, or on the ideologically volatile, or on males (far more impulsive and rebellious than females)—has led us to generalize from qualities found among a minority of the young to adolescents as a whole . . . If we examine the studies that have looked fairly closely at ordinary adolescents, we get an entirely different picture. Taken as a whole, adolescents are *not* in turmoil, *not* deeply disturbed, *not* at the mercy of their impulses, *not* resistant to parental values, *not* politically active, and *not* rebellious.

Although we now know that adolescence need not be a turbulent period, we should not lose sight of the fact that it is not always smooth. For instance, Daniel and Judith Offer (1969, 1975) studied a group of boys from early adolescence through young adulthood. They found that 80 percent of their study population could be categorized in one of three ways. Of the whole study group, 22 percent experienced **tumultuous growth**—the turbulent, crisis-filled maturation that Hall and Freud would have predicted. Virtually the same number, 23 percent, experienced **continuous growth.** For this group, adolescence was characterized by a

Figure 15.2 *Psychologists have become increasingly aware that teenagers cannot be pigeonholed according to the statistically atypical extremes of adolescent behavior. The current tendency in psychology is to view adolescent growth in terms of general patterns—i.e., tumultuous, continuous, or surgent.*

"smoothness of purpose and self-assurance" and a "mutual respect, trust, and affection" between them and their parents. Finally, 35 percent of the boys in the study group experienced **surgent growth.** They were reasonably well adjusted and coped with the tasks of adolescence quite well, but they sometimes went through periods of turmoil before reaching this level of competence. Further, those adolescents whose growth was tumultuous tended to show a history of tumult in various aspects of their upbringing, their temperament, and their social milieu. It is exceedingly rare for a well-adjusted, well-loved 10-year-old to become a severely troubled 15-year-old, unless his or her life situation has changed radically as well.

Some psychologists, parents, and journalists probably still make the mistake of generalizing about all adolescents on the basis of the behavior of the adolescents we are most likely to notice—the disrespectful, the disturbed, and the delinquent. However, as you read about the details of adolescents' physical development in this chapter, and of their cognitive and psychosocial development in the next two, keep the total picture in mind. The changes that accompany adolescence sometimes can and do cause considerable difficulty, but they need not necessarily cause havoc.

Puberty

The period of physical growth that ends childhood and brings the young person to adult size, shape, and sexual potential is called **puberty,** and normally begins sometime between ages 9 and 14.

Generally, the many changes of puberty are grouped into two categories, those that are primarily related to the overall growth of the young person's body, and those that are specifically related to the development of male or female sexual characteristics. While this distinction is convenient for the purposes of discussion, and will be used here, it is also somewhat misleading, for **sexual dimorphism,** or

Figure 15.3 *Increases in height, weight, musculature, and body fat are characteristic of all adolescents, but the range of these changes varies considerably, not only between the sexes but also between individuals of the same sex. While all the teenagers in this photo are developing normally, not all of them may feel that way at the moment. For instance, why is the boy in the center covering his chest, why is the girl on the right turning sideways, and why is the boy on the left covering his armpit? The text on pages 471–472 suggests answers.*

sex-determined physical differences, is present in every aspect of pubescent growth. Thus most physical changes are sex-related. For instance, while both sexes grow rapidly during adolescence, boys typically begin this accelerated growth about two years later, and end it with relatively more height, less fat, and stronger muscles, than girls do. The overall size and shape of a teenager's body are affected as much or more by sex hormones as by growth hormones (Petersen and Taylor, 1980).

It is also true that some of the changes that we consider sexual because we think of them as occurring exclusively in one sex—such as lowered voices in males or breast development in females—actually occur in young people of both sexes, although, obviously, by the end of puberty, such changes are markedly more pronounced in one sex than in the other. As you will soon see, the two sexes are more different in "physical" growth, and more similar in "sexual" growth, than is commonly supposed.

Physical Growth

The first signs of puberty are invisible; the next are visible to the individual but not to people in general; and, finally, puberty is apparent to everyone who looks at the young person. To be specific, the first indication of puberty is increased concentrations of male and female hormones in the bloodstream—**estrogen** (which increases somewhat in boys and markedly in girls) and **testosterone** (which increases dramatically in boys and slightly in girls). These hormonal changes generally occur at least a year before the appearance of the first signs of puberty that are perceptible as such to the young person—the initial enlargement of the girl's breasts and the boy's testes (Higham, 1980). About a year after that, the first sign of the onset of puberty that is readily observable to others occurs, a period of rapid physical growth called the **growth spurt.**

Typically, parents begin to notice that their children are emptying their plates, cleaning out the refrigerator, and straining the seams of their clothes even before they notice that their children are growing taller, for the growth spurt actually

Figure 15.4 *Many of the physical changes of puberty seem to be inevitable sources of embarrassment for the young people experiencing them. The only one at this junior-high dance who appears to be enjoying herself, for instance, is the girl whose growth spurt has not yet started.*

begins with rapid weight gain before rapid height gain. Toward the end of middle childhood, usually between the ages of 10 and 12, both boys and girls become noticeably heavier, primarily through the accumulation of fat, especially on their thighs, arms, buttocks, and abdomen.

Soon after the weight increase begins, a height increase begins, burning up some of the fat and redistributing the rest. (On the whole, a greater percentage of fat is retained by females, who naturally have a higher proportion of body fat in womanhood than in girlhood.) About a year after these weight and height increases take place, a period of muscle increase occurs: consequently, the pudginess and clumsiness exhibited by the typical child in early puberty generally has disappeared by late pubescence, a few years later. Overall, the typical girl gains about 38 pounds (17 kilograms) and 9⅝ inches (24 centimeters) between the ages of 10 and 14, while the typical boy gains the same amount of height and about 42 pounds (19 kilograms) between the ages of 12 and 16 (Lowrey, 1978).

Note, however, that this cross-sectional data, which averages out the individual growth spurts, is somewhat deceptive, because the chronological age for the growth spurt varies considerably from child to child. In any given year between ages 10 and 16, some individuals will not grow much at all because their growth spurt has not begun or is already over, while others will grow very rapidly. Records of individual growth during this period make it obvious why the word "spurt" is used to describe these increases (Tanner, 1978). During the twelve-month period of their greatest growth, many girls gain as much as 20 pounds (9 kilograms) and 3½ inches (9 centimeters), and many boys gain up to 26 pounds (12 kilograms) and 4 inches (10 centimeters).

Sequence of Growth   The growth process does not occur in every part of the body simultaneously (Katchadourian, 1977). In most cases, adolescents' hands and feet lengthen before their arms and legs do, and their torso is the last part to grow, making many adolescents temporarily big-footed, long-legged, and short-waisted. Thus, growth in puberty, unlike that of earlier periods, is distal-proximal (far to near). In addition, the nose, lips, and ears usually grow before the head itself reaches adult size and shape. The results of this uneven growth rate are often unsettling, as evidenced in the case of a 12-year-old girl who wears a woman's size in shoes while still wearing children's sizes in all her other clothes, or in the case of a 14-year-old boy who fears that his nose is the only part of his body that is getting any bigger.

Even more disturbing to the growing person can be the fact that the two halves of the body do not always grow at the same rate: one foot, breast, or ear can be temporarily larger than the other. None of these anomalies persist very long, however. Once the growth process starts, every part of the body reaches close to adult size, shape, and proportion in three or four years.

Organ Growth.   Internal organs also grow during this period (Lowrey, 1978). The lungs increase in size and capacity, allowing the adolescent to breathe more deeply and slowly, and the heart doubles in size. In addition, the total volume of blood increases. These organic changes increase endurance in physical exercise, making it possible for many teenagers to run for miles or dance for hours without stopping to rest. The digestive system increases in capacity also, so rapidly that the typical adolescent can rarely be satisfied with only three meals a day.

Figure 15.5 *Adolescents' quicker reaction time, longer legs, and increased heart and lung capacity make them much better able than children to do well in sports—from double-dutch championships to swimming and ice-skating.*

One organ system, the lymphoid system, including the tonsils and adenoids, actually decreases in size at adolescence. Consequently, teenagers are less susceptible to respiratory ailments than children. For this reason, about half the victims of childhood asthma improve markedly in adolescence (Katchadourian, 1977).

The eyes also undergo a change, as the eyeballs elongate, making many adolescents sufficiently nearsighted to require glasses.

Finally, the hormones of puberty cause many relatively minor physical changes that, despite their insignificance in the grand scheme of development, can have substantial psychic impact. For instance, oil, sweat, and odor glands become much more active during puberty. One result is acne, a problem for about two-thirds of all boys and half of all girls between the ages of 14 and 19 (Schacter et al., 1971). Another result is oilier hair and smellier bodies, which make adolescents spend more money on shampoo, soap, and deodorants than any other age group.

Figure 15.6 *Of all the parts of the body, hair is the one most subjected to change and "improvement." The typical American teenager spends many hours and dollars on shampooing, conditioning, lightening, darkening, curling, straightening, rinsing, moussing, and spraying— all in the name of achieving "natural" beauty.*

Nutrition The rapid height and weight gain of puberty obviously requires additional calories, more than during any other period of life. In addition, the adolescent body needs about 50 percent more calcium, iron, and vitamin D during the growth spurt than a year or two earlier (Sinclair, 1978). There is also a greater need for protein, though not more than the usual North American diet provides (Mellendick, 1983). The nutrient most commonly lacking in the adolescent's diet is iron (most commonly found in meat and dark-green vegetables)—a deficiency that poses a special problem for adolescent girls once menstruation begins. Iron-deficiency anemia is more common among adolescent females than among any other part of the population, so if a teenage girl seems apathetic and lazy, she should have her iron level checked before it is assumed that she suffers from a poor attitude or other psychosocial difficulties.

Figure 15.7 *The pizza shop has replaced the soda shop as the favorite food hangout of the American adolescent. Fortunately, not only is pizza relatively inexpensive, quick, and easy to share, it is also quite nutritious when compared to the many other sweet, salty, or synthetic snack foods.*

Other, less common nutritional deficiencies sometimes result from adherence to exotic eating regimens. Adolescents are particularly susceptible to the latest crash diets or food fads, in part because their level of cognitive and psychological development leads them to experiment with new ideas and life styles. Such diets can have serious consequences. For instance, the Zen macrobiotic diet—which in its final and most "purified" stage involves eating solely foods from certain grains—can result in anemia, scurvy, and kidney disease (Katchadourian, 1977). A strict vegetarian diet (no meat, fish, or eggs) often results in vitamin B-12 deficiency. Unbalanced diets are potentially harmful at any age, but they are particularly so during the rapid growth of adolescence, when the body must have sufficient nourishment for full growth potential to be realized (Mellendick, 1983).

The problem of nutrition is compounded, of course, for pregnant teenagers, who need an extraordinarily nutritious diet to provide for the full growth of their fetus as well as themselves. Malnutrition is one major reason mothers under age 16 are more than twice as likely to have premature or stillborn babies as are mothers in their twenties.

Sexual Growth

While the growth spurt is taking place, another set of changes occurs that transforms boys and girls into young men and women. As we have seen, before puberty, the physical differences between boys and girls are relatively minor—on average, boys are an inch or so taller; they also have greater arm strength, while girls have greater body flexibility. At puberty, however, many significant body differences develop, as sex organs mature and secondary sexual characteristics appear.

Changes in Sex Organs During puberty, all the sex organs become much larger. In girls, the uterus begins to grow and the vaginal lining thickens, even before there are visible signs of puberty. In boys, the testes begin to grow, and about a year later, the penis lengthens and the scrotal sac enlarges and becomes pendulous.

Toward the end of puberty, the young person's sex organs have become sufficiently mature to make reproduction possible. For girls, the specific event that is taken to indicate fertility is the first menstrual period, called **menarche.** For boys, the comparable indicator of reproductive potential is **ejaculation,** that is, the discharge of seminal fluid containing sperm. Ejaculation can occur during sleep in a nocturnal emission (a wet dream), through masturbation, or through sexual intercourse, with masturbation being the most common cause for the first ejaculation (Kinsey et al., 1948).

Actually, both menarche and ejaculation are simply one more step toward full reproductive maturity, which occurs several years later. In fact, a girl's first menstrual cycles are usually *anovulatory;* that is, they occur without ovulation. Even a year after menarche, most young women are still relatively infertile: ovulation is irregular, and if fertilization does occur, the probability of spontaneous abortion is much higher than it will be later, because the uterus is still relatively small. In the case of boys, the concentration of sperm usually necessary to fertilize an ovum is not reached until months or even years after the first ejaculation of seminal fluid (Chilman, 1983). (As many teenagers discover too late, unfortunately, this relative infertility does not mean that pregnancy is impossible at puberty; it is simply less likely than it will be a few years later.)

Secondary Sex Characteristics While maturation of the reproductive organs are the most directly sexual developments of puberty, changes in many other parts of the young person's body also indicate that sexual maturation is occurring. Most obviously, the body shape of males and females, which was almost identical in childhood, becomes quite distinct in adolescence. Males grow taller than females and become wider at the shoulders than at the hips. Females become wider at the hips, an adaptation for child-bearing that is apparent even in early puberty, and becomes increasingly so over the teenage years (Tanner, 1978).

Another obvious difference in the shape of the female body, and the one that receives the most attention in Western cultures, is the development of breasts. For most girls, the first sign that puberty is beginning is the "bud" stage of breast development, when a small accumulation of fat causes a slight rise around the nipples. From then on, breasts develop gradually for several years, with full breast growth not being attained until almost all the other changes of puberty are over (Katchadourian, 1977). Since our culture misguidedly takes breast development to be symbolic of womanhood, girls whose breasts are very small or very large often feel worry and embarrassment; small-breasted girls often feel "cheated," even disfigured; large-breasted girls may become extremely self-conscious as they find themselves the frequent object of unwanted stares and remarks.

RESEARCH REPORT   **Menarche and Self-Concept**

Menarche is often an important event in the development of the adolescent girl's self-concept, partly because it prompts her to confront her emerging womanhood. How individual girls react depends on their culture, as well as their personal experiences. As shown by Paula Weideger's (1976) study, historical and cultural attitudes toward menstruation have been predominantly negative, including such ideas as that menstruation is associated with evil spirits and that a menstruating woman is potentially dangerous to men and to growing plants. As archaic as these notions are, their effects have continued to be felt. Indeed, according to a study of young girls from several American subcultures (Henton, 1961), positive attitudes toward menstruation were rare as recently as a generation or two ago, when it was much more common for a girl to refer to her period as "the curse" rather than "my friend."

Attitudes toward menstruation and menarche have changed in recent years. Contemporary girls awaiting menarche are worried about little more than being caught by surprise in public when it occurs. Indeed, they are more likely to worry if menarche arrives later than it does for their friends rather than if it is earlier (Ruble and Brooks-Gunn, 1982). While few are surprised at menarche, many are relieved, finding that the actual experience is not as troublesome as they had thought it would be.

Most girls learn about menstruation from their mothers and teachers, and feel quite well-informed (Ruble and Brooks-Gunn, 1982). Those who are relatively uninformed, or who get a substantial part of their information from

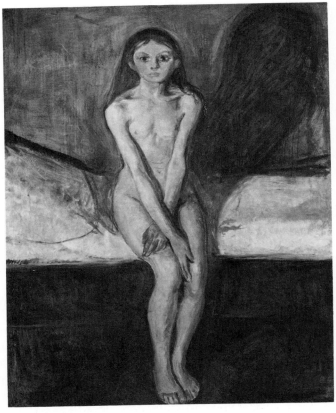

Edvard Munch's haunting image of female adolescence seems to reflect perfectly the shame and un-certainty that have characterized many young girls' entry into woman-hood.

In boys, the diameter of the areola (the dark area around the nipple) increases during puberty. Much to their consternation, many boys develop some breast tissue as well. However, their worry is needless: about 65 percent of all adolescent boys experience some breast enlargement, usually at about age 14 (Smith, 1983), but this enlargement almost always disappears by age 16.

Hair. In both sexes, head and body hair usually becomes coarser and darker during puberty. In addition, new hair growth occurs under the arms, on the face, and in the pubic area. In fact, for many young people, the appearance of a few light-colored straight strands of pubic hair is the first sign of puberty. As puberty continues, pubic hair becomes darker, thicker, and curlier, and covers a wider area. Girls reach the adult pubic-hair pattern in about three years; for boys, the process takes six years or more.

males, are more likely to be physically and psychologically distressed at menarche and during subsequent periods.

This is not to say that menstruation is necessarily a positive experience. About half of all adolescent girls experience moodiness and pain during their periods, and most feel less positive about menstruation as they become more experienced with it (Brooks-Gunn and Ruble, 1982).

To determine how the onset of menarche might affect girls' self-image, Elissa Koff and her colleagues (1978) tested and interviewed eighty-seven girls on two occasions—first when they were in seventh grade (their average age was 12) and then again half a year later.

Twenty-three of the girls had already reached menarche on the first test date, thirty reached menarche between the two test occasions, and thirty-four still had not menstruated by the second test session. By looking for differences in the test results among these three groups, the researchers hoped to discover if having had their first period made a difference in the way the girls thought about themselves and their femininity.

The results show that it did, as demonstrated by the draw-a-person test, for example. First the girls were asked to "draw a whole person . . . not a stick figure." Then they were asked to indicate the sex of the figure and to draw a second person of the opposite sex. The drawings were rated on two characteristics: which sex was drawn first, and how different the male and female figures were in terms of body shape, body parts, hair, and clothes. The girls were also asked how satisfied they were with various parts of their own bodies—seventeen parts in all, including "feminine" parts such as breasts and buttocks, as well as "nonfeminine" parts, such as hands and feet.

After menarche, girls were considerably more likely to draw a female first in the draw-a-person test (see table), and they differentiated males and females more clearly in their sketches. They also expressed more satisfaction with the feminine parts of their bodies, even though the actual change in breast size over a six-month period is small, and even though some premenarche girls were more shapely than some postmenarche girls. The authors of this study concluded that "menarche is a pivotal event for reorganization of the adolescent girl's body image and sexual identification . . . it is menarche, in particular, rather than puberty, in general, that is critical in precipitating a change in the adolescent girl's image of the body and acceptance of herself as female."

Percent of Seventh-Grade Girls Who Drew a Female Figure First, When Asked to Draw a Person

	First Test	Second Test
Group 1: Girls who had not reached menarche	68%	68%
Group 2: Girls who had reached menarche between first and second test	77%	97%
Group 3: Girls who had already reached menarche before the first test	100%	100%

Facial and body hair are considered signs of manliness in our society, a notion that is mistaken for three reasons. First, the tendency to grow facial and body hair is inherited; how often a man needs to shave is determined by his genes rather than his virility. In addition, facial hair is usually the last secondary sex characteristic to appear, sometimes long after a young male has become sexually active. Finally, girls typically develop some facial hair and more noticeable hair on their arms and legs during puberty—a sign not of masculinity but of sexual maturation.

Voice. The adolescent's voice becomes lower as the larynx grows, a change most noticeable in boys. (Even more noticeable, much to the chagrin of the young male, is his occasional loss of voice control, throwing his newly acquired baritone into a high squeak.) Girls also develop lower voices, a fact reflected in the recognition of a low, throaty female voice as "sexy."

Body Image

In a culture such as ours, which places a premium on physical attractiveness and features beautiful bodies in advertisements for everything from clothes and cosmetics to stereos and auto parts, it is no wonder that most adolescents begin spending a good deal of time every day in front of a mirror, tirelessly checking and rechecking their clothes, their physiques, their complexions, the part in their hair. As Tanner (1971) explains:

For the majority of young persons, the years from twelve to sixteen are the most eventful ones of their lives so far as their growth and development are concerned. Admittedly, during fetal life and the first year or two after birth, developments occurred still faster, and a sympathetic environment was probably even more crucial, but the subject himself was not the fascinated, charmed or horrified spectator that watches the developments, or lack of developments, of adolescence.

Psychologists generally believe that one of the tasks of adolescence is developing a **body image,** as a person's concept of his or her physical appearance is called.

In the process of acquiring this body image, most adolescents refer to the cultural body ideal—which in our society, currently, is the slim, shapely woman and the tall, muscular man promoted by movies, television, and advertising. Obviously, few people measure up to the standards of physique set by TV commercials for diet sodas or low-fat yogurt, or by the various cheesecake and beefcake stars of television soaps and series. But whereas most adults have learned to accept the discrepancy between the cultural ideal and their own appearance, few adolescents are satisfied with their looks. One nationwide study of young people between 12 and 17 years old found that 49.8 percent of the boys surveyed wanted to be taller, and 48.4 percent of the girls wanted to be thinner. A scant majority of the boys (55 percent) were reasonably satisfied with their build, as were a minority of the girls (40 percent) (Scanlan, 1975).

Other studies show that girls are dissatisfied with more parts of their bodies than boys are. Both sexes, for example, are likely to be concerned about facial features, complexion, and weight, and boys worry about the size of their penis in much the same way girls worry about the size of their breasts. But girls are much more likely to worry about the size and shape of their buttocks, legs, knees, and feet as well (Clifford, 1971).

The intense interest adolescents have in their appearance was shown in a study in which teenagers and adults were blindfolded and asked to identify an object—an upside-down mask of their own face—by touch. The younger adolescents were quicker to recognize the object than the older adolescents and adults were, despite the fact that facial shape changes most rapidly in early adolescence, theoretically making the task harder for the younger subjects. Apparently the young teenagers' preoccupation with their physiognomy compensated for the unfamiliarity of the stimulus (Collins and LaGanza, 1982).

The adolescent's concern over appearance is more than vanity—it is a recognition of the role physical attractiveness plays in gaining the admiration of the opposite sex. Hass (1979) found that the characteristics

The Timing of Puberty

The changes of puberty occur in predictable sequence and tempo. The entire process begins when hormones from the hypothalamus (a part of the brain) trigger hormones in the pituitary gland (located in the base of the skull), which in turn trigger increased hormonal production by the *gonads,* or sex glands (the testes in the male and the ovaries in the female) as well as by the adrenal glands.

For girls, the most important hormones produced by the sex glands are estrogen and progesterone, which cause, usually in sequence, the beginning of breast development, first pubic hair, widening of hips, the growth spurt, menarche, and completion of breast and pubic-hair growth. For boys, the most important hormone is testosterone, which produces, usually in sequence, growth of the testes, growth of the penis, first pubic hair, capacity for ejaculation, growth spurt, voice changes, beard development, and completion of pubic-hair growth. Once the hormonal concentrations start the biological changes of puberty, the process is rapid, with most major changes occurring within three years for girls and four years for boys (Rutter, 1980).

Given the standards of the body beautiful against which adolescents, especially girls, feel compelled to measure themselves, it is little wonder that they seem obsessively concerned with physical looks.

that boys sought in girls were, in order, good looks, a good body, friendliness, and intelligence; girls wanted boys to be intelligent, good looking, have a good body, and be good conversationalists.

The fact that physique is valued by both sexes, and that adolescents can spend hours in front of the mirror, and many dollars on clothes and cosmetics to make themselves appear more attractive, is understandable, for there is a strong relationship between how adolescents feel about their bodies and how they feel about themselves. To the adolescent, looking "terrible," or feeling regarded by others as looking "terrible," is often the same as being terrible, a feeling that may be reinforced by the fact that teenagers who are physically unattractive tend to have fewer friends than the average teenager (Rutter, 1980). Consequently, adolescents' concern for their appearance should be an occasion for adults' sympathy rather than their derision. Providing them with practical help, from cosmetic suggestions for minor flaws, to tips on diet and clothes, to medical treatment for physical abnormalities, might have far-reaching benefits for self-concept.

However, while the sequence of pubertal events is very similar for all young people, there is great variation in the age of onset. Healthy children begin puberty any time between ages 8 and 16, with ages 10, 11, or 12 being the most typical. The child's sex, genes, body type, and nourishment all affect this variation.

Factors Affecting When Puberty Occurs Male-female differences are one factor affecting when a particular person will experience puberty, although the average time differential between female and male development depends on which particular event in puberty is being compared. For example, the first signs of reproductive capability appear only a few months later in boys than in girls: the average girl reaches menarche at age 12 years, 8 months, while the average boy first ejaculates at age 13 (Zacharias et al., 1976; Schoof-Tams et al., 1976). However, since the growth spurt appears later in the sequence of pubertal changes in boys, the average boy is two years behind the average girl in this respect. Consequently, between ages 12 and 14, most girls are taller than their male classmates.

Genes are also an important factor in the age at which puberty begins. This is most clearly seen in the case of menarche, the pubertal event that is easiest to date. Although most girls reach this milestone between 11 and 14, the age of onset varies from 9 to 18. However, the difference in the age at which sisters reach menarche is, on the average, only 13 months; and the difference for monozygotic twins averages a mere 2.8 months.

Body weight and the proportion of fat are also important in determining the onset of puberty. Short, stocky children tend to experience puberty earlier than those with taller, thinner builds. Menarche in particular seems related to the accumulation of a certain amount of body fat. Females who have little body fat, such as runners and other athletes, menstruate later and more irregularly than the average girl, while those who are generally inactive menstruate earlier (Frisch, 1983). (This is one explanation for the fact that blind girls, who are usually less active than sighted girls, normally have their first period earlier than sighted girls. It may also explain why menarche is more likely to occur in winter than in spring or summer.)

Some researchers (Frisch and Revelle, 1970) believe that there is a critical weight (about 100 pounds) that young women must attain before they can reach menarche. This may or may not be the case today, for while it is true that thin girls enter puberty later, it is not clear whether weight gain promotes menarche or is merely a sign that the hormonal processes have begun. However, in earlier times, lower body weight as a result of inadequate nutrition was probably the main reason puberty occurred later than it does now. In the nineteenth century, for instance, most women had their first menstrual period between ages 15 and 17 instead of today's average of between 12 and 14.

The consequences of good nutrition, and of better health generally, are reflected in what is called the **secular trend**—the tendency of each new generation over the past hundred years or so to experience puberty earlier than their parents. (A century ago, the average male began puberty at about age 15 or 16 and the average female began it around 15.) In contemporary North America and Europe, nutrition and medical care for most children are now sufficient to allow genes and gender, rather than health and nutrition, to determine the age at which puberty begins. As a result, the average age of puberty is the same today as it was ten years ago. Although most American adults reached puberty at an earlier age than their parents and grandparents, most of today's children will experience their growth spurt and develop their sexual characteristics at about the same age their parents did.

Gender Differences in Sex Drive

The **sex drive,** that is, the need and desire to have sexual experiences, is clearly related to the hormonal changes of puberty. Typically, in boys, the wish for sexual experiences follows quite closely after the first ejaculation; for girls, the development of sex drive seems more gradual, coming a few years after menarche (Higham, 1980). Thus, there may well be a time in early adolescence when boys are more "driven" sexually than girls are.

Until recently, in fact, most people, including psychologists, believed that the sex drive is always much stronger in males than in females. This idea has been given particular support by Helene Deutsch (1944), a psychoanalyst Freud acknowledged as an expert on women. In her view, by the very nature of their genitals, females are destined to be passive and receptive, and males, to be active and aggressive.

One consequence of the idea that males have a stronger sex drive was **the double standard,** a separate code of sexual behavior for males and females. Since her sex drive was considered less strong, the female was expected to stop the sexually aggressive male rather than become carried away with passion herself. The male, on the other hand, was expected to try to get as much sexual gratification as possible. According to a study of high-school students conducted by Gary Schwartz and Don Merten (1967), the double standard was still strong among many adolescents in the mid-1960s. The students felt that a boy attained status by "providing some concrete evidence for frequent and exaggerated boasts about sexual prowess," whereas a girl "must allow herself to reach a relatively high level of sexual excitement and intimacy without giving in to what are described as persistent demands for greater sexual favors."

The view that the female sex drive was relatively weak has been challenged in recent years. One survey found that adolescent girls thought they had just as strong a sex drive as boys do (Hunt, 1970), an idea strongly supported by Gail Sheehy (1976), who quotes, as a typical case, one woman's recollection of her own teen lust:

> I remember an adolescence of absolute frenzy . . . not getting through a day without seventy-five percent of it being occupied with sexual dreaming, wishing, watching, touching if possible. [Sheehy, 1976]

Of course, it is impossible to actually measure the strength of the sex drive of either sex. We must infer the measurement from sexual behavior, which is affected by the cultural attitudes of various times. However, all available evidence does indicate that the double standard has declined considerably over the past two decades. One indicator of this is that the number of adolescent and young adult females at any given age who have experienced sexual intercourse is almost as high as the number of males who have (Hass, 1979; Sorenson, 1973; Hopkins, 1977).

This parity has been achieved mostly by the increased sexual activity among girls. For example, one study found that between 1965 and 1980 the rate of premarital intercourse among male college students increased moderately, from 65 to 77 percent, whereas it more than doubled for female students, from 29 to 64 percent (Robinson and Jedlicka, 1982). The same study found that the number of students who felt that "sexual intercourse is immoral" was down, especially among females (see Table 15.1). Another interesting trend found in the data was that, compared to attitudes in 1970, both sexes are becoming more critical of men, as well as of women, who have sexual intercourse with "a great many" partners.

TABLE 15.1 **Changing Attitudes on Premarital Intercourse**

		Percent Strongly Agreeing	
	Year	Males	Females
Premarital intercourse is immoral	1965	33%	70%
	1970	14%	34%
	1975	20%	21%
	1980	17%	25%
A man who has sexual intercourse with a great many women is immoral	1965	35%	56%
	1970	15%	22%
	1975	20%	30%
	1980	27%	39%
A woman who has sexual intercourse with a great many men is immoral	1965	42%	91%
	1970	33%	54%
	1975	29%	41%
	1980	42%	50%

Source: Robinson and Jedlicka, 1982.

Masturbation Another difference in the sexual attitudes and behaviors of adolescent boys and girls is apparent with regard to masturbation. To begin with, adolescent boys are more likely than girls to masturbate (one study found the difference to be 80 percent compared to 59 percent (Hass, 1979), and another found it to be 83 percent to 45 percent (Miller and Lief, 1976). Interestingly, boys are also more likely to feel guilty about masturbating: whereas only one-fifth of the girls who masturbated felt guilty, about half of the boys did, and those who did not feel guilty often had other negative reactions, such as feeling ashamed, stupid, or abnormal (Hass, 1979). These negative feelings may disappear as the young person becomes more mature, as was suggested by a study of West German youth between the ages of 11 and 16. This particular research found that only one boy in four under age 14 thought masturbation was "OK as often as you want," compared to 55 percent of the 15- and 16-year-olds (Schoof-Tams et al., 1976).

A review of the research on adolescent sexuality (Chilman, 1983) finds that both boys and girls are masturbating earlier in puberty, and probably in greater numbers, than they were a generation ago. These trends are particularly apparent for girls, in part because girls are more active sexually than they once were. This review also suggests that with girls, masturbation is an adjunct to an active sexual life. With boys, on the other hand, masturbation tends to be practiced when it is the only form of sexual expression available.

Storm and Stress: Who, When, and Why?

Now that we have examined the nature of physical growth and related developments during puberty, we are better able to anticipate potential problems during adolescence. And we can predict that people with certain characteristics are particularly likely to experience a stormy adolescence.

Early and Late Puberty

First let us consider the probable impact of the extreme variation in the age at which puberty begins. As we have seen, most girls begin puberty at least a year or two before most boys, and it is not uncommon for a differential as great as seven years to exist between the age early-maturing girls enter puberty and the time late-maturing boys do. In addition, within each sex, some individuals are a few years ahead of their peers and some are behind. What are the possible consequences of these variations?

Early-Maturing Girls Girls who are taller and more developed than their classmates discover that they have no peers who share their interests or problems. Prepubescent girls call them "boy crazy," and boys tease them about their big feet or developing breasts. Almost every sixth-grade class has an 11-year-old pubescent girl who slouches so she won't look so tall, wears loose shirts so no one will notice her breasts, and buys her shoes a size too small. There are additional hazards for the early maturer. If she begins dating, it will probably be with boys who are older, and her self-esteem is likely to fall for a number of reasons (Simmons et al., 1983): she may feel constantly scrutinized by her parents, criticized by her girlfriends for

Figure 15.8 *Judging by their height, shape, and carriage, you might think that these two girls are several years apart in age—yet both are 11 years old. Although for now the girl on the left may be made self-conscious by her early maturation, in a year or so she will probably find that she is the envy of her female classmates.*

not spending time with them, and pressured by her dates to be sexual. If she becomes sexually active, she is likely to become pregnant long before her body and mind are ready.

However, once the early-maturing girl has weathered the first few years, she will probably do fairly well. By seventh or eighth grade, her early maturation will have gained her increased status: she is likely to be respected and popular (Faust, 1960), and her initial problems often lead her to more mature thought as well as appearance (Livson and Peskin, 1980). Her appearance and experience gradually make her the target of envy more than scorn. After a few years of awkwardness and embarrassment, she is able to advise her less mature girl friends about topics that they find increasingly important, such as bra sizes, dating behavior, menstrual cramps, and variations in kissing.

Further research suggests that, in the long run, girls who are late to mature have more problems than girls who are early. As one review explains:

> The stress-ridden early-maturing girl in adulthood has become clearly a more coping, self-possessed and self-directed person than the later-maturing female in the cognitive and social as well as in emotional sectors. . . . By contrast, it is the late-maturing female, carefree and unchallenged in adolescence, who faces adversity maladaptively in adulthood. [Livson and Peskin, 1980]

Late-Maturing Boys By contrast to the carefree late-maturing girls, late-maturing boys tend to have many problems. They must watch themselves be outdistanced, first by the girls and then by most of the boys in their class, and they are forced to endure the patronizing scorn of those who only recently were themselves immature. Extensive longitudinal data from the Berkeley Growth Study (Jones and Bayley, 1950; Jones, 1957; Mussen and Jones, 1957; Jones, 1965) found late-maturing boys to be less poised, less relaxed, more restless, and more talkative than early-maturing boys, who were more often chosen as leaders. The late-maturing boys were more playful, more creative, and more flexible, qualities that are not usually admired by other adolescents. Another study found even worse problems associated with late maturation: a disproportionate number of late-maturers become juvenile delinquents (Wadsworth, 1979).

Follow-up studies of the Berkeley late-maturing boys when they were 33 years old, and again when they were 38, found that most of them had reached average or above-average height but that some of the personality patterns of their adolescence persisted nevertheless. Compared to early- or average-maturing boys, those who had matured late tended to be less controlled, responsible, or dominant and were less likely to hold positions of leadership in their jobs or in their social organizations. Some of them still had feelings of inferiority and rejection. However, in several positive characteristics they scored better. They were likely to have a better sense of humor and to be more egalitarian and more perceptive than their early-maturing peers. Especially in the era of greater liberation from traditional sex roles, later-maturing boys became more adaptive men (Livson and Peskin, 1980).

Of course, not all late-maturing boys feel inferior during adolescence. Some find other ways to excel, using their minds and talents to become the class scholar, or musician, or comedian. In addition, late maturation today may be less difficult than it was decades ago; for example, because of the greater freedom allowed young girls, the late-maturing boy can now gain experience with the opposite sex by dating girls several years younger than he is. If he attends a school where most students are placed in classes according to interests and abilities rather than age, he will be less likely to feel inferior and more likely to develop his creative talents.

It is also true that cultural values can intensify, or lessen, the problems of early or late maturation (Rutter, 1980). The effects of early or late maturation are more apparent, for example, among lower-class adolescents, because physique and physical prowess tend to be more highly valued among lower-class teenagers than among middle- or upper-class teenagers. Correspondingly, alternative sources of status for the early or late maturer, such as academic achievement or vocational aspiration, are less valued among lower-class adolescents.

For all these reasons, the research suggests, parents and teachers need to be particularly conscious of the special emotional needs of early- and late-maturing adolescents. Especially in adolescence, not being "on time" can make everything more difficult (Rutter, 1980).

Boys' Problems, Girls' Problems

To some extent, a person's likelihood of having problems during adolescence depends on whether that person is male or female. Certainly it would seem that many of the physical changes of puberty fall more harshly on boys than girls. For instance, boys are more likely to develop acne, and their voices are more likely to squeak before they mature.

Sexual developments can create even more problems for boys than physical growth. Many are worried that they will have a visible erection at an embarrassing moment, such as when reciting in class or dancing with a girl. As we have seen, guilt about masturbation is greater in boys than girls, and many of them worry about being oversexed (Sorensen, 1973).

Figure 15.9 *This boy, barely old enough to shave, is waiting to be booked after his arrest for delinquency. Teenage boys are three times as likely to be arrested as teenage girls are, an indication that they feel the tensions of adolescence more acutely than girls and/or that they are more likely than girls to express these tensions in acts against society.*

Since boys experience more problems as a result of the biological changes of puberty than girls do, we would expect boys, more than girls, to show signs of emotional distress during adolescence, and there is evidence for this speculation. For one thing, boys are three times as likely as girls to be arrested (ten years ago they were four times as likely to be), and they are more likely to report having difficulty with their parents and teachers (see the Closer Look on delinquency). For instance, 25 percent of the boys in Sorensen's study agreed with the statement "I have pretty much given up on ever being able to get along with my parents," compared to only 6 percent of the girls. What's more, the rate of accidental death, homicide, and suicide (the three leading causes of adolescent death) is about three times higher for boys than for girls.

Figure 15.10 *According to 1980 statistics, males (black line) 16 to 17 years old are three times more likely to die from accidents, violence, or poisoning than are females (color line) the same age. Males from 18 to 24 are four times more likely than their female counterparts to meet such untimely ends.*

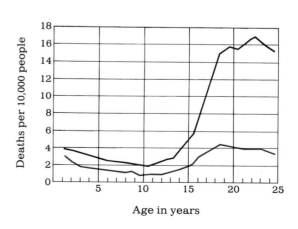

A CLOSER LOOK   **Delinquency**

Minor law-breaking seems to be part of normal adolescence. In both North America and Great Britain, at least, confidential surveys of teenagers reveal that about 80 percent of all adolescents have broken the law—mostly in minor ways, such as smoking marijuana or committing petty vandalism (Rutter and Giller, 1984). Thus, only a minority of teenagers would seem to be completely law-abiding. In fact, a person is more likely to be arrested at age 16 than at any other age.

By no means are all adolescent crimes minor, however. In the United States, 47 percent of the arrests for serious crimes, such as murder, assault, and robbery, involve youths under age 21 (U.S. Department of Justice, 1984).

Crime statistics reveal another interesting fact. Males are much more likely to be arrested than females, and they tend to be arrested for more overt crimes. The relatively rare crime of homicide is one example: males under 18 are arrested for murder eight times as often as females. In addition, boys are arrested for burglary and for robbery fifteen times more often than girls, and for vandalism ten times more often. Thus, troubled boys are more likely to lash out against someone; troubled girls are more likely to avoid confrontation (in fact, running away from home is one of the few things girls are arrested for more often than boys).

It should be pointed out that while most adolescents of both sexes are, at one time or another, delinquent in some minor way, relatively few (about one in twenty) are arrested. These few tend to be arrested repeatedly, and for them crime is not only a problem for society, but also an indication that they themselves are in trouble. To be specific, young people who become arrest statistics have lower self-esteem, poorer relationships with their family, and more difficulty in school than their peers who have not had trouble with the law. Since delinquency is both a cause and a consequence of such problems, the first offender usually needs help in order to prevent these factors from compounding each other. Almost always, when a young person is involved in a serious crime, he or she has a long history of school problems and minor offenses.

Unfortunately parents, and others, are all too likely to deny the troubled situation until it is too late. (Typifying this kind of response is the father described by Elkind [1979] as yelling "Why don't you catch some real criminals!" at a policeman who had caught his son stealing a car.) Other parents punish their child's first delinquency, but often make no attempt to strengthen family relationships and build up the young person's self-esteem, steps that would make future delinquent behavior less likely. (Interestingly, although both parents can be influential in solving this problem, closeness between mother and child seems to diminish delinquency in early adolescence, while the father-child relationship is more important after age 14 [Gold and Petronio, 1980].)

Of course, none of these statistics applies to every boy. Indeed, as the Offers (1975) found, about a fourth of their sample of boys had a smooth adolescence, and about a third had only transitory problems. Moreover, boys who are aggressive and antisocial in adolescence are usually boys who had academic and behavior problems earlier in life. Adolescence makes their behavior more troublesome, more violent, perhaps even more dangerous to themselves and to those around them, but it does not often create a serious problem where none existed before (Rutter, 1980).

For girls, the picture is somewhat different. Many develop problems that were not apparent earlier. For example, feelings of low self-esteem and moodiness are common in both sexes, and seem to be related to the biochemical changes of puberty (Rutter, 1980; Tobin-Richards, 1983; Sizer, 1985). However, girls are more likely than boys to be overwhelmed by their negative feelings: for example, they are more likely to burst into uncontrollable sobs, to avoid all social contact, to endanger their health with abnormal eating (see the Closer Look on anorexia nervosa and bulimia), and even to attempt suicide.

One longitudinal study found that, while boys with problems were more likely to improve during adolescence, girls who had problems were likely to become worse,

School achievement also seems crucial. Academic difficulty in sixth grade is one of the best predictors of delinquent behavior in ninth grade (Magnusson et al., 1975). In fact, those programs that seem to prevent chronic delinquents from becoming criminals are generally focused on developing skills in two specific areas—school and employment. If this is done in a context in which the young person can develop a relationship between himself and the teacher or a counselor, the chances are that delinquency will be an adolescent phase rather than the beginning of a criminal career (Gold and Petronio, 1980).

An additional factor influencing delinquency appears to be a socioeconomic one, since lower-class young people have somewhat higher rates of delinquency and much higher rates of arrest and incarceration than middle-class adolescents do. This difference can be explained in part by the fact that lower-class and racial-minority offenders often get arrested for acts that middle-class whites would merely get lectured for. At the same time, the incentive to commit crime, especially robbery, seems to be linked to chronic joblessness. Statistics show that the unemployment rate among black youth in the inner cities is about 50 percent, and the crime rate for this group is higher than that for any other group in the country. As one black 17-year-old boy said:

How they let this happen in a country like this, having all these kids walking around the streets, got their hands jammed down in their pockets, head down, like their necks was bent in half? What do folks think these kids gonna do, when they go month after month, year after year, without nothing that even *smells* like a job? [Quoted in Cottle, 1979]

This leads to a final question. Why are boys so much more likely to become delinquent? One major factor that influences all the other contributors to delinquency is that our culture, in some ways, tends to condone, and even encourage, minor-law-breaking in boys as a way of establishing independence and asserting masculinity. As one review explains:

If a 15-year-old manages somehow to steal the red flasher (the "bubble gum machine") off a police squad car, that act is a genuine bid for glory . . . [but] stealing the red flasher seems somehow incongruous for girls while eminently suitable for boys . . . Delinquent behavior ordinarily fails to serve adolescent girls as it serves adolescent boys to shore up a failing sense of self-esteem. [Gold and Petronio, 1980]

As with every question of sex differences, it is impossible to unravel the tangled web of nature and nurture to see precisely what accounts for the differences we see. However, as is apparent many times in this Closer Look, environment clearly contributes to delinquency at least as much as biology does.

and many girls who had earlier seemed to be untroubled later developed some problems—the end result being that, by age 18, the rate of mental health problems for girls was twice that of boys. The authors believe that the reason for the increase in problems among girls in adolescence is that females of all ages are more passive and dependent, qualities valued in children but devalued and debilitating in adolescence and adulthood (Werner and Smith, 1982). Having learned as little girls that being "good" meant doing what they were told to do, they have difficulty becoming their own person in adolescence, because they are overly dependent on others to tell them how to behave.

Of course, it is impossible to say definitively that the conflict between the developmental demand for independence and the feminine wish for approval is the root cause of the high rate of young women's problems. However, it is true that, compared to boys, girls tend to be much more self-critical, and that they will go to greater lengths to avoid the criticisms of adults and, especially, of peers (Hill and Lynch, 1983). In some cases, the avoidance of criticism may lead to withdrawal from social interaction. This may be why girls are more likely to be afraid to go to school, or to run away from home rather than taking the more direct approach of confronting their problems with their parents.

Anorexia Nervosa and Bulimia

One of the most baffling and serious problems that sometimes occurs in adolescence is **anorexia nervosa,** an eating disorder that strikes girls at least twenty times as often as boys. The roots of this disorder are emotional, not physical. ("Anorexia nervosa" means, literally, "loss of appetite due to nervous causes.") We will explore the reasons behind this disorder in a moment, but first let us describe its symptoms.

The first sign of anorexia nervosa appears in an activity almost all adolescent girls engage in—dieting. Typically, an anorexic begins to diet, loses weight, and then eats less and less until she is little more than skin and bones.

Anorexics might lose more than 30 percent of their body weight within a few months, weighing as little as 60 pounds, yet insist that they are neither hungry nor thin. Typically, they exercise daily, "to keep up muscle tone" as one patient put it as she jogged beside her hospital bed (Minuchin et al., 1978).

Often anorexia is accompanied by another bizarre eating behavior that many teenage girls engage in at least occasionally: bingeing—on, say, a whole chocolate cake and a quart of ice cream—and then purging, by ingestion of massive doses of laxatives or by intentional vomiting. When this binge-and-purge cycle becomes habitual, it is called bulimia. Without treatment, anorexia and bulimia, separately, or in combination, can be fatal.

Because there is no physical explanation for these eating disorders, there is no medical cure for the loss of appetite and weight. However, if blood pressure is very low and body fat completely gone, emergency medical treatment includes forced feeding, through the nose or veins, to prevent sudden death.

Without psychological help, about a third of all anorexic patients get better, and about 10 to 20 percent die from the effects of chronic starvation. The rest remain abnormally thin (or sometimes change to become abnormally fat) and overly dependent on others for a sense of identity throughout their lives. Bulimics sometimes become anorexic, and, even if they do not, they typically become overly concerned about eating all their lives.

The kind of psychological help anorexics receive depends on the theoretical perspective of the therapist. Psychoanalytic therapists believe that anorexics have a severe disturbance of body image. According to this theory, the anorexic is afraid of becoming a woman, so she maintains a hipless, breastless, childlike form by extreme dieting. One result is that her menstrual periods cease; another is that she becomes the center of family concern and

Unlike the retouched photo portraits used for publicity shots and album covers, this candid shot of pop singer Karen Carpenter, taken a year before her death from heart failure *brought on by anorexia nervosa, shows the gaunt appearance that hints at the underlying physical problems associated with this disorder.*

care. In these ways, the anorexic is more like a young child than a young woman. Through psychotherapy, psychiatrists try to help the patient accept her burgeoning femininity, and therefore accept food (Bruch, 1973).

Learning theorists see eating disorders as the result of maladaptive behavior (intended as a means of getting the parents' attention, for example), so they treat it by reinforcing weight gain and punishing weight loss. For example, each day that a hospitalized anorexic gains weight, she is given privileges: freedom to watch television, to make phone calls, to see visitors, to comb her hair. Each day that she loses weight, she must stay in bed, without even the right to go to the bathroom. Her only permitted activity is eating.

Two other factors are influential in the occurrence of eating disorders. One is the pattern of family interactions, which we will examine in Chapter 17. The other is the culture's inordinate emphasis on thinness. While something is clearly wrong with the psyche of the girl who starves herself to death, something is also wrong with the society that seems to encourage so many young women to be obsessed with their weight.

Once females have problems, they have more difficulty solving them, because they are more likely to blame themselves and feel helpless, while males are more likely to blame someone else and try to do something about it. In extreme cases, the masculine solution may end in jail, the female in a mental hospital, which may explain the sex differences in the proportion of males and females in these institutions, a difference already apparent by late adolescence.

In addition, as the double standard declines and adolescents of both sexes have earlier and more extensive sexual experiences, the result is increasing rates of pregnancy—a problem caused equally by both sexes but having a heavier personal price for the young woman "in trouble" than for the young man.

Having discussed adolescence in terms of the sex differences of physical development and the sex-associated problems that adolescents sometimes face, it is time to note that individual factors—personality characteristics, cognitive ability, family background—are more important than sex in determining the outcome of adolescence. As we will see in Chapter 17, while biological changes begin adolescence, culture, rather than biology, ends it. In order to reach adulthood, the young person must forge his or her own identity, which is no easy task. Those young people who do not have parental and peer support may find the psychosocial tasks of late adolescence much more difficult than the biological upheaval of early adolescence. Before discussing these problems, we should first learn about adolescent cognitive development, development that, as it progresses, makes it easier for adolescents to solve many social problems, including their own.

Figure 15.11 *This photo can be seen in two ways— as a group shot of teenagers or as a picture of thirty-two individuals, each one having unique physical characteristics, ideas, and social problems. The latter perspective is likely to lead to greater understanding of these young people.*

SUMMARY

The Stormy Decade?

1. Until recently, most psychologists believed that adolescence is inevitably a time of storm and stress, or emotional turbulence. Freudians thought that the sexual needs of the adolescent have to conflict with parental authority in order for the young person to develop normally.

2. However, recent research has shown that most adolescents, most of the time, are calm and predictable rather than turbulent and erratic. While only a minority experience a completely smooth adolescence, few are distressed most of the time.

Puberty

3. The growth spurt—first in weight, then height, then strength—is the first obvious evidence of puberty, although some hormonal changes precede it. During the year of fastest growth, an average girl grows about 3½ inches (9 centimeters) and an average boy about 4 inches (10 centimeters).

4. Growth usually begins with the extremities and proceeds toward the torso. The head, lungs, heart, and digestive system also change in size and shape during this period.

5. During adolescence, more calories and vitamins are needed than at any other time of life. Undernourishment, exotic diets, and pregnancy can all prevent normal growth during this period.

6. During puberty, all the sex organs grow larger and the young person becomes sexually mature. Menarche in girls and ejaculation in boys are the events usually taken to indicate reproductive potential, although full fertility is reached years after these initial signs of maturation.

7. Most secondary sexual characteristics—including changes in the breasts and voice and the development of pubic, facial, and body hair—appear in both sexes, although there are obvious differences in the typical development of males and females.

8. The sexual attitudes and experiences of adolescent males and females are much more similar today than they once were. For example, the double standard, still strongly in force in the 1960s, has been modified in a number of ways.

9. While the sequence of pubertal events is similar for most young people, the timing of the onset of puberty shows considerable variation. Normal young people experience their first bodily changes any time from 8 to 16. The individual's sex, genes, body type, and nutrition all affect age of puberty, with boys, thin children, and malnourished children typically reaching puberty later than their opposites.

Storm and Stress: Who, When, and Why?

10. While not all teenagers have a difficult adolescence, early-maturing girls and late-maturing boys are more likely to be distressed by their physical development or lack of it. This problem is temporary for most girls, but the lack of confidence of the typical late-maturing boy may continue into manhood.

11. Neither sex necessarily has a troubled puberty, but, in general, boys find adolescence more difficult than girls do. On the other hand, girls' problems are likely to become worse during adolescence, and girls often have more trouble solving their problems than boys do.

KEY TERMS

genital stage *(464)*
reaction formation *(464)*
tumultuous growth *(465)*
continuous growth *(465)*
surgent growth *(466)*
puberty *(466)*
sexual dimorphism *(466)*
estrogen *(467)*
testosterone *(467)*
growth spurt *(467)*

menarche *(471)*
ejaculation *(471)*
secondary sex
  characteristics *(471)*
body image *(474)*
secular trend *(476)*
sex drive *(476)*
the double standard *(476)*
anorexia nervosa *(484)*

KEY QUESTIONS

1. What was Hall's view of adolescence?

2. What is the psychoanalytic view of adolescence?

3. How "stormy" is adolescence in North America today, according to recent research?

4. What are the main nonsexual biological changes that occur during puberty?

5. What are the main sexual changes that occur during puberty?

6. What is the usual sequence of changes that occurs in puberty?

7. How can we predict when puberty will occur for a given individual?

8. What are the similarities between male and female sexual attitudes and experiences during adolescence?

9. What are the differences in male and female sexual attitudes and behavior during adolescence?

10. How can the age at which puberty occurs affect psychological development?

11. Which changes of puberty are more difficult for boys than girls, and which are more difficult for girls than boys?

12. What are the differences between the ways in which boys and girls respond to problems in adolescence?

RECOMMENDED READINGS

Group for the Advancement of Psychiatry. *Normal adolescence: Its dynamics and impact.* New York: Scribner's, 1968.

This book clearly states the view—held by many psychiatrists and psychologists until recently—that the biological changes of puberty bring a measure of disequilibrium and emotional disturbance to most young people. At the same time, the authors recognize that parents, culture, and individual personality differences play a role in the actual course of adolescence, and that even the most disturbed adolescent shows periods of "relative quiescence." This book provides the best summary of the psychoanalytic view of adolescence.

Mead, Margaret. *Culture and commitment* (Rev. ed.). Garden City, New York: Anchor Books, 1978.

Mead reflects on the nature of the generation gap that seemed to widen during the 1960s. She concludes that our society changed for the better during the 1970s because parents and adolescents began to trust each other again.

Galinsky, Ellen. *Between generations: The stages of parenthood.* New York: Berkley Books, 1982.

Galinsky discusses child development from the parents' viewpoint, showing how, at each stage, the parents' perspective and stresses change. This book is recommended here because it shows that adolescence is not characterized by emotional turbulence, rebellion, and a generation "gap," but rather that it is a stage like any other, posing somewhat different problems for parents as their children develop different needs.

Cottle, Thomas J. *Like fathers, like sons: Portraits of intimacy and strain.* Norwood, N.J.: Ablex, 1981.

Social scientists, especially those who work with delinquent youths, have recognized the special problems that boys experience in reaching manhood. However, the reasons for those problems and the ways to ameliorate them are not well understood. The father-son relationship, or lack of relationship, may be a key factor here. In this book, Cottle looks closely at several father-son relationships, providing many insights and suggestions, but no firm conclusions.

Adolescence: Cognitive Development

Chapter 16

I see no hope for the future of our people if they are dependent on the frivolous youth of today, for certainly all youth are reckless beyond words. . . . When I was a boy, we were taught to be discreet and respectful of elders, but the present youth are exceedingly wise and impatient of restraint.

Hesiod (Eighth century B.C.)

Adolescent Thought
Development of Scientific Reasoning

Logic in Other Domains

Piaget Reevaluated

Adolescent Egocentrism
Fantasies and Fables

Moral Development
Stages of Moral Development

Decision-Making: Two Contemporary Issues
Sexual Behavior

Adolescent Drug Use

Helping Adolescents Find Answers

Chapter 16

The complexity of adolescent thinking is such that although teens may wear their hearts on their sleeves or their opinions across their chests, the meaningfulness of the act may range from a deeply felt political or moral statement to an experiment with an idea to a simple shortage of other clean clothes. Adolescent thought processes, from scientific and moral reasoning to decision-making, will be the subject of this chapter.

What are the characteristics of scientific reasoning?

In which ways does egocentrism limit adolescents' ability to think rationally?

What are some of the factors that affect the development of moral judgment?

Which aspects of cognitive development interfere with the adolescent's ability to make decisions about matters with important consequences, such as drug use and sexual behavior?

The biological changes of puberty are universal and, for the most part, visible, transforming children by giving them adult size, shape, and sexuality. However, another change that typically begins in adolescence is just as important: the intellectual maturation that enables adolescents to reason and analyze much better than children.

Adolescent Thought

Piaget was the first theorist to recognize what many psychologists now consider the distinguishing feature of adolescent thought—the capacity to think in terms of possibility rather than merely concrete reality (Inhelder and Piaget, 1958). As John Flavell (1985) explains, before adolescence, the child has "an earthbound, concrete, practical-minded sort of problem solving approach . . . and speculations about other possibilities . . . occur only with difficulty and as a last resort." The adolescent, and the adult, by contrast, are more likely to approach problems "quite the other way around . . . reality is subordinated to possibility."

This means that, on the whole, adolescents are able to speculate, hypothesize, and fantasize much more readily and on a much grander scale than children who are still tied to concrete operational thinking.

By the end of adolescence, many young people can understand and create general principles or formal rules to explain many aspects of human experience. For this reason, Piaget calls the last stage of cognitive development, attained at about age 15, **formal operational thought.** At this point the adolescent "begins to build systems or theories in the largest sense of the term" about literature, philosophy, morality, love, and the world of work (Inhelder and Piaget, 1958).

**Development of
Scientific Reasoning**

One specific example of formal operational thought is the development of **scientific reasoning.** Inhelder and Piaget (1958) undertook a classic series of experiments that revealed how children between the ages of 5 and 15 reason about certain laws of physics by manipulating specific materials. Children were asked to put objects in a pail of water and explain why some sank and others floated; they were given different weights to hang on a string pendulum and asked to figure out which factors might affect the speed of the pendulum's swing (length of string, size of weight, height of release, force of release); they were asked to roll marbles down an incline onto a flat surface and estimate how far they would go. In all these experiments, Piaget and Inhelder found that reasoning abilities developed gradually in the years before adolescence, culminating at about age 14 with an understanding of the general principles involved.

For instance, the children in one experiment were asked to balance a balance scale with weights that could be hooked onto the scale's arms. This task was completely beyond the ability of most preoperational children (typically, a 4-year-old might put two weights on the same side of the scale and none on the other).

By age 7 (the usual age for the beginning of concrete operational thought), children realized that the scale could be balanced by putting the same amount of weight on both arms, but they didn't realize that the distance of the weights from the center of the scale is also an important factor.

By age 10 (near the end of the concrete operational stage), they were often able, through trial and error, to see that the farther from the fulcrum a given weight is, the more force it exerts (in one child's words, "At the end, it makes more weight"), and to find several correct combinations that would balance the scale. Note, however, that although they had discovered the importance of the weights' distance from the fulcrum in their trial-and-error experimenting, they still had to try out different weights at different distances to get the scales to balance. They could not hypothesize a general principle to guide their placement of the weights.

Finally, at about age 13 or 14, some children hypothesized the general law that there is an inverse relationship between a weight's proximity to the fulcrum and the force it exerts. Thus, they correctly concluded that if the weight on one arm of the balance is three times as heavy as the weight on the other, it has to be a third as far from the center as the other weight in order for equilibrium to be achieved, and they were able to correctly predict which other combinations of weights and distances would achieve balance.

Logic in Other Domains

Piaget's basic description of the reasoning processes that are characteristic of formal operational thinking has been tested in domains other than that of the natural sciences and, again, confirmed. For example, Peel (1971) examined the development of reasoning about social problems. He told the following story to seventy-eight children of above-average intelligence:

> Only brave pilots are allowed to fly over high mountains. This summer a fighter pilot flying over the Alps collided with an aerial cable railway, and cut a main cable causing some cars to fall to the glacier below. Several people were killed and many others had to spend the night suspended above the glacier. Was the pilot a careful airman? Why do you think so?

Despite their relatively high IQ scores, many of the children between 9 and 11 years of age gave irrelevant and inconsistent responses. Some said "Yes, he was brave," or "No, he was a showoff." Most of the 12- and 13-year-olds made their judgments solely on the basis of the content of the passage—specifically, the collision with the cable—saying such things as, "No, because if he were careful he would not have cut the cable."

Among the older subjects, however, some of the 13-year-olds and almost all of the 14- and 15-year-olds gave imaginative answers, evoking the possibility of extenuating circumstances—bad weather, sudden loss of vision, a malfunction in the plane. They usually realized that they could not decide if the pilot had been careful until they knew more about the circumstances of the accident.

Using the same technique to study logical reasoning in other areas, Peel found similar results with regard to questions demanding historical reasoning ("Why were the stones of Stonehenge placed as they were?"); ecological judgment ("What causes and prevents soil erosion?"); or sociopolitical explanations ("Were the people of Italy to blame for the water damage to art masterpieces caused by the floods in Florence?"). In addressing such questions, children younger than 13 were likely to give simple, one-option answers, whereas older adolescents were likely to see events as dynamic and consisting of many interrelated factors, and were constantly thinking of alternative possibilities.

True, False, or Impossible to Judge?   Another way to measure formal operational thinking is to look at children's ability to assess the inherent logic of various statements. In one series of experiments designed to do this, an investigator spread many solid-colored poker chips out on a table and asked adolescents and preadolescents to judge whether various statements about the chips were "true," "false," or "impossible to judge" (Osherson and Markman, 1974–1975).

For instance, the investigator hid a poker chip in his hand without letting the child see what color it was and he asked the child to judge the veracity of the statement "Either this chip is green or it is not green." Almost every preadolescent replied that the statement was "impossible to judge" rather than saying that it was true. They also thought that the statement "The chip in my hand is green and it is not green" was impossible to judge rather than false.

When the investigator held a red chip so it could be seen and said "Either the chip in my hand is green or it is not yellow," only 15 percent of the preadolescent children correctly answered "true." Beginning at age 11, however, the number of children answering correctly increased. By age 15, about half were able to accu-

Figure 16.1 *Is this demonstrator's assertion true, false, or impossible to judge? Be prepared to blush if your answer isn't "True."*

rately evaluate the logic of these either/or statements (that is, one of these statements is true if only one of the clauses is true) demonstrating what Flavell (1985) calls **the game of thinking.** That is, they were able to suspend their knowledge of reality (such as knowing that the chip is red) and think playfully about the possibilities suggested by the statement itself. Flavell gives another example of the adolescent's ability to suspend the real and think about the possible. If an impoverished college student is offered $10 to argue in favor of the position that government should *never* give or lend money to impoverished college students, chances are, he or she can earn the money. By contrast, concrete operational children have great difficulty arguing against their personal beliefs and self-interest. The ability to divorce oneself from what one believes to be the case and argue from other premises makes adolescents much more interesting and adept as participants in intellectual "bull sessions" or as partners in debate. It also opens the possibility that they can modify their own position by perceiving the merits of someone else's.

Figure 16.2 *In an attempt to score a point for her debating team, this young woman may be constructing an eloquent and logical argument for a point of view she may truly oppose. She is engaged in the game of thinking, a favorite pursuit of many adolescents but an incomprehensible puzzle for younger children.*

Piaget Reevaluated

Piaget's measures of formal operational thought have been replicated many times, with similar results. In one recent test, the balance-scale problem was re-created using a set-up more familiar to children, specifically a miniature see-saw on which pegs representing adults and children were to be placed to get the see-saw to balance. The "adults" were three times as heavy as the "children." None of the 5-year-olds could balance the see-saw, and only 23 percent of a group of second-graders (about age 7) and 24 percent of a group of fifth-graders (about age 10) could do it. Then ability began to improve, with 47 percent of eighth-graders and 90 percent of college freshmen succeeding (Surber and Gzesh, 1984). Results such as this have led not only Piaget's defenders but also his critics to agree that "children with age become increasingly systematic in their exploration of scientific-type problems," with the adolescents notably more logical and systematic than preadolescents or younger children (Braine and Rumain, 1983).

At the same time, however, the above study supports one of the major criticisms of Piaget's depiction of formal operational thinking—a criticism that has been raised in connection with earlier stages as well: When Piagetian tasks are simplified and presented as "everyday" problems, some children succeed at them at an earlier age than Piaget predicted. This study also reflects another, more significant criticism—that is, that many adolescents arrive at formal operational thinking later than Piaget predicted, if at all. In fact, many older adolescents including college students do poorly on standard tests of formal operational thought. Many adults likewise have difficulty (Neimark, 1975, 1982).

Piaget (1972) himself acknowledges that society and education are crucial factors in enabling an individual to attain formal operational thought. He believes that the maturation of brain and body that occurs at puberty makes these intellectual achievements possible, but certainly not inevitable. Without experiences such as an education, or social interactions that stress science, math, or logic, adults still think like concrete operational children.

Flavell (1982) also raises a point that has been noted with regard to Piaget's other stages: formal operational thinking is more likely to be demonstrated in certain domains than in others, depending upon an individual's intellectual endowments, experience, and interests. Flavell cites the example of an engineer whose

> use of measurement concepts and other well-practiced components of his engineering knowledge may be highly consistent across a wide variety of problems and situations in that field. However, his level of thinking is liable to appear both less mature and less consistently same-level in other areas—areas where he possesses less expertise, where his learning experiences have been less systematic, coherent, and rational, where affective and cognitive biases are likelier to intrude, etc.

However, while expertise may be part of the difference between the thinking of children and that of older adolescents and adults, it probably is not the whole explanation. Adolescents and adults are better at knowing how to confront a novel problem, or how to "think about thinking" (Flavell, 1985). As Flavell describes it, the difference between mature and childish thought is not that adults are always logical formal thinkers while children never are. Rather, it is that even when adults are not being logical, they recognize the concept of logic, whereas children do not, even when, in fact, they are being logical. According to Flavell, sometime during adolescence, people begin to understand that some statements are logical and

A CLOSER LOOK   Implications for Education

As adolescents' minds mature, the education that schools, teachers, and parents provide changes accordingly. During elementary school, the science curriculum centers on practical, visible experiences, suited to the thought patterns of the concrete operational child. An important part of elementary-school science is caring for an animal, taking nature walks, or tracing the changes in trees from fall to spring. In junior high, simple experiments such as dissecting a frog, connecting an electric circuit, or turning water into steam become possible.

Because of the young person's growing ability to think abstractly in high school and college, the study of science at these levels can include, among other things, explanation and discussion of the cell theory, calculations about the possible movements of the atom, and the working out of chemical formulas as well as the observation of visible transformations. Finally, the very idea that the theories of science are indeed theories, not established facts, is a concept that older adolescents can understand (Lovell and Shayer, 1978).

A similar shift occurs in other areas of study. High-school English no longer need center on the rules of grammar and spelling and the mechanics of reading and writing. Instead, as hypothetical thinking expands, writing becomes more creative and imaginative. Further, as students become less bound to concrete, literal thinking, metaphor, irony, and sarcasm become easier to understand, appreciate, and use. In fact, sarcasm, which is beyond most elementary-school children (Ackerman, 1978), sometimes seems to be the adolescent's favorite mode of communication.

In the social sciences, history becomes the study not only of what was but also of what might have been, and current events becomes a matter of opinion as well as of fact. Anthropology is no longer merely an account of the strange customs of strange people, but is a study of the similarities and differences of all human societies, including our own. Psychology also becomes fascinating during adolescence. It is important to remember, however, that adolescents sometimes lose sight of reality in their search for possibilities. Many young people misapply their newly acquired psychological learning to themselves and their families, deciding that they are abnormal and that their parents are to blame.

Further, as Cowan (1978) points out, since a majority of high-school students have not fully reached formal operational thought, it would be a mistake to assume that hypothetical, logical instruction should entirely replace the use of concrete examples and personal experiences.

As scholastic achievement becomes less a matter of rote learning and more a matter of the application of logic and skill, adolescents often take greater pride in their work, thus boosting their self-esteem and motivation.

In fact, a recent survey of the academic achievements of high-school students in the United States found that, while most have learned the basic skills, they have trouble applying what they know. They can read a passage, understanding the language per se, but they cannot draw implications from what they read. Similarly, they know that a square has four equal sides, and that to find the area of a rectangle one must multiply length times width—but less than half of a cross-section of 17-year-olds could find the area of a square given the length of one side (Sizer, 1985). Thus, while they have the potential to use formal operational thought, many of them do not do so, perhaps because English and math are often taught by rule or rote rather than by reasoning.

Clearly, teaching students to think logically and critically about what they know goes hand in hand with helping them to master particular academic skills and to learn specific facts (Kuhn, 1979). During adolescence, as well as later in life, the interplay of the specific and the general, the individual and the universal, and the inductive and the deductive modes of thought is at the heart of most academic, as well as personal, knowledge (Sizer, 1985).

Figure 16.3 *For parents, one of the most exasperating characteristics of adolescents is that they can reason very well in academic subjects but nevertheless may be very illogical about their own lives. The thinking that occurs in, say, carrying out an experiment in science class sometimes seems to be of an entirely different wavelength than that which occurs in establishing personal priorities.*

some are not, and they can usually recognize a logical flaw or acknowledge the truth of a law of physics if someone demonstrates it. Similarly, they are able to approach new problems with a better understanding of how to analyze, theorize, and come up with pointed questions and many possible answers—something children have difficulty doing.

As at earlier stages of cognitive development, however, there are many differences between potential and performance, as well as variations from domain to domain. These discrepancies are much more apparent during adolescence than Piaget's description of formal operational thinking would seem to suggest. While many adolescents and adults have the cognitive competence to think logically, they do not always do so, especially when thinking about themselves.

Adolescent Egocentrism

Thinking rationally about oneself is not easy at any age (Nisbett and Ross, 1980). In fact, in some ways, adolescents and adults are more likely to think irrationally than children are, because their increasing sophistication and mental agility allow them to examine all the possibilities, and thus choose versions of reality that suit their needs or confirm their suspicions (Ross, 1981).

Adolescents in particular often have difficulty thinking rationally about their immediate experiences. Their thought patterns tend to be flawed by a characteristic called **adolescent egocentrism** (Elkind, 1978). While they are long past the global egocentrism of the preschool child, adolescents tend to see themselves as much more central and significant on the social stage than they actually are. For example, the particular limits of adolescent judgment and logic often lead young people to believe that no one else has ever had the particular emotional experiences they themselves are having—that no one else, for example, has ever felt so angry, or so elated, or so misunderstood.

As David Elkind (1978) explains, this form of egocentrism occurs because adolescents fail

> to differentiate between the unique and the universal. A young woman who falls in love for the first time is enraptured with the experience, which is entirely new and thrilling. But she fails to differentiate between what is new and thrilling to herself and what is new and thrilling to humankind. It is not surprising, therefore, that this young lady says to her mother, "But Mother, you don't know how it feels to be in love."

As part of their egocentrism, adolescents often create for themselves an **imaginary audience,** as they fantasize how others will react to their appearance and behavior. For instance, adolescents are so preoccupied with their physical appearance, sometimes spending hours in front of a mirror, that they assume that everyone else judges the final result. Anticipation of a favorable judgment can cause teenagers to enter a crowded room with the air of regarding themselves as the most attractive and admired human beings alive. On the other hand, something as trivial as a slight facial blemish can make them wish that they could enter the room invisibly. Similarly, school phobia, a fear of school that often keeps the student from attending, is particularly likely in adolescence—and often centers more on worries about appearance (particularly on being viewed in the locker room) than about achievement (Rutter, 1980).

Figure 16.4 *Nearly all teenagers suffer chronic anxiety about their complexions, even if they don't actually suffer acne itself. At times their thinking is so egocentric that a single blemish is enough to make them want to go into hiding, as though the whole world were waiting to condemn them for a pimple.*

According to a questionnaire given to hundreds of normal preadolescents and adolescents, egocentrism peaks at about age 13, with girls being more self-conscious than boys (Elkind and Bowen, 1979; Gray and Hudson, 1984). It often takes several years before this egocentrism declines and the individual can walk into a crowded room without the look of one who thinks he or she owns the world or the lack of confidence of one who imagines disapproval in every gaze. Elkind explains, "Whenever the young adolescent is in public, he or she is—in his or her own mind—on stage playing before an interested critical audience. Some of the boorish behavior of young adolescents in public places has to be understood in [these] terms."

Figure 16.5 *Adolescent egocentrism sometimes makes teenagers seek public attention by almost any means at hand.*

Fantasies and Fables

Egocentrism sometimes leads past the possible into the impossible (Elkind, 1974). One example is what might be called an invincibility fable. Many young people feel that they are somehow immune to the laws of morbidity, or mortality, or probability: they take all kinds of risks, falsely secure in the notion that they will never get sick, or killed, or caught.

Another example is what Elkind (1974) calls the **personal fable,** through which adolescents imagine their own lives as heroic, or even mythical. They see themselves destined for great fame and fortune—discovering the cure for cancer or authoring a masterpiece. Piaget recognized the personal fable in the ambitions of one graduating high-school class (a dozen pupils) in a small Swiss town:

> One of them, who has since become a shopkeeper, astonished his friends with his literary doctrines and wrote a novel in secret. Another, who has since become the director of an insurance company, was interested, among other things, in the future of the theater and showed some close friends the first scene of the first act of a tragedy—and then got no further. A third, taken up with

philosophy, dedicated himself to no less a task than the reconciliation of science and religion. We do not even have to enumerate the social and political reformers found on both right and left. There were only two members of the class who did not reveal any astounding life plans. Both were more or less crushed under strong "superegos" of parental origin, and we do not know what their secret daydreams might have been. [Inhelder and Piaget, 1958]

Thus, adolescent thought processes are usually a mixture of the abilities to imagine many logical possibilities and to deny reality when it interferes with hopes and fantasies.

Moral Development

The development of formal operational thought is related to another important aspect of cognitive maturity: the development of moral reasoning. Once young people can imagine alternative solutions to various problems in science, or logic, or social studies, they can begin to be able to apply the same types of mental processes to thinking about right and wrong.

Stages of Moral Development

Remember from Chapter 14 that Lawrence Kohlberg delineated three levels of moral reasoning, with two stages at each level. Kohlberg and others have found that most children younger than 11 reason at stages 1 and 2, the preconventional stages at which the individual thinks primarily of the personal consequences of right or wrong behavior. During adolescence, however, many become capable of reasoning at stages 3 (seeking the approval of others) and 4 (recognizing that laws should be obeyed to maintain social order). During late adolescence, a minority begin to reason at stage 5 (recognizing that laws should reflect the needs of society) (Kohlberg, 1973; Kuhn et al., 1977; Colby et al., 1983).

Kohlberg and His Critics   Kohlberg's theory of moral development is a good example of the way theories develop in science. As you will remember from Chapter 2, theories help organize and clarify various observations and hypotheses, and they are made to be questioned and tested.

Originally, Kohlberg's ideas were the product of three sets of observations: Piaget's theory of cognitive development; various philosophers' systematic delineation of ethical behavior; and Kohlberg's own research on a group of eighty-four boys, ages 10, 13, and 16, who provided Kohlberg with his original empirical data on the development of moral thinking. From these three elements, Kohlberg created and validated his moral dilemmas, his stages of moral thinking, and his theory of moral development.

His theory attracted a great deal of attention, because many people had apparently been searching for a way to clarify and focus their concern about moral education and growth. However, with this attention came criticism on a number of counts:

1. Kohlberg's "universal" stages seemed to reflect liberal, Western values (Sullivan, 1977; Trainer, 1977). (In some cultures, serving the needs of kin may have a higher moral priority than observing principles that presumably apply to all of humankind.)

2. His original moral-dilemma scheme was validated only on males but was applied to females as well (Gilligan, 1982). (It may be that females are socialized to approach moral questions differently than males do.)

3. His moral stages overemphasized rational thought and underrated religious faith (Wallwork, 1980; Lee, 1980). (Some people believe that divine revelation rather than intellectual reasoning provides the best standards for moral judgment.)

4. Kohlberg's scoring guidelines for his moral dilemmas allowed many people to score quite well simply because they were verbally fluent. (Some people are able to persuasively parrot moral positions without really understanding the reasoning behind them.)

5. Finally, Kohlberg assumed moral development is sequential when, in fact, some people appeared to progress and regress in their moral reasoning (Holstein, 1976; Kuhn, 1976).

Figure 16.6 *Participation in a protest demonstration may be sparked by many reasons, some social, some personal, some superficial. However, for many older adolescents, involvement in political arguments is a response to their greater awareness of moral issues.*

Each of these criticisms has some validity. In fact, in response to some of them, Kohlberg's scoring system has been substantially revised to better distinguish moral reasoning from mere mouthing of moral clichés (Colby et al., 1983). (Many of the more verbal adolescents now score at lower stages than they would have under the old system, and no adolescents score at stage 6, the achievement of an understanding of universal principles, a level of reasoning attained only by extraordinary individuals, such as Mahatma Ghandi and Martin Luther King, Jr.) Further, some cultural differences have been found in cross-cultural work, although not as many as the critics had thought would be found (Snarey et al., 1985). More significantly, longitudinal research using the new scoring system shows moral reasoning developing in a steady, gradual progression over the years, just as Kohlberg had described it (Colby et al., 1983; Snarey et al., 1985).

Sex Differences.   Now let us consider one criticism in detail—that Kohlberg's stages of development are biased against females. The most compelling and best-known expression of this position has come from Carol Gilligan (1982).

According to Gilligan, girls and women tend to see moral dilemmas differently than boys and men do. In general, the characteristic male approach seems to be "Do not interfere with the rights of others"; the female approach, on the other hand, seems to be "Be concerned with the needs of others." Females give greater consideration to the context of moral choices, focusing on the human relationships involved. Gilligan contends that women are reluctant to judge right and wrong in absolute terms because they are socialized to be nurturant, caring, and nonjudgmental.

As evidence, Gilligan cites the responses of two bright 11-year-olds, Jake and Amy, to the dilemma of Heinz, who must decide whether to steal drugs for his dying wife (page 435). Jake considered the dilemma "sort of like a math problem with humans," and he set up an equation which showed that life is more important than property. Amy, on the other hand, seemed to sidestep the issue, arguing that Heinz "really shouldn't steal the drug—but his wife shouldn't die either." She tried to find an alternative solution (a bank loan, perhaps) and then explained that stealing wouldn't be right because Heinz "might have to go to jail, and then his wife might get sicker again, and he couldn't get more of the drug."

While Amy's response may seem equally ethical, it would be scored lower than Jake's on Kohlberg's system. Gilligan argues that this is unfair, because what appears to be women's moral weakness—their hesitancy to take a definitive position based on abstract moral premises—is, in fact,

inseparable from women's moral strength, an overriding concern with relationships and responsibilities. The reluctance to judge may itself be indicative of the care and concern that infuse the psychology of women's development. [Gilligan, 1982]

Figure 16.7 *Arguments between male and female adolescents are sometimes a form of flirtation, a way to make emotional contact while avoiding physical intimacy. However, differences in perspective affect the ways in which men and women approach many questions—from how to spend Saturday night to what to hope for in the future.*

Of course, the difference between male and female moral thinking is not absolute. Gilligan is aware that some women think about moral dilemmas the way men do, and vice versa. Nor does she think that either way of reasoning is better than the other, or even in itself sufficient. If people stress human relationships too much, they may overlook the principles involved and may be unable to arrive at just decisions; if they stress abstract principles too much, they may blind themselves to the feelings and needs of the individuals affected by their decisions. The best moral thinking synthesizes both approaches (Murphy and Gilligan, 1980; Gilligan, 1982).

While Gilligan finds both approaches valid, she contends that Kohlberg's scoring system tends to devalue the female perspective. However, an exhaustive review of sex differences in moral reasoning (Walker, 1984) finds that although females may approach moral decisions somewhat differently than males, there is no evidence that these differences systematically affect the scores on Kohlberg's dilemmas. Most studies in which males and females are compared find no sex differences at all. Among those few studies that did find adolescent and adult males scoring higher than females, the women generally had less education than the men with whom they were compared, and the old scoring system was used, which tended to favor sophisticated verbal fluency—a product of education rather than gender. Overall, then, Kohlberg's general scheme seems to apply equally to both sexes.

Conclusion Thus, it seems clear that, on the whole, Kohlberg's theory has stood the challenge of criticism, and has proved to be valid and useful in a variety of contexts with people of various ages and backgrounds (Blasi, 1980; Walker, 1982; Rest, 1983). It also seems clear that substantial moral development occurs in adolescence. In fact, young people from age 10 to 18 are more likely to progress in moral reasoning than people at any other stage in the life span (Colby et al., 1983; Damon, 1984). The likely reasons are that a variety of conditions converge. Cognitive development allows adolescents to think more abstractly; psychological maturation makes them question the moral dicta of their parents; social development exposes them to a variety of ethical values; and personal experiences compel them to make decisions on their own. As a result, adolescents gradually come to see moral questions more broadly, no longer considering only narrow personal interests (stages 1 and 2) and gradually looking at the values of their society (stages 3 and 4) and beyond (stage 5).

Note, however, that this progress takes time and experience. Many young adolescents remain at the preconventional stage of development as well as in an egocentric mode of reasoning. As we will now see, the results of such immature thinking may be disastrous when these young people are required to make decisions about certain issues they are likely to face.

Decision-Making: Two Contemporary Issues

Adolescence is typically a time when a person explores his or her sexual identity and experiments with alcohol and other drugs, often developing patterns and habits that may affect his or her entire life (Coates et al., 1982). To take one blatant and tragic example, alcohol is implicated in most of the fatal or maiming auto accidents involving drivers under the age of 20. To take another, close to 80 percent of the young females who become sexually active by age 14 will become pregnant at least once by the time they are 18.

While sexual behavior and drug use are obviously affected by a host of factors, one of the most important is the way adolescents think about sex and drugs—how they understand the various risks and evaluate the numerous moral questions. We will first look at the facts about adolescent behavior in these two areas, and then at the way adolescents think about them.

Sexual Behavior

Before evaluating the sexual behavior of today's adolescents, let us recognize that their attitudes toward sexuality are probably much healthier than those of previous generations. The decline of the double standard and the increase in sexual understanding mean that relatively few of today's young people will face the negative feelings about sexuality that pervaded our culture only two generations ago, when

> the man or woman who learned during childhood and adolescence that it was "wrong" to examine or stimulate his or her own genitals, that it was "even worse" to have any contact with those of another person, and particularly, that attempts at heterosexual relations were immoral, is expected to reverse completely at least some of these attitudes on the wedding night or shortly thereafter. This expectation is difficult to fulfill. If the initial lessons have been well learned, the unlearning is bound to take a long time and may never be completed. [Ford and Beach, 1951]

However, the behavior of today's adolescents leads to two serious problems that make many wonder if today's young people are allowed and even encouraged to have too much sexual experience too soon. Their thinking may not be as ready for sex as their bodies are.

Figure 16.8 *Norman Rockwell's* Saturday Evening Post *cover "After the Prom," which appeared in 1957, reflects a still-popular image of the wholesome innocence of young love.*

Sexually Transmitted Disease The first of these problems is **sexually transmitted disease (STD)**, a name that actually covers all the diseases that are spread by sexual contact. With the discovery of antibiotics at midcentury, many physicians thought that the problem of STD (or VD, as it then was called) could be cured once and for all. In fact, the frequency of STD did decline during the 1950s, as infected people were cured with penicillin before they could spread the disease. However, in the past twenty years, the incidence of STD has taken a marked upswing, especially among people under age 25, who now account for three-fourths of all reported cases (Green and Horton, 1982).

A major reason for this is that new STDs, and new variants of old ones, are quickly transmitted in today's sexually permissive climate. One example is herpes simplex 2, a virus closely akin to the type that causes cold sores of the mouth (Hamilton, 1980). Unlike syphilis and gonorrhea, herpes is thus far without a cure: once it has invaded the body, its symptoms (chiefly blisters and sores in the genital area) can recur indefinitely in unpredictable episodes. Herpes is now thought to have reached epidemic proportions in the United States, affecting an estimated 20 million Americans.

Another example of a rapidly spreading STD is chlamydia, a bacterial disease, which, it has been estimated, infects one out of every ten college students (Meyer, 1985). Although chlamydia can be detected by a simple laboratory test and cured by antibiotics, it remains a serious problem: very often it does not produce noticeable symptoms, increasing the likelihood of its spread; and left untreated, it can lead to sterility. Like most STDs, chlamydia is most prevalent among adolescents and young adults.

Adolescent Pregnancy The second serious consequence is adolescent pregnancy, a particularly common problem in the United States. In this country, about a million teenagers become pregnant each year, which means that almost half of all teenage girls become pregnant at least once before they are 20. Many of these pregnancies are aborted, about 10 percent spontaneously and about 40 percent by induction. Even so, 524,000 teenagers became mothers in 1983.

Following a marked increase in the rate of teenage pregnancy in the 1960s, the birth rate among teenagers has been quite stable over the past 15 years (U.S. Bureau of the Census, 1985). However, the proportion of babies born to unwed mothers has been steadily increasing. In the early 1960s, of all teenage mothers, about 18 percent gave birth out of wedlock, about 22 percent were married at the time of birth but not at the time of conception, and about 60 percent were married when their babies were conceived. In the early 1980s, the numbers were almost reversed: 48 percent of the mothers were unwed, 24 percent were wed within 7 months of their baby's birth, and 28 percent were married before the baby was conceived. A disproportionate number of unwed mothers are black, but the rate of out-of-wedlock births among black teenagers has fallen over the past twenty years. Among white teenagers, however, the rate has more than doubled.

The absence of a supportive father is only one of the many reasons that the current consequences of teenage pregnancy include lower self-esteem, less education, and reduced lifetime income for the young mother, and a higher incidence of birth complications and problems throughout childhood for the baby (Makinson, 1985). These problems are most prevalent among adolescent mothers under age 16 (Miller, 1983). Obviously, the rate of pregnancy among teenagers, like the rate of STD, is a serious developmental problem.

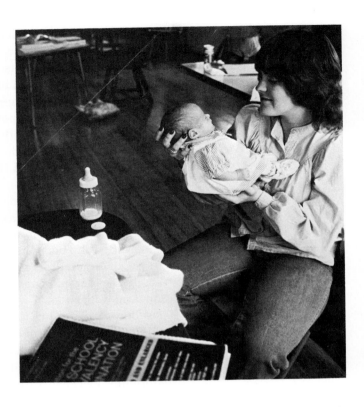

Figure 16.9 *For now, this young mother seems to be able to balance many aspects of her life. She has established a warm relationship with her infant, is pursuing her interrupted education, and even has time to enjoy some social life (as evidenced by her well-manicured fingernails). However, without either generous support from her parents or the services of an excellent day-care center, this young woman will eventually have to make sacrifices in either her education or her social life to provide for her baby's needs.*

Possible Explanations   Given the serious risks involved, what accounts for the high rate of STD and pregnancy during adolescence? At first, it might seem that the cause is simply increased sexual activity among teenagers. As we saw in Chapter 15, young people reach sexual maturity sooner today than was true of earlier generations, and an increasing proportion are sexually active. However, increased sexual activity is only part of the explanation, since the rate of STD and unwanted pregnancy for sexually active unmarried adults is much lower than for adolescents.

Another explanation commonly offered is that teenagers are poorly informed about sexual matters, or that clinics and doctors are unavailable to them. While this is certainly true in some cases, and while the quality of information and care offered to adolescents can certainly be improved, at the moment most schools provide sex education, and most sexually active teenagers can find clinics that will help them. As a leading researcher explains, "though far from perfect, the system [of education and medical help] is in place to enable adolescents to control their fertility if that is their intention" (Dryfoos, 1984).

The crux of the problem seems to be that adolescents are not very logical in their thinking about their sexual activity. As Flavell (1985) explains, many young adolescents have difficulty understanding logical hypothetical arguments. Thus, the questions "What if your partner has STD?" or "What if you become pregnant?" are not answered in rational, personal ways that would lead the young man to use a condom, or the young woman to take effective precautions, or both of them to avoid sexual intercourse until they are ready to deal with the possible consequences.

In fact, adolescents are less likely to use contraception than adults are (Bachrach, 1984). Boys typically regard pregnancy to be primarily the girl's problem. In a large sample of sexually active boys between the ages of 11 and 19, only a third said that they would be "very upset" if they got a girl pregnant, and only 46 percent said

Figure 16.10 *Finding that many boys believe birth control is the exclusive concern of women and that an unintended pregnancy is a girl's responsibility, Planned Parenthood of Central Ohio began a campaign to change young males' attitudes. Prior to the campaign, the Planned Parenthood Hotline was averaging between 200 and 300 calls a month, only about 10 or so of them from boys. After a year of public service promotions that included TV spots like the one shown here, the number of calls had risen to about 800 a month, approximately 100 of them from boys.*

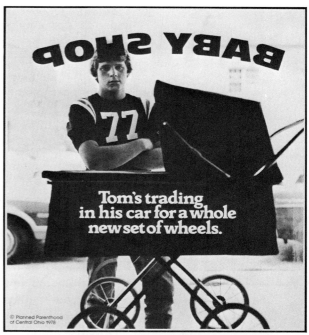

FIND OUT THE FACTS OF LIFE BEFORE EXPERIENCE BECOMES THE WORST TEACHER

they would avoid intercourse if neither they nor their partners were using contraception. This number is especially low when it is considered that a fourth of those who claimed to use contraception were actually using withdrawal as their only form of birth control. The ignorance of this group on certain matters was striking. Half of the boys mistakenly believed that they needed their parents' permission to buy condoms or contraceptive foam at a drugstore; and less than half rated any contraceptive method as "very good" at preventing pregnancy (Clark et al., 1984). Girls are somewhat more careful: about one in three sexually active teenage girls uses the most effective contraceptive methods (the pill or an IUD); another one of three uses less effective methods (such as insisting on withdrawal); and the other one-third use no method at all (Dryfoos, 1982). Not surprisingly, 36 percent of all sexually active teenage girls become pregnant within two years of first intercourse. Those under age 15 have the highest rate—41 percent (Koenig and Zelnick, 1982).

Further evidence of the adolescent's difficulty in thinking logically is shown when a pregnancy occurs. Often, girls delay facing up to the fact that they may be pregnant, which means that if they decide to have an abortion, they tend to have it relatively late, and therefore at greater risk. If they decide to have the baby, this delay means the loss of early prenatal care, and results in a rate of birth complications twice that among adult women. (Teenage girls who do get good early prenatal care have no greater rate of birth complications than adult females do [Makinson, 1985].)

Adolescent egocentrism in the form of the invincibility fable may also play a role. Many sexually active young people do not really believe that pregnancy could result from their lovemaking (Sorensen, 1973). As one pregnancy counselor put it, "The biggest thing is that they just don't think it's going to happen to them. As my mother would say 'They don't believe fat meat is greasy.' They feel they are invincible, and they are risk takers" (Shipp, 1985).

Another sign of cognitive immaturity, noted by Furstenberg (1976), is that because many young people like to think of sex as emotional and spontaneous, they feel it is not something that should be prepared for. In his study of inner-city girls, Furstenberg also found the idea that "good girls don't" was still alive to the extent that "good" girls were not supposed to be sexually active unless the passion of the moment carried them away. Forethought, such as carrying a diaphragm, or even worse, taking a pill daily, meant that a girl had sex on her mind even when she was not involved in lovemaking, and therefore was "bad."

Adolescent Drug Use

Now let us examine the scope of adolescent drug use. Researchers have studied the prevalence of drug use for the past ten years by having a large nationwide cross-section of high-school seniors fill out a detailed questionnaire (Johnston et al., 1985). The most recent results, as you can see in the chart below, show that by the time young people reach their senior year, almost all have used alcohol and a majority have tried tobacco and marijuana. With the exception of heroin, which has become decidedly unpopular among young people (Public Health Services, 1985), between one in five and one in eight have used the other illegal drugs. These rates actually underestimate the drug use of adolescents, for school drop-outs generally have higher use rates, and they are not included in this sample.

Drug use among adolescents varies from cohort to cohort, and even from year to year, with use in the mid-1980s somewhat lower than in the late 1970s. For example, daily marijuana use by high-school seniors almost doubled between 1975 and 1978, then declined each year thereafter, so that the 1983 rate of 5.5 percent was even lower than that of 1975. Use of tobacco and abuse of pills and hallucinogens has also declined, most notably with regard to PCP (Angel Dust), the use of which rose and plummeted over a five year period from 1978 to 1983. (PCP use may be on the increase, however, among school drop-outs [Public Health Service, 1985].)

These encouraging statistics are counterbalanced by two discouraging findings. First, adolescents in the 1980s are generally reporting first use of various drugs at

Figure 16.11 *Prevalence and recency of the use of eleven types of drugs, Class of 1984.*

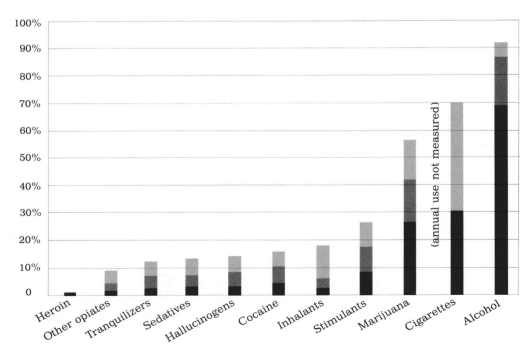

Used drug, but not in past year

Used in past year, but not in past month

Used in past month (30-day prevalence)

younger ages than in the 1970s (Johnston et al., 1985). Second, alcohol and cocaine use are increasing. More high school seniors are using alcohol in the 1980s than in the 1970s, and twice as many used cocaine in 1980 than in 1975, with the 1984 rate of cocaine use showing a continued, although more gradual increase (Johnston et al., 1985).

The specifics on cocaine use are particularly troubling. In general, drug-use rates do not vary a great deal from one part of the country to the other. Cocaine, however, does vary from region to region, with one in every four seniors in the more affluent Far West reporting having used it, compared to one in five in the North East and one in eight from the South or North Central states. Further, college-bound seniors are more likely than other young people to have tried cocaine, which is contrary to the general finding that college-bound youths are less than half as likely to use drugs as youths who are not headed for college (Johnston et al., 1985). Finally, while most adolescents consider tobacco, alcohol, and marijuana "easy to get," less than half rate cocaine so. The implications of all this are that, since cocaine is now a high-status drug that is not readily available, the use of cocaine among adolescents will increase markedly as it becomes more accessible.

Further, since wealthier and more intellectual youths are using cocaine, it is clear that the facts about the destructiveness of cocaine are not reaching even those presumably in a position to get the word first. As Lloyd Johnston and his colleagues (1985) point out, part of the problem is that the negative effects of cocaine take longer to be apparent to the user. In the words of one ex-addict:

> At first it's such a wonderful seduction, getting high, doing a few lines; no big deal. Somewhere down the path, maybe a few months or a year, the seduction turns into a nightmare. . . . Paranoia, depression, and thoughts of suicide begin to follow you around like your own shadow. [Miller, 1985]

Figure 16.12 *Cocaine's seductive effects and ease of use can lead easily to a frighteningly powerful addiction without the more common signs of drug use, such as a distinctive smell in the air or a glassy-eyed look. Symptoms of cocaine use are less direct—money spent without visible return or normal ambitions that suddenly pale in the desire for another "line."*

Why Do Adolescents Use Drugs? Adolescents certainly do not need to be told that drugs are harmful to them. For most of them, this message has come from their homes and schools since they were children. For instance, 97 percent of all adolescents report that their parents would be strongly opposed to their regular use of marijuana or daily use of alcohol, and a majority report parental opposition to even one-time use of most drugs. Given the known and suspected dangers associated with drugs, why do adolescents use them?

Given adolescents' inclination toward the imaginary audience and personal fable, some drug exploration is almost inevitable (Elkind, 1981). Indeed, two tenets of adolescent egocentrism—"I can handle anything" and "Adults don't understand my experiences"—are especially misleading for the adolescent trying to think about drugs. For instance, the cognitive confusion characteristic of regular marijuana use or the slowed reaction time after even one or two alcoholic drinks are particularly difficult to spot if one believes one is invincible.

Figure 16.13 *Despite explicit cancer warnings and drunk-driver fatality statistics, tobacco and alcohol maintain their powerful allure for the adolescent. Especially when adolescent egocentrism prevails, the risk of future danger is outweighed by the pleasures of the moment, like feeling "grown up" in the company of friends.*

The faultiness of adolescent egocentric reasoning about drug use is immediately apparent when children's and adolescents' attitudes about smoking are compared. All have heard the message about the health consequences of smoking many times. Typical school-age children take it quite literally, perhaps breaking their father's cigarettes in half and refusing to kiss their mother if she has been smoking. They nag "You're killing yourself," or cry because they don't want their parent to die. The adolescent who takes up smoking, however, believes that he or she will never have cancer or heart disease, and rather than attacking the parent who smokes, smugly argues that the parent's behavior means that the parent has no right to give advice about any drug-related matter.

**Helping Adolescents
Find Answers**

What can be done to help adolescents avoid problems with drugs or sex? Given what we know about adolescent cognition, part of the answer may simply be to do whatever might encourage adolescents to postpone drug experimentation and sexual exploration until they are more mature. While measures such as raising the drinking age, closing student smoking lounges, and ensuring the supervision of young teens' parties will obviously not stop drug use and sex experimentation among adolescents, they may slow the rate of occurrence. Also, role-playing of how to say no is useful for many adolescents who have trouble handling the social pressures to try a drug or to be sexually active.

With regard to drugs, another approach involves the testimony of peers who have given up their drug habits. Research finds that one of the best ways to help adolescents keep from smoking is to have peers who once smoked and quit tell their contemporaries what the immediate problems of smoking are (Evans and Raines, 1982). In typical adolescent fashion, teenagers seem to take the problems of yellow teeth and shortness and badness of breath more seriously than the possibility of eventual cancer or heart disease.

Further, since adolescents model their behavior after that of the adults they know best, it is probably especially important for parents and teachers of young adolescents to model responsible drug behavior. According to a number of studies, there is a significant positive correlation between parents' use of drugs (mainly tobacco, alcohol, tranquilizers, and diet pills) and their adolescents' use (primarily alcohol and illicit drugs) (Kandel, 1974; Feldman and Rosenkrantz, 1977).

In addition, despite health education in the schools, many young people are not sufficiently knowledgeable about sex (including the risks and benefits of contraception, pregnancy, and parenthood) or about the effects and dangers of drugs (including legal as well as illegal substances). Since many young people start thinking about drugs and sex and begin to experiment even before they are officially teenagers, such facts need to be provided in junior high, and perhaps even grade school, as well as high school.

However, the crucial factor in aiding adolescent cognition does not seem to be providing the facts, but helping the development of the reasoning processes that

Figure 16.14 *The SADD drinking contract is becoming increasingly popular. Such an agreement helps to diminish parents' fears about their child's safety, and it allays adolescents' fear of a bawling out in front of friends—a fear that might otherwise make them decide to try to drive home themselves. The fact that the parents make a reciprocal agreement with their children is important, because they are acknowledging their vincibility and indicating their willingness to admit when they themselves have had more than they can handle.*

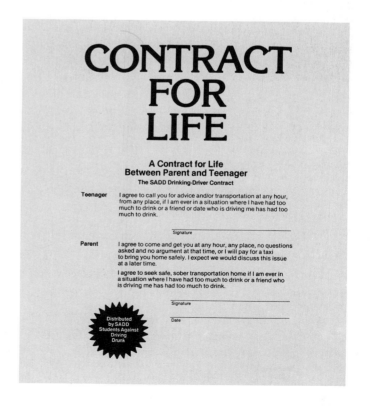

Figure 16.15 *The conversations that this young man shares with his father, other relatives, and friends are likely to be the source of greatest influence on his decision-making about social and moral issues.*

will allow adolescents to apply those facts to their own lives. Let us look again at the research on moral development, for it provides a clue about helping adolescents develop values.

Almost all developmentalists agree that adolescence, especially late adolescence, is often marked by changing values and standards. Classroom moral debates and late-night bull sessions become lively and compelling, and ethical stands passionately taken one year might be reversed by new reasoning the next (Colby et al., 1983; Damon, 1984). The solutions that young people find to social and moral dilemmas, whether actual or hypothetical, depend not only on their cognitive maturity but also on the dialogues they are able to establish with others. The adolescent who has ample opportunity to state his or her views, and to listen to the views of others, will stand a better chance of developing codes of behavior that are increasingly responsible and comprehensive.

This suggests that when parents and teachers are confronted with social or moral questions by adolescents, their best long-range strategy is to listen and debate, rather than slamming the door on open discussion or laying down the law. Given adolescent egocentrism, and the climate of our times, the more thinking adolescents can do about social and moral issues before they are confronted with the results of their behavior, the better.

SUMMARY

Adolescent Thought

1. During adolescence, young people become better able to speculate, hypothesize, and fantasize, emphasizing possibility more than reality. Unlike the younger child whose thought is tied to concrete operations, adolescents can build formal systems and general theories that transcend, and sometimes ignore, practical experience. Their reasoning is formal and abstract, rather than empirical and concrete.

2. The ability to think logically is the hallmark of formal operational thought. Between the ages of 12 and 15, many young people become able to articulate scientific principles when given Piagetian tests of formal operational thought. They are also much more able to follow logical arguments and reason about social problems.

3. Many adolescents and adults never attain formal operational thinking, as measured by Piaget's tests. However, according to Flavell, unlike children, they are able to understand general laws and logical arguments when presented with them.

Adolescent Egocentrism

4. Another characteristic of adolescent thought is a particular form of egocentrism that leads young people to overestimate their significance to others. This characteristic is sometimes expressed in a personal fable about the grand and glorious deeds they will perform in adulthood.

Moral Development

5. Moral reasoning also develops during adolescence, for the young person who can grasp general laws of physics or principles of logic is more likely to articulate moral laws and ethical principles. There is a correlation between stages of cognitive development as defined by Piaget and stages of moral development as defined by Kohlberg.

6. Most adolescents question traditional customs and laws, although none achieve an understanding of universal moral principles, the last of Kohlberg's six stages.

Decision-Making: Two Contemporary Issues

7. However, cognitive immaturity makes it difficult for adolescents to arrive at rational decisions about sexuality and drug use. Adolescents who believe that they are above many of the normal problems that humans experience may also believe that they will never be confronted with pregnancy or sexually transmitted diseases, even when they don't take precautions against them, or that they cannot become addicts even though they use addictive drugs.

8. The best way to help adolescents avoid problems with sexual behavior and drug use may be to encourage them to postpone exploration in these areas until they are able to reason more maturely about them. Role models provided by adults and peers are influential, too.

KEY TERMS

formal operational thought *(490)*
scientific reasoning *(491)*
the game of thinking *(494)*
adolescent egocentrism *(497)*
imaginary audience *(498)*
personal fable *(499)*
sexually transmitted disease (STD) *(505)*

KEY QUESTIONS

1. What are some of the tests that determine whether or not a person has attained formal operational thought?

2. According to Flavell, what are the differences between mature and childish thought?

3. What are some of the characteristics of adolescent egocentrism?

4. What stages of moral development are reached during adolescence?

5. What are some of the criticisms of Kohlberg's theory?

6. What are some of the explanations for the high rates of sexually transmitted disease and pregnancy in adolescence?

7. What are some of the factors that affect the teenager's decision to experiment with drugs?

8. What are some of the ways of helping adolescents to avoid problems with drugs and sex?

RECOMMENDED READINGS

Gilligan, Carol. *In a different voice: Psychological theory and women's development.* Cambridge, Mass.: Harvard University Press, 1983.

In her demonstration of why women understand moral issues differently than men do, Gilligan masterfully pulls together material from literary classics, quotations from many of the participants in her research on moral development, and the theories and findings of other psychologists.

Sizer, Theodore R. *Horace's compromise: The dilemma of the American high school.* Boston: Houghton Mifflin, 1985.

Although Sizer's topic is the American high school, the larger subject of the book is universal—specifically, the ways in which society transmits education, and cultural and social values to adolescents. This book should be read by everyone concerned about the ways schools do, and do not, prepare adolescents for adult life.

Lightfoot, Sara Lawrence. *The good high school.* New York: Basic Books, 1983.

In-depth portraits of six high schools—two urban, two suburban, and two "elite"—that manage to provide a good education for most of the adolescents who attend them. The author places each school in the appropriate ecological context, and then provides detailed descriptions of the formal and informal education that goes on there. A theme throughout the book is the importance of administrative and faculty leadership in creating the educational milieu in which students will flourish. One of the interesting reasons for reading this book is to see how and when Piaget's ideas of cognitive development are reflected or ignored.

Adolescence: Psychosocial Development

Chapter 17

Now watch what you say or they'll be
  calling you a radical, liberal, fanatical,
  criminal.
Won't you sign up your name, we'd like
  to feel you're acceptable, respectable,
  presentable, a vegetable!

At night, when all the world's asleep,
  the questions run too deep
  for such a simple man.
Won't you please, please
  tell me what we've learned
  I know it sounds absurd
  but please tell me who I am.

Supertramp
"The Logical Song"

Identity
Identity Statuses
Social Influences on Identity

Friends and Family
The Role of Peers
Parental Influence

Special Problems
Psychosomatic Disease
Sexual Abuse
Adolescent Suicide

Jobs and Careers
Career Selection

Conclusion

Chapter 17

One of the challenges of adolescence is to establish a sense of individual identity, to find a way to be one of the gang and yet stand out from the crowd. In meeting this challenge teenagers must make some important decisions about a wide, and sometimes bewildering, array of personal and career questions. These tasks of the teenage years, the problems they may involve, and the role of family and friends in helping adolescents confront them are among the topics discussed in this chapter.

How do changes in economic and political circumstances affect the development of identity in different generations?

In which ways does the peer group ease the transition from dependence on parents to true intimacy with a member of the opposite sex?

How wide is the "generation gap"?

What are some of the social and personal characteristics that are associated with such problems as teenage suicide and sexual abuse?

The physical changes of puberty begin the process of adolescence by transforming the child's body into an adult's, and the cognitive developments described in the preceding chapter enable the young person to begin to think logically. However, it is psychosocial development—such things as relating to parents with new independence, to friends with new intimacy, to society with new commitment, and to oneself with new understanding—that helps the young person eventually attain adult status and maturity. Taken as a whole, these aspects of psychosocial development can best be understood in terms of the adolescent's quest for identity, that is, for answers to a question that never arose in younger years: "Who am I?"

Identity

In the 1940s, Erikson became absorbed with the question of **identity,** or the individual's attempt to define himself or herself as a unique person (Coles, 1970). For Erikson, the search for identity represents a basic human need, one which, in modern society, becomes as important as food, security, and sexual satisfaction. In the past four decades, Erikson has written extensively about the search for identity as the primary task, and crisis, of adolescence, a crisis in which the young person struggles to reconcile a quest for "a conscious sense of individual uniqueness" with "an unconscious striving for a continuity of experience . . . and a solidarity with a group's ideals" (Erikson, 1968). In other words, the young person seeks to establish himself or herself as a separate individual while at the same time maintaining some connection with the meaningful elements of the past and accepting the values of a group. In the process of "finding themselves," adolescents must establish a sexual, moral, political, religious, and vocational identity that is relatively stable, consistent, and mature. This identity ushers in adulthood, as it bridges the gap between the experiences of childhood and the personal goals, values, and decisions that permit each young person to take his or her place in society (Erikson, 1975).

Figure 17.1 *The quest for identity is not always easy for adolescents. Some get themselves moving on a set track before they really know which direction they ought to head in. Others can't seem to get going at all. They may think that they should make some move forward in their lives but they are without the concrete motivation to do so.*

Identity Statuses

The ultimate goal, called **identity achievement,** occurs when adolescents achieve their new identity through "selective repudiation and mutual assimilation of childhood identifications" (Erikson, 1968). Thus, in optimal circumstances, the adolescent abandons some of the values and goals set by parents and society, while accepting others. With identity achievement, adolescents develop their own ideology and vocational goals.

Interestingly, Erikson believes that identity achievement is a prerequisite for the next stage of development, intimacy, in which the person is able to commit himself or herself to another human being. As he explains it, "true engagement with others is the result and the test of firm self-delineation" (Erikson, 1968). The idea that people must know who they are before they are truly able to love another person is one that is now commonly accepted. However, several psychologists have suggested that identity and intimacy are often closely related, as the experience of committing oneself to another person helps one understand oneself (Orlofsky, 1977; Josselson, 1980). An empirical study of college students found that for some young people, especially females—who tend to be socialized to find themselves through identification with significant others—identity and intimacy develop together, or intimacy precedes identity (Schiedel and Marcia, 1985).

For many young people, however, identity achievement is quite difficult, and even the process of accepting some parental values while rejecting others is problematic. The result often is **foreclosure,** or premature identity formation. In this case, the adolescent accepts earlier roles and parental values wholesale, never exploring alternatives or truly forging a unique personal identity. A typical example might be the young man who from childhood has thought he wanted to, or perhaps was pressured into wanting to, follow in his father's footsteps, as, say, a doctor. He might diligently study chemistry and biology in high school, take premed courses in college, and then perhaps discover in his third year of medical school (or at age 40, when his success as a surgeon seems hollow) that what he really wanted to be was a poet.

Other adolescents may find that the roles their parents and society expect them to fill are unattainable or unappealing, yet be unable to find alternative roles that are truly their own. Adolescents in this position often take on a **negative identity,** that is, an identity that is the opposite of the one they are expected to adopt. The child of a college professor, for instance, might fail high-school English and drop out of school, despite having aptitude scores that show the capacity to do college-level work. The child of devoutly religious parents might begin behaving in blatant opposition to his or her upbringing, stealing, taking drugs, and the like.

Other young people experience **identity diffusion:** they typically have few commitments to goals or values—whether those of parents, peers, or the larger society—and are often apathetic about trying to find an identity. These young people have difficulty meeting the usual demands of adolescence, such as completing school assignments, making friends, and thinking about the future. As one young man said:

> I should be getting out but I don't have the drive. Not motivated I guess. I want to move [slang for being more involved and active] too, you know. It kinda motivates me a little bit to see them [peers] going . . . I want to go too. It might motivate me for a little while. I do care but I just haven't got on it. [Quoted in Gottlieb, 1975]

Finally, instead of finding a mature identity, some young people seem to declare a **moratorium,** a kind of time-out during which they experiment with alternative identities without trying to settle on any one. In some cases, a society may provide formal moratoriums through various of its institutions. In the United States, the most obvious example of an institutional moratorium is college, which usually requires young people to sample a variety of academic areas before concentrating in any one and forestalls pressure from parents and peers to choose a career and mate. Another institution that performs a similar function is the peacetime military, which makes it possible for many young men and women to travel, acquire valuable skills, and test themselves while delaying lifetime commitments.

Figure 17.2 *There are a number of ways that young people may signal their involvement in some form of identity crisis. The adoption of a "punk" style— including wearing accessories like studded dog collars and bone earrings and engaging in such practices as slam dancing— strongly suggest the presence of a negative identity. The group on the right seems to have taken on a common identity signaled by their general grooming and choice of clothing. These symbols may be a superficial way of dealing with identity diffusion— uncertainty about who they are or what they want to be.*

In a society such as ours, where the number of possible roles seems almost infinite, Erikson believes that prolonging the final resolution of the identity crisis is often constructive. However, a moratorium can become destructive if it lasts so long that the person reaches his or her adult years without having achieved the ability to make adult commitments in terms of family, friends, vocation, and ideology.

Research on Identity Status Following Erikson's lead, many other developmentalists have found the concept of identity a useful one in understanding adolescence. Indeed, James Marcia has defined the four major identity statuses (achievement, foreclosure, diffusion, and moratorium) in sufficiently precise terms that he and other investigators can interview an adolescent and determine his or her overall identity status (Marcia, 1966). Dozens of studies that have compared adolescents' identity statuses with various measures of their cognitive or psychological development and have found that each identity status is typified by a number of distinct characteristics (see Table 17.1). For example, each of the four identity statuses correlates with a somewhat different attitude toward parents: the diffused adolescent is withdrawn, perhaps deliberately avoiding parental contact by sleeping or listening to music on headphones when the rest of the family is together; the moratorium adolescent is not withdrawn as much as independent, busy with his or her own interests; both the forecloser and achiever are loving, but the forecloser evidences more respect and deference, while the achiever treats parents with more concern, behaving toward them as an equal or even as a care-giver rather than care-receiver.

TABLE 17.1 **Characteristics of the Various Identity Statuses**

	Achievement	Foreclosure	Diffusion	Moratorium
Anxiety	moderate	repression of anxiety	moderate	high
Attitude toward parents	loving and caring	loving and respectful	withdrawn	trying to distance self
Self-esteem	high	low (easily affected by others)	low	high
Ethnic identity	strong	strong	medium	medium
Prejudice	low	high	medium	medium
Moral stage	postconventional	preconventional or conventional	preconventional or conventional	postconventional
Dependence	self-directed	very dependent	dependent	self-directed
Cognitive style	reflective	impulsive	impulsive	reflective
Cognitive complexity	medium	low	very high (confusion)	medium
College	high grades	very satisfied	variable	most dissatisfied (likely to change major)
Relations with others	intimacy	stereotyped	stereotyped or isolated	intimate

Adapted from research reviewed by Marcia, 1980

The table also shows some revealing combinations of statuses and traits. Note, for instance, that both adolescents who have achieved identity and those who have prematurely foreclosed their search for self-definition have a strong sense of ethnic identification, seeing themselves as proud to be Irish, Italian, Hispanic, or whatever. However, those who have foreclosed are relatively high in prejudice, while the identity achievers are relatively low, presumably because they are sufficiently secure in their ethnic background that they do not need to denigrate that of others.

This research, much of which is longitudinal, confirms that many adolescents go through a period of foreclosure or diffusion, and then a moratorium, before they finally achieve identity (Marcia, 1980). The process can take ten years or more (Meilman, 1979; Waterman, 1985). There is no doubt that the ease or difficulty of finding an identity is very much affected by the society, the immediate family, and the friends of the adolescent, topics we will discuss now.

A CLOSER LOOK   **The Rite of Passage**

A **rite of passage** is a ceremony or event that provides a transition from one social status or life stage to another. Weddings and funerals are two obvious examples. In many cultures, special rites of passage occur at adolescence to initiate the young person into adulthood, easing the transition from dependence on parents to adult independence. Anthropologists and sociologists have looked at adolescent rites of passage and drawn some interesting comparisons between those rites as they occur in traditional, non-Western cultures and in our own contemporary culture.

In many traditional, non-Western cultures, initiation ceremonies were both dramatic and painful, involving tests of bravery and strength, as well as separation from family and from members of the opposite sex. The young people learned religious rituals and social codes known only to adults and emerged from the process with a new status, new responsibilities, and often a new name.

For the most part, male initiation ceremonies were the more painful, often involving circumcision (cutting away the foreskin of the penis) and facial scarring. Typically, a group of boys would be separated from their families and initiated together, emphasizing their bond to their male contemporaries and their separation from their childhood home. The goal of the male initiation rite was to induct the boy as member of the larger adult community, initially as a warrior.

Female initiation rites, which occurred less commonly, were usually intended to prepare the young woman for the more personal experiences of courtship, marriage, and running a household. Typically, only one girl was initiated during a given ceremony, and her family played a major role in arranging the event. Like the male ceremony, the female initiation rite was an important function, for it announced that a future bride and potential mother was available for match-making (Paige, 1983).

Painful initiation rites such as this circumcision ritual among Australian aborigines seem repugnant to most Westerners. Yet they serve a very useful function in the cultures where they are practiced, facilitating a sudden transition from childhood to adulthood.

Social Influences on Identity

Erikson was one of the first developmental psychologists to call attention to the role of the wider society, a role now roundly emphasized by ecological and systems psychologists. In adolescence, societies provide an avenue to finding an identity primarily in two ways: by providing values that have stood the test of time and that continue to serve their function, and by providing social structures or customs that ease the transition from childhood to adulthood. Whether these factors make the search for identity easy or difficult depends primarily on the degree to which the members of the society are agreed on basic values, and the degree to which the individual is exposed to social change.

In a culture where virtually everyone holds the same religious, moral, political, and sexual values, and social change is slight, identity is easy to achieve. The young person simply accepts the only values and roles that he or she has ever known. In such cultures, the transition to the status of "adult" can be swift, often occurring through a ceremony known as a rite of passage (see Closer Look).

These distinctions will be clearer with two examples. Traditionally, at about age 15, Kikuyu boys in Kenya were circumcised, adopted by ritual parents, and anointed with a ceremonial earth. Isolated from the other members of their tribe for eight days, they sang, danced, ate special foods, and learned to be strong warriors, a role that was theirs for several years, until they married (Kenyatta, 1965; Herzog, 1970, cited in Brown, 1975). By contrast, when a Carib girl from Surinam, in South America, first menstruated, she was confined to a house for eight days so that the spirits of the river and the forest would not be offended by her bleeding and kill her (Kloos, 1969). During this period, she was dressed in old clothes and had to avoid eating certain foods. At the end of her seclusion, she was bathed by an elderly couple known to be hard-working and industrious. After her bath, a tuft of burning cotton was placed in her hands. To avoid being burned, she had to move it quickly back and forth from one hand to another, signifying that she must always keep her hands busy now that she was a woman. Then she had to put her hands into a bowl of large, biting ants, again to remind herself that she must work hard, as the ants do. Finally, she was given jewelry and special clothes, and the entire village joined in a celebration organized and financed by her parents, to acknowledge her new status.

Where they still exist, most initiation rites of this kind have been modified in recent decades. For instance, the contemporary African tribal boy is usually circumcised in a clinic under local anesthesia, and no longer emerges from the initiation rite endowed with all the independence and responsibilities of manhood. Usually he continues to live at home and to attend school. However, the rite continues to serve as a link with past generations and as a symbol of emerging manhood (Droogers, 1980).

Our own society offers dozens of rites of passage. Some are religious, such as the Catholic confirmation or the Jewish Bar Mitzvah and Bat Mitzvah; some are social, such as debutante or sweet-sixteen parties; some confer legal sanction, such as registering to vote or taking the road test for a driver's license; and some are frowned upon, such as the initiation rites practiced by some street gangs, or, at the other end of the socioeconomic spectrum, the hazing that still goes on in some college fraternities. High-school graduation, with the formal diploma and ceremony, as well as the dancing and drinking until dawn that usually follow, is probably the most common American rite of passage.

Given the complexity of our society, and the difficulty of attaining adult status, it is not surprising that our rites of passage are many and varied, and that some of their practices arise from the adolescent subculture without approval from the adult world, and that some groups of adolescents are more likely to experience them than others. Despite this variety, however, many observers believe that all these rituals further the establishment of identity by helping young people to leave childhood behind (Brown, 1975).

Identity in Modern Societies   In large, complex societies, the social influences that can affect identity formation are many and varied and often in flux. As a result, arriving at an identity in modern times is sometimes a difficult proposition, especially in periods of rapid social change. As Erikson (1968) has pointed out, following Germany's total defeat in World War I and the ensuing collapse of its economy, many Germans questioned what it meant to be a German. This "national identity crisis" continued through political chaos for nearly a generation, until Adolf Hitler rose to power by promulgating a series of myths that offered the German people a clear-cut, unifying identity—that of the Master Race, destined to rule the world once they had rearmed and rid themselves of their enemies. Young people were especially susceptible to Hitler's message, and they flocked by the hundreds of thousands to become members of official Nazi youth groups. Uniformed, indoctrinated, and regimented, they knew who they were, what they believed, and how they ought to act (see Figure 17.3).

Figure 17.3 *These photos offer an unsettling illustration of national identity taken to extremes. Hitler's Youth, for boys from 10 to 18, combined a fanatic emphasis on the collective over the individual with the ego-inflating devices of paramilitary uniform, drills, and codes of behavior to create the largest organization for youth the Western world has ever known. In 1932 the membership was 100,000, two years later, it was 3.5 million. The equivalent organization for girls was the German Girls League of Faith and Beauty, which promoted physical culture, health instruction, and domestic sciences.*

Over the past few decades, American youths have also been significantly influenced by varying social factors in their quest for identity. One example comes from some of the children whose families were hardest hit by the Great Depression in the United States. Extensive longitudinal research undertaken by Glen Elder (1974, 1980; Elder et al., 1985), as well as others (Eichorn et al., 1981), has revealed that after relatively comfortable childhoods in the pre-Depression 1920s, many of the adolescents of the 1930s had to make major adjustments in their life style and expectations of the future. In many cases, their fathers lost their jobs, and consequently their self-respect, as their role as family breadwinner vanished. Among the adult male population, the rates of alcoholism, serious depression, and suicide rose. In many cases, mothers entered the labor market for the first time to find whatever low-paying jobs were available. One consequence for the children was

(a)

(b)

(c)

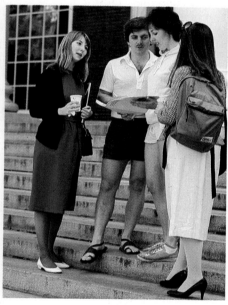

(d)

Figure 17.4 *Although no one photograph can reflect all the forces and nuances of a period in time, images such as these, all of which would be difficult to capture in other periods of time, help to illuminate some of the differences between decades. (a) During the depression of the 1930s, young men enlist in low-paying service jobs in the Civilian Conservation Corps. (b) High schoolers on a night out on the town in the 1950s. (c) Youth protests in the 1960s. (d) A 1980s coed group discussion on the steps of the Harvard Law School.*

that they had to cope with "the loss of an effective, nurturant father, and an over-burdened, dominant mother, anxiously preoccupied with matters of status and mere survival" (Elder, 1980). Another consequence was that many of them had to assume adult responsibilities. Daughters who had planned to go to college stayed home instead to manage the household and the younger children. Teenage boys took any work they could find to help their families survive.

As a result, many adolescent boys forged their identity as diligent workers who "knew the value of a dollar," while girls came to place special value on homemaking skills and "domestic bliss." It was, in fact, this very cohort that played a major role in the postwar prosperity of the late 1940s and, additionally, created the biggest "baby boom" in American history.

Quite different social factors influenced the identity formation of the children born into the "baby boom." When these babies became adolescents, in the late 1960s, their experiences were quite different from those of their parents. Not only were there many more of them; they were also affluent, a segment of the economy to be reckoned with. Indeed, they were a highly visible youth culture whose interests were flattered and catered to. For another thing, in the 1960s both birth-control and marijuana became much more available, setting the stage for a sexual and drug-use revolution. Partly because their parents regretted not having had as much higher education or economic freedom as they would have liked, this generation, far more than previous ones, attended college—a place where they could identify with their peers, and speak out on such issues as civil rights, freedom of choice in life style, and the war in Vietnam. In large measure, the identity of many of these adolescents was based on a distrust of the older generations whose values regarding sex, drugs, and politics seemed outdated and alien. The slogan "Don't trust anyone over 30" was taken seriously by a great many under 20.

As economic and political circumstances changed in the 1970s and 1980s, adolescents began to become more conservative again in their values and goals, as well as their life style. As we have already seen, daily drug use is down from a decade ago. More youths than ever before plan to attend college, primarily for the career preparation it affords, with careers in computers being the most popular of all (Gallup, 1984). More plan to marry and have children, and most are looking forward to the responsibilities of adulthood. Indeed, when a national poll in 1984 asked adolescents to cite the personal qualities they considered to be most important, the quality that rated highest was responsibility, chosen by 93 percent. The quality of independence, which was of prime importance for the adolescents of the 1960s, was much lower on the list, chosen by 68 percent of the adolescents of the 1980s (Gallup, 1984).

Such analysis highlights the importance of historical circumstances on adolescent identity formation, stamping each cohort with a particular set of values and problems that result from their experiences. This fact is now widely acknowledged by social science researchers. However, it is also important to remember that within each historical period, there are individual variations that can be greater than the differences between one cohort and another. Some families were relatively untouched by the economic depression of the 1930s, and those that were did not all respond in the same way. During the 1960s, the differences of opinion between the adolescents who were in college and those who were in the job market were far greater than the differences in opinion between one generation and another (Elder, 1980). Thus, while historical conditions do affect identity formation, the particular influences of one's family and one's peers are probably more significant than the general state of the economy, the society, or the world.

Friends and Family

Given the complexity of forming an identity in our society, whether a particular young person will be able to delay identity formation until he or she is ready to make mature decisions, or whether identity will be premature or confused, depends a great deal on family and friends.

The Role of Peers

Figure 17.5 *These photos show an activity critical to healthy adolescent development—spending time with friends. Note the sex differences here. Girls typically spend long hours simply talking to their best friends, whereas boys tend to hang out in larger groups. Further, girls tend to be more intimate with their friends, both physically and emotionally. Usually the only physical intimacy acceptable among boys occurs in horseplay or in sports, in the form of the congratulatory slap on the buttocks or the bear hug that follows a winning move.*

The socializing role of peers, which begins to emerge during the latter part of middle childhood, becomes quite prominent during adolescence.

Adolescents help each other in many ways, with identity formation, independence, and social skills. As John Coleman (1980) explains, although "the peer group has a continuous part to play in the socialization process during the whole span of school and college years . . . there are undoubtedly special factors operating during adolescence that elevate the peer group to a position of unusual prominence." Coleman finds three of these factors noteworthy. First, the physical and social changes typical of adolescence cause the young person to confront new experiences and challenges to self-esteem. At such times, the peer group can function as a self-help group, a sounding board of contemporaries who may be going through the same sorts of struggles. Second, a crucial task in adolescence is questioning the validity of adult standards and authority. As a consequence, "at a time when uncertainty and self-doubt are greatest and support is most needed, many adolescents find themselves in an emotional position where it is difficult, if not impossible, to turn to their parents. Under such circumstances, it is hardly surprising that peers play an unusually important role." Finally, adolescents need to experiment, discovering which of their personality characteristics and possible behaviors will be accepted and admired. "This process of discovery, sometimes rewarding, sometimes painful and embarrassing, is dependent on the involvement of the peer group" (Coleman, 1980).

Some of this peer-group involvement occurs casually, as a group of teenagers "hang out" together, seemingly doing nothing at the local gathering place, be it a park, a parking lot, the street corner, or a shopping mall. Most of it, however, happens through more private, self-revealing interactions with friends.

Friendship As children become adolescents, their definition of friendship changes to emphasize shared intimacy rather than mutual activities. Further, the nature of the relationship becomes less "tit for tat" and more genuinely reciprocal, involving greater loyalty and helpfulness (Berndt, 1982).

Having a close friend is sometimes crucial in helping the young person find an identity. As Osterrieth (1969) explains:

> By means of common experiences and adventures, and interminable conversations that are more or less intimate, the two partners . . . do each other the mutual favor of helping each one to know himself: they examine themselves, placing in common their experiences, their plans, their ambitions, and their most intimate secrets. In the true sense, they explain themselves to each other, and in so doing, each explains himself to himself.

The mutuality of peer friendships helps distinguish them from parent-child relationships (Youniss, 1981). Consider a study (Hunter, 1985) in which groups of adolescents rated how often they discussed various topics with their parents and with their peers, as well as the character of the conversations. As one might expect, most of the conversations about family relationships occurred with their parents, and most of their discussions about their peer relationships were with their friends. However, on academic, vocational, religious, ethical, and political topics, the young adolescents talked more with their parents, whereas older adolescents talked more about these topics with their peers.

More significant, no matter what the adolescent's age or what the issue, parents were more likely to offer and justify their own thoughts than to try to understand the adolescent's ideas. Peers, on the other hand, listened as much or more than they presented their own views. While having a parent's opinion may often be appropriate, and clarifying, at least about what the parent thinks, having a peer who listens sympathetically while a teenager gives a blow-by-blow account of a social interaction, or thinks outloud about a complex issue, helps the teen gain insight into his or her own ideas, values, and actions. In the process, self-definition, and hence identity, become strengthened.

Peer Groups Peers aid adolescents in their quest for identity in another way as well: they help them define who they are by helping them define who they are not. In our culture, every adolescent is exposed to not one peer group but many, each with distinct preferences in activities, dress, and music, and differing values about school and society (McClelland, 1982). As adolescents associate themselves with this or that subgroup (the jocks, the brains, or the punkers, for instance), they are rejecting others—and the particular self-definitions that would go with them.

Although much has been made of the influence of peer-group pressure in producing unwanted behavior, the pressure to conform to the peer group seems to be strong only for a short period, rising dramatically in early adolescence, until about age 14, and then declining (Coleman, 1980). In addition, the idea of peer-group pressure may be functional in some cases, helping to ease the transition for the young person who is trying to abandon childish modes of behavior, including dependence on parents, but who is not ready for full autonomy (Ausubel et al., 1977).

Figure 17.9 *Establishing an intimate relationship is the ultimate goal of much peer-group interaction and identity development among adolescents. Most young people spend a good deal of time talking about, horsing around with, and making eyes at, the opposite sex before reaching the point of holding hands with one of them.*

childhood, groups are formed of several individuals of the same sex. Then a particular group of girls begins to associate with a particular group of boys, at first merely seeming to appear by chance in the same vicinity at the same time. Gradually, a larger heterosexual group forms from these two groups. The members of this group "hang out" together, with most of the interaction occurring within the large group or smaller subgroups, although occasionally individuals talk briefly with individuals of the opposite sex. Dating, when and if it occurs, is more often done with several couples together. In this context, even physical affection is a semipublic affair.

This gradual transition provides peers with security and role models as well as people to talk to—avoiding the embarrassment of finding oneself alone for any period of time with a member of the other sex without knowing what to do or say. It also provides witnesses and companions of the same sex who will help the young person evaluate whether so-and-so (male) is really nice or a nerd, whether so-and-so (female) is sexy or stuck up, and, equally important, whether a particular attraction is mutual or not. If friends and the larger crowd serve to help the young person think about, talk about, and associate with members of the opposite sex without the intensity experienced in "going steady" with one person, the effect is positive in at least one sense: premarital sex and early marriage are less likely to occur (Chilman, 1983).

Finally, in late adolescence or early adulthood, true intimacy with one member of the opposite sex occurs, as people are ready for the close heterosexual friendships and sexual experiences of adulthood. No longer do they need the company of their peers, or their friends' specific reaction to each word and deed of their date, in order to validate their own feelings.

Thus, peers perform a valuable role in developing heterosexual intimacy as well as in developing identity, helping the young person reach maturity. In fact, without friends, adolescents have a much harder time coping with their immediate problems, and are more likely to have a difficult adulthood in store. The most crucial single predictor of an adolescent's future mental health and achievement is his or her ability to get along with peers (Rutter and Garmezy, 1983).

These findings help put the much overemphasized problems of "peer pressure" in perspective. Many parents worry that their children might be transformed during adolescence by the pressure of their friends, becoming, perhaps, sexually promiscuous, or drug-addicted, or delinquent. In some cases, of course, parents are right to worry, and may even have to intervene. However, while certainly some young people do things with their friends that they would not do alone or with a different peer group (the first drag on a cigarette or the first swig of beer is almost always related to the urging of friends), in general, peers are more likely to complement the influence of parents during adolescence than to pull in the opposite direction (Hartup, 1983; Fasick, 1984).

Parental Influence

According to all reports, the "generation gap," as the differences between the younger generation and the older one have been called, is not very wide at all. The younger and older generations have very similar values and aspirations. This is especially true when adolescents are compared, not with the culture as a whole, but with their own parents (McClelland, 1982).

Numerous studies have shown substantial agreement between parents and adolescents on political, religious, educational, and vocational opinions and values (Lerner et al., 1972, 1975; Feather, 1980). In all probability, this means that parental values have a powerful impact on adolescents, although, obviously, adolescents influence their parents as well.

Of course, not all adolescents have opinions similar to their parents', and even those that do tend to differ on some issues (Gallatin, 1980). Indeed, each generation in the parent-adolescent relationship has a psychic need to view that relationship somewhat differently; in effect, each group has its own "generational stake" in the family (Bengston, 1975). Parents are concerned about continuity of their own values, so they tend to minimize the import of whatever conflicts occur, blaming them on hormones or peer influences rather than anything long-lasting. Adolescents, on the other hand, are concerned with shedding many parental restraints and forging their own independent identity, so they are likely to maximize problems. Thus a conflict about a curfew may be seen by the teenager as evidence of the parents' outmoded values, or lack of trust, whereas the parents may see it merely as a problem of management, the latest version of trying to get the child in bed on time.

Nonetheless, overall agreement is apparent. Most young people, for instance, favor the same candidate for president and attend the same church as their parents do. Interestingly, daughters are even more similar to their parents on numerous value questions—from religion to drug use—than sons are (Feather, 1980).

Other similarities between parents and adolescents are apparent as well. For example, regardless of academic potential, adolescents who do relatively well in high school and college tend to be the offspring of parents who value education and did well in high school and college themselves. By contrast, most high-school drop-outs report that their parents do not understand, accept, or care about them or their education (Cervantes, 1965). Similarly, whether or not an adolescent experiments with drugs is highly correlated with his or her parents' attitudes and behavior regarding drugs (Jurich et al., 1985). Indeed, virtually every aspect of adolescent behavior is directly affected for good or ill by the family (Anolik, 1983).

Parenting Styles Beyond the generality that most parents and adolescents agree quite well, how do differing patterns of parenting affect adolescents? Glen Elder (1962), in a classic study of 7,400 adolescents from intact homes, saw parents' orientation to their children during adolescence as falling into seven possible categories, ranging from control over every aspect of the adolescent's life to no control at all:

1. *Autocratic.* Adolescents are not allowed to express opinions or make decisions about any aspect of their own lives.

2. *Authoritarian.* Although young people can contribute opinions, parents always make the final decision according to their own judgment.

3. *Democratic.* Adolescents contribute freely to the discussion of issues relevant to their behavior and make some of their own decisions, but final decisions are often formulated by the parents and always are subject to their approval.

4. *Equalitarian.* Parents and adolescents play essentially similar roles, participating equally in making decisions.

5. *Permissive.* The adolescent assumes a more active and influential position in formulating decisions, considering, but not always abiding by, parental opinions.

6. *Laissez-faire.* Parents leave it to their teenagers to decide to consider or ignore parental wishes in making their own decisions.

7. *Ignoring.* The parents take no role, nor evidence any interest, in directing the adolescent's behavior.

Elder found that the young people in his sample rated their parents in the following way:

	Mother	Father
AUTOCRATIC	9%	18%
AUTHORITARIAN	13%	17%
DEMOCRATIC	35%	31.33%
EQUALITARIAN	18%	14.33%
PERMISSIVE	24%	17.33%
LAISSEZ-FAIRE	0.6%	1%
IGNORING	0.4%	1%

It is noteworthy that about half the parents were judged to be democratic or equalitarian, the two styles recommended by most psychologists (Maccoby and Martin, 1983). Elder found that parents who were able to share power with their adolescents, neither giving up all control nor insisting on obedience, tended to have adolescents who were high achievers and unlikely to be seriously disruptive or delinquent. It is also noteworthy that if parents of adolescents err, fathers particularly are more likely to be too strict rather than too lenient, a problem discussed later.

Elder found that autocratic and authoritarian patterns were more common among large families, lower-income families, and families with younger adolescents. These generalities have been confirmed by other research, which has found reasons for these patterns.

One reason lower-income parents would be likely to cluster at the more authoritarian end of Elder's continuum is that they expect different things of their children than middle-class parents do (Kohn, 1979). While parents of all classes want their children to be honest, happy, and considerate, lower-income parents also particularly value politeness, neatness, and obedience—qualities for which many adolescents do not have equal enthusiasm. Thus lower-class parents may find themselves commanding rather than persuading their children because this seems the most effective way to make the adolescent behave as respectfully and obediently as the parents want them to (Belsky et al., 1984c). The higher the social class, the more emphasis there tends to be on self-direction and curiosity—values many adolescents do share with their parents.

Figure 17.10 Scenes such as this one bring two complementary thoughts to mind. First, common goals and pride in the accomplishments of family members are often shared by teenage children and their parents. Second, although they are temporarily disturbing to all involved, occasional angry outbursts are also typical of healthy family interaction.

Part of the reason parents of younger adolescents cluster toward greater discipline is that young people begin to become more assertive in family interactions when the physical changes of puberty occur (Steinberg, 1977). In many families, the parents' first reaction is to increase their own assertiveness, trying to insist on the parental authority and respect that their young teenager seems disinclined to give. Gradually parents tend to yield more often, in part because they recognize that their child is becoming an adult, and in part because the child is beginning to act in more mature ways.

Thus, if there is a "gap" at all, it is more likely to occur in early adolescence, and to tend to center on issues of self-discipline and self-control. During these years, teenagers and their parents are more likely to have disagreements about the adolescent's clothes, domestic neatness, and sleeping habits than about world politics or deep moral concerns. Fortunately, the bickering and alienation that occur in many families in early adolescence diminish with time (Kandel and Lesser, 1969; Offer and Offer, 1975).

Special Problems

Although most adolescents and their parents negotiate the teen years rather well, a minority of adolescents and their parents face serious problems, caused by the confluence of puberty, family difficulty, and inadequate social and cultural conditions. We will discuss three of the potentially most devastating—psychosomatic illness, sexual abuse, and suicide.

Psychosomatic Disease

One of the most puzzling problems that occurs during adolescence is the sudden development of a psychosomatic disease, that is, an illness that has psychological as well as physiological components. Typically, psychosomatic diseases occur among adolescents who have always seemed to be "good" children, but whose goodness stems from taking family restrictions and problems too seriously. Among the diseases that can have strong psychological components and that often appear or worsen at adolescence are diabetes, asthma, and eating disorders such as anorexia nervosa and bulimia. As we saw in Chapter 15, eating disorders have no apparent physiological explanation and seem to be linked to such psychological factors as a disturbed body image and a maladaptive attempt to get attention. Asthma and diabetes, while physiological in origin, can clearly be triggered by psychosocial factors (Hilliard et al., 1982; Greydanus, 1983). For example, if a mother and father begin to argue about their relationship, the normal adolescent is likely to get angry at both of them and to express that anger openly. By contrast, a child with a psychosomatic disorder is likely to have an asthma attack, a diabetic crisis, or some other sudden physical problem that forces the parents to drop their fight and come to the rescue.

Salvador Minuchin and his colleagues (1978) compared the families of young people who had psychosomatic illnesses with families where the adolescents' illnesses were organically caused. They found that the families in which psychosomatic illnesses were engendered had five characteristics:

1. *Enmeshment.* Each family member is tangled in the others' lives and problems, allowing no individuality.

2. *Overprotectiveness.* The family members elicit nurturing responses (by crying, getting sick, not eating) and the other members respond with extreme protection.

3. *Rigidity.* Change is very difficult for these families. In adolescence, the parents and the children have trouble adjusting to the development of the child.

4. *Conflict avoidance.* These families avoid conflicts, either by insisting that all is harmony, or by diffusing problems so that none are solved.

5. *Child involvement in parental conflict.* Children are called on to take sides with one parent or another. Often they become ill in order to distract their parents from problems in their marital relationship.

A systems approach to treatment of psychosomatic disorders, then, must consider the family interaction as well as the cultural context (Doherty and Baird, 1983). Thus the young anorexic is helped to develop a more balanced perspective on the merits of thinness, while the family is taught to interact in more constructive ways, allowing the adolescent to develop her own identity. Similarly, the parents of the asthmatic or diabetic child learn how to deal with the child's illness matter-of-factly, rather than with the panicky attention that the sudden crises seek to elicit.

This helps the young person achieve the self-management that is essential to controlling his or her illness and becoming independent (Travis, 1982).

Avoiding the destructive factors noted by Minuchin in connection with psychosomatic disorders can be crucial for all families with adolescents. As a series of recent studies found, adolescents who had the highest self-esteem and were closest to identity achievement tended to be in families that allowed and encouraged each member to express his or her feelings and opinions (Grotevant and Cooper, 1985). Parents who recognize their adolescents as individuals, and who realize that family disagreements may be helpful as long as the conflict is discussed and settled, will be able to help their teenagers develop a healthy identity.

Sexual Abuse

Sexual abuse of the young is a widespread problem that has only recently attracted the public attention it warrants. However, despite the publicity it has received, or perhaps because of it, most people have a distorted view of the problem.

In the public's mind, the typical case of sexual abuse involves a stranger who lures a small child away from a public place such as a playground and then forces the child to participate in some type of sex act. This, however, is the least common form of sexual abuse. In fact, relatives and family friends are the perpetrators in more than 75 percent of all cases of sexual abuse; physical force is used in only about 5 to 10 percent of all instances; and young children are the victims less often than young adolescents are (Holdern, 1980; McCabe, 1985). Incidence statistics show a marked rise of sexual abuse at puberty, and the rates continue to increase until whatever age victims are considered adults.*

As is the case with other forms of child maltreatment, precise data on sexual abuse are hard to come by because abuse is variously defined and its occurrence is, clearly, underreported. For example, some reporting agencies include only cases in which the child has been physically penetrated; most developmentalists, on the other hand, believe that "sexual abuse" is the appropriate label for any act in which an adult uses a child or adolescent for his or her own sexual needs, whether it be through some form of intercourse or a less serious act such as intentional touching of clothed breasts or genitals. Nevertheless, no matter how it is defined, sexual abuse is far more common than most people believe. As Kempe and Kempe (1984) explain:

> The lowest estimates based on official reports suggest that . . . the number of women who experienced some form of [child sexual] abuse to be well over 4 percent, or at least 4 million women in the United States. . . . these estimates are far below the actual incidence in both sexes, since most cases of sexual victimization are never reported to anyone.

Much higher estimates have resulted when adults were asked, confidentially, to recall if they themselves had ever been sexually abused as children. In one study of college students in New England, for example, 1 in every 5 (19.2 percent) women and 1 in every 12 (8.6 percent) men acknowledged that they had been abused before age 17. (Abuse in this study included the entire spectrum of sexual exploitation, from fondling and exhibitionism to rape [Finkelhor, 1979a]). A study of adult

---

*The age at which a victim of sex abuse is no longer considered a child ranges from 13 to 18 in the various states of the U.S. and 14 to 16 in Canada.

women in California found that, by the age of 14, 12 percent had experienced at least one incident of sexual abuse by a family member and 20 percent had experienced at least one incident of sexual abuse outside the family. By age 18, 16 percent had been abused by a family member and 32 percent had been abused by an outsider. (This study excluded acts—like exhibitionism—that did not involve physical contact, but included being "felt, grabbed, or kissed . . . in a way that was sexually threatening" [Russell, 1983].)

Typical Abuse As best we can tell, abuse occurs at roughly the same frequency in every region of North America, with all races represented in about the same proportion that they hold in the general population (Julian et al., 1980). Statistics show that, compared to other types of abusers, sex abusers are somewhat older (in their 30s and 40s), better educated, of higher income, and almost always male (Schlesinger, 1982; Kempe and Kempe, 1984).

Typically, abuse is perpetrated by a man the child trusts, usually the father, step-father, or other close relative or family friend. In the majority of cases, the abused child is female. The abuse often begins in childhood with sexual fondling, and, as the girl enters puberty, may include sexual intercourse. Overt force is usually not necessary at first, primarily because of the powerlessness the young girl feels vis à vis her adult male relatives. As one incest victim recalled of her father:

> When he would walk into the room it was like a sinister force. That was a world where man is boss, man is king. . . . And all he would do is lower his paper and look at me and I would just freeze. [Quoted in Armstrong, 1978]

Ironically, incest between father and daughter, the most difficult type of sexual abuse for the outsider to understand, is, in fact, the most common type of serious abuse (Kempe and Kempe, 1984). How could a father possibly use his own child as a sexual object? we wonder. In many cases, the father rationalizes his behavior by offering himself the "myth of the seductive child," according to which "children are seductive and willingly participate in or invite sexual activity with adults. This myth is . . . especially applied to adolescent victims" (McCabe, 1985). As Finklehor points out, this myth is a disastrous fabrication: no matter what their behavior, young people are clearly incapable of the informed consent that is a prerequisite for a healthy sexual relationship:

> They are unaware of the social meanings of sexuality . . . they have little way of knowing how other people are likely to react to the experience they are about to undertake, what likely consequences it will have for them in the future . . . Further, the child does not have the freedom to say yes or no. This is true in a legal sense and also in a psychological sense . . . children have a hard time saying no to adults [because] adults control all kinds of resources that are essential to them—food, money, freedom. [Finkelhor, 1979b]

The Incestuous Family. Unfortunately, in many incestuous families, incest is an integral part of the family dynamics (Jiles, 1980). The father is often introverted and immature, having little social contact outside his family. Often he is also alcoholic (Schlesinger, 1982; Justice and Justice, 1979). The mother is usually present in the household but unavailable to her husband as a sexual partner or to her daughter as a protector or confidante, often because she is ill or drug-dependent. Frequently she is consciously or unconsciously willing to ignore her daughter's well-being to protect herself or her marriage. For example, the husband's attention to the daughter may prevent him from abusing the mother or the other children, or it may keep him from leaving the family entirely. In many cases, a role-reversal occurs, with the daughter protecting the mother and younger children, while taking over much of the mother's authority and work.

Fathers manage to continue the relationship in many ways, from buying the daughter extra clothes and otherwise favoring her, to restricting her contact with peers and teachers, to using force or the threat of force. Perhaps worst of all is the use of psychological manipulation—telling the daughter that it was all her fault, that she is wrong to complain, and that no one would believe her anyway. Often there is some truth in this last threat. In about half of all cases in which incest victims tell their mothers of the abuse, their mothers refuse to believe them (McCabe, 1985). In many cases, the daughter simply leaves home as soon as she is able, coming to the attention of officials as a runaway and, far too often, as a young prostitute, rather than as a victim of sexual abuse.

Consequences of Abuse   The psychological effects of sexual abuse depend largely on the extent and duration of the abuse, and on the reaction of adults—care-givers as well as authorities—once the abuse is known. If the abuse is a single nonviolent incident, and the child tells a trusted care-giver who believes the child's account, the psychological damage may last only a few days (Schlesinger, 1982). Even with abuse that is more serious, children and adolescents can be quite resilient if they are cared for with sensitivity and respect. For instance, the child should not be required to repeat the story over and over: one private session with a professional trained in sexual trauma should be sufficient to gather whatever legal evidence is needed. Further, the incident should be kept confidential, and the victim must be reassured that it was not his or her fault.

If the abuser is a family member, and the problem has been ongoing, much damage may occur before the abuse is uncovered. As Kempe and Kempe (1984) report:

> Longstanding in-house sexual abuse with a loved person and/or relative . . . is particularly damaging for the preschool child and for the young adolescent; at these two important times both need to fulfill their sexual development in an orderly and sequential way which this misfortune totally disturbs. As a result these victims have a much higher than normal incidence of poor sexual adjustment and difficulties in sexual identity and preference. As teens they are likely to run away from an intolerable situation, become pregnant, get involved in delinquency such as theft and substance abuse (both alcohol and other drugs), engage in teenage prostitution and, as has been the experience for some of our clients, make a significant number of attempts at suicide. Some have, indeed, killed themselves . . .

Further complicating the question of recovery is the immediate reaction of outside authorities (Schlesinger, 1982). For example, about half the time the victim is removed from the home and put into foster care or an institution for troubled adolescents, which may make her feel that *she* is being punished. If the father is arrested, she feels guilty, and her mother may blame her for destroying the family.

When the family remains together, the first step in treatment is, obviously, to make sure the abuse never happens again, and this initially involves getting the abuser and the other family members to recognize the harm that has been done. As hard as it may be to believe, achieving this recognition is not easy. Many family members simply deny that the abuse could have occurred; others excuse it by saying that "no harm was done" or that it was an "expression of love" or that the girl "didn't object." As we have seen, such arguments are gross distortions of reality.

Long-term Consequences. From a developmental point of view, one of the most troubling consequences of incest is that the young person may never learn what a normal parent-child relationship should be. Kempe and Kempe (1984) report that

> child abuse is more common in mothers who were incest victims. . . . We have noted a teenage mother, who had herself been sexually abused by her father, treat her neglected 3-month-old baby in an inappropriate way during an interview with her. She called him "Lover" several times and kissed him repeatedly on his open mouth. This kind of inappropriate sexualization of a close relationship, in combination with neglectful parenting, may provide a background for future abuse.

Similar findings come from a study of mother-infant attachment patterns which focused on mothers who were under a great deal of stress because they were young, poor, and alone. About 10 percent of these mothers behaved in a seductive manner with their infant sons (Sroufe and Ward, 1980). Follow-up research found that almost half of these mothers had been sexually abused as children by family members, and, as their children grew older and entered nursery school and elementary school, they were more likely to show the kinds of inappropriate interactions with adults and other children that are symptoms of abuse, as well as to act precociously sexual with other children (Sroufe et al., 1985).

Other studies have shown that female victims of sexual abuse may have a distorted view of sexuality, and thus are more likely to marry men who are abusive. If these men begin to abuse their daughters, the mother is less alert to the problem or feels trapped again, unable to help (Kempe and Kempe, 1984). This is another explanation for the fact that children of women who have been sexually abused are more likely to be abused themselves (Goodwin, 1982). Thus, in several ways, the effects of sexual abuse may be transmitted from generation to generation.

Prevention Obviously, prevention of sexual abuse requires recognizing factors that foster sexual abuse and putting a stop to, or at least guarding against, them. As the chart on page 538 reveals, these factors begin in the macrosystem—with cultural values and practices that encourage sexual feelings toward children—and continue at each level down to the microsystem of the family.

Obviously, not all these factors can be changed or controlled. One that can be changed, however, is the culture's values about sex and about children. Already, rising awareness of the problem of sexual abuse has increased public pressure against the eroticization of children in pornography and advertising. In certain respects, another, more subtle change has been occurring by virtue of the fact that

Preconditions for Sexual Abuse of Children

1. *Adults must have sexual feelings about children.* Such feelings are encouraged by
childhood sexual experiences
exposure to child pornography
exposure to advertising that sexualizes children
male sex-role socialization that devalues nurturance and encourages sexual aggression
"successful" adult sexual experiences with children

2. *Adults must overcome internal inhibitions against abuse.* These inhibitions are
weakened by
cultural values that accept sexual interest in children
low impulse control
alcohol
stress
low self-esteem
fear of, or frustration with, sexual relationships with adults
cultural or familial values that emphasize father's unquestioned authority

3. *Adults must overcome external inhibitions to committing sexual abuse.* These obstacles
to contact with a child are minimized by
an absent, sick, or powerless mother
a mother who is neglectful, unaware of her children's need for protection
crowded living conditions or sleeping together
opportunities to be alone with the child
social isolation—family members have few friends
geographical isolation—family has few nearby neighbors

4. *Adults must overcome the child's resistance.* Overcoming this barrier is easier if the
child is
emotionally deprived
socially isolated
acquainted with the adult
fond of the adult
vulnerable to incentives offered by the adult
ignorant of what is happening
sexually repressed and sexually curious
weak and frightened of physical force

Source: Finkelhor, 1984.

fathers are more actively involved in the care of their infants than they once were. One researcher finds that incest is rare in families in which the fathers were involved in infant care-giving: presumably, these fathers see their children in protective and nurturant ways, which makes sexual feelings unlikely and inhibition against them high (Herman, 1981). This analysis would help explain why the fathers currently involved in incestuous abuse are more frequently step-fathers, whereas they were more frequently biological fathers in early cohorts (Russell, 1984; McCabe, 1985).

Certain preventive measures can be established in the social institutions of the community. Since vulnerability is fostered by ignorance, sex education in schools and churches should begin at younger ages, and should include not just the specifics of biology but also discussion of appropriate relationships between adults and children, and between men and women. This may not only prevent the children from being victims; it may also help them become adults who would not permit abuse to occur. A related step would be to make teachers and clergy aware of the

Figure 17.11 *One unfortunate consequence of the intensified publicity about child abuse is that young men are shying away from working with preschoolers. Sexual abuse is, in fact, very rare in day-care centers and does not occur if parents are as actively involved in centers as they should be. And, especially since many children have single-parent mothers, male adults who model the appropriate use of physical touch as well as social interaction are very much needed.*

preconditions for, and the symptoms of, sex abuse, so they could be alert to help victims early on.*

Finally, prevention also means empowering children so that they themselves may be able to stop sexual abuse before it begins. Knowing that it is all right to say no to adults, that one's genitals should not be touched by other people, that one's care-givers (including teachers) will listen and respond whenever the child is troubled by the sexual behavior of anyone—stranger, friend, or family member—will help children be less vulnerable.

Adolescent Suicide

One of the most perplexing problems that may occur in adolescence is suicide. From an adult's perspective, the teenager is just at the start of the many wondrous and exciting experiences that life offers. It seems inexplicable that a young person would end his or her life as it is about to really begin. Yet about one adolescent in every ten thousand does that each year, a rate double that of twenty years ago.

As can be seen in Figure 17.12, the suicide rate between ages 15 and 19 is around half that for any subsequent age group. As an index of despair, however, this differential may be misleading, because it probably results from the higher failure rate of teenagers' suicide attempts.† Further, many people who commit suicide as young adults were unsuccessful attempters as adolescents.

Contributing Factors What factors cause a young person to take his or her own life? Do adolescents who commit suicide differ in personality from normal adolescents or from disturbed nonsuicidal teenagers? And what circumstances drive a

---

*A national hotline, 1-800-422-4453, or 1-800-"4" A CHILD, is open day and night for questions and problems related to child abuse of any kind.

†Accurate statistics on attempted suicide in adolescence are hard to come by, because many attempts are hidden by embarrassed parents and many apparent accidents may actually have been suicides. However, it is generally believed that adolescents attempt suicide at least as often as adults do.

Figure 17.12 *The suicide rate for adolescents is half the rate for adults only because adolescents' attempts to kill themselves fail twice as often as those of adults. Unfortunately, the "success" rate for adolescents in the 1970s was double that of the 1960s.*

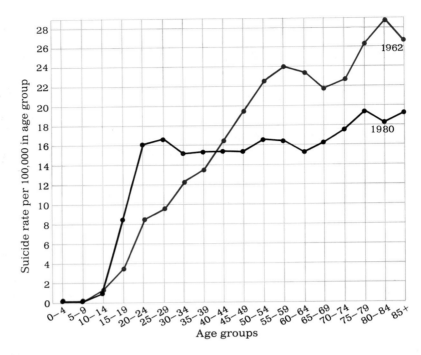

young person to the point of self-destruction? Answers to these questions are hard to arrive at. For one thing, obviously, information about suicide victims cannot be gotten directly: it must come from those acquainted with the victims, or be inferred from studies of adolescents who have failed in their attempts on their lives. The information from the former source, usually parents, may be tainted for several reasons, including grief, guilt, or a denial of, or blindness to, serious problems that may have existed. The data from the second source may also be faulty, for it simply may not be valid to generalize from studies of failed suicides to successful ones.

Allowing for these limitations in the study of teenage suicides, certain rough patterns do emerge from the research. According to a review of the psychosocial and cognitive aspects of adolescent suicide (Petzel and Riddle, 1981), suicidal behavior, and probably suicidal thoughts as well, are not normative in adolescence. Suicidal adolescents tend to be more solitary than normal adolescents and, compared to disturbed nonsuicidal adolescents, they show a greater tendency to be depressed, self-punishing, and emotional. They also seem to exhibit certain patterns according to their sex:

> Suicidal males were tense, jumpy, high strung, perfectionistic, prone to worry and suspiciousness, and had exaggerated needs for affection but few relationships with male peers; distress was channeled into projection, depression, and somatization. Suicidal males were generally less resentful than [control-group subjects] and often were referred for treatment because of impulsive behavior. Suicidal females were tearful, despondent, resentful, weak, unstable, and unpredictable. Weak defenses, poor judgment, deviant ideation, marginal control, flat affect, subjective feelings of depression, few or no friends, and sex difficulties also characterized suicidal adolescent females. [Petzel and Riddle, 1981]

Research has also shown that there is usually no single event that triggers a suicide attempt: rather, it "occurs within the context of long-standing problems," one of the most prominent of which is chronic family conflict, characterized by "anger, ambivalence, rejection, and/or communication difficulties."

Whatever the background or precipitating problems may be, one of the major factors that seems to tip the balance in the direction of suicide is the person's cognitive grasp of his or her situation. Typically, suicidal adolescents have a difficult time focusing on the future and may also have impaired problem-solving capacities. The net result is a combined sense of helplessness and hopelessness, a feeling that their suffering will be endless. As one teenager wrote in his suicide note:

> To my family and friends:
>
> I'm sorry it has to be this way. For some reason, I have set unattainable goals for myself. It hurts to live and life is full of so many disappointments and problems. . . . Please don't cry or feel badly. I know what I am doing and why I am doing it. I guess I never really found out what love or responsibility was.
>
> Bill
>
> I might also add that I had had in recent years no great desire to continue living. Saying goodbye to all of you who I was close to would only make things harder for me. Believe me, I tried to cope with my problems but I couldn't. [Jacobs, 1971]

Figure 17.13 *No one goes through life without moments of depression. It is, in part, the ability to put those times into the context of past and future that can help to diminish the hurt of painful events in the present.*

In fact, many problems of adolescence that seem insurmountable to young people like Bill have been experienced and weathered by other people many times. Without communication with parents and friends, however, the adolescent's egocentrism prevents realization of this fact, and keeps the young person imprisoned in a sense that the future will always be like the present, a dilemma to which there seems to be only one solution.

Warning Signs   A number of warning signs should alert family and friends that a young person may be becoming dangerously overwhelmed with emotional difficulties:

1. *A sudden decline in school attendance and achievement, especially in students of better-than-average ability.* Jacobs (1971) found that while about a third of the young people who attempted suicide had recently dropped out of school, only 11 percent were in serious academic difficulty. Most of them had been doing quite well before their precipitous decline.

2. *A break in a love relationship.* This is the precipitating event for many adolescent suicides. The fact that such events are relatively common in adolescence sometimes blinds parents and teachers to the pain and depression they cause, especially in the egocentric young person who believes that the lost love is the only love he or she could ever have. A sympathetic shoulder to cry on is much more helpful than a statement such as "There are other fish in the sea."

3. *Withdrawal from social relationships, especially if the adolescent seems no longer to care about social interaction.* The adolescent who decides that suicide is the solution sometimes seems less depressed than previously and may cheerfully say something to the effect of "It's been nice knowing you." A joking or serious "goodbye" accompanied by a sudden desire to be alone is a serious sign.

4. *An attempted suicide.* An attempted suicide, however weak it might seem, is an effort to communicate serious distress, and therefore must be taken seriously. If nothing changes in the adolescent's social world, an attempted suicide may turn out to have been a trial run for the real thing. Almost all adolescent suicides follow failed attempts.

When such warning signs have been detected, they must be acted upon. As Edwin Shneidman (1978) has written:

> the act of suicide is an individual's effort to stop unbearable anguish or intolerable pain by doing "something." Therefore, the way to save a person's life is also to do "something," to put your knowledge of the person's plan to commit suicide into a social network—to let others know about it, to break the secret, to talk to the person, to talk to others, to offer help, to put action around the person, to show response and concern, and, if possible, to offer love.

Professional help for suicidal adolescents and their families can often open up channels of communication that had been blocked by the self-absorption of the adolescent, and perhaps by the parents' insensitivity, as well. One important goal of therapy is to keep expectations in line with reality. Parents often demand too much. As one pediatrician explains, "A lot of families expect that the minute the youngsters become thirteen or fourteen, they should be capable of making it on their own. In reality, teenagers probably need as much support at that point in their lives as toddlers need, although of a different sort" (Langone, 1981).

Jobs and Careers

As the end of adolescence begins to approach, one of the major concerns for young people is the selection of a possible means of livelihood, a selection that involves not only one's abilities and interests but also one's sense of self. Erikson believes that, in our society, finding an occupational identity is the most difficult identity task of all. In earlier generations, young people often simply took up their parents' occupations—on the farm, or in the home, the shop, or the factory—and learned the job from their parents by working beside them. Today, however, the number of possible jobs young people must select from (most of which their parents know little about), and the time it takes to prepare for them, can make choosing a career extraordinarily difficult.

Career Selection

Given the complexity of making career choices, a rational selection process would seem to be called for. Thus, in deciding what career to pursue, a young person might first try to learn what the future job picture is likely to be, looking for occupations that will provide many employment opportunities and interesting, well-paid work. Next, that person might evaluate his or her own interests, abilities, and talents to see which careers will use them well. Personal values concerning the relative importance of money, success, fame, adventure, and other people would also be considered. All these elements would begin to point in some general direction, and the next step might be to obtain some personal experience in careers that seem possible. If experience in these fields is too hard to obtain, then talking to people already in them, and perhaps studying one aspect of them in school, would be a logical alternative.

Certainly this kind of decision-making sounds sensible, but does it sound like the kind most people usually use? Probably not. Humans have "limited computational power": they are seldom completely rational and usually make decisions after selective, somewhat random searches for information, rather than after obtaining all the facts that are relevant and calculating the advantages and disadvantages of each (Simon, 1979).

In addition, when it comes to making judgments about specific career possibilities, young people seem particularly susceptible to fantasy. All during childhood, whatever thoughts they have about a future vocation tend to be based on glamorous stereotypes that have little to do with the realities of the work involved or their own particular interests (Jordaan and Heyde, 1978). During adolescence, the element of fantasy in choosing a career diminishes somewhat, but it is still a potent factor, even by the end of college. For example, when researchers (Sarason, 1980) asked a group of college seniors who were going to be doctors and lawyers "Have you ever considered a career in business, finance, or industry?" the students' answer was,

> universally, an emphatic no, and they gave one or all of three reasons: you would be a small cog in a big wheel; it takes a long time to get to the top; and the chances are good that you will become morally corrupt in the process . . .

However, students who were actually in law or medical school realized that what the college seniors had perceived as major drawbacks to other professions were in fact to be a very real part of their lives as doctors and lawyers:

Without exception they knew that they were going to be in or around large, bureaucratically organized institutions, small cogs in the big wheel, scrambling competitively to get a place in the sun, and sensitive to the obstacles to remaining true to their ideals.

Another study, in this case of future accountants and secretaries, found that an intern program that provided on-the-job experience *decreased* motivation to learn job-related skills. Once the students knew what accountants and secretaries actually do, they were less eager to become one. Sadly, another result of the intern program was an increase in unrealistic choices for alternative careers. For instance, a student who once fantasized about becoming a secretary now fantasized about becoming a famous singer or dancer instead (Ducat, 1980).

Figure 17.14 *These students have completed an "executive internship" program in which they worked in business offices half time, while at the same time continuing their education in school. Such programs are particularly beneficial in providing adolescents with the opportunity to test their vocational fantasies before making an actual job choice.*

A second problem in career selection is that accurate knowledge about future occupations is difficult for most people to acquire, in part because the job picture changes rapidly. (The *Dictionary of Occupational Titles* lists more than 20,000 job categories, most of which did not exist twenty years ago.) In addition, college students are likely to be influenced most by their parents in making career decisions, even though parents would be unlikely to know about current job prospects (Busow and Howe, 1979).

Finally, it is not easy for young adults to set realistic goals for themselves. For instance, Buhler (1968) believes that between the ages of 15 and 25, young people are tentative and experimental in their goal-setting. Many do not really set goals at all, but rely on external circumstances (luck!) to chart their paths for them. As one researcher found after following the lives of a thousand people for ten years from age 15, there was an "almost universal period of floundering before the person settled down to a relatively permanent occupation" (Taylor, 1978). This was equally true of males and females, college graduates and high-school dropouts, professionals and the unemployed.

Figure 17.15 *Most young girls' dreams of success do not include growing up to be a welder or a plumber or an electrician. However, training in the skilled trades is one avenue to lucrative job opportunities.*

Theoretically, vocational classes and counseling in high school would seem a good source of career guidance, but in actuality they do not appear to be very effective (Lueptow, 1984; Sizer, 1985). Most high-school guidance counselors are too busy dealing with scheduling problems and disruptive students to provide the necessary individualized advice, and vocational education does not usually provide students with marketable skills, because the equipment, the techniques, and the job prospects in the labor market change much more rapidly than high-school curricula do. After visiting high schools throughout the nation, one leading educator concludes that "the best place to learn most jobs is on site . . . tomorrow's economy will be volatile and dependent on flexible workers with a high level of intellectual skills." Thus high schools should focus on the communication and thinking skills needed for the job market of the future, not for specific trades (Sizer, 1985).

Girls and Careers These problems relating to career identity are experienced by young people of both sexes. However, girls may have an additional problem. Adolescence is a time when young people of both sexes become acutely aware of the traditional male-female relationships and roles. In large measure, this has traditionally meant that whereas achievement in the outside world becomes a prime focus for boys, for girls

the establishment of successful interpersonal relationships becomes the self-defining, most rewarding, achievement task. When that change in priorities occurs—and it tends to be greatest in the later years of high school and again in the later years of college—personal qualities, such as independence, aggression and competitive achievement that might threaten success in heterosexual relationships, are largely given up. [Bardwick and Douvan, 1971]

Such feminine socialization devalues the very qualities that lead to most successful careers, especially where professional commitment, drive, and ambition are needed. This is one reason women have tended to be employed in jobs where aggression and competition are dysfunctional—and where, not just coincidentally, pay and status are low (Lueptow, 1984).

We might expect that today's young women are preparing, with specific training as well as more aggressive and self-confident personality patterns, for more responsible and prestigious careers. Although to some extent this may be true, substantial research shows that quite traditional patterns are still prevalent. One extensive study (Lueptow, 1984) compared high-school students in two cohorts, which graduated approximately five years before and five years after the peak of women's liberation in the early 1970s. There were some differences in the girls' career plans: for example, far fewer of the later cohort planned to be housewives, and a greater number of girls in the later cohort hoped to enter the white-collar professions, becoming executives and lawyers, for instance. But, just as earlier, most young women opted for careers that emphasize service and nurturance rather than individual accomplishment and achievement. Many expected to be elementary-school teachers, nurses, and secretaries. At the same time, the lucrative blue-collar skilled trades were as sex-segregated as ever, probably because girls are not encouraged to consider these vocations (Houser and Garvey, 1985).

The results of this research come as no surprise to researchers who have looked at continuing sex differences in values and personality over the past few decades (e.g., Duncan and Duncan, 1978; Veroff et al., 1981). Male and female roles and values seem not to have shifted nearly as much as one might think from the statistics on the current rate of maternal employment (62 percent) or from the news features about female coal diggers, engineers, construction workers, and the like. The sex segregation still apparent in many adolescents' career plans seems needlessly narrow.

Taken together, the evidence suggests that vocational identity is the most difficult type of identity for adolescents to achieve because, at the same time that they feel pressured to select a particular occupation, it is premature for young persons to decide on a career on the basis of the limited work knowledge and experience most of them have. Jobs and careers change throughout the life span as interests and needs change, and the job market shifts. Rather than channeling young people into vocations, or letting them select careers based on fantasy or sex-role stereotypes, we need to help them keep their options open. Adolescents need to prepare to live productive lives, perhaps anticipating many career changes as their interests and needs evolve.

Conclusion

In closing our discussion of adolescence, it would seem appropriate to reiterate a point made by Erikson (1964). Essentially, adolescence may be viewed as the dawning of commitment, to others, to ideologies, to work. And it is through these various commitments that young people begin to accomplish the task of achieving adult identity. Each family, each community, each culture, intentionally or unwittingly, works to help or hinder adolescents in their efforts to make adultlike decisions about their lives.

Within the context of the social forces that block some options and encourage others, each individual attempts to chart his or her own course. Just as each infant actively searches for cognitive equilibrium, each adolescent tries to find the identity that expresses his or her own individuality. In the process, adolescents make decisions about how to reach adulthood that may affect their entire lives. This does not mean that a person's entire future is set by the beginning of adulthood, for an individual's destiny is never fully known until the individual's life is over. However, as adolescents chart their course in one direction or another, they foreclose some options and create others. As Robert Frost wrote (1963):

Two roads diverged in a wood, and I—
I took the one less traveled by,
And that has made all the difference.

Figure 17.16 *The pathways to identity are many, and the means of arriving there, marvelously varied. How smooth the journey is depends in part on how well the route and means suit the individual's personality.*

SUMMARY

Identity

1. According to Erikson, the psychosocial crisis of adolescence is identity versus role confusion. Ideally, adolescents resolve this crisis by developing a sense of both their own uniqueness and of their relationship to the larger society, establishing a sexual, political, moral, and vocational identity in the process.

2. Sometimes the pressure to resolve the identity crisis is too great and instead of exploring alternative roles, young people foreclose their options, establishing a premature identity. Other young people simply choose values and roles opposite to those expected by parents and society, thus forming a negative identity.

3. The process of identity formation depends partly on the society: if its basic values are consistent and widely accepted, and if social change is small, the adolescent's task is fairly easy.

4. Many societies help adolescents achieve identity by providing rites of passage, or initiation ceremonies. In some cultures, these rites are painful and dramatic,

helping the young person make the transition from childhood to adolescence in a matter of days or weeks.

5. No single rite of passage can perform this function in our complex society. However, we do have institutions, such as college or the military, that help the young person declare a moratorium on final identity formation.

6. The identities chosen by large numbers of each generation are dependent, at least in part, on the economic and political experiences of each generation.

Friends and Family

7. The peer group is an important source of information and encouragement for adolescents. The adolescent subculture provides a buffer between the world of children and that of adults, allowing, for example, a social context for the beginning of heterosexual relationships.

8. Many adolescents identify strongly with their generation, believing that some ideas and experiences cannot be properly understood or appreciated by adults.

9. However, parents are the most important influence on adolescents, especially when there is discussion and respect among family members. Children, especially daughters, tend to share their parents' values.

Special Problems

10. Psychosomatic illness, sexual abuse, and suicide are among the most serious problems of adolescence. Many of these problems can be attributed to certain patterns of family interaction and also to social and cultural beliefs and patterns.

11. The most common types of sexual abuse occur between children and relatives and family friends. Patterns of family interaction may allow such abuse to continue over long periods of time. Abused children tend to develop distorted views of both parent-child relationships and adult sexuality.

12. Researchers have found that most adolescent suicides are preceded by a long sequence of negative events, including family problems and breakdowns in communication among family members. Suicide prevention requires heeding the preliminary warning signs.

Jobs and Careers

13. Particularly for today's young people, vocational identity may be the most difficult identity to achieve, in part, because of the great variety of jobs available. Girls are still especially likely to lack the necessary planning and ambition to prepare for competitive, high-status careers.

KEY TERMS

identity *(516)*
identity
  achievement *(517)*
foreclosure *(517)*
negative identity *(518)*

identity diffusion *(518)*
moratorium *(518)*
rite of passage *(520)*

KEY QUESTIONS

1. What characterizes societies in which identity formation is easy?

2. What is the function of the peer group during adolescence?

3. Which parenting styles seem least helpful to adolescents?

4. What are some family characteristics that tend to be associated with psychosomatic disease?

5. What are some of the family and social patterns that are preconditions for sexual abuse of children?

6. What are some of the psychosocial and cognitive patterns that tend to be associated with adolescent suicide?

7. Why is vocational identity considered particularly hard to achieve in the 1980s?

RECOMMENDED READINGS

Erikson, Erik. *Identity: Youth and crisis.* New York: Norton, 1968.

Erikson's detailed description of the many paths identity formation can take includes his analysis of literary figures, historical circumstances, and the American scene. His discussion of identity formation in women and blacks is one that most readers will probably find themselves alternately agreeing and disagreeing with. One question to ask as you are reading this book is how have the historical and cultural changes that have occurred in the 30 years since Erikson wrote this book altered identity formation of those in minority, or, for that matter, majority groups.

Baker, Russell. *Growing up.* New York: New American Library, 1984.

The interplay of historical, familial, and personal influences on adolescent development is well described in this account by Russell Baker, a columnist for the New York Times. Like many others of his cohort in the Great Depression, Baker's childhood and adolescence was a time of poverty, extended family support, and hard work for very little money. His account of his later life and circumstances, including his enlistment in World War II and his life with the woman that he married, help to reveal how he came to be the person he is.

York, Phillis, York, David, and Wachtel, Ted. *Toughlove.* New York: Bantam, 1983.

The essential idea of *Toughlove* is that parents need to "get tough" with their troubled and difficult adolescents, rather than trying to understand them. This idea probably meets the needs of parents who have been overly permissive, and who have neglected to establish a mutual relationship with their children, more than the needs of the children. However, the book appears on this list for three reasons. First, it reveals the difficulty some parents and adolescents have with each other. Second, it shows the value of parents' mutual support. Finally, it illustrates how fads in childrearing are affected by the overall political framework (*Toughlove* would not have been so popular before the Reagan presidency) and the values of the parental cohort, rather than by any changes in the actual nature of the child.

Many classic and contemporary novels deal with adolescence, sometimes with poignant immediacy and insight. To get an artist's view of adolescence, and to further consider the ecological setting on the adolescent experience, you might read one or more of the following:
Cather, Willa. *One of ours.* **Crane, Stephen.** *The red badge of courage.* **Hersey, John.** *Too far to walk.* **Llewellyn, Richard.** *How green was my valley.* **Knowles, John.** *A separate peace.* **Potok, Chaim.** *The chosen.* **Salinger, J.D.** *The catcher in the rye.* **Morrison, Toni.** *Song of Solomon.* **Guest, Judith.** *Ordinary people.* **Rogers, Thomas.** *At the shores.* **Brown, Rita M.** *Rubyfruit jungle.*

Part V

The Developing Person So Far: Adolescence, Ages 10–20

Physical Development

Physical Growth

At some time between the ages of 9 and 14, puberty begins with increases in male and female hormone levels. Within a year, the first perceptible physical changes appear—enlargement of the girl's breasts and the boy's testes. About a year later, the growth spurt begins. During adolescence, boys and girls gain in height, weight, and musculature. The growth that occurs during these years usually proceeds from the extremities to the torso and may be uneven.

Changes in Sex Organs and Secondary Sex Characteristics

Toward the end of puberty, the young person's potential reproductive capacity is signalled by menarche in girls and ejaculation in boys. It will take several years before full fertility is achieved.

On the whole, males become taller than females and develop deeper voices and characteristic patterns of facial and body hair. Females become wider at the hips; breast development continues for several years.

Cognitive Development

Formal Operational Thought

By the end of adolescence, many young people can understand and create general principles and use scientific reasoning. For many adolescents, cognitive advancement is also reflected in their ability to reason morally.

Adolescent Egocentrism

Adolescent egocentrism tends to prevent teenagers from thinking rationally about their own experiences. Their feelings of invincibility and uniqueness may prompt them to underestimate risks, for example, with regard to sexual relationships and drug use.

Psychosocial Development

Identity

One of the major goals of adolescence is identity achievement—the development of the young person's own sense of self. Identity formation can be affected by personal factors—including relationships with family and peers—the nature of the society, and the economic and political circumstances of the times.

Peers

During adolescence, the peer group becomes increasingly important in helping adolescents to become more independent, to "try out" new behaviors and explore different facets of their personality, and to interact with members of the opposite sex.

Parent-Child Relationships

Although in early adolescence parents and children may find themselves at odds over issues centering on the child's increased assertiveness or lack of self-discipline and self-control, these difficulties usually diminish as the parents recognize the teenager's increasing maturity and allow him or her more autonomy.

Glossary

This glossary provides brief definitions of the most important terms used in this book. To understand the terms more fully in context, consult the Index and read about the terms in the pages on which they first appear.

---

accommodation   The process of shifting or enlarging usual modes of thinking, or schemas, in order to encompass new information. For example, many Americans would have to expand their concept of food in order to be able to consider eating octopus, even though it is a delicacy in some cultures. (56)

achievement tests   Tests designed to measure how much mastery a person has in specific academic skills. (408)

activity level   A measure of the child's activity; for example, the frequency with which he or she moves from place to place. (276)

adaptation   Piaget's term for the cognitive processes through which a person adjusts to new ideas or experiences. Adaptation takes two forms, assimilation and accommodation. (56)

adolescence   The period between childhood and adulthood. Adolescence usually begins at puberty and ends at the age at which the given culture first assigns a person adult responsibilities. (516)

adolescent egocentrism   A characteristic of adolescent thought that leads the young person to think that he or she is unlike other people in many ways. (497) (See also *personal fable* and *imaginary audience*.)

age of viability   The age at which a fetus can survive outside the mother's uterus if optimal care is available (usually between twenty and twenty-six weeks after conception). (103)

aggression   Behavior that is intended to hurt or disturb another person, for example, a kick or physical assault. (336) (See also *instrumental aggression, hostile aggression*.)

amniocentesis   A prenatal diagnostic procedure in which a sample of amniotic fluid is withdrawn by syringe and tested to determine if the fetus is suffering from problems such as Down's syndrome or Tay-Sachs disease. (92)

amnion   A membrane containing the amniotic fluid that surrounds the embryo/fetus. (Also called the "bag of waters.") (100)

amniotic fluid   The liquid contained within the amnion, which cushions the growing fetus. (100)

anal stage   Sigmund Freud's term for the second stage of psychosexual development (occurring during toddlerhood), in which the anus becomes the main source of bodily pleasure, and defecation and toilet training are therefore important activities. (221)

androgyny   The tendency to incorporate both male and female qualities (as conventionally defined) into the personality. For example, an androgynous person might be both independent and nurturing. (349)

animism   The belief that inanimate objects are alive, and therefore have emotions or intentions; an idea held by many young children. (292)

anorexia nervosa   A rare disorder in which a person refuses to eat and may consequently starve. Most victims are adolescent girls. (484)

anoxia   A temporary lack of fetal oxygen during the birth process; if prolonged, it can cause brain damage. (131)

anytime malformation   A birth defect that may have occurred at any point during pregnancy. (104)

Apgar scale   A quick assessment of a newborn's heart and respiratory rate, muscle tone, color, and reflexes. This simple method is used to determine whether a newborn needs immediate medical care following birth. (126)

aptitude tests   Tests that are designed to measure potential, rather than actual, accomplishment. Intelligence tests are the aptitude tests most commonly used in childhood. (410)

articulation   The process of pronouncing a word, or making a speech sound. (306)

assimilation   Piaget's term for the inclusion of new information into already existing categories, or schemas. For example, a person may eat a new food and be unable to name it, but may nevertheless be able to guess by its taste, smell, or texture that it is, say, a fruit. In this way, a new object is placed in the preexisting category "fruit." (56)

associative play   A form of social play in which two or more children play together, but are involved in their own separate activities. They do not cooperate with each other. (322)

attachment   An affectional bond between a person and other people, animals, or objects that endures over time and produces a desire for consistent contact and feelings of distress during separation. (231)

attention deficit disorder   See *Hyperactivity*.

authoritarian parenting   A style of child-rearing in which the parents' word is law, and misconduct is punished—no excuses accepted.   *(329)*

authoritative parenting   A style of child-rearing in which the parents set limits and provide guidance, and at the same time are willing to listen to the child's ideas and make compromises.   *(329)*

autism   A serious psychological disturbance that first becomes apparent during early childhood, when a child does not initiate normal social contact. Most autistic children prefer to play with objects or by themselves, unlike normal children who enjoy company.   *(340)*

autonomy versus shame and doubt   Erikson's term for the toddler's struggle between the drive for self-control, and feelings of shame and doubt about oneself and one's abilities. This is the second of Erikson's eight stages of development.   *(222)*

autosomes   The twenty-two pairs of chromosomes that are identical in human males and females; they direct the development and functioning of much of the body, but do not determine sex.   *(72)*

babbling   Extended repetition of a combination of sounds such as "ba, ba, ba." Babbling begins at about 20 weeks of age.   *(198)*

Babinski reflex   A normal, neonatal reflex that causes the child's toes to fan upward when the sole of the foot is stroked.   *(163)*

baby talk   A term for the special form of language typically used by adults to speak with infants. Adults' baby talk is high-pitched, with many low-to-high intonations; it is simple in vocabulary and employs many questions and repetitions. (Also called *Motherese*.)   *(204)*

behaviorism   A major theory of psychology that holds that most human behavior is learned, or conditioned. Behaviorists have formulated laws of behavior that are applicable to animals and to people of all ages. Behaviorism is also called *learning theory*.   *(45)*

bilingual education   The practice of teaching minority children first in their native language and then gradually increasing their exposure to the majority language.   *(406)*

binocular vision   The coordination of both eyes that enables a person to see one, rather than two, images.   *(269)*

birth catch-up   An above-average increase in weight within the first few months of life. This phenomenon is most common among underweight newborns.   *(153)*

birth trauma   Otto Rank's term for the infant's experience of leaving the security of the womb and entering the harsh world, a shock that Rank believed causes lifelong fear and anxiety.   *(133)*

Black English   A form of English with its own rules of grammar, at variance with some rules of standard English. It is called Black English because it is a dialect spoken by many black Americans. However, many black Americans do not speak Black English, and some white Americans do.   *(404)*

blended families   Families that include a parent or child from a previous marriage or marriages, in other words, families that include step-parents, and possibly, step-siblings.   *(447)*

blind experimenters   Researchers who collect data without knowing what results to expect or without knowing which individuals have been subjected to special experimental conditions. Being unaware of the expected outcome of research, blind experimenters can be objective and reliable in reporting their findings.   *(19)*

body image   A person's concept of his or her physical appearance.   *(474)*

bone age   A measurement of a particular child's rate of ossification (hardening of cartilage into bone) as seen in terms of the average degree of ossification at any given age.   *(264)*

brain specialization   The tendency of the brain to perform certain functions with particular parts of the brain. For example, the brain center for speech is usually located in one part of the left hemisphere. As the brain matures, brain functions tend to become increasingly localized.   *(267)*

brain waves   Electrical activity in the brain as recorded on an electroencephalogram (EEG).   *(156)*

Brazelton Neonatal Behavior Assessment Scale   A rating of a newborn's responsiveness to people and the strength of his or her reflexes.   *(164)*

breathing reflex   A normal reflex that ensures that newborns (as well as older children and adults) maintain an adequate supply of oxygen by inhaling and exhaling air.   *(163)*

breech position   A birth in which the child emerges from the uterus buttocks first, instead of headfirst. About 3 percent of all births occur in the breech position.   *(131)*

bulimia   A disorder in which the person, usually female, engages repeatedly in episodes of binge eating followed by induced vomiting or use of laxatives.   *(484)*

carrier   An individual who possesses a recessive gene as part of his or her genotype (total genetic make-up). A carrier can pass on a recessive gene to his or her children, but unless the child inherits the same gene from both parents, the child will not develop the characteristic.   *(77)*

case study   The research method in which the scientist reports and analyzes the life history, attitudes, behavior, and emotions of a single individual in much more depth than is usually done with a large group of people.   *(24)*

centration   The focusing of attention on one aspect of a situation or object to the exclusion of other aspects. Young children, for example, have difficulty realizing that a mother is also a daughter, because they concentrate, or center, on one role to the exclusion of others.   *(289)*

cephalo-caudal development   Growth proceeding from the head downward (literally, from head to tail). Human growth, from the embryonic period throughout childhood, follows this pattern. *(101)*

Cesarean section   A surgical procedure in which an obstetrician cuts open the abdomen and uterus to deliver the baby. This technique is used if the fetus is unable to travel safely through the birth canal. *(132)*

child abuse   A term used to describe the many forms of maltreatment inflicted on children by parents and other caregivers; includes physical injury, emotional maltreatment, sexual abuse, and neglect of the child's basic needs. *(242)* (See also *neglect* and *sexual abuse*.)

childhood schizophrenia   An emotional disturbance that can develop during early or middle childhood. Its symptoms include an unusual difficulty with social play, conversation, and emotional expression. *(341)*

chromosome   Molecules in every cell that carry the genetic material transmitted from parents to offspring, determining their inherited characteristics. *(72)*

chunking   A memory technique that consists of grouping items to be memorized into categories. *(394)*

circular reaction   Piaget's term for an action that is repeated because it triggers a pleasing response. An example of a circular reaction would be a baby's shaking a rattle, hearing the noise, and shaking the rattle again. *(179)*

classical conditioning   The process by which an animal or person learns to associate a neutral stimulus (for example, a bell) with a meaningful one (for example, food). After training, the subject will respond in the same way to the neutral stimulus as to the meaningful one. *(47)* (Also called *respondent conditioning*.)

classification   The concept that objects can be sorted into categories or classes, as in sorting foods according to whether they are fruits, vegetables or dairy products. According to Piaget, this concept is mastered during the period of concrete operational thought. *(384)* (See also *class inclusion*.)

class inclusion   The idea that a particular object or person may belong to more than one class. For example, a father can also be someone's brother. *(384)*

code-switching   A pragmatic communication skill that comes into play when a person switches appropriately from one form of speech to another. *(403)* (See also *elaborated code, restricted code*.)

cognition   The mental processes by which the individual obtains knowledge or becomes aware of the environment, for example, perception, memory, imagination, and use of language. *(176)*

cognitive domain   That domain of human development that includes all the mental processes through which the individual obtains knowledge or becomes aware of the environment. *(3)*

cognitive theory   The theory that the way people understand and think about their experiences is an important determinant of their behavior and personality. *(54)*

cohort   A group of people who, because they were born at the same time, experience the same historical and social conditions. Differences between cohorts often complicate research that attempts to focus on differences caused by development alone, a complication known as "the cohort effect." *(26)*

collective monologue   A "conversation" between two or more children in which the participants are talking in turn, as though in conversation, but are not actually responding to the content of each other's speech. *(308)*

conception   The moment of fertilization, when a sperm and ovum join to form a zygote. *(71)*

concrete operational thought   In Piaget's theory, that stage of cognitive development in which a person understands specific logical ideas and can apply them to concrete problems but has difficulty with abstract, hypothetical thought and logic. This period usually begins at about age 7 and tends to continue to adolescence (though it sometimes ends later, or not at all). *(383)*

conditioning   In learning theory, the process of learning that occurs either through the association of two stimuli or through the use of positive or negative reinforcement. *(46)*

congenital   Present at birth, either as a result of genetic or prenatal influences or specific complications of the birth process. Not all congenital characteristics are apparent at birth. For example, diabetes is inherited and therefore congenital, but it does not appear until later in life. *(103)*

conservation   In Piagetian theory, the concept that certain properties of a given quantity of matter (volume, weight, etc.) remain constant despite changes in shape, length, or position. Preschool children usually cannot understand the concept of conservation. *(290)*

conservation of matter   The idea that the volume or weight of an object remains the same even if the form is changed. For example, when two balls of clay have the same volume rolling one ball into a long rope will not increase the amount of clay. *(290)*

conservation of number   The idea that the number of a set does not change even if the objects in it are repositioned. For example, if two sets have the same number of coins, spacing out one set so that it is distributed over a larger area will not increase the number of coins in that set. *(290)*

continuity   A term used to label development that is seen as gradual and steady. *(11)*

continuous growth   The Offers' term for the type of adolescent growth that is characterized by smooth, problem-free development. *(465)*

control group   In research, a group of subjects who are similar to the experimental group on all relevant dimensions (e.g., sex, age, educational background) but who do not experience special experimental conditions or procedures. *(19)*

conventional moral reasoning Kohlberg's term for the middle stages of moral reasoning, in which social standards are the primary moral values. (436)

cooing Infants' first noncrying vocalizations, usually uttered when they see a face or hear a voice. Cooing begins as early as 5 weeks of age. (198)

cooperative play Play in which two or more children cooperate while playing, for example, by taking turns or following rules. This form of play is difficult for many preschoolers. (322)

correlation A statistical term that indicates that two variables are somehow related. Whenever one variable changes in the same direction as another (for example, both decrease), the correlation is *positive*. Whenever one variable increases as another decreases, the correlation is *negative*. (21)

crawling A way in which babies move by getting onto their hands and knees and coordinating movement of their arms and legs to achieve locomotion. (165)

critical period Any period during which a person is especially susceptible to certain harmful or, in some instances, beneficial influences. During prenatal development, for example, the critical period is usually said to occur during the first eight weeks, when the basic organs and body structures are forming and are therefore particularly vulnerable. (104)

cross-sectional research Research involving the comparison of groups of people who are different in age but similar in other important ways (e.g., sex, socioeconomic status, level of education). Differences among the groups—as, for instance, between a group of 12-year-olds and a group of 15-year-olds—are presumably the result of development, rather than some other factor. (25)

custodial parent The parent who is granted custody and who therefore has the major responsibility for a child after a divorce. The child usually lives with the custodial parent. (445)

deep structure Noam Chomsky's term for the underlying rules of grammar and inherent meaning in each language. According to Chomsky, a child's ability to understand this structure is innate (understanding, for example, that different sentence structures indicate either a statement or a question). (196)

defense mechanisms Behavioral or thought patterns that distort one's feelings or perceptions in order to avoid unbearable inner conflicts. In psychoanalytic theory, the ego is thought to institute these defenses, involuntarily and unknowingly, when a real or imagined threat is perceived. (40)

deferred imitation The ability to re-create an action, or mimic a person, one has witnessed some time in the past. According to Piaget, infants are usually first able to do this between 18 and 24 months of age. (198)

deprivation dwarfism Retardation in a child's physical growth due to psychological factors, such as parental rejection or too much stress. (265)

depth perception The awareness of the distance between oneself and an object. Before depth perception develops, infants reach for objects that are far too distant to grasp. (161)

desensitization See *gradual desensitization*.

developmental psychology The branch of psychology that scientifically studies the changes in behavior, personality, social relationships, thought processes, and body and motor skills that occur as the individual grows older. (3)

discontinuity A term used to label development that is seen to occur in stages, or which is characterized by abrupt or uneven changes. Many developmental psychologists emphasize the discontinuity of development. (Also called the stage view of development.) (11)

disequilibrium Piaget's term for the state of conflict that results from difficulties with integrating new information into existing schemas. (55)

displacement A defense mechanism in which a feeling toward one object is shifted to another, less threatening, one (as when a person becomes angry at his boss rather than at his father, who is the original object of the anger). (41)

dizygotic twins Simultaneously born offspring who develop from two separate zygotes, each the product of a different sperm and ovum. These twins are no more similar genetically than any other two children born to the same parents. (76)

dominant gene A gene that exerts its full phenotypic effect in the offspring regardless of whether it is paired with another dominant gene or with a recessive gene. (77)

double standard The idea that males should follow one set of rules in sexual conduct, and females, another. Traditionally, females were supposed to resist the sexual advances that males were expected to make. (476)

Down's syndrome A genetic abnormality caused by an extra chromosome in the twenty-first chromosome pair. Individuals with this syndrome have round faces, short limbs, and are underdeveloped physically and intellectually. (Also called *trisomy-21.*) (81)

dramatic play Mutual fantasy play that occurs when two or more children choose roles and cooperate in acting them out. Dramatic play is an important social development of the preschool years. (324)

dwarfism Extremely short stature, caused by genetic factors, prolonged malnutrition, medical problems (such as untreated diabetes) or psychological factors (in which case the condition is called deprivation dwarfism). (265) (See also *deprivation dwarfism*.)

dyscalcula A specific learning disability involving unusual difficulty in arithmetic. (370)

dysgraphia   A specific learning disability involving unusual difficulty in handwriting.   *(370)*

dyslexia   A specific learning disability involving unusual difficulty in reading.   *(369)*

echolalia   The word-for-word repetition of what another person has just said—a speech characteristic of many autistic children.   *(340)*

eclampsia   A serious disease that can occur during the last weeks of pregnancy when a mother may have difficulty in ridding her system of fetal wastes. If not promptly treated, it can cause fetal brain damage and even death to the child and mother.   *(106)*

eclectic perspective   A view incorporating what seems to be the best, or most useful, from various theories, rather than working from a single perspective.   *(62)*

ecological approach   A way of looking at human development that emphasizes the impact of society, culture, physical setting, and other people on the development of each individual. (See *systems approach.*)   *(4)*

ego   As conceptualized by Freud, the rational, reality-oriented part of the personality.   *(40)*

egocentrism   Thought processes that are governed solely by one's own point of view. In the egocentrism of early childhood, many children believe that other people think exactly as they themselves do.   *(291)*

ejaculation   The release of seminal fluid from the penis.   *(471)*

elaborated code   This is a form of speech used by children in school and in other formal situations and is characterized by extensive vocabulary, complex syntax, lengthy sentences, and conformity to other middle-class norms for language.   *(403)* (See also *restricted code.*)

elective mutism   A psychological disorder of childhood, in which a child who is able to speak refuses to speak in nearly all social situations.   *(340)*

Electra complex   The female version of the Oedipus complex. According to psychoanalytic theory, at about age 4, girls have sexual feelings for their father and accompanying hostility toward their mother.   *(345)*

embryo   The human organism from about two to eight weeks after conception, when basic body structures and organs are forming.   *(99)*

embryonic disc   During the first weeks after conception, this flat inner structure develops into the three layers of the embryo (the ectoderm, mesoderm, and endoderm).   *(101)*

engrossment   Parents' fascination with their newborn, characterized chiefly by their continued gazing at the baby.   *(143)*

environment   The external forces, including physical surroundings, social institutions, or other individuals, that impinge on human development.   *(10)*

episiotomy   A small surgical incision in the vagina which is often made to allow the fetal head to emerge without tearing the vaginal opening.   *(132)*

equilibrium   Piaget's term for the state of mental balance achieved through the assimilation and accommodation of conflicting experiences and perceptions.   *(55)*

erythroblastosis   A condition that occurs when antibodies produced by the mother's blood damage the fetal blood supply. This disease can now be prevented. (Also called *Rh disease.*)   *(85)*

estrogen   A hormone produced primarily by the ovaries that regulates sexual development in puberty. Although boys' adrenal glands produce some estrogen, it is chiefly a female hormone.   *(467)*

ethics   In psychology, standards of conduct intended to protect subjects of research or patients in therapy from psychological or physical harm.   *(29)*

ethology   The scientific study of animal behavior. Ethological studies often shed light on human behavior.   *(259)*

experiment   (See *laboratory experiment.*)

experimental group   In research, a group of subjects who experience special experimental conditions or procedures.   *(19)*

expressive language   The use of words primarily to communicate personal desire and to interact with people.   *(202)*

farsightedness   A vision problem involving the clear perception of distant objects but difficulty in focusing on objects at close range.   *(269)*

fear of strangers   An infant's distress when confronted with a new person, especially an adult who looks unusual or who acts in an unusual way. This emotion is first noticeable at about six months, and is full-blown at a year. (Also called *stranger anxiety.*)   *(215)*

Feingold diet   A diet developed by Dr. Benjamin Feingold to treat hyperactive children, mainly by eliminating artificial colorings, flavorings, preservatives, and certain foods that are thought to produce a toxic reaction that results in hyperactivity. The effectiveness of this diet is controversial.   *(376)*

fetal alcohol syndrome (FAS)   A congenital condition characterized by a small head, abnormal eyes, malproportioned face, and retardation in physical and mental growth, that sometimes appears in children whose mothers used alcohol during pregnancy.   *(108)*

fetal monitor   A sensing device commonly used during labor that measures and records the fetal heartbeat and the strength and frequency of the mother's contractions. The fetal monitor helps determine whether medical intervention, such as a Cesarean section, is necessary to protect the health of the mother and/or the infant.   *(131)*

fetoscopy   A procedure that uses a narrow tube inserted into the uterus to view the fetus and the placenta directly.   *(92)*

fine motor skills   Skills involving small body movements, especially with the hands and fingers. Drawing, writing, and tying a shoelace demand fine motor skills.   (273)

first stage of labor   In the birth process, the period extending from the first regular uterine contraction to the full opening of the cervix to allow passage of the child's head through the vaginal canal. The first stage of labor usually lasts between four and six hours.   (125)

5-to-7 shift   The change in cognitive development between ages 5 and 7 that allows the elementary school child to think, learn, and remember in a more mature way than had been previously possible.   (383)

forceps   A large, spoonlike medical instrument sometimes used to facilitate or hasten birth. The forceps hold the fetal head and pull the baby down the vaginal canal.   (132)

foreclosure   Erikson's term for premature identity formation, in which the young person does not explore all the identities that are available.   (517)

formal operational thought   Piaget's term for the last period of cognitive development, characterized by hypothetical, logical, and abstract thought. This stage is not reached until adolescence, if at all.   (490)

fraternal twins   (See *dizygotic twins*.)

game of thinking   Flavell's term for the adolescent's ability to suspend knowledge of reality and think creatively about hypothetical possibilities.   (494)

gamete   A human reproductive cell. Female gametes are called ova, or eggs; males gametes are called spermatozoa, or sperm.   (71)

gene   The basic unit of heredity, carried by the chromosomes. Genes direct the growth and development of every organism.   (72)

generativity versus stagnation   Erikson's seventh stage of development, in which adults seek to be productive through vocation, avocation, or child-rearing. Without such productive work, adults stop developing and growing.   (42)

genetic counseling   A program of consultation and testing through which couples learn about their genetic inheritance in order to make informed decisions about childbearing.   (85)

genital stage   Freud's term for the last stage of psychosexual development, in which the primary source of sexual satisfaction is an erotic relationship with another adult.   (39)

genotype   A person's entire genetic heritage, including those characteristics carried by the recessive genes but not expressed in the phenotype.   (77)

gentle birth   Frederick Leboyer's method of childbirth in which the newborn's exposure to shocking sensory stimuli is reduced through soft lighting in the delivery room, immediate contact with the parents, and a warm bath shortly after birth.   (134)

germinal period   The first two weeks after conception, during which rapid cell division occurs. (Also called the *period of the ovum*.)   (99)

giantism   Extremely tall stature often resulting from a malfunctioning of the pituitary gland.   (263)

giftedness   A word used by educators to describe a child's unusual abilities, in intellectual work, creative thinking, or a special area, such as music or athletics.   (412)

gradual desensitization   A technique, often used by behavior therapists, to reduce a person's fear of something by gradually exposing that person to the feared object.   (339)

grammar   Structures, techniques, and rules that languages use to communicate meaning, including word order, tense, and voice.   (302)

grasping reflex   A normal, neonatal reflex that causes newborns to grip tightly when something touches their palms.   (163)

gross motor skills   Those physical skills that use large body movements. Running, jumping, and climbing involve gross motor skills.   (271)

growth spurt   The relatively rapid physical growth that occurs during puberty.   (467)

habituation   A process whereby a particular stimulus becomes so familiar that physiological responses initially associated with it are no longer present. For instance, a newborn might initially stare wide-eyed at a mobile, but gradually look at it less often as habituation occurs.   (159)

handedness   Preferential use of either the right or left hand for throwing, grasping, writing, and so on. Handedness is thought to be primarily genetic. (Also called *hand preference*)   (268)

Headstart   A special preschool educational program designed to provide culturally deprived or disadvantaged 4-year-olds with a variety of intellectual and social experiences that might better prepare them for school.   (311)

hemophilia   An X-linked blood disorder. People who suffer from this disease bleed excessively, and require periodic blood transfusions.   (89)

holistic development   A view of human development as unified and whole; this perspective emphasizes the interaction among the various physical, cognitive, and psychosocial aspects of growth.   (4)

holophrases   A single word that is intended to express a complete thought. Young children (usually about 1 year of age) use this early form of communication.   (204)

HOME   A method which measures how well the home environment of a child fosters learning. HOME looks at maternal responsiveness and involvement with the child, the child's freedom of movement, the play environment, the play materials, and the variety of activities in the child's day.   (237)

hostile aggression An attack against someone for the purpose of defending one's own self-esteem while debasing the other person's. *(336)*

hyaline membrane disease See *respiratory distress syndrome.*

hyperactivity A state of excessive activity, usually accompanied by an inability to concentrate and impulsive behavior. Also called *attention deficit disorder.* *(372)*

hypothesis A specific prediction that can be tested. Scientists reformulate their research questions into a hypothesis that is then tested in a research project. *(17)*

id As conceptualized by Freud, that part of the personality containing primitive, unconscious sexual and aggressive impulses. *(187)*

identical twins See *monozygotic twins.*

identification A defense mechanism through which a person feels like, or adopts the perspective of, someone else. Children identify with their parents for many reasons, one of them, according to psychoanalytic theory, to cope with the powerful emotions of the Oedipus (or Electra) complex. *(345)*

identity As a Piagetian term, the principle of logic which states that a given quantity of matter remains the same if nothing is added to or subtracted from it, no matter what changes occur in its shape or appearance. Before they enter the concrete operational period, children do not recognize this principle. *(291)*

identity achievement Erikson's term for a person's achievement of a sense of who he or she is as a unique individual. The main task of adolescence, according to Erikson, is the establishment of the young person's identity, including sexual, moral, political, and vocational identity. *(516)*

identity diffusion Erikson's term for the experience of a young person who is uncertain what path to take toward identity formation, and therefore becomes apathetic and disoriented. *(518)*

imaginary audience A term referring to the constant scrutiny that many adolescents typically imagine themselves to be under—from nearly everyone. *(498)*

imaginary playmate A friend who is alive only in the imagination of a child. *(339)*

implantation After conception, the burrowing of the organism into the lining of the uterus where it can be nourished and protected during growth. *(99)*

industry versus inferiority The fourth of Erikson's eight "crises," in which the school-age child busily masters many skills or develops a sense of incompetence. *(421)*

infantile sexuality The idea, held by psychoanalytic theorists, that sexual pleasures and fantasies occur in childhood. *(39)*

information processing A model of human learning that uses the functioning of the computer as an analogy for the functioning of the human mind. *(382)*

initiative versus guilt The third of Erikson's eight "crises" of psychosocial development. During this stage, the preschool child begins, or initiates, new activities—and feels guilt when efforts result in failure or criticism. *(320)*

inner speech The mental use of language to formulate ideas to oneself. Inner speech enhances memory and other cognitive abilities. *(307)*

insecure attachment A parent-child bond marked by the child's overdependence on, or lack of interest in, the parents. Insecurely attached children are not readily comforted by their parents and are less likely to explore their environment than are children who are securely attached. *(232)*

instrumental aggression Fighting over an object, a territory, or a privilege. Examples include quarreling over a toy, a seat at the front of the classroom, or a chance to wash the blackboard. (See also *hostile aggression.*) *(336)*

integrity versus despair Erikson's eighth stage of development, in which elderly people evaluate their lives to decide if they have fulfilled their potential and made a lasting contribution to their family or community. *(42)*

intelligence tests Aptitude tests, such as the Stanford-Binet and Wechsler tests, which attempt to measure such components of intelligence as general knowledge, memory, reasoning ability, and spatial perception. *(410)*

interview method The research method in which the scientist asks people specific questions designed to discover their opinions or experiences pertaining to a particular topic. Attitudes about sex, religion, or politics are often assessed by the interview method. *(24)*

intimacy versus isolation Erikson's sixth stage of development, in which young adults seek other people to share their lives with, or become isolated. *(42)*

IQ A number, or score, on an intelligence test that is designed to indicate the aptitude of a particular person for learning, especially learning in school. The average IQ is 100. *(410)*

Klinefelter's syndrome (See XXY.)

kwashiorkor A disease resulting from protein-calorie deficiency in children. The symptoms include thinning hair, paleness, and bloating of the stomach, face, and legs. *(170)*

labor The physical process of giving birth, beginning with the first uterine contractions and ending with the expulsion of the placenta. Labor is divided into three stages. *(125)*

laboratory experiment The research method in which the scientist brings people into a controlled setting, and then manipulates a variable and observes the results. For instance, children might be brought into a well-equipped playroom, and then told they can play with one, and only one, of the many toys available. (22)

Lamaze method   A technique of childbirth that involves breathing and relaxation exercises during labor. (135)

language acquisition device (LAD)   Noam Chomsky's term for an infant's inborn ability to acquire language according to a relatively stable sequence and timetable. (196)

language function   The communication of ideas and emotions through words. (197)

language structure   Particular sound combinations and rules of grammar that are at the root of any given language. (197)

latency   Freud's term for the period between the phallic stage and the genital stage. During latency, which lasts from about age 7 to age 11, the child's sexual drives are relatively quiet. (420)

learned behavior   Behavior that occurs because of specific experiences and instruction rather than because of the maturation of inborn abilities. Driving a car, solving an algebra problem, and avoiding hot stoves are all learned through some combination of personal experience, observation of others, and direct instruction. (45)

learned helplessness   The assumption that one is unable to do anything to improve one's performance or situation. For example, children who continually fail in school sometimes respond with learned helplessness. (427)

learning by association   A linking of two stimuli that causes a person or animal to respond to one stimulus as though it were the other. Having had a frightening experience during a thunderstorm might make one feel apprehensive whenever storm clouds gather, for instance. (47) (See also *classical conditioning.*)

learning disability   See *specific learning disabilities.*

learning theory   A major theory of psychology which maintains that most human behaviors are learned, or conditioned, and which formulates laws of behavior that are applicable to animals and to people of all ages. Learning theory is also called *behaviorism.* (45)

linguistics   The study of the structure and development of language. (196)

longitudinal research   A study of the same people over a long period of time. Longitudinal research is designed to measure both changes and continuity in behavior and personality over time. (26)

long-term memory   A memory storage system in which information can remain for days, months or years. (393)

low-birth-weight infant   A newborn who weighs less than 5½ pounds (2,500 grams) at birth. (127) (See also *preterm infant, small-for-dates infant.*)

mainstreaming   The practice of assigning handicapped children to regular classrooms, rather than segregating them in special classes. (367)

malnutrition   Nutrition that is so poor or insufficient that growth and health are impaired. Protein-calorie deficiency and specific vitamin or mineral deficiency are two forms of malnutrition. (168)

marasmus   A disease that afflicts infants suffering from severe malnutrition. Growth stops, body tissues waste away, and eventually death occurs. (170)

mastery play   Any form of play that leads to a mastering of new skills. During the play years, mastery play tends to develop physical skills (such as skipping or using scissors). Later, mastery play includes intellectual activities such as play with words and ideas. (257)

maturation   Changes in the body or in behavior that result from the aging process, rather than from learning. The child's ability to babble certain sounds at age 6 months and the loss of the front baby teeth at about 6 years are examples of changes that result from maturation. (10)

mean length of utterance (MLU)   The average number of utterances, or meaningful units of sound a particular person uses in sentences. In figuring MLU, the statement "I am jumping" would count as four such utterances, "-ing" being the fourth meaningful unit. (303)

meiosis   The special process of chromosome duplication and cell division that occurs only in the gametes (the reproductive cells). Meiosis produces new cells, sperm or ova, each containing half the genetic material from each parent—twenty-three chromosomes in humans. (72)

memory capacity   A measure of how much information the brain can hold, and how well it can be processed and stored. (See also *sensory register, short-term memory,* and *long-term memory.*) (393)

menarche   A female's first menstrual period. This is taken as a sign, or even as *the* sign, of puberty. (471)

mental combinations   The mental playing-out of various courses of action before actually exercising one of them. According to Piaget, this ability usually becomes apparent between 18 and 24 months of age. (185)

metacognition   The general principles and techniques of thinking and organizing information. (395)

metamemory   The ability to use and explain techniques that aid memory. (393)

milk anemia   A nutritional deficiency resulting from insufficient iron in the diet; may occur in toddlers whose diets are overly dependent on milk. (168)

minimal brain dysfunction   A tentative diagnosis for learning disabilities that appear to be organic in origin, that is, resulting from damage to and impairment of some part of the brain. (370)

mitosis   The process of chromosome duplication and cell division that creates new cells, each containing (in humans) forty-six chromosomes with genetic information identical to that of the "original" cell. (72)

mnemonic device   A memory-aiding device. *(394)* (See also *rehearsal* and *chunking*.)

modeling   The patterning of one's behavior after that of someone else. New responses can be learned, and old ones modified, through modeling. *(339)*

monologue   Speech delivered out loud but with no intent to communicate to others. This is one of the types of egocentric speech typical of preschool children. *(308)* (See also *collective monologue*.)

monozygotic twins   Two offspring who began development as a single zygote (formed from one sperm and one ovum) that subsequently divided into two zygotes. They have the same genetic make-up, are of the same sex, and look alike. *(73)*

moral development   The growth of the ability to understand, and act upon, codes of conduct, from specific rules to universal ethics. *(435)*

moratorium   Erikson's term for the informal pause in identity formation that allows young people to explore alternatives without making final choices. For many young people, college or military service provides such a moratorium. *(518)*

Moro reflex   A normal neonatal reflex in response to a sudden, intense noise or movement. In this reflex, newborns fling their arms outward, then bring them together; they may also cry with eyes wide open. *(163)*

mosaicism   A condition in which a person's cells, including reproductive cells, are a patchwork, or mosaic, of different patterns, some normal in their number of chromosomes, some not. A parent with this condition has a higher than average probability of having a child with a chromosomal defect. *(84)*

Motherese   See *baby talk*.

motor skills   Those abilities which involve body movement and physical coordination, such as walking and reaching. *(164)*

multifactorial characteristics   Those abilities or qualities that are determined by the interaction among several genetic and environmental influences. Characteristics such as intelligence, personality, and talent, are multifactorial. *(79)*

myelination   The process whereby myelin, a fatty insulating substance, is laid down on the nerve cells (neurons), facilitating quicker, more efficient transmission of neural impulses. The myelination process continues until adolescence. *(154)*

naturalistic observation   The research method in which the scientist tests a hypothesis by observing people in their usual surroundings (home, school, work place). Specific methods of data collection and special training for the observers are generally used to make this method more objective than our usual daily observations of each other. *(18)*

nature   Those innate factors that affect development. *(10)*

nature-nurture controversy   The debate within developmental psychology over the relative importance of genetically inherited capacities ("nature") and environmental influences ("nurture") in determining an individual's various traits and characteristics. *(10)*

negative identity   Erikson's term for a chosen identity that is the opposite of the identity preferred by one's parents or society. *(518)*

negative reinforcer   The removal of an unpleasant stimulus in response to a particular behavior, such removal serving to increase the likelihood that the behavior will occur again. *(48)*

neglect   A form of child abuse in which parents or caregivers fail to provide adequate or proper nutritional, supervisional, or physical care of a child. *(242)* (See also *child abuse*.)

neonate   A newborn baby. Infants are neonates from the moment of birth to the end of the first month of life. *(125)*

neural tube   The fold of cells that appears in the embryo about two weeks after conception and later develops into the head and spine. *(101)*

neurons   Nerve cells. *(154)*

noncustodial   A divorced parent who does not have the major responsibility for a child's care and for decisions affecting the child's care. *(445)*

norms   Statistical averages based on the results of research derived from a large, representative sample of a given population. Norms are not to be taken as implying "the best." For instance, the norm for an infant's first step is 12 months of age, but the infant who doesn't walk until 14 months is not necessarily less smart or less healthy than the infant who walks at 12 months. *(166)*

nurture   Environmental influences that affect development. *(10)*

obesity   Overweight to the degree that the layer of fat on the body is significantly greater than that of the average person of the same height and age. *(360)*

object permanence   The understanding that objects and people continue to exist even when they cannot be seen. This concept develops gradually between 6 and 18 months of age. *(181)*

Oedipus complex   In psychoanalytic theory, both the sexual desire that boys in the phallic stage have for their mother and the associated feelings of hostility they have toward their father. This complex is named after Oedipus, a character in ancient Greek legend who unwittingly killed his father and married his mother. *(345)*

onlooker play   "Play" that consists of one child's watching another's active play. *(322)*

open education   A form of education in which both classroom space and choice of activity are more open than they are in traditional education. The classroom has separate "areas" for each activity, and children move from one activity to another in small groups or individually. (390)

operant conditioning   A learning process, conceptualized by B. F. Skinner, through which a person or animal is more likely to perform or refrain from performing a certain behavior because of past reinforcement or punishment. Also called *instrumental conditioning*. (47)

oral stage   Freud's term for the first stage of psychosexual development, when the infant gains both nourishment and pleasure through sucking and biting. (221)

organization   Piaget's term for the process of synthesizing and analyzing perceptions and thoughts. At every stage of cognitive development, according to Piaget, people actively organize their existing ideas and adapt to new experiences. (56)

ossification   The hardening of cartilage into bones—a natural process as a child grows. (264)

ova (singular ovum)   The reproductive cells of the human female, which are present, from birth, in the ovaries. (71)

overextension   The overuse of a given word to describe several objects that share a particular characteristic. For example, toddlers often use "doggie" to label all four-legged animals. (202)

overregularization   The tendency of young children to apply grammatical rules and forms without recognizing exceptions and irregularities. Overregularization might, for example, lead a child to use the suffix "ed" to form the past tense of all verbs and say "bringed" instead of "brought." (305)

ovulation   The process (usually occurring two weeks after the beginning of each menstrual period) in which an ovum (egg) matures, is released by the ovary, and enters one of the Fallopian tubes. (71)

parallel play   Play in which two or more children simultaneously use similar toys in similar ways but do not interact. (322)

parent-infant bond   The strong feelings of attachment between parents and infants. (141)

peer group   A group of one's age-mate friends. (428)

penis envy   The psychoanalytic idea that, beginning at about age 4, girls realize that boys have a penis and become jealous because they themselves do not. (345)

perception   The processing or interpretation of sensations in order to make them comprehensible. (158)

period of the embryo   From approximately the second to the eighth week after conception, during which time the rudimentary forms of all anatomical structures develop. (99)

period of the fetus   From two months after conception until birth. In a full-term pregnancy, this period lasts seven months. (99)

period of the ovum   See *germinal period*.

permissive parenting   A style of child-rearing in which parents allow their children to do virtually anything they want to do. Permissive parents rarely punish, guide, or control their children. (329)

personal fable   The idea, held by many adolescents, that one is special—destined for great accomplishments and immune to normal troubles. (499)

personality   An individual's usual way of reacting to people and experiences. (3)

phallic stage   The third stage of psychosexual development, according to Freud, in which the penis, or phallus, is the focus of psychological concern as well as of physiological pleasure. (344)

phenotype   An individual's observable characteristics, which are the result of the interaction of the genes and the environment. (See also *genotype*.) (77)

phenylketonuria (PKU)   A genetic disease, now easily detected, in which the individual is unable to properly metabolize protein. If left untreated, mental retardation and hyperactivity result. (85)

phobia   An irrational fear that interferes with a person's normal functioning. Many phobias have specific names, such as claustrophobia (fear of enclosed places) aquaphobia (fear of water), and agoraphobia (fear of open spaces). (339)

physical domain   That domain of development that includes changes which are primarily biological. For instance, increases in height and weight, improvements in motor skills, and the development of sense organs are usually considered aspects of physical development. (3)

physique   A term that designates the height, weight, and proportions of the body. (359)

placenta   An organ made up of blood vessels leading to both the mother's and the fetus' bloodstream and having membranes to prevent mixture of the two bloodstreams. These membranes serve as screens through which oxygen and nourishment pass to the fetus and wastes pass from the fetus to the mother to be excreted through her system. (100)

play face   A facial expression, such as a smile or laugh, that accompanies playful activity. The play face helps distinguish rough-and-tumble play from real hostility. (258)

pleasure principle   In Freud's theory, the wish for immediate gratification of one's needs. This is the principle by which the id operates. (40)

pleasure smile   A relaxation of the facial muscles indicating a neonate's contentment (say, after feeding or during sleep). (198)

polygenic inheritance   The interaction of many genes to produce a particular characteristic. For example, skin color, body shape, and memory are all polygenic. (78)

positive reinforcer   A reward, or something pleasant that is given in response to a particular behavior and which increases the likelihood that that behavior will occur again. (48)

postconventional moral reasoning   Kohlberg's term for the highest stages of moral reasoning in which the person formulates and follows universal principles, realizing that the rules of society may need to be overridden.

pragmatics   In the study of language, a term for the practical aspect of communication, for example, the skill a person shows in adjusting vocabulary and grammar to fit the social context. (305)

preconventional moral reasoning   Kohlberg's term for the first stages of moral reasoning, in which the person's own welfare is paramount and the customs or mores of society are relatively unimportant. (436)

preeclampsia   A disease of pregnancy most common during the last trimester. Early signs are high blood pressure, sudden weight gain due to water retention, and protein in the urine. If left untreated, it can develop into the sometimes fatal disease, eclampsia. (106) (Also called *toxemia*.)

prenatal development   That period of development between the moment of conception and the beginning of the birth process. (98)

preoperational thought   Piaget's term for the second period of cognitive development. Children in this stage of thought, which usually occurs between the ages of 2 and 7, are unable to grasp logical concepts such as conservation, reversibility, or classification. (288)

prepared childbirth   See *Lamaze method*.

pretend play   A form of imaginative play in which the child uses symbols to fantasize and act out his or her ideas. Pretend play reflects the emergence of symbolic thought between the ages of 1 and 6. (287)

preterm infant   An infant born more than three weeks before the due date or, according to the World Health Organization, who weighs less than 5½ pounds (2500 grams) at birth. Also called premature baby. (128)

primary circular reaction   Piaget's term for a circular reaction in which the infant's body is the source of the response. In a primary circular reaction, infants repeat actions that involve their bodies—for example, sucking their thumbs or kicking their legs. Primary circular reactions occur during the second stage of sensorimotor development (usually between 1 to 4 months of age). (179)

primary motor areas of the cortex   Those parts of the brain which control simple motor abilities such as waving of the arms. (155)

primary sensory areas of the cortex   Those areas of the brain which control the five senses. (155)

prosocial behavior   Any behavior that benefits other people. Cooperation, helping, sharing, and generosity are all prosocial behaviors. (438)

provocation ecologies   Classroom environments that provoke or exacerbate hyperactive behavior in some children. (377)

proximo-distal development   Growth proceeding from the center (spine) toward the extremities (literally, from near to far). Human growth, from the embryonic period through childhood, follows this pattern. (101)

psychoanalytic theory   A theory of psychology, originated by Sigmund Freud, that stresses the influence of unconscious motivation and drives on all human behavior. (37)

psychosexual stages   The idea, held by psychoanalytic theorists, that development occurs in a series of stages (oral, anal, phallic, and genital), each of which is characterized by the focusing of sexual interest and gratification on one part of the body. (39)

psychosocial domain   The domain of human development involving emotions, personality characteristics, and relationships with other people. (3)

psychosocial theory   A theory emphasizing social and cultural effects on the individual. (43)

puberty   The period of early adolescence characterized by rapid physical growth and the attainment of the physiological capability of sexual reproduction. Puberty usually begins at about age 10 or 11 for girls, and 11 or 12 for boys, although there is much variation caused by genes and nutrition. (466)

punishment   An unpleasant event, such as a slap, which when administered in response to a particular behavior, makes it less likely that the behavior will be repeated. (48)

rarefaction ecologies   Classroom environments that ameliorate or diminish hyperactive behavior in some children. (377)

reaction formation   A defense mechanism through which a person overreacts in one direction to deny his or her feelings in the opposite direction. For instance, a couple getting a divorce, in order to deny the feelings of love they still have for each other, might convince themselves that their spouse is hateful, deceitful, and cruel. (464)

reaction time   The time it takes a person to react to a stimulus. (364)

reality principle   According to Freud, the ego's guiding principle, which tries to mediate the demands of the id and the rules of society in order to find the most rational and productive course of action. (40)

recessive gene   A gene that affects the expression of a particular phenotypic characteristic only when it is not paired with another of the same type of recessive gene, not with a dominant gene. (77)

reciprocity   A logical principle describing that a change in one dimension of an object effects a change in another direction. For example, a ball of clay, rolled out, will be both longer and thinner. According to Piaget, children begin to understand these relationships during the period of concrete operational thought. (384)

referential language   Using words primarily to identify objects and actions rather than to communicate. *(202)*

reflex   An automatic response, such as an eye blink, involving one part of the body. *(162)*

regression   A defense mechanism in which an individual under stress will temporarily revert to a more immature form of behavior (such as bed-wetting by a 12-year-old). *(40)*

rehearsal   A memory technique involving repetition of the material to be memorized. *(394)*

reinforcement   In operant conditioning, the process whereby a particular behavior is strengthened, making it more likely that the behavior will be repeated. *(48)*

reinforcer   Anything (for example, food, money, a smile) that increases the likelihood that a given response will occur again. For example, giving a child a warm hug for being polite will increase the chances that that behavior will be repeated. *(48)* (See also *positive reinforcer; negative reinforcer.*)

replicate   To repeat or duplicate. Scientists describe their experiments in detail sufficient to allow others to replicate their test procedures. *(17)*

representation   The ability, usually first evident between 18 and 24 months of age, to remember (through the creation of a mental image) an object, event, or person that has been seen or experienced at an earlier time. *(186)*

representative sample   A group of subjects in a research project who have the relevant characteristics (e.g. sex, race, socioeconomic level) of the general population or of a particular segment of the population to which the experimental results are most applicable. *(18)*

repression   A defense mechanism in which anxiety-provoking thoughts and fantasies are excluded from consciousness. *(40)*

resource room   A classroom equipped with special learning materials designed to teach children who have learning difficulties. *(367)*

respiratory distress syndrome   In neonates, irregular breathing due to insufficient surfactin. Preterm infants are at highest risk for this problem, which is the most common cause of death in otherwise normal neonates. (Also called *hyaline membrane disease.*) *(129)*

response   A behavior (either instinctual or learned) following a specific cue. (See *stimulus.*) *(46)*

restricted code   A form of speech charcterized by limited use of vocabulary and syntax. Meaning is communicated by gestures, intonation, and shared understandings. *(403)*

reversibility   The idea, described by Piaget, that something that has been changed can be returned to its original state simply be reversing the process of change. For example, a ball of clay that has been rolled out into a long, thin rope can be rerolled into a ball. Preschoolers cannot regularly apply the rule of reversibility. *(288)*

Rh disease   See *erythroblastosis.*

rite of passage   An anthropological term for a ritual that marks the transition from one stage of life to another. The initiation ceremonies at puberty are examples of a rite of passage; weddings and funerals are others. *(520)*

rooting reflex   A normal neonatal reflex that helps babies find a nipple by causing them to turn their heads toward the stimulus and start to suck whenever something brushes against their cheek. *(163)*

rough-and-tumble play   Wrestling, chasing, and hitting that occurs purely in fun, with no intent to harm. *(258)*

rubella (German measles)   A virus which, if contracted during pregnancy, can cause the fetus to develop serious handicaps, among them blindness and deafness. *(104)*

sample   In research, a group of individuals that is studied so that conclusions may be drawn about a larger group or segment of the population. (Also called *sample population.*) *(18)*

schema   Piaget's term for a general way of thinking about, or interacting with, ideas and objects in the environment. *(55)*

scientific method   A procedural model used to formulate questions, collect data, test hypotheses, and draw conclusions. Use of the scientific method helps researchers overcome biases, test assumptions, and in short, be "scientific." *(17)*

scientific reasoning   The ability to understand and use the principles of science.

secondary circular reaction   Piaget's term for infants' tendency to repeat actions to produce responses from objects or people (e.g., squeezing a rubber duck or laughing while playing with an adult). Secondary circular reactions occur during the third stage of sensorimotor development (usually between 4 and 8 months of age). *(180)*

secondary sexual characteristics   Sexual features other than the actual sex organs, such as a man's beard or a woman's breasts, that distinguish male from female. *(471)*

second stage of labor   The period during which the baby's head moves through the vaginal opening. *(125)*

secular trend   The tendency of each recent new generation to grow taller and to experience puberty earlier than their parents. *(476)*

secure attachment   A healthy parent-child bond in which the child feels comfort when the parent is present, experiences moderate distress at the parent's absence, and quickly reestablishes contact when the parent returns. *(231)*

selective attention   The ability to focus attention on particular stimuli and ignore distractions. *(393)*

self-awareness   A person's sense of himself or herself as a separate person, with particular characteristics. The development of this sense of self begins at birth, but only between 1 and 2 years of age do children begin to truly differentiate themselves from others. *(216)*

self-concept   The more clearly developed idea of the self that is acquired in early childhood. *(319)*

self-theory   The older child's or adult's complex theory about the self, based on the evidence of experience, the opinion of others, and untested assumptions about the self. *(426)*

sensation   The process by which the senses detect stimuli within the environment. *(158)*

sensorimotor intelligence   Piaget's term for the first stage of cognitive development (from birth to about 2 years old). Children in this stage primarily use the senses and motor skills (i.e., grasping, sucking, etc.) to explore and manipulate the enviroment. *(178)*

sensorimotor play   Play that captures the pleasures of using the senses, including the primary senses (touching, tasting, hearing, etc.) and the sense of motion and balance. For example, children who mash their food, or whirl their bodies around for the pure fun of it are engaging in sensorimotor play. *(256)*

sensory register   A memory system that functions for only a fraction of a second during sensory processing, retaining a fleeting impression of the stimulus that has just impinged on a particular sense organ (e.g., the eyes). If a person looks at an object, for example, and then closes his or her eyes, the visual image of the object is briefly maintained. *(393)*

separation anxiety   A child's fear of being left or abandoned by the mother or other caregiver. This emotion emerges at about 8 or 9 months, peaks at about 14 months, then gradually subsides. *(215)*

separation-individuation   A term used by Margaret Mahler to describe the period during which the child gradually develops a sense of self, apart from the mother. This period extends from about 5 months to 3 years, and is marked by the child's increasingly secure attempts to achieve psychological separation from the mother. *(223)*

seriation   The concept that items can be arranged in a logical series, as by sorting a group of sticks from longest to shortest, or arranging a group of crayons from lightest to darkest. This concept is mastered during the period of operational thought, according to Piaget. *(385)*

sex drive   The need for sexual expression. Some consider this a basic human need, like the hunger drive; others do not. *(476)*

sex-linked genes   See *X-linked* genes.

sexual abuse   The sexual exploitation of children by adults; acts range from inappropriate fondling to rape. *(534)*

sexual dimorphism   A term that refers to the differences in the form of male and female bodies not only in obvious ways, such as the difference in sex organs, but also in less apparent ways, such as the pattern of the hairline or the shape of the hands. *(466)*

sexual latency   See *latency*.

sexually transmitted diseases (STDs)   Diseases spread by sexual contact. Such diseases include syphilis, gonorrhea, herpes simplex, and AIDS. *(505)*

short-term memory   The memory sytem in which information is kept for a brief time, no longer than a minute. *(393)*

sibling   An individual's brother or sister.

sickle-cell anemia   A genetic blood disease, common among Afro-Americans, that can cause fatigue, swelling of the joints, and sometimes death. *(88)*

significance   In statistics, a term that describes whether a measured difference (for example between an experimental and control group) is a relevant scientific finding, or perhaps merely the result of chance. Usually, if the likelihood that a particular result occurred by chance is less than one chance in twenty, the result is termed significant. *(19)*

sleeper effect   An effect of an experiment or other manipulation that is not apparent for a time, but that emerges, or reemerges later. *(312)*

small-for-dates infant   An infant who is born weighing less than the average baby born after the same number of weeks of gestation. *(128)*

social cognition   A person's understanding of the dynamics of human interaction. *(424)*

social learning theory   The theory that learning occurs through imitation of, and identification with, other people. *(49)*

social play   Play involving two or more children who seem to be aware of each other. *(322)*

social reinforcers   Rewards that come from other people in response to particular behavior and increase the likelihood that that behavior will occur again. For instance, if people smile and babble in response to the infant's first babbling, the infant is likely to babble again. *(49)*

social smile   An infant's smile in response to seeing another person. In full-term infants, this kind of smile first appears at about 6 weeks after birth. *(213)*

society of children   The culture of games, sayings, and traditions passed down from one generation of children to the next. *(430)*

socioeconomic status (SES)   A measure that takes into account family income, parents' education, and father's occupation or employment. Socioeconomic status has been found to influence physical health, academic performance, and many other aspects of children's lives. *(441)*

solitary play   A form of play in which the child plays alone, seemingly unaware of other children playing nearby. *(322)*

sonogram   A method of determining the size and position of the fetus by means of sound waves. *(92)*

specific learning disabilities   Any of a number of particular difficulties in mastering basic academic skills, without apparent deficit in intelligence or impairment of sensory functions. *(369)*

spermatozoa (singular, spermatozoon)   The male reproductive cells, which begin to be produced by the testicles at puberty. *(71)*

statistics   The mathematics of the collection, organization, and interpretation of numerical data used to evaluate data and test hypotheses. *(19)*

stepping reflex   A normal neonatal reflex that causes newborns to move their legs as if to walk when their feet touch a flat surface. *(163)*

stereotype   A simplified, or conventional idea of a person or thing, based on notions of what is typical. For example, sexual stereotypes embody conventional ideas of what is "masculine" or "feminine." *(343)*

stimulus   An external condition or event that elicits a bodily response or prompts a particular action. For example, the sight or aroma of an appetizing meal is a stimulus to which the response is usually salivation. *(46)*

sucking reflex   A normal neonatal reflex that causes newborns to suck anything that touches their lips. *(163)*

sudden infant death syndrome (SIDS)   The sudden death of an apparently healthy infant (most often between the ages of 2 and 4 months). The immediate cause is that the infant stops breathing; the underlying cause is not known. *(156)*

superego   Freud's term for that part of the personality that contains the conscience, including the internalization of moral standards set by one's parents. *(187)*

surface structure   Noam Chomsky's term for the particular vocabulary and rules of grammar that differ from one language to another. The surface structure is distinct from the deep structure of language, which includes the general rules that are shared by most languages. *(196)*

surfactin   A natural substance that coats the lungs during the last weeks of fetal development and aids normal reflexive breathing during the first weeks after birth. *(129)*

surgent growth   The Offers' term for the type of adolescent development that is characterized by some emotional and social problems but on the whole is a fairly smooth progression toward adulthood. *(466)*

swimming reflex   A normal neonatal reflex that causes the newborn to make swimming motions when held aloft horizontally. *(163)*

symbiosis   A term used by Margaret Mahler to describe the period of infancy, from about 2 to 5 months, during which the infant is so entirely dependent on the mother that he or she feels literally a part of her. *(223)*

symbol   Sounds, written words, drawings, actions, or objects that stand for or signify something else. For example, a flag symbolizes a country, and the combination of the letters "d-o-g" symbolizes the spoken word "dog," which, in turn, symbolizes a particular kind of animal. *(287)*

symbolic thought   The ability to use words and images to represent objects and actions. This ability, which children usually acquire around age 2, makes it possible to remember the past, to imagine the future, and to deal with the present with more reflection and imagination. *(287)*

synchrony   Carefully coordinated interaction between infant and parent (or any other two people) in which each is exquisitely, often unknowingly, attuned to the other's verbal and nonverbal cues. *(228)*

syphilis   A sexually transmitted disease that is teratogenic to the fetus, causing serious bone, liver or brain damage. *(105)*

systems approach   An approach to human development that emphasizes the effects of the environment and that conceptualizes the environment as consisting of several levels of systems, ranging from small systems, such as the family, to large systems, for example, the cultural and political systems. (Also called the *ecological approach*.) *(4)*

temperament   The characteristic way a person responds to things and people; for example, his or her usual quality of mood, activity level, intensity of reaction, attention span. *(224)*

teratogens   External agents, such as viruses, drugs, chemicals, and radiation, which can cross the barrier of the placenta and harm the embryo or fetus. *(103)*

teratology   The scientific study of birth defects caused by genetic or prenatal problems, or by birth complications. *(103)*

tertiary circular reactions   Jean Piaget's term for the certain actions with slight variations each time (e.g. hitting a drum with a stick, then with a pencil or a hammer). Tertiary circular reactions occur during the fifth stage of sensorimotor intelligence (usually between 12 and 18 months age). *(184)*

testosterone   Hormones that are produced primarily by the testes and regulate sexual development in puberty. Although girls' adrenal glands produce some testosterone, it is chiefly a male hormone. *(467)*

thalidomide   A mild tranquilizer—now banned—which, when taken early in pregnancy, prevented normal formation of the fetus' arms, legs, and ears. *(107)*

theory   A systematic statement of hypotheses and general principles that provides a framework for future research and interpretation. *(35)*

third stage of labor   The expulsion of the placenta after a child is born. *(125)*

toddler   A child, usually between the ages of 1 and 2, who has just begun to master the art of walking. *(165)*

toxemia   See *preeclampsia*.

toxoplasmosis   A mild disease caused by a parasite often found in uncooked meat and in cat feces. If a pregnant woman contracts this disease, her fetus may suffer eye or brain damage. *(105)*

transition   The period of the birth process in which the baby's head moves through the birth canal to the vaginal opening. *(125)*

trimester   One of the three-month periods in the nine months of pregnancy. *(102)*

trisomy-21 An abnormality of the twenty-first chromosome pair that results in Down's syndrome. (See *Down's syndrome*.) (81)

trophoblast The outer cells of the developing organism during the first weeks after conception. These cells later form the four membranes (the yolk sac, amnion, allantosis, and chorion) that protect and nurture the embryo and fetus. (100)

trust versus mistrust Erik Erikson's term for the infant's basic experience of the world as either good and comfortable or as threatening and uncomfortable. Early care-giving experiences usually mold the child's viewpoint. This is the first of Erikson's eight stages of development. (221)

tumultuous growth The Offers' term for the type of adolescent development that is characterized by emotional and social problems. (465)

umbilical cord A tube connecting the developing fetus to the placenta. The cord contains a vein which carries nourishment to the fetus and two arteries which remove waste products. (100)

unconscious That part of our thoughts and memories of which we are unaware. In psychoanalytic theory, the workings of the unconscious determine much of our conscious actions and thoughts. (37)

uterus The organ in females that receives the fertilized ovum and nurtures the embryo and fetus during pregnancy. (71)

vacuum extraction tube A medical instrument that is sometimes used to facilitate or hasten birth. (132)

valid A term used in test construction to indicate that a particular test will accurately measure what it is supposed to measure. (18)

vernix A waxy, white substance that sometimes covers the skin of a preterm infant; it disappears soon after birth. (127)

visual cliff A laboratory device that consists of a ledge with an apparent drop of several feet that actually is covered by a sheet of transparent glass. Very young children will not venture beyond the end of the ledge even when coaxed by parents, a refusal that demonstrates early development of depth perception. (161)

X-linked genes Genes that are carried on the X chromosome exclusively. X-linked genes account for the fact that certain recessive genetic diseases or conditions are more likely to occur in males, who have only one X chromosome, than in females, who have two. (77)

XO (Turner's syndrome) A genetic abnormality occurring in females who inherit one rather than two X chromosomes. It results in incomplete sexual maturation and usually mental retardation as well. (80)

XX The chromosomal pair that determines that a zygote will develop into a normal female. This combination results when an ovum (which always carries an X chromosome) is fertilized by a sperm carrying an X chromosome. (72)

XXY (Klinefelter's syndrome) A group of genetic disorders present in males who inherit an extra X chromosome. This syndrome prevents the development of secondary sex characteristics. (80)

XY The chromosomal pair that determines that a zygote will develop into a normal male. This combination results when an ovum (which always carries an X chromosome) is fertilized by a sperm carrying a Y chromosome. (72)

XYY A genetic abnormality present in males who possess an extra Y chromosome. Men who have this disorder are generally taller and may be more prone to antisocial behavior than the norm. (80)

zygote The one-celled organism formed from the union of a sperm and an ovum. (71)

Bibliography

Abraham, Kitty G., and **Christopherson, Victor A.** (1984). Perceived competence among rural middle school children: Parental antecedents and relation to locus of control. *Journal of Early Adolescence, 4,* 343–351.

Abraham, Sidney, Lowenstein, Frank W., and **Johnson, Clifford L.** (1974). *First health and nutrition survey, United States, 1971–1972: Dietary intake and biochemical findings.* Washington, DC: National Center for Health Statistics.

Abravanel, Eugene, and **Sigafoos, Ann D.** (1984). Exploring the presence of imitation during early infancy. *Child Development, 55,* 381–392.

Achenbach, Thomas M. (1982). *Developmental psychopathology* (2nd ed.). New York: Wiley.

Achenbach, Thomas M., and **Edelbrock, Craig S.** (1981). Behavioral problems and competencies reported by parents of normal and disturbed children aged four through sixteen. *Monographs of the Society for Research in Child Development, 46* (Serial No. 188).

Ackerman, B.P. (1978). Children's comprehension of presupposed information: Logical and pragmatic inferences to speaker belief. *Journal of Experimental Child Psychology, 26,* 92–114.

Adelson, Joseph. (1979). Adolescence and the generalization gap. *Psychology Today. 12*(9), 33–37.

Agathanos, Helen, and **Stathakopoulous, Nella.** (1983). Life events and child abuse: A controlled study. In Jerome E. Leavitt (Ed.), *Child abuse and neglect: Research and innovation.* The Hague: Martinus Nijhoff.

Ainsworth, Mary D. Salter. (1967). *Infancy in Uganda: Infant care and the growth of love.* Baltimore: Johns Hopkins Press.

Ainsworth, Mary D. Salter. (1973). The development of infant-mother attachment. In Bettye M. Caldwell and Henry N. Ricciuti (Eds.), *Review of child development research.* Vol. III. Chicago: University of Chicago Press.

Ainsworth, Mary D. Salter, and **Bell, Silvia M.** (1970). Attachment, exploration, and separation: Illustrated by the behavior of one-year-olds in a strange situation. *Child Development, 41,* 49–67.

Ainsworth, Mary D.S., Blehar, M., Waters, Everett, and **Wall, S.** (1978). *Patterns of attachment.* Hillsdale, NJ: Erlbaum.

Akiyama, M. Michael. (1984). Are language acquisition strategies universal? *Developmental Psychology, 20,* 219–228.

Aldis, Owen. (1975). *Play fighting.* New York: Academic Press.

Aleksandrowicz, Malca K., and **Aleksandrowicz, Dov. R.** (1974). Obstetrical pain-relieving drugs as predictors of infant behavior variability. *Child Development, 45,* 935–945.

Alexander, James F., and **Malouf, Roberta E.** (1983). Problems in personality and social development. In Paul H. Mussen (Ed.), *Handbook of child psychology: Vol. 4. Socialization, personality and social development.* New York: Wiley.

Ali, Z., and **Lowry, M.** (1981). Early maternal-child contact: Effects on later behavior. *Developmental Medicine and Child Neurology, 23,* 337–345.

Allard, Alexander Jr. (1983). *Playing with form.* New York: Columbia University Press.

Allen, J.R., Barsotti, D.A., and **Carsten, L.A.** (1980). Residual effect of polychlorinated biphenyls on adult nonhuman primates and their offspring. *Journal of Toxicology and Environmental Health, 6,* 55–66.

Amabile, Teresa M. (1983). *The social psychology of creativity.* New York: Springer-Verlag.

Ambert, Anne-Marie. (1982). Differences in children's behavior toward custodial mothers and custodial fathers. *Journal of Marriage and the Family, 44,* 73–86.

Anastasi, Anne. (1982). *Psychological testing* (5th ed.). New York: Macmillan.

Anderson, Christine Warren, Nagle, Richard J., Roberts, William A., and **Smith, James W.** (1981). Attachment to substitute caregivers as a function of center quality and caregiver involvement. *Child Development, 52,* 53–61.

Anderson, W. French. (1984). Prospects for human gene therapy. *Science, 226,* 401–409.

Anglin, Jeremy M. (1977). *Word, object, and conceptual development.* New York: Norton.

Anolik, Steven A. (1983). Family influence upon delinquency: Biosocial and psychosocial perspectives. *Adolescence, 18,* 489–498.

Apgar, Virginia. (1953). A proposal for a new method of evaluation in the newborn infant. *Current Research in Anesthesia and Analgesia, 32,* 260.

Apgar, Virginia, and **Beck, Joan.** (1973). *Is my baby all right?* New York: Trident Press.

Appel, Lynne F., Cooper, Robert G., McCarrell, Nancy, Sims-Knight, Judith, Yussen, Steven R., and **Flavell, John H.** (1972). The development of the distinction between perceiving and memorizing. *Child Development, 43,* 1365–1381.

Applebaum, Mark I., and **McCall, Robert B.** (1983). Design and analysis in developmental psychology. In Paul H. Mussen (Ed.), *Handbook of Child Psychology: Vol 1. History, theory, and methods.* New York: Wiley.

Archer, Cynthia. (1984). Children's attitudes toward sex-role divisions in adult occupational roles. *Sex Roles, 10,* 1–10.

Arend, Richard, Gove, Frederick L., and **Sroufe, L. Alan.** (1979). Continuity of individual adaptation from infancy to kindergarten: A predictive study of ego-resiliency and curiosity in preschoolers. *Child Development, 50,* 950–959.

Ariès, Philippe. (1962). *Centuries of childhood: A social history of family life.* Robert Baldick (trans). New York. Knopf.

Armstrong, Louise. (1978). *Kiss daddy goodnight.* New York: Hawthorn Books.

Asch, S.E., and **Nerlove, H.** (1960). The development of double function terms in children: An exploratory investigation. In Bernard Kaplan and Seymour Wapner (Eds.), *Perspectives in psychological theory: Essays in honor of Heinz Werner.* New York: International Universities Press.

Asher, J.J., and **Garcia, R.** (1969). The optimal age to learn a foreign language. *Modern Language Journal, 53,* 334–341.

Asher, Steven R., and **Renshaw, Peter D.** (1981). Children without friends: Social knowledge and social skill training. In Steven R. Asher and John M. Gottman (Eds). *The development of children's friendships.* Cambridge: Cambridge University Press.

Åstrand, Per-Olof. (1976). The child in sport and physical activity: Physiology. In J.G. Albinson and G.M. Andrew (Eds.), *Child in sport and physical activity.* Baltimore: University Park Press, 19–33.

Ausubel, David P., Montemayor, Raymond R., and **Svajian, Pergrouhi (Najarian).** (1977). *Theory and problems of adolescent development* (2nd Ed.) New York: Grune and Stratton.

Axia, Giovanna, and **Baroni, Rosa.** (1985). Linguistic politeness at different age levels. *Child Development, 56,* 918–927.

Bachrach, Christine A. (1984). Contraceptive practice among American women, 1973–1982. *Family Planning Perspectives, 16,* 253–259.

Bailey, D.A. (1977). The growing child and the need for physical activity. In Russell C. Smart and Mollie S. Smart (Eds.), *Readings in child development and relationships* (2nd ed.). New York: Macmillan.

Bakeman, R., and **Brown, J.V.** (1980). Early interaction: Consequences for social and mental development at three years. *Child Development, 51,* 437–447.

Baker, S. Josephine. (1923). Healthy children. Boston: Little-Brown.

Baker, J.L., and **Gottlieb, Jay.** (1980). Attitudes of teachers toward mainstreaming. In Jay Gottlieb (Ed.), *Educating mentally retarded persons in the mainstream.* Baltimore: University Park Press.

Bandura, Albert. (1969). *Principles of behavior modification.* New York: Holt.

Bandura, Albert. (1977). *Social learning theory.* Englewood Cliffs, NJ: Prentice-Hall.

Bandura, Albert. (1981). Self-referent thought: A developmental analysis of self-efficacy. In John H. Flavell and Lee Ross (Eds.), *Social cognitive development: Frontiers and possible futures.* Cambridge: Cambridge University Press.

Bank, Stephen P., and **Kahn, Michael D.** (1982). *The sibling bond.* New York: Basic Books.

Bard, B., and **Sachs, J.** (1977). *Language acquisition patterns in two normal children of deaf parents.* Paper presented at the meeting of the Boston University Conference on Language Acquisition.

Bardwick, Judith M., and **Douvan, Elizabeth.** (1971). Ambivalence: The socialization of women. In Vivian Gornick and Barbara K. Moran (Eds.), *Woman in sexist society.* New York: Basic Books.

Barkley, R.A. (1977). A review of stimulant drug research with hyperactive children. *Journal of Child Psychology and Psychiatry, 18,* 137–165.

Barnard, Kathryn E., and **Bee, Helen L.** (1983). The impact of temporally patterned stimulation on the development of preterm infants. *Child Development, 54,* 1156–1167.

Barrera, Maria E., and **Maurer, Daphne.** (1981a). The perception of facial expressions by the three-month-old. *Child Development, 52,* 203–206.

Barrera, Maria E., and **Maurer, Daphne.** (1981b). Discrimination of strangers by the three-month-old. *Child Development, 52,* 558–563.

Bartel, Nettie R. (1971). Locus of control and achievement in middle- and lower-class children. *Child Development, 42,* 1099–1107.

Baruch, G., Barnett, R., and **Rivers C.** (1983). *Lifeprints: New patterns of work and love for today's women.* New York: McGraw-Hill.

Baskin, Yvonne. (1984). *The gene doctors.* New York: Morrow.

Bates, E. (1976). Acquisition of polite forms: Longitudinal evidence. In E. Bates (Ed.), *Language and context: The acquisition of pragmatics.* New York: Academic Press.

Baum, Cynthia G. (1984). Social factors associated with adolescent obesity. *Journal of Pediatric Psychology, 9,* 293–302.

Baumrind, Diana. (1967). Child-care practices anteceding three patterns of preschool behavior. *Genetic Psychology Monographs, 75,* 43–88.

Baumrind, Diana. (1971). Current patterns of parental authority. *Developmental Psychology, 4* (Monograph I), 1–103.

Baumrind, Diana. (1982). Are androgynous individuals more effective persons and parents? *Child Development, 53,* 44–75.

Bayer, Leona M., and **Snyder, Margaret M.** (1971). Illness experience of a group of normal children. In Mary Cover Jones, Nancy Bayley, Jean Walker Macfarlane, and Marjorie

Pyles Honzik (Eds.), *The course of human development*. Waltham, Mass.: Xerox College Publishing, 91–103.

Bayley, Nancy. (1935). The development of motor abilities during the first three years. *Monographs of the Society for Research in Child Development, 1.*

Bayley, Nancy. (1955). On the growth of intelligence. *American Psychologist, 10,* 805–818.

Beal, Carole R., and **Flavell, John H.** (1982). Effect of increasing the salience of message ambiguities on kindergartners' evaluations of communication success and message adequacy. *Developmental Psychology, 18,* 43–48.

Beal, Carole R., and **Flavell, John H.** (1983). Young speakers' evaluation of their listeners' comprehensions in a referential communication task. *Child Development, 54,* 148–153.

Behrman, Richard E., and **Vaughn, Victor C. III.** (1983). *Pediatrics.* Philadelphia: Saunders, 1983.

Bell, Richard Q., and **Harper, Lawrence V.** *Child effects on adults.* Hillsdale, NJ: Erlbaum, 1977.

Bell, Richard Q., and **Waldrop, M.F.** (1982). Temperament and minor physical anomalies. In R. Porter and G.M. Collins (Eds.), *Temperamental differences in infants and young children.* London: Pittman

Beller, E. Kuno. (1979). Early intervention programs. In Joy D. Osofsky (Ed.), *Handbook of infant development.* New York: Wiley.

Belsky, Jay. (1984). The determinants of parenting: A process model. *Child Development, 55,* 83–96.

Belsky, Jay, Steinberg, Laurence D., and **Walker, Ann.** (1982). The ecology of day care. In Michael Lamb (Ed.), *Nontraditional families: Parenting and child development.* Hillsdale, NJ: Erlbaum.

Belsky, Jay, Gilstrap, Bonnie, and **Rovine, Michael.** (1984b). The Pennsylvania Infant and Family Development Project I: Stability and change in mother-infant and father-infant interaction in a family setting at one, three, and nine months. *Child Development, 55,* 692–705.

Belsky, Jay, Robins, Elliot, and **Gamble, Wendy.** (1984c). The determinants of parental competence: Toward a contextual theory. In Michael Lewis (Ed.), *Beyond the dyad.* New York: Plenum.

Belsky, Jay, Taylor, Dawn G., and **Rovine, Michael.** (1984a). The Pennsylvania Infant and Family Development Project II: The development of reciprocal interaction in the mother-infant dyad. *Child Development, 55,* 706–717.

Bem, Sandra L. (1974). The measurement of psychological androgyny. *Journal of Consulting and Clinical Psychology, 42,* 155–162.

Bem, Sandra L. (1981). Gender-schema theory: A cognitive account of sex-typing. *Psychological Review. 88,* 354–364.

Benbow, C.P., and **Stanley, J.C.** (1980). Sex differences in mathematical ability: Fact or artifact. *Science, 210,* 1262.

Bender, Lauretta. (1973). The life course of children with schizophrenia. *American Journal of Psychiatry, 130,* 783–786.

Bengston, Vernon L. (1975). Generation and family effects in value socialization. *American Sociological Review. 40,* 358–371.

Bennett, Neville. (1976). *Teaching styles and pupil progress.* Cambridge, MA.: Harvard University Press.

Berezin, Nancy. (1980). *The gentle birth book: A practical guide to Leboyer family-centered delivery.* New York: Pocket Books.

Berk, Laura E., and **Garvin, Ruth A.** (1984). Development of private speech among low-income Appalachian children. *Developmental Psychology, 20,* 271–286.

Berkowitz, Leonard. (1973). Control of aggression. In Bettye M. Caldwell and Henry N. Ricciuti (Eds.), *Review of child development research.* Vol. III. Chicago: University of Chicago Press.

Berndt, Thomas J. (1981). Relations between social cognition, nonsocial cognition, and social behavior. In John H. Flavell and Lee Ross (Eds.), *Social cognitive development: Frontiers and possible futures.* Cambridge: Cambridge University Press.

Berndt, Thomas J. (1982). The features and effects of friendship in early adolescence. *Child Development, 53,* 1447–1460.

Bernstein, Basil. (1971, 1973). *Class, codes, and control* (Vols. 1, 2). London: Routledge and Kegan Paul.

Bierman, Karen Lynn, and **Furman, Wyndol.** (1984). The effects of social skills training and peer involvement on the social adjustment of preadolescents. *Child Development, 55,* 151–162.

Bigelow, Ann E. (1983). Development of the use of sound in the search behavior of infants. *Developmental Psychology, 19,* 317–321.

Bigelow, B.J. (1977). Children's friendship expectations: A cognitive developmental study. *Child Development, 48,* 246–253.

Bigelow, B.J., and **La Gaipa, J.J.** (1975). Children's written descriptions of friendship: A multidimensional analysis. *Developmental Psychology, 11,* 857–858.

Biggs, John B., and **Collis, K.F.** (1982). *Evaluating the quality of learning: The SOLO taxonomy (Structure of the Observed Learning Outcome).* New York: Academic Press.

Bijou, Sidney W., and **Baer, Donald M.** (1965). *Child development: Vol. 2. Universal stage of infancy.* New York: Appleton-Century-Crofts.

Biller, Henry B. (1981). Father absence, divorce and personality development. In Michael E. Lamb (Ed.), *The role of the father in child development.* New York: Wiley.

Binet, Alfred. (1909). *Les idées modernes sur les enfants.* Paris: Schleicher.

Bing, Elizabeth D. (1970). *Adventure of birth.* New York: Simon and Schuster.

Bing, Elizabeth D. (1983). *Dear Elizabeth Bing: We've had our baby.* New York: Pocket Books.

Black, Rebecca, and **Mayer, Joseph.** (1980). Parents with special problems: Alcoholism and opiate addiction. In C. Henry

Kempe and Ray E. Helfer (Eds.), *The battered child* (3rd ed.). Chicago: The University of Chicago Press.

Blake, J. (1981). The only child in America: Prejudice versus performance. *Population and Development Review, 1*, 25–44.

Blasi, Augusto. (1980). Bridging moral cognition and moral action: A critical review of the literature. *Psychological Bulletin, 88*, 593–637.

Blewitt, Pamela. (1982). Word meaning acquisition in young children. A review of theory and research. In H.W. Reese and L.P. Lipsitt (Eds.), *Advances in child development and behavior*. New York: Academic Press.

Block, Jeanne. (1971). *Lives through time*. Berkeley, CA: Bancroft Books.

Block, Jack H., and **Block, Jeanne.** (1980). The role of ego control and ego-resiliency in the organization of behavior. In W. Andrew Collins (Ed.), *Development of cognitive affect, and social relations*. Minnesota symposium on child psychology (Vol. 13). Hillsdale, NJ: Erlbaum.

Bloom, Benjamin S. (1964). *Stability and change in human characteristics*. New York: Wiley.

Bloom, Lois. (1975). Language development. In Frances Degan Horowitz (Ed.), *Review of child development research* (Vol. IV). Chicago: University of Chicago Press, 245–303.

Bloom, Lois, Merkin, Susan, and **Wootten, Janet.** (1982). Wh-Questions: Linguistic factors that contribute to the sequence of acquisition. *Child Development, 53*, 1084–1092.

Blos, Peter. (1962). *On adolescence: A psychoanalytic interpretation*. New York: Free Press.

Boffey, Philip M. (1983, August 2). "Safe" form of radiation arouses new worry. *The New York Times*, p. C1.

Bogin, Barry, and **MacVean, Robert B.** (1983). The relationship of socioeconomic status and sex to body size, skeletal maturation, and cognitive status of Guatemala City schoolchildren. *Child Development, 54*, 115–128.

Bolton, Brian E. (1976). *Psychology of deafness for rehabilitation counselors*. Baltimore: University Park Press.

Bond, Guy L., Tinker, Miles A., Wasson, Barbara B. (1979). *Reading difficulties: Their diagnosis and correction* (4th ed.). Englewood Cliffs, NJ: Prentice Hall.

Bonvillian, John D., Orlansky, Michael D., and **Novack, Lesley Lazin.** (1983). Developmental Milestones: Sign language acquisition and motor development. *Child Development, 54*, 1435–1445.

Borke, Helene. (1975). Piaget's mountains revisited: Changes in the egocentric landscape. *Developmental Psychology, 11*, 240–243.

Borstelmann, L.J. (1983). Children before psychology: Ideas about children from antiquity to the late 1800's. In Paul H. Mussen (Ed.), *Handbook of child psychology: Vol. 1. History, theory, and methods*. New York: Wiley.

Bouchard, Thomas. (1981, August). *The Minnesota study of twins reared apart: Description and preliminary findings*. Paper presented at the annual meeting of the American Psychological Association.

Boukydis, C.F. Zachariah, and **Burgess, Robert L.** (1982). Adult physiological response to infant cries: Effects of temperament of infant, parental status, and gender. *Child Development, 53*, 1291–1298.

Bower, Bruce. (1985). Kids and the bomb: Apocalyptic anxieties. *Science News, 128*, 106–107.

Bower, T.G.R. (1977). *A primer of infant development*. San Francisco: Freeman.

Bower, T.G.R. (1979). *Human Development*. San Francisco: Freeman.

Bower, T.G.R., and **Wishart, J.G.** (1979). Towards a unitary theory of development. In E.B. Thomas (Ed.), *Origins of the infant's social responsiveness*. Hillsdale, NJ: Erlbaum.

Bowerman, Melissa. (1982). Reorganizational processes in lexical and syntactic development. In Eric Wanner and Lila R. Gleitman (Eds.), *Language acquisition: The state of the art*. Cambridge, England: Cambridge University Press.

Bowlby, John. (1969, 1973). *Attachment* (Vol. I) and *Loss* (Vol. II). New York: Basic Books.

Bowlby, John. (1980). *Attachment and loss: Vol. 3. Loss, sadness, and depression*. New York: Basic Books.

Boxer, Andrew M., Gershenson, Harold P., and **Offer, Daniel.** (1984). Historical time and social change in adolescent experience. *New Directions for Mental Health Services, 22*, 83–95.

Bradley, Robert H., and **Caldwell, Bettye M.** (1976). The relation of infants' home environments to mental test performance at fifty-four months: A follow-up study. *Child Development, 47*, 1172–1174.

Bradley, Robert H., and **Caldwell, Bettye M.** (1980). The relation of home environment, cognitive competence, and IQ among males and females. *Child Development, 51*, 1140–1148.

Bradley, Robert H., and **Caldwell, Bettye M.** (1984). The HOME inventory and family demographics. *Developmental Psychology, 20*, 315–320.

Bradley, Robert H., and **Caldwell, Bettye M.** (1984). The relation of infant's home environments to achievement test performance in first grade: A follow-up study. *Child Development, 55*, 803–809.

Bradshaw, John L. (1983). *Human cerebral asymmetry*. Englewood Cliffs, NJ: Prentice Hall.

Braine, Martin D.S., and **Rumain, Barbara.** (1983). Logical reasoning. In Paul H. Mussen (Ed.), *Handbook of child psychology: Vol. 3. Cognitive development*. New York: Wiley.

Brainerd, Charles J. (1983). Working memory systems and cognitive development. In Charles J. Brainerd (Ed.), *Recent advances in cognitive-developmental theory: Progress in cognitive development research*. New York: Springer-Verlag.

Brazelton, T. Berry. (1978). Introduction. In Arnold J. Sameroff (Ed.), Organization and stability of newborn behavior: A commentary on the Brazelton Neonatal Behavior Assessment Scale. *Monographs of the Society for Research in Child Development, 43* (Serial No. 177).

Brazelton, T. Berry, Koslowski, Barbara, and **Main, Mary.** (1974). The origins of reciprocity. The early mother-infant interaction. In Michael Lewis and Leonard A. Rosenblum

(Eds.), *The effect of the infant on its caregiver*. New York: Wiley.

Brazelton, T. Berry, Yogman, Michael, Als, Heidelise, and **Tronick, Edward.** (1979). The infant as a focus for Family Reciprocity. In Michael Lewis and Leonard A. Rosenblum (Eds.), *The child and his family*. New York: Plenum.

Bretherton, Inge, and **Waters, Everett.** (1985). Growing points of attachment theory and research. *Monographs of the Society for Research in Child Development, 50* (1, 2, Serial No. 209).

Brim, Orville G. (1976). Life span development of the theory of oneself: Implications for child development. In Haynes W. Reese (Ed.), *Advances in child development and behavior* (Vol. 2). New York: Academic Press.

Broman, S.H., Nichols, P.L., and **Kennedy, W.A.** (1975). *Preschool I.Q.: Prenatal and early developmental correlates*. New York: Erlbaum.

Bronfenbrenner, Urie. (1974). *A report on the longitudinal evaluations of preschool programs. Vol. II.: Is early intervention effective?* U.S. Department of Health, Education, and Welfare. DHEW Publication No. OHD 74–24. Washington, DC: Office of Child Development, 1974.

Bronfenbrenner, Urie. (1975). Is early intervention effective? In M. Guttenberg and E.L. Struening (Eds.), *Handbook of evaluation research* (Vol. 2). Beverly Hills, CA: Sage.

Bronfenbrenner, Urie. (1977). Toward an experimental ecology of human development. *American Psychologist, 32*, 513–531.

Bronfenbrenner, Urie. (1979). *The ecology of human development: Experiments by nature and design*. Cambridge, MA: Harvard University Press.

Bronfenbrenner, Urie, and **Crouter, Ann C.** (1983). The evolution of environmental models in developmental research. In Paul H. Mussen (Ed.), *Handbook of child psychology: Vol. 1. History, theory, and methods*. New York: Wiley.

Bronson, Wanda C. (1985). Growth in the organization of behavior over the second year of life. *Developmental Psychology, 21*, 108–117.

Brook, Danae. (1976). *Naturebirth: You, your body, and your baby*. New York: Pantheon.

Brooks, Jeanne, and **Lewis, Michael.** (1976). Infants' responses to strangers. Midget, adult and child. *Child Development, 47*, 323–332.

Brooks-Gunn, Jeanne, and **Ruble, Diane N.** (1982). The development of menstrual related beliefs and behaviors during early adolescence. *Child Development, 53*, 1578–1588.

Brown, Ann L., and **De Loache, Judy S.** (1978). Skills, plans, and self-regulation. In Robert S. Siegler (Ed.), *Children's thinking: What develops*. Hillsdale, NJ: Erlbaum.

Brown, Ann L., Bransford, John D., Ferrara, Roberta, and **Campione, Joseph.** (1983). Learning, Remembering, and Understanding. In Paul H. Mussen (Ed.), *Handbook of child psychology: Vol. 3. Cognitive development*. New York: Wiley.

Brown, B.J., and **Lloyd, H.A.** (1975). A controlled study of children not speaking at school. *Journal of the Association of Workers for Maladjusted Children, 3*, 49–63.

Brown, Bertram S. (1983). The impact of political and economic changes upon mental health. *American Journal of Orthopsychiatry, 53*, 583–592.

Brown, Judith K. (1975). Adolescent initiation rites: Recent interpretations. In Robert E. Grinder (Ed.), *Studies in adolescence: A book of readings in adolescent development* (3rd ed.). New York: Macmillan.

Brown, Larry. (1983). Status of child protective services in the United States: An analysis of issues and practice. In Jerome E. Leavitt (Ed.), *Child abuse and neglect: Research and innovation*. The Hague: Martinus Nijhoff.

Brown, Roger A. (1973). *A first language: The early stages*. Cambridge, Harvard University Press.

Bruch, Hilda. (1973). *Eating disorders: Obesity, anorexia nervosa, and the person within*. New York: Basic Books.

Bruner, Jerome Seymour. (1964). The course of cognitive growth. *American Psychologist, 19*, 1–15.

Bruner, Jerome Seymour. (1973). *Beyond the information given: Studies in the psychology of knowing*. Jeremy M. Anglin (Ed.) New York: Norton.

Bruner, Jerome Seymour. (1974–1975). From communication to language: A psychological perspective. *Cognition, 3*, 255–287.

Bruner, Jerome Seymour. (1983). *Child's talk: Learning to use language*. New York: Norton.

Bryan, James H. (1975). Children's cooperation and helping behaviors. In E. Mavis Hetherington (Ed.), *Review of child development research* (Vol. V). Chicago: University of Chicago Press, 127–181.

Buhler, Charlotte. (1968). Introduction. In Charlotte Buhler and Fred Massarick (Eds.), *The course of human life: A study of goals in the humanistic perspective*. New York: Springer.

Burelson, Brant R. (1982). The development of comforting communication skills in childhood and adolescence. *Child Development*, 1578–1588.

Busow, S.A., and **Howe, K.G.** (1979). Model influences on career choices of college students. *The Vocational Guidance Quarterly, 27*, 239–243.

Buss, Ray R., Yussen, Steven R., Mathews, Samuel R. II, Miller, Gloria E., and **Rembold, Karen L.** (1983). Development of children's use of a story scheme to retrieve information. *Developmental Psychology, 19*, 22–28.

Butler, John A., Starfield, Barbara, and **Stemark, Suzanne.** (1984). Child health policy. In Harold W. Stevenson and Alberta E. Siegel (Eds.), *Child development research and social policy*. Chicago: University of Chicago Press.

Butler, Neville. (1974). Late postnatal consequences of fetal malnutrition. In Myron Winick (Ed.), *Nutrition and fetal development*. New York: Wiley.

Cairns, Robert B. (1983). The emergence of developmental psychology. In Paul H. Mussen (Ed.), *Handbook of child psychology: Vol. 1. History, theory, and methods*. New York: Wiley.

Caldwell, Bettye M. (1964). The effects of infant care. In Martin L. Hoffman and Lois Wladis Hoffman (Eds.), *Review of child development research,* Vol. I. New York: Russell Sage.

Caldwell, Bettye M., and **Bradley, Robert H.** (1984). Home observation for the measurement of the environment. New York: Dorsey.

Campos, Joseph J., and **Stenberg, Carl.** (1981). Perception, appraisal and emotion: The onset of social referencing. In Michael E. Lamb and L. R. Sherrod (Eds.), *Infant social cognition: Empirical and theoretical considerations.* Hillsdale, NJ: Erlbaum.

Campos, Joseph J., Barrett, Karen C., Lamb, Michael L., Goldsmith, H. Hill, and **Stenberg, Craig.** (1983). Socioemotional development. In Paul H. Mussen (Ed.), *Handbook of child psychology: Vol. 2. Infancy and developmental psychobiology.* New York: Wiley.

Campos, Joseph J., Hiatt, Susan, Ramsay, Douglas, Henderson, Charlotte, and **Svejda, Marilyn.** (1978). The emergence of fear on the visual cliff. In Michael Lewis and Leonard A. Rosenblum (Eds.), *The development of affect.* New York: Plenum.

Campos, Joseph J., Langer, Alan, and **Krowitz, Alice.** (1970). Cardiac responses on the visual cliff in prelocomotor human infants. *Science, 170,* 195–196.

Cantwell, Dennis P. (1975). *The hyperactive child: Diagnosis, management, current research.* New York: Spectrum.

Cantwell, Hendrika B. (1980). Child neglect. In C. Henry Kempe and Ray E. Helfer (Eds.), *The battered child* (3rd ed.). Chicago: University of Chicago Press.

Cárdenas, Jose A. (1977). Response I. in Noel Epstein (Ed.), *Language, ethnicity and the schools.* Washington D.C.: Institute for Educational Leadership.

Carew, Jean V. (1980). Experience and the development of intelligence in young children at home and in day care. *Monographs of the Society for Research in Child Development, 45* (Serial No. 187).

Carew, Jean V., and **Lightfoot, Sarah L.** (1979). *Beyond bias: Perspectives on classrooms.* Cambridge, MA: Harvard University Press.

Carey, Susan. (1978). The child as word learner. In Morris Halle, J. Bresman, and G.A. Miller (Eds.), *Linguistic theory and psychological reality.* Cambridge, MA: MIT Press.

Carey, William B., and **McDevitt, Sean C.** (1978). Stability and change in individual temperament diagnoses from infancy to early childhood. *Journal of the American Academy of Child Psychiatry, 17,* 331–337.

Carlberg, C. and **Kavale, Kenneth.** (1980). The efficacy of special versus regular class placement for exceptional children: A meta-analysis. *Journal of Special Education, 14,* 296–309.

Carlson, Bonnie E. (1984). The father's contribution to child care: Effects on children's perceptions of parental roles. *American Journal of Orthopsychiatry, 54,* 123–136.

Carlsson, S.G., Fagerberg, H., Horneman, G. Hwang, P., Larson, K., Rodholm, M., Schaller, J., Daniellson, B., and **Gundewal, C.** (1979). Effects of various amounts of contact between mother and child on the mother's nursing behavior:

A follow-up study. *Infant Behavior and Development, 2,* 209–214.

Caron, Albert J., and **Caron, Rose F.** (1981). Processing of relational information as an index of infant risk. In S.L. Friedman and M. Sigman (Eds.), *Preterm birth and psychological development.* New York: Academic Press.

Caron, Albert J., and **Caron, Rose F.** (1982). Cognitive development in infancy. In Tiffany M. Field, Aletha Huston, Herbert C. Quay, Lillian Troll, and Gordon E. Finley (Eds.), *Review of Human Development.* New York: Wiley.

Caron, Albert J., Caron, Rose F., Caldwell, Roberta C., and **Weiss, Sandra J.** (1973). Infant perception of the structural properties of the face. *Developmental Psychology, 9,* 385–399.

Carter-Saltzman, Louise. (1980). Biological and sociocultural effects on handedness: Comparison between biological and adoptive families. *Science, 209,* 1263–1265.

Case, Robbie. (1985). *Intellectual development: Birth to adulthood.* Orlando: Academic Press.

Cassill, Kay. (1982). *Twins reared apart.* New York: Atheneum.

Cazden, Courtney B. (1976). The neglected situation in child language research and education. In Arlene Skolnik (Ed.), *Rethinking childhood.* Boston: Little, Brown, (originally published in *Language and poverty,* Frederick Williams (Ed.), University of Wisconsin Press, 1970).

Cervantes, Lucius F. (1965) *The dropout: Causes and cures.* Ann Arbor: University of Michigan Press.

Chapman, Michael. (1979). Listening to reason: Children's attentiveness and parental discipline. *Merrill-Palmer Quarterly, 25,* 251–263.

Charlesworth, William R. (1984, February 27). Personal correspondence.

Cherry, Louise, and **Lewis, Michael.** (1976). Mothers and two-year-olds: A study of sex-differentiated aspects of verbal interaction. *Developmental Psychology, 12,* 278–282.

Chess, Stella, and **Thomas, Alexander.** (1982). Infant bonding: Mystique and reality. *American Journal of Orthopsychiatry, 52,* 213–222.

Chess, Stella, Korn, Sam J., and **Fernandez, Paulina B.** (1971). *Psychiatric disorders of children with congenital rubella.* New York: Brunner/Mazel.

Chi, Michelene T.H. (1976). Short-term memory limitations in children: Capacity or processing deficits? *Memory and Cognition, 4,* 559–572.

Chi, Michelene T.H. (1978). Knowledge structures and memory development. In Robert S. Siegler (Ed.), *Children's thinking: What develops?* Hillsdale, NJ: Erlbaum.

Chi, Michelene T.H. (1981). Knowledge development and memory performance. In M. Friedman, J.P. Das, and N. O'Conner (Eds.), *Intelligence and learning.* New York: Plenum.

Chilman, Catherine S. (1983). *Adolescent sexuality in a changing American society* (2nd ed.). New York: Wiley.

Chira, Susan. (1984, February 11). Town experiment cuts TV. *The New York Times.*

Chivian, Eric, Mack, John E., Waletzsky, Jeremy, P. Lazaroff, Cynthia, Doctor, Ronald and **Goldering, John M.** (1985). Soviet children and the threat of nuclear war: A preliminary study. *American Journal of Orthopsychiatry, 55,* 484–502.

Chomsky, Carol. (1969). *The acquisition of syntax in children from five to ten.* Cambridge, MA: MIT Press.

Chomsky, Noam. (1968). *Language and mind.* New York: Harcourt, Brace, World.

Chomsky, Noam. (1980). *Rules and representations.* New York: Columbia University Press.

Chukovsky, Korneǐ Ivanovich. (1968). *From two to five.* Berkeley: University of California Press.

Cicourel, Aaron V., Jennings, Kenneth H., Jennings, Sybillyn H.M., Leiter, Kenneth C.W., Mackay, Robert, Mehan, Hugh, and **Roth, David. R.** (1974) *Language use and school performance.* New York: Academic Press.

Clarizio, H.F. (1979). In defense of the I.Q. test. *School Psychology Digest, 8,* 79–88.

Clark, Eve V. (1982). The young word maker: A case study of innovation in the child's lexicon. In Eric Wanner and Lila R. Gleitman (Eds.), *Language acquisition: The state of the art.* Cambridge, England: Cambridge University Press.

Clark, Kenneth B. (1965) *Dark ghetto: Dilemmas of social power.* New York: Harper & Row.

Clark, Samuel D. Jr., Zabin, Laurie S., and **Hardy, Janet B.** (1984). Sex, contraception and parenthood: Experiences and attitudes among urban black young men. *Family Planning Perspectives, 16,* 77–82.

Clarke, Ann M., and **Clarke, A.D.B.** (Eds.).(1976). *Early experience: Myth and evidence.* New York: Free Press.

Clarke-Stewart, K. Alison. (1982). *Daycare.* Cambridge, MA: Harvard University Press.

Clarke-Stewart, K. Alison. (1984). Day Care: A new context for research and development. In Marion Perlmutter (Ed.), Parent-child interactions and parent-child relations in child development. *The Minnesota Symposia on Child Psychology,* Vol. 17, Hillsdale, NJ: Erlbaum.

Clarke-Stewart, K. Alison, and **Fein, Greta G.** (1983). Early childhood programs. In Paul H. Mussen (Ed.), *Handbook of Child Psychology: Vol. 2. Infancy and developmental psychobiology.* New York: Wiley.

Clarkson, Marsha G., and **Berg, W. Keith.** (1983). Cardiac orienting and vowel discrimination in newborns: Crucial stimulus parameters. *Child Development, 54,* 162–171.

Clifford, Edward. (1971). Body satisfaction in adolescence. *Perceptual and Motor Skills, 33,* 119–125.

Clingempeel, W.G., and **Reppucci, N.D.** (1982). Joint custody after divorce: Major issues and goals for research. *Psychological Bulletin, 91,* 102–127.

Coates, Thomas J., Petersen, Anne C., and **Perry, Cheryl.** (1982). Crossing the barriers. In Thomas J. Coates, Anne C. Petersen, and Cheryl Perry, (Eds.). *Promoting adolescent health: A dialogue on research and practice.* New York: Academic Press.

Coffield, Frank. (1983). "Like father, like son": The family as a potential transmitter of deprivation. In Nicola Madge (Ed.), *Families at risk.* London: Heinemann.

Cohen, Sarale E., and **Parmalee, Arthur H.** (1983). Prediction of five year Stanford-Binet scores in preterm infants. *Child Development, 54,* 1242–1253.

Cohen, Leslie B., DeLoache, Judy S., and **Strauss, Mark S.** (1979). Infant visual perception. In Joy D. Osofsky (Ed.), *Handbook of infant development.* New York: Wiley.

Cohen, Stephen M., Allen, Martin G., Pollin, William, and **Hrubec, Zdenek.** (1972). Relationship of schizo-affective psychosis to manic depressive psychosis and schizophrenia. *Archives of General Psychiatry, 26* (6), 539–545.

Cohn, Anne H. (1983). The prevention of child abuse: What do we know about what works. In Jerome E. Leavitt (Ed.), *Child abuse and neglect: Research and innovation.* The Hague: Martinus Nijhoff.

Cohn, Jeffrey F. and **Tronick, Edward Z.** (1983). Three-month-old infants' reaction to simulated maternal depression. *Child Development, 54,* 185–193.

Coie, John D., and **Krehbiel, Gina.** (1984). Effects of academic tutoring on the social status of low-achieving, socially rejected children. *Child Development, 55,* 1465–1478.

Colby, Anne, Kohlberg, Lawrence, Gibbs, John, and **Lieberman, Marcus.** (1983). A longitudinal study of moral development. *Monographs of the Society for Research in Child Development, 48* (1–2, Serial No. 200).

Coleman, John C. (1980). Friendship and the peer group in adolescence. In Joseph Adelson, (Ed.), *Handbook of adolescent psychology.* New York: Wiley.

Coles, Robert. (1970) *Erik H. Erikson: The growth of his work.* Boston: Little, Brown.

Collins, J.K., and **LaGanza, S.** (1982). Self-recognition of the face: A study of adolescent narcissism. *Journal of Youth and Adolescence, 11,* 317–328.

Colman, Arthur, and **Colman, Libby.** (1977). *Pregnancy: The psychological experience.* New York: Bantam.

Colton, Raymond H., and **Steinschneider, A.** (1981) The cry characteristics of an infant who died of the Sudden Infant Death Syndrome. *Journal of Speech and Hearing Disorders, 46,* 359–363.

Condron, John C., and **Bode, Jerry G.** (1982). Rashomon, working wives, and family division of labor: Middletown, 1980. *Journal of Marriage and the Family, 44,* 421–439.

Conners, C.K. (1980). *Food additives and hyperactive children.* New York: Plenum.

Cook, Thomas D., Appleton, Hilary, Conner, Ross F., Shaffer, Ann, Tamkin, Gary, and **Weber, Stephen J.** (1975). *"Sesame Street" revisited.* New York: Russell Sage.

Cooley, Charles H. (1902). *Human nature and the social order.* New York: Scribners.

Cooper, Catherine R., Grotevant, Harold D., Moore, Mary Sue, and **Condon, Sherri M.** (1984). Predicting adolescent role-taking and identity exploration from family communication patterns: A comparison of one- and two-child families. In Toni Falbo (Ed.), *The single-child family*. New York: Guilford.

Coopersmith, Stanley. (1967). *The antecedents of self-esteem*. San Francisco: Freeman.

Corballis, Michael C. (1983). *Human Laterality*. New York: Academic Press.

Cordes, Colleen. (1985, June). Fields cooperate to study surveys. *APA Monitor, 16* (6), p. 32.

Cornell, Edward H. (1980). Distributed study facilitates infants' delayed recognition memory. *Memory and Cognition, 8,* 539–542.

Corrigan, Roberta L. (1978). Language development as related to Stage 6 object permanence development. *Journal of Child Language, 5,* 173–189.

Corrigan, Roberta L. (1983). The development of representational skills. In Kurt W. Fischer (Ed.), *Levels and transitions of children's development*. New Directions for Child Development, No. 21. San Francisco: Jossey-Bass.

Corter, Carl, Abramovitch, Rona, and **Pepler, Debra J.** (1983). The role of the mother in sibling interaction. *Child Development, 54,* 1599–1605.

Cottle, Thomas J. (1979). Adolescent voices. *Psychology Today, 12*(9), 43–44.

Cowan, Philip A. (1978). *Piaget, with feeling: Cognitive, social, and emotional dimensions*. New York: Holt, Rinehart and Winston.

Cox, Kathleen. (1983). Sex, adolescents, and the schools. In Geoff Lindsay (Ed.), *Problems of adolescence in the secondary school*. London: Croom Healm.

Crnic, Keith A., Ragozin, Arlene S., Greenberg, Mark T., Robinson, Nancy M., and **Basham, Robert B.** (1983). Social interaction and developmental competence of preterm and full term infants during the first year of life. *Child Development, 54,* 1199–1210.

Crockenberg, Susan. (1983). Early mother and infant antecedents of Bayley Scale Performance at 21 months. *Developmental Psychology, 19,* 727–730.

Cronbach, Lee J. (1984). *Essentials of Psychological Testing* (4th ed.). New York: Harper and Row.

Cunningham, C.E. and **Barkeley R.A.** (1978). The role of academic failure in hyperactive behavior. *Journal of Learning Disabilities, 11,* 15–21.

Curtiss, Susan R. (1977). *Genie: A linguistic study of a modern-day "wild child."* New York: Academic Press.

Damon, William. (1977). *The social world of the child*. San Francisco: Jossey-Bass.

Damon, William. (1984). Self understanding and moral development from childhood to adolescence. In William M. Kurtines and Jacob L. Gewirtz (Eds.), *Morality, moral behavior, and moral development*. New York: Wiley.

Danforth, David N. (Ed.). (1977). *Obstetrics and gynecology*, 3rd ed. New York: Harper & Row.

Daniels, Denise, and **Plomin, Robert.** (1985). Origins of individual differences in infant shyness. *Developmental Psychology, 21,* 118–121.

Daniels, Denise, Dunn, Judy, Furstenberg, Frank F., Jr., and **Plomin, Robert.** (1985). Environmental differences within the family and adjustment difference within pairs of adolescent siblings. *Child Development, 56,* 764–774.

Dasen, P. R. (Ed.).(1977). *Piagetian psychology: Cross-cultural contributions*. New York: Gardner.

Dasen, P.R., and **Heron A.** (1981). Cross-cultural tests of Piaget's theory. In Harry C. Triandis and A. Heron, (Eds.), *Handbook of cross-cultural psychology: Vol. 4. Developmental psychology*. Boston: Allyn and Bacon.

Davenport-Slack, Barbara, and **Boylan, Claire Hamblin.** (1974). Psychological correlates of childbirth pain. *Psychosomatic Medicine 36,* 215–223.

Davies, P.A. (1976). Infants of very low birth weight: An appraisal of some aspects of their present neonatal care and of their later prognosis. In D. Hull (Ed.), *Recent advances in pediatrics*. Edinburgh: Churchill Livingstone.

Davis, Elizabeth. (1983). *A Guide to midwifery: Heart and hands*. New York: Bantam.

Davis, Janet M., and **Rovee-Collier, Carolyn K.** (1983). Alleviated forgetting of a learned contingency in 8-week-old infants. *Developmental Psychology, 19,* 353–365.

DeCasper, Anthony J., and **Fifer, William P.** (1980). Of human bonding: Newborns prefer their mothers' voices. *Science, 208,* 1174–1175.

de Hirsch, Katrina, Jansky, Jeannette Jefferson, and **Langford, William S.** (1966). *Predicting reading failure: A preliminary study of reading, writing, and spelling disabilities in preschool children*. New York: Harper and Row.

deMause, Lloyd. (1975). The evolution of childhood. In Lloyd deMause (Ed.), *The history of childhood*. New York: Harper and Row.

Denney, Nancy Wadsworth, Zeytinoglu, Sezen, and **Selzer, S. Claire.** (1977). Conservation training in four-year-old children. *Journal of Experimental Child Psychology, 24,* 129–146.

Dennis, Wayne. (1973). *Children of the crèche*. New York: Appleton-Century-Crofts.

Deno, E.N. (Ed.).(1973). *Instructional alternatives for exceptional children*. Arlington, VA: Council for Exceptional Children.

Derdeyn, Andre, and **Scott, Elizabeth.** (1984). Joint custody: A critical analysis and appraisal. *American Journal of Orthopsychiatry, 54,* 199–209.

DeStefano, C.T., and **Mueller, E.** (1982). Environmental determinants of peer social activity in 18-month-old males. *Infant Behavior and Development, 5,* 175–183.

Deutsch, Helene. (1944–1945). *The psychology of women: A psychoanalytic interpretation*. (Vol. 2). New York: Grune and Stratton.

de Villiers, J.G. (1980). The process of rule learning in children: A new look. In K. E. Nelson (Ed.), *Children's language* (Vol. 2). New York: Gardner Press.

de Villiers, Jill G., and **de Villiers, Peter A.** (1973). A cross-sectional study of the acquisition of grammatical morphemes in child speech. *Journal of Psycholinguistic Research, 2,* 267–278.

de Villiers, Jill G., and **de Villiers, Peter A.** (1978). *Lanugage acquisition.* Cambridge, MA: Harvard University Press.

de Villiers, Peter A., and **de Villiers, Jill G.** (1979). *Early language.* Cambridge, MA: Harvard University Press.

Diaz, Rafael M. (1985). Bilingual cognitive development: Addressing three gaps in current research. *Child Development, 56,* 1376–1388.

Dick-Read, Grantly. (1972). *Childbirth without fear: The original approach to natural childbirth.* Rev. ed. Helen Wessel and Harlan F. Ellis (Eds.). New York: Harper & Row.

Dietz, William H., Jr., and **Gortmaker, Steven L.** (1985). Do we fatten our children at the television set? Obesity and television viewing in children and adolescents. *Pediatrics, 75,* 807–812.

DiGeorge, Angelo M. (1983). The endocrine system. In Richard E. Behrman and Victor C. Vaughn III (Eds.), *Pediatrics.* Philadelphia: Saunders.

DiPietro, Janet Ann. (1981). Rough and tumble play. A function of gender. *Developmental Psychology, 17,* 50–58.

Dockrell, J., Campbell, R., and **Neilson, I.** (1980). Conservation accidents revisited. *International Journal of Behavioral Development, 3,* 423–439.

Dodge, Kenneth A., Murphy, Roberta R., and **Buchsbaum, Kathy.** (1984). The assessment of intention-cue detection skills in children: Implications for developmental psychopathology. *Child Development, 55,* 163–173.

Doherty, William J., and **Baird, Macaran A.** (1983). *Family therapy and family medicine.* New York: Guilford.

Doman, Glenn. (1980) *Teach your baby to read:* Chatto Bodley Jonathan.

Donaldson, Margaret. (1978). *Children's minds.* London: Fontana.

Donaldson, Margaret. (1982). Conservation: what is the question? *British Journal of Educational Psychology, 73,* 199–207.

Donaldson, Margaret, Grieve, Robert, and **Pratt, Chris.** (1983). General introduction. In Margeret Donaldson, Robert Grieve, and Chris Pratt (Eds.), *Early childhood development and education: Readings in psychology.* New York: Guilford.

Donovan, Bonnie. (1977). *The Cesarean birth experience: A practical, comprehensive, and reassuring guide for parents and professionals.* Boston: Beacon Press.

Douvan, Elizabeth, and **Adelson, Joseph.** (1966). *The adolescent experience.* New York: Wiley.

Dronamraju, Krishna R. (1974). Multigenic inheritance. In Daniel Bergsma (Ed.), *Medical genetics today.* Baltimore: Johns Hopkins Press, 250–254.

Droogers, Andre. (1980). *The dangerous journey: Symbolic aspects of boys' initiation among the Wagenia of Kisangani, Zaire.* The Hague: Mouton.

Dryfoos, Joy G. (1982). Contraceptive use, pregnancy intentions, and pregnancy outcomes among U.S. women. *Family Planning Perspectives, 14* (2), 81–94.

Dryfoos, Joy G. (1984). A new strategy for preventing unintended teenage childbearing. *Family Planning Perspectives, 16,* 193–195.

Dubey, Dennis R., O'Leary, Susan G., and **Kaufman, Kenneth F.** (1983). Training parents of hyperactive children in child management: A comparative outcome study. *Journal of Abnormal Child Psychology, 11,* 229–246.

Ducat, Diane E. (1980). Cooperative education, career exploration and occupational concepts for community college students. *Journal of Vocational Behavior, 17,* 195–203.

Duckworth, Eleanor. (1972). The having of wonderful ideas. *Harvard Educational Review, 42,* 217–231.

Duffey, James, Salvia, John, Tucker, James, and **Ysseldyke, James E.** (1981). Nonbiased assessment: A need for operationalism. *Exceptional Children, 47,* 427–434.

Duncan, Beverly, and **Duncan, Otis Dudley.** (1978). *Sex typing and social roles: A research report.* New York: Academic Press.

Dunn, Lloyd M. (Ed.). (1973). *Exceptional children in the schools: Special education in transition* (2nd Ed.). New York: Holt, Rinehart and Winston.

Dunn, Judy, and **Kendrick, Carol.** (1982). Siblings: *Love, envy and understanding.* Cambridge, MA: Harvard University Press.

Dunn, Judy, and **Kendrick, Carol.** (1982). The speech of two- and three-year-olds to infant siblings: "Baby talk" and the context of communication. *Journal of Child Lanugage, 9,* 579–595.

Dunn, Judy, and **Kendrick, Carol.** (1982). *Siblings: Love, envy and understanding.* Cambridge: Harvard University Press.

Dunn, Judy, and **Munn, Penny.** (1985). Becoming a family member: Family conflict and the development of social understanding in the second year. *Child Development, 56,* 480–492.

Dunphy, Dexter C. (1963). The social structure of urban adolescent peer groups. *Sociometry, 26,* 230–246.

Dutcher, Nadine. (1981). *The use of first and second languages in primary education: Selected case studies.* Education Department of the World Bank. (Cited in Rotberg, 1982).

Dweck, Carol S. and **Elliott, Elaine S.** (1983). Achievement motivation. In Paul H. Mussen (Ed.), *Handbook of child psychology: Vol. 4. Socialization and personality development.* New York: Wiley.

Eaton, Warren O. *Motor activity from fetus to adult.* Paper, 1983.

Eckholm, Erick. (1985, October 20). Experts predict almost every child will be vaccinated by 1990. *The New York Times,* p.16.

Edgerton, Robert B. (1979). *Mental Retardation.* Cambridge, MA: Harvard University Press.

Egan, Jane (1976). Object-play in cats. In Jerome S. Bruner, Alison Jolly, and Kathy Sylva (Eds.), *Play.* New York: Basic Books.

Egeland, Brian and **Farber, Ellen A.** (1984). Infant-mother attachment: Factors related to its development and changes over time. *Child Development, 55,* 753-771.

Eichorn, Dorothy H. (1979). Physical development: Current foci of research. In Joy D. Osofsky (Ed.) *Handbook of infant development.* New York: Wiley.

Eichorn, Dorothy H., Clausen, John A., Haan, Norma, Honzick, Marjorie P., and **Mussen, Paul H.** (Eds.). (1981). *Present and past in middle life.* New York: Academic Press.

Eimas, Peter D., Sigueland, Einar R., Jusczyk, Peter, and **Vigorito, James.** (1971). Speech perception in infants. *Science, 171,* 303-306.

Eisenberg, Nancy. (1982). *The development of prosocial behavior.* New York: Academic Press.

Eisenberg, Nancy, Lunch, Teresa, Shell, Rita, and **Roth,Karlsson.** (1985). Children's justifications for their adult and peer-direction compliant (prosocial and nonprosocial) behaviors. *Developmental Psychology, 21,* 325-331.

Eisenberg-Berg, Nancy, Boothby, Rita, and **Matson, Tom.** (1979). Correlates of preschool girls feminine and masculine toy preferences. *Developmental Psychology, 48,* 1411-1416.

Ekholm, Mats. (1984). Readiness to help others and tolerance: Attitude development during the school years and a ten-year comparison. *Scandinavian Journal of Educational Research, 28,* 71-86.

Ekman, P., and **Freisen W.** (1976). Measuring facial movement. *Environmental Psychology and Verbal Behavior, 1,* 56-75.

Ekman, P., and **Friesen, W.** (1978). *Facial action coding system.* Palo Alto, CA: Consulting Psychologists Press.

Ekman, P., Sorenson, E., and **Friesen, W.** (1969). Pancultural elements in the facial expression of emotion. *Science, 164,* 86-88.

Elardo, Richard, Bradley, Robert, and **Caldwell, Bettye M.** (1975). The relation of infants' home environments to mental test performance from six to thirty-six months. A longitudinal analysis. *Child Development, 46,* 71-76.

Elardo, Richard, Bradley, Robert, and **Caldwell, Bettye M.** (1977). A longitudinal study of the relation of infants' home environments to language development at age three. *Child Development,48,* 595-603.

Elder, Glen H., Jr. (1962) Structural variations in the child-rearing relationship. *Sociometry, 25,* 241-262.

Elder, Glen H., Jr. (1974). *Children of the Great Depression.* Chicago: University of Chicago Press.

Elder, Glen H., Jr. (1980). *Family structure and socialization.* New York: Arno Press.

Elder, Glen H., Jr. (1980). Adolescence in historical perspective. In Joseph Adelson, (Ed.), *Handbook of adolescent psychology.* New York: Wiley.

Elder, Glen H., Jr., Nguyen, Tri Van, and **Caspi, Avshalom.** (1985). Linking family hardship to children's lives. *Child Development, 56,* 361-375.

Elkind, David. (1969). Piagetian and psychometric conceptions of intelligence. *Harvard Educational Review, 39,* 319-337.

Elkind, David. (1974). *Children and adolescents: Interpretive essays on Jean Piaget.* New York: Oxford University Press.

Elkind, David. (1978). *The child's reality: Three developmental themes.* Hillsdale, NJ: Erlbaum.

Elkind, David. (1979). *The child and society.* New York: Oxford University Press.

Elkind, David. (1981). *The hurried child: Growing up too fast too soon.* Reading, MA: Addison-Wesley.

Elkind, David. (1981). *Children and adolescents: Interpretive essays on Jean Piaget* (3rd ed.). New York: Oxford University Press.

Elkind, David, and **Bowen, R.** (1979). Imaginary audience behavior in children and adolescents. *Developmental Psychology, 15,* 38-44.

Emde, Robert N., and **Harmon, R.J.** (1972). Endogenous and exogenous smiling systems in early infancy. *Journal of the American Academy of Child Psychiatry, 11,* 77-100.

Emery, Alan E.H. (1983). *Elements of medical genetics* (6th ed.) Edinburgh: Churchill Livingstone.

Emery, Donald G. (1975). *Teach your preschooler to read.* New York: Simon and Schuster.

Emery, Robert E., Hetherington, E. Mavis, and **Dilalla, Lisabeth F.** (1984). Divorce, children, and social policy. In Harold W. Stevenson and Alberta E. Siegel (Eds.), *Child development research and social policy.* Chicago: University of Chicago Press.

Endo, R., Sue, S., and **Wagner, N.N.** (Eds.). (1980). *Asian-Americans: Social and psychological perspectives.* Palo Alto, CA: Science and Behavior Books.

Enkin, M.W., Smith, S.L., Dermer, S.W., and **Emmett, J.O.** (1972). An adequately controlled study of the effectiveness of PPM training. In Norman Morris (ed.), *Psychosomatic medicine in obstetrics and gynecology.* Basel: Karger.

Entwisle, Doris R., and **Baker, David P.** (1983). Gender and young children's expectations for performance in arithmetic. *Developmental Psychology, 19,* 200-209.

Erikson, Erik H. (1963). *Childhood and society.* (2nd ed.). New York: Norton.

Erikson, Erik H. (1964). A memorandum on identity and Negro youth. *Journal of social issues, 20,* 29-42.

Erikson, Erik H. (1968). *Identity, youth, and crisis.* New York: Norton.

Erikson, Erik H. (1975). *Life history and the historical moment.* New York: Norton.

Eriksson, Bengt O. (1976). The child in sport and physical activity: Medical aspects. In J.G. Albinson and G.M. Andrew (Eds.), *Child in sport and physical activity.* Baltimore: University Park Press, 43-66.

Erlenmeyer-Kimling, L. and **Jarvik, Lissy F.** (1963). Genetics and intelligence: A review. *Science, 142,* 1477–1479.

Eron, Leonard D., Huesmann, L. Rowell, Brice, Patrick, Fischer, Paulette, and **Mermelstein, Rebecca.** (1983). Age trends in the development of aggression, sex typing, and related television habits. *(Developmental Psychology, 19,* 71–77.

Ervin, Susan. (1964). Imitation and structural change in children's language. In Eric Lenneberg (Ed.), *New directions in the study of language.* Cambridge, MA: MIT Press.

Espenshade, T.J. (1979). The economic consequences of divorce. *Journal of Marrriage and the Family, 41,* 615–625.

Etaugh, Claire. (1974). Effects of maternal employment on children: A review of recent research. *Merrill-Palmer Quarterly, 20,* 71–98.

Evans, D. (1983). *Understanding infinity and zero in the early school years.* Doctoral dissertation, University of Pennsylvania. [Cited in Gelman and Baillargeon (1983).]

Evans, Richard I., and **Raines, Bettye E.** (1982). Control and prevention of smoking in adolescents. In Thomas J. Coates, Anne C. Petersen, and Cheryl Perry (Eds.), *Promoting adolescent health: A dialogue on research and practice.* New York: Academic Press.

Eveleth, Phillis B., and **Tanner, James M.** (1976). *Worldwide variation in human growth.* Cambridge, England: Cambridge University Press.

Fabricius, William V., and **Wellman, Henry M.** (1983). Children's understanding of retrieval cue utilization. *Developmental Psychology, 19,* 15–21.

Fagot, Beverly L. (1978). The influence of sex of child on parental reactions to toddler children. *Child Development, 49,* 459–465.

Fagot, Beverly L. (1982). Adults as socializing agents. In Tiffany M. Field, Aletha Huston, Herbert C. Quay, Lillian Troll, Gordon E. Finley (Eds.), *Review of human development,* New York: Wiley.

Falbo, Toni. (1984). Only children: A review. In Toni Falbo (Ed.), *The single-child family.* New York: Guilford.

Fantz, Robert. (1961). The origin of form perception. *Scientific American, 204* (5), 66–72.

Fantz, Robert L., Fagan, J.F., and **Miranda, S.B.** (1975). Early visual selectivity. In Leslie B. Cohen and Philip Salapatek (Eds.), *Infant perception: From sensation to cognition.* New York: Academic Press.

Farel, Anita M. (1980). Effects of preferred maternal roles, maternal employment, and socio-demographic status on school adjustment and competence. *Child Development, 51,* 1179–1186.

Farkas, G., Smith, D.A., and **Stromsdorfer, E.W.** (1983). The youth entitlement demonstration: Subsidized employment with a schooling requirement. *Journal of Human Resources, 18,* 557–573.

Farnham-Diggory, Sylvia. (1978). *Learning disabilities.* Cambridge, Mass.: Harvard University Press.

Fasick, Frank A. (1984). Parents, peers, youth culture and autonomy in adolescence. *Adolescence, 19,* 143–157.

Faust, Margaret S. (1983). Alternative constructions of adolescent growth. In Jeanne Brooks-Gunn and Anne C. Petersen (Eds.), *Girls at puberty: Biological and psychosocial aspects.* New York: Plenum.

Feather, Norman T. (1980). Values in adolescence. In Joseph Adelson (Ed.), *Handbook of adolescent psychology.* New York: Wiley.

Featherstone, Helen. (1980). *A difference in the family.* New York: Basic Books.

Featherstone, Joseph. (1971). *Schools where children learn.* New York: Liveright.

Fein, Greta G., Schwartz, Pamela M., Jacobson, Sandra W., and **Jacobson, Joseph L.** (1983). Environmental toxins and behavioral development: A new role for psychological research. *American Psychologist, 38,* 1188–1197.

Feingold, Benjamin F. (1974). *Why your child is hyperactive.* New York: Random House.

Feiring, Candice, and **Lewis, Michael.** (1984). Changing characteristics of the U.S. family: Implications for family networks, relationships, and child development. In Michael Lewis (Ed.), *Beyond the dyad.* New York: Plenum.

Feldman, David Henry. (1980). *Beyond universals in cognitive development.* Norwood, NJ: Ablex.

Feldman, Ben H., and **Rosenkrantz, Arthur L.** (1977). Drug use by college students and their parents. *Addictive Diseases: An International Journal, 3,* 235–241.

Feldman, S. Shirley, Biringen, Zeynap C., and **Nash, Sharon Churnin.** (1981). Fluctuations of sex-related self-attributions as a function of stage of family life cycle. *Developmental Psychology, 17,* 24–35.

Feldstein, Jerome H., and **Feldstein, Sandra.** (1982). Sex differences on televised toy commercials. *Sex Roles, 8,* 581–587.

Felton, Gary, and **Segelman, Florrie.** (1978). Lamaze childbirth training and change in belief about personal control. *Birth and the family journal, 5,* 141–150.

Ferguson, Charles A. (1977). Baby talk as a simplified register. In Catherine E. Snow and Charles A. Ferguson (Eds.), *Talking to children: Language input and requisition.* Cambridge, England: Cambridge University Press.

Ferree, Myra M. (1976). Working class jobs: Housework and paid work as sources of satisfaction. *Social Problems, 23,* 431–441.

Ferster, Charles B., and **Skinner, B. F.** (1957). *Schedules of reinforcement.* New York: Appleton-Century-Crofts.

Field, Dorothy. (1981). Can preschool children really learn to conserve? *Child Development, 52,* 326–334.

Field, Tiffany M. (1977). Effects of early separation, interactive deficits, and experimental manipulation on mother-infant face-to-face interaction. *Child Development, 48,* 763–771.

Field, Tiffany M. (1979). Infant behavior directed at peers in the presence and absence of mother. *Infant behavior and development, 2,* 47–54.

Field, Tiffany M. (1980). Interactions of high risk infants: Quantitative and qualitative differences. In D.B. Sawin, R.C. Hawkins, L.P. Walker, and J.H. Penticuff (Eds.), *Exceptional infant: Vol. 4. Psychosocial risks in infant environmental transactions*. New York: Brunner/Mazel.

Field, Tiffany M. (1981). Gaze behavior of normal and high-risk infants during early interactions. *Journal of the American Academy of Child Psychiatry, 20*, 308–317.

Field, Tiffany M. (1982). Individual differences in the expressivity of neonates and young infants. In R. Feldman (Ed.), *Development of nonverbal behavior in children*. New York: Springer-Verlag.

Field, Tiffany M., and **Reite, Martin.** (1984). Children's responses to separation from mother during the birth of another child. *Child Development, 55*, 1308–1316.

Field, Tiffany M., and **Roopnarine, Jaipaul L.** (1982). Infant-peer interactions. In Tiffany M. Field, Aletha Huston, Herbert C. Quay, Lillian Troll, and Gordon E. Finley (Eds.), *Review of Human Development*, New York: Wiley.

Field, Tiffany M., Dempsey, J.R., and **Shuman, H.H.** (1981). Developmental follow-up of preterm and post term infants. In S.L. Friedman and Marian Sigman (Eds.), *Preterm birth and psychological handicap*. New York: Academic Press.

Field, Tiffany M., Gewirtz, Jacob L., Cohen, Debra, Garcia, Robert, Greenberg, Reena, and **Kerry, Collins.** (1984). Leave-takings and reunions of infants, toddlers, preschoolers, and their parents. *Child Development, 55*, 628–634

Field, Tiffany M., Schanberg, Saul M., Scafidi, Frank, Bauer, Charles R., Vega-Lahr, Nitza, Garcia, Robert, Nystrom, Jerome, and **Kuhn, Cynthia M.** (1985). Effects of tactile/kinesthetic stimulation on preterm neonates. *Pediatrics*, in press.

Fincher, Jack. (1977). *Sinister people: The looking-glass world of the left-hander: A scientific shaggy-dog story*. New York: Putnam.

Finkelhor, David. (1979a). *Sexually victimized children*. New York: Free Press.

Finkelhor, David. (1979b). What's wrong with sex between adults and children? Ethics and the problems of sexual abuse. *American Journal of Orthopsychiatry, 49*, 692–697.

Finkelhor, David. (1984). *Child sexual abuse: New theory and practice*. New York: Free Press.

Fischer, Kurt W. (1980). A theory of cognitive development: The control of hierarchies of skill. *Psychological Review, 87*, 477–531.

Fischer, Kurt W., and **Roberts, R.J.** (1983). *A developmental sequence of classification skills in preschool children*. Unpublished. Cited in Gelman and Baillargeon.

Fisher, W. M., Huttel, F. A., Mitchell, I., and **Meyer, A. E.** (1972). The efficacy of the psychoprophylactic method of prepared childbirth. In Norman Morris (Ed.), *Psychosomatic medicine in obstetrics and gynecology*. Basel: Karger.

Fitzgerald, Hiram E., and **Brackbill, Yvonne.** (1976). Classical conditioning in infancy: Development and constraints. *Psychological Bulletin, 83*, 353–376.

Flavell, John H. (1963). *The developmental psychology of Jean Piaget*. Princeton, NJ: Van Nostrand.

Flavell, John H. (1975). *The development of role-taking and communication skills in children*. Huntington, NY: Krieger (originally published by Wiley, 1968).

Flavell, John H. (1970). Developmental studies of mediated memory. In Hayne W. Reese and Lewis P. Lipsitt (Eds.), *Advances in child development and behavior* (Vol. 5). New York: Academic Press, 182–211.

Flavell, John H. (1977). *Cognitive development*. Englewood Cliffs, NJ: Prentice-Hall.

Flavell, John H. (1982). Structures, stages, and sequences in cognitive development. In W. Andrew Collins (Ed.), *The concept of development: The Minnesota symposia on child psychology*. Vol. XV. Hillsdale, NJ: Erlbaum.

Flavell, John H. (1985). Cognitive development (2nd ed.). Englewood Cliffs, NJ: Prentice-Hall.

Flavell, John H., and **Markman, Ellen M.** (1983). Preface to Volume III. Paul H. Mussen (Ed.), *Handbook of child psychology: Vol. 3. Cognitive development*. New York: Wiley.

Flavell, John H., and **Ross, Lee** (Eds.). (1981). *Social cognitive development: Frontiers and possible futures*. Cambridge: Cambridge University Press.

Flavell, John H., Speer, James Ramsey, Green, Frances L., August, Diane L. (1981). The development of comprehension monitoring and knowledge about communication. *Monograph of the Society for Research in Child Development*. Serial no. 192, *46* (5).

Flynn, T. M., and **Flynn, L. A.** (1978). Evaluation of the predictive ability of five screening measures administered during kindergarten. *Journal of Experimental Education, 46*, 65–69.

Foege, William H. (1985). Preface. National Research Council (Ed.). Injury in America: A continuing public health problem. Washington DC: National Academy Press.

Ford, Clellan S., and **Beach, Frank A.** (1951). *Patterns of sexual behavior*. New York: Harper.

Forness, Steven R., Sinclair, Esther, and **Russell, Andrew T.** (1984). Serving children with emotional or behavior disorders: Implications for educational policy. *American Journal of Orthopsychiatry, 54*, 22–32.

Fraiberg, Selma. (1968). *The magic years*. New York: Scribner.

Frankenburg, William K., and **Dodds, Josiah B.** (1967). The Denver Developmental Screening Test. *Journal of Pediatrics, 71*(3), 181–191.

Frankenburg, W.K., Frandal, A. Sciarillo, W., and **Burgerss, D.** (1981). The newly abbreviated and revised Denver Developmental Screening Test. *Journal of Pediatrics, 99*, 995–999.

Franklin, Deborah. (1984). Rubella threatens unborn in vaccine gap. *Science News, 125*, 186.

French, Doran C. (1984). Children's knowledge of the social functions of younger, older, and same-age peers. *Child Development, 55*, 1429–1433.

Freud, Anna. (1968). Adolescence. In A.E. Winder and D.L. Angus (Eds.), *Adolescence: Contemporary studies*. New York: American Books.

Freud, Sigmund. (1963). *Three case histories.* New York: Collier. (Originally published 1918).

Freud, Sigmund. (1965). *New introductory lectures on psychoanalysis.* James Strachey (Ed. and Trans.). New York: Norton, 1965. (Original work published 1933.)

Freud, Sigmund. (1960). *A general introduction to psychoanalysis,* Joan Riviare (Trans.). New York: Washington Square Press. (Original work published 1935.)

Freud, Sigmund. (1938). *The basic writings of Sigmund Freud.* A.A. Brill (Ed. and Trans.). New York: Modern Library.

Freud, Sigmund. (1964). *An outline of psychoanalysis: Vol. 23, The standard edition of the complete psychological works of Sigmund Freud.* J. Strachey (Ed. and Trans.), London: Hogarth Press. (Original work published 1940.)

Freud, Sigmund. (1947). *On war, sex, and neurosis.* New York: Arts and Sciences Press.

Frisch, Rose E. (1983). Fatness, puberty, and fertility: The efects of nutrition and physical training on menarche and ovulation. In Jeanne Brooks-Gunn and Anne C. Petersen (Eds.), *Girls at puberty: Biological and psychosocial aspects.* New York: Plenum.

Frisch, Rose E., and **Revelle, Roger.** (1970). Height and weight at menarche and a hypothesis of critical body weights and adolescent events. *Science, 169,* 397–399.

Fritz, Janet, and **Wetherbee, Sally.** (1982). Preschoolers' beliefs regarding the obese individual. *Canadian Home Economics Journal, 33,* 193–196.

Fuhrmann, Walter, and **Vogel, Friedrich.** (1983). *Genetic counseling* (3rd. ed.). New York: Springer-Verlag.

Furstenberg, Frank F., Jr. (1976). *Unplanned parenthood: The social consequences of teenage childbearing.* New York: Free Press.

Furstenberg, Frank F., Jr., Spanier, G.B., and **Rothschild, N.** (1982). Patterns in parenting in the transition from divorce to remarriage. In P.W. Berman and E.R. Ramey (Eds.), *Women in a developmental perspective.* (NIH publication no. 82-2298) Washington DC.

Gadverry, Sharon. (1980). Effects of restricting first graders' TV viewing on leisure time use, IQ change, and cognitive style. *Journal of Applied Developmental Psychology, 1,* 45–57.

Gaensbauer, Theodore J. (1980). Anaclitic depression in a three-and-a-half month old child. *American Journal of Psychiatry. 137,* 841–842.

Galambos, N.L., and **Garbarino, John.** (1983, July-August). Identifying the missing links in the study of latchkey children. *Children Today,* pp. 2–4, 40–41.

Galinsky, Ellen. (1981). *Between generations: The six stages of parenthood.* New York: Berkley.

Gallatin, Judith. (1980). Political thinking in adolescence. In Joseph Adelson (Ed.), *Handbook of adolescent psychology.* New York: Wiley.

Gallup, Gordon G., Jr., (1977). Self-recognition in primates: A comparative approach to the bidirectional properties of consciousness. *American Psychologist, 32,* 329–338.

Gallup, George, Jr. (1984, March). *Religion in America.* Gallup Report No. 222.

Garbarino, James. (1976). A preliminary study of some ecological correlates of child abuse: The impact of socioeconomic stress on mothers. *Child Development, 47,* 178–185.

Garbarino, James, Sebes, Janet, and **Schellenbach, Cynthia.** (1984). Families at risk for destructive parent-child relations in adolescence. *Child Development, 55,* 174–183.

Gardner, Howard. (1980). *Artful scribbles: The significance of children's drawings.* New York: Basic Books.

Gardner, Howard. (1982). *Art, mind and brain: A cognitive approach to creativity.* New York: Basic Books.

Gardner, Howard. (1983). *Frames of mind: The theory of multiple intelligences.* New York: Basic Books.

Gardner, Lytt I. (1972). Deprivation dwarfism. *Scientific American, 227* (1), 76–82.

Gardner, William I. (1977). *Learning and behavior characteristics of exceptional children and youth: A humanistic behavioral approach.* Boston: Allyn & Bacon.

Garmezy, Norman. (1976). Vulnerable and invulnerable children: Theory, research, and intervention. Abstracted in the Journal Supplement Abstract Service, *Catalog of Selected Documents in Psychology, 6* (4), 96.

Garmezy, Norman, Masten, Ann, Nordstrom, Lynn, and **Ferrarese, Michael.** (1979). The nature of competence in normal and deviant children. In Martha Whalen Kent and Jon E. Rolf (Eds.), *Primary prevention of psychopathology: Vol. III. Social competence in children.* Hanover, NH: University Press of New England.

Garvey, Catherine. (1976). Some properties of social play. In Jerome S. Bruner, Alison Jolly, and Kathy Sylva (Eds.), *Play.* New York: Basic Books.

Garvey, Catherine. (1977). *Play.* Cambridge, MA: Harvard University Press.

Garvey, Catherine. (1984). *Children's talk.* Cambridge, MA: Harvard University Press.

Gasser, R.D., and **Taylor, C.M.** (1976). Role adjustment of single parent fathers with dependent children. *Family Coordinator, 25,* 397–401.

Gelles, Richard J. (1975). Violence and pregnancy: A note on the extent of the problem and needed services. *Family Coordinator, 24,* 81–86.

Gelles, Richard J. (1978). Violence toward children in the United States. *American Journal of Orthopsychiatry, 48,* 580–592.

Gelman, Rochel. (1982). Assessing one-to-one correspondence: Still another paper on conservation. *British Journal of Psychology, 73,* 209–220.

Gelman, Rochel, and **Baillargeon, Renee.** (1983). A review of some Piagetian Concepts. In Paul H. Mussen (Ed.), *Handbook of child psychology: Vol. 3. Cognitive development.* New York: Wiley.

Gelman, Rochel, and **Gallistel, C.R.** (1978). The child's understanding of number. Cambridge, MA: Harvard University Press.

Gelman, Rochel and **Spelke, Elizabeth.** (1981). The development of thoughts about animate and inanimate objects: Implications for research on social cognition. In John H. Flavell and Lee Ross (Eds.), *Social cognitive development: Frontiers and possible futures.* Cambridge, England: Cambridge University Press.

Gelman, Rochel, Maccoby, Eleanor, and **LeVine, Robert.** (1982). Complexity in development and developmental studies. In W. Andrew Collins (Ed.), *The concept of development.* Minnesota Symposia on Child Psychology (Vol. 15), Hillsdale, NJ: Erlbaum.

Genishi, Celie, and **Dyson, Anne Haas.** (1984). *Language Assessment in the Early Years.* Norwood, NJ: Ablex.

George, Victor, and **Wilding, Paul.** (1972). *Motherless families.* London: Routledge and Kegan Paul.

Gesell, Arnold. (1926). *The Mental Growth of the Pre-school child: A psychological outline of normal development from birth to the sixth year including a system of developmental diagnosis.* New York: Macmillan.

Gesell, Arnold, and **Amatruda, Catherine S.** (1947). *Developmental diagnosis: Normal and abnormal child development, clinical methods and pediatric applications.* 2nd ed. New York: Hoeber.

Gesell, Arnold, and **Ilg, Frances L.** (1946). *The child from five to ten.* New York: Harper.

Gesell, Arnold, Ames, Louise Bates, and **Ilg, Frances L.** (1977). *The child from five to ten.* (Rev. ed.). New York: Harper & Row.

Gibson, Eleanor J. (1982). The concept of affordances in Development: The renascence of functionalism. In W. Andrew Collins (Ed.), *The Concept of Development: The Minnesota Symposia on Child Psychology,* (Vol. 15), Hillsdale, NJ: Erlbaum.

Gibson, James J. (1979). The ecological approach to visual perception. Boston: Houghton-Mifflin.

Gibson, Eleanor J. and **Levin, Harry.** (1975). *The psychology of reading.* Cambridge, MA: MIT Press.

Gibson, Eleanor J., and **Walk, Richard D.** (1960). The "visual cliff." *Scientific American, 202* (4), 64–72.

Giles-Sims, Jean, and **Finkelhor, David.** (1984). Child abuse in stepfamilies. *Family Relations, 33,* 407–413.

Gilligan, Carol. (1982). *In a different voice: Psychological theory and women's development.* Cambridge, MA: Harvard University Press.

Gilmartin, Brian G. (1985). Some family antecedents of severe shyness. *Family Relations, 34,* 429–438.

Ginsburg, Harvey J., and **Miller, Shirley M.** (1982). Sex differences in children's risk-taking behavior. *Child Development, 53,* 426–428.

Gleason, Jean Berko. (1967). Do children imitate? *Proceedings of the International Conference on Oral Education of the Deaf, 2,* 1441–1448.

Glick, Paul C. (1979). Children of divorced parents in demographic perspective. *Journal of Social Issues, 32,* 112–125.

Glick, Paul C. (1984). Marriage, divorce, and living arrangements: Prospective changes. *Journal of Family Issues, 5,* 7–26.

Goad, Walter B., Robinson, Arthur, and **Puck, Theodore T.** (1976). Incidence of aneuploidy in a human population. *American Journal of Human Genetics, 28,* 62–68.

Goertzel, Mildred, and **Goertzel, Victor.** (1978). *Three hundred eminent personalities: A psychosocial analysis of the famous.* San Francisco: Jossey Bass.

Goetz, T.E., and **Dweck, Carol.** (1980). Learned helplessness in social situations. *Journal of Personality and Social Psychology, 39,* 246–255.

Gold, Delores, and **Andres, David.** (1978). Developmental comparisons between ten-year-old children with employed and nonemployed mothers. *Child Development, 49,* 75–84.

Gold, Martin, and **Petronio, Richard J.** (1980). Delinquent behavior in adolescence. In Joseph Adelson (Ed.), *Handbook of adolescent psychology.* New York: Wiley.

Goldberg, Susan. (1983). Parent-infant bonding: Another look. *Child Development, 54,* 1355–1382.

Goldberg, Susan, and **Lewis, Michael.** (1969). Play behavior in the year-old infant: Early sex differences. *Child Development, 40,* 21–31.

Goldberg, Susan, LaCombe, Suzanne, Levinson, Dvora, Parker K., Ross, Christopher, and **Goldenring, John M.** (1985). Thinking about the threat of nuclear war: Relevance to mental health. *American Journal of Orthopsychiatry, 55,* 502–512.

Golden, M., and **Birns, B.** (1976). Social class and infant intelligence. In Michael Lewis (Ed.), *Origins of intelligence.* New York: Plenum.

Goldman, Ronald, and **Goldman, Juliette.** (1982). *Children's sexual thinking.* London: Routledge and Kegan Paul.

Goldsmith, H. Hill. (1983). Genetic influences on personality from infancy to adulthood. *Child Development, 54,* 331–355.

Goldsmith, H. Hill, and **Campos, Joseph J.** (1982). Toward a theory of infant temperament. In R.N. Emde and R.J. Harmon, (Eds.), *The development of attachment and affiliative systems: Psychobiological aspects.* New York: Plenum.

Goldsmith, H. Hill, and **Gottesman, I.I.** (1981). Origins of variation in behavioral style: A longitudinal study of temperament in young twins. *Child Development, 52,* 91–103.

Goodnow, Jacqueline J. (1976). The nature of intelligent behavior: Questions raised by cross-cultural studies. In Lauren B. Resnick (Ed.), *The nature of intelligence.* New York: Wiley, 169–188.

Goodnow, Jacqueline J. (1977). *Children drawing.* Cambridge, MA: Harvard University Press.

Goodson, Barbara Dillon, and **Hess, Robert D.** (1978). The effects of parent training programs on child performance and behavior. In Bernard Brown (Ed.), *Found: Long-term gains from early intervention.* Boulder, CO: Westview Press.

Goodwin, J. (1982). *Sexual abuse: Incest victims and their families.* Boston: John Wright.

Gordon, I.J. (1969) *Early childhood stimulation through parent education.* Final report to the Children's Bureau, Social and Rehabiliation Service, Department of Health, Education, and Welfare, Gainesville, FL, University of Florida, Institute for the Development of Human Resources, ED 038 166.

Gottfredson, Denise C. (1985). Youth employment, crime and schooling: A longitudinal study of a national sample. *Developmental Psychology, 21,* 419–432.

Gottfried, Allen W., and **Bathurst, Kay.** (1983). Hand preference across time is related to intelligence in young girls, not boys. *Science, 221,* 1074–1075.

Gottlieb, Benjamin H. (1975). The contribution of natural support systems to primary prevention among four social subgroups of adolescent males. *Adolescence, 10,* 207–220.

Gottlieb, Jay, and **Leyser, Yona.** (1981). Friendship between mentally retarded and nonretarded children. In Steven R. Asher and John M. Gotman (Eds.), *The Development of Children's Friendships.* Cambridge, England: Cambridge University Press.

Gottman, John M. (1983) How children become friends. *Monographs of the Society for Research in Child Development, 48* (3, Serial No. 201).

Gottman, John M., and **Parkhurst, J.T.** (1980). A developmental theory of friendship and acquaintanceship processes. In W. Andrew Collins (Ed.), Development of cognitive affect and social relations. *Minnesota Symposia on Child Psychology* (Vol. 13). Hillsdale, NJ:Erlbaum.

Gottman, John M., Gonzo, J., and **Rasmussen, B.** (1975). Social interaction, social competence, and friendship in children. *Child Development, 45,* 709–718.

Grant, James P. (1982). *The state of the world's children: 1982–1983.* New York: UNICEF and Oxford University Press.

Gratch, Gerald. (1979). The development of thought and language in infancy. In Joy D. Osofsky (Ed.), *Handbook of infant development.* New York: Wiley.

Gray, Jane, and **Kaplan, Betty.** (1980). The lay health visitor program: An eighteen month experience. In C. Henry Kempe and Ray E. Helfer (Eds.), *The battered child* (3rd ed.). Chicago: The University of Chicago Press.

Gray S.W., and **Wandersman, L. P.** (1980). The methodology of home-based intervention studies: Problems and promising strategies. *Child Development, 51,* 993–1009.

Gray, William M., and **Hudson, Lynne M.** (1984). Formal operations and the imaginary audience. *Developmental Psychology, 20,* 619–627.

Green, Lawrence W., and **Horton, Denise.** (1982). Adolescent health: Issues and challenges. In Thomas J. Coates, Anne C. Petersen, and Cheryl Perry (Eds.), *Promoting adolescent health: A dialogue on research and practice.* New York: Academic Press.

Greenberg, Martin, and **Morris, Norman.** (1974). Engrossment: The newborn's impact upon the father. *American Journal of Orthopsychiatry, 44.* 520–531.

Greenberger, E. (1983). A researcher in the policy area: The case of child labor. *American Psychologist, 38,* 106–111.

Greenfeld, Josh. (1978). *A place for Noah.* New York: Holt, Rinehart, and Winston.

Greenspan, Stanley, and **Greenspan, Nancy T.** (1985). *First Feelings,* New York: Viking.

Greer, Douglas, Potts, Richard, Wright, John C., and **Huston, Aletha C.** (1982). The effects of television commercial form and commercial placement on children's social behavior and attention. *Child Development, 53,* 611–619.

Grief, Esther Blank. (1976). Sex-role playing in pre-school children. In Jerome S. Bruner, Alison Jolly, and Kathy Sylva (Eds.), *Play.* New York: Basic Books.

Gresham, Frank M. (1982). Misguided mainstreaming: The case for social skills training with handicapped children. *Exceptional Children, 48,* 422–433.

Greydanus, Donald E., and **Hofman, Adele.** (1983). Endocrine disorders, In Adele Hofmann (Ed.), *Adolescent medicine,* Menlo Park, CA: Addison-Wesley.

Grinker, Joel A. (1981). Behavioral and metabolic factors in childhood obesity. In Michael Lewis and Leonard A. Rosenblum (Eds.), *The uncommon child.* New York: Plenum Press.

Grobstein, Clifford, Flower, Michael, and **Mendeloff, John.** (1983). External Human Fertilization: An evaluation of policy. *Science, 222,* 127–133.

Grosjean, Francois. (1982). *Life with two languages: An introduction to bilingualism.* Cambridge, MA: Harvard University Press.

Grossman, F.K., Eichler, L.S., and **Winickoff, S.A.** (1980). *Pregnancy, birth, and parenthood.* San Francisco: Jossey-Bass.

Grotevant, Harold D., and **Cooper, Catherine R.** (1985). Patterns of interaction in family relationships and the development of identity exploration in adolescence. *Child Development, 56,* 415–428.

Guilleminault, C., Boeddiker, Margaret Owen, and **Schwab, Deborah.** (1982). Detection of risk factors for "near miss SIDS" events in full-term infants. *Neuropediatrics, 13,* 29–35.

Giunagh, B. J., and **Gordon, I.J.** (1976). *School performance as a function of early stimulation.* Final report to the Office of Child Development.

Gump, Paul V. (1975). Ecological psychology and children. In E. Mavis Hetherington (Ed.), *Review of child development research* (Vol. V). Chicago: University of Chicago Press.

Gunnar, Megan R., and **Stone, Cherly.** (1984). The effect of positive maternal affect on infant responses to pleasant, ambiguous, and fear-provoking toys. *Child Development, 55,* 1231.

Gupta, Chhanda, Yaffe, Sumner J., and **Shapiro, Bernard H.** (1982). Prenatal exposure to phenobarbital permanently decreases testosterone and causes reproductive dysfunction. *Science, 216.* 640–642.

Guskin S., and **Spiker H.H.** (1968). Educational research in mental retardation. In N.E. Ellis (Ed.), *International review of research in mental retardation* (Vol. 3). New York: Academic Press.

Guthrie. D.M. (1980). *Neuroethology.* New York: Halsted Press.

Guthrie, Robert V. (1976). *Even the rat was white: A historical view of psychology.* New York: Harper and Row.

Gutmann, David. (1975). Parenthood: Key to the comparative psychology of the life cycle. In Nancy Datan and L. Ginsberg (Eds.), *Life span developmental psychology,* New York: Academic Press.

Haaf, Robert A., Smith, P. Hull, and **Smitley, Suzanne.** (1983). Infant response to facelike patterns under fixed-trial and infant-control procedures. *Child Development, 54,* 172–177.

Haas, Linda. (1981). Domestic role sharing in Sweden. *Journal of Marriage and the Family, 43,* 957–967.

Habicht, Jean-Pierre, Yarbrough, Charles, Lectig, Aaron, and **Klein, Robert.** (1974). Relation of maternal supplementary feeding during pregnancy to birth weight and other socio-biological factors. In Myron Winick (Ed.), *Nutrition and fetal development.* New York: Wiley.

Haddad, Gabriel G., Walsh, Ellen M., Leistene, Heidi L., Grodin, Warren K., and **Mellins, Robert B.** (1981). Abnormal maturation of sleep state in infants with aborted Sudden Infant Death Syndrome. *Pediatric Research, 15,* 1055–1057.

Hagen, John W., Jongeward, Robert H., Jr., and **Kail, Robert V., Jr.** (1975). Cognitive perspectives on the development of memory. In Hayne W. Reese (Ed.), *Advances in child development and behavior.* Vol. X. New York: Academic Press.

Haith, Marshall M., Bergman, Terry, and **Moore, Michael J.** (1977). Eye contact and face scanning in early infancy. *Science, 198,* 853–854.

Hale, Janice E. (1982). *Black children: Their roots, culture, and learning styles.* Provo, UT: Brigham Young University Press.

Halford, Graeme S., and **Boyle, Frances M.** (1985). Do young children understand conservation of number? *Child Development, 56,* 165–176.

Hall, G. Stanley. (1883). The contents of children's minds. *Princeton Review.* 2, 249–272.

Hall, G. Stanley. (1904). *Adolescence: Its psychology and its relations to physiology, anthropology, sociology, sex, crime, religion and education.* New York: Appleton.

Halliday, M.A.K. (1979). One child's protolanguage. In Margaret Bullowa (Ed.), *Before Speech: The beginning of interpersonal communication.* Cambridge, England: Cambridge University Press.

Halpern, Robert. (1984). Lack of effects for home-based early intervention? Some possible explanations. *American Journal of Orthopsychiatry, 54,* 33–42.

Hamilton, Richard. (1980). *The herpes book.* New York: St. Martin.

Hanson, James W., Streissguth, Ann P., and **Smith, David W.** (1978). The effects of moderate alcohol consumption during pregnancy on fetal growth and morphogenesis. *The Journal of Pediatrics, 92,* 457–460.

Harada, M. (1976). Intrauterine poisoning: Clinical and epidemiological studies and significance of the problem. *Bulletin of the Institute of Constitutional Medicine, Kumamoto University.*

Hardy, Janet B. (1973). Clinical and developmental aspects of congenital rubella. *Archives of Otolaryngology, 98,* 230–236.

Hardy, Janet B., McCracken, George H., Jr., Gilkeson, Mary Ruth, and **Sever, John L.** (1969). Adverse fetal outcome following maternal rubella *after* the first trimester of pregnancy. *Journal of the American Medical Association, 207,* 2414–2420.

Hardy-Brown, Karen. (1983). Universals and individual difference: Disentangling two approaches to the study of language acquisition. *Developmental Psychology, 19,* 610–624.

Hardyck, Curtis, and **Petrinovich, Lewis F.** (1977). Left-handedness. *Psychological Bulletin, 84,* 385–404.

Harlow, Harry F., and **Harlow, Margaret.** (1962). Social deprivation in monkeys. *Scientific American, 207* (5), 136–146.

Harlow, Harry F., and **Mears, Clara.** (1979). *The human model: Primate perspectives.* New York: Wiley.

Harlow, Harry F., and **Suomi, Stephen J.** (1971). Social recovery by isolation reared monkeys. *Proceedings of the National Academy of Science, 68,* 1534–1538.

Harper, Lawrence V., and **Huie, Karen S.** (1985). The effects of prior group experience, age, and familiarity on the quality and organization of preschoolers' social relationships. *Child Development, 56,* 704–717.

Harper, Lawrence V., and **Sanders, Karen M.** (1975). Preschool children's use of space: Sex differences in outdoor play. *Developmental Psychology, 11,* 119.

Harper, R.M., Leake, B., Hoffman, H., Walter, D.O., Hoppenbrouwers, T., Hodgman, J., and **Sternman, M.B.** (1981). Periodicity of sleep states is altered in infants at risk for the sudden infant death syndrome. *Science, 213,* 1030–1032.

Harris, Florence R., Wolf, Montrose M., and **Baer, Donald M.** (1964). Effects of adult social reinforcement on child behavior. *Young Children* (Formerly *The Journal of Nursery Education*), 20(1), 8–17.

Harrison, Algea, Serafica, Felicisima, and **McAdoo, Harriette.** (1984). Ethnic families of color. In Ross D. Parke (Ed.), *Review of Child Development Research* (Vol. 7). Chicago: University of Chicago Press.

Harsanyi, Zsolt, and **Hutton, Richard.** (1981). *Genetic prophecy: Beyond the double helix.* New York: Rawson Wade.

Harter, Susan. (1982). Children's understanding of multiple emotions: A cognitive developmental approach. In W.F. Overton (Ed.), *The relationship between social and cognitive development.* Hillsdale, NJ: Erlbaum.

Harter, Susan. (1983). Developmental perspectives on the self-system. In Paul H. Mussen (Ed.), *Handbook of child psychology: Vol. 4. Socialization, personality and social development.* New York: Wiley.

Harter, Susan, and **Pike, Robin.** (1984). The pictorial scale of perceived competence and social acceptance for young children. *Child Development, 55,* 1969–1982.

Harter, Susan, and **Ward, C.** (1978). A factor-analysis of Coopersmith's self-esteem inventory. Unpublished manuscript, University of Denver. (Cited in Harter, 1983)

Hartshorne, Hugh, May, Mark A., and **Maller, J.B.** (1929). *Studies in service and self-control.* New York: Macmillan.

Hartsough, Carolyn S., and **Lambert, Nadine M.** (1985). Medical factors in hyperactive and normal children: Prenatal, developmental, and health history findings. *American Journal of Orthopsychiatry, 55,* 190–201.

Hartup, Willard W. (1974). Aggression in childhood: Developmental perspectives. *American Psychologist, 29,* 336–341.

Hartup, Willard W. (1983). Peer relations. In Paul H. Mussen (Ed.), *Handbook of child psychology: Vol. 4. Socialization, personality and social development.* New York: Wiley.

Hass, Aaron. (1979). *Teenage sexuality: A survey of teenage sexual behavior.* New York: Macmillan.

Hatano, Giyoo, Miyake, Kazuno, and **Nobumoto, Tajima.** (1980). Mother behavior in an unstructured situation and child's acquisition of number conservation. *Child Development, 51,* 379–385.

Hawkins, J., Pea, R.D., Glick, J., and **Scribner, S.** (1984). "Merds that laugh don't like mushrooms": Evidence for deductive reasoning in preschooler. *Developmental Psychology, 20,* 584–594.

Hay, D.F., and **Ross, H.S.** (1982). The social nature of early conflict. *Child Development, 53,* 105–113.

Heald, Felix P. (Ed.). (1969). *Adolescent nutrition and growth.* New York: Appleton-Century-Crofts.

Heald, Felix P. (1975). Juvenile obesity. In Myron Winick (Ed.), *Childhood obesity.* New York: Wiley.

Heinonen, Olli P., Slone, Dennis, and **Shapiro, Samuel.** (1977). *Birth defects and drugs in pregnancy.* Littleton, MA: Publishing Sciences Group.

Helfer, Ray E. (1980). Developmental deficits which limit interpersonal skills. In C. Henry Kempe and Ray E. Helfer (Eds.), *The battered child* (3rd ed.). Chicago: The University of Chicago Press.

Helton, George B., Workman, Edward A., and **Matuszek, Paula A.** (1982). *Psychoeducational assessment: Integrating concepts and techniques.* New York: Grune and Stratton.

Henderson, Edmund. (1985). *Teaching spelling.* Boston: Houghton Mifflin.

Henneborn, William James, and **Cogan, Rosemary.** (1975). The effect of husband participation on reported pain and probability of medication during labor and birth. *Journal of Psychosomatic Research, 19,* 215–222.

Henton, Comradge L. (1961). The effect of socio-economic and emotional factors on the onset of menarche among Negro and White girls. *Journal of Genetic Psychology, 98,* 255–264.

Herman, Judith. (1981). *Father-daughter incest.* Cambridge, MA: Harvard University Press.

Hermelin, Beate, and **O'Connor, N.** (1971). Functional asymmetry in the reading of Braille. *Neuropsychologia, 9,* 431–435.

Hershorn, Michael, and **Rosenbaum, Alan.** (1985). Children of marital violence: A closer look at the unintended victims. *American Journal of Orthopsychiatry, 55,* 260–266.

Herzog, A. Regula. (1982). High school seniors' occupational plans and values: Trends in sex differences 1976 through 1980. *Sociology of Education, 55,* 1–13.

Hess, Robert D., and **Shipman, Virginia C.** (1965). Early experience and the socialization of cognitive modes in children. *Child Development, 36,* 869–886.

Hetherington, E. Mavis. (1972). Effects of parental absence on personality development of adolescent daughters. *Developmental Psychology, 7,* 313–326.

Hetherington, E. Mavis, and **Camara, Kathleen A.** (1984). Families in transition: The process of dissolution and reconstitution. In Ross D. Parke (Ed.), *Review of child development research* (Vol. 7). Chicago: University of Chicago Press.

Hetherington, E. Mavis and **McIntyre, C.W.** (1975). Developmental psychology. In M.R. Rosenzweig and L.W. Porter (Eds.), *Annual Review of Psychology,* Palo Alto, CA: Annual Reviews.

Hetherington, E. Mavis, Camara, Kathleen A., and **Fetherman D.L.** (1981). Achievement and intellectual functioning of children in one-parent households. In J. Spence, (Ed.), *Assessing achievement.* New York: Freeman.

Hetherington, E. Mavis, Cox, Martha, and **Cox, Roger.** (1979). Play and social interaction in children following divorce. *Journal of Social Issues, 35,* 26–49.

Hetherington, E. Mavis, Cox, Martha, and **Cox, Roger.** (1982). Effects of divorce on parents and children. In Michael E. Lamb (Ed.), *Nontraditional families: Parenting and child development.* Hillsdale, NJ: Erlbaum.

Hier, Daniel B., Atkins, L., and **Perlo, U.P.** (1980). Learning disorders and sex chromosome aberrations. *Journal of Mental Deficiency Research, 24,* 17–26.

Higgins, Anne T., and **Turnure, James E.** (1984). Distractability and concentration of attention in children's development. *Child Development, 55,* 1799–1810.

Higgins, E. Tory. (1981). Role taking and social judgment: alternative developmental perspectives and processes. In John H. Flavell and Lee Ross (Eds.), *Social cognitive development: Frontiers and possible futures.* Cambridge, England: Cambridge University Press.

Higham, Eileen. (1980). Variations in adolescent psychohormonal development. In Joseph Adelson (Ed.), *Handbook of adolescent psychology.* New York: Wiley.

Hill, John P., and **Lynch, Mary Ellen.** (1983). The intensification of gender-related role expectations during early adolescence. In Jeanne Brooks-Gunn and Anne C. Petersen (Eds.), *Girls at puberty: Biological and psychosocial aspects.* New York: Plenum.

Hillerich, Robert L. (1983). The principal's guide to improving reading instruction. Newton, MA: Allyn and Bacon.

Hilliard, Jomary P., Fritz, Gregory K., and **Lewiston, Norman J.** (1982). Goal-setting of asthmatic, diabetic and healthy children. *Child Psychiatry and Human Development, 13,* 35–47.

Hinde, Robert A. (1983). Ethology and Child Development. In Paul H. Mussen (Ed.), *Handbook of child psychology: Vol. II. Infancy and developmental psychobiology*. New York: Wiley.

Hindley, C.B., Filliozat, A.M., Klackenberg, G., Nicolet-Meister, D., and **Sand, E.A.** (1966). Differences in age of walking in five European longitudinal samples. *Human Biology, 38,* 364–379.

Hirschi, Travis. (1969). *Causes of delinquency*. Berkeley, CA: University of California Press.

Hoffman, Lois Wladis, and **Nye, F. Ivan.** (1974). *Working mothers*. San Francisco: Jossey-Bass.

Hoffman, Lois Wladis. (1977). Changes in family roles, socialization, and sex differences. *American Psychologist, 32,* 644–657.

Hoffman, Lois Wladis. (1984). Work, family, and the socialization of the child. In Ross D. Parke (Ed.), *Review of child development research* (Vol. 7). Chicago: University of Chicago Press.

Hoffman, Martin L. (1981). Perspectives on the difference between understanding people and understanding things: The role of affect. In John H. Flavell and Lee Ross (Eds.), *Social cognitive development: Frontiers and possible futures*. Cambridge: Cambridge University Press.

Hoffman, Martin L. (1984). Empathy, its limitations, and its role in a comprehensive moral theory. In William M. Kurtines and Jacob L. Gewirtz (Eds.), *Morality, moral behavior, and moral development*. New York: Wiley.

Holden, George W. (1983). Avoiding conflict: Mothers as tacticians in the supermarket. *Child Development, 54,* 233–240.

Holdern, William A. (1980). *Sexual abuse of children*. Englewood, CO: American Humane Society.

Hollander, P. (1982). Legal context of educational testing. In National Research Council, Committee on Ability Testing, *Ability testing: Uses, consequences and controversies*. Washington DC: National Academy Press.

Hollingworth, Leta S. (1942). *Children above 180 I.Q. Stanford-Binet origin and development*. Yonkers-on-Hudson, New York: World Book.

Holmberg, M.C. (1980). The development of social interchange patterns from 12 to 42 months. *Child Development, 51,* 448–456.

Holstein, C. (1976). Development of moral judgment: A longitudinal study of males and females. *Child Development, 47,* 51–61.

Holzman, Mathilda. (1983). The language of children: Development in home and in school. Englewood Cliffs, NJ: Prentice-Hall.

Hooker, J.G., Lucas, M., Richards, B.A., Shirley, I.M., Thompson, B.D., and **Ward, R.H.** (1984). Is maternal alpha-fetoprotein screening still of value in a low risk area for neural tube defects. *Prenatal Diagnosis, 4,* 29–33.

Hoorweg, Jan. (1976). *Protein-energy malnutrition and intellectual abilities: A study of teen-age Ugandan children*. The Hague: Mouton.

Hopkins, J. Roy. (1977). Sexual behavior in adolescence. *Journal of Social Issues, 33*(2), 67–85.

Horner, Thomas M. (1985). The psychic life of the young infant: Review and critique of the psychoanalytic concepts of symbiosis and infantile omnipotence. *American Journal of Orthopsychiatry, 55,* 324–344.

Horney, Karen. (1967). *Feminine psychology*. Harold Kelman (Ed.), New York: Norton.

Horowitz, Frances Degen, and **Paden, Lucile York.** (1973). The effectiveness of environmental intervention programs. In Bettye M. Caldwell and Henry N. Ricciuti (Eds.), *Review of child development research:* Vol. III. *Child development and social policy*. Chicago: University of Chicago Press, 331–402.

Houser, Betsy Bosak, and **Garvey, Chris.** (1985). Factors that affect nontraditional vocational enrollment among women. *Psychology of Women Quarterly, 9,* 105–117.

Hoving, K.L., Spencer, T., Robb, K., and **Schulte, D.** (1978). Developmental changes in visual information processing. In P.A. Ornstein (Ed.), *Memory development in children*. Hillsdale, NJ: Erlbaum.

Howes, Carolyn. (1983). Patterns of friendship. *Child Development, 54,* 1041–1053.

Howes, Virgil M. (1974). *Informal teaching in the open classroom*. New York: Macmillan.

Hubert, Nancy C., Wachs, Theodore D., Peters-Martin, Patricia, and **Gandour, Mary Jane.** (1982). The study of early temperament: measurement and conceptual issues. *Child Development, 53,* 571–600.

Hughes, A., and **Trudgill, Peter.** (1979). *English accents and dialects*. London: Edward Arnold.

Hughes, Martin, and **Donaldson, Margaret.** (1979). The use of hiding games for studying coordination of viewpoints. *Educational Review, 31,* 133–140.

Hughes, Martin, and **Grieve, Robert.** (1980). On asking children bizarre questions. *First Language, 1,* 149–160.

Humphreys, Lloyd G., Rich, Susan A., and **Davey, Timothy C.A.** (1985). Piagetian test of intelligence, *Developmental Psychology, 21,* 872–877.

Hunt, J. McVicker. (1961). *Intelligence and experience*. New York: Ronald Press.

Hunt, M. (1970). Special sex education survey. *Seventeen,* (Jul.), 94ff.

Hunter, Fumiyo Tao. (1985). Adolescents' perception of discussion with parents and friends. *Developmental Psychology, 21,* 433–440.

Huston, Aletha C. (1983). Sex-typing. In Paul H. Mussen (Ed.), *Handbook of child psychology: Vol. 4. Socialization, personality and social development*. New York: Wiley.

Huston, Aletha C. (1985). The development of sex-typing: Themes from recent research. *Developmental Review, 5,* 1–17.

Ilg, Frances L., and **Ames, Louise Bates.** (1965). *School readiness: Behavior tests used at the Gesell Institute*. New York: Harper & Row.

Ilg, Frances L., Ames, Louise Bates, and Baker, Sidney M. (1981). *Child behavior* (Rev. Ed.). New York: Harper and Row.

Inhelder, Bärbel, and Piaget, Jean. (1958). *The growth of logical thinking from childhood to adolescence.* New York: Basic Books.

Inhelder, Bärbel, and Piaget, Jean. (1970). *The early growth of logic in the child: Classification and seriation.* New York: Humanities Press, (Original work published 1964)

Inhelder, Bärbel, Sinclair, Hermine, and Bovet, Magal. (1974). *Learning and the development of cognition.* Susan Wedgwood (Trans.). Cambridge, MA: Harvard University Press.

Innovation. (1983, November 3). *The new womb.* Public Broadcasting Television.

Isaacs, N. (1974). *A brief introduction to Piaget.* New York: Schocken.

Ives, William. (1980). Preschool children's ability to coordinate spatial perspectives through language and pictures. *Child Development, 51,* 1303–1306.

Izard, C.E. (1978). On the ontogenesis of emotions and emotion-cognition in infancy. In Michael Lewis and Leonard Rosenblum (Eds.), *The development of affect.* New York: Plenum.

Izard, C.E. (1980). *The maximally discriminative facial movement scoring system.* Unpublished manuscript, University of Delaware.

Jacklin, Carol Nagy and Maccoby, Eleanor E. (1978). Social behavior at 33 months in same-sex and mixed-sex dyads. *Child Development, 49,* 557–569.

Jackson, Brian, and Jackson, Sonia. (1979). *Childminder: A study in action research.* London: Routledge and Kegan Paul.

Jackson, George D. (1975). On the report of the ad hoc committee on educational uses of tests with disadvantaged students: Another psychological view from the Association of Black Psychologists. *American Psychologist. 30,* 88–93.

Jacobs, Blanche S., and Moss, Howard A. (1976). Birth order and sex of sibling as determinants of mother-infant interaction. *Child Development, 47,* 315–322.

Jacobs, Jerry. (1971). *Adolescent suicide.* New York: Wiley.

Jacobson, Joseph L., Boersma, David C., Fields, Robert B., and Olson, Karen L., (1983). Paralinguistic features of adult speech to infants and small children. *Child Development. 54.* 436–442.

Jacobson, Joseph L., Jacobson, Sandra W., Fein, Greta G., Schwartz, Pamela M., and Dowler, Jeffrey K. (1984). Prenatal exposure to an environmental toxin: A test of multiple effects. *Developmental Psychology, 20,* 523–532.

Jahoda, Marie. (1981). Work, employment and unemployment. *American Psychologist, 36,* 184–191.

James, William. (1950). *The principles of psychology.* (Vol. I) New York: Dover (Original work published 1890)

Jelliffe, Derrick B., and Jelliffe, E.F. Patrice. (1977). Current concepts in nutrition: "Breast is best": Modern meanings. *New England Journal of Medicine, 297,* 912–915.

Jencks, Christopher, Smith, Marshall, Acland, Henry, Bane, Mary Jo, Cohen, David, Gintis, Herbert, Heyns, Barbara, and Michelson, Stephan. (1972). *Inequality: A reassessment of the effect of family and schooling in America.* New York; Basic Books.

Jiles, Darrel. (1980). Problems in the assessment of sexual abuse referrals. In William A. Holdern (Ed.), *Sexual abuse of children.* Englewood, CO: American Humane Society.

Jirásek, Jan E. (1976). Principles of reproductive embryology. In J. L. Simpson (Ed.), *Disorders of sexual differentiation: Etiology and clinical delineation.* New York: Academic Press, 52–109.

Johnson, Elmer. J. (Ed.). (1983). *International handbook of contemporary developments in criminology: Europe, Africa, the Middle East, and Asia.* Westport, CT: Greenwood Press.

Johnson, Russell R., Greenspan, Stephen, and Brown, Gwyn M. (1984). Children's ability to recognize and improve upon socially inept communications. *Journal of Genetic Psychology, 144,* 255–264.

Johnston, Lloyd D., O'Malley, Patrick M., and Bachman, Jerald G. (1985). *Use of licit and illicit drugs by American high school students, 1975–1984.* National Institute of Drug Abuse, United States Department of Health and Human Services. Washington, DC.

Johnston, Robert B. (1976). Motor function: Normal development and cerebral palsy. In Robert B. Johnston and Phyllis R. Magrab (Eds.), *Developmental disorders: Assessment, treatment, education.* Baltimore: University Park Press.

Jones, Kenneth Lyons (1975). The fetal alcohol syndrome. In Raymond D. Harbison (Ed.), *Perinatal addiction.* New York: Halsted Press.

Jones, Mary Cover. (1957). The later careers of boys who were early- or late-maturing. *Child Development, 28,* 113–128.

Jones, Mary Cover. (1965). Psychological correlates of somatic development. *Child Development, 36,* 899–911.

Jones, Mary Cover, and Bayley, Nancy. (1950). Physical maturing among boys as related to behavior. *Journal of Educational Psychology. 41,* 129–248.

Jones, N. Burton. (1976). Rough-and-tumble play among nursery school children. In Jerome S. Bruner, Alison Jolly, and Kathy Sylva (Eds.) *Play.* New York: Basic Books.

Jordaan, Jean Pierre, and Heyde, Martha Bennett. (1978). *Vocational maturity during the high school years.* New York: Teachers College Press.

Joreskog, K. G. (1973). A general method for estimating a linear structural equation system. In A.S. Goldberger and O.D. Duncan (Eds.), *Structural equation models in the social sciences.* New York: Seminar Press.

Josselson, Ruthellen L. (1980). Ego development in adolescence. In Joseph Adelson (Ed.), *Handbook of adolescent psychology.* New York: Wiley.

Juel-Nielsen, Neils. (1980). *Individual and environment: Monozygotic twins reared apart.* New York: International Universities Press.

Julian, Valerie, Moher, Cynthia and Lapp, Jane. (1980). Father-daughter incest. In William A. Holdern (Ed.), *Sexual* *abuse of children*. Englewood, CO: American Humane Society.

Jurich, Anthony P., Polson, Cheryl J., Jurich, Julie A., and **Bates, Rodney A.,** (1985). Family factors in the lives of drug users and abusers. *Adolescence. 20,* 143-159.

Justice, Blair, and **Justice, Rita.** (1979). *The broken taboo: Sex in the family.* New York: Human Sciences Press.

Kadushin, Alfred. (1970). *Adopting older children.* New York: Columbia University Press.

Kagan, Jerome. (1971). *Change and continuity in infancy.* New York: Wiley.

Kagan, Jerome. (1978). The baby's elastic mind. *Human Nature. 1.* 66–73.

Kagan, Jerome. (1979). Overview: Perspectives on human infancy. In Joy D. Osofsky (Ed.), *Handbook of infant development.* New York: Wiley.

Kagan, Jerome. (1981). The second year: The emergence of self-awareness. Cambridge, MA: Harvard University Press.

Kagan, Jerome. (1983). Preface to the second edition. In Jerome Kagan and Howard Moss, *Birth to maturity* (2nd ed.). New Haven: Yale University Press.

Kagan, Jerome, Kearsley, Richard B., and **Zelazo, Philip R.** (1977). The effects of infant day care on psychological development. *Evaluation Quarterly, 1,* 109–142.

Kagan, Jerome, and **Klein, Robert E.** (1973). Cross-cultural perspectives on early development. *American Psychologist. 28,* 947–961.

Kandel, Denise. (1974). Inter- and intragenerational influences on adolescent marijuana use. *Journal of Social Issues. 30*(2), 107–135.

Kandel, Denise, and **Lesser, Gerald S.** (1969), Parent-adolescent relationships and adolescent independence in the United States and Denmark. *Journal of Marriage and the Family. 31,* 348–358.

Karmel, Marjorie. (1959). *Thank you Dr. Lamaze.* Philadelphia: Lippincott.

Katchadourian, Herant A. (1977). *The biology of adolescence.* San Francisco: Freeman.

Kaye, Kenneth. (1982). *The mental and social life of babies: How parents create persons.* Chicago: University of Chicago Press.

Keller, W.D., Hildebrandt, K.A., and **Richards, M.** (1981, April). *Effects of extended father-infant contact during the newborn period.* Paper presented at the biennial meeting of the Society for Research in Child Development, Boston.

Kellogg, Rhoda. (1970). *Analyzing children's art.* Palo Alto, CA: Mayfield.

Kempe, C. Henry. (1980). Incest and other forms of sexual abuse. In C. Henry Kempe and Ray E. Helfer (Eds.), *The battered child* (3rd ed.). Chicago: University of Chicago Press.

Kempe, Ruth S., and **Kempe, C. Henry.** (1978). *Child abuse.* Cambridge, MA: Harvard University Press.

Kempe, Ruth S., and **Kempe, C. Henry.** (1984). *The common secret: Sexual abuse of children and adolescents.* New York: Freeman.

Keniston, Kenneth, and **The Carnegie Council on Children.** (1977). *All our children: The American family under pressure.* New York: Harcourt, Brace, Jovanovich.

Kennel, John H., Jerauld, Richard, Wolfe, Harriet, Chesler, David, Kreger, Nancy C., McAlpine, Willie, Steffa, Meredith, and **Klaus, Marshall H.** (1974). Maternal behavior one year after early and extended post-partum contact. *Developmental Medicine and Child Neurology, 16,* 172–179.

Kenyatta, Jomo. (1965). *Facing Mount Kenya: The tribal life of the Gikuyu.* New York: Vintage Books.

Kett, Joseph F. (1977). *Rites of passage: Adolescence in America, 1790 to the present.* New York: Basic Books.

Kinsbourne, Marcel, and **Hiscock, Merrill.** (1983). The normal and deviant development of functional lateralization of the brain. In Paul H. Mussen (Ed.), *Handbook of child psychology: Vol. 2. Infancy and developmental psychobiology.* New York: Wiley.

Kinsbourne, Marcel and **Swanson, J.M.** (1979). Models of hyperactivity. In R.L. Trites (Ed.), *Hyperactivity in children.* Baltimore: University Park Press.

Kinsey, Alfred C., Pomeroy, Wardell B., and **Martin, Clyde E.** (1948). *Sexual behavior in the human male.* Philadelphia: Saunders.

Kirk, L. (1977). Maternal and subcultural correlates of cognitive growth rate: The GA pattern. In P.R. Dasen (Ed.), *Piagetian psychology: Cross-cultural contributions.* New York: Halsted.

Kitzinger, Sheila. (1983). *The complete book of pregnancy and childbirth.* New York: Knopf.

Klaus, Marshall H., and **Kennel, John H.** (1976). *Maternal-infant bonding. The impact of early separation or loss on family development.* St. Louis: Mosby.

Klaus, Marshall H., and **Kennell, John H.** (1982). *Parent-infant bonding.* St. Louis: Mosby.

Kleck, Robert E., Richardson, Stephen A., and **Ronald, Linda.** (1974). Physical appearance cues and interpersonal attraction in children. *Child Development, 45,* 305–310.

Klein, Melanie. (1957). *Envy and gratitude.* New York: Basic Books.

Klein, Robert P. (1985). Caregiving arrangements by employed women with children under 1 year of age. *Developmental Psychology, 21,* 403–406.

Kloos, Peter. (1969). Female initiation rites among the Maroni River Caribe. *American Anthroplogist. 71,* 898–905.

Klug, William S., and **Cummings, Michael R.** (1983). *Concepts of genetics.* Columbus, OH: Merrill.

Knapp, Mary, and **Knapp, Herbert.** (1976). *One potato, two potato: The secret education of American children.* New York: Morton.

Knight, G.P., and **Kagan, S.** (1977). Development of prosocial and competitive behaviors in Anglo-American and Mexican-American children. *Child Development, 48,* 1385–1394.

Koch, Kenneth. (1970). *Wishes, lies, and dreams: Teaching children to write poetry.* New York: Chelsea House.

Koenig, Michael A., and **Zelnik, Melvin.** (1982). The risk of premarital first pregnancy among metropolitan-area teenagers: 1976 and 1979. *Family Planning Perspectives, 14,* 239–247.

Koff, Elissa, Rierdan, Jill, and **Silverstone, Esther.** (1978). Changes in representation of body image as a function of menarcheal status. *Developmental Psychology, 14,* 635–642.

Kohlberg, Lawrence. (1963). Development of children's orientation towards a moral order (Part I). Sequence in the development of moral thought. *Vita Humana, 6,* 11–36.

Kohlberg, Lawrence. (1966). A cognitive developmental analysis of children's sex-role concepts and attitudes. In Eleanor Maccoby (Ed.), *The development of sex differences.* Stanford, CA: Stanford University Press, 82–172.

Kohlberg, Lawrence. (1969). Stage and sequence: The cognitive developmental approach to socialization. In D.A. Goslin (Ed.), *Handbook of socialization theory and research.* Chicago: Rand McNally, 347–408.

Kohlberg, Lawrence. (1971). Stages of moral development as a basis for moral education. In C.M. Beck, B.S. Crittenden, and E.V. Sullivan (Eds.), *Moral education: Interdisciplinary approaches.* Toronto: University of Toronto Press.

Kohlberg, Lawrence. (1973). Continuities in childhood and adult moral development revisited. In Paul B. Baltes and K. Warner Schaie (Eds.), *Life-span developmental psychology: Personality and socialization.* New York: Academic Press.

Kohlberg, Lawrence. (1981). *The philosophy of moral development.* New York: Harper and Row.

Kohlberg, Lawrence, Levine, C., and **Hewer, A.** (1983). *Moral stages: A current formulation and a response to critics.* Basel, Switzerland: Karger.

Kohlberg, Lawrence, and **Elfenbein, Donald.** (1975). The development of moral judgments concerning capital punishment. *American Journal of Orthopsychiatry, 45,* 614–640.

Kohlberg, Lawrence, and **Ullian, Dorothy, Z.** (1974). Stages in the development of psychosexual concepts and attitudes. In Richard C. Friedman, Ralph M. Richart, and Raymond L. VandeWiele (Eds.), *Sex differences in behavior: A conference.* New York: Wiley, 209–231.

Kohlberg, Lawrence, Yaeger, Judy, and **Hjertholm, Else.** (1968). Private speech: Four studies and a review of theories. *Child Development, 39,* 691–736.

Kohn, Robert R. (1979). Biomedical aspects of aging. In David D. Van Tassel (Ed.), *Aging, death, and the completion of being.* Philadelphia: University of Pennsylvania Press.

Kolata, Gina Bari. (1979). Scientists attack report that obstetrical medications endanger children. *Science, 204,* 391–392.

Kolata, Gina Bari. (1981). Fetal alcohol advisory debated. *Science, 214,* 642–645.

Kolata, Gina Bari. (1983). First trimester prenatal diagnosis. *Science, 221,* 1031–1032.

Kolata, Gina Bari. (1985). Down Syndrome—Alzheimer's linked. *Science, 230,* 1152–1153.

Kontos, Donna. (1978). A study of the effects of extended mother infant contact on maternal behavior at one and three months. *Birth and Family Journal, 5,* 133–140.

Korbin, Jill E. (1981). Introduction. In Jill E. Korbin (Ed.), *Child abuse and neglect: Cross-cultural perspectives.* Berkeley, CA: University of California Press.

Korbin, Jill E. (1981). "Very few cases": Child abuse and neglect in the people's republic of China. In Jill E. Korbin (Ed.), *Child abuse and neglect: Cross-cultural perspectives.* Berkeley, CA: University of California Press.

Korner, Anneliese F., Zeanah, Charles H., Linden, Janine, Berkowitz, Robert I., Kraemer, Helena C., and **Agras, W. Stewart.** (1985). The relation between neonatal and later activity and temperament. *Child Development, 56,* 38–42.

Kornhaber, Arthur, and **Woodward, Kenneth L.** (1981). *Grandparents/grandchildren: The vital connection.* Garden City, NJ: Anchor.

Kornhaber, R.C., and **Schroeder, H.E.** (1975). Importance of model similarity on extinction of avoidance behavior in children. *Journal of Consulting and Clinical Psychology, 43,* 601–607.

Koslowski, Barbara. (1980). Quantitative and qualitative changes in the development of seriation. *Merrill-Palmer Quarterly, 26,* 391–405.

Kotelchuck, Michael. (1976). The infant's relationship to the father: Experimental evidence. In Michael E. Lamb (Ed.), *The role of the father in child development.* New York, Wiley.

Kramer, Judith A., Hill, Kennedy T., and **Cohen, Leslie B.** (1975). Infants' development of object permanence: A refined methodology and new evidence for Piaget's hypothesized ordinality. *Child Development, 46,* 149–155.

Krantz, Murray, Webb, Sally D., and **Andrews, David.** (1984). The relationship between child and parental social competence. *Journal of Psychology, 118,* 51–56.

Kratochwill, T.R. (1981). *Selective mutism: Implications for research and treatment.* Hillsdale, NJ: Erlbaum.

Kravitz, Ruth I., and **Driscoll, James M.** (1983). Expectations for childhood development among child-abusing and nonabusing parents. *American Journal of Orthopsychiatry, 53,* 336–344.

Kuczaj, Stan A., and **Lederberg, A.R.** (1977). Height, age and function: Differing influences on children's comprehension of "older" and "younger." *Journal of Child Language, 4,* 395–416.

Kuczaj, Stan A., and **Maratsos, Michael P.** (1983). Initial verbs of yes-no questions: A different kind of general grammatical category. *Developmental Psychology, 19,* 440–444.

Kuhn, Deanna. (1976). Short-term longitudinal evidence for the sequentiality of Kohlberg's early stages of moral judgment. *Developmental Psychology, 12,* 162–166.

Kuhn, Deanna. (1978). Mechanisms of cognitive and social development: One psychology or two? *Human Development, 25,* 233–249.

Kuhn, Deanna. (Ed.) (1979). *Intellectual development beyond childhood. New Directions in Child Development: Vol. 5.* San Francisco: Jossey-Bass.

Kuhn, Deanna, Langer, Jonas, Kohlberg, Lawrence, and **Haan, Norma S.** (1977). The development of formal operations in logical and moral judgment. *Genetic Psychology Monographs, 95,* 97–188.

Kuhn, Deanna, Nash, Sharon Churnin, and **Brucken, Laura.** (1978). Sex role concepts of two- and three-year-olds. *Child Development, 49,* 445–451.

Kurokawa, Minako. (1969). Acculturation and childhood accidents among Chinese and Japanese Americans. *Genetic Psychology Monographs, 79,* 89–159.

Labov, William. (1972). *Language in the inner city: Studies in the black English vernacular.* Philadelphia: University of Pennsylvania Press.

La Freniere, Peter, Strayer, F.F., and **Gauthier, Roger.** (1984). The emergence of same-sex affiliative preferences among preschool peers: A developmental/ethological perspective. *Child Development, 55,* 1958–1965.

Lamb, David R. (1984). *Physiology of exercise: Response and adaptation* (2nd ed.). New York: Macmillan.

Lamb, Michael E. (1977). The development of parental preferences in the first two years of life. *Sex Roles, 5,* 495–497.

Lamb, Michael E. (1978). Interactions between 18-month-olds and their preschool-aged siblings. *Child Development, 49,* 51–59.

Lamb, Michael E. (1981). The development of father-infant relationships. In Michael E. Lamb (Ed.), *The role of the father in child development* (Rev. Ed.). New York: Wiley.

Lamb, Michael E. (1982). Maternal employment and child development: A review. In Michael E. Lamb (Ed.), *Nontraditional families: Parenting and child development.* Hillsdale, NJ: Erlbaum.

Lamb, Michael E., Frodi, Majt, Hwang, Carl-Philip, and **Frodi, Ann M.** (1983). Effects of paternal involvement on infant preferences for mothers and fathers. *Child Development, 54,* 450–458.

Lamb, Michael E., and **Hwang, C.P.** (1982). Maternal attachment and mother-neonate bonding: A critical review. In Michael E. Lamb and Ann L. Brown (Eds.), *Advances in developmental psychology* (Vol. 2). Hillsdale, NJ: Erlbaum.

Lamb, Michael E., and **Sutton-Smith, Brian** (Eds.). (1982). *Sibling relationships: Their nature and significance across the life-span.* Hillsdale, NJ: Erlbaum.

Lambert, Nadine M., and **Hartsough, Carolyn S.** (1984). Contribution of predispositional factors to the diagnosis of hyperactivity. *American Journal of Orthopsychiatry, 54,* 97–109.

Lambert, Nadine M., Sandoval, Jonathan, and **Sassone, Dana.** (1978). Prevalence of hyperactivity in elementary school children as a function of social system definers. *American Journal of Orthopsychiatry, 48,* 446–463.

Lambert, Wallace, and **Tucker, G. Richard.** (1972). *Bilingual education of children.* Rowley, MA: Newbury House.

Lamm, Stanley S., and **Fisch, Martin L.** (1982). *Learning disabilities explained.* Garden City, NY: Doubleday.

Langlois, J.H., and **Downs, A.C.** (1980). Mothers, fathers, and peers as socialization agents of sex-typed play behaviors in young children. *Child Development, 51,* 1237–1247.

Langone, John. (1981). Too weary to go on. *Discover, 2,* (11), 72–77.

Laosa, Luis. (1980). Maternal teaching strategies in Chicano and Anglo-American families: The influence of culture and education on maternal behavior. *Child Development, 51,* 759–765.

Laosa, Luis. (1984). Social policies toward children of diverse ethnic racial and language groups in the United States. In Harold W. Stevenson and Alberta E. Siegel (Eds.), *Child development research and social policy.* Chicago: University of Chicago Press.

Laosa, Luis M., and **Brophy, Jere E.** (1972). Effects of sex and birth order on sex-role development and intelligence among kindergarten children. *Developmental Psychology, 6,* 409–415.

Larsen, John W. (1982). Toxoplasmosis. In John T. Queenan and John C. Hobbins (Eds.), *Protocols for high-risk pregnancies.* Oradell, NJ: Medical Economics Books.

Larsen, Spencer A., and **Homer, Daryl R.** (1978). Relation of breast versus bottle feeding to hospitalization for gastroenteritis in a middle-class U.S. population. *The Journal of Pediatrics, 92,* 417–418.

Lazar, Irving, and **Darlington, Richard.** (1982). Lasting effects of early education: A report from the consortium for longitudinal studies. *Monographs of the Society for Research in Child Development,* Serial No. 195, Vol. 47, Nos. 2–3.

Leavitt, Jerome E. (1983). Preface. In Jerome E. Leavitt (Ed.). *Child abuse and neglect: Research and innovation.* The Hague: Martinus Nijhoff.

Leboyer, Frederick. (1975). *Birth without violence.* New York: Knopf.

Lee, James Michael. (1980). Christian religious education and moral development. In Brenda Munsey (Ed.), *Moral development, moral education and Kohlberg: Basic issues in philosophy, psychology, religion and education.* Birmingham, AL: Religious Education Press.

Lee, Lee C. (1976). *Personality development in childhood.* Monterey, CA: Brooks/Cole.

Lefkowitz, Monroe M. (1981). Smoking during pregnancy: Long-term effects on offspring. *Developmental psychology, 7,* 192–194.

Leifer, A.D., Leiderman, P.H., Barnett, C.R., and **Williams, J.A.** (1972). Effects of mother-infant separation on maternal attachment behavior. *Child Development, 43,* 1203–1218.

Leifer, Myra. (1980). *Psychological effects of motherhood: A study of first pregnancy.* New York: Praeger.

Lenneberg, Eric H. (1967). *Biological foundations of language.* New York: Wiley.

Lepper, M.R., and **Greene, D.** (Eds.). (1978). *The hidden costs of reward.* Hillsdale, NJ: Erlbaum.

Lerner, H.E. (1978). Adaptive and pathogenic aspects of sex-role stereotypes: Implications for parenting and psychotherapy. *American Journal of Psychiatry, 135*, 48–52.

Lerner, Richard M., Karson, M., Meisels, M., and **Knapp, J.R.** (1975). Actual and perceived attitudes of late adolescents and their parents: The phenomenon of the generation gap. *Journal of Genetic Psychology, 126*, 195–207.

Lerner, Richard M., Schroeder, C., Rewitzer, M., and **Weinstock, A.** (1972). Attitude of high-school students and their parents toward contemporary issues. *Psychology Reports, 31*, 255–258.

Lerner, Richard M., and **Spanier, G.B.** (1978). *Child influences on marital and family interaction.* New York: Academic Press.

Lesser, Gerald S. (1984). A world of difference. *Action for Children's Television Magazine, 13*, 8.

Lester, Barry M., Als, Heidelise, and **Brazelton, T. Berry.** (1982). Regional obstetric anesthesia and newborn behavior: A reanalysis toward synergistic effects. *Child Development, 53*, 687–692.

Lester, Barry M., and **Zeskind, Philip Sanford.** (1982). A biobehavioral perspective on crying in early infancy. In H. Fitzgerald, Barry Lester, and Micheal W. Yogman (Eds.), *Theory and research in behavioral pediatrics* (Vol. 1). New York: Plenum.

Levenstein, Phyllis. (1970). Cognitive growth in preschoolers through verbal interaction with mothers. *American Journal of Orthopsychiatry, 40*, 426–432.

Levenstein, Phyllis, Kochman, Arlene, and **Roth, Helen.** (1973). From laboratory to real world: Service delivery of the mother-child home program. *American Journal of Orthopsychiatry, 43* (1).

Lever, Janet. (1976). Sex differences in the games children play. *Social Problems, 23*, 478–487.

Levine, Laura E. (1983). Mine: Self-definition in 2-year-old boys. *Developmental Psychology, 19*, 544–549.

Lewis, Michael, and **Brooks, Jeanne.** (1978). Self-knowledge and emotional development. In Michael Lewis and Leonard A. Rosenblum (Eds.), *The development of affect.* New York: Plenum, 205–226.

Lewis, Michael, Brooks, Jeanne, and **Haviland, Jeannette.** (1978). Hearts and faces: A study in the measurement of emotion. In Michael Lewis and Leonard Rosenblum, (Eds.), *The development of affect.* New York: Plenum.

Lewis, Michael, and **Brooks-Gunn, Jeanne.** (1979). *Social cognition and the acquisition of self.* New York: Plenum.

Lewis, Michael, Feiring, Candace, McGuffog, Carolyn, and **Jaskir, John.** (1984). Predicting psychopathology in six-year-olds from early social relations. *Child Development, 55*, 123–136.

Lewis, Michael, and **Michalson, Linda.** (1983). *Children's emotions and moods.* New York: Plenum.

Lewis, Richard. (1977). *Miracles: Poems by children of the English-speaking world.* New York: Bantam.

Lewis, Richard. (1978). *Journeys.* New York: Bantam.

Liben, Lynn S. (1982). The developmental study of children's memory. In Tiffany M. Field, Aletha Huston, Herbert C. Quay, Lillian Troll, and Gordon E. Finley (Eds.), *Review of human development.* New York: Wiley.

Lidz, Theodore. (1976). *The person: His and her development throughout the life cycle* (Rev. Ed.). New York: Basic Books.

Liebert, Robert M. (1984). What develops in moral development. In William M. Kurtines and Jacob L. Gewirtz (Eds.), *Morality, moral behavior, and moral development.* New York: Wiley.

Liebert, Robert M., Neale, John M., and **Davidson, Emily S.** (1973). *The early window: Effects of television on children and youth.* New York: Pergamon Press.

Liebert, Robert M., Sprafkin, Joyce, and **Davidson, Emily S.** (1982). *The early window: Effects of television on children and youth* (2nd ed.). New York: Pergamon Press.

Light, P.H., Buckingham, N., and **Robbins, A.H.** (1979). The conservation task as an interactional setting. *British Journal of Educational Psychology, 49*, 304–310.

Lindblad-Goldberg, Marion, and **Dukes, Joyce Lynn.** (1985). Social support in black, low-income, single-parent families: Normative and dysfunctional patterns. *American Journal of Orthopsychiatry, 55*, 42–58.

Linde, Shirley M. (1972). *Sickle cell: A complete guide to prevention and treatment.* New York: Pavilion.

Lindquist, G.T. (1982). Preschool screening as a means of predicting later reading achievement. *Journal of Learning Disabilities, 15*, 331–332.

Linksz, Arthur. (1973). *On writing, reading, and dyslexia.* New York: Grune and Stratton.

Lipsitt, Lewis P. (1978). Perinatal indicators, and psychophysiological precursors of crib death. In Frances Degen Horowitz (Ed.), *Early developmental hazards: Predictors and precautions.* Boulder, CO: Westview Press.

Lipsitt, Lewis P. (1982). Infant learning. In Tiffany M. Field, Aletha Huston, Herbert C. Quay, Lillian Troll, and Gordon E. Finley (Eds.), *Review of human development.* New York: Wiley.

Livesley, W.J., and **Bromley, D.B.** (1973). *Person perception in childhood and adolescence.* London: Wiley.

Livson, Norman, and **Peskin, Harvey.** (1980). Perspectives on adolescence from longitudinal research. In Joseph Adelson, (Ed.), *Handbook of adolescent psychology.* New York: Wiley.

Lock, A. (1980). *The guided reinvention of language.* New York: Academic Press.

Locksley, A., and **Colten, M.E.** (1979). Psychological androgyny: A case of mistaken identity. *Journal of Personality and Social Psychology, 37*, 1017–1031.

Loehlin, John C., Willerman, Lee, and **Horn, Joseph M.** (1982). Personality resemblances between unwed mothers and their adopted-away offspring. *Journal of Personality and Social Psychology, 42*, 1089–1099.

Longstreth, Langdon E. (1980). Human handedness: More evidence for genetic involvement. *Journal of Genetic Psychology, 137*, 275–283.

Lovell, Kenneth, and **Shayer, Michael.** (1978). The impact of the work of Piaget on science curriculum development. In Jeanette McCarthy Gallagher and J.A. Easley, Jr. (Eds.), *Knowledge and development: Vol. 2. Piaget and education.* New York: Plenum Press.

Lowe, Marianne. (1975). Trends in the development of representational play in infants from one to three years—An observational study. *Journal of Child Psychology, 16,* 33–48.

Lowrey, George H. (1978). *Growth and development of children* (7th ed.). Chicago: Year Book Medical Publishers.

Lueptow, Lloyd B. (1984). *Adolescent sex role and social change.* New York: Columbia University Press.

Lynch, Margaret A., and **Roberts, Jacquie.** (1983). A follow-up study of abused children and their families. In Jerome E. Leavitt (Ed.), *Child abuse and neglect: Research and innovation.* The Hague: Martinus Nijhoff.

Lynn, R. (1982). IQ in Japan and the United States shows a growing disparity. *Nature, 297,* 222–223.

Lytton, Hugh, Conway, Dorice, and **Sauvé, Reginald.** (1977). The impact of twinship on parent-child interaction. *Journal of Personality and Social Psychology, 35,* 97–107.

Maccoby, Eleanor Emmons. (1980). *Social development: Psychological growth and the parent-child relationship.* New York: Harcourt Brace Jovanovich.

Maccoby, Eleanor Emmons. (1982). Let's not over-attribute to the attribution process. In E. Tory Higgens, Diane N. Rubble, and Willard W. Hartup (Eds.), *Social cognition and social behavior: Developmental processes.* Cambridge, England: Cambridge University Press.

Maccoby, Eleanor Emmons. (1983). In Norman Garmezy and Michael Rutter (Eds.), *Stress, coping, and development in children.* New York: McGraw-Hill.

Maccoby, Eleanor Emmons. (1984). Socialization and developmental change. *Child Development, 55,* 317–328.

Maccoby, Eleanor Emmons, and **Jacklin, Carol Nagy.** (1980). Sex differences in aggression: A rejoinder and a reprise. *Child Development, 51,* 964–980.

Maccoby, Eleanor Emmons, and **Martin, John A.** (1983). Socialization in the context of the family: Parent-child interaction. In Paul H. Mussen (Ed.), *Handbook of child psychology: Vol. 4. Socialization, personality and social development.* New York: Wiley.

Maccoby, Eleanor Emmons, and **Hagen, John W.** (1965). Effect of distraction upon central versus incidental recall: Developmental trends. *Journal of Experimental Child Psychology, 2,* 280–289.

Maccoby, Eleanor Emmons, and **Jacklin, Carol Nagy.** (1974). *The psychology of sex differences.* Stanford: Stanford University Press.

Macfarlane, Aidan. (1977). *The psychology of childbirth.* Cambridge, MA: Harvard University Press.

Mack, John E. (1981). Psychosocial effects of the nuclear arms race. *Bulletin of Atomic Science, 37,* 18–23.

Mack, John E., and **Hickler, Holly.** (1981). *Vivienne: The life and suicide of an adolescent girl.* Boston: Little, Brown.

Mackenzie, Thomas B., Collins, Nancy M., and **Popkin, Michael E.** (1982). A case of fetal abuse? *American Journal of Orthopsychiatry, 52,* 699–703.

Mackworth, N.H., and **Bruner, Jerome S.** (1970). How adults and children search and recognize pictures. *Human Development, 13,* 149–177.

Madden, John, Levenstein, Phyllis, and **Levenstein, Sidney.** (1976). Longitudinal I.Q. outcomes of the mother-child home program. *Child Development, 47,* 1015–1025.

Madden, John, O'Hara, John, and **Levenstein, Phyllis.** (1984). Home again: Effects of the mother-child home program on mother and child. *Child Development, 55,* 636–647.

Madsen, M.C., and **Shapira, A.** (1977). Cooperation and challenge in four cultures. *Journal of Social Psychology, 102,* 189–195.

Maehr, Martin L. (1974). Culture and achievement motivation. *American Psychologist, 29,* 887–896.

Magnusson, D., Duner, A., and **Zetterblom, G.** (1975). *Adjustment.* New York: Wiley.

Mahler, Margaret. (1968). *On human symbiosis and the vicissitudes of individuation.* New York: International Universities Press.

Mahler, Margaret S., Pine, Fred, and **Bergman, Anni.** (1975). *The psychological birth of the human infant: Symbiosis and individuation.* New York: Basic Books.

Mahoney, Maurice J. (1984). Quoted in Early prenatal diagnosis: How safe? *Science News, 125,* 360.

Main, Mary, and **George, Carol.** (1985). Responses of abused and disadvantaged toddlers to distress in agemates: A study in the day care setting. *Developmental Psychology, 21,* 407–412.

Makinson, Carolyn. (1985). The health consequences of teenage fertility. *Family Planning Perspectives, 17,* 132–139.

Malcolm, Andrew H. (1985, October 20). New generation of poor youths emerges in U. S., *The New York Times,* p. 1.

Malson, M. (1983). The social support systems of black families. *Marriage and Family Review, 5,* 37–57.

Maqsud, M. (1983). Relationship of locus of control to self-esteem, academic performance, and prediction of performance among Nigerian secondary school pupils. *British Journal of Educational Psychology, 53,* 215–221.

Maratsos, Michael. (1982). The child's construction of grammatical categories. In Eric Wanner and Lila R. Gleitman (Eds.), *Language acquistion: The state of the art.* Cambridge, England: Cambridge University Press.

Marcia, James E. (1966). Developmental and validation of ego identity status. *Journal of Personality and Social Psychology, 3,* 551–558.

Marcia, James E. (1980). Identity in adolescence. In Joseph Adelson (Ed.), *Handbook of adolescent psychology.* New York: Wiley.

Marcia, James E., and **Schiedel, Don G.** (1985). Ego identity, intimacy sex role orientation, and gender. *Developmental Psychology, 21*, 149–160.

Margolis, Lewis H., and **Runyan, Carol W.** (1983). Accidental policy: An analysis of the problem of unintended injuries of childhood. *American Journal of Orthopsychiatry, 53*, 629–644.

Markell, Richard A., and **Asher, Steven R.** (1984). Children's interactions in dyads: interpersonal influence and sociometric status. *Child Development, 55*, 1412–1424.

Martin, Barclay. (1975). Parent-child relations. In Frances Degan Horowitz (Ed.), *Review of child development research* (Vol. IV.) Chicago: University of Chicago Press.

Martin, Harold P. (1980). The consequences of being abused and neglected: How the child fares. In C. Henry Kempe and Ray E. Helfer (Eds.), *The battered child* (3rd ed.). Chicago: University of Chicago Press.

Martin, John A. (1981). A longitudinal study of the consequences of early mother-infant interaction: A microanalytic approach. *Monographs of the Society for Research in Child Development, 46* (3, Serial No. 190).

Martinez, G.A., and **Nalezienski, J.P.** (1981). 1980 update: The recent trend in breastfeeding. *Pediatrics, 67*, 260.

Masters, William H., and **Johnson, Virginia E.** (1966). *Human sexual response.* Boston: Little, Brown.

Matarazzo, Joseph D. (1982). Behavioral health's challenge to academic, scientific, and professional psychology. *American Psychologist, 37*, 1–14.

Maugh, Thomas H., III. (1981). A new understanding of sickle cell emerges. *Science, 211*, 265–267.

Mayer, Jean. (1968). *Overweight: Causes, costs, and control.* Englewood Cliffs, NJ: Prentice-Hall.

McAdoo, Harriette. (1979, May). Black kinship. *Psychology Today.*

McAuliffe, Kathleen, and **McAuliffe, Sharon.** (1983, November 6). Keeping up with the genetic revolution. *The New York Times Magazine*, pp. 40–44, 92–97.

McCabe, Maryann. (1985). Dynamics of child sexual abuse. In Maryann McCabe, Ronald E. Cohen, and Victor Weiss (Eds.), *Child sexual abuse.* New York: Goldner Press.

McCall, Robert B. (1979). The development of intellectual functioning in infancy and the prediction of later I.Q. In Joy D. Osofsky (Ed.), *Handbook of infant development.* New York: Wiley.

McCall, Robert B. (1981). Nature-nurture and the two realms of development: A proposed integration with respect to mental development. *Child Development, 52*, 1–12.

McCall, Robert B. (1983). Environmental effects on intelligence: The forgotten realm of discontinuous nonshared within-family factors. *Child Development, 54*, 408–415.

McCall, Robert B. (1984). Developmental changes in mental performance: The effect of the birth of a sibling. *Child Development, 55*, 1317–1321.

McCarthy, Dorothea. (1954). Language development in children. In Leonard Carmichael (Ed.), *Manual of child psychology.* (2nd ed.). New York: Wiley.

McCartney, Kathleen. (1984). Effect of quality of day care environment on children's language development. *Developmental Psychology, 20*, 244–260.

McCleary, Elliott H. (1974). *New miracles of childbirth.* New York: McKay.

McClelland, David C., Constantian, Carol A., Regalado, David, and **Stone, Carolyn.** (1978). Making it to maturity. *Psychology Today, 12* (1), 42–53, 114.

McClelland, Kent A. (1982). Adolescent subculture in the schools. In Tiffany Field, Aletha Huston, Herbert C. Quay, Lillian Troll, and Gordon E. Finley (Eds.), *Review of human development.* New York: Wiley.

McGarrigle, J., and **Donaldson, Margaret.** (1974). Conservation "accidents." *Cognition, 3*, 341–350.

McGhee, Paul H. (1971). Cognitive development and children's comprehension of humor. *Child Development, 42*, 123–138.

McGlaughin, Alex, and **Empson, Janet M.** (1983). Sisters and their children. Implications for a cycle of deprivation. In Nicola Madge (Ed.), *Families at risk.* London: Heinemann.

McGurk, Harry, and **Lewis, Michael.** (1974). Space perception in early infancy: Perception within a common auditory-visual space? *Science, 186*, 649–650.

McIntire, Roger W. (1973). Parenthood training or mandatory birth control: Take your choice. *Psychology Today, 7* (5), 34–39, 132–133, 143.

McKusick, Victor A. (1979). *Mendelian inheritance in man: Catalog of autosomal dominant, autosomal recessive, and X-linked phenotypes* (5th ed.). Baltimore: Johns Hopkins Press.

McLaughlin, Barry. (1984). *Second language acquisition in childhood: Vol. 1. Preschool children* (2nd ed.). Hillsdale, NJ: Erlbaum.

McNeill, David. (1970). Language development in children. In Paul Mussen (Ed.), *Handbook of child psychology* (3rd ed.). New York: Wiley.

McRoy, Ruth G. and **Zurcher Louis A.** (1983). *Transracial and interracial adoptees: The adolescent years.* Springfield IL: Thomas.

Mead, George Herbert. (1934). *Mind, self, and society.* Chicago: University of Chicago Press.

Meadow, Kathryn P. (1975). The development of deaf children. In E. Mavis Hetherington (Ed.), *Review of child development research*, (Vol. V.). Chicago: University of Chicago Press.

Meilman, Phillip W. (1979). Cross-sectional age changes in ego identity status during adolescence. *Developmental Psychology, 15*, 230–231.

Mellendick, George J.D. (1983). Nutritional issues in adolescence. In Adele D. Hofmann (Ed.), *Adolescent medicine.* Reading, MA: Addison-Wesley.

Meltzoff, Andrew N. and **Moore, M. Keith.** (1983). Newborn infants imitate adult facial gestures. *Child Development, 54*, 702–709.

Mendelsohn, Eve, Robinson, Susan, Gardner, Howard, and **Winner, Ellen.** (1984). Are preschoolers renaming intentional category violations? *Developmental Psychology, 20*, 187–192.

Mercer, Jane F. (1979). *System of multicultural pluralistic assessment (SOMPA) technical manual.* New York: Psychological Corporation.

Meredith, Howard V. (1978). Research between 1960 and 1970 on the standing height of young children in different parts of the world. In Hayne W. Reese and Lewis P. Lipsitt (Eds.), *Advances in child development and behavior* (Vol. 12, pp. 2–59). New York: Academic Press.

Mervis, Carolyn B., and **Mervis, Cynthia A.** (1982). Leopards are kitty-cats: Object labeling by mothers for their thirteen-month-olds. *Child Development, 53,* 267–273.

Messick, Samuel. (1980). Test validity and the ethics of assessment. *American Psychologist, 35,* 1012–1027.

Messick, Samuel. (1983). Assessment of children. In Paul H. Mussen (Ed.), *Handbook of child psychology: Vol. 3. Cognitive development.* New York: Wiley.

Meyer, Thomas J. (1985, December 4). 1 in 10 students said to suffer from sexual disease chlamydia. *Chronicle of Higher Education,* pp. 33, 35.

Michel, George F. (1981). Right-handedness: A consequence of infant supine head-orientation preference? *Science, 212,* 685–687.

Miller, C. Arden. (1985). Infant mortality in the U.S. *Scientific American, 235* (1), 31–37.

Miller, George L. (1985, June). Cocaine. In U.S. Public Health Services, *Patterns and trends in drug abuse: A national and international perspective.* Department of Health and Human Services, Washington DC.

Miller, Louise B., and **Bizzell, Rondeall P.** (1983). Long-term effects of four preschool programs: Sixth, seventh, and eighth grades. *Child Development, 54,* 727–741.

Miller, Louise B., and **Dyer, Jean L.** (1975). Four preschool programs: Their dimensions and effects. *Monographs of the Society for Research in Child Development, 40* (5&6).

Miller, Patricia H. (1983). *Theories of developmental psychology.* San Francisco: Freeman.

Miller, Peter, Smith, David W., and **Shepard, Thomas H.** (1978). Maternal hyperthermia a possible cause of anencephaly. *Lancet, I,* 8076, 519–521.

Miller, Shelby H. (1983). *Children as parents: Final report on a study of childbearing and child rearing among 12–15 year-olds.* New York: Child Welfare League of America.

Miller, William R., and **Lief, Harold I.** (1976). Masturbatory attitudes, knowledge, and experience: Data from the sex knowledge and attitude test (SKAT). *Archives of Sexual Behavior, 5,* 447–467.

Milne, Conrad, Seefeldt, Vern, and **Reuschlein, Philip.** (1976). Relationship between grade, sex, race, and motor performance in young children. *Research Quarterly, 47,* 726–730.

Milunsky, Aubrey. (1977). *Know your genes.* Boston: Houghton Mifflin.

Minuchin, Patricia P. (1977). *The middle years of childhood.* Monterey, CA: Brooks/Cole.

Minuchin, Patricia, and **Shapiro, Edna K.** (1983). The school as a context for social development. In Paul H. Mussen (Ed.), *Handbook of child psychology: Vol. 4. Socialization, personality and social development.* New York: Wiley.

Minuchin, Salvador, Rosman, Bernice L., and **Baker, Lester.** (1978). *Psychosomatic families: Anorexia nervosa in context.* Cambridge, MA: Harvard University Press.

Mischel, Walter. (1970). Sex typing and socialization. In Paul H. Mussen (Ed.), *Carmichael's manual of child development* (Vol. II). New York: Wiley.

Mischel, Walter. (1977). On the future of personality measurement. *American Psychologist, 32,* 246–254.

Mischel, Walter. (1979). On the interface of cognition and personality: Beyond the person-situation debate. *American Psychologist, 34,* 740–754.

Mitchell, G., and **Shively, C.** (1984). Naturalistic and experimental studies of nonhuman primate and other animal families. In Ross D. Parke (Ed.), *Review of child development research: Vol. 7. The family.* Chicago: University of Chicago Press.

Miyake, Kazuo, Chen, Shing-jen, and **Campos, Joseph J.** (1985). Infant temperament, mother's mode of interaction, and attachment in Japan: An interim report. In Inge Bretherton and Everett Waters, (Eds.), *Growing points of attachment theory and research. Monographs of the Society for Research in Child Development, 50* (1–2, Serial No. 209).

Moen, Phyllis. (1982). The two-provider family: Problems and potentials. In Michael E. Lamb (Ed.), *Nontraditional families: Parenting and child development.* Hillsdale, NJ: Erlbaum.

Moore, Keith L. (1982). *The developing human: Clinically oriented embryology* (3rd ed.). Philadelphia: Saunders.

Moore, Raymond S., and **Moore, Dorothy N.** (1975). *Better late than early.* New York: Reader's Digest Press.

Morgan, Brian L.G. (1982). Effects of hormonal and other factors on growth and development. In John W.T. Dickerson and Harry McGurk, (Eds.), *Brain and behavioral development: Interdisciplinary perspectives on structure and function.* London: Surrey University Press.

Moss, Melvin. (February 19, 1979). Director of Medical Research for Muscular Dystrophy Foundation. Personal communication.

Mukherjee, Anil B., and **Hodgen, Gary D.** (1982). Maternal ethanol exposure induces transient impairment of umbilical circulation and fetal hypoxia in monkeys. *Science, 218,* 700–702.

Muller-Schwarze, Dietland, Stagge, Barbara, and **Muller-Schwarze, Christine.** (1982). Play behavior: Persistence, decrease, and energetic compensation during food shortage in deer fawns. *Science, 215,* 85–87.

Murphy, John M., and **Gilligan, Carol.** (1980). Moral development in late adolescence and adulthood: A critique and reconstruction of Kohlberg's theory. *Human Development, 23,* 77–104.

Murphy, Lois Barclay, and **Moriarty, Alice E.,** (1976). *Vulnerability, coping, and growth: From infancy to adolescence.* New Haven: Yale University Press.

Murray, Ann D., Dolby, Robyn M., Nation, Roger L., and **Thomas, David B.** (1981). Effects of epidural anesthesia on newborns and their mothers. *Child Development, 52,* 71–82.

Mussen, Paul Henry, and **Eisenberg-Berg, Nancy.** (1977). *Roots of caring, sharing, and helping: The development of prosocial behavior in children.* San Francisco: Freeman.

Mussen, Paul Henry, and **Jones, Mary Cover.** (1957). Self-conceptions, motivations, and interpersonal attitudes of late- and early-maturing boys. *Child Development, 28,* 243–256.

Myers, Barbara J. (1982). Early intervention using Brazelton training with middle-class mothers and fathers of newborns. *Child Development, 53,* 462–471.

Myers, Barbara J. (1984). Mother-infant bonding: the status of this critical period hypothesis. *Developmental Review, 4,* 240–274.

Myers, H.F. (1982). Research on the Afro-American family: A critical review. In B. Bass, G. Wyatt, and G. Powell (Eds.), *The Afro-American family: Assessment, treatment and research issues.* New York: Grune and Stratton.

National Center for Health Statistics. (1971). *Parent ratings of behavioral patterns of children* (Series 11, No. 108). United States Department of Health, Education and Welfare, Rockville, MD.

National Center for Health Statistics. (1976). NCHS Growth Charts, *Vital Statistics, 253* (Supp.). U.S. Department of Health, Education, and Welfare.

National Center for Health Statistics. (1979). *Trends in breast-feeding among American mothers* (Series 23, No. 3). Division of Vital Statistics, National Center for Health Statistics, Washington DC.

National Center for Health Statistics. (1984a). *Vital statistics of the United States, 1979: Vol. 2. Mortality (Part A).* United States Department of Health and Human Services, Hyattsville, MD.

National Center for Health Statistics. (1984b). Advance report of final mortality statistics, 1982. *Monthly Vital Statistics, 33,* (9).

National Center for Health Statistics. (1984c). Multiple causes of death in the United States. *Monthly Vital Statistics, 32,* (10, Supplement 2).

National Institute of Child Health. (1979). *Antenatal diagnosis.* United States Department of Health, Education, and Welfare, NIH publication No. 80-1973.

National Research Council. (1985). *Injury in America: A continuing public health problem.* Washington DC: National Academy Press.

Neimark, Edith D. (1975). Intellectual development during adolescence. In Frances Degan Horowitz (Ed.), *Review of research in child development* (Vol. IV). Chicago: University of Chicago Press.

Neimark, Edith D. (1982). Cognitive development in adulthood: Using what you've got. In Tiffany M. Field, Aletha Huston, Herbert C. Quay, Lillian Troll, and Gordon E. Finley (Eds.), *Review of human development.* New York: Wiley.

Nelson, Katherine. (1973). Structure and strategy in learning to talk. *Monographs of the Society for Research in Child Development, 38* (1 & 2, Serial No. 149).

Nelson, Katherine. (1981). Individual differences in language development: Implications for development and language. *Developmental Psychology, 17,* 170–187.

Nelson, Katherine, and **Gruendel, Janice M.** (1981). Generalized event representations: Basic building blocks of cognitive development. In Ann Brown and Michael Lamb (Eds.), *Advances in developmental psychology* (Vol. 1). Hillsdale, NJ: Erlbaum.

Nelson-Le Gall, Sharon A., and **Gumerman, Ruth A.** (1984). Children's perceptions of helpers and helper motivation. *Journal of Applied Developmental Psychology, 5,* 1–12.

Nettlebladt, Per, Fagerstrom, Carl-Fredrik, and **Uddenberg, Nils.** (1976). The significance of reported childbirth pain. *Journal of Psychosomatic Research, 20,* 215–221.

Newberger, Carolyn Moore, Newberger, Eli H., and **Harper, Gordon P.** (1976). The social ecology of malnutrition in childhood. In John D. Lloyd-Still (Ed.), *Malnutrition and intellectual development* (pp. 160–186). Littleton, MA: Publishing Sciences Group.

Newberry, Phillis, Weissman, Myrna, and **Myers, Jerome K.** (1979). Working wives and housewives: Do they differ in mental status and social adjustment? *American Journal of Orthopsychiatry, 49,* 282–291.

Newbrun, Ernest. (1982). Sugar and dental caries: A review of human studies. *Science, 217,* 418–423.

Newcomer, Susan F., and **Udry, J. Richard.** (1985). Parent-child communication and adolescent sexual behavior. *Family Planning Perspectives, 17,* 169–174.

Nisbett, R.E., and **Ross, Lee.** (1980). *Human inference: Strategies and shortcomings of social judgment.* Englewood Cliffs, NJ: Prentice-Hall.

Nix, Gary W. (Ed.). (1976). *Mainstream education for hearing impaired children and youth.* New York: Grune & Stratton.

Novak, M.A., and **Harlow, Harry F.** (1975). Social recovery of monkeys isolated for the first year of life: 1. Rehabilitation and therapy. *Developmental Psychology, 11,* 453–465.

Nyhan, William L., (1976). *The heredity factor: Genes, chromosomes and you.* New York: Grosset and Dunlop.

O'Brien, Marion, and **Huston, Aletha C.** (1985). Development of sex-typed play behavior in toddlers. *Developmental Psychology, 21,* 866–871.

O'Brien, Marion, Huston, Aletha C., and **Risley, Todd R.** (1983). Sex-typed play of toddlers in a day care center. *Journal of Applied Developmental Psychology, 4,* 1–9.

O'Brien, Thomas E. and **McManus, Carol E.** (1978). Drugs and the fetus. A consumer's guide by generic and brand name. *Birth and the Family Journal, 5,* 58–86.

O'Conner, S., Vietze, P.M., Sherrod, K.B., Sandler, H.M., and **Altermeiner, W.A.** (1980). Reduced incidence of parenting inadequacy following rooming-in. *Pediatrics, 66,* 176–182.

Offer, Daniel (1969). *The psychological world of the teenager: A study of normal adolescent boys.* New York: Basic Books.

Offer, Daniel, and **Offer, Judith** (1975). *From teenage to young manhood.* New York: Basic Books.

Ogra, Pearay L. and **Greene, Harry L.** (1982). Human milk and breast feeding: An update on the state of the art. *Pediatric Research, 16,* 266–271.

Ollendick, Thomas H., Francis, Greta, and **Hart, Kathleen J.** (1985). Correlates of adult and child perception of social competency. *Journal of Abnormal Child Psychology, 13,* 129–141.

Olson, Emelie A. (1981). Socioeconomic and psychocultural contexts of child abuse and neglect in Turkey. In Jill E. Korbin (Ed.), *Child abuse and neglect: Cross-cultural perspectives.* Berkeley, CA: University of California Press.

Olson, Lawrence. (1983). *Costs of children.* Lexington, MA: Lexington Books.

Omenn, Gilbert S. (1978). Prenatal diagnosis of genetic disorders. *Science, 200,* 952–958.

Opie, Iona, and **Opie, Peter** (1959). *The lore and language of schoolchildren.* Oxford: The Clarendon Press.

Orlofsky, J.L. (1977). Sex role orientation, identity formation, and self-esteem in college men and women. *Sex roles, 3,* 561–575.

Ornitz, Edward M. and **Ritvo, Edward R.** (1976). The syndrome of autism: A critical review. *American Journal of Psychiatry, 133,* 609-621.

Osherson, Daniel N., and **Markman, Ellen** (1974–1975). Language and the ability to evaluate contradictions and tautologies. *Cognition, 3,* 213–226.

Osman, Betty B. (1979). *Learning disabilities: A family affair.* New York: Random House.

Oster, Harriet (1978). Facial expression and affect development. In Michael Lewis and Leonard A. Rosenblum (Eds.), *The development of affect.* New York: Plenum.

Osterrieth, Paul A. (1969). Adolescence: Some psychological aspects. In Gerald Caplan and Serge Lebovici (Eds.), *Adolescence: Psychosocial perspectives.* (pp. 11–21). New York: Basic Books.

Ostrea, Enrique M., Jr., and **Chavez, Cleofe J.** (1979). Perinatal problems (excluding neonatal withdrawal) in maternal drug addiction: A study of 830 cases. *The Journal of Pediatrics, 94,* 292–295.

Oyama, S. (1976). A sensitive period for the acquisition of non-native phonological system. *Journal of Psycholinguistic Research, 5,* 261-284.

Paige, Karen Eriksen. (1983). A bargaining theory of menarcheal responses in preindustrial cultures. In Jeanne Brooks-Gunn and Anne C. Petersen (Eds.), *Girls at puberty: Biological and psychosocial perspectives.* New York: Plenum.

Palmer, Frances H. (1978). The efects of early childhood intervention. In Bernard Brown (Ed.), *Found: Long-term gains from early intervention.* Boulder, CO: Westview Press.

Papousek, Hanus, and **Papousek, Mechthild.** (1982). Infant-adult social interactions: Their origins, dimensions, and failures. In Tiffany M. Field, Aletha Huston, Herbert C. Quay, Lillian Troll, and Gordon E. Finley (Eds.), *Review of human development.* New York: Wiley.

Parke, Ross D. (1977). Punishment in children: Effects, side effects, and alternative strategies. In Harry L. Hom, Jr. and Paul A. Robinson (Eds.), *Psychological processes in early education* (pp. 71–97). New York: Academic Press.

Parke, Ross D. (1979). The father of the child. *The Sciences, 19*(4), 12–15.

Parke, Ross D. (Ed.) (1984). *Review of child development research: (Vol. 7) The family.* Chicago: University of Chicago Press.

Parke, Ross D. and **Sawin, Douglas B.** (1975, April). *Infant characteristics and behavior as elicitors of maternal and paternal responsivity in the newborn period.* Paper presented at the biennial meeting of the Society for Research in Child Development, Denver.

Parke, Ross D., and **Slaby, Ronald G.** (1983). The development of aggression. In Paul H. Mussen (Ed.), *Handbook of child psychology: Vol. 4. Socialization and personality development.* New York: Wiley.

Parke, Ross D., and **Tinsley, Barbara R.** (1981). The father's role in infancy: Determinants of involvement in caregiving and play. In Michael E. Lamb (Ed.), *The role of the father in child development* (2nd ed.). New York: Wiley.

Parmelee, Arthur H., Jr., and **Sigman, Marian D.** (1983). Perinatal brain development and behavior. In Paul H. Mussen (Ed.), *Handbook of child psychology: Vol. 2. Infancy and developmental psychobiology.* New York: Wiley.

Parten, Mildred B. (1932). Social particpation among preschool children. *Journal of Abnormal and Social Psychology, 27,* 243–269.

Patterson, Gerald R. (1980). Mothers: The unacknowledged victims. *Monographs of the Society for Research in Child Development, 45,* (5, Serial No. 186).

Patterson, Gerald R. (1982). *Coercive family processes.* Eugene, OR: Castalia Press.

Patterson, Gerald R., Littman, R.A., and **Bricker, W.** (1967). Assertive behavior in children: A step toward a theory of aggression. *Monographs of the Society for Research in Child Development, 32* (Serial No. 113).

Paulston, Christina Bratt. (1978). Bilingual/bicultural education. In Lee S. Shulman (Ed.), *Review of research in education.* Itasca, IL: Peacock.

Pawson, M., and **Morris, Norman.** (1972). The role of the father in pregnancy and labor. In Norman Morris (Ed.), *Psychosomatic medicine in obstetrics and gynecology.* Basel, Switzerland: Karger.

Pederson, Frank A., Yarrow, Leon J., Anderson, Barbara J., and **Cain, Richard L., Jr.** (1979). Conceptualization of father influences in the infancy period. In Michael Lewis and Leonard A. Rosenblum (Eds.), *The Child and his family.* New York: Plenum.

Peel, E.A. (1971). *The nature of adolescent judgment.* New York: Wiley.

Pelton, Leroy H. (1978). Child abuse and neglect: The myth of classlessness. *American Journal of Orthopsychiatry, 48,* 608-617.

Pennington, Bruce F., Bender, Bruce, Puck, Mary, Salbenblatt, James, and **Robinson, Arthur.** (1982). Learning disabilities in children with sex chromosomal anomalies. *Child Development, 53,* 1182-1192.

Persaud, T.V.N. (1977). *Problems of birth defects: From Hippocrates to thalidomide and after: Original papers.* Baltimore: University Park Press.

Petersen, Anne C., and **Taylor, Brandon.** (1980). The biological approach to adolescence. In Joseph Adelson (Ed.), *Handbook of adolescent psychology.* New York: Wiley.

Peters-Martin, Patricia, and **Wachs, Theodore D.** (1984). A longitudinal study of temperament and its correlates in the first 12 months. *Infant Behavior and Development, 7,* 285-298.

Petzel, Sue V., and **Riddle, Mary.** (1981). Adolescent suicide: Psychosocial and cognitive aspects. In Feinstein, Looney, Schwartzberg, and Sorosky (Eds.), *Adolescent psychiatry: Developmental and clinical studies.* Chicago and London: The University of Chicago Press. (pp. 343-398).

Phipps-Yonas, Susan. (1980). Teenage pregnancy and motherhood: A review of the literature. *American Journal of Orthopsychiatry, 50,* 403-431.

Piaget, Jean. (1952a). *The origins of intelligence in children.* Margaret Cook (Trans.). New York: International Universities Press.

Piaget, Jean. (1952b). *The child's conception of number.* London: Routledge and Kegan Paul.

Piaget, Jean. (1959). *The language and thought of the child* (3rd ed.). Marjorie and Ruth Gabain (Trans.). London: Routledge and Kegan Paul.

Piaget, Jean. (1962). *Judgment and reasoning in the child.* Marjorie Warden (Trans.). London: Routledge and Paul. (Original work published 1928)

Piaget, Jean. (1965). *The moral judgment of the child.* Marjorie Gabain (Trans.). New York: The Free Press. (Original work published 1932)

Piaget, Jean. (1967). *Six psychological studies.* New York: Random House. (Originally published as *Six Etudes de Psychologie,* 1964).

Piaget, Jean. (1970a). *The child's conception of time,* A.J. Pomerans (Trans.). New York: Basic Books.

Piaget, Jean. (1970b). *The child's conception of movement and speed,* G.E.T. Holloway and M.J. Mackenzie (Trans.). New York: Basic Books.

Piaget, Jean. (1972). Intellectual evolution from adolescence to adulthood. *Human Development, 15,* 1-12.

Piaget, Jean. (1976). *The grasp of consciousness: Action and concept in the young child,* Susan Wedgwood (Trans.). Cambridge, MA: Harvard University Press.

Piaget, Jean. (1983). Piaget's theory. In Paul H. Mussen (Ed.), *Handbook of child psychology: Vol. 1. History, theory, and methods.* New York: Wiley. (Original work published 1970)

Piaget, Jean and **Inhelder, Bärbel.** (1963). *The child's conception of space,* F.J. Langdon and J.L. Lunzer (Trans.). London: Routledge and Paul.

Piaget, Jean, and **Inhelder, Bärbel.** (1969). *The psychology of the child,* Helen Weaver (Trans.). New York: Basic Books.

Piaget, Jean, and **Inhelder, Bärbel.** (1974). *The child's construction of quantities: Conservation and atomism.* London: Routledge and Kegan Paul.

Piaget, Jean, and **Szeminska, Aline.** (1965). *The child's conception of number,* Caleb Gattegno and F. Hodgson (Trans.). New York: Norton.

Pick, Anne D., Frankel, Daniel G., and **Hess, Valerie.** (1975). Children's attention: The development of selectivity. In E. Mavis Hetherington (Ed.), *Review of child development research* (Vol. V). Chicago: University of Chicago Press.

Pines, Maya. (1978). Invisible playmates. *Psychology Today, 12* (4), 38-42, 106.

Pines, Maya. (1984). In the shadow of Huntington's. *Science 84, 5,* (4), 32-39.

Pissanos, Becky W., Moore, Jane B., and **Reeve, T. Gilmour.** (1983). Age, sex, and body composition as predictors of children's performance on basic motor abilities and health-related fitness items. *Perceptual and Motor Skills, 56,* 71-77.

Poffenberger, Thomas. (1981). Child rearing and social structure in rural India: Toward a cross-cultural definition of child abuse and neglect. In Jill E. Korbin (Ed.), *Child abuse and neglect: Cross-cultural perspectives.* Berkeley, CA: University of California Press.

Polit, Denise. (1984). The only child in single-parent families. In Toni Falbo (Ed.), *The single-child family.* New York: Guilford.

Powers, Stephen, and **Wagner, Michael J.** (1984). Attributions for school achievement of middle school students. *Journal of Early Adolescence, 4,* 215-222.

Prescott, G.A., Balow, I.H., Hogan, T.P., and **Farr, R.C.** (1978). *Teacher's manual of administering and interpreting complete survey battery, Metropolitan Achievement Test: Elementary.* New York: Harcourt, Brace, Jovanovich.

Pringle, Mia Kellmer. (1974). Reducing the costs of raising children in inadequate environments. In Nathan B. Talbot (Ed.), *Raising children in modern America: Problems and prospective* (pp. 189-215). Boston: Little Brown.

Provence, Sally. (1978). A clinician's view of affect development in infancy. In Michael Lewis and Leonard Rosenblum, (Eds.), *The development of affect.* New York: Plenum.

Public Health Services. (1985, June). *Patterns and trends in drug abuse: A national and international perspective.* U.S. Department of Health and Human Services, Washington, D.C.

Queenan, John T., and **Hobbins, John C.** (Eds.). (1982). *Protocols for high-risk pregnancies.* Oradell, NJ: Medical Economics Books.

Radin, Norma. (1982). Primary caregiving and role-sharing fathers. In Michael E. Lamb (Ed.), *Nontraditional families: Parenting and child development.* Hillsdale, NJ: Erlbaum.

Radke-Yarrow, Marian, Zahn-Waxler, Carolyn, and **Chapman, Michael.** (1983). Children's prosocial dispositions and behavior. In Paul H. Mussen (Ed.), *Handbook of child psychology: Vol. 4. Socialization and personality development.* New York: Wiley.

Ramey, C.T., and **Haskins, Ron.** (1981). The causes and treatment of school failure: Insights from the Carolina Abecedarian Project. In M.J. Begab, H. Garber, and H.C. Haywood (Eds.), *Psychosocial influences in retarded performance: Vol. 2. Strategies for improving competence.* Baltimore: University Park Press.

Ramsay, Douglas S. (1980). Onset of unimanual handedness in infants. *Infant Behavior and Development, 3,* 377–385.

Ramsay, Douglas S. (1984). Onset of duplicated syllable babbling and unimanual handedness in infancy: Evidence for developmental change in hemispheric specialization? *Developmental Psychology, 20,* 64–71.

Rank, Otto. (1929). *The trauma of birth.* New York: Harcourt Brace.

Raring, Richard H. (1975). *Crib death.* Hicksville, NY: Exposition Press.

Ravitch, Diane. (1983). *The troubled crusade: American education 1945–1980.* New York: Basic Books.

re:act. (1984). Viewing goes up. *Action for Children's Television Magazine, 13,* p. 4.

Rebelsky, Freda G., Starr, Raymond H., Jr., and **Luria, Zella.** (1967). Language development: The first four years. In Yvonne Brackbill (Ed.), *Infancy and early childhood.* New York: The Free Press.

Reinis, Stanislav, and **Goldman, Jerome.** (1980). *The development of the brain: Biological and functional perspectives.* Springfield, IL: Thomas.

Resnick, Lauren B. (1983). Mathematics and science learning: A new conception. *Science, 220,* 477–478.

Rest, James R. (1983). Morality. In Paul H. Mussen (Ed.), *Handbook of child psychology: Vol. 3. Cognitive development.* New York: Wiley.

Rholes, William S., Blackwell, Janette, Jordan, Carol, and **Walters, Connie.** (1980). A developmental study of learned helplessness. *Developmental Psychology, 16,* 616–624.

Rice, Mabel L. (1982). Child language: What children know and how. In Tiffany Field, Aletha Huston, Herbert C. Quay, Lillian Troll, and Gordon E. Finley (Eds.), *Review of human development.* New York: Wiley.

Rice, Mabel L. (1984). Cognitive aspects of communicative development. In Richard L. Schiefelbusch and Joanne Pickar (Eds.), *The acquisition of communicative competence.* Baltimore: University Park Press.

Riordan, Jan. (1983). *A practical guide to breastfeeding.* St. Louis, MO: Mosby.

Ritchie, Jane, and **Ritchie, James.** (1981). Child rearing and child abuse: The Polynesian context. In Jill E. Korbin (Ed.), *Child abuse and neglect: Cross-cultural perspectives.* Berkeley, CA: University of California Press.

Roberts, Jean, and **Baird, James T., Jr.** (1972). National Center for Health Statistics. *Behavior patterns of children in school.* Series 11–#113, DHEW Publication No. 72–1042.

Roberts, J. Fraser. (1973). *An introduction to medical genetics* (6th ed.). London: Oxford University Press.

Robinson, E.J. and **Robinson, W.P.** (1981). Ways of reacting to communication failure in relation to the development of the child's understanding about verbal communication. *European Journal of Social Psychology, 11,* 189–208.

Robinson, Halbert B. (1981). The uncommonly bright child. In Michael Lewis and Leonard A. Rosenblum (Eds.), *The uncommon child.* New York: Plenum.

Robinson, Ira E., and **Jedlicka, Davor.** (1982). Change in sexual behavior of college students from 1965 to 1980: A research note. *Journal of Marriage and the Family, 44,* 237–240.

Robinson, Nancy, and **Robinson, Halbert.** (1976). *The mentally retarded child: A psychological approach.* New York: McGraw-Hill.

Roche, Alex F. (1981). The adipocyte-number hypothesis. *Child Development, 52,* 31–43.

Rodholm, M. (1981). Effects of father-infant post-partum contact on their interaction 3 months after birth. *Early Human Development, 5,* 79–86.

Rodman, Hyman, Pratte, David J., and **Nelson, Rosemary Smith.** (1985). Child care arrangements and children's functioning: A comparison of self-care and adult care children. *Developmental Psychology, 21,* 413–418.

Rogers, Sinclair. (1976). The language of children and adolescents and the language of schooling. In Sinclair Rogers, (Ed.), *They don't speak our language.* London: Edward Arnold.

Romaine, Suzanne. (1984). *The language of children and adolescents: the acquisition of communication competence.* Oxford: Blackwell.

Romalis, Shelly. (1981). *Childbirth: Alternatives to medical control.* Austin: University of Texas Press.

Roman, Mel, and **Haddad, William.** (1978). *The disposable parent: The case for joint custody.* New York: Holt, Rinehart and Winston.

Roopnarine, Jaipual L. (1984). Sex-typed socialization in mixed-age preschool classrooms. *Child Development, 55,* 1078–1084.

Roper, R., and **Hinde, R.A.** (1978). Social behavior in a play group: Consistency and complexity. *Child Development, 49,* 570–579.

Rose, Susan A. (1983). Differential rates of visual information processing in full-term and preterm infants. *Child Development, 54,* 1189–1198.

Rose, Susan A. (1984). Developmental changes in hemispheres specialization for tactile processing in very young children: Evidence from cross-modal transfer. *Developmental Psychology, 20,* 568–574.

Rosenbach, John H., and **Mowder, Barbara A.** (1981). Test bias: The other side of the coin. *Psychology in the Schools, 18*, 450–454.

Ross, Bruce M., and **Kerst, Stephen M.** (1978). Developmental memory theories: Baldwin and Piaget. In Hayne W. Reese and Lewis P. Lipsitt (Eds.), *Advances in child development and behavior* (Vol. XII). New York: Academic Press.

Ross, Dorothea M., and **Ross, Sheila A.** (1982). *Hyperactivity: Current issues, research, and theory* (2nd ed.). New York: Wiley.

Ross, Lee. (1981). The "intuitive scientist" formulation and its developmental implications. In John H. Flavell and Lee Ross (Eds.), *Social cognitive development: Frontiers and possible futures.* Cambridge: Cambridge University Press.

Rotberg, Iris C. (1981). Federal policy issues in elementary and secondary education. In Robert A. Miller (Ed.), *The federal role in education: New directions for the eighties.* Washington DC: Institute for Educational Leadership.

Rotberg, Iris C. (1982). Some legal and research considerations in establishing federal policy in bilingual education. *Harvard Educational Review, 52*, 149–168.

Rothbart, M.K., and **Derryberry, D.** (1981). Development of individual differences in temperament. In Michael E. Lamb and Ann L. Brown (Eds.), *Advances in developmental psychology (Vol. 1).* Hillsdale, NJ: Erlbaum.

Rother, Larry. (1985, July 30). Full-day kindergarten is gaining in popularity. *The New York Times,* pp. C 1, 9.

Routh, Donald K., Schroeder, Carolyn S., and **O'Tuama, Lorcan A.** (1974). Development of activity level in children. *Developmental Psychology, 10*, 163–168.

Rubin, Kenneth H. (1977). The social and cognitive value of preschool toys and activities. *Canadian Journal of Behavioral Science, 9*, 382–385.

Rubin, Kenneth H., Fein, Greata G., and **Vandenberg, Brian.** (1983). Play. In Paul H. Mussen (Ed.), *Handbook of child psychology: Vol. 4. Socialization, personality and social development.* New York: Wiley.

Rubin, Zick. (1980). *Children's friendships.* Cambridge, MA: Harvard University Press.

Rubin, Zick, and **Sloman, Jane.** (1984). How parents influence their children's friendships. In Michael Lewis (Ed.), *Beyond the dyad.* New York: Plenum.

Ruble, Diane N., Balaban, Terry, and **Cooper, Joel.** (1981). Gender constancy and the effects of sex-typed televised toy commercials. *Child Development, 52*, 667–673.

Ruble, Diane N., and **Brooks-Gunn, Jeanne.** (1982). The experience of menarche. *Child Development, 53*, 1557–1577.

Ruddy, Margaret G., and **Bornstein, Marc H.** (1982). Cognitive correlates of infant attention and maternal stimulation over the first year of life. *Child Development, 53*, 183–188.

Rudel, Harry W., Kinel, Fred A., and **Henzl, Milan R.** (1973). *Birth control: Contraception and abortion.* New York: Macmillan.

Ruff, Holly A. (1982). The development of object perception in infancy. In Tiffany M. Field, Aletha Huston, Herbert C.

Quay, Lillian Troll, and Gordon E. Finley (Eds.), *Review of human development.* New York: Wiley.

Rush, David, Stein, Zena, and **Sudder, Mervyn.** (1980). *Diet in pregnancy: A randomized controlled trial of nutritional supplements.* New York: Liss.

Russell, Diana E.H. (1983). The incidence and prevalence of intrafamilial and extrafamilial sexual abuse of female children. *Child Abuse and Neglect, 7*, 133–146.

Russell, Diana E.H. (1984). Sexual exploitation: Rape, child sexual abuse, and workplace harassment. *Sage Library of Social Research, 155.* Beverly Hills, CA: Sage Publications.

Russell, Graeme. (1978). The father role and its relation to masculinity, femininity, and androgyny. *Child Development, 49*, 1174–1181.

Russell, Michael J. (1976). Human olfactory communication. *Nature, 260*, 520–522.

Rutter, Michael. (1975). *Helping troubled children.* London: Penguin.

Rutter, Michael. (1979). Protective factors in children's responses to stress and disadvantage. In Martha Whalen Kent and Jon E. Rolf (Eds.), *Primary prevention of psychopathology: Vol. III. Social competence in children.* Hanover, N.H.: University Press of New England.

Rutter, Michael. (1980). *Changing youth in a changing society: Patterns of development and disorder.* Cambridge, MA: Harvard University Press.

Rutter, Michael. (1981). *Maternal deprivation reassessed.* 2nd ed. Middlesex, England: Penguin.

Rutter, Michael. (1982). Epidemiological-longitudinal approaches to the study of development. In W. Andrew Collins (Ed.), *The concept of development. Minnesota symposium on child psychology,* (Vol. 15). Hillsdale, NJ: Erlbaum.

Rutter, Michael. (1982). Socio-emotional consequences of day care for preschool children. In E.F. Zigler and E.W. Gordon (Eds.), *Day care: Scientific and social policy issues.* Boston: Auburn House.

Rutter, Michael, and **Garmezy, Norman.** (1983). Developmental psychopathology. In Paul H. Mussen (Ed.), *Handbook of child psychology: Vol. 4. Socialization, personality and social development,* New York: Wiley.

Rutter, Michael, and **Giller, Henri.** (1984). *Juvenile delinquency: Trends and perspectives.* New York: Guilford.

Rutter, Michael, Maughan, Morimore, Peter, and **Ouston, Janet.** (1979). *Fifteen thousand hours: Secondary schools and their effects on children.* Cambridge, MA: Harvard University Press.

Rutter, Michael, Quinton, David, and **Liddle, Christin.** (1983). Parenting in two generations: Looking backwards and looking forwards. In Nicola Madge (Ed.), *Families at risk.* London: Heinemann.

St. Clair, K.L. (1978). Neonatal assessment procedures: A historical overview. *Child Development, 49*, 280–292.

Salapatek, Philip. (1977). Stimulus determinants of attention in infants. In Benjamin B. Wolman (Ed.). *International encyclopedia of psychiatry, psychology, psychoanalysis, and neurology* (Vol. X). New York: Aesculapius.

Salter, Alice. (1978). Birth without violence: A medical controversy. *Nursing Research, 27,* 84–88.

Saltz, Eli, Campbell, Sarah, and **Skotko, David.** (1983). Verbal control of behavior: The effects of shouting. *Developmental Psychology, 19,* 461–464.

Sameroff, Arnold J. (1978). Summary and conclusions: The future of newborn assessment. In Arnold J. Sameroff (Ed.), *Organization and stability of newborn behavior: A commentary on the Brazelton Neonatal Behavior Assessment Scale. Monographs of the Society for Research in Child Development, 43,* (Serial No. 177).

Sameroff, Arnold J. (1982). Development and the dialectic: The need for a systems approach. In W. Andrew Collins (Ed.), *The concept of development. Minnesota Symposia on Child Psychology* (Vol. 15.) Hillsdale, NJ: Erlbaum.

Sameroff, Arnold J. (1983). Developmental systems: contexts and evolution. In Paul H. Mussen (Ed.), *Handbook of child psychology: Vol. 1. History, theory, and methods.* New York: Wiley.

Sameroff, Arnold J., and **Chandler, Michael J.** (1975). Reproductive risk and the continuum of caretaking casualty. In Frances D. Horowitz, Mavis Hetherington, Sandra Scarr-Salapatek, and G. Siegel (Eds.), *Review of child development research.* Vol. IV. Chicago: University of Chicago Press.

Sameroff, Arnold J., and **Cavanaugh, Patrick J.** (1979). Learning in infancy: A developmental perspective. In Joy D. Osofsky (Ed.), *Handbook of infant development.* New York: Wiley.

Sameroff, Arnold J., and **Seifer, Ronald.** (1983). Familial risk and child competence. *Child Development, 54,* 1254–1268.

Samuelson, Franz, J.B. (1980). Watson's little Albert, Cyril Burt's twin, and the need for a critical science, *American Psychologist, 35,* 619–625.

Santrock, John E., Warshak, Richard A., and **Elliott, Gary L.** (1982). Social development and parent-child interaction in father-custody and stepmother families. In Michael E. Lamb (Ed.), *Nontraditional families: Parenting and child development.* Hillsdale, NJ: Erlbaum.

Santrock, John W. (1972). Relation of type and onset of father absence to cognitive development. *Child Development, 43,* 455–469.

Sarason, Seymour B. (1980). Individual psychology: An obstacle to comprehending adulthood. In Lynne A. Bond and James C. Rosen (Eds.), *Competence and coping during adulthood.* Hanover, N.H.: University Press of New England.

Satterfield, J.H., Satterfield, B.T., and **Cantwell, D.P.** (1981). Three-year multimodality treatment study of 100 hyperactive boys. *Journal of Pediatrics, 98,* 650–655.

Sattler, Jerome M. (1982). *Assessment of children's intelligence and special abilities.* Boston: Allyn and Bacon.

Satz, P., Taylor, A.G., Friel, L., and **Fletcher, J.** (1978). Some developmental and predictive precursor of reading disabilities: A six year follow-up. In A.L. Benton and D. Pearl (Eds.), *Dyslexia: An appraisal of current knowledge.* New York: Oxford University Press.

Saville-Troike, Muriel, McClure, Erica, and **Fritz, Mary.** (1984). Communicative tactics in children's second language acquisition. In Fred R. Eckman, Lawrence H. Bell, and Diane Nelson (Eds.), *Universals of second language acquisition.* Rowley, MA: Newbury House.

Savin-Williams, Ritch C., and **Demo, David H.** (1984). Developmental change and stability in adolescent self-concept. *Developmental Psychology, 20,* 1100–1110.

Scanlan, James V. (1975). *Self-reported health behavior and attitudes of youths 12–17 years.* U.S. Department of Public Health Service. Health Education and Welfare, Series 11, Number 147, Publication No. (HRA) 75–1629.

Scarr, Sandra. (1984). *Mother care/Other care.* New York: Basic Books.

Scarr, Sandra. (1985). Constructing psychology: Making facts and fables for our times. *American Psychologist, 40,* 499–512.

Scarr, Sandra, and **McCartney, Kathleen.** (1983). How people make their own environments: A theory of genotype/environment effects. *Child Development, 54,* 424–435.

Scarr, Sandra, and **Weinberg, Richard A.** (1980). Calling all camps! The war is over. *American Sociological Review, 45,* 859–865.

Scarr, Sandra, and **Weinberg, Richard A.** (1983). The Minnesota adoption studies: Genetic differences and malleability. *Child Development, 54,* 253–259.

Scarr-Salapatek, Sandra, and **Williams, Margaret L.** (1973). The effects of early stimulation on low-birth-weight infants. *Child Development, 44,* 94–101.

Schachter, Rubin J., Pantel, Ernestine S., Glassman, George M., and **Zweibelson, Irving.** (1971). Acne Vulgaris and psychological impact on high school students. *New York State Journal of Medicine, 71,* 2886–2890.

Schaffer, H. Rudolf. (1984). *The child's entry into a social world.* New York: Academic Press.

Schanberg, Saul M., Evonick, G., and **Kuhn, Cynthia M.** (1984). Tactile and nutritional aspects of maternal care: Specific regulators of neuroendocrine function and cellular development. *Proceedings of the Society for Experimental Biology and Medicine, 175,* 135.

Schanberg, Saul M., and **Kuhn, Cynthia M.** (1980). Maternal deprivation: An animal model of psychosocial dwarfism. In E. Usdin, T.L. Sourkes, and M.B.H. Youdim (Eds.), *Enzymes and neurotransmitters in mental disease.* New York: Wiley.

Schardein, James. L. (1976). *Drugs as teratogens.* Cleveland: CRC Press.

Scheinfeld, Amram. (1973). *Twins and supertwins.* Baltimore: Penguin.

Scher, Jonathan, and **Dix, Carol.** (1983). *Will my baby be normal?: Everything you need to know about pregnancy.* New York: Dial Press.

Schexnider, Virginia Y.R., Bell, Richard Q., Shebilske, Wayne L. and **Quinn, Patricia.** (1981). Habituation of visual attention in infants with minor physical anomalies. *Child Development, 52*, 812–818.

Schick, Bela, and **Rosenson, William.** (1932). *Child care today.* New York: Greenberg.

Schiefelbusch, Richard L. (1984). Assisting children to become communicatively competent. In Richard L. Schiefelbusch and Joanne Pickar (Eds.), *The acquisition of communicative competence.* Baltimore: University Park Press.

Schiefelbusch, Richard L., and **Pickar, Joanne** (Eds.). (1984). *The acquisition of communicative competence.* Baltimore: University Park Press.

Schieffelin, Bambi B. and **Eisenberg, Ann R.** (1984). Cultural variation in children's conversations. In Richard L. Schiefelbusch and Joanne Pickar (Eds.), *The acquisition of communicative competence.* Baltimore: University Park Press.

Schlesinger, Benjamin. (1982). *Sexual abuse of children.* Toronto: University of Toronto Press.

Schlesinger, Hilde S., and **Meadow, Kathryn P.** (1972). *Sound and sign: Childhood deafness and mental health.* Berkeley: University of California Press.

Schmitt, Barton D. (1980). The child with nonaccidental trauma. In C. Henry Kempe and Ray E. Helfer (Eds.), *The battered child* (3rd ed.). Chicago: The University of Chicago Press.

Schoof-Tams, Karin, Schlaegel, Jürgen, and **Walezak, Leonhard.** (1976). Differentiation of sexual morality between 11 and 16 years. *Archives of Sexual Behavior, 5*, 353–370.

Schull, William J., Otake, Masanori, and **Neel, James V.** (1981). Genetic effects of the atomic bombs: A reappraisal. *Science, 213*, 1220–1227.

Schulte, F.J., Albani, M., Schnizer, H., Bentele, K., and **Klingspron, R.** (1982). Neuronal control of neonatal respiration—sleep apnea and the Sudden Infant Death Syndrome. *Neuropediatrics, 13*, 3–14.

Schwartz, Gary, and **Merten, Don.** (1967). The language of adolescence: An anthropological approach to the youth culture. *The American Journal of Sociology, 72*, 453–468.

Schwartz, Marvin. *Physiological psychology* (2nd ed.). (1978). Englewood Cliffs, N.J.: Prentice Hall.

Schwartz, M., and **Day, R.H.** (1979). Visual shape perception in infancy. *Monographs of the Society for Research in Child Development, 44* (7, Serial No. 182).

Schweinhart, L.J., and **Weikart, D.** (1983). The effects of the Perry Preschool Program on youths through age 15—A summary. In Consortium for Longitudinal Studies, *As the twig is bent... Last effects of preschool programs.* Hillsdale, NJ: Erlbaum.

Schwertzbeck. (1983). In Jerome E. Leavitt (Ed.), *Child abuse and neglect: Research and innovation.* The Hague: Martinus Nijhoff.

Scribner S., and **Cole, M.** (1981). *The consequences of literacy.* Cambridge, MA: Harvard University Press.

Sears, Pauline S., and **Barbee, H.B.** (1977). Career and life satisfactions among Terman's gifted women. In J.C. Stanley (Ed.), *The gifted and the creative: A fifty-year perspective.* Baltimore: Johns Hopkins Press.

Sears, Robert R. (1977). Sources of life satisfaction of the Terman gifted men. *American Psychologist, 32*, 119–138.

Sears, Robert R., Rau, Lucy, and **Alpert, Richard.** (1965). *Identification and child rearing.* Stanford, CA: Stanford University Press.

Seashore, Marjorie J., Leifer, Aimee Dorr, Barnett, Clifford R., and **Leiderman, P. Herbert.** (1973). The effects of denial of early mother-infant interaction on maternal self-confidence. *Journal of Personality and Social Psychology, 26*, 369–378.

Segall, M.H. (1980). *Cross-cultural psychology: An introduction.* Monterey, CA: Brooks/Cole.

Seitz, Victoria, Rosenbaum, Laurie K., and **Apfel, Nancy H.** (1985). Effects of family support intervention: A ten year follow-up. *Child Development, 56*, 376–391.

Serbin, L.A., Tronick, I.J., and **Sternglanz, S.** (1977). Shaping cooperative cross-sex play. *Child Development, 48*, 924–929.

Seymour, Dorothy. (1971). Black children, black speech. *Commonweal*, 175–178.

Shantz, Carolyn Uhlinger. (1983). Social cognition. In Paul H. Mussen (Ed.), *Handbook of child psychology: Vol. 3. Cognitive development.* New York: Wiley.

Shay, Sharon Williams. (1980). Community Council for child abuse prevention. In C. Henry Kempe and Ray E. Helfer (Eds.), *The battered child* (3rd ed.). Chicago: The University of Chicago Press.

Shea, John D.C. (1981). Changes in interpersonal distances and categories of play behavior in the early weeks of preschool. *Developmental Psychology, 17*, 417–425.

Sheehy, Gail. (1976). *Passages: Predictable crisis of adult life.* New York: Dutton.

Shephard, Roy J. (1976). Physiology—Comment. In J.G. Albinson and G.M. Andrew (Eds.), *Child in sport and physical activity* (pp. 35–40). Baltimore: University Park Press.

Sherman, Julia. (1982). Continuing in mathematics: A longitudinal study of the attitudes of high school girls. *Psychology of Women Quarterly, 7*, 132–140.

Sherman, Julia. (1983). Factors predicting girls and boys enrollment in college preparatory mathematics. *Psychology of Women Quarterly, 7*, 272–281.

Sherrod, Kathryn B., O'Connor, Susan, Vietze, Peter M., and **Altermeier, William A.** (1984). Child health and maltreatment. *Child Development, 55*, 1174–1183.

Shields, James. (1962). *Monozygotic twins, brought up apart and brought up together: An investigation into the genetic and environmental causes of variation in personality.* London: Oxford University Press.

Shinn, Marybeth. (1978). Father absence and children's cognitive development. *Psychological Bulletin, 85*, 295–324.

Shipp, E.E. (1985, November 4). Teen-agers taking risks: When pregnancy is the result. *The New York Times*, p. A 16.

Shirley, Mary M. (1933). The first two years: A study of twenty-five babies. *Institute of Child Welfare Monograph No. 8*. Minneapolis: University of Minnesota Press.

Shneidman, Edwin S. (1978). Suicide. In Gardner Lindzey, Calvin S. Hall, and Richard F. Thompson, *Psychology* (2nd ed.). New York: Worth.

Siegal, Michael. (1984). Economic deprivation and the quality of parent-child relations: A trickle-down framework. *Journal of Applied Developmental Psychology, 5,* 127–144.

Siegel, Linda S. (1982). Reproductive, perinatal, and environmental factors as predictors of the cognitive and language development of preterm and full-term infants. *Child Development, 53,* 963–973.

Siegel, Susan. (1981). Infant tests as predictors of cognitive and language development at two years. *Child Development, 52,* 545–557.

Siegler, Robert S. (1983). Five generalizations about cognitive development. *American Psychologist, 38,* 263–277.

Sigel, Irving E., Dreyer, Albert S., and **McGillicuddy-DeLisi, Ann V.** (1984). Psychological perspectives on the life course. In Ross D. Parke (Ed.), *Review of child development research: Vol. 7. The family.* Chicago: University of Chicago Press.

Silberman, Charles. (1970). *Crisis in the classroom: The remaking of American education.* New York: Random House.

Silverman, W.A. (1980). *Retrolental fibroplasia: A modern parable.* New York: Grune and Stratton.

Simmons, Roberta G., Blyth, Dale A., and **McKinney, Karen L.** (1983). The social and psychological effects of puberty on white females. In Jeanne Brooks-Gunn and Anne C. Petersen (Eds.), *Girls at puberty: Biological and psychosocial aspects.* New York: Plenum.

Simmons, Roberta G., Rosenberg, Florence, and **Rosenberg, Morris.** (1973). Disturbance in the self-image at adolescence. *American Sociological Review, 38,* 553–568.

Simon, Herbert A. (1979). *Models of thought.* New Haven: Yale University Press.

Simon, Rita J., and **Altstein, Howard.** (1981). *Transracial adoption: A follow up.* Lexington MA: Lexington Books.

Sinclair, Caroline B. (1973). *Movement of the young child: Ages two to six.* Columbus, Ohio: Merrill.

Sinclair, David. (1978). *Human growth after birth* (3rd ed.). London: Oxford University Press.

Singer, Dorothy G., and **Singer, Jerome L.,** (1977). *Partners in play: A step-by-step guide to imaginative play in children.* New York: Harper & Row.

Siqueland, Einar R., and **Lipsitt, Lewis P.,** (1966). Conditioned headturning in human newborns. *Journal of Experimental Child Psychology, 3,* 356–376.

Sizer, Theodore R. (1985). *Horace's compromise: The dilemma of the American high school.* Boston: Houghton Mifflin.

Skinner, B.F. (1953). *Science and human behavior.* New York: Macmillan.

Skinner, B.F. (1957). *Verbal behavior.* New York: Appleton-Century-Crofts.

Skinner, B.F. (1972). *Beyond freedom and dignity.* New York: Knopf.

Skinner, B.F. (1980). The experimental analysis of operant behavior: A history. In R.W. Riebes and K. Salzinger (Eds.), *Psychology: Theoretical–historical perspective.* New York: Academic Press.

Skinner, B.F. (1983). *A matter of consequences: Part 3 of an autobiography.* New York: Knopf.

Slaughter, Diana T. (1983). Early intervention and its effects on maternal and child development. *Monographs of the Society for Research in Child Development, 48* (Serial No. 202).

Slobin, Dan I. (1971). *Psycholinguistics.* Glenview, IL: Scott Foresman.

Slobin, Dan I. (1982). Universal and particular in the acquisition of language. In Eric Wanner and Lila R. Gleitman (Eds.), *Language acquisition: The state of the art.* Cambridge, England: Cambridge University Press.

Smith, David W., Clarren, Sterling K., and **Sedgwick, Mary Ann Harvey.** (1978). Hyperthermia as a possible teratogenic agent. *Journal of Pediatrics, 92,* 878–883.

Smith, Mark Scott (Ed.). (1983). *Chronic disorders in adolescence.* Littleton, MA: Wright.

Smith, M. Brewster. (1983). Hope and despair: Keys to the socio-psychodynamics of youth. *American Journal of Orthopsychiatry, 53,* 388–399.

Smith, Nils V. (1973). *The acquisition of phonology: A case study.* Cambridge, England: Cambridge University Press.

Smith, Peter K. (1978). A longitudinal study of social participation in preschool children: Solitary and parallel play reexamined. *Developmental Psychology, 12,* 517–523.

Smith, Peter K. (1979). The ontogeny of fear in children. In W. Sluckin (Ed.), *Fear in animals and man.* New York: Van Nostrand Reinhold.

Smith, Peter K. (1984). *Play in animals and humans.* Basil: Blackwood.

Smith, R. Jeffrey. (1978). Agency drags its feet on warning to pregnant women. *Science, 199,* 748–749.

Smokler, C.S. (1982). Self-esteem in preadolescent and adolescent females. Unpublished doctoral dissertation, University of Michigan, 1975. Cited in Michael E. Lamb, Maternal employment and child development: A review. In Michael E. Lamb (Ed.), *Nontraditional families: Parenting and child development.* Hillsdale, NJ: Erlbaum.

Snarey, John R., Reimber, Joseph, and **Kohlberg, Lawrence.** (1985). Development of social-moral reasoning among Kibbutz adolescents: A longitudinal cross-cultural study. *Developmental Psychology, 21,* 3–17.

Snow, Catherine E. (1984). Parent-child interaction and the development of communicative ability. In Richard L. Schiefelbusch and Joanne Pickar (Eds.), *The acquisition of communicative competence.* Baltimore: University Park Press.

Snow, Catherine E., and **Ferguson, Charles A.** (Eds.), (1977). *Talking to children*. Cambridge, England: Cambridge University Press.

Snyder, Lynn S. (1984). Communicative competence in children with delayed language development. In Richard L. Schiefelbusch and Joanne Pickar (Eds.), *The acquisition of communicative competence*. Baltimore: University Park Press.

Snyder, S. (1978). Dopamine and schizophrenia. In L. Wynne, R. Cromwell, and S. Matthysse (Eds.), *The nature of schizophrenia: New approaches to research and treatment*. New York: Wiley.

Society for Research in Child Development. (1973). Committee on ethics research with children. *SRCD Newsletter.* (Winter), 3–4.

Solnit, Albert J. (1980). Preface to the third edition. In C. Henry Kempe and Ray E. Helfer (Eds.), *The battered child* (3rd ed.). Chicago: The University of Chicago Press.

Sonnenschein, Susan. (1984). How feedback from a listener affects children's referential communication skills. *Developmental Psychology, 20,* 287–292.

Sorce, James F., **Emde, Robert N.**, and **Campos, Joseph J.** (1985). Maternal emotional signaling: Its effects on the visual cliff behavior of 1-year-olds. *Developmental Psychology, 21,* 195–200.

Sorensen, Robert C. (1973). *Adolescent sexuality in contemporary America: Personal values and sexual behavior, ages thirteen to nineteen.* New York: World.

Sosa, R., **Kennell, J.**, **Klaus, Marshall**, and **Urutia, J.** (1976). The effects of early mother-infant contact on breast-feeding, infection, and growth. In *Breast-feeding and the mother. CIBA Foundation Symposium No. 45.* Amsterdam: Associated Scientific.

Spache, George D. (1976). *Investigating the issues of reading disabilities.* Boston: Allyn and Bacon.

Spelke, Elizabeth S., and **Owsley, Cynthia.** (1979). Intermodal exploration and knowledge in infancy. *Infant Behavior and Development, 2,* 13–27.

Spence, Janet T., and **Helmreich, Robert L.** (1978). *Masculinity and femininity: Their psychological dimensions, correlates, and antecedents.* Austin, TX: University of Texas Press.

Spitz, René Arpad. (1945). Hospitalism: An inquiry into the genesis of psychiatric conditions in early childhood. *Psychoanalytic Study of the Child, 1,* 53–74.

Spock, Benjamin. (1976). *Baby and child care.* New York: Pocket.

Sprafkin, Joyce N., **Swift, Carolyn**, and **Hess, Robert** (Eds.). (1983). Rx television: Enhancing the preventive impact of TV. *Prevention in human services* (Vol. 2, Nos. 1-2). New York: Haworth Press.

Sprague, R.L., and **Ullman, R.K.** (1981). Psychoactive drugs and child management. In J.M. Kaufman and D.P. Hallahan (Eds.), *Handbook of special education*. New York: Prentice-Hall.

Sroufe, L. Alan. (1978). Attachment and the roots of competence. *Human Nature, 1978, 1,* 50–57.

Sroufe, L. Alan. (1979). Socioemotional development. In Joy Osofsky (Ed.), *Handbook of infant development.* New York: Wiley.

Sroufe, L. Alan. (1985). Attachment classification from the perspective of infant-caregiver relationships and infant temperament. *Child Development, 56,* 1–14.

Sroufe, L. Alan, **Fox, Nancy E.**, and **Pancake, Van R.** (1983). Attachment and dependency in developmental perspective. *Child Development, 54,* 1615–1627.

Sroufe, L. Alan, **Jacobvitz, Deborah**, **Mengelsdorf, Sarah**, **DeAngelo, Edward**, and **Ward, Mary Jo.** (1985). Generational boundary dissolution between mothers and their preschool children: A relationship systems approach. *Child Development, 56,* 317–325.

Sroufe, L. Alan, and **Ward, Mary Jo.** (1980). Seductive behavior of mothers of toddlers: Occurrence, correlates, and family origins. *Child Development, 51,* 1222–1229.

Sroufe, L. Alan, and **Waters, Everett.** (1976). The ontogenesis of smiling and laughter: A perspective on the organization of development in infancy. *Psychological Review, 83,* 173–189.

Staffiere, J. Robert. (1967). A study of social stereotype of body image in children. *Journal of Personality and Social Psychology, 7,* 101–104.

Stark, C.R., **Orleans, M.**, **Haverkamp, A.D.**, and **Murphy, J.** (1984). Short and long term risks after exposure to diagnostic ultrasound in utero. *Obstetrical Gynecology, 63,* 194–200.

Steele, Brandt. (1980). Psychodynamic factors in child abuse. In C. Henry Kempe and Ray E. Helfer (Eds.), *The battered child* (3rd ed.) Chicago: The University of Chicago Press.

Stein, Aletha Huston, and **Friedrich, Lynette Kohn.** (1975). Impact of television on children and youth. In E. Mavis Hetherington (Ed.), *Review of child development research* (Vol. V). Chicago: University of Chicago Press.

Stein, Zena A., and **Susser, Mervyn W.** (1976). Prenatal nutrition and mental competence. In J. D. Lloyd-Still (Ed.), *Malnutrition and intellectual development.* Littleton, MA: Publishing Sciences Group.

Steinberg, Laurence D. (1977). *A longitudinal study of physical growth, intellectual development, and family interaction in early adolescence.* Unpublished doctoral dissertation. Cornell University.

Steinberg, Laurence D., **Greenberger, Ellen**, **Garduque, Laurie**, **Ruggiero, M.**, and **Vaux, Allen.** (1982). Effect of working on adolescent development. *Developmental Psychology, 18,* 385–395.

Steinman, S. (1981). The experience of children in a joint custody arrangement: A report of a study. *American Journal of Orthopsychiatry, 51,* 403–414.

Steinmetz, S.K. (1977). *The cycle of violence: Assertive, aggressive and abusive family interaction.* New York: Praeger.

Stenberg, Craig, and **Campos, Joseph J.** (1983). The development of the expression of anger in human infants. In Michael Lewis and C. Saarni, Carolyn (Eds.), *The socialization of affect.* New York: Plenum.

Stern, Daniel (1977). *The first relationship: Mother and infant.* Cambridge, MA: Harvard University Press.

Stern, J.A., Oster, P.J., and **Newport, K.** (1980). Reaction time measures, hemispheric specialization, and age. In Leonard W. Poon (Ed.), *Aging in the 80's: Psychological issues.* Washington, DC: American Psychological Association.

Stern, Leonard. (1985). *The structures and strategies of human memory.* Homewood, IL: Dorsey Press.

Stevenson, Harold. (1983). How children learn—the quest for a theory. In Paul H. Mussen (Ed.), *Handbook of child psychology: Vol. 1. History, theory, and methods.* New York: Wiley.

Stevenson, Harold W., Stigler, James W., Lee, Shin-ying, and **Lucker, G. William.** (1985). Cognitive performance and academic achievement of Japanese, Chinese, and American children. *Child Development, 56,* 718–734.

Stewart, A., and **Kneale, G.W.** (1970). Radiation dose effects in relation to obstetric X-rays and childhood cancers. *Lancet, I,* 1495.

Stipek, Deborah J. (1984). Sex differences in children's attributions of success and failure on math and spelling tests. *Sex Roles, 11,* 969–981.

Stipek, Deborah J., and **Hoffman, J.** (1980). Development of children's performance-related judgments. *Child Development, 51,* 912–914.

Stipek, Deborah J., Roberts, Theresa A., and **Sanborn, Mary E.** (1984). Preschool-age children's performance expectations for themselves and another child as a function of the incentive value of success and the salience of past performance. *Child Development, 55,* 1983–1989.

Stoddart, Trish, and **Turiel, Elliot.** (1985). Children's concepts of cross-gender activities. *Child Development, 56,* 1241–1252.

Stone, L. Joseph, and **Church, Joseph.** (1973). *Childhood and adolescence: A psychology of the growing person* (3rd ed.). New York: Random House.

Strain, Phillip S., and **Shores, Richard E.** (1983). A reply to "misguided mainstreaming." *Exceptional Children, 50,* 271–273.

Strauss, Murray A., Gelles, Richard J., and **Steinmetz, Suzanne K.** (1980). *Behind closed doors: Violence in the American family.* New York: Anchor Doubleday.

Streissguth, Ann Pytkowicz, Barr, Helen M., and **Martin, Donald C.** (1983). Maternal alcohol use and neonatal habituation assessed with the Brazelton scale. *Child Development, 54,* 1109–1118.

Streissguth, Ann Pytkowicz, Martin, Donald C., Barr, Helen M., Sandman, MacGregor, Beth, Kirshner, Grace L., and **Darby, Betty L.** (1984). Intrauterine alcohol and nicotine exposure: Attention and reaction time in 4-year-old children. *Developmental Psychology, 20,* 533–541.

Sulik, Kathleen K., Johnston, Malcolm C., and **Webb, Mary A.** (1981). Fetal alcohol syndrome: Embryongenesis in a mouse model. *Science, 214,* 936–938.

Sullivan, Edmund V. (1977). A study of Kohlberg's structural theory of moral development: A critique of liberal social science ideology. *Human Development, 20,* 352–376.

Sullivan, Margaret Wolan. (1982). Reactivation: Priming forgotten memories in human infants. *Child Development, 53,* 516–523.

Sun, Marjorie. (1983). FDA draws criticism on prenatal test. *Science, 221,* 440–442.

Suomi, Stephen J., and **Harlow, Harry F.** (1976). Monkeys without play. In Jerome S. Bruner, Alison Jolly, and Kathy Sylva (Eds.), *Play.* New York: Basic Books.

Super, Charles M. (1976). Environmental effects on motor development: The case of African infant precocity. *Developmental Medicine and Child Neurology, 18,* 561–567.

Super, Charles M., and **Harkness, Sara.** (1982). The development of affect in infancy and early childhood. In Daniel A. Wagner and Harold W. Stevenson (Eds.), *Cultural perspectives on child development.* San Francisco: Freeman.

Surber, Colleen F., and **Gzesh, Steven M.** (1984). Reversible operations in the balance scale task. *Journal of Experimental Child Psychology, 38,* 254–274.

Sutcliffe, D. (1982). *British Black English.* Oxford: Blackwell.

Sutker, Patricia B. (1982). Adolescent drug and alcohol behaviors. In Tiffany M. Field, Aletha Huston, Herbert C. Quay, Lillian Troll, Gordon E. Finley (Eds.), *Review of human development,* New York: Wiley.

Swanson, J.M., and **Kinsbourne, Marcel.** (1980). Artificial color and hyperactive behavior. In R.M. Knights and D.J. Bakker (Eds.), *Treatment of hyperactive and learning disordered children.* Baltimore: University Park Press.

Swartzbach. (1983). In Nicola Madge (Ed.), *Families at risk.* London: Heinemann.

Szalai, Alexander, Converse, Philip E., Feldheim, P., Scheuch, E.K., and **Stone, P.J.** (Eds.). (1972). *The use of time: Daily activities of urban and suburban populations in twelve countries.* The Hague, The Netherlands: Mouton.

Tan, Lesley E. (1985). Laterality and motor skills in four-year-olds. *Child Development, 56,* 119–124.

Tannenbaum, Abraham J. (1983). *Gifted Children: Psychological and educational perspectives.* New York: Macmillan.

Tanner, James M. (1970). Physical growth. In Paul H. Mussen (Ed.), *Carmichael's manual of child psychology* (3rd ed.). Vol. I. New York: Wiley.

Tanner, James M. (1971). Sequence, tempo, and individual variation in the growth and development of boys and girls aged twelve to sixteen. *Daedalus, 100,* 907–930.

Tanner, James M. (1978). *Fetus into man: Physical growth from conception to maturity.* Cambridge, MA: Harvard University Press.

Tanzer, Deborah, and **Block, Jean Libman.** (1976). *Why natural childbirth? A psychologist's report on the benefits to mothers, fathers and babies.* New York: Schocken.

Taylor, Brian. (1981). *Perspectives on paedophilia.* London: Batsford.

Taylor, Leona. (1978). Do we have to have compulsory education for adolescents? In John C. Flanagan (Ed.), *Perspectives* *on improving education: Project TALENTS, young adults look back*. New York: Praeger.

Taylor, P.M., Taylor, F.H., Campbell, S.B., Maloni, J., and Dickey D. (1979, March). *Effects of extra contact on early maternal attitudes, perceptions, and behaviors*. Paper presented at the biennial meeting of the Society for Research in Child Development, San Francisco.

Telegdy, G.A. (1975). The effectiveness of four readiness tests as predictors of first grade academic achievement. *Psychology in the Schools, 12*, 4–11.

Terman, Lewis M., and Oden, Melita H. (1959). *Genetic studies of genius Vol. 5: The gifted group at mid-life: Thirty-five years' follow-up of the superior child*. Stanford, CA: Stanford University Press.

Tesfaye, Andargatchew. (1976). Ethiopia. In Dea H. Chang (Ed.), *Criminology in a cross-cultural perspective*. Durham, NC: Carolina Academic Press.

Thoman, E.B. (1975). Sleep and wake behaviors in neonates: Consistencies and consequences. *Merrill Palmer Quarterly, 21*, 295–314.

Thomas, Alexander. (1981). Current trends in developmental theory. *American Journal of Orthopsychiatry, 51*, 580–609.

Thomas, Alexander, and Chess, Stella. (1977). *Temperament and development*. New York: Brunner/Mazel.

Thomas, Alexander, and Chess, Stella. (1980). *The dynamics of psychological development*. New York: Brunner/Mazel.

Thomas, Alexander, Chess, Stella, and Birch, Herbert G. (1963). *Behavioral individuality in early childhood*. New York: New York University Press.

Thomas, Alexander, Chess, Stella, and Birch, Herbert G. (1968). *Temperament and behavior disorders in children*. New York: New York University Press.

Thomas, Alexander, Chess, Stella, and Mendez, O. (1974). Cross-cultural study of behavior in children with special vulnerabilities to stress. In D. Ricks, Alexander Thomas, and M. Roff (Eds.), *Life history research in psychopathology* (Vol. 3.). Minneapolis: University of Minnesota Press.

Thompson, Jean R., and Chapman, Robin S. (1977). Who is "Daddy" revisited: The status of two-year-olds' overextended words in use and comprehension. *Journal of Child Language, 4*, 359–375.

Thompson, Michael. (1983). Organizing a human services network for primary and secondary prevention of the emotional and physical neglect and abuse of children. In Jerome E. Leavitt (Ed.), *Child abuse and neglect: Research and innovation*. The Hague: Martinus Nijhoff.

Thompson, M.E., Hartsock, G., and Farson, C. (1979). The importance of immediate postnatal contact: Its effect on breast-feeding. *Canadian Family Physician, 25*, 1374–1378.

Thompson, R.A., Lamb, Michael E., and Estes, D. (1982). Stability of infant-mother attachment and its relationship to changing life circumstances in an unselected middle class sample. *Child Development, 53*, 144–148.

Thompson, Spencer K. (1975). Gender labels and early sex role development. *Child Development, 46*, 339–347.

Tieger, T. (1980). On the biological basis of sex differences in aggression. *Child Development, 51*, 943–963.

Tizard, Barbara. (1977). *Adoption: A second chance*. New York: Free Press.

Tobin-Richards, Maryse H., Boxer, Andrew M, and Petersen, Anne C. (1983). The psychological significance of pubertal change: Sex difference in perceptions of self during early adolescence. In Jeanne Brooks-Gunn and Anne C. Petersen (Eds.), *Girls at puberty: Biological and psychosocial aspects*. New York: Plenum.

Tomasello, Michael, and Mannle, Sara. (1985). Pragmatics of sibling speech to one-year-olds. *Child Development, 56*, 911–917.

Tonkova-Yampol'skaya, R.V. (1973). Development of speech intonation in infants during the first two years of life. In Charles A. Ferguson and Dan Isaac Slobin (Eds.), *Studies of child language development*. New York: Holt, Rinehart and Winston.

Torrence, F. Paul. (1972). Characteristics of creatively gifted children and youth. In E. Philip Trapp, and Philip Himelstein (Eds.), *The exceptional child*. New York: Appleton Century Crofts, pp. 273–291.

Touliatos, John, and Compton, Norma H. (1983). *Approaches to child study*. Minneapolis, MN: Burgess.

Tower, Roni Beth, Singer, Dorothy G., Singer, Jerome L., and Biggs, Ann. (1979). Differential effects of television programming on preschoolers' cognition, imagination, and social play. *American Journal of Orthopsychiatry, 49*, 265–281.

Trainer, F.E. (1977). A critical analysis of Kohlberg's contributions to the study of moral thought. *Journal for the Theory of Social Behavior, 7*, 41–63.

Travis, Luther B. (1982). The child with diabetes. In J. David Schantz and Oscar B. Crofford (Eds.), *Diabetes mellitus: Problems in management*. Menlo Park, CA: Addison-Wesley.

Tronick, Edward Z., Als, H. Adamson, L., Wise, S., and Brazelton, T.B. (1978). The infant's response to entrapment between contradictory measures in face-to-face interaction. *Journal of the American Academy of Child Psychiatry, 17*, 1–13.

Turiel, Elliot. (1974). Conflict and transition in adolescent moral development. *Child Development, 45*, 14–29.

Turiel, Elliot. (1983). *The development of social knowledge: Morality and convention*. Cambridge: Cambridge University Press.

Turiel, Elliot, and Smetana, Judith G. (1984). Social knowledge and action: The coordination of domains. In William M. Kurtines and Jacob L. Gewirtz (Eds.), *Morality, moral behavior, and moral development*. New York: Wiley.

Turkington, Carol. (1983, November). Lifetime of fear may be the legacy of latchkey children. *APA Monitor*, p. 19.

Ungerer, Judy A. and Sigman, Marian. (1983). Developmental lags in preterm infants from one to three years. *Child Development, 54*, 1217–1228.

U.S. Department of the Census. (1985). *Statistical Abstract of the United States*. United States Department of Commerce, Washington, D.C.

U.S. Department of Health, Education, and Welfare. (1979, March 5–7). *Antenatal Diagnosis*. Report of a conference sponsored by the National Institute of Child Health and Human Development. NIH Publication No. 80-1973.

U.S. Department of Justice. (1984). *Crime in the United States*. Federal Bureau of Investigation, Washington, DC.

Universals of Second Language Acquisition. (1984). Rowley, MA: Newbury House.

Uzgiris, Ina C., and **Hunt, J. McVicker.** (1975). *Assessment in infancy: Ordinal scales of psychological development*. Urbana, IL: University of Illinois Press.

Vandell, Deborah L. (1980). Sociability with peers and mothers in the first year. *Developmental Psychology, 16*, 355–361.

Vandenberg, Brian. (1978). Play and development from an ethological perspective. *American Psychologist, 33*, 724–738.

Van Oeffelen, Michiel P., and **Vos, Peter G.** (1984). The young child's processing of dot patterns: A chronometric and eye movement analysis. *International Journal of Behavioral Development, 7*, 53–66.

Vaughan, Victor C. III. (1983). Developmental pediatrics. In Richard E. Behrman and Victor C. Vaughan, III (Eds.), *Pediatrics*. Philadelphia: Saunders.

Vaughn, Brian, Egeland, Bryan, Sroufe, L. Alan, and **Waters, Everett.** (1979). Individual differences in mother-infant attachment at twelve and eighteen months: Stability and change in families under stress. *Child Development, 50*, 971–975.

Veroff, Joseph, Douvan, Elizabeth, and **Kulka, Richard A.** (1981). *The inner American: A self-portrait from 1957 to 1976*. New York: Basic Books.

Visher, J.S., and **Visher, E.B.** (1982). Stepfamilies and stepparenting. In R. Walch (Ed.), *Normal family processes*. New York: Guilford.

von Hofsten, Claes. (1983). Catching skills in infancy. *Journal of Experimental Psychology: Human Perception and Performance, 9*, 75–85.

Vurpillot, Elaine. (1968). The development of scanning strategies, and their relation to visual differentiation. *Journal of Experimental Child Psychology, 6*, 632–650.

Vygotsky, Lev Semenovich. (1962). *Thought and language*. Cambridge, MA: MIT Press.

Waber, Deborah P. (1976). Sex differences in mental abilities: A function of maturation rate? *Science, 192*, 572–574.

Wachs, Theodore D. (1975). Relation of infant performance on Piaget scales between twelve and twenty-four months and their Stanford-Binet performance at thirty-one months. *Child Development, 46*, 929–935.

Wadsworth, M.E.J. (1979). *Roots of delinquency: Infancy, adolescence, and crime*. Oxford: Martin Robertson.

Waldrop, M.F., and **Halverson, C.F. Jr.** (1971). Minor physical anomalies and hyperactive behavior in young children. In J. Hellmuth (Ed.), *The exceptional infant* (Vol. 2). New York: Brunner/Mazel.

Walker, Elaine, and **Emory, Eugene.** (1983). Infants at risk for psychopathology: Offspring of schizophrenic parents. *Child Development, 54*, 1254–1285.

Walker, Lawrence J. (1982). The sequentiality of Kohlberg's stages of moral development. *Child Development, 53*, 1330–1336.

Walker, Lawrence J. (1984). Sex differences in the development of moral reasoning: A critical review. *Child Development, 55*, 677–691.

Wallace, James R., Cunningham, Thomas F., and **Del Monte, Vickie.** (1984). Change and stability in self-esteem between late childhood and early adolescence. *Journal of Early Adolescence, 4*, 253–257.

Wallach, Michael A., and **Kogan, Nathan.** (1965). *Modes of thinking in young children: A study of the creativity-intelligence distinction*. New York: Holt, Rinehart, and Winston.

Wallerstein, Judith S. (1984). Children of divorce: Preliminary report of a ten year follow-up of young children. *American Journal of Orthopsychiatry, 54*, 444–458.

Wallerstein, Judith S., and **Kelly, Joan Berlin.** (1980). *Surviving the breakup: How children and parents cope with divorce*. New York: Basic Books.

Wallwork, Ernest. (1980). Morality, religion and Kohlberg's theory. In Brenda Munsey (Ed.), *Moral development, moral education and Kohlberg: Basic issues in philosophy, psychology, religion and education*. Birmingham, AL: Religious Education Press.

Walters, William, and **Singer, Peter.** (1982). *Test-tube babies: A guide to moral questions, present techniques, and future possibilities*. Melbourne: Oxford University Press.

Ward, Elizabeth. (1984). *Father-daughter rape*. London: The Women's Press.

Ward, M.C. (1982). *Them children: A study in language learning*. New York: Irvington Press. (Original work published 1971)

Waterman, Alan S. (1985). Identity in the context of adolescent psychology. In Alan S. Waterman (Ed.), *Identity in adolescence: Processes and contents. New directions in child development* (Vol. 30). San Francisco: Jossey-Bass.

Watson, John B. (1925). *Behaviorism*. New York: Norton.

Watson, John B. (1928). *Psychological care of the infant and child*. New York: Norton.

Watson, John B. (1967). *Behaviorism*. (rev. ed.). Chicago: University of Chicago Press. (Original work published 1930)

Watson, John R., and **Raynor, Rosalie.** (1920). Conditioned emotional reactions. *Journal of Experimental Psychology, 3*, 1–14.

Watson, Malcolm W. (1981). The development of social roles: A sequence of social-cognitive development. In Kurt W.

Fischer (Ed.), *Cognitive development. New directions for child development,* (Vol. 12). San Francisco: Jossey-Bass.

Watson, Malcolm W. (1984). Development of social role understanding. *Developmental Review, 4,* 192–213.

Watson, Malcolm W., and Amgott-Kwan, Terry. (1983). Transitions in children's understanding of parental roles. *Developmental Psychology, 19,* 659–666.

Weideger, Paula. (1976). *Menstruation and menopause: The physiology and psychology, the myth, and the reality.* New York: Knopf.

Weil, William B., Jr. (1975). Infantile obesity. In Myron Winick (Ed.), *Childhood obesity.* New York: Wiley.

Weinraub, M., and Lewis, Michael. (1977). The determinants of children's responses to separation. *Monographs of the Society for Research in Child Development, 42* (4, Serial no. 172.)

Weiss, Bernard. (1982). Food additives and environmental chemicals as sources of childhood behavior disorders. *Journal of the American Academy of Child Psychiatry, 21,* 144–152.

Weiss, B., Williams, J.H., Margen, S., Abrams, B., Caan, B., Citron, L.J., Cox, C., McKibben, J., Oga, D., and Schultz, S. (1980). Behavioral responses to artificial food colors. *Science, 207,* 1487–1489.

Weiss, R.S. (1975). *Marital separation.* New York: Basic Books.

Weissbluth, Marc, Brouillete, Robert T., Liu, Kiang, and Hunt, Carl E. (1982). Sleep apnea, sleep duration, and infant temperament. *Journal of Pediatrics, 101,* 307–310.

Wells, J.C. (1982). *Accents of English* (Vols. 1–3). Cambridge, England: Cambridge University Press.

Werner, Emmy E., Bierman, J.M., and French, F.E. (1971). *The children of Kauai: A longitudinal study from the prenatal period to age ten.* Honolulu: University of Hawaii Press.

Werner, Emmy E., and Smith, Ruth S. (1982). *Vulnerable but invincible: A study of resilient children.* New York: McGraw-Hill.

Werner, J.S., and Perlmutter, Marion. (1979). Development of visual memory in infants. In Haynes W. Reese and Lewis P. Lipsitt (Eds.), *Advances in child development and behavior* (Vol. 14). New York: Academic Press.

Werry, John S. (1972). Childhood psychosis. In Herbert C. Quay and John S. Werry (Eds.), *Psychopathological disorders of childhood* (pp. 173–233). New York: Wiley.

Werry, John S. (1977). The use of psychotropic drugs in children. *American Academy of Child Psychiatry, 16,* 446–468.

Westbrook, Mary T. (1978). The effects of the order of a birth on women's experience of childbearing. *Journal of Marriage and the Family, 40,* 165–172.

Westinghouse Learning Corporation. (1969). *The impact of Head Start: An evaluation of the Head Start experience on children's cognitive and affective development.* Athens, OH: Ohio University Press.

Westoff, Charles F., Calot, Gerard, and Foster, Andrew D. (1983). Teenage fertility in developed nations: 1971–1980. *Family Planning Perspectives, 15,* 105–110.

Whalen, C.K., Henker, B., Collins, B.E., Finck, D., and Dotemoto, S. (1979). A social ecology of hyperactive boys: Medication effects in systematically structured classroom environments. *Journal of Applied Behavioral Analysis, 12,* 65–81.

White, Burton L. (1975). *The first three years of life.* Englewood Cliffs, NJ: Prentice-Hall.

White, Burton L. (1979). *The origins of human competence: Final report of the Harvard Preschool Project.* Lexington, MA: Lexington Books.

White, Burton L., and Carew-Watts, Jean. (1973). *Experience and environment: Major influences on the development of the young child.* Englewood Cliffs, NJ: Prentice-Hall.

White, Robert W. (1959). Motivation reconsidered: The concept of competence. *Psychological Review, 66,* 297–333.

White, Robert W. (1979). Competence as an aspect of personal growth. In Martha Whalen Kent and Jon E. Rolf (Eds.), *Primary prevention of psychopathology:* Vol. III. *Social competence in children* (pp. 5–22). Hanover, NH: University Press of New England.

White, Sheldon H. (1965). Evidence for a hierarchical arrangement of learning processes. In Lewis P. Lipsitt and Charles C. Spiker (Eds.), *Advances in child development and behavior.* Vol. II. New York: Academic Press.

Whiten, A. (1977). Assessing the effects of perinatal events on the success of the mother-infant relationship. In H.R. Shaffer (Ed.), *Studies of mother-infant interaction.* New York: Academic Press.

Whiting, Beatrice B., and Whiting, John W.M. (1975). *Children of six cultures.* Cambridge, MA: Harvard University Press.

Wiggins, Jerry S., and Holzmuller, Ana. (1978). Psychological androgyny and interpersonal behavior. *Journal of Consulting and Clinical Psychology, 46,* 40–52.

Willatts, Peter. (1984). Stages in the development of intentional search by young infants. *Developmental Psychology, 20,* 389–396.

Williams, R., and Mitchell, H. (1977). What happened to ABPsi's moratorium on testing: A 1968 to 1977 reminder. *Journal of Black Psychology, 4,* 25–42.

Wilson, James Q. (1983). Raising Kids. *The Atlantic Monthly, 252*(4), 45–56.

Wilson, Ronald S. (1983). The Louisville twin study: Developmental synchronies in behavior. *Child Development, 54,* 298–316.

Wilson, Ronald S., and Harpring, E.B. (1972). Mental and motor development in infant twins. *Developmental Psychology, 7,* 277–297.

Winer, G.A. (1980). Class inclusion reasoning in children. *Child Development, 51,* 309–328.

Winick, Myron (Ed.). (1975). *Childhood obesity.* New York: Wiley.

Winn, Marie. (1977). *The plug-in drug.* New York: Viking.

Witelson, Sandra F. (1985). The brain connection: The corpus callosum is larger in left-handers. *Science, 229,* 665–668.

Wohlwill, J.F. (1973). *The study of behavioral development.* New York: Academic Press.

Wolff, Georg, and **Money, John.** (1980). Relationship between sleep and growth in patient with reversible somatotropin deficiency (Psychosocial dwarfism). In Gertrude J. Williams and John Money (Eds.), *Traumatic abuse and neglect of children at home.* Baltimore: Johns Hopkins University Press.

Wolff, Jurgen M., and **Lipe, Dewey.** (1978). *Help for the overweight child.* New York: Penguin.

Wolff, Peter. (1969). The natural history of crying and vocalization in early infancy. In B.M. Foss (Ed.), *Determinants of infant behavior* (Vol. IV). London: Methuen.

Wolfram, W., and **Christian, D.** (1976). *Appalachian speech.* Center for Applied Linguistics: Washington, DC.

Wolock, Isabel, and **Horowitz, Bernard.** (1984). Child maltreatment as a social problem: The neglect of neglect. *American Journal of Orthopsychiatry, 54,* 530–543.

Wolpe, J. (1969). *The practice of behavior therapy.* Elmsford, NY: Pergamon.

Wong Fillmore, Lily. (1976). *The second time around: Cognitive and social strategies in second language acquisition.* Doctoral Dissertation, Stanford University. (Cited in McLaughlin, 1984)

Worobey, John, and **Belsky, Jay.** (1982). Employing the Brazelton Scale to influence mothering: A experimental comparison of three strategies. *Developmental Psychology, 18,* 736–743.

Yakovlev, P.I., and **Lecours, A.R.** (1967). The myelogenetic cycles of regional development of the brain. In A. Minkowski (Ed.), *Regional development of the brain in early life: Symposium.* Oxford: Blackwell.

Yalisove, Daniel. (1978). The effect of riddle-structure on children's comprehension and appreciation of riddles. Doctoral dissertation, New York University. *Dissertation Abstracts International, 36,* 6.

Yalisove, Daniel. (1978). The effect of riddle structure on children's comprehension of riddles. *Developmental Psychology, 14,* 173–180.

Yang, Raymond K. (1979). Early infant assessment: An overview. In Joy D. Osofsky (Ed.), *Handbook of infant development.* New York: Wiley.

Yarrow, Marian Radke, Campbell, John D., and **Burton, Roger V.** (1968). *Child-rearing: An inquiry into research and methods.* San Francisco: Jossey-Bass.

Yeater, Keith Owen, MacPhee, David, Campbell, Frances A., and **Ramey, Craig T.** (1979). Maternal IQ and Home Environment as determinants of early childhood intellectual competence: A developmental analysis. *Developmental Psychology, 15,* 731–739.

Young, Andrew W. (1982). Asymmetry of cerebral hemispheric function during development. In John W.T. Dickerson and Harry McGurk, (Eds.), *Brain and behavioral development: Interdisciplinary perspectives on structure and function.* London: Surrey University Press.

Younger, Alastair J., Schwartzman, Alex E., and **Ledingham, Jane E.** (1985). Age-related changes in children's perceptions of aggression and withdrawal in their peers. *Developmental Psychology, 21,* 70–75.

Youniss, James. (1980). *Parents and peers in social development: A Sullivan-Piaget perspective.* Chicago: University of Chicago Press.

Zacharias, L., Rand, W.M., and **Wurtman, R.J.** (1976). A prospective study of sexual development and growth in American girls: The statistics of menarche. *Obstetrical and Gynecological Survey, 31,* 325–337.

Zahr, Lina. (1985). Physical attractiveness and Lebanese children's school performance. *Psychological Reports, 56,* 191–192.

Zegiob, Leslie E., and **Forehand, Rex.** (1975). Maternal interactive behavior as a function of race, socioeconomic status, and sex of the child. *Child Development, 46,* 564–568.

Zelazo, P.R. (1979). Infant reactivity to perceptual-cognitive events: Application for infant assessment. In Richard B. Kearsley and Irving E. Sigel (Eds.), *Infants at risk: Assessment of cognitive functioning.* Hillsdale, NJ: Erlbaum.

Zeskind, Philip Sanford. (1983). Cross-cultural differences in maternal perceptions of high and low risk infants. *Child Development, 54,* 1119–1128.

Zeskind, Philip Sanford, and **Lester, Barry M.** (1978). Acoustic features and auditory perceptions of the cries of newborns with prenatal and perinatal complications. *Child Development, 49,* 580–589.

Zeskind, Philip Sanford, Sale, Jean, Maio, Mary Lisa, Huntington, Lee, and **Weiseman, Julie R.** (1985). Adult perceptions of pain and hunger cries: A syncrony of arousal. Child Development, 56, 549–554.

Zigler, Edward, Abelson, Willa D., and **Seitz, Victoria.** (1973). Motivational factors in the performance of economically disadvantaged children on the Peabody Picture Vocabulary Test. *Child Development, 44,* 294–303.

Zigler, Edward, Abelson, Willa, D., Trickett, Penelope K., and **Seitz, Victoria.** (1982). Is an intervention program necessary in order to improve economically disadvantaged children's I.Q. scores? *Child Development, 53,* 340–348.

Zigler, Edward, and **Berman, Winnie.** (1983). Discerning the future of early childhood intervention. *American Psychologist, 38,* 894–906.

Zill, N. (1983). *Happy, healthy, and insecure.* New York: Doubleday.

Zimmerman, Barry J. (1983). Social learning theory: A contextualist account of cognitive functioning. In Charles J. Brainerd (Ed.), *Recent advances in cognitive developmental theory.* New York: Springer-Verlag.

Acknowledgments

Part Openers

Part I   Prenatal photographs: Landrum B. Shettles; newborn: © Erika Stone 1981
Part II   *all*: © Joel Gordon
Part III   *all*: © Elizabeth Crews
Part IV   *all*: © Pam Hasegawa/Taurus Photos
Part V   *all*: © Elizabeth Crews

Chapter 1

Opener and p. 2   © Shirley Zeiberg
1.2   © Shirley Zeiberg
1.3   © Michal Heron/Woodfin Camp & Associates
1.4   © Hazel Hankin
1.5   © Shirley Zeiberg
1.6   © Hazel Hankin
A Closer Look, pp. 14–15   *left*, The Bettmann Archive; *center*, The Bettmann Archive; *top right*, © James Carroll; *bottom right*, © Leo Chopin/Black Star
1.8   © Elizabeth Crews
1.9   © Charles Gatewood/Stock, Boston
Research Report, p. 18,   © L.J. Weinstein/Woodfin Camp & Associates
A Closer Look, p. 21,   © Ira Berger/Woodfin Camp & Associates
1.11   © Jim Anderson/Woodfin Camp & Associates
1.12   © Beryl Goldberg
1.13   © Discover Magazine 12/84, Time Inc.
1.14   © The Bettmann Archive

Chapter 2

Opener and p. 34,   © Erika Stone
2.2   *left*, © Sybil Shelton/Peter Arnold, Inc.; *right*, © Shirley Zeiberg
2.3   Culver Pictures
2.4   © F. D. Bodin/Stock, Boston
2.6   © Olive R. Pierce/Black Star
2.7   *left*, © Paul S. Conklin; *right*, © Alan Carey/The Image Works
2.8   The Bettmann Archive
2.9   © Joe McNally/Wheeler Pictures
2.10   *left*, © Mimi Cotter/Int'l. Stock Photo; *right*, © Hazel Hankin
2.11   *left*, © Erika Stone; *right*, © Elizabeth Crews/Stock, Boston
2.12   © Bill Anderson/Monkmeyer Press Photo Service
2.13   © Sybil Shelton/Peter Arnold, Inc.
2.14   © David A. Krathwohl/Stock, Boston
Research Report, p. 59,   *left*, Courtesy Jeremy Bernstein; *right*, Courtesy Erika Bernstein
2.15   © Elizabeth Crews/Stock, Boston

Chapter 3

Opener and p. 68,   From Lennart Nilsson, *A child is born*. Copyright © 1978 Delacorte Press, New York. Photograph courtesy Lennart Nilsson, Bonnier Fakta, Stockholm.
3.1   The Granger Collection
3.3   © Erika Stone
3.5   Courtesy The March of Dimes
A Closer Look, p. 74,   Courtesy Jack Solomon, P.C.; p. 75, Courtesy Thomas J. Bouchard
3.7   *left*, © Erika Stone; *right*, © Michal Heron/Woodfin Camp & Associates
3.9   UPI/Bettmann Newsphotos
3.10   © Erika Kroll/Taurus Photos
Research Report, p. 82,   Chart adapted from R.S. Wilson, "Twins: Patterns of cognitive development as measured on the Wechsler Preschool and Primary Scale of Intelligence." *Development Psychology*, 1975, *11*. Copyright © 1975 by the American Psychological Association. Adapted by permission of the author.
A Closer Look, p. 89, *left*,   © R. Kolberg/Taurus Photos; *right*, © Neal T. Nichols/Taurus Photos
3.11   Courtesy Victor A. McKusick
3.12   Sepp Seitz/Woodfin Camp & Associates
3.13   *photo* © Mimi Cotter Int'l. Stock Photo

Chapter 4

Opener and p. 98,   From Lennart Nilsson, *A child is born*. Copyright © 1978 Delacorte Press, New York. Photograph courtesy Lennart Nilsson, Bonnier Fakta, Stockholm.
4.1   © Per Sundström/Gamma Liaison
4.2   Landrum B. Shettles
4.4   (a) (b) (c) © Claude Edelmann/Black Star; (d) © Donald Yeager/Camera MD Studios
4.5   © S.J. Allen/Int'l. Stock Photo
4.6   Carolina Biological Supply Co.
4.7   Milwaukee Sentinel/UPI, Bettmann Newsphoto
4.8   *all*, Carnegie Institute of Washington, Department of Embryology, Davis Division
4.9   Adapted from Keith L. Moore, *The developing human* (3rd ed.), Fig. 8.14, p. 152. Philadelphia: W.B. Saunders Company, 1982.
4.10   From "Fetal alcohol syndrome experience with 41 patients." *Journal of the American Medical Association*, *235*(14). Courtesy James W. Hanson, M.D., Department of Pediatrics, College of Medicine, the University of Iowa.
4.11   © Robin Schwartz/Int'l. Stock Photo
4.12   © W. Eugene Smith, Courtesy of Center for Creative Photography, University of Arizona
4.13   © Joel Gordon 1982

4.14 © Alan Carey/The Image Works
4.15 © Hazel Hankin
4.16 © Elizabeth Crews
4.17 © Marilyn Sanders/Peter Arnold, Inc.

Chapter 5
Opener and p. 124, © Jim Harrison/Stock, Boston
5.2 © Joel Gordon 1984
5.3 © Erika Stone
Research Report, p. 129, © Jim Anderson/Woodfin Camp & Associates
5.4 © Elizabeth Crews
5.5 © Gabor Demjen/Stock, Boston
5.7 From Frederick Leboyer, *Birth without violence.* Copyright © 1975 by Alfred A. Knopf, Inc. Reprinted by permission of the publisher. Photographs courtesy Editions du Seuil, Paris.
5.8 © Jim Harrison/Stock, Boston
A Closer Look, p. 136, © Martin A. Levick/Black Star
5.9 *all*, © Mimi Cotter/Int'l. Stock Photo
5.10 © Gabor Demjen/Stock, Boston
A Closer Look, p. 143 © Jim Harrison/Stock, Boston
5.11 © Alice Kandell/Kay Reese & Associates
5.12 © Joel Gordon 1984

Chapter 6
Opener, p. 152, and p. 251 *top*: © Hazel Hankin
6.1 National Center for Health Statistics
6.2 Adapted from W.J. Robbins and others, *Growth.* Copyright © 1929 by Yale University Press. Reprinted by permission.
6.3 (d) (e) (f) Adapted from J.L. Conel, *The postnatal development of the human cerebral cortex* (7 vols.). Cambridge, MA: Harvard University Press, 1939-1963.
6.4 From Paul H. Mussen (Ed.), *Handbook of child psychology* (4th ed.), Vol. II. Marshall M. Haith and Joseph J. Campos (Volume Eds.), *Infancy and developmental psychobiology.* New York:Wiley, 1983
6.5 © Jason Laure/Woodfin Camp & Associates
6.6 Adapted from Robert L. Fantz, "The origin of form perception." Copyright © 1961 by Scientific American, Inc. All rights reserved.
Research Report, p. 161, *both*, Courtesy Dr. Joseph J. Campos, University of Denver
6.8 *left*, © Jeffrey D. Smith/Woodfin Camp & Associates; *center*, © Marc & Evelyne Bernheim/Woodfin Camp & Associates; *right*, © Bill Wrenn/Int'l, Stock Photo
6.9 *all*, © Ken Karp
6.10 *all*, © Elizabeth Crews
6.11 © Joel Gordon 1983
6.12 © Alice Kandell/Rapho, Photo Researchers
Table 6.1 Adapted from W. K. Frankenburg and J.B. Dodds, "The Denver developmental screening test." *Journal of Pediatrics*, 1967, *71*(2), 181-191.
A Closer Look, p. 169 *left*, © Ellis Herwig/Stock, Boston; *right*, © Michal Heron/Woodfin Camp & Associates
6.13 (a) AP/Wide World Photos; (b) Reuters/Bettmann Newsphotos
6.14 © Marc & Evelyne Bernheim/Woodfin Camp & Associates

Chapter 7
Opener, p. 176, and p. 251 *center*: © Erika Stone
7.1 © Shirley Zeiberg

7.2 © Shirley Zeiberg
7.3 © Mimi Cotter/Int'l. Stock Photo
A Closer Look, p. 183 © Hazel Hankin
7.4 © Mimi Cotter/Int'l. Stock Photo
7.5 © Elizabeth Crews
7.6 © Abigail Heyman/Archive Pictures
7.7 © George Ancona/Int'l. Stock Photo
7.8 © Jason Laure/Woodfin Camp & Associates
Research Report, p. 191 From C.K. Rovee-Collier, "Reactivation of infant memory." *Science*, 6 June 1980, *208*(4448), pp. 1159–1161. Copyright © 1980 by the American Association for the Advancement of Science.
7.9 © Michael Douglas/The Image Works
7.10 © Erika Stone
7.11 © Erika Stone
7.12 © Erika Stone/Peter Arnold, Inc.
7.13 © Erika Stone
A Closer Look, p. 199 © Alan Carey/The Image Works
7.14 *left*, © Beryl Goldberg; *right*, © Elizabeth Crews
7.15 Adapted from R.V. Tonkova-Yanpol'skaya, "Development of speech intonation in infants during the first two years of life." *Soviet Psychology*, 1969, *7*(3), 48–54. Reprinted with permission of M.E. Sharpe, Inc.
7.16 © Erika Stone/Peter Arnold, Inc.

Chapter 8
Opener, p. 212, and p. 251 *bottom*: © Michael Hayman/Stock, Boston
8.1 © Mimi Cotter/Int'l. Stock Photo
Research Report, p. 214, after photo by Carroll Izard, University of Delaware
8.2 © Ken Karp
8.3 ® Erika Stone
8.4 © Erika Stone
A Closer Look, p. 219: *left*, © Erika Stone; *right* © Shirley Zeiberg
8.5 © Erika Stone/Peter Arnold, Inc.
8.6 © Erika Stone
8.7 © Frank Siteman/Taurus Photos
8.8 © Linda Ferrer/Woodfin Camp & Associates
8.9 © Elizabeth Crews
Research Report, p. 234 © Beryl Goldberg; p. 235, © Mimi Cotter/Int'l. Stock Photo
8.10 © Marion Bernstein
8.11 © *left*, © Beryl Goldberg; *right*; © Erika Stone
8.12 © Tim Kelly/Black Star
8.13 AP/Wide World Photos
8.14 © Beatriz Schiller/Int'l. Stock Photo

Chapter 9
Opener, p. 256, and p. 353 *top*: © Elizabeth Crews
9.1 © Elizabeth Crews
9.2 © Elizabeth Crews
9.3 © Michael D. Sullivan/TexaStock
9.4 National Center for Health Statistics
9.5 © Shirley Zeiberg/Taurus Photos
9.6 © Michael D. Sullivan/TexaStock
9.7 UPI/Bettmann Newsphotos
A Closer Look, p. 267, © Hazel Hankin
9.8 © David A. Krathwohl/Stock, Boston
A Closer Look, p. 271, © Elizabeth Crews
9.9 *left*, © Alan Carey/The Image Works; *right*, © Michael Weisbrot and family/Int'l. Stock Photo

9.10 *left*, © Laima Druskis/Taurus Photos; *right*, © Elizabeth Crews

A Closer Look, p. 275, Courtesy Larry Fenson, San Diego State University

9.11 © Joseph Schuyler/Stock, Boston

9.12 © Jeff Albertson/Stock, Boston

9.13 © George Ancona/Int'l. Stock Photo

Research Report, p. 280, © Ginger Chih/Peter Arnold, Inc.

9.15 © Elizabeth Crews

Chapter 10

Opener, p. 286, and p. 353 *center*: © Elizabeth Crews

10.1 From Celia Genishi and Anne Haas Dyson, *Language assessment in the early years.* Copyright © 1984 Ablex Publishing Corporation. Reprinted by permission of the publisher.

10.2 *left*, © Elizabeth Crews; *right*; © Shirley Zeiberg

10.4 © Mimi Forsyth/Monkmeyer Press Photo Service

Chart, p. 291, adapted from Howard Gardner, *Developmental psychology.* Copyright © 1978 by Little, Brown and Company. Reprinted by permission of the publisher.

10.5 Adapted from Howard Gardner, *Developmental psychology*, Fig. 7.3. Copyright © 1978 by Little, Brown and Company. Reprinted by permission of the publisher.

10.7 From Jane G. Martel, *Smashed potatoes.* Copyright © 1974 by Jane G. Martel. Reprinted by permission of Houghton Mifflin Company.

10.7 Adapted from Martin Hughes and Margaret Donaldson, "The use of hiding games for studying coordination of viewpoints." *Educational Review*, 1979, *31*, 133–140

A Closer Look, p. 196, © Michael Weisbrot and family

10.8 © Shirley Zeiberg

Research Report, p. 300, From Susan Curtiss, *Genie: A psycholinguistic study of a modern-day "wild child."* New York: Academic Press, 1977.

p. 302 "Little stones…," "The world is so…," and "A hole is to dig" from Ruth Krauss, *A hole is to dig*, illustrated by Maurice Sendak. Text © 1952 by Ruth Krauss. Illustrations © 1952 by Maurice Sendak. Reproduced by permission of Harper & Row, Publishers, Inc.

10.10 © Alan Carey/The Image Works

10.11 © Susan Lapides 1981/Design Conceptions

10/13 © Elizabeth Crews

Chapter 11

Opener, p. 318, and p. 353 *bottom*: © Alan Carey/The Image Works

11.1 © Ken Karp

11.2 © David M. Grossman

11.3 (a) © Mimi Cotter/Int'l. Stock Photo; (b) © Mike Mazzaschi/Stock Boston; (c) © Judith Aronson/Peter Arnold, Inc.; (d) © White and Pite/Int'l. Stock photo; (e) © Hazel Hankin

11.4 © Pellegrini/Int'l. Stock Photo

11.5 © Mimi Cotter/Int'l. Stock Photo

Research Report, pp. 326–327, Harry F. Harlow, University of Wisconsin Primate Laboratory

11.7 *left*, © Ed Lettau/Photo Researchers; *right*, © Erika Stone

Research Report, p. 334 © Joel Gordon 1979

11.8 *left*, © J. Berndt/Stock, Boston; *right*, © Shirley Zeiberg

11.10 © Alan Carey/The Image Works

11.11 © Joanne Leonard/Woodfin Camp & Associates

11.12 *left*, © James Holland/Stock, Boston; *right*, © Burk Uzzle/Woodfin Camp & Associates

11.13 *left*, © Shirley Zeiberg; *right*, © Michael Weisbrot and family

Chapter 12

Opener, p. 358, and p. 457 *top*: © Mimi Cotter/Int'l. Stock Photo

12.1 © Elizabeth Crews

12.2 © Shirley Zeiberg

12.3 left, © Mike Mazzaschi/Stock, Boston; right, © Elizabeth Crews

12.4 © Alan Carey/The Image Works

12.5 (a) © Joan Menschenfreund; (b) © R.S. Uzzell III/Woodfin Camp & Associates

12.6 © David Strickler/Monkmeyer Press Photo Service

12.7 © Will McIntyre/Photo Researchers

12.8 © Beryl Goldberg

12.9 © Alice Kandell/Photo Researchers

Chapter 13

Opener, p. 382, and p. 457 *center*: © Donald Dietz/Stock, Boston

13.1 © Ingeborg Lippmann/Peter Arnold, Inc.

13.2 © Marion Bernstein

13.3 © Bruce Roberts/Photo Researchers

13.4 © Susan Berkowitz/Taurus Photos, Courtesy of the Teachers' Room

A Closer Look, p. 391: *top*, © Robert Kalman/The Image Works; *bottom*, © Elizabeth Crews

13.6 © Michael Weisbrot and family/Stock, Boston

13.7 © Ken Karp

13.8 © Elizabeth Crews

13.9 © Sybil Shelton/Peter Arnold, Inc.

13.10 © Sybil Shelton/Peter Arnold, Inc.

A Closer Look, p. 401, © Charles Harbutt/Archive Pictures

Chart, p. 402 Based on data from C. Chomsky, *The acquisition of syntax in children from five to ten.* Copyright © 1969 by the Massachusetts Institute of Technology. Adapted by permission of the MIT Press.

13.11 © Erika Stone

13.12 © Elizabeth Crews/Stock, Boston

13.13 © Elizabeth Crews

13.14 © Elizabeth Crews

13.15 © Mimi Forsyth/Monkmeyer Press Photo Service

A Closer Look, p. 412, The Bettmann Archive

13.16 © Marion Bernstein

13.17 © George Roos/Peter Arnold, Inc.

Chapter 14

Opener, p. 420, and p. 457 *bottom*: © Ken Karp

14.1 ® Joan Menschenfreund/Taurus Photos

14.2 © Charles Gupton/Stock, Boston

14.3 *both*, © Michal Heron/Woodfin Camp & Associates

14.4 (a) © John Curtis/Taurus Photos; (b) © Peter Symasko/Int'l. Stock Photo; (c) © Marc & Evelyne Bernheim/Woodfin Camp & Associates; (d) © Tony Howarth/Woodfin Camp & Associates; (e) © Scott Thode/Int'l. Stock Photo

14.5 © Jean-Claude Lejeune/Stock, Boston

14.6 *left*, © Martha Bates/Stock, Boston; *right*, © Sybil Shelton/Peter Arnold, Inc.

14.8 *left*, Michael Weisbrot and family/Int'l. Stock Photo; *right*, © Elizabeth Crews

14.9 © Elizabeth Crews

14.10 ® Jehangir Gazdar/Woodfin Camp & Associates
14.11 © Erika Stone/Peter Arnold, Inc.
14.12 *left*, © Elizabeth Crews; *right*, © David M. Grossman
14.13 © Joel Gordon 1980
14.14 © Michael Weisbrot and family/Int'l. Stock Photo
14.15 From Michael Rutter, "Protective factors in children's responses to stress and disadvantage." In Whalen and Rolf (Eds.), *Primary prevention of psychopathology*, Vol. III: *Social competence in children*. Reprinted by permission of the University Press of New England. Copyright © 1970 by the Vermont Conference on the Primary Prevention of Psychopathology.
14.16 © Alan Carey/The Image Works

Chapter 15
Opener, p. 462, and p. 549 *top*: © Bill Ross/West Light, Woodfin Camp & Associates
15.1 The Granger Collection
15.2 © James Carroll
15.3 © Alan Carey/The Image Works
15.4 © Donald Dietz/Stock, Boston
15.5 © Barbara Pfeffer/Peter Arnold, Inc.
15.6 © Sybil Shelton/Peter Arnold, Inc.
15.7 © Elizabeth Crews
Research Report, p. 472 Edvard Munch, *Puberty*, 1895. Nasjonalgalleriet, Oslo
A Closer Look, p. 475; *left*, © Charles Gatewood; *right*, © Andy Levin/Black Star
Table 15.1 From Ira E. Robinson and Davor Jedlicka, "Change in sexual behavior of college students from 1965 to 1980: A research note." *Journal of Marriage and the Family*, 1982, *44*, 237–240.
15.8 © Ken Karp
15.9 © Paul S. Conklin/Monkmeyer Press Photo Service
15.10 © National Center for Health Statistics
A Closer Look, p. 484 AP/Wide World Photos
15.11 © Shirley Zeiberg

Chapter 16
Opener, p. 490, and p. 549 *center*: © Marcia Weinstein
16.2 © Elizabeth Crews
A Closer Look, p. 496, © Michal Heron/Woodfin Camp & Associates

16.3 © Michal Heron
16.4 © Elizabeth Crews
16.5 © Christopher Morrow/Black Star
16.6 © Beatriz Schiller/Int'l. Stock Photo
16.7 Susan Meiselas/Magnum Photos
16.8 Reprinted by permission of the Estate of Norman Rockwell. Photograph courtesy Harry N. Abrams, Inc.
16.9 © Susan Lapides 1981/Design Conceptions
16.10 Courtesy Planned Parenthood of Central Ohio
16.11 National Institute of Drug Abuse, U.D. Department of Health and Human Services, 1985.
16.12 © R.D. Ullmann/Taurus Photos
16.13 *left*, © Joseph Szabo/Photo Researchers; *right*, © Alan Carey/The Image Works
16.14 Courtesy SADD
16.15 © Joan Menschenfreund/Taurus Photos

Chapter 17
Opener, p. 516, and p. 549 *bottom*: © Joel Gordon 1983
17.1 © Joel Gordon 1979
17.2 © *left*, © Susan Lapides 1981/Design Conceptions; *right*, © Michael D. Sullivan
A Closer Look, p. 520 Fritz Goro, LIFE Magazine © 1955 Time Inc.
17.3 *both*, The Bettmann Archive
17.4 (a) The Bettmann Archive; (b) Elliott Erwitt/Magnum Photos; (c) © Michael Abramson/Black Star; (d) © Richard Howard/Black Star
17.5 *left*, © Joel Gordon 1980; *right*, © Shirley Zeiberg
17.6 © Joel Gordon 1980
17.7 © Edward Lettau/Photo Researchers
17.8 © Elizabeth Crews
17.9 © Edward Lettau/Photo Researchers
17.10 © William Hubbell/Woodfin Camp & Associates
17.11 © Shirley Zeiberg
17.12 © National Center for Health Statistics
17.13 © Joel Gordon 1980
17.14 © Joel Gordon 1984
17.15 © Susan Lapides 1983/Design Conceptions
17.16 © Joel Gordon 1979

Name Index

Abraham, Kitty G., 427
Abraham, Sidney, 262
Abravanel, Eugene, 190
Achenbach, Thomas M., 262, 341, 371
Ackerman, B.P., 496
Adelson, Joseph, 465
Agathanos, Helen, 245
Ainsworth, Mary D. Salter, 167, 231, 232, 236
Akiyama, M. Michael, 304
Aldis, Owen, 259
Aleksandrowicz, Dov R., 133
Aleksandrowicz, Malca K., 133
Ali, Z., 142
Allard, Alexander, Jr., 274
Allen, J.R., 110
Altstein, Howard, 145
Amabile, Theresa M., 413
Amatruda, Catherine S., 167
Ambert, Anne-Marie, 448
Ames, Louise Bates, 270, 279
Amgott-Kwan, Terry, 424
Anastasi, Anne, 16, 274, 409, 415, 416
Anderson, Christine Warren, 236
Andres, David, 450
Anglin, Jeremy M., 300, 388
Anolik, Steven A., 531
Apgar, Virginia, 87, 95, 97, 110, 126, 127, 145, 146
Appel, Lynne F., 394
Applebaum, Mark I., 26
Archer, Cynthia, 425
Arend, Richard, 237
Aries, Philippe, 14
Armstrong, Louise, 535
Asche, S.E., 302
Asher, J.J., 306
Asher, Steven R., 433, 434
Åstrand, Per-Olof, 364
Auden, W.H., 175
Ausubel, David P., 526, 527
Axia, Giovanna, 403

Bachrach, Christine A., 506
Baer, Donald M., 50
Bailey, D.A., 365
Baillargeon, Renée, 187, 287
Baird, James T., Jr., 428
Baird, Macaran A., 534
Bakeman, R., 129
Baker, David P., 11
Baker, J.L., 368
Baker, S. Josephine, 220
Bandura, Albert, 50, 334, 347, 422
Bank, Stephen P., 453

Bard, B., 335
Bardwick, Judith M., 545
Barkley, R.A., 371
Barnard, Kathryn E., 128
Barnett, R., 449
Baroni, Rosa, 403
Barrera, Maria E., 160
Bartel, Nettie R., 442
Baskin, Yvonne, 93
Bathurst, Kay, 266
Baumrind, Diana, 328–330, 331, 350
Bayer, Leona M., 269
Bayley, Nancy, 13, 480
Beach, Frank A., 504
Beal, Carole R., 308
Beck, Joan, 87, 95, 97, 110
Bee, Helen L., 128
Behrman, Richard E., 106, 129, 130
Bell, Richard Q., 5, 328, 330, 375
Bell, Silvia M., 231
Beller, E. Kuno, 192
Belsky, Jay, 233, 234, 313, 330, 446, 532
Bem, Sandra, 349, 350
Benbow, C.P., 11
Bender, Lauretta, 341
Bengsten, Vernon L., 530
Bennett, Neville, 397
Berezin, Nancy, 134, 138, 146
Berg, Alan, 160, 204
Berk, Laura, 307
Berkowitz, Leonard, 337
Berman, Winnie, 311
Berndt, Thomas J., 431, 526
Bernstein, Basil, 403
Bettelheim, Bruno, 352
Bierman, Karen Lynn, 434
Bigelow, Ann, 182
Bigelow, B.J., 431
Biggs, John B., 384
Bijou, Sidney W., 50
Biller, Henry B., 444, 446
Bing, Elizabeth D., 118, 135, 136, 137, 146
Birch, Herbert G., 224
Bizzell, Rondeall P., 273
Black, Rebecca, 246
Blasi, Augusto, 503
Blewitt, Pamela, 300
Block, Jack, 452
Block, Jeanne, 138, 330, 452
Bloom, Benjamin S., 300
Bloom, Lois, 299, 300
Blos, Peter, 463
Bode, Jerry, 24, 348

Boffey, Philip M., 92
Bogin, Barry, 171
Bond, Guy L., 269
Bonvillian, John D., 199
Borke, Helene, 294
Borstelmann, L.J., 28
Bouchard, Thomas, 74, 75
Boukydis, C.F. Zachariah, 213
Bowen, R., 499
Bower, T.G.R., 164, 179, 188, 440
Bowerman, Melissa, 303
Bowlby, John, 236
Boxer, Andrew M., 15, 27
Boylan, Claire Hamblin, 137
Brackbill, Yvonne, 189
Bradley, Robt. H., 237, 238
Bradshaw, John L., 268
Braine, Martin D.S., 495
Brainerd, Charles J., 177
Brazelton, T. Berry, 164, 173, 228, 230, 234
Bretherton, Inge, 232
Brill, A.A., 463
Brim, Orville G., 426
Broman, S.H., 129
Bromley, D.B., 425
Bronfenbrenner, Urie, 4, 24, 31, 312
Bronson, Wanda C., 225
Brooks, Jeanne, 215, 217
Brooks-Gunn, Jeanne, 472, 473
Brophy, Jere E., 279
Brown, Ann L., 393
Brown, B.J., 340
Brown, Bertram S., 392, 442
Brown, J.V., 129
Brown, Judith K., 521
Brown, Larry, 242, 243
Brown, Roger, 303, 304
Bruch, Hilda, 484
Bruner, Jerome Seymour, 61, 205, 269, 299
Bryan, James H., 439
Buhler, Charlotte, 544
Burelson, Brant R., 439
Burgess, Robert L., 213
Busow, S.A., 544
Buss, Ray R., 395
Butler, John A., 277
Butler, Neville, 109

Cairns, Robert B., 29, 45, 53, 61, 62
Caldwell, Bettye M., 45, 221, 237, 238
Calvin, W.H., 63
Camara, Kathleen A., 443, 449

Campos, Joseph J., 161, 212, 213, 214, 216, 218, 224, 226, 320
Canter, Pamela, 497
Cantwell, Dennis P., 243, 374
Cárdenas, Jose A., 406
Carew, Jean V., 240, 241
Carew-Watts, Jean V., 238–240
Carey, Susan, 300
Carlberg, C., 368
Carlson, Bonnie E., 449
Carlsson, S.G., 142
Caron, Albert J., 160, 176, 188, 189
Caron, Rose F., 160, 176, 188, 189
Carter-Saltzman, Louise, 266
Case, Robbie, 288
Cassill, Kay, 75, 76
Cavanaugh, Patrick J., 190
Cazden, Courtney B., 309
Cervantes, Lucius F., 531
Chandler, Michael J., 113
Chapman, Michael, 203, 332
Charlesworth, William R., 29
Chavez, Cleofe J., 109
Cherry, Louise, 310
Chess, Stella, 7, 106, 142, 224, 225, 227, 465
Chilman, Catherine S., 471, 478, 529
Chivian, Eric, 440
Chomsky, Carol, 400, 401, 402
Chomsky, Noam, 196, 197
Christian, D., 404
Christopherson, V.A., 427
Chukovsky, Korneĭ Ivanovich, 302
Church, Joseph, 308, 342
Churchill, Winston, 373, 413
Cicourel, Aaron V., 270
Clarizio, H.F., 415
Clark, Eve V., 303
Clark, Kenneth B., 416
Clark, Samuel D., 507
Clarke-Stewart, K. Alison, 235, 236, 313
Clarkson, Marsha G., 160, 204
Clifford, Edward, 474
Clingempeel, W.G., 445
Coates, Thomas J., 503
Cogan, Rosemary, 138
Cohen, Stephen M., 79, 160, 350
Cohn, Anne H., 244, 245
Cohn, Jeffrey F., 213
Coie, John D., 434
Colby, Anne, 437, 500, 501, 503, 512
Cole, M., 395
Coleman, John C., 525, 526
Coleridge, Samuel Taylor, 97
Coles, Robert, 516
Collins, J.K., 474
Collis, K.F., 384
Colman, Arthur, 116, 118
Colman, Libby, 116, 118
Compton, Norma H., 228
Condron, John C., 24, 348
Conners, C.K., 376
Cook, Thomas D., 335
Cooper, Catherine R., 534
Coopersmith, Stanley, 427
Corballis, Michael C., 266, 267
Cornell, Edward H., 191
Corrigan, Robert L., 201, 288
Corter, Carl, 326
Cottle, Thomas J., 483
Cowan, Philip A., 54, 59, 63, 203, 290, 294, 383, 496

Crnic, Keith A., 129
Cronbach, Lee J., 416
Crouter, Ann C., 4
Cummings, Michael R., 73
Cunningham, C.E., 371
Curtiss, Susan R., 300

Damon, William, 437, 503, 512
Danforth, David N., 125, 126
Daniels, Denise, 226, 227
Darlington, Richard, 312
Dasen, P.R., 294
Davenport-Slack, Barbara, 137
Davies, P.A., 128
Davis, Elizabeth, 126, 132, 133, 147
Day, D., 188
DeCasper, Anthony J., 160
de Hirsch, Katrina, 270, 274
De Loache, Judy S., 393
DeMause, Lloyd, 28
Demo, David H., 426
Denney, Nancy Wadsworth, 295
Dennis, Wayne, 21
Deno, E.N., 367
Derdeyn, Andre, 445
Derryberry, D., 226
Deutsch, Helene, 41, 476
de Villiers, Jill G., 302, 304, 305
de Villiers, Peter A., 306, 400, 402
Diaz, Rafael M., 406
Dick-Read, Grantly, 135
Dietz, William H., Jr., 363
diGeorge, Angelo M., 264
DiPietro, Janet Ann, 259, 279
Dix, Carol, 92, 107, 109, 131, 132
Dockrell, J., 297
Dodds, Josiah B., 165, 167
Dodge, Kenneth A., 433
Doherty, William J., 534
Doman, Glenn, 270
Donaldson, Margaret, 294, 295, 297, 308
Donovan, Bonnie, 132
Douvan, Elizabeth, 465, 545
Dronamraju, Krishna R., 91
Droogers, Andre, 521
Dryfoos, Joy G., 506, 507
Dubey, Dennis R., 377
Ducat, Diane E., 544
Duckworth, Eleanor, 390
Duffey, James, 416
Dukes, Joyce Lynn, 453
Duncan, Beverly, 546
Duncan, Otis Dudley, 546
Dunn, Lloyd M., 140, 218, 325, 326, 367
Dunphy, Dexter, 528
Dutcher, Nadine, 406
Dweck, Carol S., 427, 434
Dyer, Jean L., 273
Dyson, Anne Haas, 299, 310

Eaton, Warren O., 276
Edelbrock, C.S., 262
Edison, Thomas, 413
Edgerton, Robert B., 84
Egan, Jane, 259
Egeland, Bryan, 233
Eichorn, Dorothy H., 168, 263, 362
Eimas, Peter D., 160

Eisenberg, Nancy, 310, 327, 438
Eisenberg-Berg, Nancy, 342, 438, 439
Ekholm, Mats., 438
Ekman, P., 214
Elardo, Richard, 237
Elder, Glen H., Jr., 522, 523, 531
Elfenbein, Donald, 437
Eliot, T.S., 1
Elkind, David, 192, 271, 390, 482, 497, 498, 499, 510
Elliot, Elaine S., 427
Elster, Arthur B., 234
Emde, Robert N., 213
Emery, Alan E.H., 73, 84
Emery, Donald G., 270
Emery, Robert E., 443, 444, 445
Emory, Eugene, 79
Endo, R., 16
Enkin, M.W., 135
Entwisle, Doris R., 11
Erikson, Erik, 41, 42, 43, 44, 45, 62, 63, 211, 221, 222, 223, 224, 249, 319, 320, 351, 421, 424, 427, 442, 455, 516, 517, 519, 521, 522, 546, 547
Eriksson, Bengt O., 359
Erlenmeyer-Kimling, L., 82
Eron, Leonard D., 441
Ervin, Susan, 304
Espenshade, T.J., 445
Etaugh, Claire, 449
Etzioni, Amitai, 95
Evans, Richard I., 511
Eveleth, Phillis B., 261, 262, 359

Fabricius, William V., 394
Fagot, Beverly I., 345
Falbo, Toni, 124, 326
Fantz, Robert, 159
Farber, Ellen A., 233
Farel, Anita M., 449
Farnham-Diggory, Sylvia, 370, 371, 379
Fasick, Frank A., 530
Faust, Margaret Siler, 479
Feather, Norman T., 530
Featherstone, Helen, 6, 352
Featherstone, Joseph, 390
Fein, Greta G., 111
Feingold, Benjamin F., 376–377
Feiring, Candice, 447
Feldman, S. Shirley, 348, 511
Feldstein, Jerome H., 334
Feldstein, Sandra, 334
Felton, Gary, 135
Ferenzi, S., 463
Ferguson, Charles A., 205, 206
Ferree, Myra M., 449
Ferster, Charles B., 49
Field, Tiffany, 22, 128, 129, 140, 190, 213, 296
Fifer, William P., 160
Fincher, Jack, 266, 267
Finkelhor, David, 448, 534, 535, 538
Fisch, Martin L., 372
Fischer, Kurt W., 61, 187
Fisher, W.M., 135
Fitzgerald, Hiram E., 189
Flavell, John H., 12, 54, 61, 178, 187, 287, 289, 307, 308, 388, 389, 423, 424, 490, 494, 495, 506, 513
Flynn, L.A., 270
Flynn, T.M., 270
Foege, William H., 277

Ford, Clellan S., 504
Forehand, Rex, 310
Forness, Steven R., 368
Fox, Greer Litton, 95
Fraiberg, Selma, 339
Frankenburg, William K., 165, 167
Franklin, Deborah, 106
French, Doran C., 439
Freud, Anna, 41, 42, 464
Freud, Sigmund, 38, 39, 40, 41, 42, 44, 45, 60,
    62, 63, 220, 221, 222, 223, 224, 249, 344, 345,
    346, 351, 420, 424, 455, 463, 464, 465, 476
Friedrich, Lynette Kohn, 246, 334, 335
Friesen, W., 214
Frisch, Rose E., 476
Fritz, Janet, 360
Frost, Robert, 547
Fuhrmann, Walter, 84, 90
Furman, Wyndol, 434
Furstenberg, Frank F., Jr., 444, 449, 508

Gadverry, Sharon, 335
Gaensbauer, Theodore J., 213
Galambos, N.L., 450
Galinsky, Ellen, 113, 114, 115, 464
Gallatin, Judith, 530
Gallistel, C.R., 298
Gallup, George, Jr., 524
Garbarino, John, 31, 442, 450
Garcia, R., 306
Gardner, Howard, 61, 80, 193, 268, 274, 275,
    287, 301, 322
Gardner, Lytt I, 22, 265
Gardner, William I., 367
Garland, Eddy, 74
Garmezy, Norman, 337, 340, 341, 374, 376, 451,
    452, 453, 530
Garvey, Catherine, 259, 260, 307, 324, 325, 343,
    352, 546
Garvin, Ruth A., 307
Gasser, R.D., 446
Gelles, Richard, J., 117, 245
Gelman, Rochel, 187, 287, 298, 423
Genishi, Celie, 299, 310
George, Victor, 338, 446
Gesell, Arnold, 13, 16, 19, 167, 363
Ghandi, Mahatma, 501
Gibson, Eleanor, 161, 188, 189, 271
Gibson, James, 188
Giles-Sims, Jean, 448
Giller, Henri, 482
Gilligan, Carol, 16, 31, 281, 501, 502, 503
Ginsberg, Harvey J., 18, 19, 20
Gleason, Jean Berko, 304
Glick, Paul C., 69, 443
Goad, Walter B., 80, 81
Goertzel, Mildred, 413
Goertzel, Victor, 413
Goetz, T.E., 434
Gold, Delores, 450
Gold, Martin, 482, 483
Goldberg, Susan, 142, 310, 440
Goldman, Juliette, 58, 349, 425
Goldman, Ronald, 58, 349, 425
Goldsmith, H. Hill, 79, 226
Gonzo, J., 425, 434, 438
Goodnow, Jacqueline J., 274, 275
Goodwin, J., 537
Gordon, John E., 192
Gortmaker, Steven L., 363

Gottesman, Irving I., 226
Gottfried, Allen W., 266
Gottlieb, Benjamin H., 8, 368
Gottlieb, Jay, 518
Gottman, John, 425, 434, 438
Gould, Stephen J., 63
Grant, James P., 170
Gratch, Gerald, 189
Gray, S.W., 248, 313
Gray, William M., 499
Green, Lawrence, 505
Greenberg, Martin, 143
Greene, Walter H., 168, 422
Greenfeld, Josh, 342, 352
Greenspan, Nancy T., 237
Greenspan, Stanley, 237
Greer, Douglas, 335
Gregg, McAllister, 106
Greif, Esther Blank, 347
Gresham, Frank M., 368
Greydanus, Donald E., 533
Grieve, Robert, 307
Grinker, Joel A., 360, 361, 362
Grobstein, Clifford, 99
Grosjean, Francois, 406
Grotevant, Harold D., 534
Gruendel, Janice M., 306
Guinagh, B.J., 192
Gumerman, Ruth A., 429
Gump, Paul V., 272
Gunnar, Megan R., 219
Gupta, Chhanda, 107
Guthrie, D.M., 154
Guthrie, Robert V., 16
Gutmann, David, 348, 350
Gzesh, Steven M., 495

Haaf, Robert A., 160
Haas, Linda, 348
Habicht, Jean-Pierre, 119
Haddad, Gabriel G., 445
Hagen, John W., 393, 395
Haith, Marshall M., 160
Hale, Janice E., 16, 31
Hall, Calvin S., 63
Hall, G. Stanley, 13, 29, 462, 463, 464
Halliday, M.A.K., 201, 207
Halpern, Robert, 192
Halverson, C.F., 375
Hamilton, Richard, 505
Hanson, James W., 108
Hardy, Janet B., 5, 106, 505
Hardyck, Curtis, 266
Harkness, Sara, 16
Harlow, Harry F., 260, 326, 327
Harlow, Margaret, 260, 326, 327
Harmon, Lenore W., 213
Harper, Lawrence V., 5, 156, 279, 322, 328, 330
Harpring, E.B., 167
Harris, Florence R., 46
Harrison, Algea, 453
Harsanyi, Zsolt, 88
Harter, Susan, 289, 318, 319, 345, 422, 426
Hartshorne, Hugh, 438
Hartsough, Carolyn S., 375
Hartup, Willard W., 216, 321, 327, 336, 360, 371,
    432, 530
Haskins, Ron, 312
Hass, Aaron, 474, 477, 478
Hawkins, J., 396

Hay, D.F., 337
Heald, Felix P., 362
Heinonen, Olli P., 103, 104
Helmreich, Robt. L., 349, 350
Helton, George B., 416
Henderson, Edmund, 395
Henneborn, William James, 138
Henton, Comradge L., 472
Herman, Judith, 538
Hermelin, Beate, 268
Hershorn, Michael, 443
Herzog, A. Regula, 521
Hess, Robert D., 310
Hetherington, E. Mavis, 51, 443, 444, 446, 447,
    448, 449
Heyde, Martha Bennett, 543
Hiatt, Susan, 213
Hier, Daniel B., 81
Higgens, E. Tory, 266, 426
Higham, Eileen, 467, 476
Hill, John P., 483
Hillerich, Robert L., 269, 270, 271
Hilliard, Jomary P., 533
Hinde, Robert A., 322
Hindley, C.B., 166
Hirschi, Travis, 52
Hiscock, Merrill, 266, 267
Hobbins, John C., 116, 131
Hodgen, Gary D., 108
Hoffman, J., 319
Hoffman, Lois Wladis, 449, 450
Hoffman, Martin L., 424
Holden, George, 74, 333
Holdern, William A., 534
Hollander, P., 16
Holmberg, M.C., 322
Holstein, C., 501
Holzman, Mathilda, 399, 403
Holzmuller, Ana, 349
Homer, Daryl R., 168
Hooker, J.G., 92
Hoorweg, Jan, 171
Hopkins, J. Roy, 477
Horner, Thomas M., 224
Horney, Karen, 41, 346
Horowitz, Frances Degan, 243, 312
Horton, Denise, 505
Houser, Betsy Bosak, 546
Hoving, K.L., 393
Howe, K.G., 544
Howes, Carolyn, 327
Howes, Virgil M., 390
Hubert, Nancy C., 226
Hudson, Lynne M., 499
Hughes, A., 404
Hughes, Martin, 294, 295, 307
Huie, Karen S., 322
Humphreys, Lloyd G., 410
Hunt, J. McVicker, 187, 300
Hunter, Fumiyo Tao, 526
Huston, Althea C., 342, 344, 349
Hutton, Richard, 88
Huxley, Aldous, 67
Hwang, Carl-Philip, 141

Ilg, Frances L., 270, 279
Inhelder, Bärbel, 55, 63, 292, 384, 385, 490, 491,
    500
Isaacs, N., 289

Ives, William, 294
Izard C.E., 213, 214, 216

Jacklin, Carol Nagy, 11, 19, 280, 337, 347
Jackson, George D., 416
Jacobs, Blanche S., 310
Jacobs, Jerry, 541, 542
Jacobson, Joseph L., 111, 205
Jahoda, Marie, 449
James, William, 158, 261
Jarvik, Lissy F., 82
Jedlicka, Davor, 477
Jelliffe, Derrick B., 168
Jelliffe, E.F. Patrice, 168
Jencks, Christopher, 411, 442
Jiles, Darrel, 535
Jimenez, Sherry Lynn Mims, 95
Jirasek, Jan E., 102
Johnson, Elmer J., 15
Johnson, Russell R., 425
Johnson, Virginia E., 114, 117
Johnston, Lloyd D., 508, 509
Johnston, Malcolm C., 165
Jones, Ernest, 463
Jones, Kenneth Lyons, 108
Jones, Mary Cover, 480
Jones, N. Burton, 258, 259
Jordaan, Jean Pierre, 543
Josselson, Ruthellen, 517
Juel-Nielson, Neils, 74, 83
Julian, Valerie, 535
Jung, Carl, 463
Jurich, Anthony P., 531
Justice, Blair, 535
Justice, Rita, 535

Kadushin, Alfred, 144
Kagan, Jerome, 61, 187, 194, 215, 220, 224, 227, 439
Kahn, Michael D., 453
Kandel, Denise, 511, 532
Kaplan, Betty, 248
Karmel, Marjorie, 136, 147
Katchadourian, Herant A., 468, 469, 470, 471
Kavale, Kenneth, 368
Kaye, Kenneth, 207, 213, 230
Keller, W.D., 142
Kelly, Joan Berlin, 26, 296, 297, 443, 444, 445, 452
Kempe, C. Henry, 245, 247, 248, 534, 535, 536, 537
Kempe, Ruth S., 245, 246, 248, 534, 535, 536, 537
Kendrick, Carol, 140, 325, 326
Keniston, Kenneth, 442
Kennel, John H., 141, 142, 143
Kerst, Stephen M., 393
Kett, Joseph F., 14, 31
Kinsbourne, Marcel, 266, 267, 376
Kinsey, Alfred C., 471
Kitzinger, Sheila, 92, 110, 112, 119, 137
Klaus, Marshall H., 141, 142, 143
Kleck, Robert E., 434
Klein, Robert P., 194, 236, 346
Kloos, Peter, 521
Klug, William S., 73
Knapp, Herbert, 430
Knapp, Mary, 430

Kneale, G.W., 110
Knight, G.P., 439
Koch, Kenneth, 398
Koenig, Michael A., 507
Koff, Elissa, 473
Kogan, Nathan, 413
Kohlberg, Lawrence, 16, 307, 344, 348, 435, 436, 437, 500, 501, 503, 513
Kohn, Robert R., 532
Kolata, Gina Bari, 91, 92, 108, 133
Kontos, Donna, 142
Korbin, Jill E., 262
Kornhaber, Arthur, 5, 124
Kornhaber, R.C., 339
Koslowski, Barbara, 388
Kramer, Judith A., 187
Krantz, Murray, 434
Kratochwill, T.R., 340
Krehbiel, Gina K., 434
Kuczaj, Stan A., 289
Kuhn, Deanna, 22, 62, 343, 496, 500, 501
Kurokawa, Minako, 277

Labov, William, 404
La Gaipa, J.J., 431
LaGanza, S., 474
La Freniere, Peter, 280
Lamaze, Fernand, 136, 137, 146
Lamb, Michael E., 5, 140, 141, 234, 235, 236, 326, 360, 361, 365, 449, 450
Lambert, Nadine M., 373, 375
Lambert, Wallace, 406
Lamm, Stanley S., 372
Langlois, J.H., 345
Langone, John, 542
Laosa, Luis M., 16, 279, 407
Larsen, John W., 105
Larsen, Spencer A., 168
Lazar, Irving, 312
Leavitt, Jerome E., 242
Leboyer, Frederick, 123, 124, 134, 138, 146
Lecours, A.R., 268
Lee, James Michael, 501
Lee, Lee C., 37
Lefkowitz, Monroe M., 109
Leifer, A.D., 142
Leifer, Myra, 112, 137
Lenneberg, Eric H., 198, 201, 300
Lepper, M.R., 422
Lerner, H.E., 346
Lerner, Richard M., 5, 530
Lesser, Gerald S., 335, 532
Lester, Barry M., 133, 157, 228, 231
Levenstein, Phyllis, 313, 314
Lever, Janet, 432
Levin, Harry, 271
Levine, Laura E., 320, 321
Lewis, Michael, 179, 215, 216, 217, 219, 310, 447
Lewis, Richard, 398
Leyser, Yona, 8
Liben, Lynn S., 393
Liebert, Robert M., 51, 334, 438
Lief, Harold I., 478
Light, P.H., 297
Lindblad-Goldberg, Marion, 453
Linde, Shirley M., 88
Lindquist, G.T., 270
Linksz, Arthur, 267
Lipe, Dewey, 362, 379

Lipsitt, Lewis P., 157, 190, 191
Livesley, W.J., 425
Livson, Norman, 479, 480
Lloyd, H.A., 340
Locksley, A., 350
Loehlin, John C., 79, 80
Longstreth, Langdon E., 266
Lovell, Kenneth, 496
Lowe, Marianne, 288
Lowrey, George H., 152, 158, 168, 261, 262, 263, 264, 269, 279, 358, 362, 363, 468
Lowry, M., 142
Lueptow, Lloyd B., 545, 546
Lynch, Margaret A., 247
Lynn, R., 414
Lytton, Hugh, 310

Maccoby, Eleanor Emmons, 11, 19, 51, 258, 280, 328, 331, 333, 337, 347, 393, 422, 531
MacDonald, Paul C., 107
Macfarlane, Aidan, 141, 147
Mack, John E., 440
Mackenzie, Thomas B., 116
Mackworth, N.H., 269
Madden, John, 314
Madsen, M.C., 439
Maehr, Martin L., 442
Magnusson, D., 483
Mahler, Margaret, 41, 221, 223, 224, 237, 249
Mahoney, Maurice J., 92
Main, Mary, 237, 338
Makinson, Carolyn, 507
Malcom, Andrew H., 441, 446, 453
Malouf, Roberta E., 342
Malson, M., 453
Maqsud, M., 442
Marcia, James E., 517, 519
Margolis, Lewis H., 277
Markell, Richard A., 433
Markman, Ellen, 493
Martel, Jane, 293
Martin, Barclay, 45, 51, 221, 531
Martin, Harold P., 243
Martin, John, 328, 331, 333, 422, 531
Masters, William H., 114, 117
Maugh, Thomas H., 88
Mayer, Jean, 246, 361
McAdoo, Harriette, 453
McAuliffe, Kathleen, 91
McAuliffe, Sharon, 91
McCabe, Maryann, 534, 535, 536, 538
McCall, Robert B., 26, 74, 79, 140, 187, 193
McCarthy, Dorothea, 13
McCartney, Kathleen, 75, 313
McCleary, Elliot H., 131
McClelland, David C., 331, 526, 530
McGarrigle, J., 297
McGurk, Harry, 179
McIntire, Roger N., 88
McIntyre, C.W., 51
McKusick, Victor A., 91
McLaughlin, Barry, 300, 311, 406
McManus, Carol E., 105, 107
McNeill, David, 196
McRoy, Ruth G., 145
McWhorter, DeAnna, 103
Meadow, Kathryn, 199
Mears, Clara, 326
Meilman, Phillip W., 520
Mellendick, Geroge J.D., 470

Meltzoff, Andrew N., 190
Mercer, Jane F., 415
Meredith, Howard V., 261
Merten, Don, 477
Mervis, Carolyn B., 205
Mervis, Cynthia A., 205
Messick, Samuel, 415
Meyer, Thomas J., 505
Michaelson, Linda, 216, 219
Michel, George F., 266
Miller, Arden C., 505
Miller, George L., 509
Miller, Louise B., 273
Miller, Patricia H., 37, 63
Miller, Peter, 114
Miller, Shelby H., 18, 19, 20
Miller, William R., 478
Milne, Conrad, 278
Milunsky, Aubrey, 84, 87, 88, 110
Minuchin, Patricia, 397, 430, 434, 444, 452
Minuchin, Salvador, 484, 533, 534
Mischel, Walter, 61, 347
Mitchell, G., 260, 416
Money, John, 265
Montessori, Maria, 273
Moore, Dorothy, 270
Moore, Keith L., 80, 81, 87, 99, 101, 102
Moore, Keith M., 190
Moore, Raymond, 270
Moriarty, Alice E., 227, 272, 306, 451, 452, 453
Morris, Norman, 138, 143
Moss, Melvin, 87, 310
Mowder, Barbara A., 416
Mukherjee, Anil B., 108
Munn, Penny, 218
Murphy, John M., 503
Murphy, Lois Barclay, 227, 272, 306, 451, 452, 453, 503
Murray, Ann D., 133
Mussen, Paul Henry, 438, 439, 480
Myers, H.F., 16

Naeye, Richard L., 118
Neimark, Edith D., 495
Nelson, Katherine, 201, 202, 203, 306
Nelson-Le Gall, Sharon A., 429
Nerlove, H., 302
Nettlebladt, Per, 137
Newberger, Carolyn Moore, 171
Newberry, Phillis, 449
Newbrun, Ernest, 263
Nietzsche, Friedrich, 255
Nisbett, R.E., 497
Nix, Gary W., 367
Novak, M.A., 327
Nye, F. Ivan, 449
Nyhan, William L., 87, 88

O'Brien, Marion, 342, 349
O'Brien, Thomas E., 105
O'Connor, N., 268
Oden, Melita H., 26, 412
Offer, Daniel, 465, 482, 532
Offer, Judith, 465, 482, 532
Ogra, Pearay L., 168
Ollendick, Thomas H., 434
Omenn, Gilbert S., 87

Opie, Iona, 430
Opie, Peter, 430
Orlofsky, J.L., 517
Ornitz, Edward M., 340
Osherson, Daniel N., 493
Osman, Betty B., 372, 373
Oster, Harriet, 198, 214
Osterreith, Paul A., 526
Ostrea, Enrique M., Jr., 109
Owsley, Cynthia, 161
Oyama, S., 306

Paige, Karen Eriksen, 520
Palmer, Frances, H., 313
Parke, Ross D., 234, 235, 333, 335, 336, 337, 440
Parkhurst, J.T., 438
Parmelee, Arthur H., Jr., 103, 155, 156
Parten, Mildred B., 322
Patterson, Gerald R., 52, 53, 333, 337, 377, 422
Paulston, Christina Bratt, 406
Pavlov, Ivan, 47, 136
Pawson, M., 138
Pederson, Frank A., 235
Peel, E.A., 493
Pelton, Leroy H., 244
Pennington, Bruce F., 81
Perlmutter, Marion, 191
Peskin, Harvey, 479, 480
Petersen, Anne C., 467
Peters-Martin, Patricia, 225
Petrinovich, Lewis F., 266
Petronio, Richard J., 482, 483
Petzel, Sue V., 540
Piaget, Jean, 54, 55, 56, 58, 60, 61, 62, 63, 177, 178, 179, 180, 181, 182, 185, 186, 187, 188, 189, 192, 193, 198, 201, 208, 287, 289, 290, 291, 292, 294, 296, 298, 299, 308, 311, 315, 348, 383, 384, 385, 386, 387, 388, 389, 390, 391, 392, 415, 416, 435, 437, 455, 490, 491, 493, 495, 497, 499, 500, 512, 513
Pickar, Joanne, 299
Pike, Robin, 319
Pines, Maya, 339
Pissanos, Becky W., 278
Plomin, Robert, 226, 227
Poffenberger, Thomas, 262
Polit, Denise, 446
Powers, Stephen, 426
Prescott, G.A., 409
Pringle, Mia Kellmer, 144
Pritchard, Jack, 107

Queenan, John T., 116, 131

Radke-Yarrow, Marian, 438, 439
Raines, Bettye, E., 511
Ramey, C.T., 312
Ramsay, Douglas S., 266
Rank, Otto, 41, 133
Raring, Richard H., 156
Ravitch, Diane, 389, 391
Rebelsky, Freda G., 309
Reite, Martin, 140
Renshaw, Peter D., 433, 434
Reppucci, N.D., 445
Resnick, Lauren B., 396, 398
Rest, James R., 437, 438

Revelle, Roger, 476
Rholes, William S., 427
Rice, Mabel L., 305, 306
Richardson, Ken, 95
Riddle, Mary, 540
Riordan, Jan, 169
Ritchie, James, 244
Ritchie, Jane, 244
Ritvo, Edward R., 340
Roberts, Jacquie, 247
Roberts Jean, 428
Roberts J. Fraser, 84
Robinson, E.J., 309
Robinson, Halbert B., 271, 411, 412
Robinson, Ira E., 477
Robinson, Nancy, 411
Robinson, W.P., 309
Roche, Alex F., 363
Rockefeller, Nelson, 373
Rodholm, M., 142
Rodman, Hyman, 450
Rogers, Sinclair, 403
Romaine, Suzanne, 400, 401, 403, 404
Romalis, Shelly, 137
Roman, Mel, 445
Roopnarine, Jaipual L., 344
Roper, R., 322
Rose, Susan A., 268
Rosenbach, John H., 416
Rosenbaum, Alan, 443
Rosenkrantz, Arthur L., 511
Rosenson, William, 218
Ross, Bruce M., 393
Ross, Dorothea M., 108, 226, 372, 375, 376, 377
Ross, H.S., 337
Ross, Lee, 425, 497
Ross, Sheila A., 108, 226, 372, 375, 376, 377
Rotberg, Iris C., 397, 406, 407
Rothbart, M.K., 225
Rousseau, Jean-Jacques, 28
Routh, Donald K., 276
Rovee-Collier, Carolyn K., 191
Rubin, Kenneth H., 260, 279, 287, 288, 324
Rubin, Zick, 321, 323, 431, 433, 434, 439
Ruble, Diane N., 349, 472
Rudel, Harry W., 69
Ruff, Holly A., 187
Rumain, Barbara, 495
Runyan, Carol W., 277
Rush, David, 119
Russell, Diana E.H., 535, 538
Russell, Michael J., 162
Rutter, Michael, 143, 226, 313, 337, 340, 341, 374, 376, 442, 443, 444, 447, 451, 452, 465, 474, 475, 480, 482, 498, 530
Ryan, Bruce P., 164, 165

Sachs, J. 335
St. Clair, K.L., 226
Salapatek, Philip, 159
Salter, Alice, 134
Sameroff, Arnold J., 5, 62, 113, 129, 190
Sanders, Karen M., 279
Santrock, John E., 443, 444, 446, 448
Santrock, John W., 444
Sarason, Seymour B., 543
Sattler, Jerome M., 416
Satz, P., 270
Saville-Troike, Muriel, 407
Savin-Williams, Ritch C., 426

Scanlan, James V., 474
Scarr, Sandra, 17, 21, 75, 78, 83, 313
Scarr-Salapatek, Sandra, 192
Schacter, Rubin J., 469
Schaffer, H. Rudolph, 228
Schanberg, Saul M., 22
Schardein, James L., 107
Scheinfeld, Amram, 76
Scher, Jonathan, 92, 107, 109
Schick, Bela, 218
Schiedel, Don G., 517
Schiefelbusch, Richard L., 299, 310
Schieffelin, Bambi B., 310
Schlesinger, Benjamin, 535, 536
Schlesinger, Hilde S., 199
Schoof-Tams, Karin, 475, 478
Schroeder, H.E., 339
Schulte, F.J., 157
Schwartz, Gary, 477
Schwartz, M., 188
Schwartz, Marvin, 154, 155
Schweinhart, L.J., 312
Scott, Ralph, 445
Scribner, S., 395
Sears, Robert R., 51, 332, 347, 412
Seashore, Marjorie J., 142
Segall, M.H., 16
Segelman, Florrie, 135
Seifer, Ronald, 129
Seitz, Victoria, 313
Serbin, L.A., 280
Seymour, Dorothy, 405
Shantz, Carolyn Uhlinger, 425
Shapira, Ariella, 439
Shapiro, Edna K., 428, 434, 444, 452
Shay, Sharon Williams, 248
Shayer, Michael, 496
Shea, John D.C., 259
Sheehy, Gail, 477
Sherman, Julia, 11
Sherrod, Kathryn B., 171
Shields, James, 74, 82
Shinn, Marybeth, 444, 447
Shipman, Virginia C., 310
Shipp, E.E., 507
Shirley, Mary M., 19, 166, 167
Shirely, C., 260
Shneidman, Edwin S., 542
Shores, Richard E., 368
Siegel, Michael, 442
Sigafoos, Ann D., 190
Sigel, Irving, E., 5
Sigman, Marian D., 103, 128, 155, 156
Silberman, Charles, 390
Silverman, W.A., 128
Simmons, Roberta G., 426, 478
Simon, Herbert A., 543
Simon, Rita James, 145
Sinclair, Caroline B., 271, 279
Sinclair, David, 260, 264, 470
Singer, Dorothy G., 335
Singer, Jerome L., 335
Singer, Peter, 95
Siqueland, Einar R., 190
Sizer, Theordore R., 482, 496, 545
Skinner, B.F., 47, 48, 48, 49, 63, 195, 197, 208
Slaby, Ronald G., 335, 336, 337, 440
Slaughter, Diana T., 310, 314
Slobin, Dan I., 204, 304
Sloman, Jane, 434
Smetana, Judith G., 438

Smith, David W., 114
Smith, Herbert A., 215
Smith, Jeffrey R., 107
Smith, M. Brewster, 440, 472
Smith, Nils V., 306
Smith, Peter K., 260, 322
Smith, Ruth S., 26, 227, 451, 452, 453, 454, 483
Smokler, C.S., 450
Snarey, John R., 501
Snow, Catherine E., 206, 228, 310
Snyder, Lynn S., 310
Snyder, Margaret M., 269
Snyder, S., 224
Solnit, Albert J., 242
Sonnenschein, Susan, 309
Sorce, James F., 219
Sorensen, Robert C., 477, 480, 507, 528
Sosa, R., 142
Spache, George D., 267
Spanier, G.B., 5
Spears, David, 95
Spelke, Elizabeth S., 161, 423
Spence, Janet T., 349, 350
Spitz, René Arpad, 22
Spock, Benjamin, 176
Sprafkin, Joyce N., 51
Sprague, R.L., 377
Sroufe, L. Alan, 213, 216, 232, 233, 236, 237
Staffieri, J. Robert, 360
Stanley, J.C., 11
Stark, C.R., 92
Stathakopoulous, Nella, 245
Steele, Brandt, 246
Stein, Althea Huston, 171, 334, 335
Stein, Zena A., 119
Steinberg, Laurence D., 532
Steinman, S., 445
Steinmetz, S.K., 337
Stenberg, Craig, 213
Stern, Daniel, 206, 228, 229, 230, 231
Stern, J.A., 364
Stern, Leonard, 393, 395
Stevenson, Harold W., 53, 409, 414
Stevenson, R.L., 1
Stewart, A., 110
Stipek, Deborah J., 319, 426
Stoddart, Trish, 425
Stone, L. Joseph, 219, 308, 342
Strain, Phillip S., 368
Strauss, Murray A., 337
Streissguth, Ann Pytkowicz, 107, 108, 375
Sulik, Kathleen K., 108
Sullivan, Edmund V., 191, 501
Sun, Marjorie, 92
Suomi, Stephen J., 326, 327
Super, Charles M., 16, 167
Surber, Colleen F., 495
Susser, Mervyn W., 119
Sutcliffe, D., 404
Sutker, Patricia B., 51, 531
Sutton-Smith, Brian, 5
Swanson, J.M., 376
Szalai, Alexander, 429
Szeminska, Aline, 386

Tan, Lesley E., 266
Tannenbaum, Abraham J., 413
Tanner, James M., 22, 79, 153, 171, 261, 262, 264, 265, 266, 278, 359, 468, 471, 474
Tanzer, Deborah, 138

Tayler, Leona, 544
Taylor, Brandon, 467
Taylor, C.M., 446
Taylor, P.M., 142
Telegdy, G.A., 270
Terman, Lewis M., 26, 412
Tesfaye, Andargatchew, 15
Thoman, E.B., 156
Thomas, Alexander, 61, 142, 224, 225, 227, 375, 465
Thompson, Cherry, 157
Thompson, Jean R., 203
Thompson, M.E., 142
Thompson, Michael, 244, 245, 246
Thompson, R.A., 234
Thompson, Spencer K., 342
Tieger, T., 337
Tinsley, Barbara R., 234, 235
Tizard, Barbara, 144
Tobin-Richards, Maryse H., 482
Tonkova-Yampol'skaya, R.V., 200
Torrence, E. Paul, 413
Touliatos, John, 228
Tower, Roni Beth, 335
Trainer, F.E., 501
Tronick, Edward Z., 213
Trudgill, Peter, 404
Tucker, G. Richard, 406
Turiel, Elliot, 425, 437, 438, 513
Turkington, Carol, 450
Turnure, James E., 266

Ullian, Dorothy Z., 348
Ullman, R.K., 377
Ungerer, Judy A., 128
Uzgiris, Ina C., 187

Vandenberg, Brian, 260
Van Oeffelen, Michiel P., 269
Vaughan, Victor C. III, 106, 129, 130
Vaughn, Brian, 233
Veroff, Joseph, 546
Visher, E.B., 448
Visher, J.S., 448
Vivaldi, Antonio, 193
Vogel, Friedrich, 84, 90
von Hofsten, Claes, 165
Vos, Peter G., 269
Voyat, Gilbert, 415
Vurpillot, Elaine, 269
Vygotsky, Lev Semenovich, 299

Waber, Deborah P., 11
Wachs, Theodore D., 187
Wadsworth, M.E.J., 480
Wagner, Michael J., 426
Waldrop, M.F., 375
Walk, Richard D., 161
Walker, Elaine, 79
Walker, Lawrence J., 503
Wallace, James R., 426
Wallach, Michael A., 413
Wallerstein, Judith S., 26, 296, 297, 443, 444, 445, 452
Wallwork, Ernest, 501
Walters, William, 95
Wandersman, L.P., 313

Ward, C., 426
Ward, Mary Jo, 537
Ward, M.C., 310
Waterman, Alan S., 520
Waters, Everett, 216, 232
Watson, John B., 45, 220, 249
Watson, Malcolm W., 288, 424
Weideger, Paula, 472
Weikart, D., 312
Weil, William B., Jr., 362
Weinberg, Richard A., 78, 83
Weinraub, M., 215
Weiss, B., 376
Weiss, R.S., 445
Weissbluth, Marc, 157
Wellman, Henry M. 394
Wells, J.C., 404
Werner, Emmy E., 26, 227, 451, 452, 453, 454, 483
Werner, J.S., 191
Werry, John S., 341, 377
Westbrook, Mary T., 112
Wetherbee, Sally, 360
Whalen, Carol K., 377

White, Burton L., 181, 193, 202, 238–241, 310
White, Robert W., 202, 422, 434
White, Sheldon H., 320
Whiten, A., 142
Whiting, Beatrice Blyth, 271, 337, 428
Whiting, John W.M., 271, 337, 428
Wiggins, Jerry S., 349
Wilding, Paul, 446
Willatts, Peter, 187
Williams, Margaret L., 192
Williams R., 416
Wilson, James Q., 53
Wilson, Ronald S., 82, 167
Winer, G.A., 388
Winick, Myron, 361
Winn, Marie, 335
Wishart, J.G., 188
Wohlwill, J.F., 27
Wolff, Georg, 265
Wolff, Jurgen M., 362, 379
Wolff, Peter, 197, 213
Wolfram, W., 404
Wolock, Isabel, 243
Wolpe, J., 339

Wong Fillmore, Lily, 407
Woodward, Kenneth L., 5, 124

Yakovlev, P.I., 268
Yalisove, Daniel, 400, 403
Yarrow, Marion Radke, 332
Younger, Alastair J., 433
Youniss, James, 327, 434, 526

Zacharias, L., 475
Zahr, Lina, 434
Zegiob, Leslie, E., 310
Zelazo, P.R., 216
Zelnik, Melvin, 507
Zeskind, Philip Sanford, 157, 213
Zigler, Edward, 309, 311
Zill, N., 446
Zimmerman, Barry J., 422
Zurcher, Louis A., 145

Subject Index

Abortion, 115
  and adolescent pregnancy, 507
  and prenatal diagnosis, 92–93
  spontaneous, 92, 103, 110, 114, 115, 471
Abuse, child (*see* Child abuse)
Accelerated infant development programs, 192
  Better Baby Institute, 192
  evaluations of, 193–194
  Suzuki method of musical training, 193
Accidents:
  and adolescent drinking, 503
  and adult supervision, 277
  rates for children, 276–277
  research on prevention, 277
Accommodation, 56–57
Achievement tests, 408–409
  California Achievement Tests, 409
  Iowa Tests of Basic Skills, 409
  Metropolitan Achievement Test, 409
  construction of, 409
Acne, adolescent, 469, 498
Action for Children's Television, (ACT), 335
Activity level, 276–277
Adaptation of thought, 56
Adolescence:
  and abortion, 507
  and alcohol abuse, 17, 503, 508–512
  American experience of, 14–15, 27
  and body image, 474
  and career selection, 543–546
  and contraception, 506–508
  and delinquency, 15, 482–483
  and drug abuse, 17, 503, 508–512
  and egocentrism, 497–500, 507–508, 510, 512
  and formal operational thought, 490–493, 495, 497
  and growth spurt, 467–468
  and identity formation, 516–524
  and imaginary audience, 498, 510
  and moral development, 500–503
  and nutrition, 470
  and parental influence, 530–532
  and peer group, 525–530
  and pregnancy, 485, 504, 505–508
  and psychosomatic disease, 533–534
  and rites of passage, 520–521
  and school phobia, 498
  and scientific reasoning, 491–492
  and sex drive, 476–478
  and sex education, 506
  and sexual behavior, 504–508

  and sexually-transmitted disease (STD), 505
  (*see also* Puberty)
Adoption, 144–145
  and infant temperament, 227
  interracial, 144–145
  intraracial, 83, 144–145
  and IQ, 82–83
Age of viability in fetus, 103
Aggression, 336
  adult intervention and, 337
  between siblings, 337
  hostile, 336
  imitative, 258
  instrumental, 336
  reactions to, 330–331, 337
  and television, 51
Alcohol:
  abuse of, by adolescents, 503, 508–512
  and birth defects, 107–108, 375
  and child abuse, 246
Allantois membrane, 100
Alphafetoprotein assay, 92
Ambidexterity, 267, 301
American sign language (Ameslan), 199
"American Question," The, 189–194
Amniocentesis, 92
Amniotic fluid, 100, 102, 115, 134
Amniotic sac, 125
Anal stage of development
  (*see also*, Psychoanalytic theory), 39, 42, 220–221
Androgyny theory:
  flexible sex roles, 349–350
  self-esteem and, 350
  and traditional sex-role patterns, 349–350
Anemia, iron deficiency:
  in adolescent females, 470
  in children, 263
Anencephaly, 82, 92
Anesthesia and childbirth, 132, 135–136
Anger, 215–216, 218
Animism, concept of, 293
Anorexia nervosa, 484, 533
Anoxia, 131
Anticipation of events (by infants), 183–184
Anxiety:
  separation, 215
  stranger, 215
Apgar scale, 126
Appearance:
  adolescent concern with, 498
  and changing body proportions, 154
  and Downs syndrome, 84

  importance of, in middle childhood, 360
  of neonate, 125
Aptitude tests, 410–416
  caution in using, 416
  IQ tests, 410
    Goodenough-Harris test, 410
    Peabody Picture Vocabulary test, 410
    purpose of, 412–414
    Stanford-Binet test, 410, 414
    Wechsler tests, 410, 414
  meaning of scores, 410–411, 415–416
  scoring of, 410–411, 415
  SOMPA (System of Multicultural Pluralistic Assessment), 415
  validity of, 414
Art, children's, 274–275
  artistic development, stages of, 274
  communication skills, development of, 275
  as form of mastery play, 274
  and intelligence, 274
Arteries, hardening of, 91
Asian-American children, 16
Assimilation, 56–57
Asthma, 469
Attachment:
  impact on personality development, 236
  in parent-child interaction, 231–237
  insecure, 232
  secure, 232
Attention deficit disorder, 373
  (*see also* Hyperactivity)
Aunts, 439, 453
Autism, 340–341, 342
Autonomy versus shame and doubt, 222
  (*see also* Erikson, Psychosocial theory)
Autosomes, 80–81

Babbling, 198
  and deaf infants, 199
Baby Boom, postwar, 523–524
Baby talk, 204, 206
  (*see also* Language development)
"Back to Basics" educational movement, 391
Bedwetting, 269
Behaviorism (*see* Learning Theory)
Better Baby Institute, 192, 270
Bilingualism:
  advantages of, 406
  methods of teaching, 406–408
  strategies for learning, 407–408
Binocular vision, 269

Birth:
   and anesthesia, 132, 135–136
   and birth attendants, 137, 139
   and birth places, 137, 139
   and birthing positions, 137
   breech position of baby, 131
   Cesarean section, 132, 135, 138
   and classical conditioning, 136
   and episiotomy, 137
   fathers and, 124, 125, 135–137
   Lamaze method, 135–137
   Leboyer gentle birth, 134
   and prepared parents, 135–340
   and siblings, 140–141
   stress of, 131–133
   and trauma, 133
Birth catch-up, 153
Birth control (see Contraception)
Birth defects, 104
   critical periods for malformations, 104–
      105
   and disease, 104
   and teratogens, 104
Birth order, 202, 309, 310
Birth problems, 26
Birth trauma, 133
Birth weight, 127–128
   average, 127
   birth catch-up, 153
   low birth weight, 130
   teenage mothers and, 130
Black American children, 404–406, 453
   and adoption, interracial, 144–145
   and achievement tests, 414–415
   and family support systems, 453
   and group identification, 528
   and walking, age of, 166
Black English, 404–406
Blastocyst, 99
Blended families, 447–449
   (see also Family)
Blind experimenters, 19, 216
Blood pressure, high, 91
Body image, 474
Body proportions, 154, 260
Body temperature, 269
Bonding:
   in animals, 141
   in humans, 141–144
Bone age, 264
Bottle-feeding, 169–170
   (see also Breast-feeding, Nutrition)
Brain:
   growth and maturation, 154–157, 164–167,
      265–269
   and hand preference, 266–267, 268
   hemispheres, 267–268
   and infant state regulation, 156–157
   myelination, 266, 268
   primary motor areas, 155
   primary sensory areas, 155, 164–167
Brain waves, 156
Brazelton Neonatal Behavior Assessment
   Scale, 164
Breast development in adolescence, 471–
   472, 474
Breast-feeding;
   advantages of, 168
   infant nutrition and, 168
   versus bottle feeding, 169–170
   (see also Bottle-feeding, Nutrition)

Breech birth position, 131
Brothers (see Siblings)
Bulimia, 484

Caffeine, 109
Cancer, 91, 277, 511
Carbon monoxide, 110
Career selection, 543–546
   and girls, 545
   and identity, 543
Care-givers
   behavior with toddlers, 240–241
   generating intellectual experiences, 240
   and infant attachment, 233–235
   and intellectual stimulation, 240–241
   (see also Fathers, Mothers)
Case study as research method, 24
Cause and effect, concept of, 289–290
Centration, concept of, 289–290
Cephalo-caudal development, 164
Cervix, 124–125
Cesarian section, 132, 135
   with father present, 138
Child abuse and neglect, 237–238, 244–247
   causes of, 244–247
   and child's aggressive behavior, 337–338
   definition of, 242–243
   and parental drug abuse, 245–246
   factors associated with, 246
   and family history of, 245
   first U.S. cases of, 14
   Genie, story of, 300–301
   and historical views of punishment, 28
   hot line for help, 539
   incidence of, 242
   intervention and treatment for, 247–248
   neglect, 243
   Parents Anonymous, 247
   Polynesians and, 244
   prevention of, 248
   signs of physical abuse, 242–243
   and single parents, 235
   and social isolation, 245
   and teenage parents, 248
   (see also Sexual abuse)
Childbirth (see Birth)
Childhood:
   differing views of, 28
   as a life stage, 14
   modern American attitudes toward, 14, 28
   view of in Middle Ages, 14
Chlamydia, 505
Chomsky, Noam, 10
   deep language structure, 196
   language acquisition device (LAD), 196–
      197
   and language development, 196–197
   surface structure of language, 196
Chorion membrane, 100
Chorion villi sampling, 92
Chromosomes, 72
   abnormalities of, 80–93
   autosomes, 72
   prenatal diagnosis of abnormalities, 92
   sex chromosomes, 72–73, 77–78, 80
Chunking, 394–395
Cigarettes:
   and birth defects, 109
   and breast-feeding, 169
Circular reactions, 179–180

   primary, 180
   secondary, 180–181
   tertiary, 184
Circumcision, 133
Classification, 384–385
Class inclusion, 384
Cleft lip, 85, 91
Cleft palate, 84, 86, 91, 126
Club foot, 84, 86, 91
Cocaine, 109, 509
Cohort, 26
Cognitive domain of development, 3
Cognitive theory, 54–62
   basic concepts of development, 54, 56
   clinical method, 58–59
   conservation, concept of, 55–56
   disequilibrium, 55
   in early childhood, 55, 177–194
   equilibrium, 55
   evaluation of cognitive theories, 60–61
   intelligence, adaptation, 56–57
   intelligence, organization, 56–57
   in middle childhood, 55, 287–299, 423–424
   schemas, 55
   and sex–role development, 348–349
   and stages of development:
      concrete operational, 54–55
      formal operational, 54–55
      preoperational, 54–55
      sensorimotor, 54–55
   thirst for knowledge, 56
   (see also Piaget)
Color-blindness, 78, 90
"Combat crisis," 44
Competent children:
   characteristics of, 239
   role of parents, 239–241, 427
   role of school, 427, 452
Conception:
   biology of, 68, 71
   culture and, 69–70
Concrete operational thought, 383–391
   (see also Piaget, Cognitive theory)
Conditioning, 46–49
   and childbirth, 136
   classical, 47
   and infants, 189–191
   and language development, 195–196
   operant, 47–48
   Pavlov and, 47
   and punishment, 49
   and social reinforcement, 49
Congenital problems (see Birth defects)
Conscience, development of, 40–41
Conservation, problems of, 290–291, 295–298
   of liquid, 290–291, 295–298, 383, 384
   of matter, 290–291, 295–298
   of number, 290–291, 295–298
Continuity, 11
Contraception, 169, 506, 507, 508, 511, 524
Control group, 19
Cooing, 198
Cooley's anemia (Thalassemia), 87
Correlation:
   definition of, 20
   negative, 21
   positive, 21
   zero, 21
Crawling, 165
Crib death (see Sudden infant death
   syndrome)

Cries, 197–198
  classification of, 213
Cross-cultural research:
  and best-friend characteristics, 431
  and child abuse, 244
  and cooperative behavior, 439
  and fears about nuclear war, 440
  and infant formula, 170
  and language development, 197
  and mother-infant attachment, 231
  and mother-infant contact, 142
  and playmate choice, 280
  and reading and math achievement and
    aptitude, 409, 414
  and walking-age norms, 166
Cross-sectional research, 25
Cystic fibrosis, 84, 86

Day care, 233, 240, 311–315
Deaf infants, 198–199
Deaf parents, 199
Death:
  accidental, 276–277, 481
  preoperational concept of, 296–297
  Sudden Infant Death Syndrome (SIDS),
    156–157
Deep structure of language, 196
Defense mechanisms, 40–41
  displacement, 41
  regression, 40
  repression, 40–41
Delinquency, 15, 482–483
Depression, in adolescence, 464, 540–542
Depth perception:
  in infants, 161
  visual-cliff experiment, 161, 219
Diabetes, 86, 91, 264
Diets:
  and anorexia nervosa, 484
  in early childhood, 262–263
  Feingold diet, 376–377
  for hyperactive children, 376–377
  and obesity, 360–362
  for toddlers, 168
  vegetarian, 470
  Zen macrobiotic, 470
  (see also Breast-feeding, Malnutrition,
    Nutrition)
Discipline, effective methods of, 333
  problems with, 330–332
  and punishment, 48–49, 330–331
Discontinuity, 11
Disequilibrium, 55
Displacement defense mechanism, 41
Divorce:
  children's adjustment to, 26, 443–445, 452
  and custodial-parent remarriage, 448
  and non-custodial-parent remarriage,
    448–449
  preoperational concept of, 296–297
Dizygotic twins, 76
  (see also Multiple births, Twins)
Dolls, and pretend play, 288
Double standard, 504
Down's syndrome
  autosomal abnormality, 81
  distinguishing features of, 84
Dramatic play, 324–325
Drug abuse, 503, 524
  alcohol, 107–108, 375, 508–512

cocaine, 109, 509
hallucinogens, 508
heroin, 109, 508
marijuana, 109, 508, 509, 510
PCP (angel dust), 508, 509
tobacco, 109, 508, 509, 510, 511
Drugs and birth defects, 107–109
Drugs and childbirth, 132–133
Dwarfism, 263–264
  deprivation dwarfism, 263–264, 265
Dyscalcula, 370
Dysentery, 264
Dysgraphia, 370
Dyslexia, 369, 372

Echolalia, 340
Eclampsia, 106–107
Eclectic perspective on development, 62
Ecological approach to development, definition, 4–5
Ectoderm, 101
Education:
  and adolescent drug abuse, 511
  college as institutional moratorium, 518
  and enrichment programs for deprived
    infants, 191
  of gifted children, 412–413
  and handicapped children, 366–378
  mainstreaming, 367–369
  Piaget in the classroom, 390–391
  preschool, 311–314
  Project Headstart, 311–314
  resource room, 367
  and sex education, 506, 511, 538
  (see also Teaching)
Ego, 40–41, 291
  (see also Freud, Psychoanalytic theory)
Egocentrism, adolescent, 497–500, 507–508,
  510, 512
Egocentrism, concept of, 291–292, 308
Ejaculation, 471, 475
Elective mutism, 340
Electra complex, 345, 346
Electroencephalogram (EEG), 156
Embryo, 99, 100, 101
Emotional development, 212–218
  anger, 215–216
  fears, 215–216, 440, 498
  measuring infant emotion, 214
  self-awareness, 216–218
  social smile, 213
Emphysema, 91
Endoderm, 101
Engrossment, of fathers with newborn, 143
Environment, impact on development,
  78–80
Environmental hazards and birth defects,
  109
Episiotomy, 132, 137
Equilibrium, cognitive, 55
Erikson, Erik:
  case study of "combat crisis," 44
  psychosocial theory, 41–45
    evaluation of, 44–45
  (see also Psychosocial theory)
Erythroblastosis (RH disease), 85
Estrogen, 467
Ethology, 259
Exercise, and childhood obesity, 361
Experimental group, 19
Eyes:

changes at puberty, 469
vision in infancy, 159–160
visual examination, 269

FACS scoring system, 214
Fallopian tubes, 71, 99
Family:
  and adolescent self-esteem, 534
  and the aggressive child, 52–53
  and anorexia nervosa, 48–49
  and birth of child, 124
  Black American, 453
  blended by remarriage, 447–449
  effect of divorce on children, 443–445, 452
  and handicapped child, 5–9
  and hyperactive child, 375–377
  and incest, 536–537
  and latchkey children, 450
  and maternal employment, 449–450
  planning of, 69, 70
  and preterm infants, 128–129
  and psychosomatic illness in adolescents,
    533–534
  single-parent, 446–447
  size of, 69
  and social-support network, 454
  (see also Fathers, Mothers, Parents,
    Siblings)
Family support systems, 454
Fantasy in childhood, 339–340
Fathers:
  and adolescent delinquency, 482
  and aggressive child, 53
  attachment to their infants, 235
  and birth of child, 124, 135
  and bonding with newborn, 142–144
  as custodial parent, 448
  and engrossment with newborn, 143
  and first-born child, 143, 234
  and incest with daughters, 535–536, 537,
    538
  and infant care, 164, 213, 234–235, 538
  and maternal employment, 449–450
  as Lamaze coaches, 135–137
  and play patterns with children, 234–235
  and pregnancy, 113–119
  and presence in the home, 454
  and single-parent households, 446–447
  and sons, 234–235
  as stepfathers, 448
    and sex abuse, 538
  and time spent with children, 429
  (see also Family, Parents)
Fear, in childhood, 339–340
  of strangers, 215
  of nuclear war, 440
Feingold diet, the, 376–377
Fetal alcohol syndrome (FAS), 108
Fetal monitor, 131
Fetoscope, 92, 115, 116
Fetus, 99
  birth position of, 124
  development periods of, 104
  health of:
    detection of, 116
    tests for, 115
  monitoring of, 131–132
  period of, 99, 102, 103
  reaction to alcohol, 108
  rights of, 116–117

sex-organ development, 102, 104
  surgery on, 116
  viability, age of, 103, 115
Fine motor skills, 273–275
  and children's art, 274–275
  and school readiness, 271–275
Five-to-seven shift, 383
Florida Parent Education Program, 192
Fontanelles, 127
Football, 364, 365
Forceps, 132
Foreclosure, 517, 519
Formal operational thought, 490–492
  (see also Scientific reasoning)
Freud, Sigmund
  child-mother relationship, 220
  defense mechanisms, 40–41
  female sexual development, theory of,
    345, 346
  psychoanalytic theory, development of,
    38–39
  psychoanalytic theory, evaluation of,
    44–45
  psychosexual stages of development,
    39, 42
  (see also Psychoanalytic theory)
Friendship, 431–433, 453, 526
  and physical appearance, 360
  and rejection, 433–435
  (see also Peer group)

Game of thinking, 494
Games (see Play)
Gametes:
  ova, 71
  spermatozoa, 71
Gastrula, 99
Genes, 72
  abnormal, 80–93
  dominant, 77–78
  harmful, 84
  and IQ, 82–83
  recessive, 77
  X-linked recessive, 77–78
Genetic carrier, 77
Genetic counseling, 85–93
  recommendations for, 88
Genetic disorders:
  dominant gene disorder, 91
  erythroblastosis (RH disease), 85
  mutation and, 91
  PKU (phenylketonuria), 85
  prediction of, 90–91
  recessive, 85
  sex-linked, 90–91
Genetic engineering, 93
Genetic inheritance, 71–78
Genetics, 71–93
Genetic testing:
  blood test for, 89–90
  cell-scraping for, 89–90
  compulsory, 88
  and family medical history, 90
  by physical observation, 89–90
Genetic uniqueness, 73
  and twins, 73–76
Genital stage of development, 39, 464
"Genius" children, 26
Genotype, 77
Gentle birth, 134

Germinal period, 99–100
Gesell Institute (Center for the Study of
  Child Development at Yale University),
  270
Giantism, 263–264
Gifted children:
  creativity, 412–413
  educational support for, 412–413
  intellect, 412
  skills, 412
Gonad, indifferent, 102
Gonorrhea, 505
Goodenough-Harris Drawing Test, 274
Grammar, 196, 299, 302–305, 400–402
  (see also Language development)
Grandparents, 5, 439, 453
Grasping in infants, 57, 165, 178, 189
Gross motor skills, 270–272
Growth problems:
  dwarfism, 263
  giantism, 263
  and ossification, 264
  treatment of, 264–265

Handicapped children, 366–378
  effect on family, 5–9
  and hyperactivity, 372–378
  and mainstreaming, 7–8, 367–369
  and resource rooms, 367
  and separate education, 8–9, 366–367
Hands:
  and infant grasping, 57, 165, 178, 189
  and motor skills, 257, 273
  stages in fetal development, 104
Headstart program, 311–314
  IQ scores for attendees, 311–312
  long-term benefits, 312–313
  sleeper effect of, 312
Hearing impairment, 199
  and American Sign Language (Ameslan),
    199
  and infant babbling, 199
  and infant language development, 199
Heart, growth at puberty, 468
Height:
  in adolescence, 468
  at birth, 152
  in early childhood, 152–154
  in middle childhood, 261–262, 264, 358–360
  as multifactorial characteristic, 79
Hemophilia, 86, 90
Heredity (see Genes, Genetics)
Heredity/environment controversy (see
  Nature versus nurture)
Heroin and birth defects, 109
Herpes simplex 2, and birth defects, 104
Holistic view of development, 4
Holophrases, 204
HOME (Home Observation for the Measure-
  ment of the Environment), 237–238
Home birth, 137
Homicide, adolescent, 481
Homunculus, 98
Hookworm, 264
Hormones:
  and adolescent acne, 469
  and growth problems, 264–265
  at puberty, 467, 469, 474
Humor:
  absurdity riddles, 400–401

  adolescent sarcasm, 496
  joke-telling skill, 403
  language-ambiguity jokes, 400
  middle-childhood jokes, 400–401
  reality riddles, 400
Huntington's disease, 86, 91
Hyaline membrane disease, 129
Hydrocephalus, 86, 92, 116
Hyperactive children, 372–378
  attention deficit disorder, 374
  causes of, 375–376
  and diet for, 376–377
  help for, 376–378
  and sex-differences, 374
Hypnotic suggestion, 38
Hysteria, 37–38

Id, 40–41, 345
Identity, cognitive concept of, 291, 383–385
Identity, psychosocial:
  achievement of, 516–524
  and career selection, 543
  diffusion, 518, 519
  Erikson's concept of,
  negative, formation of, 518–519
  social influences on, 521–524
Illness, preoperational concept of, 296–
  297
Imaginary audience, 498, 510
Imaginary playmates, 339
Imitation, deferred, 186
Implantation of embryo, 99
Industry versus inferiority, 421
  (see also Erikson, Psychosocial theory)
Infant carriers, 162
Infant formula, 169–170
  contamination of, 170
Infantile sexuality, 39
Infant mortality rate (U.S.), 128–129
Infants:
  accelerated development programs for,
    192–194
  and attachment to parents, 231–237
  body language, 230–231
  brain development, 154–157
  communication, 197–198, 213
  definition of, 165
  emotional development of, 213–216
  growth, 152–153, 159
  habituation to stimulus, 159
  hearing-impaired, 199
  locomotion, 165–168
  low birth weight, 127–128
  malnutrition, 170–171
  memory capacity, 191
  nutrition, 168–172
  and parents' emotional cues, 219
  and parents' voice recognition, 161
  play with parents, 234–235
  psychological states, 156
  reflexes, 162–163, 164
  self-awareness, 216–218
  senses, development of, 160–162
  separation anxiety, 215
  size and proportions, 152, 154
  and synchrony of interaction with parents,
    228–231
  vocabulary, 201, 202
  (see also Fathers, Mothers, Parents)
Infant-state regulation, 156–157

Infant vocalizations, 181
Information-processing theory, 392–398
    chunking, 394–395
    cognitive framework, 395
    memory capacity, 393
    memory, long-term, 393
    memory, short-term, 393
    memory techniques, 394
    metacognition, 395
    metamemory, 394
    mnemonic devices, 394
    "readiness," 397
    rehearsal, 394
    selective attention, 393–394
    sensory register, 393
Inner speech, 24
Intellectual development, 82–83
    environmental influences, 82–83
    genetic influences, 82–83
Interview method, 24
Intonation as communication, 200
"Invulnerable" (stress-resistant) children,
    451
    (see also Stress)
IQ:
    and birth of sibling, 140–141
    heritability of, 82–83
    in infants, 193–194
    and Project Headstart, 311–312
    scores and categories, 82
    tests for, 410
        scoring, 410
IQ tests:
    and black childrens' scores, 16
    determining scores, 410
    established norms, 16
    first test, 29
    and infants, 193–194
    meaning of scores, 410
    and non-English-speaking children, 415
    and white middle-class children, 415

Kleinfelter's syndrome, 8
Kohlberg, Lawrence:
    levels of moral reasoning, 436, 500
        conventional, 436
        preconventional, 436
        postconventional, 436
Kwashiorkor, 170

Labor (see Birth)
Laboratory experiment, 22
Lamaze method of childbirth, 135–137
Language development:
    articulation, 306
    babbling, 198–199
    baby talk, 204, 206
    bilingualism, 406–408
    black English, 404–406
    code-switching, 403–404
    collective monologue, 308
    comprehension, 201
    cooing, 198
    creating words, 303
    critical period for, 300–301
    crying, 197–198
    in deaf infants, 199
    difficulties with, 304–305

during preschool years, 299–311
    egocentric speech, 308
    elaborated code, 403
    first spoken words, 201
    grammar, 196, 299, 302–305, 400–402
    holophrases, 204
    humor, 400–401, 403
    inner speech, 307
    intonation, 200–201
    language acquisition device, 196–197
    language function, 197
    language and thought, relationship, 299
    monologue, 308
    nonstandard English, 404–406
    overextension of vocabulary, 202
    overregularization of grammar rules, 304
    pragmatics, 305–306, 402–404
    preschool programs for, 311–314
    restricted code, 403
    smile, pleasure, 198
    stages of, 196
    structure, deep, 196
    structure, surface, 196
    turn-taking ritual, 205
    vocabulary, 201–204, 300–302, 398–399
    word combinations, 204
Language, expressive, 202–203
Language, referential, 202–203
Lanugo, 128
Latchkey children, 450
Lead and birth defects, 110
Lead poisoning, 277
    and hyperactivity, 375
Learned helplessness, 426–427
Learning disabilities:
    causes of, 370–371
    dyscalcula, 370
    dysgraphia, 370
    dyslexia, 369
    help for, 370–371
    and school experiences, 372–373
    specific learning disabilities, 369, 374
Learning theories, 45–53
    behavior, laws of, 46–49
    behaviorism, 45–48
    Pavlov, Ivan, 47
    Skinner, B.F., 48
    social learning theory, 50–53
    (see also Reinforcement)
Leboyer gentle-birth method, 138
Left-handedness, 266–268
    and brain development, 266–268
    and genetic origin, 266
    and handwriting, 267
    historical consideration of, 266
Leukemia, childhood, 110
"Little Scientist," The, 185, 237
Logical thought:
    in adolescence, 490–494
    classification, 384
    class inclusion, 384–385
    logical ideas, development of, 383–384
    mathematics, 386
    and scientific reasoning, 491–492
    seriation, 385
    time and distance, 387
    (see also Concrete operational thought)
Longitudinal research, 26
Low birth weight infants, 127–128
    causes of, 130
    consequences of, 130

teenage mothers and, 130
Lungs, growth during puberty, 468
Lymphoid system, 469

Macrosystem, 5, 440
Mahler, Margaret, 223–224
Mainstreaming, 7–8, 367–369
    advantages of, 366–367
    difficulties with, 368
    resource room, 367
    (see also Handicapped children)
Malnutrition (see also Nutrition):
    in Africa, 171
    in infants, 170–172, 262
    and growth problems, 264, 265
    long-term effects of, 171
    in middle childhood, 359
Marasmus, 170
Marfan's syndrome, 86
Marijuana, 524
    and birth defects, 109
Mastery (of new skills) play, 257–258
Masturbation, 478, 480
Maternal body temperature and birth
    defects, 114
Maternal employment, 454
    and infant attachment, 233
    and latchkey children, 450
    sex differences in children's reaction to,
    454
    and shared housework, 348
Mathematical aptitude, 11
Mathematics and concrete concepts, 386
Maximally Discriminative Facial Move-
    ments Codes (MAX), 214
Mean length of utterance (MLU), 303
Meiosis, 72–73
Memory:
    adult, 191
    capacity, 393
    chunking, 394–395
    cognitive framework, 395
    infant, 191
    long-term, 393
    mnemonic devices and, 394
    rehearsal and, 394
    selective attention and, 393–394
    sensory register and, 393
    short-term, 393
    techniques, 394
Menstruation:
    adolescent girls' attitudes toward, 472
    cultural and historical view of, 471
    menarche, 471
    menarche and self-concept, 472–473
    onset of, 471
    and rites of passage, 521
Mental combinations, 185
Mental retardation:
    and fetal alcohol syndrome, 107–108
    genetic causes of, 81, 85, 86–87
    and mainstreaming, 366
    (see also Down's syndrome)
Mercury poisoning and birth defects, 110
Mesoderm, 101
Mesosystem (defined), 5
    (see also School, Teaching)
Methadone and birth defects, 109
Microsystem, defined, 5
    (see also Family)

Midwifery, 137, 139
Milk anemia, 168
Minamata disease, 110
Minimal brain dysfunction, 370
Minority children:
  and achievement tests, 414–416
  and bilingual education, 406–408
  and black English, 404–405
  and code-switching, 405
  and group identification, 528
  and non-standard English, 404–405
  and peer group, 527
  and segregation in special classes, 367
  and stress, 454
Mirror experiment of infant self-awareness,
  217, 320
Miscarriage, 114–115
  (see also Abortion, spontaneous)
Mitosis, 72
Mnemonic devices, 394
Modeling, 50–51, 347–348, 422, 511
Montessori schools, 313
  and development of fine motor skills, 273
Moral development, 435–438
  in adolescence, 500–503
  and cross-cultural research, 439, 501
  Kohlberg's stages of, 435–437
  in middle childhood, 435–438
  moral behavior, 438–440
  and prosocial behavior, 438
  sex differences, 502–503
Mosaicism, 84
Mothers:
  and adolescent delinquency, 482
  and adoption, 144
  and aggressive child, 52–53
  attachment to child, 231–234
  bonding with infants, 141–144
  and bottle-feeding, 169
  breast-feeding, 169
  and childbirth experience, 135–140
  of competent children, 238–240
  and childhood fears, 339–340
  as custodial parent, 448
  Erikson's view of, 221–223
  and father-daughter incest, 536–537
  and Florida Parent Education Program,
    192
  Freud's view of, 220
  and infant learning, 192
  and language development, 202–203,
    313–314
  employment, 449–450, 454, 546
  and personality development, 218, 220
  and play with children, 234–235
  and pregnancy, 113–119
  and preterm infants, 22, 23, 142
  and responsiveness to infants, 330
  and separation-individuation, 223–224
  and sibling rivalry, 326
  and single-parent households, 446–447
  as step-mothers, 448
  and Suzuki musical training, 193
  and symbiosis, 223–224
  and temperament of child, 224–225
  and toddlers, 218, 238–240
  (see also Family, Fathers, Parents)
Motor skills:
  development:
    cephalo-caudal, 164
    proximo-distal, 164

fine motor skills, 273
  articulation of, 306
  value of, 273–274
gross motor skills, 270–272
  in infants, 164–167
  in middle childhood, 270–276, 362–365
  and norms of mastery, 166
  and reaction time, 364
  and regular physical activity, 365
  and sex-based differences, 364
  and sports, 364–365
  in twins, 164–167
  variations in timing, 166–168
Multifactorial characteristics, 79
Multiple births, 73–76
  factors affecting incidence of, 76
  health and emotional patterns of, 341
  language proficiency of, 309
  and low birth weight, 130
  and motor skills, 164–167
  prenatal diagnosis of, 92
  (see also Twins)
Mumps and birth defects, 104
Muscular dystrophy, 87
Myelin, 154
Myelination, 266, 273

Native American infants, 166
Naturalistic observation, 18
Nature versus nurture controversy, 10–11,
  22, 78–79, 177, 344
  and adolescent delinquency, 482–483
  and temperament, 227
  and twins, 74–75
Naziism, 522
Neo-Freudians, 41, 44–45, 221
Neonates, 125
  appearance of, 127
  selective perception of, 158
  sensation in, 158
Neo-Piagetian research:
  on adolescents, 495–496
  and cognitive heterogeneity, 388
  on conservation, 295–298
  on infants, 187–188
  on number, children's recognition of,
    297–298
  on object permanence, 187
  on perspective-taking, 294–295
  on preschoolers, 294–298
  on school-age children, 388
Neural-tube development, 101
Neurons, 154
New York Longitudinal Study
  (of temperament), 224–227
Norms, 166
  for motor-skill development, 167
  variations, 167
Nuclear war, children's fears about, 440
Nutrition:
  and bottle-feeding, 168–170
  and breastmilk, 168–170
  and eating habits, 168, 262–263
  and infants, 168–170
  and iron-deficiency anemia, 168, 263, 470
  and malnutrition, 170–172, 262
  and marasmus, 170
  and tooth decay, 263
  and vitamin deficiencies, 168

Obesity:
  causes of, 362–363
  help for, 360–361
  in middle childhood, 360–361
  and self-concept, 360
  and television, 363
  in toddlers, 168
Object permanence, 181, 186–187
Oedipus complex, 345, 346, 421, 464
Open classroom, 390
Oral stages of development, 39, 220–221
Organization of thought, 56
Ossification, 264
Ova, 71
  and chromosomal abnormalities, 84
Ovaries, 71
Ovist, 98

Parental criticism, effects of, 331–332
Parent-infant interaction:
  attachment, insecure, 231–237
  attachment, secure, 232–233
  synchrony, 228–231
Parenting styles, 328–330
  and adolescents, 531–532
  and income, 532
Parents:
  and adolescent delinquency, 482, 483
  and adolescent drug abuse, 17, 510, 511, 531
  and moral questions, 510, 511
  and adolescent psychosomatic illness,
    533–534
  and adolescent self-doubt, 525
  and adolescent suicide, 540, 542
  and aggression, 337
  and attachment to infant, 231–237
  and bilingualism, 407
  and birth of child, 124
  and bonding with newborn, 141–144
  and childbirth, 135
  and custody and visitation rights, 445
  effect of divorce, 452
  and handicapped child, 5–9
  and incest, 534–536
  and infant cognitive growth, 194
  and infant emotion, 213
  and infant temperament, 226–227
  and language development, 194–207, 305,
    306, 309, 310
  and learning disabilities, 371–373
  and modeling techniques, 339
  and moral questions, 510, 511
  and obesity, 361–363
  and positive reinforcement, 333
  and preschool education programs,
    313–314
  and psychoanalytic theory, 345
  and school readiness, 270–271
  and self-esteem, 427, 434, 534
  and sex abuse, 534–539
  and sex-role development, 345, 347–350
  and sibling rivalry, 326
  and single-parent households, 345, 348,
    446–447
  and smoking, 510
  and social children, 434
  and synchrony, 228–231
  and values, 530–53
  (see also Family, Fathers, Mothers)
Parents Anonymous, 247

Pavlov, Ivan, 47
  (*see also* Conditioning)
PCBs and birth defects, 110–111
Peer groups:
  in adolescence, 525–530
  clubs and gangs, 430, 431
  dependence on, 429
  and friendship, 431–433, 438–439
  and rejection, 433–436
  and the "society of children," 430
Penis envy, 345
Perception, infant, 158–159
  of depth, 161
Period of the fetus, 99, 102–103
Personal fable, 499, 510
Personality development, 218–220
  autonomy versus shame and doubt, 222
  cross-cultural differences, 16
  psychosexual stages, 220–221
  separation-individuation, 223–224
  symbiosis, 223
  temperament, 224–227
  trust versus mistrust, 221–222
  (*see also* Psychosocial theory,
    Temperament)
Phallic stage of development, 39
Phenotype, 77
Phenylketonuria (PKU), 85, 87, 90
Phobia, 339
Physical development:
  and activity level, 276–278
  in adolescence, 466–476
  cephalo-caudal, 101, 153
  and accident rates, 276–277
  in early childhood, 260–270
  in infancy, 152–154
  in middle childhood, 358–363
  and obesity, 168, 360–361, 363
  and peer comparisons, 360
  and physique variations, 359–360
  prenatal, 99–103
  proximo-distal development, 101, 153
  and readiness for school, 270–271
  and sensorimotor play, 256–257
Physical domain of development, 3
Piaget, Jean:
  and the "American question," 189–194
  and circular reactions, 179
  and cognitive theory, 187–189
  and cognitive development, 54–59
  and the clinical method, 58–59
  and concrete operational thought,
    383–389
  and conservation problems, 290–291,
    295–298
  and deferred imitation, 186
  and formal operational thought, 490–497
  and intelligence, concept of, 56–57
  and logical ideas, 383–384
  and metal combinations, 185
  and moral development, 435
  and object permanence, 181–182
  and sensorimotor intelligence, stages of,
    178–187
  and symbolic thought, 287
  and three mountains experiment, 293–
    295
  (*see also* Cognitive theory, Neo-Piagetian
    research)
PKU (phenylketonuria), 85, 87, 90
Placenta, 100, 103, 105, 125, 132–133

Play:
  in animals, 259–260
  categories of, 322–324
  and developing motor skills, 270–272, 365
  and developing self-concept, 321
  dramatic play, 324–325, 327
  and gender stereotypes, 343
  and language competence, 310, 322–324
  and mastery of new skills, 257–258
  and motor skills, 259–260
  and nurturant behavior, 259–260
  and play face, 259
  rough-and-tumble play, 258–260
    sex differences in, 259
  and safe play areas, 272
  and sex-appropriate toys and play pat-
    terns, 342, 344
  and sex-role development, 344, 347
  and sex-typed toys, 345
  and social cognition, 425
  and social skills, 259–260
  sports, 364–365
  symbolic play, 287–288
  value of, in childhood, 326–327
Play face, 258–259
Pleasure principle, 40–41
Polio and birth defects, 104
Polygenic inheritance, 78
Pragmatics, 305–306, 402–404
  (*see also* Language development)
Pregnancy:
  adolescents and, 470, 485, 505–508
  first trimester of, 113
  and nutrition, 118–119
  psychological impact of, 112
  second trimester of, 115–117
  and stress, 112–113, 114
  third trimester of, 118–119
Premature birth (*see* Preterm infants)
Prenatal diagnosis, 92
Preoperational thought, 54–55, 288–294
  (*see also* Piaget, Cognitive theory)
Preschool education, 311–314
  benefits, 313–314
  parental involvement, 313–314
  Project Headstart, 311–313
  (*see also* Day care)
Pretending, 186
Pretend play, 287–288
Preterm infants, 128
  and contact with mother, 142
  and home environment, 129
  and hospital environment, 129
  and physical stimulation, 22–23
  and reflexes, 163
  and special stimulation, 192
Pride, in toddlers, 218
Primates:
  and aggression, 337
  and play, 259–260
  and social behavior, 326–327
Project Headstart, 311–314
Proportions, body, 154, 260
Proximo-distal development, 164
Psychoanalytic theory:
  and adolescence, 463–464
  development of, 38–39
  and early childhood, 344–345
  evaluation of, 44–45
  and infancy, 220–224
  and middle childhood, 420–421

  (*see also* Erikson, Freud)
Psychological disturbances:
  autism, 340
  causes of, 341
  childhood schizophrenia, 341
  echolalia, 340
  elective mutism, 340
  parenting and, 341
  treatments and cures of, 341
Psychological dwarfism, 22
Psychosexual stages of development,
    defined, 39–42
  in adolescence, 463–464
  anal stage, 220
  in infancy, 220–221
  in early childhood, 344–345
  genital stage, 464
  latency, 420
  in middle childhood, 420
  oral stage, 220
  phallic stage, 344
Psychosocial domain of development, 3
Psychosocial theory:
  aspects of, 43
  comparison to Freudian theory, 42–45
  cultural differences, 43
  (*see also* Erikson)
Psychosomatic illness, 533–534
Puberty:
  in boys, 479–482
  and ejaculation, 471, 475
  in girls, 478–485
  and hormones, 467, 474
  and masturbation, 478
  and menarche, 471, 472–473, 474, 475, 476
  nutrition during, 470
  onset of, 359, 475–476
  organ growth during, 468–469
  physical growth during, 467–468
  secular trend of, 476
  and sex drive, 476–477
  sexual activity during, 477, 485
  sexual dimorphism, 466–467
  sexual growth during, 471–473
Punishment:
  effectiveness as discipline, 27–28, 51
  historical methods of, 27–28
  learning theory and, 48–49
Pyloric stenosis, 87

Radiation and birth defects, 110
Reading readiness, 270–271
Reality principle, 40–41
Recipes, children's, 293
Reciprocity, 384, 386
Reflexes, neonatal, 128–129, 162–163, 178
  Babinski, 163
  breathing, 162
  crying, 163
  grasping, 163, 178
  Moro, 163
  rooting, 163, 190
  stepping, 163
  sucking, 163, 178, 179
  swallowing, 163
  swimming, 163
Regression, 40
Rehearsal, 394
Reinforcement:
  laws of, 48–49

negative reinforcer, 48
positive reinforcer, 48
and punishment, 48
rewards, 421–422
Rejected children, 433–435
characteristics of, 433
help for, 434–435
Replication, of test results, 17
Representation, 186
Representative sample, 18
Repression, 40
Resource room, 367
Respiratory distress syndrome (hyaline membrane disease), 129
Restricted code, 403
Reversibility, concept of, 289
Rh disease (erythroblastosis), 85
Rites of passage, 520–521
Rough-and-tumble play, 258–259
Rubella (German measles):
and autism, 341
and birth defects, 104–105, 106
and damage to developing embryo, 5, 104–105, 106

SADD (Students Against Drunk Driving), 511
Sadness in infancy, 213
Sample size, 18
Schema, 55, 178, 182, 201
Schizophrenia:
multifactorial causation, 79
in childhood, 341
School:
and mainstreaming, 367–369
as mesosystem, 4
readiness, 271, 275
as social support system, 452
and self-esteem, 427, 452
(see also Education, Teaching)
Scientific investigation:
and blind experimenters, 19
case studies, 24
cohort effects in, 26–27
and control group, 19
cross-sectional research, 25–26
determining significance of, 19
ethics and values of, 29–30
and experimental group, 19
interview method, 24
laboratory experiment, 22–24
longitudinal research, 26–27
naturalistic observation, 18, 20–21
representative sample, 18–19
sample size, 18
Scientific Method, the, 17
Scientific reasoning, 491–492
Secondary sex characteristics, 471–473
Secular trend, 476
Self-awareness, in infancy, 216–218
Self-concept:
in adolescents, 464
and Erikson's theories, 319–320
in infants, 216–218, 221, 223
initiative versus guilt, 319–320
at menarche, 471–472
and social skills, 320–322
socioeconomic status and, 441–442
and self-theory, 426
Self-doubt, 525

Self-esteem, 427–429
and parental influence, 534
and peer group, 428–429
and school, 427, 452
and useful work, 428
Sensation in infants, 158–161
hearing, 160–161
pain, 161
smell, 162
taste, 161
vision, 159–160
Sensorimotor play, 256–257
Separation-individuation in early childhood, 223
Seriation, 384, 385, 388
Sex differences:
and adolescent acne, 469
and adolescent body image, 474–475
and adolescent delinquency, 482–483
and adolescent growth, 467–468
and adolescent sexuality, 506, 507
and adolescent suicide, 481, 540
and aggression, 337
and androgyny theory, 349–350
and birth order, 454
and childhood accidents, 277
and dramatic play, 325
and father's presence, 454
and friendship preferences, 432
and height and weight, 262
and hyperactivity, 374
and language proficiency, 309
and learning disabilities, 369
and left-handedness, 266
and maternal employment, 454
and math aptitude, 11
and moral reasoning, 16, 501, 502, 503
and motor skills, 279
and onset of puberty, 475–476
and permissive parenting, 330
and playmate preference, 279–280
and play patterns, 259, 279–280
and punishment, 331
and reaction to parents' divorce, 444
and risk-taking, 18–20
and rites of passage, 521–522
and temperament, 227
and toys, 342
Sex education, 506, 511
and sex abuse, 538
Sex roles:
and career choices, 545–546
children's perceptions of, 51
and cognitive theory, 348–349
cultural influence on, 51
development of, 320
and division of household tasks, 24
and the double standard, 476–477, 485
and early-maturing boys, 480
and early-maturing girls, 478–479
and Electra complex, 345
learning theory and, 51, 345–348
and Oedipus complex, 345
and psychoanalytic theory, 344–345
and sex drive, 476–477
and sexual activity, 477, 485
and working mothers, 449–450
Sexual abuse, 534–539
of adolescents, 534
of children, 234
consequences of, 536–537

definitions of, 534
and eroticization of children, 537
within the family, 534, 535, 536
father-daughter incest, 535
frequency of, 534–535
national hotline for, 539
preconditions for, 535, 538
prevention of, 537–539
and sex education, 538
and teenage prostitution, 537
Sexual dimorphism, 466–467
Sexual growth during puberty, 471–473
breast development, 471
ejaculation, 471
facial hair, 473
fertility, 471
menarche, 471, 472–473
pubic hair, 472–473
secondary sex characteristics, 471
sex organs, 471
voice changes, 473
Sexual latency, 39
Sexually-transmitted disease (STD), 505, 506
chlamydia, 505
gonorrhea, 505
herpes simplex 2, 505
syphilis, 505
Shame in toddlers, 218
Siblings:
aggression, 337
birth of, 124
effect on child's development, 326
experience of childbirth, 140–141
and handicapped child, 7–9
influence on each other, 5
interaction between, 325–326
and learning disabilities, 370
and sense of responsibility, 422
and stress, 453
Piaget's study of, 58–59
rivalry between, 236, 241
(see also Family)
Sickle-cell anemia, 87, 88, 89, 90, 92
Single-parent households, 21, 446–447
and black American families, 453
financial difficulties of, 446
"role-overload", 446
and sex-role difficulties for children, 446
social support network for, 447
Sisters (see Siblings)
Skin color, 78
Skinner, B.F., 47–49, 195–196
Sleep:
abnormal patterns of, 265
in infants, 156
Sleeper effect, 312
Small-for-dates infants, 128
Smile:
pleasure, 198
social, 213
Soccer, 364
Social cognition, 424–435
Social isolation, 326–327
Social learning theory, 49–50, 347–348, 422
effects of, 51
evaluations of, 51–53
and infants, 190–191
modeling, 50
Society of children, 430
Society for Research in Child Development, 29

Socioeconomic factors:
  and childhood accidents, 2–7
  and childhood obesity, 362
  and health care, 262
  effects on children, 441–442
  and height, 262
  and HOME evaluation, 237–238
  and infant attachment, 233
  and language development, 309–310
  and mother-infant interaction, 314
  and play areas, 272
  and puberty onset, 480
  and teenage pregnancy, 505
Socioeconomic status (SES), 441–442
Softball, 365
Sonogram, 92, 115, 116
  and Cesarean section, 132
Special-needs children, 366–378
Spermatozoa, 71
Spina bifida, 87, 91, 92
Sports, 363, 364–365
Step-families, 447–449
Stress:
  and adolescence, 464, 480-485
  and childbirth, 131–133
  competence and, 452
  and fears of nuclear war, 440
  and "invulnerable" children, 451
  in middle childhood, 402, 451–455
  and parent-child attachment, 233
  during pregnancy, 112–114
  school and, 452
  social support and, 453
Sudden infant death syndrome (SIDS), 156–157
Suicide, adolescent, 481, 539, 542
  behavior prior to, 540
  incidence of, 539
  professional help for, 542
  warning signs of, 542
Superego, 40–41, 345
Surface structure of language, 196
Surfactin, 129
Surgent growth, 466
Suzuki musical training, 193
Symbiosis, 223
Symbol, 287
Synchrony, 228–231
Syphilis, 105, 505
Systems approach to development, defined, 4–5

Tay-Sachs disease, 87, 90, 92
Teaching:
  and adolescent abilities, 496
  and adolescent delinquency, 482–483
  and adolescent maturation, 480
  and adolescent moral questions, 512
  and behaviorists, 391
  and bilingual education, 406–408
  and childhood obesity, 361

and handicapped children, 366–369
and hyperactive children, 374, 377
and infants, 189–194
and learning disabilities, 369–374
and learning theorists, 391
and mainstreaming, 7–8, 367–369
and modeling, 50
and special education, 367–369
  (see also Education)
Teenage parents and child abuse, 248
Teenage pregnancy, 504, 505–507
Teenage prostitution and sexual abuse, 534–539
Television:
  Action for Children's Television (ACT), 335
  adverse effects of, 51, 335, 363, 440–441
  average amount watched, 334
  cartoons and preschool children, 334
  and childhood obesity, 363
  commercials and preschool children, 334
  reform of children's programming, 335
  and sex-role development, 347
  and social-skills development, 335
  and verbal-skills development, 335
  and violence, 334–335
Temperament, 224–229
  and genetic influence, 225–227
  New York Longitudinal Study of, 224–225
  and parental response, 225–227
Teratogens, 103–104, 105
  environmental, 110
  and hyperactive children, 375
  risk factors, 111
Teratology, 103–104
Testosterone, 467
Thalassemia, 89, 90
Thalidomide and birth defects, 107–108
Ticklishness, 181
Toddlers:
  cognitive development, 184–194
  emotional development, 231–238
  and fathers' role, 234–235
  language development, 201–204
  nutrition, 168, 170
  and pretending, 186
  and teaching, 192–194
  and walking, 166–167
Toilet-training:
  and psychosexual theory, 221
  and toddler autonomy, 222
Tooth decay, 263
Toxoplasmosis, 105
Transition, in birth process, 125, 131
Trophoblast, 100, 101
Trust versus mistrust in early childhood, 221
Tumultuous growth, 465
Turner's syndrome, 81
Twins:
  dizygotic, 73–74, 76
    IQ of, 82
    motor skills of, 164–167

monozygotic, 72, 73–74
    IQ of, 82
    menarche, age of, 476
    motor skills of, 164–167
    and schizophrenia, 79
  and nature-versus-nurture controversy, 74–75
  (see also Multiple births)

Umbilical cord, 100, 124, 125, 130, 131, 134, 138
Uncles, 439, 453
Uterus, 99, 124–125

Vaccines and birth defects, 105
Vacuum extraction, 132
Vernix, 127, 128
Vision:
  at birth, 159
  in infants, 159–160
Visual-cliff experiment, 161
Vitamin deficiencies, 168
Vitamins and birth defects, 107
Vocabulary:
  in the first two years, 201–204
  in the play years, 300–302
  in the school years, 398–399
  (see also Language development)

Walking:
  norms for, 166–167
  and black children, 167
  variations, reasons for, 167
Watson, John, 45, 220
Weaning, 168
Weight:
  in adolescence, 467–468
  at birth, 152
  in early childhood, 152–154
  in middle childhood, 261–262, 358–362
Working mothers, effects on children, 454
  (see also Mothers)

X-rays and birth defects, 110

Yolk sac, 100
Youth culture, 524

Zygote, 71–72, 99, 101
  and genetic information, 72
  and sex determination, 72–73